The Income Taxation of Trusts and Estates

The Income Taxation of Trusts and Estates

SECOND EDITION

Jay A. Soled
DISTINGUISHED PROFESSOR AND DIRECTOR
MASTER OF ACCOUNTANCY IN TAXATION
RUTGERS BUSINESS SCHOOL

Alan S. Acker
LAWYER, CARLILE PATCHEN & MURPHY

Jeremiah W. Doyle, IV
SENIOR VICE PRESIDENT/FAMILY WEALTH STRATEGIST
BNY MELLON WEALTH MANAGEMENT
LECTURER, BOSTON UNIVERSITY SCHOOL OF LAW

Steven G. Siegel
PRESIDENT, THE SIEGEL GROUP
ADJUNCT PROFESSOR OF LAW
GRADUATE TAX PROGRAM
UNIVERSITY OF ALABAMA

Sean R. Weissbart
PARTNER, BLANK ROME LLP
ADJUNCT PROFESSOR OF LAW
NEW YORK UNIVERSITY SCHOOL OF LAW

CAROLINA ACADEMIC PRESS
Durham, North Carolina

LCCN 2023937999
ISBN 978-1-5310-2808-4
eISBN 978-1-5310-2809-1

Carolina Academic Press
700 Kent Street
Durham, North Carolina 27701
(919) 489-7486
www.cap-press.com

Printed in the United States of America

Contents

Table of Cases

Table of Statutes and Regulations

Internal Revenue Code (cont'd)

Federal Regulations

Federal Tax Court Rules

Revenue Proceedings

State Materials

Restatements

Acknowledgments

Thank you to my wife, Amy, my children, Derek, Amanda, and Heather, my daughter-in-law, Beret, my parents, Myron and Marion, and my in-laws, Paul and Sandra. Without their support, attainment of my goals would have remained distant dreams.

JAY SOLED 2023

For my mom and dad, my wife, JoDee, and my sons, Will and Cam.

JEREMIAH DOYLE 2023

It is always extremely gratifying when one's teaching, speaking and writing are appreciated by students and professional audiences. What contributes significantly to this work are the understanding and sacrifices of time made by our families.

I want to thank my wife Jane, children Lori and Dana, sons-in-law Jared and Bret and grandchildren Sophie, Nessa, Samantha, and Archie for their love and support. Knowing you are with me makes all of the effort worthwhile.

STEVEN SIEGEL 2023

Thank you to my family and mentors for all their support along the way and to my colleague, Kyle Durante, for his valuable input with the chapter on foreign trusts.

SEAN WEISSBART 2023

The Income Taxation of Trusts and Estates

Introduction

The Internal Revenue Code ("Code") is complex, and Subchapter J, which encapsulates the income taxation of trusts and estates, is no exception. However, through a combination of hard work and perseverance, mastery is achievable. And that is where this textbook comes into play. We have designed it to facilitate the learning process. If you diligently work through each chapter, while we can't promise proverbial gold, we can offer you something much more valuable: a knowledge base that you can carry with you throughout the rest of your career.

The textbook is framed in the following fashion. First, in Chapter 1, we proceed down the following dual path: (A) we set forth the fundamentals of the nation's transfer tax system, namely, its gift, estate, and generation-skipping transfer taxes and (B) we examine salient elements of a decedent's final income tax return and important elections every executor must consider making. Basic knowledge of this overall landscape is pivotal to understanding the motivation behind inter vivos trust establishment, testamentary trust establishment, and the settling of a decedent's final affairs. Next, in Chapter 2, we explore how trusts and estates share many tax attributes with individual taxpayers and, likewise, how they differ. In Chapter 3, we detail the concept of distributable net income ("DNI"), a defining characteristic of trusts and estates that distinguishes them from all other legal entities under the Code. With this knowledge base in hand, Chapters 4 and 5 investigate what are known as simple and complex trusts (the latter category of which includes estates). In Chapters 6 and 7, we then turn your attention to trusts that have unique characteristics, namely, grantor and charitable trusts. Chapter 8 tackles a pervasive issue in the trusts and estates area, namely, income with respect to decedent and how it is taxed. In the last substantive chapter, Chapter 9 investigates how the Code taxes income earned by foreign trusts. Finally, at the end of the textbook, we conclude.

At the outset, we want to acknowledge that this textbook is not some sort of a magic carpet. You cannot simply hop on and enjoy the ride. Instead, you must be willing to commit yourself and your time to understanding the difficult concepts this textbook presents and seeks to impart. Assuming you are willing to devote yourself and your energies to achieve mastery, upon completion of this textbook, we are confident that you can immediately begin to practice in this area of the law.

But kindly bear in mind that this is an introductory textbook, not an exhaustive treatise. That being the case, in your practice, please be well aware of the fact that you're apt to come across issues and concepts that this textbook does not cover.

Fear not, there are at least four excellent resources you may wish to add to your tax library. They are as follows:

- Byrle M. Abbin & Frances Way Schafer, Income Taxation of Fiduciaries and Beneficiaries (Wolters Kluwer 2022)
- Alan Acker, Bloomberg Tax Portfolio, Income Taxation of Trusts and Estates, No. 852-4th T.M.
- Howard M. Zaritsky, Norman Lane, & Robert Danforth, Federal Income Taxation of Estates and Trusts (Thomson Reuters 2023)
- Grayson McCouch, Federal Income Taxation of Trusts, Estates, and Beneficiaries in a Nutshell (Nutshell Series 3d 2023)

For those students who this Introduction hasn't frightened off, brace yourselves for a stupendous journey, one punctuated with adventure and, yes, periodic frustration. By semester's end, if you've marked up the text, been a fastidious reader, and challenged yourself with the problems, you will be ready to help other taxpayers fulfill their civic duty to meet their appropriate taxes — the financial engine that keeps our society humming. And you should be proud of achieving this milestone.

Chapter 1

The Basics

I. Introduction

As we embark on this journey of discovery, it's important to understand how the nation's transfer tax system, the decedent's final tax return, and tax elections underlie Subchapter J and shape its contours. Taxpayers admittedly create trusts for many reasons, ranging from protecting young descendants to ensuring a new spouse can't wreak financial havoc; however, potential income and transfer tax savings are motivating reasons that also lead to trust formation. Also, how executors and personal representatives handle decedents' final income tax returns and various tax elections may affect the estate administration and trust funding processes.

Before diving headfirst into Subchapter J, we thus pause. Every student of Subchapter J should have a basic understanding of the nation's transfer tax system and, in addition, know how to address commonplace issues that confront executors and personal representatives regarding the filing of a decedent's final income tax return and tax elections that must be considered.

In Section II below, we explore the fundamentals of the nation's transfer tax system, comprised by its gift, estate, and generation-skipping taxes. Next, in Section III, we address those issues and concerns that typically beset practitioners regarding the filing of a decedent's final income tax return (Form 1040 (U.S. Individual Income Tax Return)) and those tax elections that executors and personal representatives must ponder.

II. The Nation's Transfer Tax System

The United States has a three-part transfer tax system. It is comprised of a gift tax, estate tax, and generation-skipping transfer tax. The historic goals of the transfer tax system are essentially twofold in nature: to protect against too much power being concentrated in the hands of wealthy taxpayers and to raise revenue. Whether the nation's transfer tax system actually achieves these objectives has been the fodder of many political debates; although we will not enter this debate, we will only comment that over the course of the last two decades, Congress has emasculated the transfer tax system (with a much larger exemption and lower tax rates), leaving the long-term prospects of the transfer tax system remaining intact somewhat in doubt.

Notwithstanding the transfer tax system's ever-changing political favor, it would be foolhardy to ignore the impact it has had in shaping trust formation and estate administration. After all, the gift, estate, and generation-skipping transfer taxes have been part of the nation's tax fabric for many decades and, in the case of the estate tax, for well over a century. And, on the one hand, although we don't anticipate that the transfer tax system will return to its broader reach anytime soon, on the other hand, we do not expect that Congress will ultimately repeal it. Thus, all Subchapter J students should study the basics of the nation's transfer tax system; indeed, without such a basic understanding, students would lack an important vantage point and could feel unmoored. In particular, the transfer tax regime has played a pivotal roles in shaping how estate planners strategically use trusts to avoid transfer taxes on their clients' behalf and how the estate administration process is conducted.

So get ready to be tethered to Subchapter J with a firmer grip. Regarding transfer taxes, your ticket to that tighter grip is set forth in Subsections A, B, and C below, which respectively explore the gift tax, estate tax, and generation-skipping transfer tax.

A. The Gift Tax

Internal Revenue Code: Sections 2501(a)(1), 2502(a), 2503(a)-(e), 2505(a), 2511(a), 2512(a)-(b), 2513(a).

Treasury Regulations: Section 25.2512-1(a).

Chapter 12 of the Code encapsulates the nation's gift tax system. Let's first consider its basic structure, and then we can observe commonplace strategies tax practitioners have employed to mitigate their clients' gift tax exposure.

The starting point of Chapter 12 is found in Code § 2511. It defines the meaning of "transfer" and broadly declares that the nation's gift tax applies to all gratuitous transfers "whether the transfer is in trust or otherwise, whether the gift is direct or indirect, and whether the property is real or personal, tangible or intangible. . . ." Very, very broad, right? And the value of such gift? Not surprisingly, it's the "amount of the gift." Code § 2512(a), which the Treasury regulations amplify with the following familiar definition: "The value of the property is the price at which such property would change hands between a willing buyer and a willing seller, neither being under any compulsion to buy or to sell, and both having reasonable knowledge of relevant facts." Treas. Reg. § 25.2512-1(a). In many situations, application of this Code section and accompanying Treasury regulation is simple enough: a taxpayer buys her daughter a new $50,000 car, making thereby a taxable gift of the same amount (the taxpayer's daughter has no income because of Code § 102(a)).

A taxable gift also extends to exercising powers of appointment. For example, a taxpayer who exercises a *general power of appointment*, defined as the ability to vest property to oneself, one's estate, one's creditors, or the creditors of one's estate, has made a taxable gift. Code § 2514(b).

An example of a general power of appointment trust provision is set forth below:

Sample general power of appointment:

> LIFETIME GENERAL POWER OF APPOINTMENT. With respect to any trust being held for the benefit of a child of mine, the Trustee will distribute so much or all of the principal of such child's trust to or for the benefit of any person or persons, including such child, as such child appoints by a signed writing to that effect delivered to the Trustee during such child's lifetime.

By exercising this power, the trust beneficiary will make a taxable gift. Code § 2514(b).[1]

In contrast, a taxpayer who exercises what are non-general powers of appointment, also known as *special powers of appointment* (i.e., whereby the person exercising the power cannot vest property to oneself, one's estate, one's creditors, or to the creditors of one's estate), is not deemed to have made a taxable gift. Code § 2514(c).

Examples of a special power of appointment trust provision are set forth below. The first is narrow in scope and the second is broader.

Sample special power of appointment (<u>limited</u> in scope to beneficiary's issue):

> LIFETIME SPECIAL POWER OF APPOINTMENT. With respect to any trust being held for the benefit of a child of mine, the Trustee will distribute so much or all of the principal of such child's trust to or for the benefit of **any one or more of my child's descendants**, as my child appoints by a signed writing to that effect delivered to the Trustee during such child's lifetime. (Emphasis added.)

Under the specified terms, since the trust beneficiary has a limited power to appoint principal and undistributed income only to his or her descendants, it makes this power of appointment a limited one. By exercising this power which is limited in scope, the trust beneficiary will not have made a gift. See Code § 2514(c).

Example of special power of appointment (<u>broad</u> in scope):

> **LIFETIME SPECIAL POWER OF APPOINTMENT.** With respect to any trust being held for the benefit of a child of mine, the Trustee will distribute so much or all of the principal of such child's trust to or for the benefit of **anyone other than such child, such child's estate, such child's creditors, or the creditors of such child's estate**, as my child appoints by a signed writing to that effect delivered to the Trustee during such child's lifetime.

Under the terms specified, the trust beneficiary has a limited power to appoint principal to anyone other than himself or herself, his or her estate, his or her creditors,

---

1. To the extent that the trust beneficiary dies without having exercised the power, then the trust property will be included in the trust beneficiary's gross estate. 26 U.S.C. § 2041.

or the creditors of his or her estate; that being the case, this also makes this power of appointment a limited one. Similar to the example in the paragraph above, by exercising this power which, although broad in scope, is not a general power of appointment, the trust beneficiary will not have made a gift. See Code § 2514(c).

Taxpayers must remember that donative intent is "not an essential element in the application of the gift tax to the transfer."[2] Treas. Reg. § 25.2511-1(g)(1). As the Treasury Regulation explains:

> Transfers reached by the gift tax are not confined to those only which, being without a valuable consideration, accord with the common law concept of gifts, but embrace as well sales, exchanges, and other dispositions of property for a consideration to the extent that the value of the property transferred by the donor exceeds the value in money or money's worth of the consideration given therefor.

Once the taxpayer has made a gratuitous transfer, there are several steps tax practitioners should follow. The first is to determine if any exclusions or deductions are applicable. Second, exemptions and tax rates should be considered. Next, filing requirements and deadlines must be met. Finally, thought should be given to popular gift tax minimization strategies that taxpayers may undertake.

Consider each of the foregoing steps.

Exclusions. The Code specifies three important exclusions.

The first is the so-called "annual exclusion" found in Code § 2503(b). To "obviate the necessity of keeping an account of and reporting numerous small gifts," Congress provided taxpayers with the opportunity to make gifts of relatively small value that would not be included in the gift tax base.[3] It provides that present interest gifts (defined as an "unrestricted right to the immediate use, possession, or enjoyment of property or the income from property"[4]), such as birthday, graduation, and wedding presents, are not included in the gift tax base. This exclusion is subject to important limitations, however: it is capped at a relatively low dollar amount (in 2023, the annual exclusion amount was $17,000, but this dollar figure is adjusted annually for inflation); in addition, future interest gifts (i.e., those wealth transfers "limited to commence in use, possession, or enjoyment at some future date or time"[5]) do not qualify for this exclusion.

---

2. *See generally Duberstein v. Commissioner*, 363 U.S. 278 (1960).

3. S. Rep. No. 665, 72d Cong., 1st Sess. (1932), reprinted in 1931-1 (Part 2) C.B. 496, 525.

4. Treas. Reg. § 25.2503-3(b). To broaden this exclusion's utility, Congress also treats as "present interests" deferred payments made to taxpayers under the age of 21 (usually to a Uniform Transfer to Minors Account (UTMA)) as long as the following three conditions are met: (i) the gifted property can be expended solely for the donee's benefit; (ii) if the donee dies before attaining age 21, the property is payable to the donee's estate; and (iii) the property vests in the donee when the donee reaches age 21. Code section 2503(c).

5. Treas. Reg. § 25.2503-3(a).

The second important exclusion is found in Code § 2503(c). It essentially provides that gifts made to minors that vest when the minor attains age 21 qualify as a present, rather than a future, interest. Therefore, taxpayers who make transfers pursuant to a state's Uniform Transfers to Minors Act (UTMA) or Uniform Gifts to Minors Act (UGMA), in which the property being transferred vests when the minor attains age 21, qualify for the annual exclusion (subject to the same dollar caps set forth above).

The third and final exclusion is found in Code § 2503(e). This Code section excludes from the gift tax base a person's gratuitous payment of another's tuition and medical care expenses. In order to qualify for this exclusion, the payments in question must be made directly to the educational institution or the health provider, as the case may be.

Deductions. There are two important deductions that many taxpayers seek to capitalize upon.

The first is the gift tax charitable deduction. The general rule permits taxpayers to make transfers to both charitable organizations and governmental entities, and such transfers will qualify for the unlimited gift tax charitable deduction. Code § 2522(a). The same is not true with respect to contributions made into trust in which charitable organizations and governmental entities are designated beneficiaries; unless certain terms and conditions are met (see Chapter 7), such contributions will not qualify for the gift tax charitable deduction. Code § 2522(c).

The second is the unlimited marital gift tax deduction found in Code § 2523. In its simplest form, any outright transfer of property to a spouse qualifies for this deduction. To illustrate, if one spouse transfers $100 million to another spouse, there would be a $100 million gift but a dollar-for-dollar marital deduction offset. (However, gifts made to a non-citizen spouse do not qualify for the unlimited gift tax marital deduction. Code § 2523(i).)

The Code treats spouses essentially as a single economic unit, and hence, tax-free transfers made between spouses are sanctioned. If, however, one spouse transfers property to another spouse that will not ultimately be included in the transfer tax base in the recipient spouse's hands, the transferred property will not qualify for the unlimited gift tax marital deduction.

In order for any transfer in trust to qualify for the unlimited gift tax marital deduction, it must meet the conditions set forth in Code § 2523. Two types of trusts meet these conditions: (i) a "qualified terminal-interest trust" (a QTIP trust) and (ii) a general power of appointment trust.

A QTIP trust is one in which the property being transferred into trust meets the following three criteria: (i) the donor spouse transfers property into trust; (ii) the donee spouse has a qualifying income interest for life in the trust; and (iii) a proper election is made that will cause the trust property to be included in the surviving spouse's estate. Code § 2523(f)(2). A general power of appointment trust vests the recipient spouse during her lifetime or upon her demise with the power to vest the trust property to herself or to her estate. Code § 2523(e). Both QTIP and general power appointment trusts ensure the integrity of the transfer tax base insofar as assets transferred into either trust remain in the transfer tax base.

A significant difference between the two types of trusts—QTIP and general power of appointment trusts—is that under a QTIP trust, the creator of the trust can control the ultimate distribution of the trust funds after the spouse's death, while under a general power of appointment trust, the surviving spouse can control the ultimate distribution of the trust funds after such spouse's death. Which trust is best will depend on the particular facts and circumstances of the couple.

Rates and Exemptions. Congress imposes a flat 40% tax rate on taxable gifts. Code § 2502. In reality, however, few taxpayers actually pay gift tax.[6] The reason for the absence of gift tax payments is simple: Congress provides a large exclusion from the gift tax base ($12,920,000 in 2023 (which is annually adjusted for inflation)). Code § 2505(a). In addition, a surviving spouse can be credited with the deceased spouse's unused exclusion (DSUE) amount, thus increasing the surviving spouse's own exclusion amount. Code § 2010(c)(4). Although a taxpayer's own exclusion amount is indexed to inflation, the DSUE amount does not receive an annual inflation adjustment. Thus, if a deceased spouse has not used any of his or her applicable exclusion for estate or gift taxes, the deceased spouse's entire available exclusion may be added to the surviving spouse's remaining exclusion provided that a timely federal estate tax return is filed for the deceased spouse.

Filing Requirements and Deadlines. The Code requires that taxpayers who make taxable gifts file a Form 709 (U.S. Gift (and Generation-Skipping Transfer) Tax Return). Code § 6019. The filing due date for such gift tax returns is on or before April 15 of the year following the date the gift was made. Code § 6075(b)(1). Taxpayers who secure extensions to file their income tax returns automatically extend their gift tax return filing deadline to the designated extension date. Code § 6075(b)(2).[7] In any tax year that includes the date of the taxpayer's death, the gift tax return filing deadline is no later than the time (including extensions) for filing the estate tax return with respect to the donor. Code § 6075(b)(3). Married taxpayers who thus consent can elect to treat any gift as if made one half by each. Code § 2513(a).

Strategies. Taxpayers often structure their affairs to reduce their transfer tax burdens, employing different tax-planning devices to achieve this objective. Here we explore three such devices: (i) the Crummey trust; (ii) the grantor retained annuity trust; and (iii) minority and marketability valuation discounts.

---

6. In 2020, for example, the IRS reported 174,026 gift tax returns filed; however, only 516 resulted in the payment of tax. See IRS, Statistics of Income, available at https://www.irs.gov/statistics/soi-tax-stats-total-gifts-of-donor-total-gifts-deductions-credits-and-net-gift-tax. Put somewhat differently, .00016% of the U.S. population of 330 million paid a gift tax.

7. However, the Code grants no extensions to pay any gift tax owed.

(i) The Crummey Trust. Transfers into trust generally give beneficiaries future interests in the trust property (i.e., they often do not have the immediate right to the use or enjoyment of all of the trust property). That being the case, in the absence of tax planning, trust contributions would not qualify for the gift tax annual exclusion, which is only available for gifts of present interests: taxpayers making trust contributions would therefore either expend part of their lifetime exclusion or, if it has already been expended, be obligated to pay gift tax.

To transform what otherwise would be gifts of future interests into gifts of present interests, taxpayers can provide in their trust instrument terms that grant trust beneficiaries the right to immediately withdraw contributed trust funds. This right to withdraw gifts made to the trust by the trust beneficiaries often is limited as to time and amount. By adding a right-to-withdraw window, taxpayers transform otherwise future interests into present interests. If the trust beneficiary fails to exercise the withdrawal right, the contributed trust property is added to trust principal and available for the trustee to distribute at a future date in accordance with the trust terms.

In *Crummey v. Commissioner*, 397 F.2d 82 (9th Cir. 1968), the validity of this tactic was tested and approved. Note that the opinion did not require that the beneficiaries had to know about their right to withdraw contributions made to the trust. Notwithstanding, trust instruments giving beneficiaries a limited right to withdraw gifts made to the trust routinely require that the beneficiaries be informed of their right to withdraw such gifts. Accordingly, any time trust contributions are made, trustees will routinely scramble to give notice to trust beneficiaries of their limited withdrawal rights.

The *Crummey* decision opened the proverbial doors for taxpayers to use trusts to capitalize upon the use of the annual exclusion from which they would otherwise be precluded. Time and time again, estate planners eponymously reference Crummey powers in their trust documents; indeed, Crummey powers have become a ubiquitous feature in most, but not all, inter vivos irrevocable trusts. And, despite their ubiquity in inter vivos trust instruments, Crummey powers are virtually never exercised (can you suspect why?).

Below is a sample Crummey withdrawal right and how it effectively transforms a future property right into a present property right.

WITHDRAWAL RIGHTS.

> A: Following any gift made to the trust by any donor in any calendar year, the beneficiary shall have the right, during the beneficiary's lifetime, upon the beneficiary's written request to the Trustee, to receive from the trust property outright and free from this trust, an amount in each calendar year not exceeding the lesser of (a) the total amount of gifts made by a donor for that calendar year, (b) if the donor was not married at the time of the gift, the amount of the annual exclusion from federal gift tax

> available to the donor under Section 2503 of the Internal Revenue Code of 1986, as amended or recodified (the "Code") (currently $17,000), or (c) if the donor was married at the time of any gift, the aggregate amount of the annual exclusions from federal gift tax available to the donor and the donor's spouse under Section 2503 of the Code (currently $34,000), with respect to gifts of present interests made in such calendar year by the donor to the trust.
>
> Such amounts shall be payable, at the Trustee's discretion, in cash or in property having a fair market value equal to the amount determined above. The right to demand payment pursuant to this Paragraph shall not be cumulative from year to year but shall exist for 30 days from the date of notice of the gift but not beyond December 31 of such year. Such right of withdrawal shall be exercisable only by written notice to the Trustee of the amount the beneficiary wishes to withdraw, and the amount so demanded shall be paid by the Trustee promptly upon receipt of such notice.
>
> B: Following any actual or deemed transfer to the trust on behalf of the beneficiary, the Trustee shall promptly give written notice to the beneficiary of any such transfer, the amount of such transfer, and the amount which the beneficiary may withdraw pursuant to this Paragraph.
>
> C: If the beneficiary is a minor or otherwise fails in legal capacity at the time any gift to the trust is received, notice of the transfer shall be given to the guardian of the beneficiary's estate, or, if there is no such guardian, to any other person (other than me) designated by the Trustee, and such guardian or other designated person may make the demand for withdrawal on behalf of the beneficiary. Any property received pursuant to the demand shall be held by the guardian or other designated person for the sole benefit and use of the beneficiary.
>
> D: In order to effect the right of withdrawal conferred by this Article, the Trustee shall retain in trust (except as distributed in satisfaction of such withdrawal rights) for at least 30 days, any cash or property received in trust and giving rise to a right of withdrawal under this Article. Retention of such property shall be required, however, only if, and to the extent that, other assets then held in trust or received by the Trustee in exchange for the cash or property would be insufficient to fund the right of withdrawal attributable to such cash or property.

Consider an example of how Crummey withdrawal rights effectively transfer wealth free of gift tax. Suppose a married taxpayer establishes an irrevocable trust, the terms of which have Crummey withdrawal rights for the benefit of his wife and three children. In 2023, the taxpayer can contribute $119,000 to the trust and not exhaust any part of his lifetime exemption. More specifically, he will be deemed to have made a $17,000 gift to his spouse and gifts of $34,000 to each of his three children (which the taxpayer and his spouse may elect to treat as split gifts on their respective gift tax returns).[8] Assuming none of the beneficiaries exercise their Crummey withdrawal rights, the trust contribution will be added to trust corpus and, going forward, invested by the trustee.

(ii) The Grantor Retained Annuity Trust. Prior to the introduction of Chapter 14 to the Code, entitled "Special Valuation Rules," taxpayers could establish trusts with significant contributions, retain the right to receive trust income for a term of years, and give the future interest to another family member (often a child or grandchild of the transferor). For gift tax purposes, the transferor has made a gift of the remainder interest in the trust, and the fair market value of such gift was equal to the total amount contributed to the trust reduced by the actuarial value of the transferor's retained right to the income. As part of this overall strategy, the trustee would make trust investments designed to generate little or no trust income so that the amount ultimately passing to the trust's designated remainder beneficiaries would be greater than the amount reportable for gift tax purposes—the difference amounted to a tax-free transfer of wealth. These trusts, known as grantor retained income trusts, or the acronym GRITs, came at the expense of greatly narrowing the nation's transfer tax base.

Over three decades ago, Congress sought to end this perceived abuse of GRITs by enacting Code § 2702. This provision essentially declares that the fair market value of the retained interest will be zero unless the retained interest is "qualified" or the trust does not benefit family members (as defined) of the grantor. While so-called "qualified interests" come in a variety of forms, the most commonly used is an annuity amount. Code § 2702(b)(1). Under the protection of Code § 2702, taxpayers are at liberty to make a trust contribution, retain the right to receive an annuity amount (as opposed to simply the income) for a term of years ((a) for the life of the term holder, (b) for a term of years, or (c) for the shorter of (a) or (b)), and have the trust remainder interest vest with whomever the settlor designates. Such a trust is known as a grantor retained annuity trust or GRAT. Similar to GRITs, the value of the gift of the remainder interest in a GRAT for gift tax purposes is equal to the amount contributed to the trust reduced by the actuarial value of the retained annuity. Because the settlor determines both the duration and amount of the annuity, the settlor can design the GRAT to have the remainder interest be valued at whatever amount is desired by the settlor.

With the help of their advisors, many taxpayers have instituted GRATs in which they calibrate the fair market value of the retained annuity interest to equal the fair market value of the contributed trust property. This valuation exercise negates the presence of a taxable gift. If the return on the contributed trust property exceeds the assumed rate of return determined in accordance with Code § 7520, then whatever remains in the trust after the trust term ends passes tax-free to the trust

8. This trust contribution does not qualify for the gift tax marital deduction. This is because the spousal beneficiary has a terminal interest (but the trust contribution will nevertheless qualify for the annual exclusion).

remainder beneficiaries; if, instead, the return on the contributed trust property fails to perform in excess of the Code § 7520 rate and nothing remains in the trust when its term ends, the taxpayer has lost nothing in the process and can commence the formation of a new GRAT. This technique, known as a zeroed-out GRAT, was given the imprimatur of judicial approval in *Walton v. Commissioner*, 115 T.C. 589 (2000).

(iii) Minority and Marketability Valuation Discounts. Ownership interests in business enterprises come in many forms (e.g., limited liability company membership interests and corporate stock) and varieties (e.g., common versus preferred stock and voting interests versus non-voting interests). Notwithstanding these forms and varieties, minority ownership interests in business enterprises often have a fair-market value less than the pro rata value of the underlying property owned by such entities because the lack of control places the economic interests of the minority owner in potential jeopardy. To illustrate, if a taxpayer owns 10% of a business enterprise, and the other 90% is held by an unrelated third party, the latter can dictate important business decisions such as salary determinations, timing of profit distributions, and the like. The lack of control thus diminishes the value of minority interests to a potential buyer.

Another factor that diminishes value of an ownership interest in a closely held business is the absence of a readily available market to sell such business interest. This diminution in value is related to the anticipated costs associated with marketing the business and identifying viable buyers.

When making intra-family transfers, taxpayers often take advantage of minority and marketability valuation discounts, which often may exceed 30% in total.[9] In a simple scenario, assume that a taxpayer owns all 100 shares of the outstanding stock of a corporation that owns as its sole asset a building worth $1 million and has no liabilities. If the taxpayer transfers 40 shares of stock in this corporation to her daughter, for gift tax purposes and assuming aggregate valuation discounts of 30%, the taxpayer would not have to report a gift of $400,000 (i.e., .40 × $1,000,000). Instead, the taxpayer may report a gift equal to $280,000 (($1,000,000 ×.40) less ($400,000 ×.30)), assuming a combined 30% minority and marketability discount is apropos.

Over the course of many decades, the IRS and taxpayers have battled over the size and permissibility of valuation discounts. In Revenue Ruling 93-12, 1993-1 C.B. 202 below, the IRS finally conceded that valuation discounts in the context of family gifts are permissible, but did not set forth the numerical boundaries of what these discounts should be.

9. The actual amount of valuation discount will depend upon the particular facts and circumstances of the business transaction contemplated.

Revenue Ruling 93-12

Issue

If a donor transfers shares in a corporation to each of the donor's children, is the factor of corporate control in the family to be considered in valuing each transferred interest, for purposes of section 2512 of the Internal Revenue Code?

Facts

P owned all of the single outstanding class of stock of X corporation. P transferred all of P's shares by making simultaneous gifts of 20 percent of the shares to each of P's five children, A, B, C, D, and E.

Law and Analysis

Section 2512(a) of the Code provides that the value of the property at the date of the gift shall be considered the amount of the gift.

Section 25.2512-1 of the Gift Tax Regulations provides that, if a gift is made in property, its value at the date of the gift shall be considered the amount of the gift. The value of the property is the price at which the property would change hands between a willing buyer and a willing seller, neither being under any compulsion to buy or to sell, and both having reasonable knowledge of relevant facts.

Section 25.2512-2(a) of the regulations provides that the value of stocks and bonds is the fair market value per share or bond on the date of the gift. Section 25.2512-2(f) provides that the degree of control of the business represented by the block of stock to be valued is among the factors to be considered in valuing stock where there are no sales prices or bona fide bid or asked prices.

Rev. Rul. 81-253, 1981-1 C.B. 187, holds that, ordinarily, no minority shareholder discount is allowed with respect to transfers of shares of stock between family members if, based upon a composite of the family members' interests at the time of the transfer, control (either majority voting control or de facto control through family relationships) of the corporation exists in the family unit. The ruling also states that the Service will not follow the decision of the Fifth Circuit in *Estate of Bright v. United States*, 658 F.2d 999 (5th Cir. 1981).

In *Bright*, the decedent's undivided community property interest in shares of stock, together with the corresponding undivided community property interest of the decedent's surviving spouse, constituted a control block of 55 percent of the shares of a corporation. The court held that, because the community-held shares were subject to a right of partition, the decedent's own interest was equivalent to 27.5 percent of the outstanding shares and, therefore, should be valued as a minority interest, even though the shares were to be held by the decedent's surviving spouse as trustee of a testamentary trust. See also, *Propstra v. United States*, 680 F.2d 1248 (9th Cir. 1982). In addition, *Estate of Andrews v. Commissioner*, 79 T.C. 938 (1982), and *Estate of Lee v. Commissioner*, 69 T.C. 860 (1978), nonacq., 1980-2 C.B. 2, held that the corporation shares owned by other family members cannot be attributed to an individual family member for determining whether the individual family member's shares should be valued as the controlling interest of the corporation.

After further consideration of the position taken in Rev. Rul. 81-253, and in light of the cases noted above, the Service has concluded that, in the case of a corporation with a single class of stock, notwithstanding the family relationship of the donor, the donee, and other shareholders, the shares of other family members will not be aggregated with the transferred shares to determine whether the transferred shares should be valued as part of a controlling interest.

In the present case, the minority interests transferred to A, B, C, D, and E should be valued for gift tax purposes without regard to the family relationship of the parties.

Holding

If a donor transfers shares in a corporation to each of the donor's children, the factor of corporate control in the family is not considered in valuing each transferred interest for purposes of section 2512 of the Code. For estate and gift tax valuation purposes, the Service will follow *Bright*, *Propstra*, *Andrews*, and *Lee* in not assuming that all voting power held by family members may be aggregated for purposes of determining whether the transferred shares should be valued as part of a controlling interest. Consequently, a minority discount will not be disallowed solely because a transferred interest, when aggregated with interests held by family members, would be a part of a controlling interest. This would be the case whether the donor held 100 percent or some lesser percentage of the stock immediately before the gift.

What the IRS left unsaid was whether, from a public policy perspective, minority and marketability valuation discount retention makes sense. When business and investment interests are transferred and exchanged between unrelated parties, discounting plays a potentially prominent role in the valuation process; however, when the donor and donee are family members, query whether it is appropriate to permit such discounting. For the time being, congressional reticence has been construed as sanctioning this transfer tax minimization technique and its existence continues unabated.

Questions

1. A single taxpayer has six children. What is the maximum aggregate dollar amount she may give her children in 2023 and still be within the scope of the annual exclusion?
2. Regarding question 1, if the taxpayer were married, what is the maximum aggregate dollar amount she may give her children to still be within the scope of the annual exclusion?

3. What is the maximum dollar amount a taxpayer may gift in 2023 without having to pay gift tax? What does your answer implicitly assume?
4. Suppose a taxpayer has a teenage grandchild. What common techniques may the taxpayer employ to minimize potential gift tax exposure?
5. Why is the use of Crummey withdrawal rights such a common feature in inter vivos irrevocable trusts?
6. Why might a person favor a QTIP trust over another form of marital trust?
7. Why do wealthy taxpayers relish GRAT use?
8. If a taxpayer exercises a special power of appointment, does the taxpayer need to file a gift tax return? Why might a settlor hesitate before granting a trust beneficiary a special power of appointment?

B. The Estate Tax

Internal Revenue Code: Sections 2001(a)-(c), 2010(a), (c), 2031(a), 2032(a), 2033, 2035(a), 2036(a), 2037(a), 2038(a)(2), 2039(a), 2040(a), 2041(a)(2), (b), 2042, 2043, 2044, 2051, 2053(a), 2054, 2055(a), 2056(a), (b)(1), (b)(5), (b)(7), 2058(a).

Treasury Regulations: Section 20.2031-1(b).

When a taxpayer dies, the Code currently imposes an estate tax upon the "fair market value" of assets owned in a decedent's estate. Here, as with the gift tax, fair market value of property included in the gross estate is defined as "the price at which the property would change hands between a willing buyer and a willing seller, neither being under any compulsion to buy or sell and both having reasonable knowledge of relevant facts." Treas. Reg. § 20.2031-1(b). The valuation of assets in the gross estate is generally determined either on the date of the decedent's death or six months after the decedent's death.[10]

Below we consider (a) what the Code requires to be included in a decedent's gross estate, (b) those items that are deductible, (c) exclusion amounts, tax rates, and filing requirements, and (d) estate tax minimization strategies.

(a) Estate Tax Inclusion. Like its gift tax counterpart, the breadth of the estate tax is substantial. For starters, Code § 2031 makes the following declaration: "The value of the gross estate of the decedent ... [shall include] the value at the time of his death of all property, real or personal, tangible or intangible, wherever situated." Its scope, of course, includes all those interests in which a decedent held a direct ownership interest. For example, if a taxpayer dies owning title to a personal residence, its fair market value is included in the value of the taxpayer's gross estate.

---

10. In those instances when there would be an overall reduction in the amount of estate tax due, the Code permits executors to elect the so-called *alternate valuation date*. If this election is made, executors assess the fair market value of a decedent's assets six months after the decedent's death or, if earlier, when assets are sold or otherwise disposed of. Code § 2032(a).

But the scope of the estate tax inclusion extends well beyond direct property ownership. It includes certain property interests which were relinquished, owned jointly with others, and indirectly held, a list of which are enumerated below:

- Transfers within Three Years of Death (Code § 2035(a), (b)). A taxpayer's gross estate includes those property interests described below (enumerated under Code §§ 2036, 2037, 2038, or 2042) if the taxpayer transfers or relinquishes them within three years of death.
  - **Example:** Two years before a taxpayer dies, she transfers the ownership of a $1 million life insurance policy on her life to her son (i.e., she completes a change of ownership that the underwriting insurance company provides, submits the completed form to the company, and the company thereafter effectuates the ownership change). For purposes of the estate tax, the full $1 million of life insurance proceeds is includible in the taxpayer's gross estate.

  Furthermore, a taxpayer's gross estate also includes any gift tax paid with respect to any gifts made within three years of the taxpayer's death.[11]
  - **Example:** Two years before a taxpayer dies, she transfers $20 million to her son and pays $2,832,000 of gift tax ($20 million–$12,920,000 exclusion × 40% tax rate). The gift tax paid of $2,832,000 is deemed includible in the taxpayer's gross estate.
- Transfers with Retained Life Estates (Code § 2036(a)). Requires inclusion if a taxpayer transfers property outright or in trust and retains the right to "possession or enjoyment of, or the right to the income from, the property, or the right, either alone or in conjunction with any person, to designate the persons who shall possess or enjoy the property or the income therefrom." This inclusion rule aims to include those property interests in which the taxpayer would like to "have his cake and eat it, too." What this means in the parlance of the estate tax is that the taxpayer wants to enjoy the indicia of property ownership (e.g., cash flow), but ultimately not have such property includible in his gross estate. The Code denies this privilege.
  - **Example:** A taxpayer makes a transfer into trust and retains a lifetime income interest. Upon death, the full fair market value of the trust assets would be includible in the taxpayer's gross estate.
- Transfers Taking Effect at Death (Code § 2037(a)). If the taxpayer has retained a reversionary interest in property (the actuarial value of which exceeds 5%), the fair market value of the underlying property is included in the taxpayer's gross estate.

11. The estate tax is tax inclusive (the estate tax burden is levied on tax dollars that are used to pay the estate tax); in contrast, the gift is tax exclusive (the gift tax burden is not levied on tax dollars that are used to pay the gift tax). The estate tax thus results in a heavier tax burden than the gift tax. The three-year look-back at gift tax paid resulting in estate tax inclusion aims to curtail taxpayers from making death-bed gifts to minimize their overall transfer tax burden.

- **Example:** Suppose a taxpayer transfers property to his 90-year-old mother with a reversionary right to receive it back if his mother predeceases him. Since the taxpayer's actuarial right of reversion exceeds 5%, the fair market value of the transferred property is includible in the taxpayer's estate even if his mother survives him.

- Revocable Transfers (Code § 2038(a)). A taxpayer's gross estate includes all property over which a taxpayer has at the time of his death the right "to alter, amend, revoke, or terminate" beneficial enjoyment. Via this Code section, not surprisingly, Congress has declared that the ability to control the disposition of property is tantamount to direct property ownership.
  - **Example:** Taxpayer establishes a revocable trust. Upon the taxpayer's demise, the fair market value of the trust assets are includible in the taxpayer's gross estate.
  - **Example:** Taxpayer establishes an irrevocable trust for the benefit of his son and daughter, naming himself as trustee. Three years later, the taxpayer resigns as trustee, and the successor named in the trust agreement accepts the appointment as trustee. Five years later, the taxpayer dies. The fair market value of the assets is not includible in the taxpayer's gross estate.

- Annuities (Code § 2039(a)). A taxpayer's gross estate includes the actuarial value of any annuity paid for by the taxpayer (including IRAs and qualified plans) and directed or passed to others upon a taxpayer's demise.
  - **Example:** Taxpayer purchases a joint annuity for herself and her daughter. Upon the taxpayer's passing, the fair market value of the remaining annuity interest is includible in the taxpayer's gross estate.

- Joint Interests (Code § 2040(a), (b)). The Code requires that the entire fair market value of any joint ownership interest be includible in the taxpayer's gross estate. This rule is subject to two limitations: to the extent the other joint property owner can prove contribution, that proportion of the jointly held interest is not included in the taxpayer's gross estate. The Code also creates a presumption that spouses, who are joint owners, contributed equally to the property's purchase and thus, in those cases, only one-half of the property's fair market value is included in the decedent's gross estate.
  - **Example:** The taxpayer dies holding title to real estate jointly with his son. Unless the taxpayer's son can prove his contribution, the full fair market value of this real estate is includible in the taxpayer's estate. Had ownership been with the taxpayer's spouse, only one-half of the fair market value of such property would have been includible in the taxpayer's gross estate, regardless of which spouse furnished the consideration for the property.

- Powers of Appointment (Code § 2041(a)). If a taxpayer possesses a general power of appointment over property (i.e., exercisable in favor of the taxpayer, his estate, his creditors, or the creditors of his estate), the fair market value of the property over which such power can be exercised is includible in the taxpayer's gross estate.

- **Example:** A trust gives the taxpayer a general power of appointment over all the trust assets. The fair market value of the trust assets are thus includible in the taxpayer's estate.

The Code broadly defines the exercise of a general power of appointment to include the release or lapse of such power. Code § 2041(a)(2). However, the Code carves out an important exception to this inclusion rule. This exception specifies that no lapse of a power of appointment over property will be deemed to exist to the extent it doesn't exceed the greater of "(i) $5,000 or (ii) 5 percent of the aggregate value, at the time of such lapse, of the assets out of which, or the proceeds of which, the exercise of the lapsed powers could have been satisfied." Code § 2041(b)(2).[12] As a result of this exception, trust settlors often accord trust beneficiaries what are commonly known as "5 and 5 Powers" that grant responsible trust beneficiaries added latitude during the trust term.

A sample "5 and 5 Power" appears immediately below:

> **RIGHT OF WITHDRAWAL.** In any tax year of the Family Trust, my wife, **JANE SMITH**, shall have the non-cumulative right, in her absolute discretion, to withdraw from the trust principal, (1) an amount not exceeding $5,000 in value and, (2) if my spouse is living on December 1 of such year, to withdraw from the trust principal during that month an amount not exceeding the amount, if any, by which five percent of the market value of the net principal of the trust determined at the time of the withdrawal request is made (not reduced by any income taxes chargeable to principal) exceeds the value of the property previously withdrawn by my wife for such year. My wife will make any request for withdrawal by delivering to the Trustee a signed writing to that effect and the Trustee will satisfy such withdrawal request within 30 days of its receipt, even if such 30 day period ends after the close of such year.

Note that in the provision set forth above, in any year that Jane dies, if she dies before December, she will include $5,000 in her gross estate (assuming she has not exercised her right of withdrawal), and if she dies in December, she will include five percent of the value of the trust principal in her gross estate, because she has a general power of appointment over these amounts at the time of her death.

12. In the realm of the gift tax, the lapse of a general power of appointment is considered a property transfer. Code § 2514(a). This rule likewise does not apply to the extent the power that is allowed to lapse does not exceed the greater of "(1) $5,000 or (2) 5 percent of the aggregate value of the assets out of which, or the proceeds of which, the exercise of the lapsed powers could be satisfied." Code § 2514(e).

- Proceeds of Life Insurance (Code § 2042). Life insurance proceeds payable to a taxpayer's estate as well as the proceeds of any insurance policy over which the taxpayer had "incidents of ownership, exercisable alone or in conjunction with any other person" are includible in the taxpayer's estate.
  - **Example:** Taxpayer dies owning a life insurance policy the proceeds of which are payable to his granddaughter. Due to the taxpayer's ability to control the ultimate enjoyment of the life insurance proceeds (a clear incident of ownership), such life insurance proceeds are includible in the taxpayer's gross estate.
- Transfers for Insufficient Consideration (Code § 2043). Transfers of interests, rights, or powers described in Code §§ 2035, 2036, 2037, 2038, and 2041 (see above) for insufficient consideration are included in a taxpayer's gross estate to the extent the fair market value of the interest, right, or power transferred exceeds the amount of consideration paid.
  - **Example:** Taxpayer sells a retained reversionary trust interest with an actuarial value of $1 million for $700,000. Upon the taxpayer's demise, the $300,000 difference between the fair market value and the amount paid is includible in the taxpayer's estate.
- Certain Property for which Marital Deduction Was Previously Allowed (Code § 2044). If a taxpayer had a "qualifying income interest for life" and there was a prior marital estate or gift tax deduction taken with respect to such property (see below), its fair market value is included in the taxpayer's gross estate.
  - **Example:** Five years earlier, husband dies bequeathing $5 million into a trust in which a QTIP election was made (see below regarding the estate tax marital deduction). The wife now dies when the QTIP trust has assets with a fair market value of $8 million. The Code requires the inclusion of the $8 million of trust assets in the wife's estate.

(b) Estate Tax Deductions. Notwithstanding the broad breadth of estate tax inclusion, the Code also allows numerous deductions. A summary of the most salient deductions is set forth in the bullet points below:

- Expenses, Indebtedness, and Taxes (Code § 2053(a)). The Code permits deductions for funeral expenses, administrative expenses (e.g., attorney and accountant fees), claims against the estate, and unpaid mortgages and tax debts.
- Losses (Code § 2054). Uncompensated losses incurred by an estate "arising from fires, storms, shipwrecks, or other casualties" are deductible.
- Transfers for Public, Charitable, and Religious Uses (Code § 2055). Bequests made to governmental and charitable organizations are generally deductible; in the case of so-called split interest trusts (e.g., situations in which there are charitable and noncharitable trust beneficiaries), special rules enumerated in Chapter 7 apply.

- Bequests, Etc., to Surviving Spouse (Code § 2056). Amounts directly passing to a surviving spouse or held in trust for the primary benefit of the surviving spouse and that meet certain conditions qualify for the unlimited marital estate tax deduction. This treatment is consistent with the Code's treatment of spouses as a single economic unit. However, "terminable interests" passing for a surviving spouse's benefit generally do not qualify for the estate tax marital deduction. A terminable interest is one that terminates with respect to the surviving spouse "on the lapse of time, on the occurrence of an event or contingency, or on the failure of an event or contingency to occur," and then passes to someone other than the surviving spouse. Code § 2056(b)(1). This limitation makes sense, because the termination of the surviving spouse's interest means that nothing is includible in the surviving spouse's gross estate when the interest passes to the next person.
  - **Example:** A husband dies leaving a will that establishes a testamentary trust with an income interest to his wife and grants a discretionary right to the trustee to make principal distributions to the children of his first marriage. Under the trust, when the wife dies, the trust assets pass to the husband's children from his first marriage. The wife's interest in this trust is a terminable interest, because it terminates upon the occurrence of an event — her death — and passes to persons other than the surviving spouse — the decedent's children from a prior marriage. As such, the fair market value of assets passing into this trust would not qualify for the estate tax marital deduction.

  There are two exceptions to the terminable interest rule: (1) a bequest that is conditioned on the spouse surviving for six months or less, and (2) an interest held in trust for the benefit of the surviving spouse that meets the qualified terminable interest trust (QTIP) rules found in Code § 2056(b)(7) (the spouse must have the right to all income during the spouse's life, no distribution of trust principal may be made to anyone other than the surviving spouse, and the executor must elect to have the trust treated as a QTIP trust).

  - **Example:** A husband dies with a will that establishes a testamentary trust for his wife's benefit. The trust terms provide that the trustee must distribute the income to the wife at least annually for life, that no principal distributions may be made to anyone other than the wife, and that, upon the wife's death, the trustee must distribute the principal to the husband's children from a prior marriage. The husband's executors make a QTIP election on the husband's estate tax return. Under these circumstances, the fair market value of the trust assets will qualify for the estate tax marital deduction.[13]

13. And recall that, under Code § 2044, when the wife later dies, this property will be included in her gross estate, because it previously qualified for the estate tax marital deduction.

- State Death Taxes (Code § 2058). In 2023, there were sixteen states that levied an estate tax or an inheritance tax. On the federal estate tax return, these taxes remain deductible.

(c) Exclusion Amounts, Tax Rates, and Filing Requirements. There are several remaining facets of the federal estate tax that require further explication, including the exclusion amount, tax rates, and filing requirements.

The applicable exclusion amount (i.e., the amount the Code excludes from estate tax) starts with a fixed dollar amount (in 2023, it was $12,920,000), known as the basic exclusion amount, which is annually adjusted for inflation. The applicable exclusion amount also will include, if applicable, a deceased spouse's unused exclusion amount. To illustrate, if a husband predeceases his wife, and if the husband's executor files an estate tax return and does not elect out of portability, the surviving wife will also have her husband's unused exclusion amount. Thus, in the case in which a husband dies in 2023, and assuming he had not made any prior taxable gifts and he bequeaths his entire estate to his wife, assuming a timely filed estate tax return is filed for the husband, the surviving spouse's applicable exclusion amount would be $25,840,000.

Over the course of the past century, tax rates and tax rate schedules related to the estate tax have varied tremendously. For the last several years, however, despite its historic progressive rate structure, the estate tax rate has remained at a flat 40%. Also, another important item to bear in mind is that the computation of the estate tax requires a de facto two-step process: first, all prior taxable gifts made after 1976 must be added to the estate tax base (i.e., the property owned by the decedent at death) and a tentative estate tax computed on this amount (Code § 2001(b)(1)(B)), and from this tentative tax is then subtracted "the aggregate amount of tax which would have been payable under Chapter 12 with respect to gifts made by the decedent." Code § 2001(b)(2). Do you understand why Congress instituted this two-step process?

Estate tax returns are filed on a Form 706 (U.S. Estate (and Generation-Skipping Transfer) Tax Return) and such returns are due 9 months after a decedent's death. Code § 6075(a). Taxpayers may, however, obtain an automatic six-month extension of time to file (6081(a)) and, in cases of undue hardship, extend the time for payment up to ten years. Code § 6161(a)(2).

(d) Estate Tax Minimization Strategies. Since 1981 when the estate tax marital deduction became unlimited, taxpayers' testamentary estate plans have been commonly populated with two kinds of trusts: Marital Trusts and Bypass Trusts. Although each trust form may share common characteristics and terms, each aims to achieve different objectives.

Consider first a Marital Trust. Its central purpose is to establish a trust for the primary benefit of the surviving spouse and to comply with the statutory requirements to qualify for the estate tax marital deduction. While the assets comprising a marital trust will not be subject to the estate tax when the first spouse dies, the assets comprising such trust when the surviving spouse dies will be included in his or her estate for estate tax purposes.

Here's an example of what the salient provisions of a QTIP trust (one type of marital trust) may look like:

> **ADMINISTRATION OF THE MARITAL TRUST.** The Trustee will administer the Marital Trust in accordance with the following terms and conditions:
>
> **(i) PAYMENT OF INCOME.** During the life of my wife, Elaine, my Trustee shall pay to Elaine or apply for her benefit all of the net income of the Marital Trust, in convenient installments, but not less frequently than quarter-annually.
>
> **(ii) PAYMENT OF PRINCIPAL.** During Elaine's life my Trustee shall pay to Elaine or apply for her benefit such amounts from the principal of the Marital Trust as my Trustee considers desirable for Elaine's health, education, support, and maintenance.
>
> **(iii) TERMINATION OF THE MARITAL TRUST.**
>
> **(a) Distribution of Income and Principal.** Upon Elaine's death, all accrued and undistributed income and all principal of the Marital Trust remaining upon Elaine's death shall be added to the principal of the By-Pass Trust and administered in accordance with its terms and provisions as set forth below.
>
> **(b) Taxes Attributable to QTIP Property.** Prior to the termination of the Marital Trust, my Trustee shall pay, either directly to the appropriate taxing authority or to the executors or personal representatives of Elaine's estate, as my Trustee considers advisable, the amount requested and certified by such executors or personal representatives as being equal to the amount by which the estate and inheritance taxes assessed by reason of Elaine's death are increased as a result of the inclusion of the principal and undistributed income of the Marital Trust in Elaine's estate for such tax purposes.

Next consider a By-Pass Trust. The primary purpose of a by-pass trust is to hold in trust an amount equal to the first decedent spouse's applicable exclusion amount and to structure such trust so that it will not be included in the surviving spouse's estate. (Prior to portability, if the first decedent spouse did not use his or her applicable exclusion amount, the ability to shelter such amount from the estate tax was wasted.) A by-pass trust enables a decedent spouse to place assets in trust that will not be subject to the estate tax because of the decedent's available exclusion amount and will not be included in the surviving spouse's estate upon his or her later death. Thus, this trust may be said to "by-pass" the surviving spouse's estate. This type of trust sometimes is referred to as a "credit-shelter" trust. With the advent of portability (whereby a decedent spouse's unused exclusion amount can be transferred to a surviving spouse), by-pass trusts do not enjoy the same popularity that they once had. (They do remain popular, however, in those states which have retained their estate tax regimes and have thus far eschewed portability.)

The following example provides terms that one may find in a bypass trust:

> **ADMINISTRATION OF THE BY-PASS TRUST.** The Trustee will administer the By-Pass Trust in accordance with the following terms and conditions:
>
> **(i) PAYMENT OF INCOME AND PRINCIPAL.** During the life of my wife, Elaine, my Trustee shall pay to or apply on benefit of (i) Elaine or (ii) my issue such amounts of income and principal of the By-Pass Trust as my Trustee considers desirable to provide for Elaine's health, education, support and maintenance.
>
> **(ii) TERMINATION OF THE BY-PASS TRUST.** Upon Elaine's death, all accrued and undistributed income and all principal of the By-Pass Trust remaining upon Elaine's death shall be distributed to my then living issue, per stirpes. If no issue of mine survives Elaine, then the Trustee will distribute such property to those persons who would have taken, and in such shares as they would have taken, such property as if I had owned only such property and died intestate a resident of the State of New Jersey immediately after Elaine.

Questions

1. Suppose a taxpayer has exhausted her lifetime exclusion amount and has $14 million. Assuming a flat 40% gift tax rate, what is the maximum amount the taxpayer may transfer to her daughter (and still have the necessary liquidity to pay any gift tax owed)? Assuming a flat 40% estate tax rate, what is the maximum amount this same taxpayer can bequeath to her daughter? Does this example help illustrate why the estate tax is often referred to as being tax inclusive while the gift tax is often referred to as being tax exclusive?
2. In question 1 above, would your answer change if the taxpayer was ever married? What, if anything, would you need to know?
3. To what extent, if any, are the following assets / interests includible in the taxpayer's gross estate?
    a. Taxpayer owns title to a personal residence with a fair market value of $1 million jointly with his sister.
    b. Same as a., but joint title is held with his wife.
    c. Taxpayer owns title to a $50,000 painting which is insured against theft. Would your answer change if the painting had not been insured?

d. Taxpayer is the income beneficiary of a trust that holds $1 million of assets. Would your answer change if the taxpayer also held a lifetime special power of appointment? Would your answer change if, in addition to the lifetime right to income and the possession of the special power of appointment, the taxpayer also held a testamentary general power of appointment?

e. The taxpayer establishes a revocable trust and names herself a beneficiary. Would your answer change if the taxpayer didn't name herself a beneficiary?

4. In 2023, a never-married taxpayer dies with a gross estate of $22,120,000 and $200,000 of deductible estate administration expenses. Compute the estate tax due. On what form is the estate tax reported and when is this return due?

5. Why might someone prefer a QTIP trust over a general power of appointment trust?

6. Specify one major advantage and disadvantage associated with a by-pass trust.

7. In light of congressional tax reforms that significantly increased the applicable exclusion amount, what effect might this have on lifetime and testamentary trust formation?

C. The Generation-Skipping Transfer Tax

Internal Revenue Code: Sections 2601, 2602, 2611(a), 2612(a), (b), (c), 2613(a), (b), 2621(a), 2622(a), 2623, 2631(a), 2632(a), 2641(a), 2642(a)(1)-(2), 2651(a)-(b).

The generation-skipping transfer (GST) tax is levied, in addition to the gift and estate tax, on transfers made to so-called skip persons. Skip persons come in the following two varieties:

- Any "natural person which is 2 or more generations below the generation assignment of the transferor." Code § 2613(a)(1).
- A trust in which "all interests in such trust are held by skip persons" or "there is no person holding an interest in such trust, and at no time after such transfer may a distribution . . . be made from such trust to a non-skip person." Code § 2613(a)(2).

Using the two aforementioned definitions, for purposes of learning and this textbook, skip persons are thus either (i) grandchildren or more remote lineal descendants (e.g., great grandchildren) or (ii) trusts established in which grandchildren (or more remote lineal descendants) are the only beneficiaries.

A little history explains the origin of the GST tax. Over a century ago, when the estate tax was enacted, wealthy taxpayers decided that rather than gift or bequeath their assets to their children (aka non-skip persons) they would instead establish lifetime trusts for the benefit of their children and, due to the Rule Against

Perpetuities,[14] the trust corpus would ultimately vest with their grandchildren or great-grandchildren. By going through this exercise, no part of the trust would be included in a child's gross estate, because each child only possessed a life estate, thereby escaping the reach of the estate tax at the generational level of their children, potentially saving vast sums of tax dollars. Many states have modified their Rule Against Perpetuities making it easier for these types of trusts to continue for many generations, thereby allowing wealthy families to escape the reach of the estate tax for multiple generations; these types of trusts are sometimes referred to as "dynasty trusts." To prevent the easy escape from the estate tax, in 1986, Congress enacted Chapter 13 to the Code (an earlier attempt to address this problem in 1976 was retroactively repealed). Aptly entitled "Generation-Skipping Transfer Tax," the imposition of this tax was designed to ensure that a transfer tax was levied at each generational level. This sentiment is eloquently captured in a one-paragraph summary regarding the origin of the GST tax.

The Estate Tax: Ninety Years and Counting[15]

By Darien B. Jacobson, Brian G. Raub & Barry W. Johnson

> The 1976 tax reform package [the forerunner to the 1986 reform package] introduced a tax on generation-skipping transfer trusts (GSTs). Prior to passage of the act, a transferor, for example, could create a testamentary trust and direct that the income from the trust be paid to his or her children during their lives and then, upon the children's deaths, that the principal be paid to the transferor's grandchildren. The trust assets included in the transferor's estate would be taxed upon the transferor's death. Then, any trust assets included in the grandchildren's estates would be taxed at their deaths. However, the intervening beneficiaries, the transferor's children in this example, would pay no estate tax on the trust assets, even though they had enjoyed the income derived from those assets. Congress responded to the GST tax leakage by creating a series of rules that were designed to treat the termination of the intervening beneficiaries' interests as a taxable event. Under these rules, a grantor was allowed to transfer up to $1,000,000 to a GST tax-free, with amounts over that taxed at the highest marginal estate tax rate. As with the gift tax exclusion, married persons may combine their GST tax exemptions, allowing couples a $2-million exemption. Overall, the GST tax "ensures that the transmission of hereditary wealth is taxed at each generation level." Boris I. Bittker & Elias Clark, Federal Estate and Gift Taxation (1990), p. 30.

---

14. This rule essentially declares that property interests must vest within a life in being at the time of trust creation plus 21 years. *See, e.g.*, William B. Stoebuck & Dale A. Whitman, The Law of Property § 3.17 (3d. ed. 2000) ("[n]o interest is good unless it must vest, if at all, no later than twenty-one years after some life in being at the creation of the interest.").

15. SOI Bulletin (2007), p. 123, available at https://www.irs.gov/pub/irs-soi/ninetyestate.pdf.

Taxable Events and Tax Base. The Code triggers application of the GST tax when one of three events occurs. The first, known as a *direct skip*, is when a transfer is made directly to a skip person (e.g., a taxpayer makes a $100,000 gift to a grandchild or a trust established for that grandchild's benefit). Code § 2612(c). The second, known as a *taxable distribution*, is when a transfer is made from a trust to a skip person (e.g., a trust established for the benefit of the taxpayer's descendants makes a distribution to one of the taxpayer's grandchildren). Code § 2612(b). The third, known as a *taxable termination*, is when a trust terminates ("by death, lapse of time, release of power, or otherwise") and the trust property vests with one or more skip persons (e.g., upon the death of the taxpayer's child, the trust continues for the benefit of the taxpayer's grandchildren). Code § 2612(a).

The GST tax is levied on the taxable amount. In the case of direct skips, the taxable amount is "the value of property received by the transferee." Code § 2623. In the case of taxable distributions, the taxable amount is "the value of property received by the transferee, reduced by expenses incurred by the transferee in connection with the determination, collection, or refund of the tax. . . ." Code § 2621. In the case of taxable terminations, the taxable amount is "the value of all property with respect to which the taxable termination has occurred reduced by [traditional trust administration expenses]." Code § 2622.

Exemptions and Tax Rates. The Code provides a generous GST tax exemption currently equal to the "basic exclusion amount." Code § 2631(c). This amount is set forth in Code § 2010(c) and is equal to $12,920,000 (2023) and annually adjusted for inflation. Taxpayers are at liberty to allocate this exemption amount to lifetime and testamentary transfers that are made outright or in trust (Code § 2632(a)); to safeguard against taxpayer mistakes, the Code also has an elaborate system of automatically allocating GST tax exemption that is beyond the scope of this textbook. Code § 2632(b)–(c).

The GST tax rate is unique. It engenders a computational process that is intertwined with the exemption amount. More specifically, there is no one tax rate or schedule. Instead, the Code defines the "applicable rate" in terms of the following formula:

$$\text{The maximum Federal estate tax rate (currently 40\%)} \times \text{the inclusion ratio with respect to the transfer}$$

Code § 2641(a). A prerequisite to being able to compute the applicable rate is to know the *inclusion ratio*, which the Code defines as follows: One less the applicable fraction (albeit a bit oversimplified, the numerator of this fraction is equal to the GST exemption allocated to the transfer and the denominator is equal to the fair market value of the property the taxpayer is transferring). Code § 2642(a).

An example helps illustrate how to compute the GST tax. Suppose a taxpayer transfers $15 million outright to her granddaughter. Suppose further that, at the time, the basic exclusion amount was $10 million. Under this set of assumptions, the inclusion ratio would equal 1/3 (i.e., 1–$10 million / $15 million) and thus the applicable rate would be .40 × 1/3 or approximately 13.33%. Accordingly, this transfer would generate a $2 million GST tax burden (i.e., $15 million × .1333). (Had this transfer been made in trust for the benefit of the skip person (here, the taxpayer's granddaughter) rather than outright, the same GST tax consequences would have befallen the taxpayer.)

Filing Requirements and Deadlines. The filing requirements associated with GST transfer tax compliance vary depending upon the nature of the GST tax transfer.

In the case of direct skips during lifetime, taxpayers who make such gifts must complete a Form 709 (United States Gift (and Generation-Skipping Transfer) Tax Return) reflecting the transfer; decedents who make direct skip bequests trigger the responsibility of their executors or personal representatives to complete a Form 706 (United States Estate (and Generation-Skipping Transfer) Tax Return) reflecting the transfer. (The filing deadlines for gift and estate tax returns are specified above.)

In the case of taxable distributions, the administrative compliance burden is bifurcated: the trustee must file an informational Form 706-GS(D-1) (Notification of Distribution From a Generation-Skipping Trust) by April 15 of the year following the calendar year in which the distribution was made and provide a copy to each distributee; once in hand, each distributee must file Form 706-GS(D) (Generation-Skipping Transfer Tax Return for Distributions) by the fifteenth day of the fourth month after the close of the taxable year of the taxable distribution.

Finally, in the case of taxable terminations, the administrative compliance burden falls on the trustee, who must file Form 706-GS(T) (Generation-Skipping Transfer Tax Return For Terminations) by the fifteenth day of the fourth month after the close of the trust's taxable year, unless an extension is granted.

Tax Planning Strategies. While there are many ways in which taxpayers seek to best use their GST tax exemption, a popular technique is the use of so-called dynasty trusts.[16] This technique has become increasingly popular as many states have either eliminated their rules against perpetuities or greatly elongated permissible trust terms.

Dynasty trusts share many of the same characteristics of other trusts. The trust terms, for example, typically contain Crummey withdrawal rights and grant a trust beneficiary a right to trust income. In addition, the trustee is often instructed to make distributions in accordance with a beneficiary's need to meet expenses for health, education, maintenance, and support (colloquially known as a HEMS standard, and these are "ascertainable standards" under Code § 2041).

---

16. Robert H. Sitkoff & Max M. Schanzenbach, *Perpetuities or Taxes? Explaining the Rise of the Perpetual Trust*, 27 Cardozo L. Rev. 2465 (2006).

But there is one characteristic that truly distinguishes a dynasty trust from other trusts, namely, its longevity. At no point during a trust beneficiary's lifetime do the assets of the trust vest; instead, the trust assets cascade down to the next generation and are once again held for the benefit of the next generation in such a manner so as to avoid the trust assets being included in any beneficiary's gross estate. And so on and so forth down the generational line. Taxpayers who initially establish such trusts allocate sufficient GST exemption to ensure that such trusts have a zero inclusion ratio; a zero inclusion ratio insulates the trust assets from ever bearing transfer tax after the initial funding, regardless of their future value. Furthermore, because the vast majority of states have repealed or extended the duration of their Rules Against Perpetuities,[17] these trusts may theoretically remain in existence for many millennia to come.

Questions

1. In general terms, describe each of the following events:
   a. Direct Skip
   b. Taxable Distribution
   c. Taxable Termination
2. Why do taxpayers seek to ensure that the trusts they create have a zero inclusion ratio?
3. In each of the following scenarios, discuss whether and when a GST tax may be applicable:
   a. A taxpayer transfers $1 million to his great-granddaughter.
   b. A taxpayer transfers $1 million into a trust that is established for the benefit of the taxpayer's son and, upon the son's demise, the trust assets then pass in further trust for the benefit of the son's children.
   c. During the son's lifetime, the trustee in problem 4b distributes $100,000 to each of the son's children.
4. What two factors have made dynasty trusts increasingly popular in the last twenty years?
5. When selecting trustees for a dynasty trust, what considerations come into play?
6. Assume the GST tax exemption is equal to $10 million. If the taxpayer makes a $25 million gift to his grandson, how much GST tax must he remit? How much gift tax does the taxpayer owe (assuming the lifetime exclusion amount at the time of the gift were also $10 million)? What tax form does the taxpayer use to report this gift and when is it due?

---

17. Robert H. Sitkoff & Max M. Schanzenbach, *Jurisdictional Competition for Trust Funds: An Empirical Analysis of Perpetuities and Tax*, 115 Yale L.J. 356 (2005).

7. Assume the GST tax exemption is equal to $10 million. If the taxpayer dies with a $25 million net estate and bequeaths the entirety of it to his grandson, how much estate and GST tax must his estate remit (assuming the lifetime exclusion amount at the time of death were also $10 million)? What tax form does the estate use to report the transfer and when is it due?

III. Decedent's Final Income Tax Return and Important Elections

When taxpayers die, new taxpayers, namely, their estates, come into existence. To handle estate affairs, a fiduciary must ordinarily be appointed. To fulfill this role, if the taxpayer dies testate (i.e., with a will), an appropriate court will appoint an executor or personal representative (to "execute" the will); conversely, if a taxpayer dies intestate (i.e., without a will), an appropriate court will appoint an administrator (to "administer" the estate). For purposes of the rest of this Chapter, we will assume that the decedent died testate and the court appointed executors to handle the estate's affairs, although, had the decedent instead died intestate and the court appointed an administrator or administrators to handle the estate's affairs, our analysis would be identical.

Once estate executors have been appointed, they should immediately submit a Form SS-4 (Application for an Employer Identification Number) to the IRS. Submission of this form will enable estate executors to secure a taxpayer identification number which they can then furnish to all income payers with whom the decedent held investments (e.g., banks and brokerage firms). Another item executors should submit to the IRS is Form 56 (Notice Concerning Fiduciary Relationship). Submission of this form puts the IRS on notice that the estate executors have all of the same powers, rights, duties, and privileges of the decedent and that, going forward, the IRS should send all tax notices to them.

Among the many responsibilities estate fiduciaries are charged with, for purposes of this Chapter, two are paramount. First, as discussed below in Subsection A, executors must timely prepare and complete a taxpayer's final income tax return. Second, as discussed below in Subsection B, executors must consider the advantages and disadvantages associated with making myriad important elections.

A. Taxpayer's Final Income Tax Return

Internal Revenue Code: Sections 443(a)(2), 6012(a), 6081(a).

Treasury Regulations: Sections 1.443-1(a)(2), 1.6012-3(b)(1), 1.6013-1(a)(1), 1.6153-1(a)(4), 1.6654-2(e)(7)(i).

One responsibility charged to executors is that they are liable for failing to file a decedent's final income tax return (Form 1040 (U.S. Income Tax Return)). This return is due April 15th of the year following death. Code § 6012(a). However, executors who timely submit a Form 4868 (Application for Automatic Extension of Time to File U.S. Individual Income Tax Return), are able to extend the return due date to October 15. Code § 6081(a).

There are two items that distinguish a decedent's final income tax return from his prior tax returns and two items that remain constant.

Differences:

1. First, whereas a normal tax year is 365 days, here, the tax year is shorter (unless the decedent died on December 31). It starts on January 1 and ends on the date of death. Code § 443(a)(2).
2. Second, the Code eschews the need to make estimated tax payments after the date of death. Treas. Reg. § 1.6153-1(a)(4); Treas. Reg. § 1.6654-2(e)(7)(i).

Similarities:

1. First, the decedent's final tax return should include all income and deductions based on the accounting method used by the decedent while living. Treas. Reg. § 1.443-1(a)(2), Treas. Reg. § 1.6012-3(b)(1).
2. Second, assuming the decedent taxpayer was on the cash method of accounting (as are the vast majority of taxpayers), all cash actually or constructively received before death should be reported, including uncashed checks (e.g., *Commissioner v. Kahler*, 18 T.C. 31 (1952)), credited interest (Treas. Reg. § 1.451-2(a), (b)), and declared dividends made subject to the demand of the shareholder (Treas. Reg. § 1.451-2(b)).

In terms of actual tax return submission, the governing rules are fairly straightforward. The decedent's executors should file the income tax return in question and sign their names in their fiduciary capacities (e.g., John and Jane Smith, Co-Executors of the Estate of Mary Smith, Deceased). If a surviving spouse has not remarried by the end of year which includes decedent's date of death, the estate executors and the surviving spouse may file a joint tax return (query whether this is a wise decision since the filing of a joint return triggers joint and several liability). Treas. Reg. § 1.6013-1(a)(1). Usually, executors write "Deceased" twice: first, along the top of decedent's final tax return and, second, in the block where the taxpayer's name is ordinarily placed (along with the date of death).

With these basics now in mind, consider a series of special rules. These rules pertain to items of income and deductions, the application of which depend upon each decedent taxpayer's unique circumstances.

- Pass-Through Entity Ownership: Executors must allocate income and deductions between the decedent shareholder/member and his estate. S corporations and partnerships have the following choice:
  - They may elect to pro-rate the income and deductions based on the number of days during the tax year before and after death occurred (Code § 1377(a)(1) and Treas. Reg. § 1.706-(c)(2)(ii)).

  - Alternatively, they may hypothetically close the entity's books on the date of death and specifically allocate income and deductions accordingly. Code § 1377(a)(2) and Treas. Reg. § 1.706-1(c)(2)(ii)).
- Trust Income: Executors must only include those trust distributions that were made prior to death and which were comprised of distributable net income (see Chapter 3).
- Wages / Salaries / IRAs / Retirement Plans: Amounts paid before death are included on the decedent's final tax return (Code § 61); amounts paid after a decedent's death are commonly known as Income in Respect of a Decedent (see Chapter 8) and reported by the recipient of such income. Code § 691(a).
- Series E and EE Bonds: Assuming the decedent taxpayer had elected to report the interest each year it accrued, the decedent's final income tax return must include the increase in value of such bonds. 31 C.F.R. § 351.8(b).
- Medical Expenses: The decedent's medical expenses paid (i) during the year of death or (ii) within one year of death are deductible. Code § 213(a), (c). (To claim this deduction on the decedent's final income tax return, the decedent's executors must supply a written statement that affirms that such deductions have neither been taken nor will they be taken on the decedent's estate tax return.) Code § 213(c)(2); Treas. Reg. § 1.213-1(d)(2).
- Capital Loss Carryovers and Net Operating Losses: Executors may use these losses on the decedent's final income tax return; however, whichever losses cannot be used are extinguished and do not pass to the estate or any other putative estate beneficiary. Treas. Reg. § 1.1212-1(c), Rev. Rul. 74-175, 1974-1 C.B. 52.
- Passive Loss Deductions: Such losses are permitted on a decedent's final income tax return, but to the extent the property giving rise to the loss had a basis increase due to the application of Code § 1014, the amount of the allowable loss is correspondingly reduced. Code § 469(g)(2).
- Annuity Deductions: Executors of a decedent who has not recovered his full investment may deduct the unrecovered investment as an allowable itemized deduction. Code § 72(b)(3). (Note that for tax years 2018 through 2025, miscellaneous itemized deductions are disallowed.)
- Charitable Contributions: Charitable contributions that exceed certain thresholds under the Code can be carried forward up to five years and used in future years (Code § 170(d)); however, in the year of a decedent's death, these unused carryforwards must either be used or they are extinguished. Treas. Reg. § 1.170A-10(d)(4)(iii).
- Tax Credits: The executors may use available tax credits on the decedent's final income tax return; however, to the extent they are not so used, the Code does not provide that they carry over to any other taxpayer (i.e., they are thus lost).

When executors must prepare the decedent's final income tax return, consider one of the most critical issues that may arise. Many payers who owe the decedent money (e.g., banks, investment companies, and employers) may not know of the taxpayer's death until weeks or months after death has occurred. As a result, tax information returns such as Form 1099s and W-2s are often inaccurate; they report income inuring to the decedent after the decedent's date of death.[18] These inaccurate information returns should be handled in one of two ways:

- Consistent with the amounts specified on these information returns, these dollar figures should be reported in their entirety on the decedent's final income tax return. The decedent executors should then subtract the amounts that accurately belong on the estate's income tax return (Form 1041). (This subtraction process is usually done either on a Schedule B of the Form 1040 or, alternatively, by attaching a schedule to the tax return which shows the allocation process.)
- Sometimes erroneous information returns are issued in the year following the decedent's death (when the decedent's final income tax return has already been filed), inaccurately portraying that the decedent had earned income. In those cases, the income reflected on these information returns should instead populate the estate's income tax return (Form 1041), with a statement attached indicating the decedent's Social Security number and specifying that its proper inclusion is on the estate's income tax return because the decedent's final income tax return (Form 1040) had already been filed.

B. Elections That Estate Executors Must Make or Consider

Internal Revenue Code: Sections 441(a), (b), 642(g), 645.

Treasury Regulations: Sections 1.441-1(b), (c), 1.642(g)-2, 1.662(c)-1.

When a taxpayer dies and a new taxpayer comes into existence, namely, the decedent's estate, there are myriad elections that an executor must consider. These elections often will have tax consequences, and executors risk being surcharged by estate beneficiaries if they fail to give proper consideration to tax elections and such failure causes taxes or expenses to otherwise be incurred.

Below are three important elections that every executor must consider.

Fiscal vs. Calendar Year Election. When an estate comes into existence, the executors can elect to be either a calendar or fiscal year taxpayer. If the latter is chosen, the initial fiscal year cannot be longer than a 12-month period and must end on the last day of a month (other than December). Treas. Reg. § 1.441-1(b), (c). For example, if a decedent dies on July 17, 2024, his executors can choose to be a calendar year taxpayer or, alternatively, a fiscal year taxpayer, but not a fiscal year ending later than on June 30, 2025.

18. In the vast majority of cases, this income constitutes income in respect of a decedent (IRD) (see Chapter 8) and, as such, should be reported on the estate's Form 1041.

The tax year selected by an executor will have consequences to the estate beneficiaries. More specifically, beneficiaries must report their share of estate income resulting from distributions to them in the tax year within which the estate tax year ends. Treas. Reg. §1.662(c)-1.

For example, suppose a decedent dies on February 1, 2024, and the estate elects to use a January 31 fiscal year and invests in interest-bearing certificates of deposit. Also suppose that the executor makes a distribution to the estate's sole beneficiary in November 2024, and the amount distributed is greater than all of the estate income ultimately earned by the estate for its tax year ending January 31, 2025. The beneficiary will be deemed to have received the estate's income on the last day of the estate's fiscal year (i.e., January 31, 2025) and, as a result, the beneficiary will report this income on the beneficiary's 2025 tax return notwithstanding that the beneficiary received the distribution in 2024. As such, even though the majority of such income was largely earned in 2024, the tax on such income is deferred to the due date of the beneficiary's 2025 income tax return (i.e., April 15, 2026).

The Qualified Revocable Trust Election. By way of background, in many places throughout the country, taxpayers actively seek to avoid probate (probate is the process by which a decedent's estate and final affairs are administered). Depending upon the state and county in which the taxpayer was domiciled at death, the reasons for avoiding probate can vary (i.e., for a whole host of reasons, the process can be long, expensive, and cumbersome).

A common mechanism to avoid the probate process is the use of a revocable trust, because assets owned by the trustee of a revocable trust are not subject to the probate process.[19] Because taxpayers can and often do serve as sole trustees and beneficiaries of such trusts and can revoke them at any time, they maintain complete asset control. For tax purposes, since the taxpayer and the trust are truly one another's alter egos, the Code ignores the trust's independent existence (see Chapter 6) and the taxpayer must, on his own tax return, report all of the trust's income, deductions, and credits.

Like all mortal beings, taxpayers who establish revocable trusts ultimately die. By its terms, a revocable trust then becomes irrevocable. As such, the Code treats the trust as a new taxpayer, subject to the same tax fate of all trusts under Subchapter J.

But estates have some favorable tax provisions not available to trusts. For example, an estate may elect a fiscal tax year, while a trust must have a calendar tax year. (This sentiment probably reflects congressional sympathies that a taxpayer's death is occasion to be magnanimous.) This bias puts taxpayers who used a revocable trust to avoid the probate process possibly at a tax disadvantage relative to those who did not.

---

19. Decedents who have established a revocable trust also will have a "pour over" will. The terms of a pour over will essentially declare that any assets a decedent owns and are subject to the terms of the will are to be transferred into the revocable trust and administered in accordance with its terms.

To level the playing field, Code § 645 permits taxpayers to elect to treat a decedent's revocable trust as part of the estate, rather than as a stand-alone irrevocable trust. Taxpayers choosing to make this election use Form 8855. The trustee should submit this form by the related estate's tax return submission due date and, if there is no estate (i.e., all of the decedent's assets were titled in the name of the trust, obviating the probate process and negating the need to create an estate), by the due date of the Form 1041 for the first tax year of the electing trust,[20] including extensions. Once this election is made, it is irrevocable.

The advantages associated with making this election are numerous and include, but are not limited to, the following:

- The trust, as part of the estate, will be on the same tax year as the estate, which may be a fiscal year rather than being forced to be a calendar year taxpayer;
- Eliminates the need to make estimated payments for two years (Code § 6654(l); Treas. Reg. § 1.645-1(e)(4));
- If the trust owns shares in an S corporation, it does not have to make a special qualified subchapter S election or an electing small business trust election while it is considered part of the estate (Code § 1361(b)(1));
- Since the trust is treated as part of the estate, the charitable set aside deduction is available (Code § 642(c));
- Up to $25,000 of passive loss deductions is permitted for rental real estate activities (Code § 469(i)(4));
- The satisfaction of a pecuniary bequest with loss property (i.e., tax basis in excess of fair market value) will not be disallowed (Code § 267(b)(13));
- The income, deductions, and credits of the estate and electing trust can be combined and a single fiduciary income tax return filed for the combined entities; and
- The estate can claim the $600 deduction afforded to estates in Code § 642(b)(1).[21]

If a Code § 645 election is made, it remains effective for the longer of (i) two years from the decedent's date of death or (ii) in cases when an estate tax return is filed, until six months after the date of the final determination of the federal estate tax liability. Code § 645(b)(2); Treas. Reg. § 1.645-1(f)(2).

When the election term expires, and assuming the trust continues in existence, the electing trust and estate (if any) are treated as distributing their assets to a new trust. All of the items of income, including capital gains, that are attributable to the electing trust are deemed distributed to the new trust and included in

---

20. As indicated by the section entitled "Fiscal vs. Calendar Year," estates may elect a fiscal tax-year while trusts must have a calendar tax year.

21. Note that, in some instances, making the election may prove disadvantageous because if the trust stayed separate, the estate would still get the $600 deduction, but the trust would get either a $100 or $300 deduction as well.

its Distributable Net Income (DNI) (see Chapter 3). Going forward, the new trust should secure and use its own Taxpayer Identification Number for income tax reporting purposes.

Administration Expense Deduction Election. When a taxpayer dies, there are many administrative expenses estates incur. Some of these expenses are personal in nature (e.g., casket purchase, gravestone, and funeral flower arrangements); other expenses are more generic in nature (e.g., accounting expenses to prepare the estate's income tax return, heating costs to ensure that the water pipes in the decedent's home do not freeze, and executor commissions to remunerate the fiduciary for faithfully overseeing the estate's proper administration).

A preliminary question is what estate administration expenses are deductible. In the income tax sphere, Code § 212 permits the deductibility of many administration expenses. Code § 212 reads as follows:

SEC. 212. EXPENSES FOR PRODUCTION OF INCOME.

In the case of an individual, there shall be allowed as a deduction all the ordinary and necessary expenses paid or incurred during the taxable year—

(1) for the production or collection of income;

(2) for the management, conservation, or maintenance of property held for the production of income; or

(3) in connection with the determination, collection, or refund of any tax.

In the estate tax sphere, relative to its income tax counterpart (i.e., Code § 212), Code § 2053(a) provides a broader range of deductions. It states as follows:

SEC. 2053. EXPENSES, INDEBTEDNESS, AND TAXES.

(a) General Rule—For purposes of the tax imposed by section 2001, the value of the taxable estate shall be determined by deducting for the value of the gross estate such amounts—

(1) for funeral expenses,

(2) for administration expenses,

(3) for claims against the estate, and

(4) for unpaid mortgages on, or any indebtedness in respect of, property where the value of the decedent's interest therein, undiminished by such mortgage or indebtedness, is included in the value of the gross estate, as are allowable by the laws of the jurisdiction, whether within or without the United States, under which the estate is being administered.

In light of the differences between Code §§ 212 and 2053(a), there are some deductions that may only appear on the estate tax return of the estate. In particular, funeral expenses, such as those associated with the casket, flowers, and repast are deductible on the estate tax return (if any), but never on the estate's income tax return. *Estate of Orville F. Yetter*, 35 T.C. 737 (1961).

But with respect to many other administration expenses (accounting fees, appraisal fees, attorney fees, fiduciary fees, and investment management expenses), an executor may deduct such expenses on either the decedent's estate tax return or the estate's income tax return. Code § 642(g). Indeed, executors are at liberty to take a portion of such fees on one return and the balance on the other return. Treas. Reg. § 1.642(g)-2.

To make a Code § 642(g) election requires more than proper numerical reporting. In addition, the Treasury regulations require that "a statement, in duplicate" be submitted that declares that the same expenses will not also appear on the decedent's estate tax return. Treas. Reg. § 1.642(g)-1. (Neither the Code nor Treasury regulations require that a similar sort of statement appear on or with a decedent's estate tax return (Form 706).) The regulations simply require that this statement be filed any time prior to the expiration of the statute of limitations with respect to the income tax return on which the expenses were deducted. Commentators have noted that the requirement to file the statement may be illusory, because non-compliance means that the statute of limitations has expired.[22]

All of this information still leaves unanswered the important question on which tax return should these administration expenses be deducted. Depending upon decedent's particular circumstances, answers will vary. If no estate tax return needs to be filed or, alternatively, there is no estate tax due (e.g., due to use of the estate tax marital or charitable deductions), the answer is almost always on the estate's income tax return. However, if an estate tax return needs to be filed and estate taxes are due, the decision whether to deduct estate administration expenses on the estate tax return will vary based upon a number of factors. Such factors to consider include, but are not limited to, whether there is also a state estate tax return due and whether the income the estate generates is also subject to state income tax. In the Technological Age that we now exist in, most practitioners will often prepare "dummy returns" of both the Forms 706 and 1041 and elect to deduct administrative expenses on the tax return that yields the greater tax savings.

Questions

1. A taxpayer dies on June 30. Regarding the items below, how should the executor treat them for tax purposes:
    a. For the first half of the year, the taxpayer earned $100,000 salary, $10,000 of which was direct deposited in the taxpayer's bank account after death.
    b. Over the course of the full calendar year, taxpayer earned $100,000 of income interest invested in a certificate of deposit.
    c. The taxpayer was an LLC member and receives a Form K-1 reflecting $100,000 of limited liability company earnings for the year.

22. Reg. § 1.642(g)-1(a)(2) provides that the statement should be filed no later than "any time before the expiration of the statutory period applicable to the taxable year the deduction is sought."

   d. To treat the taxpayer's medical ailment, for the first six months of the year, he received experimental medical treatment that cost $100,000 and which the taxpayer's executors paid in mid-July.
   e. Under Code § 1212, in the year of death, the taxpayer had a $100,000 capital loss carryforward.
   f. Under Code § 172, in the year of death, the taxpayer had a $100,000 net operating loss.
   g. Under Code § 469, in the year of death, the taxpayer had a $100,000 passive activity loss from a prior tax year that had been suspended from a partnership investment in which the taxpayer had a $50,000 adjusted basis and the date of death value was $75,000.
2. Since the vast majority of income tax returns are now filed electronically, what is the protocol for an executor "signing" a decedent's final tax return?
3. Elections:
   a. What factors should an executor consider when choosing whether an estate should be a fiscal or calendar year taxpayer?
   b. Making a Code § 645 election appears to always make sense. Nevertheless, are there circumstances when not making such an election makes sense, too?
   c. Assuming a taxpayer's estate incurs legal and accounting fees that total $100,000, on which tax return should an executor deduct these fees and why?

Chapter 2

Subchapter J: The Basics

I. Introduction

Once you understand the tax-related and other forces driving trust formation and the direction estate planning may take, it is time to stretch your knowledge base and grasp the fundamentals of Subchapter J. Subchapter J starts with a simple supposition: trusts and estates should be taxed in the same manner as an individual taxpayer. But the stark reality is that trusts and estates are not individuals, and their distinguishing features require careful consideration.

This chapter's goal is to highlight many of the fundamental distinctions between how, for income tax purposes, the Code treats individual taxpayers versus its treatment of trusts and estates. Some of these distinctions are relatively easy to identify and to master how they apply; other distinctions do not share these features (i.e., they are difficult to recognize and challenging to apply). We save for Chapter 3 the defining characteristic — namely, the concept of Distributable Net Income (or DNI) — that truly differentiates the tax treatment of trusts and estates from that of individual taxpayers.

A breakdown of this Chapter's salient provisions is as follows. Section II delves into the elementary aspects of Subchapter J. Section III next considers how the deduction related to the production of income applies and how the receipt of tax-exempt income bears on this deduction. Section IV then explores the role of the passive activity loss limitation rule in the context of Subchapter J. Section V follows, investigating how the somewhat newly-minted twenty percent business deduction related to the receipt of flow-through business income applies. Finally, Section VI discusses the charitable deduction and how it functions in the context of Subchapter J.

Since 1954, while the contours of Subchapter J have remained fairly constant, Congress has reformed many of the Code's other salient features. These reforms have had significant rippling effects upon Subchapter J. Among other objectives, this Chapter explores these rippling effects. Be brave: mastering the basics of Subchapter J will dissipate the fear and trepidation that sometimes haunts students in the chapters that follow.

II. Elementary Aspects of Subchapter J

Internal Revenue Code: Sections 1(e), 642(b), 1411(a).

Regulations: Section 1.1411-3(e)(5), Example 1.

In many respects, trusts and estates are taxed in a manner similar to that as an individual taxpayer. Consider three similar attributes, namely, (A) Tax Rate Structure, (B) Application of the Net Investment Tax, and (C) Personal Exemption.

A. Tax Rate Structure

Internal Revenue Code: Section 1(e).

The income that trusts and estates generate is subject to its own tax rate schedule. The tax rates, found in Code § 1(e) (and adjusted annually for inflation), are specified below for 2023:

Taxable Income	Taxes
Up to $2,900	10% of taxable income
Over $2,900 but not over $10,550	$290 plus 24% of the excess over $2,900
Over $10,550 but not over $14,450	$2,126 plus 35% of the excess over $10,550
Over $14,450	$3,491 plus 37% of the excess over $14,450

What is apparent from the foregoing tax rate schedule is the phenomenon of so-called tax-bracket compression (i.e., virtually no income is taxable at the lower tax rates and the vast majority of income is taxable at the highest stated tax rate). What this tax-bracket compression signifies is something highly important: while trusts and estates can achieve many different objectives, they are no longer used as a vehicle to save income taxes. (Practice point: if prospective clients come to you wishing to establish one or more inter vivos trusts as an income tax savings device, you should quickly debunk them of their benighted understanding of the law.)[1]

B. Net Investment Tax

Internal Revenue Code: Section 1411(a).

1. If a taxpayer attempts to establish multiple trusts with an income tax minimization goal in mind, the Code will void this objective. Code § 643(f) declares that, under Regulations prescribed by the Secretary, two or more trusts will be treated as one trust if "(1) such trusts have substantially the same grantor or grantors and substantially the same primary beneficiary or beneficiaries, and (2) a principal purpose of such trusts is the avoidance of the tax imposed by this chapter." The flush language of this Code section adds that "[f]or purposes of the preceding sentence, a husband and wife shall be treated as 1 person."

Regulations: Section 1.1411-3(e)(5), Example 1.

Just like an individual, trust and estate income has potential exposure to the alternative minimum tax (Code § 59(c)), and also, its undistributed net investment income is subject to the 3.8% Medicare contribution tax. Code § 1411(a)(2). While a detailed discussion of the alternative minimum tax is beyond the scope of this book, an exposition of the tax levied upon net investment income is a worthwhile endeavor.

The net investment income tax, equal to a flat 3.8%, is in addition to the income tax. In the case of trusts and estates, the tax base is equal to the **lesser** of the following:

(1) The undistributed net investment income for the year, or

(2) The excess (if any) of:

  a. Adjusted gross income (AGI) (as defined in Code § 67(e)) for the year, over

  b. The dollar amount at which begins the highest income tax bracket in Code § 1(e) for the tax year.

Code § 1411(a)(2).

In terms of comprehending the scope of this tax base, there is one phrase—namely, "undistributed net investment income"—and one cross reference—namely, to Code § 67(e)—that each requires further explanation.

Consider first undistributed net investment income. The Code defines three baskets of net investment income: (1) gross income from interest, dividends, annuities, royalties, and rents, other than such income which is derived in the ordinary course of a trade or business; (2) income derived from a passive activity or a trade or business of trading in financial instruments or commodities; and (3) investment net gains. Code § 1411(c)(1)(A). The *undistributed net investment income* is simply the net investment income that a trustee or executor retains rather than distributes to designated beneficiaries.

Consider next the role of Code § 67(e). This Code provision determines the AGI of trusts and estates. It states that AGI is computed in the same way as that of an individual taxpayer, except it permits deductions for each of the following: (1) those unique costs associated with being a trust or estate (e.g., trustee and executor commissions);[2] (2) the personal exemption under Code § 642(b); and (3) the distribution deduction allowable under Code §§ 651 and 661.

In computing undistributed net investment income and the role AGI plays, consider a detailed example found in Treas. Reg. § 1.1411-3(e)(5).[3]

---

2. Technically, these are costs that would not be incurred if the property were not held in a trust or an estate. The U.S. Supreme Court has noted that this determination requires a fact-specific inquiry into whether the existence of a trust or estate was the catalyst behind the cost being incurred (*Knight v. Commissioner*, 552 U.S. 181, 128 S. Ct. 782 (2008), reprinted below). See Treas. Reg. § 1.67-4 (elaborating the application of this rule).

3. Admittedly, this example incorporates several concepts such as distributable net income and fiduciary accounting income which are discussed in later chapters. Notwithstanding, students

Example: (i) In Year 1, the Trust has dividend income of $15,000, interest income of $10,000, capital gain of $5,000, and $75,000 of taxable income relating to a distribution from an individual retirement account (as defined under Code § 408). The Trust has no expenses and distributes $10,000 of its current year trust accounting income to A, a beneficiary of Trust.

Composition of Trust Accounting Income	
Category	**Dollar Amount**
Dividend	$15,000
Interest	$10,000
IRA Distribution	$75,000
TOTAL	$100,000

(ii) Under Code § 643, the Trust's distributable net income is $100,000 ($15,000 in dividends plus $10,000 in interest plus $75,000 of taxable income from an individual retirement account), from which the $10,000 distribution to A is paid. The Trust's distribution deduction under Code § 661 is $10,000. Under Treas. Reg. § 1.662(b)-1, the deduction reduces each class of income comprising distributable net income on a proportional basis. The $10,000 distribution equals 10% of distributable net income ($10,000 divided by $100,000). Therefore, the distribution consists of dividend income of $1,500, interest income of $1,000, and ordinary income attributable to the individual retirement account of $7,500. Because the $5,000 of capital gain allocated to principal for trust accounting purposes did not enter into distributable net income, no portion of that amount is included in the $10,000 distribution, nor does it qualify for the distribution deduction under section 661.

Composition of $10,000 Distribution	
Category	**Dollar Amount**
Dividend	$1,500
Interest	$1,000
IRA Distribution	$7,500
TOTAL	$10,000

should persevere and try to comprehend this material; they will be richly rewarded for their efforts (and will achieve even greater mastery if they subsequently revisit this material).

(iii) The Trust's net investment income is $30,000 ($15,000 in dividends plus $10,000 in interest plus $5,000 in capital gain); however, $75,000 of taxable income attributable to the individual retirement account is excluded income under § 1.1411-1(d)(4). The Trust's undistributed net investment income under paragraph (e)(2) of this section is $27,500, which is Trust's net investment income ($30,000) less the amount of dividend income ($1,500) and interest income ($1,000) distributed to A. The $27,500 of undistributed net investment income is comprised of the capital gain allocated to principal ($5,000), the remaining undistributed dividend income ($13,500), and the remaining undistributed interest income ($9,000).

Composition of Net Investment Income	
Category	**Dollar Amount**
Dividend	$15,000
Interest	$10,000
Capital Gain	$ 5,000
TOTAL	$30,000

Composition of Undistributed Net Investment Income	
Category	**Dollar Amount**
Dividend	$13,500 ($15,000 – $1,500)
Interest	$ 9,000 ($10,000 – $1,000)
Capital Gain	$ 5,000
TOTAL	$27,500

(iv) Under paragraph (e)(3) of this section and pursuant to Treas. Reg. § 1.1411-4(a)(1), A's net investment income includes dividend income of $1,500 and interest income of $1,000, but does not include the $7,500 of ordinary income attributable to the individual retirement account because it is excluded from net investment income under Treas. Reg. § 1.1411-8.

Composition of Distributed Net Investment Income	
Category	**Dollar Amount**
Dividend	$1,500
Interest	$1,000
TOTAL	$2,500

The example in the Treasury Regulation ends here. However, an exact computation of the net investment income tax would be the **lesser** of the following:

(1) The undistributed net investment income for the year (**$27,500**), or

(2) The excess (if any) of:

a. Adjusted gross income (AGI) (as defined in Code § 67(e)) for the year (i.e., **$94,900** ($105,000 – $100 (personal exemption for complex trust) – $10,000 (Code § 661 deduction))), over

b. The dollar amount at which the highest income tax bracket in Code § 1(e) begins for the tax year (**$14,450**).

Code § 1411(a)(2).

Applying this formula, the lesser dollar amount is equal to $27,500 and application of the 3.8% tax rate would yield a $1,045 tax burden (3.8% × $27,500).[4]

C. Personal Exemption

Internal Revenue Code: Section 642(b).

Aside from the basic tax structure applicable to trusts and estates, they, too, can deduct a personal exemption amount—a deduction that is no longer available to individual taxpayers. Code § 67(e)(2). In the chart below, the personal exemption deduction amounts are specified.

	Personal Exemption Dollar Amount
Estate	$600
Trust which is required to distribute income currently	$300
Complex trusts	$100

Code § 642(b).[5]

4. The foregoing example is of somewhat limited help, because it assumes that the trust has no expenses—an unlikely scenario in the real world. If the trust had paid $4,000 in trustee fees, the trustee must allocate such deduction proportionately between the net investment income and the excluded income. Treas. Reg. § 1.1411-4(g)(1). Thus, for § 1411 purposes, this allocation process can be achieved by any reasonable method to determine the net investment income of the trust, but should align with the trust's DNI computation.

5. A discussion of a *qualified disability trust* is beyond the scope of this book. Such trusts are described in Section 1917(c)(2)(B)(iv) of the Social Security Act (42 U.S.C. § 1396p(c)(2)(B)(iv)). Code § 642(b)(2)(C)(ii)(1). In 2023, it qualifies for a $4,700 exemption, but this dollar figure is annually adjusted for inflation.

Problems

1. In 2023, a trustee of a discretionary trust that is not required to distribute income invests its principal in a certificate of deposit. The trust earns $100,000 of interest income and incurs no expenses. Using the rate schedule posited in the textbook, compute the income tax that would be due. What is the trust's effective tax rate?
2. Suppose in problem 1, the trustee, in addition to having a discretionary right to distribute principal, is required under the trust terms to annually distribute trust income. Aside from the trust now qualifying for a distribution deduction, what other tax effect will the mandatory income distribution requirement have?
3. Suppose a trust earns income from the following sources: $10,000 dividend; $20,000 interest; $30,000 capital gain; $40,000 IRA distribution; and $50,000 from an investment as a limited partner in a partnership. Assume that the trust incurs no expenses and distributes $30,000 to a designated trust beneficiary. In addition to the income tax the trust would owe, compute its net investment income tax burden.

III. Deductions Related to the Production of Income

Internal Revenue Code: Sections 67(e), 212.

Regulations: Section 1.67-4.

This section considers how the deduction related to the production of income applies (A) to the receipt of taxable income and (B) the receipt of tax-exempt income.

A. Receipt of Taxable Income

Let's start with the basics. If a taxpayer spends money to produce more income, the Code permits the taxpayer to deduct the associated expenses and report the net dollar amount as part of the tax base. In the trade and business context, Code § 162 provides the "bridge" that enables taxpayers to achieve this objective and, in the investment context, Code § 212 does the same. In a simple case scenario, assume a taxpayer invests $1 million to own title to a condominium unit which produces $100,000 of rental income. If the associated management fees equal $10,000, the taxpayer may deduct these management fees against the rental income and report the $90,000 he nets (i.e., $100,000 – $10,000). Code § 212(1), (2).

Four cases are provided below to assist in defining the contours of Subchapter J's application to Code § 212 expenses. The first, *Trust of Bingham v. Commissioner*, is one of the chestnut cases in the realm of Subchapter J; it sets forth the nature of deductible investment and management expenses when incurred by a trust or estate. By way of contrast, the second case, *Alfred I. duPont Testamentary Trust v. Commissioner*, warns that not all expenses that trusts and estates incur are deductible; instead, some expenses are tantamount to being personal in nature and, as such, are nondeductible under Code § 212. The third case, *Knight v. Commissioner*, analyzes when a section 212 expense will be considered a miscellaneous itemized deduction subject to a two percent floor of AGI.[6] The fourth case, *Manufacturers Hanover Trust Co. v. United States*, analyzes when a trust must capitalize expenses associated with securing bona fide title to property.

Trust of Bingham v. Commissioner

325 U.S. 365 (1945)

Petitioners are the trustees of a testamentary trust created for a term of twenty-one years under the will of Mary Lily (Flagler) Bingham. The testatrix bequeathed to the trustees the residue of her estate, including a large number of securities. The trustees were empowered in their discretion to sell any of the property held in trust (except certain securities of two companies designated as the "principal properties"), to invest and reinvest the proceeds and the income from the trust fund, and to use the proceeds and the income for the benefit of the principal properties and for the "maintenance, administration or development of the said principal or subsidiary properties." The trustees were to pay specified amounts annually to certain legatees. When the niece of the testatrix reached a certain age, she was to receive from the trust a specified amount in cash or securities. At the end of twenty-one years, the trustees were directed to pay other legacies, and to distribute the remainder of the fund in equal parts to a brother and two sisters of the testatrix.

In 1935 petitioners paid the bequest to the niece partly in securities. The Commissioner assessed a deficiency of over $365,000 for income tax upon the appreciation in value of the securities while they were in petitioner's hands. In contesting unsuccessfully this deficiency, petitioners paid out in the year 1940 approximately $16,000 in counsel fees and expenses. In that year, also, petitioners paid out about $9,000 for legal advice in connection with the payment of one of the cash legacies, and in connection with tax and other problems arising upon the expiration of the trust and relating to the final distribution of the trust fund among the three residuary legatees.

The question is whether these legal expenses, paid in 1940, are deductible from gross income in the computation of the trust's income tax, as "non-trade" or "non-business" expenses within the meaning of § 23(a)(2) of the Internal Revenue Code. That section, added by § 121 of the Revenue Act of 1942, and made applicable to

6. Note that until 2026, miscellaneous itemized deductions cannot be deducted at all. Code § 67(g). After this time, unless Congress takes further action, trusts and estates can take these deductions to the extent they exceed two percent of adjusted gross income.

tax years "beginning after December 31, 1938," authorizes the deduction of "all the ordinary and necessary expenses paid or incurred during the taxable year for the production or collection of income, or for the management, conservation, or maintenance of property held for the production of income." Section 162 of the Code, so far as now relevant, makes § 23(a)(2) applicable to the income taxation of trusts.

Petitioners, in their income tax return for 1940, took deductions for the legal expenses. The Commissioner disallowed the deductions and assessed a tax deficiency, and petitioners filed the present suit in the Tax Court to set aside the assessment. That Court, after finding the facts as we have stated them, found that the trust property was held for the production of income; that all the items in question were ordinary and necessary expenses of the management of the trust property; and that the fees and expenses for contesting the income tax deficiency assessment were also for the conservation of the trust property. It therefore concluded that all were rightly deducted in calculating the taxable net income of the trust. 2 T.C. 853.

On the Government's petition for review, the Court of Appeals for the Second Circuit reversed. *Com'r v. Kenan*, 145 F.2d 568. We granted certiorari, 324 U.S. __, 65 S.Ct. 861, on a petition which asserted as grounds for the writ that the decision of the Court of Appeals departed from the principles laid down in *Dobson v. Commissioner*, 320 U.S. 489, 64 S.Ct. 239, 88 L.Ed. 248, governing review of decisions of the Tax Court, and that the decision conflicted in principle with *Commissioner v. Heininger*, 320 U.S. 467, 64 S.Ct. 249, 88 L.Ed. 171, and *Kornhauser v. United States*, 276 U.S. 145, 48 S.Ct. 219, 72 L.Ed. 505.

The Court of Appeals left undisturbed the Tax Court's findings that the questioned items were ordinary and necessary expenses for the management or conservation of the trust property, but it held that the fees for contesting the tax deficiency were nevertheless not deductible under § 23(a)(2). It thought that the expenses of contesting the income tax had nothing to do with the production of income and hence were not deductible as expenses "for the production of income" within the meaning of the statute. The court also thought that these expenses were not deductible, because they were paid in connection with property held by the trustees "ready for distribution", and hence not "for the production of income." Similarly it held that the fees for professional services rendered in connection with the payment of legacies and the distribution of the trust fund, were not expenses relating to the management of property held for the production of income, since they were rendered after the trust term had expired and when the property was ready for distribution.

The Government makes like arguments here. In addition it urges that the expenses in connection with the distribution of the trust fund were not expenses of management of the trust property held for the production of income but only expenses relating to its devolution; and that the expenses are not deductible under § 23(a)(2) because there was no proximate relationship between the expenses when paid and the property then held in trust.

We think that these objections to the deductions fail to take proper account of the plain language of § 23(a)(2), and the purpose of the section as disclosed by its statutory setting and legislative history; and that notwithstanding the weight of the Tax Court's decision against them, they raise questions of law reviewable by the Circuit Court of Appeals and by this Court.

The requirement of § 23(a)(2) that deductible expenses be "ordinary and necessary" implies that they must be reasonable in amount and must bear a reasonable and proximate relation to the management of property held for the production of income. See H.Rep. No. 2333, 77th Cong., 2d Sess., p. 75; Sen.Rep. No. 1631, 77th Cong., 2d Sess., p. 88. Ordinarily questions of reasonableness and proximity are for the trier of fact, here the Tax Court. *Commissioner v. Heininger, supra*, 320 U.S. 475, 64 S.Ct. 254, 88 L.Ed. 171; *McDonald v. Commissioner*, 323 U.S. 57, 64, 65, 65 S.Ct. 96, 99; see *Commissioner v. Scottish American Inv. Co.*, 323 U.S. 119, 65 S.Ct. 169. And even when they are hybrid questions of "mixed law and fact," their resolution, because of the fact element involved, will usually afford little concrete guidance for future cases, and reviewing courts will set aside the decisions of the Tax Court only when they announce a rule of general applicability, that the facts found fall short of meeting statutory requirements. *Dobson v. Commissioner, supra*, 320 U.S. 502, 64 S.Ct. 247, 88 L.Ed. 248; *Commissioner v. Estate of Bedford*, 325 U.S. 283, 65 S.Ct. 1157; cf. Paul, "Dobson v. Commissioner," 57 Harv.Law Rev. 753, at 828-832, 836, 837. But whether the applicable statutes and regulations are such as to preclude the decision which the Tax Court has rendered, is, as was recognized in *Dobson v. Commissioner, supra*, 320 U.S. 492, 493, 64 S.Ct. 242, 88 L.Ed. 248, a question of law reviewable on appeal. See also *Commissioner v. Heininger, supra*, 320 U.S. 475, 64 S.Ct. 254, 88 L.Ed. 171.

Here the decision of the Court of Appeals was that the expenses were not deductible because they were not for the purpose of producing income or capital gain, and because the trust property, being ready for distribution, was no longer held for the production of income. The terms of the trust, the nature of the property, and the duties of the trustees with respect to it, were all found by the Tax Court and are not challenged. The questions whether, on the facts found, the expenses in question are nondeductible, either because they were not to produce income or because they were related to the management of property which was not held for the production of income, turn in this case on the meaning of the words of § 23(a)(2), "property held for the production of income." They are therefore questions of law, decision of which is unembarrassed by any disputed question of fact or any necessity to draw an inference of fact from the basic findings. See *Commissioner v. Scottish American Inv. Co., supra.* They are "clear cut" questions of law, decision of which by the Tax Court does not foreclose their decision by appellate courts, as in other cases, *Dobson v. Commissioner, supra*, 320 U.S. 492, 493, 64 S.Ct. 242, 88 L.Ed. 248, although their decision by the Tax Court is entitled to great weight. *Dobson v. Commissioner, supra*, 320 U.S. 501, 502, 64 S.Ct. 246, 247, 88 L.Ed. 248, and cases cited; cf. *Medo Photo Supply Corp. v. Labor Board*, 321 U.S. 678, 681, 682, n. 1, 64 S.Ct. 830-832, 88 L.Ed. 1007, and cases cited.

Since our decision in the *Dobson* case we have frequently reexamined, as matters of law, determinations by the Tax Court of the meaning of the words of a statute as applied to facts found by that court. A question of law is not any the less such because the Tax Court's decision of it is right rather than wrong. Whether or not its decision is "in accordance with law" is a question which the statute, Int.Rev.Code, § 1141(c)(1), expressly makes subject to appellate review. Congress, when it thus authorized review of questions of law only, was not unaware of the difficulties of such a review of the decisions of a tribunal, which decides questions both of law and of fact. But Congress did not dispense with such review.

Hence the statute does not leave the Tax Court as the final arbiter of the issue whether its own decisions of questions of law are right or wrong. That can only be ascertained upon resort to the prescribed appellate process by a consideration of the merits of the point of law involved, and by its decision at the conclusion of the process, not before it begins. The fact that the Court of Appeals, below, while accepting the Tax Court's findings of fact, has nevertheless reversed its decision, would seem not to leave the question of law decided so free from doubt that the mandate of the statute could rightly be disregarded on any theory. If review were to be denied in this case, it would be difficult to say that any construction of a taxing statute by the Tax Court would be subject to appellate review.

We turn to the first ground for reversal relied on by the Court of Appeals, that the property was held for distribution, and no longer for the production of income. The fact that the trustees, in the administration of the trust, were required to invest its corpus for the production of income and to devote the income to the purposes of the trust, establishes, as the Tax Court held, that the trust property was held for the production of income during the stated term of the trust. The decisive question is whether the property ceased to be held for the production of income because, as the trust term reached its expiry date, the trustees were under a duty to distribute the property among the remaindermen.

It is true that expiration of the trust operated to change the beneficiaries entitled to receive the income of the trust property, from those entitled to the income during the term of the trust to the remaindermen. But the duty of the trustees to hold and conserve the trust property, and until distribution, to receive income from it, continued. The property did not cease to be held for the production of income because, upon the expiration of the trust and until distribution, the trustees were under an additional duty to distribute the trust fund, or because the trustees, upon distribution, were then accountable to new and different beneficiaries, the residuary legatees, both for the principal of the fund and any income accumulating after the expiry date. To exclude from the deduction privilege, expenses which the Tax Court has held to be expenses of management of the trust, on the ground that the trust fund, upon the expiration of the trust, ceased to be "held for the production of income" would be to disregard the Tax Court's findings of fact and the words of the statute, and would defeat its obvious purpose.

Nor is there merit in the court's conclusion that the expenses were not deductible because they were not for the production of income. Section 23(a)(2) provides for two classes of deductions, expenses "for the production of income" and expenses of "management, conservation, or maintenance of property held for the production of income." To read this section as requiring that expenses be paid for the production of income in order to be deductible, is to make unnecessary and to read out of the section the provision for the deduction of expenses of management of property held for the production of income.

There is no warrant for such a construction. Section 23(a)(2) is comparable and in pari materia with § 23(a)(1), authorizing the deduction of business or trade expenses. Such expenses need not relate directly to the production of income for the business. It is enough that the expense, if "ordinary and necessary," is directly connected with or proximately results from the conduct of the business. *Kornhauser v. United States, supra*, 276 U.S. 152, 153, 48 S.Ct. 219, 72 L.Ed. 505; *Commissioner v. Heininger, supra*, 320 U.S. 470, 471, 64 S.Ct. 252, 88 L.Ed. 171. The effect of § 23(a)(2) was to provide for a class of non-business deductions co-extensive with the business deductions allowed by § 23(a)(1), except for the fact that, since they were not incurred in connection with a business, the section made it necessary that they be incurred for the production of income or in the management or conservation of property held for the production of income. *McDonald v. Commissioner, supra*, 323 U.S. 61, 62, 66, 65 S.Ct. 96, 97, 98, 100; and see H.Rep. No. 2333, 77th Cong., 2d Sess., pp. 46, 74-76; S. Rep. No. 1631, 77th Cong., 2d Sess., pp. 87–88.

Since there is no requirement that business expenses be for the production of income, there is no reason for that requirement in the case of like expenses of managing a trust, so long as they are in connection with the management of property which is held for the production of income. Section 23(a)(2) thus treats the trust as an entity for producing income comparable to a business enterprise, and like § 23(a)(2) permits deductions of management expenses of the trust, even though the particular expense was not an expense directly producing income. It follows that all of the items of expense here in question are deductible if, as the Tax Court has held, they are expenses of management or conservation of the trust fund, whether their expenditure did or did not result in the production of income.

The Government contends that the expenses incurred in connection with the distribution of the corpus of the trust to legatees, are not deductible, because they are not expenses of managing income producing property, but expenses in connection with the devolution of the property. If the suggestion is correct, it would follow that expenses incurred in distributing the income of the trust to the income beneficiaries are likewise not deductible, since the distribution of income is also a devolution of trust property. But the duties of the trustees were not only to hold the property for the production of income and to collect the income, but also, in administering the trust, to distribute the income and the principal so held from time to time, and the remainder of the principal at the expiration of the trust. Performance of each of these duties is an integral part of carrying out the trust enterprise. Accordingly, as the Tax Court held, the costs of distribution here were quite as much expenses of a function of "management" of the trust property as were expenses incurred in producing the trust income; and if "ordinary and necessary," they were deductible.

In support of its contention, the Government relies upon a part of the House Committee Report, accompanying the bill which became the Revenue Act of 1942, see H. Rep. No. 2333, 77th Cong., 2d Sess., p. 75, and upon Treas. Regs. 103, § 19.23(a)-15, neither of which was mentioned by the Court of Appeals. They state that an administrator or executor may not deduct expenses incurred in the administration of the estate of a decedent, including those of distributing assets to the beneficiaries. It is argued that by analogy like expenses of trustees should not be deductible. But it is to be noted that there is no such statement in the Report or Regulations as to the distribution expenses of trustees. On the contrary, the Regulations, § 19.23(a)-15, in dealing specifically with expenses of trustees, provides only that their expenses of management and conservation of the trust property held for the production of income are deductible. And the references in the Report to the non-deductibility of expenses of administrators and executors were in explanation of the Congressional purpose to prevent the specified administration expenses from being deductible both for income and estate taxation. To accomplish that purpose the Report recommended an amendment, which became § 161(a) of the Revenue Act of 1942, adding § 162(e) to the Internal Revenue Code. Section 162(e) provides, with immaterial exceptions, that "amounts allowable under section 812(b) as a deduction in computing the net estate of a decedent shall not be allowed as a deduction under section 23." Here, as the Tax Court found, there is no possibility of such a double deduction, since the expenses were not deductible under the decedent's estate tax return.

What we have said applies with equal force to the expenses of contesting the tax deficiency. Section 23(a)(2) does not restrict deductions to those litigation expenses which alone produce income. On the contrary, by its terms and in analogy with the rule under § 23(a)(1), the business expense section, the trust, a taxable entity like a business, may deduct litigation expenses when they are directly connected with or proximately result from the enterprise—the management of property held for production of income. *Kornhauser v. United States, supra*, 276 U.S. 152, 153, 48 S.Ct. 220, 72 L.Ed. 505; *Commissioner v. Heininger, supra*, 320 U.S. 470, 471, 64 S.Ct. 252, 88 L. Ed. 171. The Tax Court could find as a matter of fact, as it did, that the expenses of contesting the income taxes were a proximate result of the holding of the property for income. And we cannot say, as a matter of law, that such expenses are any less deductible than expenses of suits to recover income. Cf. *Commissioner v. Heininger, supra*.

The Government relies on Treas. Regs. 103, § 19.23(a)-15, which provide that "expenditures incurred for the purpose of recovering taxes (other than recoveries required to be included in income), or for the purpose of resisting a proposed additional assessment of taxes (other than taxes on property held for the production of income) are not deductible expenses under this section [§ 23(a)(2) of the Code], except that part thereof which the taxpayer clearly shows to be properly allocable to the recovery of interest required to be included in income." So far as this regulation purports to deny deduction of litigation expense unless it is to produce income, it is not in conformity to the statute, for the reasons already stated, or with the Regulation already mentioned, which provides that in addition to expenses for the production or collection of trust income, expenses of management or conservation of trust property held for the production of income are also deductible. To that extent and to the extent that it departs from the rule of *Kornhauser v. United States, supra*, it conflicts with the meaning and purpose of § 23(a)(2), and so is unauthorized. *Helvering v. Reynolds Tobacco Co.*, 306 U.S. 110, 59 S.Ct. 423, 83 L.Ed. 536.

We find no error of law in the judgment of the Tax Court. Its judgment will be affirmed and that of the Court of Appeals reversed.

View of one building and fountain on the duPont estate.

Alfred I. duPont Testamentary Trust v. Commissioner

514 F.2d 917 (5th Cir. 1975)

CLARK, Circuit Judge:

The Commissioner disallowed deductions claimed by the taxpayer, a testamentary trust created under the will of Alfred I. duPont, in the tax years 1966 and 1967 for expenses of maintaining an estate owned by the taxpayer but which was then being used as Mrs. duPont's home [which is pictured above]. The expense deductions were claimed to be ordinary and necessary expenses under Int. Rev. Code of 1954 § 212 because the estate was rental property or alternatively because the estate was part of an income producing entity comprised of the estate and securities owned by taxpayer. The Tax Court upheld the Commissioner. *Alfred I. duPont Testamentary*

Trust, 62 T.C. 36 (1974). On this appeal, taxpayer urges error in the Tax Court's § 212 reasoning and also urges alternate theories of deductibility specifically related to operating trusts. We affirm in part and remand.

About 1910 Alfred I. duPont built a mansion on a 300 acre tract in Brandywine Hundred, New Castle County, Delaware which he named "Nemours." Mr. duPont lived at Nemours with his wife, Jessie Ball duPont, from their marriage in 1921 until 1926. After 1926 they resided principally in Florida, but spent an average of two months a year at Nemours. By the time of [Mr. duPont's] death in 1935 Nemours included formal gardens, man-made lakes, a greenhouse, large monuments built in honor of Mr. duPont's ancestors, an extensive system of roadways, bridges, walkways, stables, and various other buildings.

In 1925 Mr. duPont organized Nemours, Inc. (the corporation) and transferred to it full title to the mansion house and grounds in exchange for all of the corporation's stock. Subsequently Mr. and Mrs. duPont leased Nemours for the term of their joint lives plus the life of the survivor. The agreed rental was one dollar a year. The duPonts were required by the lease agreement to pay all taxes and the expense of the upkeep of the buildings and grounds. In January 1929 Mr. duPont transferred to the corporation 20,000 shares of preferred stock of Almour Securities, Inc. valued at 2,000,000 dollars. In exchange for this transfer, the lease agreement was amended to provide that the corporation would pay taxes and expenses of upkeep.

Beginning in 1929, the corporation listed the value of the Almour stock on most of its income tax returns as "paid in surplus" or "surplus." In 1932 and again in 1937 (the year the corporation was dissolved) respectively, the stock value was reflected in "undivided profits" and in "earned surplus and undivided profits." The Almour stock represented the largest asset value of the corporation. Its other assets, the land and improvements comprising Nemours, were valued at 572,215 dollars in 1929 and at over 1,000,000 dollars in 1936 and 1937. The corporation never reported any rental income from the lands and buildings, but did report dividend income of about 100,000 dollars per year from the Almour stock.

The corporation claimed deductions each year from 1929-37 for the expenses of maintaining Nemours. Most of the deductions were challenged by the government as not incurred in connection with property held for the production of income. Pursuant to an agreement between the corporation and the Revenue Service, no deduction was allowed for most of the expenses claimed. Since the dividend income reported in each of the years prior to 1935 was offset by the 100 percent deduction allowed for dividends paid by domestic corporations, the real property maintenance deduction allowed in those years had no tax consequence. The business of the corporation was shown in its tax returns as "Owners and Operators of Real Estate," until Mr. duPont's death at which time its business was designated as "Holding Real Estate For Charitable Foundation."

Mr. duPont died in 1935 survived by his wife. His will vested title to the stock of the corporation in his executors who were instructed by the will to set up a trust to continue the maintenance of the grounds. The stock of the corporation was to comprise the corpus of this testamentary trust along with large blocks of other securities. Mrs. duPont was a trustee and the principal income beneficiary for her life. The trust was to pay her 200,000 dollars plus any income remaining after the payment of specified annuities. The trustees were directed to organize a charitable foundation at the death of Mrs. duPont and to transfer to it the trust assets. This foundation, to be designated the Nemours Foundation, was to be operated in memory of duPont ancestors for the treatment of crippled children or old people. The mansion house was to be maintained in its then state and opened to the public. The trust became operative in 1937.

In valuing the corporation's stock for estate tax purposes, the executors subtracted a reserve fund representing the anticipated maintenance cost of Nemours for the projected life expectancy of Mrs. duPont (19½ years). Subsequent income tax deductions by Mr. duPont's estate for maintenance of Nemours were challenged by the Revenue Service as duplicating the estate tax deductions. An agreement was reached between the parties whereby a portion of each year's maintenance expense would be deducted from the reserve. When the reserve was depleted in the early 1950's the trust began to deduct the full amount of the expenses incurred in maintaining Nemours. These deductions were not challenged.

From 1962 until her death in 1970, Mrs. duPont resided full time at Nemours. The mansion house was not then and has not yet been opened to the public. A hospital for crippled children, built sometime after Mr. duPont's death, occupies 22 acres of the Nemours estate grounds.

During 1966 and 1967, the tax years in question, the gross income of the trust was 13,000,000 dollars. Of this sum 11,000,000 dollars was distributed to Mrs. duPont. The trust spent 255,753 dollars in 1966 and 274,451 dollars in 1967 for general maintenance of the Nemours estate. An additional 114,284 dollars was expended during 1967 for repaving existing paved roadways and walkways; paving existing unpaved roadways; rehabilitating various structures such as a classical temple, ornamental balustrades, steps, fountains, terraces, flagstones, and urns; and purchasing a jeep and a dump truck. The Commissioner disallowed all of these deductions. The reasons given were that (1) the property was not held for the production of income; (2) the expenditures did not qualify as administration expenses; and (3) the expenditures did not qualify as charitable deductions. Alternatively he contended that the 114,284 dollar outlay represented capital expenditures which were not allowable as deductions.

Prepaid Rent

The taxpayer maintains that the deductions were proper under Int.Rev.Code of 1954 § 212(1), which provides a deduction for "all the ordinary and necessary expenses paid or incurred during the taxable year . . . for the production or collection of income. . . ."

Taxpayer contends that under the 1929 amendment to the 1925 lease to the duPonts, the transfer of the 2,000,000 dollars worth of Almour securities constituted pre-paid rent, and therefore that, insofar as the corporation and the trust were concerned, Nemours was income producing rental property.

The attempt to characterize the transfer of the Almour securities as pre-paid rent was correctly rejected by the Tax Court both as a matter of form and of substance. No part of these assets or the dividends therefrom were ever reported as taxable rental income on the corporation's income tax returns. The 1929 agreement clearly establishes that Mr. duPont conveyed the Almour securities to the corporation which he continuously owned and controlled until the time of his death, to enable it to pay taxes and maintenance expenses he had previously borne personally. The only payment specified as rent in the initial agreement and in the 1929 amendment was a token 1 dollar a year. The record contains no other indication that the conveyance of Almour stock was intended to constitute pre-paid rent. Neither the documentation or the conduct of the parties indicates that the securities were transferred for any purpose other than to relieve the duPonts of the day-to-day burdens of administering the estate.

No attempt was made to show what the anticipated expenses of maintaining the estate might be as compared to the income produced by or the total value of Almour securities. In short, the taxpayer trust simply failed to carry its burden of proving that Nemours was rental property in these tax years. This failure of affirmative proof controls our decision here. See *Mayrath v. Commissioner of Internal Revenue*, 357 F.2d 209 [17 AFTR 2d 375] (5th Cir. 1966); and *International Trading Co. v. Commissioner of Internal Revenue*, 275 F.2d 578 [5 AFTR 2d 970] (7th Cir. 1960).

Property Held for the Production of Income

Alternatively, the taxpayer urges the upkeep and maintenance expense was deductible under section 212(2) which allows a deduction for "all the ordinary and necessary expenses paid or incurred . . . for the management, conservation or maintenance of property held for the production of income. . . ."

To support this argument before us, taxpayer relies principally on *Bingham's Trust v. Commissioner of Internal Revenue*, 325 U.S. 365 [33 AFTR 842] 65 S.Ct. 1232, 89 L.Ed. 1670 (1945) in which the Court held that legal fees incurred to contest an income tax deficiency were deductible since they were funds expended for the conservation of trust property which was held for the production of income. The taxpayer asserts that *Bingham*'s rationale covers the expenses incurred in maintaining Nemours even though Nemours was not strictly property held for the production of income.

The thrust of the argument is that the taxpayer trust, an entity for the production of income comparable to a business enterprise, could deduct these expenses as maintenance expenses even though Nemours did not directly produce income, because payment of the maintenance and upkeep expense was a fundamental duty of the trustees in the administration of the trust. This interpretation glosses over the fact that a threshold determination in *Bingham* was that the property which the expenditure protected was held for the production of income. Although it was the duty of the trustees to maintain Nemours, Nemours was not property held for the production of income. See *Estate of Mortimer B. Fuller*, 9 T.C. 1069 (1947), aff'd per curiam 171 F.2d 704 [37 AFTR 685] (3d Cir. 1948). In the case at bar, the question which concerned the Court in *Bingham* — whether the expense incurred was connected with, or proximately resulted from, the management of property held for production of income — is never reached.

Despite the lease agreements between the wholly-owned corporation and the duPonts and the controlling terms of Mr. duPont's testamentary trust, Nemours remained the duPonts' personal residence. It was the antithesis of income producing property. The expenses incurred in the maintenance and upkeep of this private residence never were deductible expenses relating to property held for the present or future production of income. See *Eugene H. Walet, Jr.*, 31 T.C. 461 (1958), aff'd per curiam 272 F.2d 694 [4 AFTR 2d 5955] (5th Cir. 1959).

Alternative Trust Deductions

As an alternative to its section 212 contentions, the taxpayer seeks deductiblity under section 642(c) or section 170(a). It asserts that if the expenses are not deductible as expenses paid for the benefit of Mrs. duPont, the life beneficiary, then they were incurred for the benefit of the remainderman, the Nemours Foundation, a charitable organization. Since the Nemours Foundation was a validly existing organization in the years in question, section 170(a) would provide a deduction for amounts distributed currently for the benefit of a charitable organization.

Section 642(c) speaks of amounts to be "paid or permanently" set aside during the current year pursuant to the terms of the governing instrument for a charitable purpose. Mrs. duPont was in possession of Nemours for the years in question, and the expenses were for current maintenance. The Nemours Foundation did not receive Nemours until 1970. It is true that 22 acres of the grounds were being used as a children's hospital, but this fact is of no moment since the expenses sought to be deducted were not in any way connected with the hospital. Further, the trust instrument itself did not provide that any amounts be expended for the foundation until after Mrs. duPont's death. The charitable purpose was too remote to cause these expenses for present maintenance to be deductible as paid or permanently set aside during the taxable years for charitable purposes.

The taxpayer makes a second arguendo assertion, if the deductions are denied under section 212, that the Tax Court erred in not treating them as deductions allowable under section 651 or 661 because they were amounts expended by a trust for its beneficiary. Section 651 permits a trust to deduct current income required by the terms of the trust to be distributed currently. Its companion, section 652, provides that such required amount shall be included in the gross income of the beneficiary.

Section 661 permits a deduction by a trust where accumulated income is required to be distributed, paid or credited in the current tax year, such as the year in which a trust is terminated. Its companion, section 662, requires such distribution, payment or credit to be reported as a part of the gross income of the beneficiary. The Tax Court did not mention this contention in its opinion.

The obligation to maintain Nemours was created by the 1929 amendment to the lease agreement. It was, in that year, a commitment by a wholly owned corporation to pay personal living expenses of Mr. and Mrs. duPont which he funded by the conveyance of Almour stock. It primarily retained this same personal expense character in 1966 and 1967 as to Mrs. duPont, a trustee as well as the principal beneficiary of the trust. The record before us does not reveal whether Mrs. duPont reported any part of these payments as income to her in either tax year. She would have been required to do this by sections 652 and 662, if the payments had qualified for deductions by the trust as funds distributed to her pursuant to the trust agreement under section 651 or 661. Cf. *Commissioner of Internal Revenue v. Plant,* 76 F.2d 8 (2d Cir. 1935).

We are unsure of the basis for the Commissioner's action in recognizing for estate tax purposes the creation and amortization of a maintenance reserve fund for Nemours and his failure to challenge the trust's annual maintenance deductions from the time this reserve had been depleted until the 1966 and 1967 tax years. Nor do we know how these amounts were treated by Mrs. duPont in connection with her personal income tax returns for these tax years. We decline to determine the right of the trust to deduct these challenged amounts under section 651 or 661 until the matter has been squarely presented to and decided by the Tax Court. Except as expressly set out herein, we intimate no views on this issue.

Conclusion

Deductions are a matter of legislative grace. See *Deputy v. Du Pont,* 308 U.S. 488 [23 AFTR 808], 60 S.Ct. 363, 84 L.Ed. 416 (1940). The deductions claimed by the taxpayer here must fit into a statutory category of deductibility, else the trustees must carry out their fiduciary duty at the expense of the trust, rather than the public fisc.

We agree with the Tax Court that the trustees were entitled to no deduction for the expenses incurred in the maintenance and upkeep of Nemours during Mrs. duPont's life under sections 212, 642(c) or 170(a). We reach no conclusion as to deductibility under section 651 or 661, nor as to the collateral effect the allowance of such deductions would have had on Mrs. duPont's tax liability under section 652 or 662, nor whether limitations would bar the present assessment or allocation of such amounts to her personally. The cause is remanded for such further proceedings as the Tax Court may determine are necessary to enable it to consider and decide these issues.

Affirmed in part and remanded.

Once trustees and executors determine whether the investment and management expenses the trusts and estates incur are deductible investment or management expenses or non-deductible personal expenses, they face another limitation. The Code specifies that those expenditures that constitute what are known as "miscellaneous itemized expenses" are not deductible.[7] Included in the category of disallowed miscellaneous itemized expenses are Code § 212 investment and management expenses. However, Code § 67(e)(1) carves out an important exception to this limitation, permitting "deductions for costs which are paid or incurred in connection with the administration of the estate or trust and which would not have been incurred if the property were not held in such trust and estate." In other words, if the very existence of the trust and estate leads to an expense being incurred (e.g., trustee and executor commissions), then the expense remains deductible.

Deciding which investment and management expenses are unique to trusts and estates and which are not is a challenging exercise. At least insofar as investment advisory fees are concerned, the U.S. Supreme Court has explored this issue below in *Knight v. Commissioner.* In the aftermath of this case, the Treasury Department promulgated regulations which further amplify the meaning of the Code § 67(e) statutory language and added a deeper hue to the Supreme Court's analysis.

Knight v. Commissioner

552 U.S. 181 (2008)

Chief Justice Roberts delivered the opinion of the Court.

Under the Internal Revenue Code, individuals may subtract from their taxable income certain itemized deductions, but only to the extent the deductions exceed 2% of adjusted gross income. A trust may also claim those deductions, also subject to the 2% floor, except that costs incurred in the administration of the trust, which would not have been incurred if the trust property were not held by a trust, may be deducted without regard to the floor. In the case of individuals, investment advisory fees are subject to the 2% floor; the question presented is whether such fees are also subject to the floor when incurred by a trust. We hold that they are and therefore affirm the judgment below, albeit for different reasons than those given by the Court of Appeals.

I

The Internal Revenue Code imposes a tax on the "taxable income" of both individuals and trusts. 26 U.S.C. § 1(a). The Code instructs that the calculation of taxable income begins with a determination of "gross income," capaciously defined as "all income from whatever source derived." § 61(a). "Adjusted gross income" is then calculated by subtracting from gross income certain "above-the-line" deductions, such as trade and business expenses and losses from the sale or exchange of property. § 62(a). Finally, taxable income is calculated by subtracting from adjusted gross

7. After December 31, 2025, this law is supposed to sunset, and taxpayers will be able to deduct such expenses to the extent they exceed 2% of a taxpayer's AGI. Code § 67(g).

income "itemized deductions"—also known as "below-the-line" deductions—defined as all allowable deductions other than the "above-the-line" deductions identified in § 62(a) and the deduction for personal exemptions allowed under § 151 (2000 ed. and Supp. V). § 63(d) (2000 ed.).

Before the passage of the Tax Reform Act of 1986, 100 Stat. 2085, below-the-line deductions were deductible in full. This system resulted in significant complexity and potential for abuse, requiring "extensive [taxpayer] recordkeeping with regard to what commonly are small expenditures," as well as "significant administrative and enforcement problems for the Internal Revenue Service." H.R. Rep. No. 99-426, p. 109 (1985).

In response, Congress enacted what is known as the "2% floor" by adding § 67 to the Code. Section 67(a) provides that "the miscellaneous itemized deductions for any taxable year shall be allowed only to the extent that the aggregate of such deductions exceeds 2 percent of adjusted gross income." The term "miscellaneous itemized deductions" is defined to include all itemized deductions other than certain ones specified in § 67(b). Investment advisory fees are deductible pursuant to 26 U.S.C. § 212. Because § 212 is not listed in § 67(b) as one of the categories of expenses that may be deducted in full, such fees are "miscellaneous itemized deductions" subject to the 2% floor. 26 CFR § 1.67-1T(a)(1)(ii) (2007).

Section 67(e) makes the 2% floor generally applicable not only to individuals but also to estates and trusts, with one exception relevant here. Under this exception, "the adjusted gross income of an estate or trust shall be computed in the same manner as in the case of an individual, except that . . . the deductions for costs which are paid or incurred in connection with the administration of the estate or trust and which would not have been incurred if the property were not held in such trust or estate . . . shall be treated as allowable" and not subject to the 2% floor. § 67(e)(1).

Petitioner Michael J. Knight is the trustee of the William L. Rudkin Testamentary Trust, established in the State of Connecticut in 1967. In 2000, the Trustee hired Warfield Associates, Inc., to provide advice with respect to investing the Trust's assets. At the beginning of the tax year, the Trust held approximately $2.9 million in marketable securities, and it paid Warfield $22,241 in investment advisory fees for the year. On its fiduciary income tax return for 2000, the Trust reported total income of $624,816, and it deducted in full the investment advisory fees paid to Warfield. After conducting an audit, respondent Commissioner of Internal Revenue found that these investment advisory fees were miscellaneous itemized deductions subject to the 2% floor. The Commissioner therefore allowed the Trust to deduct the investment advisory fees, which were the only claimed deductions subject to the floor, only to the extent that they exceeded 2% of the Trust's adjusted gross income. The discrepancy resulted in a tax deficiency of $4,448.

The Trust filed a petition in the United States Tax Court seeking review of the assessed deficiency. It argued that the Trustee's fiduciary duty to act as a "prudent investor" under the Connecticut Uniform Prudent Investor Act, Conn. Gen. Stat.

§§ 45a-541a to 45a-541l (2007), required the Trustee to obtain investment advisory services, and therefore to pay investment advisory fees. The Trust argued that such fees are accordingly unique to trusts and therefore fully deductible under 26 U.S.C. § 67(e)(1). The Tax Court rejected this argument, holding that § 67(e)(1) allows full deductibility only for expenses that are not commonly incurred outside the trust setting. Because investment advisory fees are commonly incurred by individuals, the Tax Court held that they are subject to the 2% floor when incurred by a trust. *Rudkin Testamentary Trust v. Commissioner*, 124 T. C. 304, 309–311 (2005).

The Trust appealed to the United States Court of Appeals for the Second Circuit. The Court of Appeals concluded that, in determining whether costs such as investment advisory fees are fully deductible or subject to the 2% floor, § 67(e) "directs the inquiry toward the counterfactual condition of assets held individually instead of in trust," and requires "an objective determination of whether the particular cost is one that is peculiar to trusts and one that individuals are incapable of incurring." 467 F.3d 149, 155 [98 AFTR 2d 2006-7368], 156 (2006). The court held that because investment advisory fees were "costs of a type that could be incurred if the property were held individually rather than in trust," deduction of such fees by the Trust was subject to the 2% floor. *Id.*, at 155–156.

The Courts of Appeals are divided on the question presented. The Sixth Circuit has held that investment advisory fees are fully deductible. *O'Neill v. Commissioner*, 994 F.2d 302, 304 [71 AFTR 2d 93-2052] (1993). In contrast, both the Fourth and Federal Circuits have held that such fees are subject to the 2% floor, because they are "commonly" or "customarily" incurred outside of trusts. See *Scott v. United States*, 328 F.3d 132, 140 [91 AFTR 2d 2003-2100] (CA4 2003); *Mellon Bank, N.A. v. United States*, 265 F.3d 1275, 1281 [88 AFTR 2d 2001-5800] (CA Fed. 2001). The Court of Appeals below came to the same conclusion, but as noted announced a more exacting test, allowing "full deduction only for those costs that *could not* have been incurred by an individual property owner." 467 F.3d, at 156 (emphasis added). We granted the Trustee's petition for certiorari to resolve the conflict, 551 U.S. __ (2007), and now affirm.

II

"We start, as always, with the language of the statute." *Williams v. Taylor*, 529 U.S. 420, 431 (2000). Section 67(e) sets forth a general rule: "[T]he adjusted gross income of [a] . . . trust shall be computed in the same manner as in the case of an individual." That is, trusts can ordinarily deduct costs subject to the same 2% floor that applies to individuals' deductions. Section 67(e) provides for an exception to the 2% floor when two conditions are met. First, the relevant cost must be "paid or incurred in connection with the administration of the . . . trust." § 67(e)(1). Second, the cost must be one "which would not have been incurred if the property were not held in such trust." *Ibid.*

In applying the statute, the Court of Appeals below asked whether the cost at issue could have been incurred by an individual. This approach flies in the face of the statutory language. The provision at issue asks whether the costs "would not have been incurred if the property were not held" in trust, *ibid.*, not, as the Court of Appeals would have it, whether the costs "could not have been incurred" in such a case, 467 F.3d, at 156. The fact that an individual could not do something is one reason he would not, but not the only possible reason. If Congress had intended the Court of Appeals' reading, it easily could have replaced "would" in the statute with "could," and presumably would have. The fact that it did not adopt this readily available and apparent alternative strongly supports rejecting the Court of Appeals' reading.

Moreover, if the Court of Appeals' reading were correct, it is not clear why Congress would have included in the statute the first clause of § 67(e)(1). If the only costs that are fully deductible are those that could not be incurred outside the trust context — that is, that could only be incurred by trusts — then there would be no reason to place the further condition on full deductibility that the costs be "paid or incurred in connection with the administration of the . . . trust," § 67(e)(1). We can think of no expense that could be incurred exclusively by a trust but would nevertheless not be "paid or incurred in connection with" its administration.

The Trustee argues that the exception in § 67(e)(1) "establishes a straightforward causation test." Brief for Petitioner 22. The proper inquiry, the Trustee contends, is "whether a particular expense of a particular trust or estate was caused by the fact that the property was held in the trust or estate." *Ibid.* Investment advisory fees incurred by a trust, the argument goes, meet this test because these costs are caused by the trustee's obligation "to obtain advice on investing trust assets in compliance with the Trustees' particular fiduciary duties." *Ibid.* We reject this reading as well.

On the Trustee's view, the statute operates only to distinguish costs that are incurred by virtue of a trustee's fiduciary duties from those that are not. But all (or nearly all) of a trust's expenses are incurred because the trustee has a duty to incur them; otherwise, there would be no reason for the trust to incur the expense in the first place. See G. Bogert & G. Bogert, Law of Trusts and Trustees § 801, p. 134 (2d rev. ed. 1981) ("[T]he payment for expenses must be reasonably necessary to facilitate administration of the trust"). As an example of a type of trust-related expense that would be subject to the 2% floor, the Trustee offers "expenses for routine maintenance of real property" held by a trust. Brief for Petitioner 23. But such costs would appear to be fully deductible under the Trustee's own reading, because a trustee is obligated to incur maintenance expenses in light of the fiduciary duty to maintain trust property. See 1 Restatement (Second) of Trusts § 176, p. 381 (1957) ("The trustee is under a duty to the beneficiary to use reasonable care and skill to preserve the trust property").

Indeed, the Trustee's formulation of its argument is circular: "Trust investment advice fees are caused by the fact the property is held in trust." Brief for Petitioner 19. But "trust investment advice fees" are only aptly described as such because the property is held in trust; the statute asks whether such costs would be incurred by an individual if the property were not. Even when there is a clearly analogous category of costs that would be incurred by individuals, the Trustee's reading would exempt most or all trust costs as fully deductible merely because they derive from a trustee's fiduciary duty. Adding the modifier "trust" to costs that otherwise would be incurred by an individual surely cannot be enough to escape the 2% floor.

What is more, if the Trustee's position were correct, then only the first clause of § 67(e)(1) — providing that the cost be "incurred in connection with the administration of the . . . trust" — would be necessary. The statute's second, limiting condition — that the cost also be one "which would not have been incurred if the property were not held in such trust" — would do no work; we see no difference in saying, on the one hand, that costs are "caused by" the fact that the property is held in trust and, on the other, that costs are incurred "in connection with the administration" of the trust. Thus, accepting the Trustee's approach "would render part of the statute entirely superfluous, something we are loath to do." *Cooper Industries, Inc. v. Aviall Services, Inc.*, 543 U.S. 157, 166 (2004).

The Trustee's reading is further undermined by our inclination, "[i]n construing provisions . . . in which a general statement of policy is qualified by an exception, [to] read the exception narrowly in order to preserve the primary operation of the provision." *Commissioner v. Clark*, 489 U.S. 726, 739 [63 AFTR 2d 89-860] (1989). As we have said, § 67(e) sets forth a general rule for purposes of the 2% floor established in § 67(a): "For purposes of this section, the adjusted gross income of an estate or trust shall be computed in the same manner as in the case of an individual." Under the Trustee's reading, § 67(e)(1)'s exception would swallow the general rule; most (if not all) expenses incurred by a trust would be fully deductible. "Given that Congress has enacted a general rule . . . , we should not eviscerate that legislative judgment through an expansive reading of a somewhat ambiguous exception." *Ibid.*

More to the point, the statute by its terms does not "establis[h] a straightforward causation test," Brief for Petitioner 22, but rather invites a hypothetical inquiry into the treatment of the property were it held outside a trust. The statute does not ask whether a cost was incurred because the property is held by a trust; it asks whether a particular cost "would not have been incurred if the property were not held in such trust," § 67(e)(1). "Far from examining the nature of the cost at issue from the perspective of whether it was caused by the trustee's duties, the statute instead looks to the counterfactual question of whether individuals would have incurred such costs in the absence of a trust." Brief for Respondent 9.

This brings us to the test adopted by the Fourth and Federal Circuits: Costs incurred by trusts that escape the 2% floor are those that would not "commonly" or "customarily" be incurred by individuals. See *Scott*, 328 F.3d, at 140 [91 AFTR 2d 2003-2100] CA4, 5/1/2003 ("Put simply, trust-related administrative expenses are subject to the 2% floor if they constitute expenses commonly incurred by individual taxpayers"); *Mellon Bank* [88 AFTR 2d 2001-5800], 265 F.3d, at [red. Cir. Sept. 7, 2001] (§ 67(e) "treats as fully deductible only those trust-related administrative expenses that are unique to the administration of a trust and not customarily incurred outside of trusts"). The Solicitor General also accepts this view as an alternative reading of the statute. See Brief for Respondent 20–21. We agree with this approach.

The question whether a trust-related expense is fully deductible turns on a prediction about what would happen if a fact were changed—specifically, if the property were held by an individual rather than by a trust. In the context of making such a prediction, when there is uncertainty about the answer, the word "would" is best read as "express[ing] concepts such as custom, habit, natural disposition, or probability." *Scott, supra*, at 139. See Webster's Third New International Dictionary 2637–2638 (1993); American Heritage Dictionary 2042, 2059 (3d ed. 1996). The Trustee objects that the statutory text "does not ask whether expenses are 'customarily' incurred outside of trusts," Reply Brief for Petitioner 15, but that is the direct import of the language in context. The text requires determining what would happen if a fact were changed; such an exercise necessarily entails a prediction; and predictions are based on what would customarily or commonly occur. Thus, in asking whether a particular type of cost "would not have been incurred" if the property were held by an individual, § 67(e)(1) excepts from the 2% floor only those costs that it would be uncommon (or unusual, or unlikely) for such a hypothetical individual to incur.

III

Having decided on the proper reading of § 67(e)(1), we come to the application of the statute to the particular question in this case: whether investment advisory fees incurred by a trust escape the 2% floor.

It is not uncommon or unusual for individuals to hire an investment adviser. Certainly the Trustee, who has the burden of establishing its entitlement to the deduction, has not demonstrated that it is. See *INDOPCO, Inc. v. Commissioner*, 503 U.S. 79, 84 [69 AFTR 2d 92-694] (1992) (noting the "'familiar rule' that 'an income tax deduction is a matter of legislative grace and that the burden of clearly showing the right to the claimed deduction is on the taxpayer'" (quoting *Interstate Transit Lines v. Commissioner*, 319 U.S. 590, 593 [30 AFTR 1310] (1943))); Tax Court Rule 142(a)(1) (stating that the "burden of proof shall be upon the petitioner," with certain exceptions not relevant here). The Trustee's argument is that individuals cannot incur trust investment advisory fees, not that individuals do not commonly incur investment advisory fees.

Indeed, the essential point of the Trustee's argument is that he engaged an investment adviser because of his fiduciary duties under Connecticut's Uniform Prudent Investor Act, Conn. Gen. Stat. § 45a-541a(a) (2007). The Act eponymously requires trustees to follow the "prudent investor rule." To satisfy this standard, a trustee must "invest and manage trust assets *as a prudent investor would*, by considering the purposes, terms, distribution requirements and other circumstances of the trust." § 45a-541b(a) (emphasis added). The prudent investor standard plainly does not refer to a prudent *trustee*; it would not be very helpful to explain that a trustee should act as a prudent trustee would. Rather, the standard looks to what a prudent investor with the same investment objectives handling his own affairs would do—*i.e.*, a prudent individual investor. See Restatement (Third) of Trusts (Prudent Investor Rule) Reporter's Notes on § 227, p. 58 (1990) ("The prudent investor rule of this Section has its origins in the dictum of *Harvard College v. Amory*, 9 Pick. (26 Mass.) 446, 461 (1830), stating that trustees must 'observe how men of prudence, discretion, and intelligence manage their own affairs, not in regard to speculation, but in regard to the permanent disposition of their funds, considering the probable income, as well as the probable safety of the capital to be invested'"). See also, *e.g.*, *In re Musser's Estate*, 341 Pa. 1, 9–10, 17 A.2d 411, 415 (1941) (noting the "general rule" that "a trustee must exercise such prudence and diligence in conducting the affairs of the trust as men of average diligence and discretion would employ in their own affairs"). And we have no reason to doubt the Trustee's claim that a hypothetical prudent investor in his position would have solicited investment advice, just as he did. Having accepted all this, it is quite difficult to say that investment advisory fees "would not have been incurred"—that is, that it would be unusual or uncommon for such fees to have been incurred—if the property were held by an individual investor with the same objectives as the Trust in handling his own affairs.

We appreciate that the inquiry into what is common may not be as easy in other cases, particularly given the absence of regulatory guidance. But once you depart in the name of ease of administration from the language chosen by Congress, there is more than one way to skin the cat: The Trustee raises administrability concerns in support of his causation test, Reply Brief for Petitioner 6, but so does the Government in explaining why it prefers the Court of Appeals' approach to the one it has successfully advanced before the Tax Court and two Federal Circuits. Congress's decision to phrase the pertinent inquiry in terms of a prediction about a hypothetical situation inevitably entails some uncertainty, but that is no excuse for judicial amendment of the statute. The Code elsewhere poses similar questions—such as whether expenses are "ordinary," see §§ 162(a), 212; see also *Deputy, Administratrix v. Du Pont*, 308 U.S. 488, 495 [23 AFTR 808] (1940) (noting that "[o]rdinary has the connotation of normal, usual, or customary")—and the inquiry is in any event what § 67(e)(1) requires.

As the Solicitor General concedes, some trust-related investment advisory fees may be fully deductible "if an investment advisor were to impose a special, additional charge applicable only to its fiduciary accounts." Brief for Respondent 25. There is nothing in the record, however, to suggest that Warfield charged the Trustee anything extra, or treated the Trust any differently than it would have treated an individual with similar objectives, because of the Trustee's fiduciary obligations. See App. 24–27. It is conceivable, moreover, that a trust may have an unusual investment objective, or may require a specialized balancing of the interests of various parties, such that a reasonable comparison with individual investors would be improper. In such a case, the incremental cost of expert advice beyond what would normally be required for the ordinary taxpayer would not be subject to the 2% floor. Here, however, the Trust has not asserted that its investment objective or its requisite balancing of competing interests was distinctive. Accordingly, we conclude that the investment advisory fees incurred by the Trust are subject to the 2% floor.

The judgment of the Court of Appeals is affirmed.

In the aftermath of the *Knight* decision, the Treasury Department has promulgated instructive regulations. The demarcation test for whether an investment or management expenditure incurred by an estate or trust is deductible is whether "it commonly or customarily would be incurred by a hypothetical individual owning the same property." Treas. Reg. § 1.67-4(a). If such expense would be commonly or customarily incurred by an individual, it is not deductible; conversely, if such expense would not commonly or customarily be incurred by an individual, it would be deductible. The Treasury Regulations then elaborate those expenses which would **not** be deductible, including, but not limited to, the following:[8]

- Ownership costs such as condominium fees, insurance premiums, maintenance and lawn services, and automobile registration and insurance costs. Treas. Reg. § 1.67-4(b)(2). (However, if such expenses are incurred to produce income (e.g., rent generation) rather than merely to preserve property, such expenses would be deductible.)
- All tax preparation fees aside from those related to estate and generation-skipping transfer tax returns, fiduciary income tax returns, and the decedent's final individual income tax returns. Treas. Reg. § 1.67-4(b)(3).
- Investment advisory fees except for "certain incremental costs of investment advice beyond the amount that normally would be charged to an individual investor." Treas. Reg. § 1.67-4(b)(4).
- Appraisal fees (e.g., for insurance coverage), but not those "to determine the fair market value of assets as of the decedent's date of death (or the alternate valuation date), to determine value for purposes of making distributions, or as otherwise required to properly prepare the estate's or trust's tax returns, or a generation-skipping transfer tax return. . . ." Treas. Reg. § 1.67-4(b)(5).

All fiduciary expenses that individuals would not normally incur and that are unique to trusts and estates (e.g., probate court fees and costs; fiduciary bond premiums; legal publication costs of notices to creditors or heirs; the cost of certified copies of the decedent's death certificate; and costs related to fiduciary accounts) are deductible. Treas. Reg. § 1.67-4(a)(6).

---

8. If the trust or estate incurs a bundled fee that has a component that would be disallowed and a component that would be allowed, the taxpayer should "unbundle" and allocate the expense using a "reasonable method." Treas. Reg. § 1.67-4(c).

Once an investment or management expense is determined to be deductible under Code § 212, yet more analysis awaits. More specifically, a determination must be made if the expense in question should be capitalized under Code § 263. Code § 263 declares that no deduction is allowed for "[a]ny amount paid out for new buildings or for permanent improvements or betterments made to increase the value of any property or estate." Code § 263(a). The Treasury Regulations amplify the statute and state "[e]xpenses paid or incurred in defending or perfecting title to property, in recovering property . . . , or in developing or improving property, constitute a part of the cost of the property and are not deductible expenses." Treas. Reg. § 1.212(k).

In the case below, the Court of Claims goes through two different analytic exercises. Part one of the case, presented immediately below, analyzes whether certain expenses related to securing bona fide title to property that a trust incurs must be capitalized (i.e., whether Treas. Reg. § 1.212(k) limits the availability of a deduction). Part two of the case, presented in the next subsection of the textbook, examines how the receipt of tax-exempt income may curtail the availability of otherwise deductible expenses. Because the familial relationships in the case below present their own challenge, we have supplied what we hope will prove to be a useful family tree.

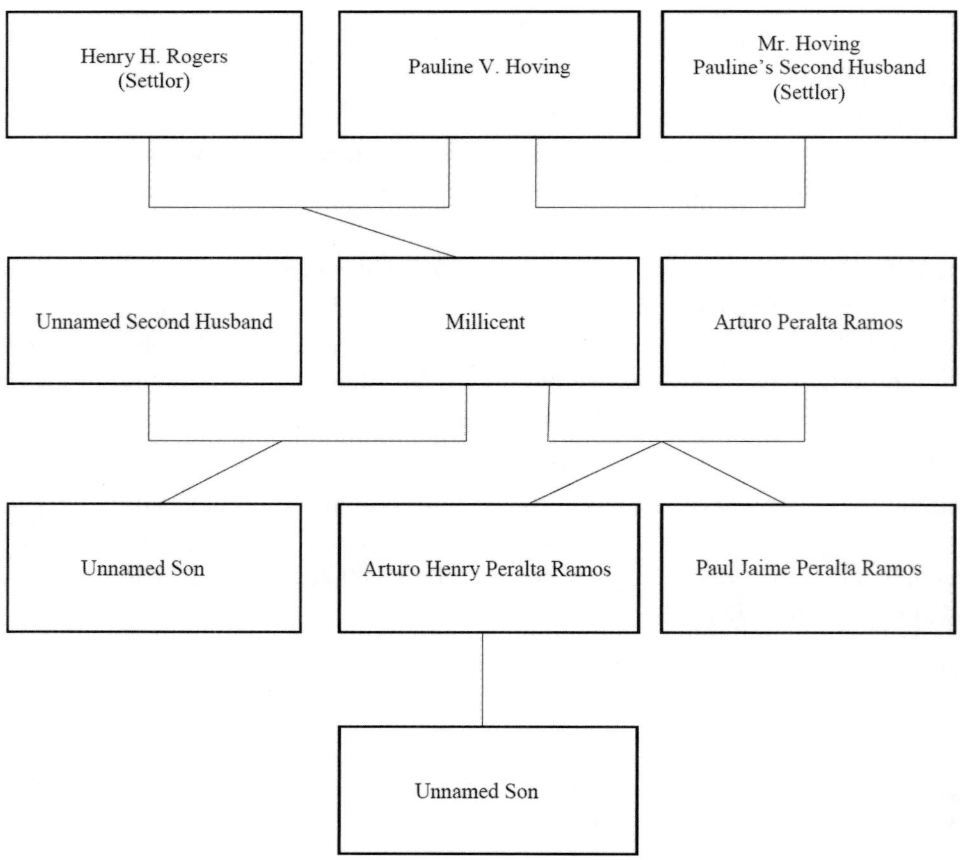

Manufacturers Hanover Trust Co. v. United States

160 Ct. Cl. 582, 312 F.2d 785 (1963)

Davis, Judge, delivered the opinion of the court:

This is a suit brought by plaintiff, as trustee under a trust indenture executed by Henry H. Rogers on November 5, 1927, to obtain a refund of income taxes and interest in the amount of $23,008.89, which was paid by the trust for calendar year 1954. The case is before the court on plaintiff's motion and defendant's cross-motion for summary judgment, and presents three issues which call for resolution: (1) whether attorneys' fees incurred by the taxpayer in certain trust litigation are deductible as ordinary and necessary expenses for the management, conservation, or maintenance of property held for the production of income, or whether the expenses were capital expenditures incurred in defending or perfecting title to property; (2) whether capital gains and other gross income allocated to trust principal are to be taken into account in determining the amount of expenses, otherwise deductible by the trust, which are rendered nondeductible because allocable to tax-exempt income; and (3) whether taxpayer, in its claim for refund, made a sufficient demand for a deduction for the amount of income which it was required to distribute currently to the beneficiaries.

Plaintiff is a corporation organized under New York law for the conduct of a banking and trust business. On November 5, 1927, Henry H. Rogers executed an indenture transferring property in trust to an individual trustee, since deceased, and to plaintiff's predecessor, in contemplation of his daughter Millicent's forthcoming marriage to Arturo Peralta Ramos. The marriage took place two days later. Under the terms of the indenture, the net income of the trust was payable to Millicent for life, and at her death the trust was to be divided into equal shares (after making provision for her husband, if he survived her and had the marriage not terminated in divorce—as it did), one share to be held in trust for and the net income paid for life to each surviving child of the marriage. Thereafter, the corpus was to be paid to that child's issue per stirpes; or, in default of issue, to his brothers or sisters or their issue; and in case of default of such beneficiaries, to the grantor or those entitled to take under his will. The indenture also contained reservations of reversionary interests in the event that Millicent might be survived by only one child, or by no children, but these provisions never came into effect, for at her death on January 1, 1953, she was survived by two sons of her marriage to Ramos—Arturo Henry Peralta Ramos and Paul Jaime Peralta Ramos, who were born on November 14, 1928, and February 18, 1931, respectively. The grantor, Henry H. Rogers, died testate on July 25, 1935, leaving a part of his residuary estate in trust for his widow, Pauline. She survived him, and by remarriage became Pauline V. Hoving.

After the death of Millicent, early in 1953, there was uncertainty as to the validity of the continuing trusts to Arturo Henry and Paul under Section 11 of the New York Personal Property Law, which prohibits suspension of the absolute power of alienation for more than two lives in being. On January 7, 1954, the plaintiff filed a petition in the Supreme Court of the State of New York for an order settling its account as trustee and fixing and allowing its commissions, and also construing the trust indenture and the grantor's will and instructing plaintiff as to the disposition of the trust assets. Millicent's executors, her two sons born of the marriage with Ramos, the infant son of Arturo Henry Ramos, another son of Millicent by a later marriage, and Mrs. Hoving were among those made parties to the proceeding, and they, as well as plaintiff, participated and prepared briefs on the issue of the validity of the trust. The position of Mrs. Hoving, residuary legatee of Henry Rogers, was that under New York law the continuing trusts for Arturo Henry and Paul were illegal and void, and she may also have attacked the entire inter vivos trust indenture of November 5, 1927. The other participants, opposing the interpretation advanced by Mrs. Hoving, contended that the trust indenture was wholly valid.

On November 29, 1954, before the cause was decided by the state court, the parties settled the proceeding by stipulation, after extended negotiations. Under the terms of this agreement, Mrs. Hoving withdrew her answer, consented that an order be entered construing the secondary trusts as valid, and assigned any rights of hers to the assets of these trusts to Arturo Henry and Paul in return for their paying her from their own funds the sum of $40,000. The parties also stipulated, subject to court approval, the various allowances to be paid to the different attorneys (and to the guardian ad litem of the infant respondent), and that all such allowances should be paid by the trust. The court entered a final order on December 6, 1954, in conformity with the stipulations, that plaintiff's accounts as trustee were approved and settled; that the trusts to commence upon the death of Millicent for the benefit of Arturo Henry and Paul were valid and enforceable; and that the trustee was to pay out of the trust corpus $49,000 in attorneys' fees and $15.25 as disbursements.

When it filed its fiduciary income tax return for 1954, plaintiff claimed a deduction of the entire $49,015.25 paid out in the trust litigation. Upon audit, the Commissioner of Internal Revenue disallowed the deduction "to the extent of $35,315.25 for the reason that to that extent the expenditures were not deductible under section 212 of the Internal Revenue Code of 1954 but should be capitalized under section 263 as an expenditure to perfect title." The $13,700 allowed by the Commissioner was attributed by him to the accounting aspect of the litigation and therefore allowable as an ordinary and necessary expense of the trust. Plaintiff paid the deficiency and then filed a refund claim asserting that the entire amount of attorneys' fees was deductible (except to the extent, if any, allocable to tax-exempt income) as an ordinary and necessary expense. Rejection of the refund claim brings the matter before us.

There is no dispute as to the allocation of these litigation fees between the accounting and the trust-construction phases. Plaintiff's position is the broader one that the sums attributable to the construction aspect of the suit must also be allowed as a deduction under Section 212 of the Internal Revenue Code of 1954 (26 U.S.C. § 212 (1958 ed.)), authorizing the deduction of "all the ordinary and necessary expenses paid or incurred during the taxable year for the production or collection of income

[or] for the management, conservation, or maintenance of property held for the production of income," and more particularly by Treasury Regulation § 1.212-1(i), which says that "reasonable amounts paid or incurred by the fiduciary of an estate or trust on account of administration expenses, *including fiduciaries' fees and expenses of litigation*, which are ordinary and necessary in connection with the performance of the duties of administration are deductible under section 212" (emphasis added). On the other hand, defendant relies, of course, on Treasury Regulation § 1.212-1(k):

> Expenses paid or incurred *in defending or perfecting title to property*, in recovering property (other than investment property and amounts of income which, if and when recovered, must be included in gross income), or in developing or improving property, constitute a part of the cost of the property and are not deductible expenses. Attorneys' fees paid in a suit to quiet title to lands are not deductible * * * (emphasis added).

As we have recently noted with respect to comparable provisions under the 1939 Code, these sections of the statute and the regulations, taken together, require that, before the expenditures can be deductible, they must be (a) "ordinary and necessary"; (b) "paid or incurred during the taxable year"; (c) "for the production or collection of income," or "for the management, conservation, or maintenance of property held for the production of income"; and (d) other than capital expenditures, including expenditures incurred in "defending or perfecting title to property." See *California and Hawaiian Sugar Refining Corp. v. United States*, No. 287-59, Ct. Cl., decided December 5, 1962, slip op. at 10-11 [10 AFTR 2d 6078]; *Industrial Aggregate Co. v. United States*, 284 F.2d 639, 644 [6 AFTR 2d 5959] (C.A. 8, 1960). In this case the critical question is whether the expenditures were incurred in the defense or perfection of title.

The binding effect of the rule that expenditures incurred in defending or perfecting title must be capitalized has long been recognized, and often applied. See, for example, *Bowers v. Lumpkin*, 140 F.2d 927 [32 AFTR 201] (C.A. 4, 1944); *Roberts v. United States*, 115 Ct. Cl. 428, 87 F. Supp. 935 [38 AFTR 1312] (1950); *Vernor v. United States*, 87 Ct. Cl. 435, 23 F. Supp. 532 [21 AFTR 485] (1938); *United States v. St. Joe Paper Co.*, 284 F.2d 430 [6 AFTR 2d 6058] (C.A. 5, 1960); *Brown v. Commissioner*, 215 F.2d 697 [46 AFTR 580] (C.A. 5, 1954); *Safety Tube Corp. v. Commissioner*, 168 F.2d 787 [36 AFTR 1120] (C.A. 6, 1948); *Johnson v. Commissioner*, 162 F.2d 844 [35 AFTR 1568] (C.A. 5, 1947); *Jones' Estate v. Commissioner*, 127 F.2d 231 [29 AFTR 226] (C.A. 5, 1942); *Boulder Building Corp v. United States*, 125 F. Supp. 512 (W.D. Okla., 1954); *Coughlin v. Commissioner*, 3 T.C. 420 (1944). The validity of the rule is settled but problems continue to arise in its application to the varieties of particular circumstance. See e.g., the various opinions in *Ruoff v. Commissioner*, 277 F.2d 222 [5 AFTR 2d 1181] (C.A. 3, 1960), and 30 T.C. 204 (1958). When is an expenditure merely conservative, and when does it exceed this line and become an element of title perfection or defense? The subsidiary principles are not fully developed; the answer often depends, also, on a weighing of the individual facts. There is as yet "no hard and fast rule" by which deductibility can "easily be determined" (*Brown v. Commissioner, supra*, 215 F.2d 697, 699 [46 AFTR 580] (C.A. 5, 1954)); but certain helpful guidelines have been fixed, even though there may still be dispute as to others.

In ascertaining the character of an expenditure for legal fees, the courts uniformly look first to the primary purpose of the litigation. "[I]f the primary purpose was title, then the expenditure is capital in nature and must be capitalized; if the aspect of title is only incidental to the primary purpose of the litigation, then the expense is deductible as such and need not be capitalized." *Loyd v. United States*, 139 Ct. Cl. 626, 632, 153 F. Supp. 416, 419 [52 AFTR 201] (1957); *Industrial Aggregate Co. v. United States, supra*, 284 F.2d at 645 [6 AFTR 2d 5959]; *Ruoff v. Commissioner, supra*, 277 F.2d 222 [5 AFTR 2d 1181] (C.A. 3, 1960). It makes no difference that the expenditures were ordinary and necessary in the colloquial sense, or that they affected the possibility of obtaining income, or even that they arose from following the only feasible course open to the taxpayer. If the primary purpose of the proceeding was defense or perfection of title to property, the expenses must be capitalized. Especially in this area is it true that "not every expenditure can be claimed as a deduction and this is so whatever may be the effect of the expenditure upon the profit-seeking activities of the taxpayer." *Lewis v. Commissioner*, 253 F.2d 821, 825 [1 AFTR 2d 1355] (C.A. 2, 1958). Moreover, contrary to plaintiff's assertion, section 1.212-1(i) of the Treasury Regulations, quoted above, does not "flatly allow" all fiduciaries' expenses of litigation as deductions. Such expenses are allowed only so long as they do not fall within the proscription of subsection (k) of the same regulation (and Section 263 of the Code and its regulations), pertaining to non-deductible capital expenditures. We find nothing in the 1954 Code or regulations indicating that fiduciaries, when faced with the necessity of making capital expenditures, should be afforded treatment so radically different from that accorded other taxpayers. Neither Congress nor the Treasury has purported to authorize a fiduciary to consider all of its litigation expenditures as "ordinary and necessary expenses."

Attempting to show that, in any case, the trust-construction proceeding did not have as its primary goal the defense of the trust's title to its assets, the plaintiff asserts that under New York law it had acquired an unimpeachably valid title to the entire trust property upon creation of the trust in 1927, and that the litigation was simply to determine the proper disposition in 1954 of the property committed to its care, i.e., whether after the death of Millicent Rogers in 1953 the trust assets should be used for the secondary trusts created for Arturo Henry and Paul Ramos or should be paid to the residuary legatees of Henry Rogers. Plaintiff says that under New York law the trust was indisputably lawful throughout the life of Millicent, and the only question which could possibly arise would be the continuing validity of the trusts for her sons after her death in 1953. The Government counters that the litigation was primarily to determine the initial validity of the trust's title to the property beginning with 1927; the brief points to certain principles of New York law holding that, if a grant violates the New York rules against perpetuities and the suspension of the power of alienation, it may be void from its inception and title, by operation of law, will remain in the grantor despite the trust agreement. Mrs. Hoving's challenge to the trust's title, the Government says, was of this fundamental character, raising the issue of whether the trustee ever had any valid title to the trust assets.

It is unnecessary, we think, to determine whether the question of New York law involved in the state litigation was the trust's right to the property ab initio, or solely the trust's continued legal title after the death of Millicent. A decision adverse to the plaintiff, rendered on either of these theories, would have deprived it of the title to the property, which it would certainly have claimed and retained if it were not for this or comparable litigation. There was much more to the case than a mere request by plaintiff for directions as to the future distribution of trust assets which the trustee admittedly owned. The plaintiff was, at the least, seeking to perfect (and to defend) its very title to the property from and after January 1, 1953, when Millicent died; the minimal issue in the proceeding was a possible defect which would have voided the trustee's title on that date and would have required the property to revert back to the grantor's residuary estate. There was a direct challenge to the trustee's continued title, not simply a dispute between beneficiaries of the trust. Moreover, this defect, if it existed under New York law, was already inherent in the title when the trustee acquired the assets under the trust indenture in 1927; it was a substantial pre-existing flaw in the basic indenture, not a subsequent cloud upon a once perfect and unquestioned title. Thus, it seems to us plain that, even on plaintiff's understanding of the precise issue in the construction proceeding, the perfection and defense of the trustee's claimed title to the trust property under the trust indenture was the essence of that suit. The litigation costs are therefore capital expenditures, rather than expenses deductible as ordinary and necessary under section 212. See *Parkway Realty Corp. v. Commissioner*, T.C. Mem. Dec., March 16, 1959; *Brown v. Commissioner*, 215 F.2d 697, 699-701 [46 AFTR 580] (C.A. 5, 1954); *Lewis v. Commissioner*, 253 F.2d 821, 827-28 [1 AFTR 2d 1355] (C.A. 2, 1958); *Wilson v. Commissioner*, 37 T.C. 230–34 (1961).

This situation is to be distinguished from that which would arise if a fiduciary sought to deduct expenses incurred in determining which of several potential beneficiaries was entitled to receive trust property. There the fiduciary's title would not be at issue, and it would not be engaged in perfecting or defending title. In *Trust of Bingham v. Commissioner*, 325 U.S. 365 [33 AFTR 842] (1945), expenses were incurred in winding up the trust after its expiration; the Court held that the costs of distribution, if ordinary and necessary, were deductible expenses incurred in the management of the trust property. *Trust of Spero v. Commission*, 30 T.C. 845, 855–56 (1958), is also a case in which the court felt itself to be dealing with expenses incurred in deciding which beneficiaries were the proper recipients of assets to be distributed by a fiduciary, as opposed to determining whether the trust had itself lost title to the property. Here the facts are the reverse.

Plaintiff argues that, nevertheless, we are compelled by our decision in *Loyd v. United States*, 139 Ct. Cl. 626, 153 F. Supp. 416 [52 AFTR 201] (1957), to rule in its favor. That case involved the deductibility of legal fees by the executors of a daughter's estate, which were paid to counsel for litigating the validity of a charitable bequest by her mother, the amounts of which would be included in the estate of the daughter, as sole heir of the grantor, if the mother's charitable grant was invalid under state law. As a result of this litigation holding the charitable bequest partly invalid, most of the property was delivered to the executors of the daughter. While recognizing the validity of the rule requiring capitalization of the expenses of title, the court interpreted the record as indicating that "the primary purpose, or at least the motivating force, of the litigation was not the question of who had title to the property, rather it was that the proper distribution of the estate's assets could not have been had without a prior determination by the court of the validity of the gift." *Loyd v. United States, supra*, 139 Ct. Cl. at 634, 153 F. Supp. at 421. Although title to certain property was one aspect of the litigation, it was incidental to the primary purpose of settling the two estates. The daughter's executors had a disputed claim to the assets marked for the charitable gift, but the overriding concern of the litigation, the court held (139 Ct. Cl. at 633-34), was not the issue of title but the proper administration of the daughter's estate which could not have been had without "first obtaining the answer to the question of validity of the grant to the church." In the present case, unlike *Loyd*, there is no showing, and on this record no reason to believe, that the proceeding by plaintiff in the New York Supreme Court was instituted because it was absolutely essential to the further management of the trust. There was no impending marshalling and distribution of the assets held by plaintiff; the trust could well have gone on, as provided by the indenture, until challenged by a proper adverse party. In this light, the litigation voluntarily begun after Millicent's death had for its direct, if not sole, purpose a legal declaration, helpful but not mandatory, whether the indenture was effective to give the trust continued title to the property. The costs of this type of quiet-title proceeding are capital expenditures rather than deductible expenses of trust administration.

B. Receipt of Tax-Exempt Income

The Code precludes deductions associated with the production of tax-exempt income. In other words, expenses incurred to generate tax-exempt income are not deductible. Code § 265(a). The reason for this limitation is obvious: the expenses associated with the production of tax-exempt income would otherwise offset taxable income earned by the taxpayer. Consider a corporate taxpayer which invests $1 million in tax-free bonds that pay $50,000 of interest income. Assume the corporate taxpayer pays a $10,000 annual fee to investment experts who manage the aforementioned bond portfolio. Since the interest income the bonds generate is exempt from tax, allowing the taxpayer to use this $10,000 expense elsewhere on its tax return would impermissibly shelter the receipt of taxable income.

When it comes to the income taxation of trusts and estates and the receipt of tax exempt income, determining the amount of the disallowed deduction presents a unique set of challenges. Consider first the concept of Distributable Net Income (DNI), which will be explored in depth in the next chapter. In a nutshell, DNI is the taxable income a trust and estate earns subject to several modifications, two of which are the general exclusion of capital gains and losses and the inclusion of net tax-exempt income. Code § 643.

The Code and regulations draw a relationship between DNI and allowable deductions. This relationship requires further explication beginning with the fact that deductions, including those found under Code § 212, are generally grouped into the following three baskets:

1. Direct Deductions: Those deductions directly related to one class of income (interest, rents, dividends, capital gains, etc.) are allocated to that class (e.g., rental repairs would be deducted directly against rental income). Treas. Reg. § 1.652(b)-3(a).
2. Excess Direct Deductions: So-called excess direct deductions may be allocated in any manner the taxpayer wishes (except for those expenses directly related to the production of tax-exempt income which cannot be allocated to any other class of income). Treas. Reg. § 1.652(b)-3(d). Unlike the rule for indirect deductions below, no portion of excess direct deductions needs to be allocated to tax-exempt income.
3. Indirect Deductions: These deductions, which include fiduciary commissions, costs of accountings, and the preparation of fiduciary tax returns, can be allocated to any class of income with two important limitations: first, they can only be allocated to items which are included in DNI (which generally does not include capital gains and losses) and second, a reasonable proportion must be allocated to tax-exempt income (and, thus, such proportion is not deductible). Treas. Reg. § 1.652(b)-3(b); Treas. Reg. § 1.265-1(c).

Determining the amount of the disallowed expense related to the generation of tax-exempt income boils down to the following disallowance ratio:

$$\frac{\text{Tax-exempt income}}{\text{Total amount of the gross income comprising DNI}} \times \text{Indirect Deduction} = \text{Disallowed Section 265 Deduction}$$

A salient feature of this disallowance ratio is that its denominator, like the concept of DNI, often excludes capital gains.[9] Notice that if capital gains were included in the denominator, it would be numerically larger and, as such, the amount of disallowed expenditure correspondingly smaller. In the continuation of the *Manufacturers Hanover Trust Co.* case below, taxpayers argued this exact point (i.e., the denominator should include all trust income, including capital gains, thereby yielding a smaller disallowance dollar figure), but the Court of Claims soundly rejected the taxpayers' position.

---

9. As discussed in the next chapter, while capital gains often are excluded from DNI, there are situations when DNI can be comprised of capital gain income.

Manufacturers Hanover Trust Co. v. United States

160 Ct. Cl. 582, 312 F.2d 785

[Continued]

The second issue relates to the allocation of the legal fees and trustee's commissions paid or incurred by the taxpayer, and otherwise allowable as "ordinary and necessary" deductions under Section 212, between taxable income and tax-exempt income (here, tax-exempt interest) received by the trust in 1954. Section 265 provides that no deduction shall be allowed for any amount allocable to a class of income wholly exempt from income tax. Treasury Regulation § 1.265-1 (c), promulgated under this section of the Code, sets forth, in general terms, the method by which this allocation is to be made.

Plaintiff reported the receipt of $8,370.85 during 1954 as interest wholly exempt from federal income taxes. The defendant allocated the indirect expenses (legal fees and commissions) between tax-exempt interest, on the one hand, and dividends and taxable interest, on the other, but, in so doing, excluded from the allocation base capital gains and taxable stock dividends, both of which, although elements of the trust's taxable income, were allocable to the principal of the trust under local law and the trust indenture. By the exclusion of these elements of taxable income from the base, the portion of the indirect expenses allocable to tax-exempt interest, and hence not deductible, was significantly increased. It is this refusal of the Internal Revenue Service to consider all the elements of the trust's taxable income, in making the allocation, which prompts plaintiff's complaint.

Since trust income is involved, it will help to begin with a brief outline of the special taxing system established by subchapter J of chapter 1 of the 1954 Code, the portion dealing with the income taxation of estates, trusts, beneficiaries, and decedents. "The basic principle underlying the taxation of ordinary trusts is that all the taxable income is to be taxed as income only once — either to the trust, or to the beneficiary, or in part to each. This is accomplished by allowing the estate or trust a deduction for certain amounts distributed or required to be distributed [whether or not actually distributed], and taxing the beneficiary on such amounts." Montgomery's Federal Taxes, 20.1 (38th ed. 1961). In general, this scheme of taxation is implemented by treating a trust as a separate taxable entity, the taxable income of which is computed in the same manner, and taxed to the same extent, as the taxable income of an individual — with certain exceptions set forth in the Code. §§ 641, 642, 651, 1954 I.R.C. Chief among these exceptions is the authorization of a deduction for that "income" of the taxable year which is required to be distributed currently. § 651(a), 1954 I.R.C. This deduction is designed to avoid the double taxation that would result if the income required to be distributed were first taxed to the trust, and then taxed again when distributed to the beneficiaries. So that the income not go untaxed, the Code requires that the beneficiaries include in their gross incomes the trust income distributable to them, whether it is actually distributed or not. § 652(a), 1954 I.R.C.

The central device utilized to effectuate this "flow-through" scheme of taxation is "distributable net income" — a crucial term in the present case. This is defined by Section 643(a) as the taxable income of the trust with certain important modifications, the most pertinent of which are:

1. Distributions to beneficiaries are not deducted.
2. Capital gains allocable to corpus (as here), and not paid, credited, or required to be distributed to any beneficiary, or paid or permanently set aside for charitable purposes, are excluded.
3. For trusts like plaintiff's which distribute current income only, extraordinary dividends or taxable stock dividends not paid or credited to any beneficiary because allocated by the fiduciary (in good faith) to principal, are *excluded.*
4. Tax-exempt interest, "reduced by any amounts which would be deductible in respect of disbursements allocable to such interest but for the provisions of section 265 (relating to disallowance of certain deductions)," is *included.*

Around this concept of "distributable net income" the Code builds its provisions for (a) the deduction allowed the trust for its current distributions to the beneficiaries, and (b) the distributions which the beneficiaries must include in their own gross incomes. "Thus, distributable net income has been termed the measuring rod or yardstick to be employed in determining, on the one hand, the maximum deduction for distributions which may be allowed to the estate or trust and for gauging, on the other hand, the extent to which beneficiaries may be taxable on the distributions." 6 Mertens "Law of Federal Income Taxation" § 36.04.

"Distributable net income" first appears on our stage in plaintiff's claim that, by excluding capital gains and taxable stock dividends from the allocation base used in determining the amount of administration expenses deductible, the Commissioner of Internal Revenue followed Special Instruction 39 of the instructions to Form 1041, the fiduciary income tax return. Instruction 39 applies to the separate schedule on the form to be used for the computation of "distributable net income," and says that for this purpose tax-exempt interest is to be reduced by

> any amounts which, but for the provisions of Section 265, would be deductible in respect of disbursements, expenses, losses, etc., of the trust or estate, directly or indirectly allocable to such interest. The amount of the indirect disbursements, etc., allocable to tax-exempt interest is that amount which bears the same ratio to the total disbursements, etc., of the trust or estate not directly attributable to other items of income as the total tax-exempt interest received bears to the total of all the items of gross income (including tax-exempt interest * * *) entering into *distributable net income* (emphasis added).

By including only those items of gross income which enter into distributable net income, this instruction excludes capital gains and taxable stock dividends (both allocable to corpus). The plaintiff says that the Commissioner also presumably relied on the examples in section 1.652 (c)-4 of the Treasury Regulations, which similarly determine the amount of administration expenses allocable to tax-exempt interest. The argument is that the instruction and the regulation are unreasonable in arbitrarily ignoring large classes of income, and that this exclusion will result, through the years, in the over-collection of tax. Plaintiff urges that, although the "artificial concept" of distributable net income may be suited to the determination of the maximum amount of income taxable to beneficiaries, "it is peculiarly ill-adapted to answer the far more simple and truly unrelated question of what general administration expenses are allocable to tax-exempt interest."

The defendant's reply is that Instruction 39 to Form 1041, and the examples set forth in various regulations under subchapter J, are irrelevant to the question of allocation of deductions by the trust; they relate to the computation of distributable net income, and "although in such computation capital gains and losses are also excluded, this has only an indirect bearing upon the reasonableness of the allocation under Section 265 (1) which is here involved." Thus abandoning the stance taken by the Commissioner, the Government proposes a new theory which in this case (it says) would reach approximately the same result as that of the Commissioner and would therefore deprive the plaintiff of its claimed refund. Plaintiff, in turn, attacks the defendant's substitute theory as wholly unwarranted.

On the narrowest view of the question presented to us by this case, we would not have to resolve these controversies. Strictly, only the trust's taxable income is before us. And where, as here, the allowable deductions are insufficient to absorb the distributable net income of the trust (excluding tax-exempt income and deductions allocable thereto) the result of the subchapter J system of taxation is that the taxable income of the trust is unchanged, whether or not income allocable to principal account is included in the base for the allocation of otherwise deductible expenses between taxable and tax-exempt income. This is true because the deduction for income required to be distributed currently — which in this case equals (and can never exceed) the distributable net income reduced by tax-exempt income and the deductions allocable thereto — and the allowable operating expenses are both proper deductions, in themselves, from the trust's taxable income, but at the same time the expense deductions are also proper deductions in computing distributable net income itself. Since the expense deductions enter into the computation of taxable income, and distributable net income (which here equals the current distribution deduction) is a function of taxable income, the two types of deduction are intimately related, varying inversely with each other. If plaintiff is right and capital gains allocable to principal are included in the allocation base, the deduction for legal fees (and trustee's commissions) will be increased, but that increase will necessarily push down the taxable income (before deduction for current distributions), and therefore the current distribution deduction, by the same amount. Since the adjusted distributable net income limits the deduction available to the trust for amounts of income required to be distributed currently, the changes in the amount of expenses deductible by the trust will be offset by countervailing changes in the amount of the deduction for distributions, and the taxable income of the trust will be static. So far as the trust is concerned, we could, therefore, under the present circumstances, abstain from deciding the exact make-up of the deductions.

However, it will not do to stop so short of giving a response to the issue argued to us. While in these circumstances the inclusion of capital gains (and other amounts not includible in the computation of distributable net income) in the allocation base does not alter the taxable income of the trust, it would decrease the tax liability of the income beneficiaries. This would be the direct result of the decrease in distributable net income stemming from that inclusion, for distributable net income limits the amount required to be included in gross income by the income beneficiaries. It seems appropriate, therefore, to take the step of answering on its merits the allocation issue posed by the parties.

Returning then to the arguments on allocation, we find it necessary to consider the plaintiff's attack on the Commissioner's method of allocation because we cannot agree with the defendant's assertion that Instruction 39 and the regulations under subchapter J are irrelevant to the reasonableness of the allocation of trust expenses under Section 265(1). Treasury Regulation 1.652(c)-4, to which taxpayer refers, furnishes an example of the application of the rules for trusts required to distribute all income currently. Sub-paragraph (e) of this example consists of a computation of the taxable income of a trust, and the allocation of indirect expenses to the taxable and nontaxable portions of the trust's income is made, without discussion, on a distribution base from which capital gains allocable to corpus have been excluded. This is a plain enough indication, which we cannot ignore, of the specific method the Commissioner has chosen, by regulation, for the allocation of the expenses of trusts. Instruction 39, which by its terms purports to operate within the boundaries of Section 265, simply follows suit. More generally, the over-all regulation on allocation of expenses between taxable and tax-exempt income (Section 1.265-1(c), quoted above) requires that allocation of indirect expenses should be made "in the light of all facts and circumstances in each case." When the income of a trust is involved, the concept of distributable net income, as well as the special system of taxation in subchapter J, is an important component "of all the facts and circumstances." That concept and system are, as we have said, the primary mechanisms by which the income of a trust is taxed but once, either to the trust or to its beneficiaries; as the Tax Court has held, they should not be disregarded in applying the general allocation provisions of Section 265 to the particular problems of trust income. See *Tucker v. Commissioner, supra* [38 T.C. 955 (1962)].

Since the challenged regulation and instruction are thus applicable, we are controlled by their provisions unless we can agree with plaintiff that they are unreasonable as applied to the case before us. *Estate of Bahen v. United States*, Ct. Cl. No. 144-60, decided July 18, 1962, slip op. 4, 13, 305 F.2d 827, 829, 835 [10 AFTR 2d 6195]. But in the present circumstances—where the deductible expenses fall short of absorbing the distributable net income—the regulation and the instruction do not unfairly ignore large classes of income in making the expense allocation. The income beneficiaries are taxable only to the extent of distributable net income, which excludes gains attributable to corpus. It is not out of key, therefore, to insist that the allocation of expenses between taxable and tax-exempt income should be restricted to the same type of non-corpus gains. This is all the more so since, under Section 652 (b), the amounts included in the income beneficiary's gross income have the same character in his hands—e.g., as taxable dividends or tax-exempt interest—as in the hands of the trust. Moreover, under the 1954 Code, as a result of the structure of distributable net income (which has as its starting point the taxable income of the trust), the tax benefit of deductions allocable to corpus is generally shifted to the income beneficiaries. See *Tucker v. Commissioner, supra*. The challenged regulation and instruction allowably balance this incongruity—that the income beneficiary, not the corpus beneficiary, receives the tax benefit of expenses allocable to corpus—by providing that those indirect expenses which are usually chargeable against capital gains must be allocated by the income beneficiary to all the income (both taxable and tax-exempt) required to be distributed to him. All the income required to be distributed currently by the trust and "included" in gross income by the beneficiary (particularly tax-exempt income), rather than just the taxable elements, bears the burden of the expenses attributable to capital gain. The tax benefit of the portion of these expenses assigned to tax-exempt income is loss, but this is not unfair to a taxpayer who has the special advantage of deductions attributable to gains he does not receive. Perhaps there may be other trust situations in which the Commissioner's regulations on allocation are unreasonable, but they are not so in the circumstances we have here. Plaintiff cannot recover the tax computed under those regulations.

In partial answer, plaintiff relies strongly on a twenty-year old internal directive of the Revenue Service to its agents (Field Procedure Memorandum No. 232, dated October 30, 1942), which authorized capital gains to be taken into account in full for trust allocation purposes. We doubt the weight to be given at this time to such non-public internal instructions, but in any event it must be recognized that the memorandum was addressed to agents charged with the administration of a law prohibiting the tax benefit of deductions chargeable to corpus from being enjoyed by the income beneficiaries, and the system of allocation of expenses it suggested was tailored to that need. The changed system of taxing fiduciaries set forth in subchapter J of the 1954 Code robs the memorandum of continued persuasiveness in this field.

[Before handling a third issue, the Claims Court upheld the Commissioner's position on this second issue.]

Is the formula to determine the expense disallowance amount announced in *Manufacturers Hanover Trust Co.* fair, bearing in mind that it produces an outcome in which a larger amount of the investment and management expense is disallowed? In the court's mind, this is the appropriate result, because the trust's DNI will thus be comprised of a larger portion of taxable income (a point which will be illustrated in more detail in the next chapter). As a result, the current trust income beneficiary will bear a larger income tax burden (as the composition of income distributed is deemed to be comprised of taxable, not tax-exempt, income); however, the very same trust income beneficiary is able to capture tax benefits that truly burden the trust remainder beneficiary (e.g., the charging of a portion of the commissions against the principal of the trust).[10] In the court's mind, these disparate tax treatments between current and remainder trust beneficiaries essentially function to cancel each other out, producing an outcome that should be palatable to everyone.[11]

But sometimes indirect expenses, such as termination commissions, relate to time periods that extend beyond the immediate tax year. In those cases, using the fractional method described in *Manufacturers Hanover Trust Co.* to compute the amount of the disallowed expenses does not make sense and could be easily manipulated (e.g., in the year of termination, the taxpayer trustee might strategically eschew the receipt of tax-exempt income). That being the case, the IRS and courts allow a different approach in computing the amount of disallowed expense when addressing termination commissions, embodied in the fraction below:

$$\frac{\text{Tax-exempt income (earned over time period in question)}}{\begin{array}{c}\text{Total amount of income comprising}\\ \text{the gross amount of DNI}\\ \text{(earned over time period in question)}^{12}\end{array}} \times \text{Indirect Deduction} = \begin{array}{c}\text{Disallowed Section}\\ \text{265 Deduction}\end{array}$$

Whittemore v. United States, 383 F.2d 824 (8th Cir. 1967). Another court, *Fabens v. Commissioner*, 519 F.2d 1310 (1st Cir. 1975), added an important refinement to the

10. For example, assume under the Principal and Income Act that fiduciary commissions are chargeable one-half to income and one-half to principal. If the annual trustee commissions are $10,000, the current income beneficiary bears a $5,000 burden and the remainder beneficiary bears a $5,000 burden; however, the entire $10,000 is deductible in the current tax year, potentially sheltering otherwise taxable income. Another court, which had the same holding as *Manufacturers Hanover Trust Co.*, echoed this identical sentiment: "the income beneficiary receives the benefit of all the deductions of the trust not attributable to tax-exempt interest, including those deductions, if any, properly allocable to capital gains." *Tucker v. Commissioner*, 322 F.2d 86, Ft. 2 (2d Cir. 1963).

The Uniform Principal and Income Act was drafted by the National Conference of Commissioners on Uniform State Laws (now known as the Uniform Law Commission) as last amended or revised in 2008. In October 2018, the Uniform Law Commission issued the Uniform Fiduciary Income and Principal Act. The 2018 Act is available at the Uniform Law Commission website, www.uniformlaws.org. To date, six states have adopted it and several other states are on the verge of enacting it.

11. One caveat: no trust or estate beneficiary financially benefits by the imposition of a larger tax burden.

12. Because in the year of termination, DNI will include capital gains and losses (see Chapter 3), they should not be excluded from the denominator.

foregoing formula, requiring that unrealized gains and losses should also be taken into account with respect to indirect expenses incurred over an elongated time period:

$$\frac{\begin{array}{c}\text{Tax-exempt income}\\ \text{(earned over time period in question)}\\ \text{PLUS unrealized gains/losses}\end{array}}{\begin{array}{c}\text{Total amount of income comprising}\\ \text{the gross amount of DNI}\\ \text{(earned over time period in question)}\\ \text{PLUS unrealized gains/losses}^{13}\end{array}} \times \text{Indirect Deduction} = \begin{array}{c}\text{Disallowed Section}\\ \text{265 Deduction}\end{array}$$

After reading these formulations, if you feel a bit lost, you are not alone. What is difficult is that you do not yet have command of the difficult concept of DNI, which is presented in the next chapter. Once you peruse Chapter 3 and master its intricacies, we invite you to reread this section of the textbook. Doing so will further solidify your knowledge base.

Problems

1. A trustee incurs several expenditures that are listed below. Which expenditures are deductible and why?
   a. As part of the trust corpus, a trust owns title to a personal residence in which one of the trust beneficiaries resides rent-free. The trust pays $5,000 seasonally for landscape costs.
   b. As part of the trust corpus, a trust owns title to a personal residence in which one of the trust beneficiaries resides and pays fair-market rent. The trust pays $5,000 seasonally for landscape costs.
   c. The trust pays $5,000 in legal fees to an attorney to secure a new rental building.
   d. The trust pays $5,000 in income commissions to the trustee.
   e. The trust pays $5,000 in corpus commissions to the trustee.
   f. The trust pays $5,000 to a brokerage house as part of the latter's investment advisory fee.
   g. The trustee pays $5,000 to an appraisal firm to value a piece of real estate that it plans to distribute.
   h. The trustee pays $5,000 to an appraisal firm to value a piece of real estate that it plans to sell.

13. Because in the year of termination, DNI will include capital gains and losses (see Chapter 3), they are included in the denominator.

2. A trust earns the amounts delineated below and, in years 1 and 2, incurs $20,000 of annual trustee commissions (under the Principal and Income Act, one-half of the commissions is charged against the income beneficiary and the other one-half against the remainder beneficiary). Assume further that the trust owns X company stock, Y company stock, and Z company stock; the stock shares of each company appreciate $50,000 annually. Stock X is sold at the end of year 1 ($50,000 capital gain); stock Y is sold at the beginning of year 3 ($100,000 capital gain); and stock Z has appreciated (total appreciation is $150,000). Finally, assume that in year 3, the trust is terminated, and $40,000 of trust termination commissions is paid.

   Determine the amount of Trustee commissions that are disallowed in tax years 1, 2, and 3. By way of contrast, had the taxpayer prevailed in *Manufacturers Hanover Trust Co.*, what dollar amount would have been disallowed in year 1?

Year 1		Year 2		Year 3	
Rental	$10,000	Rental	$10,000	Rental	$10,000
Capital Gain	$50,000	Capital Gain	$0	Capital Gain	$100,000
Tax-exempt	$10,000	Tax-exempt	$10,000	Tax-exempt	$10,000

3. Assume the terms of the trust in problem 2 require that all of its income be paid out currently. For year 1, compute (i) fiduciary accounting income, (ii) gross income, (iii) tentative taxable income, and, (iv) albeit a bit premature, consider computing the trust's DNI under the IRS's and taxpayer's approach in the *Manufacturers Hanover* case.

IV. Loss Limitations

Internal Revenue Code: Sections 461(l) and 469

Regulations: Section 1.469-5T(a)

By way of background, the Code has many hurdles before taxpayers can secure allowable losses. The first limitation is found in Code § 165(c) which declares allowable losses are those limited to "(1) losses incurred in a trade or business; (2) losses incurred in any transaction entered into for profit, though not connected with a trade or business; and (3) . . . losses [that] arise from fire, storm, shipwreck, or other casualty, or from theft."[14] Another limitation, found in Code § 465, limits deductions to amounts taxpayers have "at risk" which is defined as the amount of money

14. Until 2026, a personal casualty loss will be deductible "only to the extent it is attributable to a Federally declared disaster. . . ." I.R.C. § 165(h)(5)(A).

and the adjusted basis of other property contributed by the taxpayer to the activity plus amounts borrowed for which the taxpayer is personally liable or has pledged property. Code § 465(b).

Assuming taxpayers, including trusts and estates, surmount the loss limitation rules found in Code §§ 165(c) and 465, there are two more that may apply and which require enumeration: (1) the passive loss limitation rules found in Code § 469 and (2) the overall loss limitation rules found in Code § 461(l).

A. The Passive Activity

In an attempt to curtail tax shelter activity, Congress enacted Code § 469. This Code § declares that passive losses are only deductible against passive income, with any excess suspended and eligible to be carried forward to the next tax year (Code § 469(a), (b)) where the process repeats itself until such time as when the taxpayer generates passive income (Code § 469(d)) or, alternatively, the taxpayer disposes of the passive activity. Code § 469(g).

The Code and Treasury regulations provide elaborate definitions of what constitutes a passive activity. Yet, in its simplest form, a passive activity means "any activity (A) which involves the conduct of any trade or business, and (B) in which the taxpayer does not materially participate." Code § 469(c). Since the phrase "materially participate" is itself amorphous, the Code amplifies its meaning with yet another definition: "A taxpayer shall be treated as materially participating in an activity only if the taxpayer is involved in the operations of the activity on a basis which is—(A) regular, (B) continuous, and (C) substantial." Code § 469(h).

Because many trusts and estates own rental real estate, there is a special rule that applies in this context that warrants attention. The Code generally treats all rental activities as being per se passive. Code § 469(c)(2). There is an important exception to this rule applicable to real estate professionals who meet the following conjunctive test: "(i) more than one-half of the personal services performed in trades or businesses by the taxpayer during such taxable year are performed in real property trades or businesses in which the taxpayer materially participates, and (ii) such taxpayer performs more than 750 hours of services during the taxable year in real property trades or businesses in which the taxpayer materially participates." Code § 469(c)(7)(B). If a real estate professional meets this conjunctive test, then the losses generated from the rental real estate activities are deemed active in nature.

In light of the fact that trusts and estates are inanimate, determining exactly how the passive activity limitation applies to them (including the professional real estate exception delineated in the paragraph above) is unclear. And while the Treasury Department seems poised to issue regulations that would elucidate how these rules would apply, it has yet to do so (i.e., Treas. Reg. § 1.469-5T(g), adopted in 1992, under the heading of "Material participation of trusts and estates" is the word "reserved").

Thus the responsibility of defining the phrase "material participation" and how it applies to trusts and estates has been de facto delegated to the judiciary. In a case of first impression, *Mattie K. Carter Trust v. Commissioner*,[15] a District Court had to determine whether the losses a trust sustained were active or passive. The facts of the case involved a trustee who managed a 15,000-acre ranch and who employed "a full-time ranch manager and other full- and part-time employees who performed essentially all of the activities of the ranch." The IRS argued that the sole metric to analyze the trust's activities was the trustee's activity in his fiduciary capacity; in contrast, the taxpayer contended that the court should look beyond the trustee's activities and include those who were employed by and agents of the trust. Embracing the taxpayer's position, the District Court ruled that common sense dictated that "the participation of Carter Trust in the ranch operations should be scrutinized by reference to the trust itself, which necessarily entails an assessment of the activities of those who labor on the ranch, or otherwise in furtherance of the ranch business on behalf of the Carter Trust."

Needless to say, the IRS was not a fan of the *Carter* decision and thought it was incorrectly decided. A series of post-*Carter* administrative rulings make this point. *See* T.A.M. 200733023 (because the trustee of the testamentary trust in question was not himself involved in the partnership's business dealings, the IRS ruled that the trust was not a material participant); Priv. Ltr. Rul. 201029014 ("[I]t is appropriate in the trust context to look only to the activities of the trustee. Thus, the sole means for a trust to establish material participation is if its fiduciary is involved in the operations of the activity on a regular, continuous, and substantial basis."); Chief Counsel Advice 201244017 (same); T.A.M. 201317010 (same).

But taxpayers did not subscribe to the IRS position and have continued to challenge it. And they again met with success, most recently in the Tax Court.

Aragona Trust v. Commissioner

142 T.C. 165 (2014)

The respondent (referred to here as the "IRS") issued a notice of deficiency to the Frank Aragona Trust (sometimes referred to here as the "trust"), determining the following deficiencies in federal income tax and the following penalties:

Year	Deficiency	Accuracy-related penalty sec. 6662(a)
2003	$86,289.00	$17,257.80
2004	421,292.00	84,258.40
2005	-0-	-0-
2006	84,540.00	16,908.00

15. 256 F. Supp. 2d 536 (N.D. Tex. 2003).

The trust filed a petition as permitted by section 6213(a).[16] We have jurisdiction to redetermine the deficiencies and penalties under section 6214(a). After concessions,[17] the two issues remaining for decision are:

(1) Does section 469(c)(7) apply to the trust? Yes.

(2) Are the fees that the trust paid to its trustees properly characterized as expenses of the trust's rental real-estate activities? We need not reach this issue because of our resolution of the first issue.

Findings of Fact

Some facts have been stipulated by the parties. The stipulated facts are incorporated in the Court's findings of fact. The trust is a complex residuary trust that owns rental real-estate properties and is involved in other real-estate business activities such as holding real estate and developing real estate. Its principal place of business was in Michigan when it filed the petition. In 1979 Frank Aragona formed the trust with him as grantor and trustee and with his five children as beneficiaries. According to the trust instrument, the five children share equally in the income of the trust. Frank Aragona died in 1981. He was succeeded as trustee by six trustees. One of the six trustees was an independent trustee.[18] The other five trustees were Frank Aragona's five children, including Paul V. Aragona, the executive trustee.[19] Although the trustees formally delegated their powers to the executive trustee (in order to facilitate daily business operations), the trustees acted as a management board for the trust and made all major decisions regarding the trust's property. During 2005 and 2006 the board met every few months to discuss the trust's business. Each of the six trustees was paid a fee directly by the trust (referred to here as a "trustee fee" or collectively as "trustee fees") in part for the trustee's attending board meetings. Three of the children — Paul V. Aragona, Frank S. Aragona, and Annette Aragona Moran — worked full time for Holiday Enterprises, LLC, a Michigan limited liability company that is wholly owned by the trust. Holiday Enterprises, LLC, is a disregarded entity for federal income tax purposes. Holiday Enterprises, LLC, managed most of the trust's rental real-estate properties. It employed several people in addition to Paul V. Aragona, Frank S. Aragona, and Annette Aragona Moran, including a controller, leasing agents, maintenance workers, accounts payable clerks, and accounts receivable clerks. In addition to receiving a trustee fee, Paul V. Aragona,

---

16. Even though the petition was filed by Paul V. Aragona, the executive trustee, for ease of reference we refer to the trust as having filed the petition. In any event we do not mean to suggest whether the petitioner in this case is the trustee or the trust. See sec. 7482(b)(1)(A) (providing that default appellate venue for deficiency cases is the circuit in which is located the legal residence of the petitioner). We do not reach that particular question. All references to sections are to the Internal Revenue Code of 1986, as in effect for the years at issue.

17. The IRS conceded that the trust is not liable for any accuracy-related penalties for the 2003, 2004, and 2006 tax years. (The notice of deficiency did not determine a penalty for 2005.)

18. The trust instrument gives the independent trustee the power to distribute the principal of the trust under limited circumstances.

19. When the petition was filed, Paul V. Aragona was a resident of Michigan.

Frank S. Aragona, and Annette Aragona Moran each received wages from Holiday Enterprises, LLC.

The trust conducted some of its rental real-estate activities directly, some through wholly owned entities, and the rest through entities in which it owned majority interests and in which Paul V. and Frank S. Aragona owned minority interests. It conducted its real-estate holding and real-estate development operations through entities in which it owned majority or minority interests and in which Paul V. and Frank S. Aragona owned minority interests.

The table below summarizes the activities of the six trustees on behalf of the trust during 2005 and 2006:

Name of Trustee	Role	Annual trustee fee
Salvatore S. Aragona	Full-time dentist; limited involvement in trust's business	$72,000
Paul V. Aragona	Executive trustee; full-time employee of Holiday Enterprises, LLC	72,000
Anthony F. Aragona	Disabled; limited involvement in trust's business	72,000 /a/
Frank S. Aragona	Full-time employee of Holiday Enterprises, LLC	72,000
Annette Aragona Moran	Full-time employee of Holiday Enterprises, LLC	72,000
Charles E. Turnbull	Independent trustee; attorney with O'Reilly Rancilio, P.C.; limited involvement in trust's business	14,400
Total		374,400

/a/ The $72,000 annual trustee fee for Anthony F. Aragona was reported as a distribution from the trust for tax purposes.

During the 2005 and 2006 tax years, the trust incurred losses from its rental real-estate properties. The losses were reported on the trust's income-tax returns, Forms 1041, "U.S. Income Tax Return for Estates and Trusts" and on Schedules E, "Supplemental Income and Loss", and were reflected on line 5. Some of the losses were reported as being associated with Holiday Enterprises, LLC, including $302,400 (the $374,400 in trustee fees minus the $72,000 in trustee fees paid to Anthony F. Aragona). The losses reported as being associated with Holiday Enterprises, LLC, were subdivided into various categories of expenses; the $302,400 was reported in the category of "other" expenses. On its returns the trust treated its rental real-estate activities, in which it engaged both directly and through its ownership interests in a number of entities, as non-passive activities. So treated, the losses from these activities contributed to the amounts of net operating losses, which the trust carried back to its 2003 and 2004 tax years.

While reporting losses for its rental real-estate activities, the trust also reported gains from its other (non-rental) real-estate activities. The trust owned interests in a number of entities engaged in real-estate holding activities and real-estate development projects.

On its Form 1041 for each year, the trust did not enter an amount on line 12, the line for deductions for "Fiduciary fees".

In the notice of deficiency, the IRS determined that the trust's rental real-estate activities were passive activities,[20] a determination that increased the passive-activity losses for 2005 and 2006.[21] The increase in the passive-activity losses resulted in a decrease in the allowable deductions from gross income for each of those years,[22] which decreased the net-operating-loss carrybacks to the 2003 and 2004 years. The notice of deficiency determined that for each of 2005 and 2006 the trust should be allowed a deduction of $302,400 for "Fiduciary fees". The notice of deficiency also determined that the trust's Schedule E expenses, which, as reported on the returns, included the $302,400 in trustee fees, should be reduced by $302,400. Thus, the notice of deficiency reclassified the $302,400 amounts as fiduciary fees to be deducted on line 12 of Form 1041 instead of expenses deducted against rental income on Schedule E (and reflected on line 5 of Form 1041). In explaining the reclassification of the $302,400 in fees, the notice of deficiency stated:

> It is determined your fiduciary fees of $302,400.00 and $302,400.00, should be reported on line 12 on the face of the return Form 1041 instead of $302,400.00 and $302,400.00 shown as a rental expense deduction on the Schedule E for taxable years 2005 and 2006, respectively.
>
> The adjustment was made to the rental loss claimed by Holiday Enterprises to disallow the trustee fees as an "other" expense and the expense was moved to Line 12 on the face of the return where they are required to be shown as "fiduciary fees".

Computationally, the notice of deficiency did not include the $302,400 in the amount of the trust's passive-activity-loss deductions for each year.

Opinion

The petitioner generally bears the burden of proof (and therefore must prove the relevant facts by the preponderance of the evidence) except when the conditions of section 7491(a) are satisfied. Tax Ct. R. Pract. & Proc. 142(a); *Welch v. Helvering*, 290 U.S. 111, 115 [12 AFTR 1456] (1933); *Bronstein v. Commissioner*, 138 T.C. 382, 384 (2012). Our findings of fact in this Opinion are based on the preponderance of the

20. The notice of deficiency stated that "[t]he rental losses incurred are deemed passive".

21. A passive-activity loss is the amount by which aggregate losses from all the taxpayer's passive activities for the year exceed the aggregate income from all the taxpayer's passive activities for the year. Sec. 469(d)(1). The trust's losses from its rental real-estate activities exceeded its income from the activities. Therefore, characterizing the trust's rental real-estate activities as passive resulted in a net increase in the trust's passive-activity loss for each year.

22. The existence of a passive-activity loss for the year results in the disallowance of current deductions in the amount of the passive-activity loss for the year. Sec. 1.469-1T(a)(1)(i), Temporary Income Tax Regs., 53 Fed. Reg. 5701 (Feb. 25, 1988).

evidence. Thus, it is unnecessary to determine which party (i.e., the trust or the IRS) has the burden of proof. See *Estate of Bongard v. Commissioner*, 124 T.C. 95, 111 (2005).

1. Does the section 469(c)(7) exception apply to the trust?

In 1986 Congress enacted section 469. Tax Reform Act of 1986, Pub. L. No. 99-514, sec. 501(a), 100 Stat. at 2233. Section 469(a)(1) provides that a taxpayer's passive-activity loss is disallowed for the year if the taxpayer is "described in" section 469(a)(2).[23] The following taxpayers are "described in" section 469(a)(2): individuals, estates, trusts, closely held C corporations, and personal service corporations. A passive-activity loss is the amount by which the aggregate losses from all the taxpayer's passive activities for the year exceeds the aggregate income from all the taxpayer's passive activities for such year. Sec. 469(d)(1); see also sec. 1.469-2T(b)(1), Temporary Income Tax Regs., 53 Fed. Reg. 5711 (Feb. 25, 1988). A passive activity is any activity which involves the conduct of any trade or business in which the taxpayer does not materially participate. Sec. 469(c)(1). Under section 469(c)(2), any rental activity is considered a passive activity, even if the taxpayer materially participates in the activity. Sec. 469(c)(4). Thus, any rental activity is passive per se.

In 1993 Congress enacted section 469(c)(7), which provides that section 469(c)(2) does not apply to the rental real-estate activity of any taxpayer who meets the requirements of section 469(c)(7)(B). Omnibus Budget Reconciliation Act of 1993, Pub. L. No. 103-66, sec. 13143(a) and (b), 107 Stat. at 440, 441.[24] Section 469(c)(7)(B) consists of two tests. The first test is met if more than one-half of the "personal services" performed in trades or businesses by the taxpayer during the taxable year is performed in real-property trades or businesses in which the taxpayer materially participates. Sec. 469(c)(7)(B)(i). The second test is met if the taxpayer performs more than 750 hours of "services" during the year in real-property trades or businesses in which the taxpayer materially participates. Sec. 469(c)(7)(B)(ii). Both tests must be met.[25]

---

23. A loss from an activity disallowed under sec. 469(a) is treated as a deduction allocable to such activity for the next tax year. Sec. 469(b).

24. The following reason was given for the amendment:

> The passive loss rules limit deductions and credits from passive trade or business activities. Deductions attributable to passive activities, to the extent they exceed income from passive activities, generally may not be deducted against other income, such as wages, portfolio income, or business income that is not derived from a passive activity.
>
> * * *
>
> The committee considers it unfair that a person who performs personal services in a real estate trade or business in which he materially participates may not offset losses from rental real estate activities against income from nonrental real estate activities or against other types of income such as portfolio investment income.
>
> * * *

H. R. Rept. No. 103-111, at 612–613 (1993), 1993-3 C.B. 1, 188-189.

25. Sec. 469(c)(7)(B) provides in part:

This paragraph shall apply to a taxpayer for a taxable year if—

Section 469(c)(7)(D)(i) provides a special rule for determining whether a closely held C corporation meets the requirements of section 469(c)(7)(B):

> In the case of a closely held C corporation, the requirements of subparagraph (B) shall be treated as met for any taxable year if more than 50 percent of the gross receipts of such corporation for such taxable year are derived from real property trades or businesses in which the corporation materially participates.

Thus, the determination of whether a closely held C corporation meets the requirements of section 469(c)(7)(B) does not involve the one-half-of-personal-services test and the 750-hour test.

The requirements of section 469(c)(7)(B) can be met only by a taxpayer who materially participates in a real-property trade or business. This is because the one-half-of-personal-services test, the 750-hour test, and the special rule for closely held C corporations all presuppose that the taxpayer materially participates in real-property trades or businesses. Sec. 469(c)(7)(B)(i) and (ii); see sec. 469(c)(7)(D); see also sec. 1.469-9(c)(3), Income Tax Regs.

The term "real property trade or business" is defined as any real-property development, redevelopment, construction, reconstruction, acquisition, conversion, rental, operation, management, leasing, or brokerage trade or business. Sec. 469(c)(7)(C).

Regulatory guidance regarding the section 469(c)(7) exception is found in section 1.469-9, Income Tax Regs. This regulation states that only a "qualifying taxpayer" falls within the exception. Sec. 1.469-9(e)(1), Income Tax Regs. ("Section 469(c)(2) does not apply to any rental real estate activity of a taxpayer for a taxable year in which the taxpayer is a qualifying taxpayer[.]"). The term "qualifying taxpayer" is defined by the regulation as "a taxpayer that owns at least one interest in rental real estate and meets the requirements of paragraph (c) of this section." Sec. 1.469-9(b)(6), Income Tax Regs. Section 1.469-9(c), Income Tax Regs. (the paragraph (c) provision referred to in the quotation above) provides: "(1) In general.—A qualifying taxpayer must meet the requirements of section 469(c)(7)(B)." Thus, to be a "qualifying taxpayer" within the meaning of the regulation a taxpayer must own at least one interest in rental real estate and satisfy the requirements of section 469(c)(7)(B). Two other aspects of the regulation are of note. First, section 1.469-9(b)(4), Income Tax Regs., provides, in part, that "[p]ersonal services means any work performed by an individual in connection with a trade or business." This is an interpretation of the term "personal services" used in the first test of section 469(c)(7)(B). Second,

---

(i) more than one-half of the personal services performed in trades or businesses by the taxpayer during such taxable year are performed in real property trades or businesses in which the taxpayer materially participates, and

(ii) such taxpayer performs more than 750 hours of services during the taxable year in real property trades or businesses in which the taxpayer materially participates.

section 1.469-9(c)(2), Income Tax Regs., provides that "[a] closely held C corporation meets the requirements of paragraph (c)(1) of this section by satisfying the requirements of section 469(c)(7)(D)(i)."

Section 469(h) provides that for the purposes of section 469 a taxpayer is treated as materially participating in an activity only if the taxpayer is involved in the operation of the activity on a basis which is regular, continuous, and substantial. The test in section 469(h) has two functions. First, it is used to determine whether a particular activity is a passive activity. See sec. 469(c)(1) (defining passive activity as an activity, involving the conduct of a trade or business, in which the taxpayer does not materially participate). Second, it is used to determine whether a taxpayer materially participates in real-property trades or businesses. See sec. 469(c)(7)(B)(i) and (ii). Thus, a taxpayer is treated as materially participating in real-property trades or businesses if the taxpayer is involved in the operation of real-property trades or businesses on a basis which is regular, continuous, and substantial.

a. Can a trust qualify for the section 469(c)(7) exception?

i. The IRS's arguments

For the section 469(c)(7) exception to apply, there must be "personal services performed * * * by the taxpayer". Sec. 469(c)(7)(B)(i). Because "[p]ersonal services" are defined by regulation as "work performed by an individual in connection with a trade or business", the IRS contends that a trust cannot perform personal services. See sec. 1.469-9(b)(4), Income Tax Regs. Therefore, the IRS contends, a trust cannot qualify for the section 469(c)(7) exception.

The IRS asserts that the legislative history of section 469(c)(7) supports its view that Congress did not intend the section 469(c)(7) exception to apply to trusts. In describing the provision in the bill that would be adopted by the House, and enacted by Congress in amended form as section 469(c)(7), the report of the House Ways and Means Committee stated that the provision "applies to individuals and closely held C corporations." H.R. Rept. No. 103-111, at 614 (1993), 1993-3 C.B. 167, 190. The report further stated that an "individual taxpayer" meets the requirements of the exception "if more than half of the personal services the taxpayer performs in a trade or business are in real property trades or businesses in which he materially participates." *Id.* (The bill adopted by the House had provided that the section 469(c)(7) exception was applicable "if more than one-half of the personal services performed in trades or businesses by the taxpayer * * * are performed in real property trades or businesses in which the taxpayer materially participates." H.R. 2264, 103d Cong., sec. 14143 (1993). The bill did not yet include the 750-hour test now codified in section 469(c)(7)(B)(ii). The report also stated that a closely held C corporation meets the requirements of the section 469(c)(7) exception "if more than 50 percent of its gross receipts for the taxable year are derived from real property trades or businesses in which the corporation materially participates (within the meaning of sec. 469(h)(4))." H.R. Rept. No. 103-111, *supra* at 614, 1993-3 C.B. at 190. The report did not describe how any class of taxpayer other than an individual or a closely held

C corporation meets the requirements of the exception. *Id.* The report of the conference committee, also describing the bill adopted by the House, similarly stated that an "individual taxpayer" meets the requirements of the exception "if more than half of the personal services the taxpayer performs in trades or businesses during the taxable year are in real property trades or businesses in which he materially participates." H.R. Conf. Rept. No. 103-213, at 546 (1993), 1993-3 C.B. 393, 424. The conference report further stated that a closely held C corporation meets the requirements of the exception "if more than 50 percent of its gross receipts for the taxable year are derived from real property trades or businesses in which the corporation materially participates." *Id.* The conference report also discussed the final version of the bill. *Id.* at 547, 1993-3 C.B. at 425. It described the section 469(c)(7) exception thus:

> The conference agreement follows the House bill, with a modification. Under the conference agreement, an individual taxpayer meets the eligibility requirements if (1) more than half of the personal services the taxpayer performs in trades or businesses during the taxable year are performed in real property trades or businesses in which the taxpayer materially participates, and (2) such taxpayer performs more than 750 hours of services during the taxable year in real property trades or businesses in which the taxpayer materially participates. * * *

Id.

ii. Analysis

The IRS argues that a trust is incapable of performing "personal services" because the regulation defines "personal services" to mean "any work performed by an individual in connection with a trade or business". Sec. 1.469-9(b)(4), Income Tax Regs. We reject the IRS's argument. A trust is an arrangement whereby trustees manage assets for the trust's beneficiaries. 1 Restatement, Trusts 3d, sec. 2 (2003) (a trust "is a fiduciary relationship with respect to property, * * * subjecting the person who holds title to the property to duties to deal with it for the benefit of" others); see also sec. 301.7701-4(a), Proced. & Admin. Regs. ("In general, the term 'trust' as used in the Internal Revenue Code refers to an arrangement created either by will or by an inter vivos declaration whereby trustees take title to property for the purpose of protecting or conserving it for the beneficiaries under the ordinary rules applied in chancery or probate courts."). If the trustees are individuals, and they work on a trade or business as part of their trustee duties, their work can be considered "work performed by an individual in connection with a trade or business." Sec. 1.469-9(b)(4), Income Tax Regs. We conclude that a trust is capable of performing personal services and therefore can satisfy the section 469(c)(7) exception.

Indeed, if Congress had wanted to exclude trusts from the section 469(c)(7) exception, it could have done so explicitly by limiting the exception to "any natural person". In section 469(i), the Internal Revenue Code does exactly that. Section 469(i) grants a $25,000 allowance to "any natural person" who fulfills certain requirements. That Congress did not use the phrase "natural person" but instead used the word "taxpayer" in section 469(c)(7) suggests that Congress did not intend to exclude trusts from the section 469(c)(7) exception, despite what the IRS argues here.

We need not address the trust's arguments regarding the regulation, which are that:

(1) the word "individual" in the regulation should be interpreted to include a trust, and

(2) in the alternative, even if the word "individual" does not include a trust, then the regulation is inapplicable to taxpayers that are trusts.

We now turn to the legislative history of the section 469(c)(7) exception, which the IRS contends shows that trusts cannot qualify for that exception. The Ways and Means Committee report states that the section 469(c)(7) exception applies to individuals and closely held C corporations. H.R. Rept. No. 103-111, *supra* at 614, 1993-3 C.B. at 190. The report does not say that the exception applies only to individuals and closely held C corporations. Therefore, the report does not compel the conclusion that only individuals and closely held C corporations can qualify for the section 469(c)(7) exception.

The legislative history states that an individual meets the requirements of section 469(c)(7) by meeting the one-half-of-personal-services test and, in discussing the final version of the legislation, the 750-hour test. *Id.*; H.R. Rept. No. 103-213, *supra* at 546, 1993-3 C.B. at 424. It is true that an individual falls within the section 469(c)(7) exception by meeting the two tests. But this does not mean that other types of taxpayers cannot fall within the exception.

b. Does the trust qualify for the section 469(c)(7) exception?

The IRS's fallback position is that even if some trusts can qualify for the section 469(c)(7) exception, the trust does not qualify because it did not materially participate in real-property trades or businesses. The IRS concedes that the trust's real-estate operations qualify as real property trades or businesses. Therefore the question to be resolved is whether the trust materially participated in its real-estate operations. We hold that it did so.

Section 469(h) supplies the definition of what it means to materially participate in an activity. By that definition, a taxpayer is treated as materially participating in an activity only if the taxpayer is involved in the operations of the activity on a basis which is regular, continuous, and substantial. Sec. 469(h). Interpreting section 469(h), the Department of the Treasury has promulgated regulations for determining whether taxpayers who are individuals materially participate in an activity. See sec. 1.469-5T(a), (b), (c), and (d), Temporary Income Tax Regs., 53 Fed. Reg. 5725 (Feb. 25, 1988). Section 469(h)(4) provides a method for determining whether certain types of corporations[26] have met the tests for material participation. The statute

26. The IRS does not take the position that the trust should be treated as a corporation. See sec. 301.7701-4(b), Proced. & Admin. Regs. (business trusts, defined as devices created by

does not provide a method for determining how a trust may materially participate in an activity, and no regulations have yet been promulgated for taxpayers that are trusts. See sec. 1.469-5T(g), Temporary Income Tax Regs., 53 Fed. Reg. 5727 (Feb. 25, 1988) (reserving a place for a regulation to be titled "Material participation of trusts and estates"). Therefore, we must make the determination of whether a trust materially participates in an activity in the absence of regulatory guidance.[27]

The IRS argues that in determining whether a trust is materially participating in an activity, only the activities of the trustees can be considered and the activities of that trust's employees must be disregarded. In support, the IRS cites S. Rept. No. 99-313, at 735 (1986), 1986-3 C.B. (Vol. 3) 1, 735, which states that a trust "is treated as materially participating in an activity * * * if an executor or fiduciary, in his capacity as such, is so participating." The Senate committee report also stated that "the activities of * * * [employees] are not attributed to the taxpayer".[28]

On the basis of these legal principles, the IRS would have us ignore the activities of the trust's non-trustee employees.[29] Additionally, the IRS would have us ignore the activities of the three trustees who are employees of Holiday Enterprises, LLC. It reasons that the activities of these three trustees should be considered the activities of employees and not fiduciaries because (1) the trustees performed their activities as employees of Holiday Enterprises, LLC, and (2) it is impossible to disaggregate the activities they performed as employees of Holiday Enterprises, LLC, and the activities they performed as trustees.

---

beneficiaries to carry on profit-making businesses, are to be treated for federal tax law purposes as corporations or partnerships).

27. A number of commentators have argued that there is a need for a regulation that resolves questions regarding material participation of trusts and generally coordinates the passive-activity-loss rules of sec. 469 with the rules on taxation of trusts in subch. J. See, e.g., 1 Byrle K. Abbin, David K. Carlson, and Mark L. Vorsatz, Income Taxation of Fiduciaries and Beneficiaries, sec. 801, at 8003 to 8004 (2012 ed.) ("Section 469 does not easily comport with subchapter J. To date no regulatory explanation has been forthcoming * * * [on questions including] where and how material participation is measured[.]"); M. Carr Ferguson, James J. Freeland, and Mark L. Ascher, Federal Income Taxation of Estates, Trusts, and Beneficiaries, para. 8.01, at 8-1 to 8-8 (3d ed. 2003); Leo L. Schmolka, "Passive Activity Losses, Trusts, and Estates: The Regulations (If I Were King)", 58 Tax L. Rev. 191 (2005).

28. The Senate committee report stated:

> The fact that a taxpayer utilizes employees or contract services to perform daily functions in running the business does not prevent such taxpayer from qualifying as materially participating. However, the activities of such agents are not attributed to the taxpayer, and the taxpayer must still personally perform sufficient services to establish material participation.

S. Rept. No. 99-313, at 735 (1986), 1986-3 C.B. (Vol. 3) 1, 735.

29. The IRS disagrees with *Carter Trust v. United States*, 256 F. Supp. 2d 536, 541 [91 AFTR 2d 2003-1946] (N.D. Tex. 2003), which held that the activities of the trust's non-trustee employees (and of the trustee) are considered in determining whether the trust materially participated in ranching activity.

If the Court adopts all these arguments made by the IRS, then it should ignore the activities of the 20 or so non-trustee employees and the 3 trustee-employees (Paul V. Aragona, Frank S. Aragona, and Annette Aragona Moran). This would leave only the relatively insignificant activities of the trustees who are not employees (Salvatore S. Aragona, a dentist, Anthony F. Aragona, who is disabled and unable to work, and Charles E. Turnbull, an outside attorney who is the independent trustee).

Even if the activities of the trust's non-trustee employees should be disregarded,[30] the activities of the trustees — including their activities as employees of Holiday Enterprises, LLC — should be considered in determining whether the trust materially participated in its real-estate operations. The trustees were required by Michigan statutory law to administer the trust solely in the interests of the trust beneficiaries, because trustees have a duty to act as a prudent person would in dealing with the property of another, i.e., a beneficiary. Mich. Comp. Laws sec. 700.7302 (2001) (before amendment by 2009 Mich. Pub. Acts No. 46); see also *In re Estate of Butterfield*, 341 N.W.2d 453, 459 (Mich. 1983) (construing Mich. Comp. Laws sec. 700.813 (1979), a statute in effect from 1979 to 2000 that was a similarly-worded predecessor to Mich. Comp. Laws sec. 700.7302). Trustees are not relieved of their duties of loyalty to beneficiaries by conducting activities through a corporation wholly owned by the trust. Cf. *In re Estate of Butterfield*, 341 N.W.2d at 457 ("Trustees who also happen to be directors of the corporation which is owned or controlled by the trust cannot insulate themselves from probate scrutiny [i.e., duties imposed on trustees by Michigan courts] under the guise of calling themselves corporate directors who are exercising their business judgment concerning matters of corporate policy."). Therefore their activities as employees of Holiday Enterprises, LLC, should be considered in determining whether the trust materially participated in its real-estate operations.[31]

Considering the activities of all six trustees in their roles as trustees and as employees of Holiday Enterprises, LLC, the trust materially participated in its real-estate operations. Three of the trustees participated in the trust's real-estate operations full time. The trust's real-estate operations were substantial. The trust had practically no other types of operations. The trustees handled practically no other businesses on behalf of the trust. The IRS argues that because Paul V. Aragona and

30. We need not and do not decide whether the activities of the trust's non-trustee employees should be disregarded.

31. We need not consider the effect of sec. 469(c)(7)(D)(ii), which provides that for purposes of sec. 469(c)(7)(B) personal services performed as an employee are generally not treated as performed in real-property trades or businesses. This rule has no application to the resolution of this case because, as we explain infra, the IRS has confined its challenges to the trust's qualification for sec. 469(c)(7) treatment to two challenges: (1) that trusts are categorically barred from sec. 469(c)(7) treatment, and (2) the trust did not materially participate in real-property trades or businesses. Thus, we need not, and do not, determine how many hours of personal services were performed by the trust in real-property trades or businesses. We also note that the IRS does not cite sec. 469(c)(7)(D)(ii) in its brief.

Frank S. Aragona had minority ownership interests in all of the entities through which the trust operated real-estate holding and real-estate development projects and because they had minority interests in some of the entities through which the trust operated its rental real-estate business, some of these two trustees' efforts in managing the jointly held entities are attributable to their personal portions of the businesses, not the trust's portion. Despite two of the trustees' holding ownership interests, we are convinced that the trust materially participated in the trust's real-estate operations. First, Frank S. and Paul V. Aragona's combined ownership interest in each entity was not a majority interest—for no entity did their combined ownership interest exceed 50%. Second, Frank S. and Paul V. Aragona's combined ownership interest in each entity was never greater than the trust's ownership interest. Third, Frank S. and Paul V. Aragona's interests as owners were generally compatible with the trust's goals—they and the trust wanted the jointly held enterprises to succeed. Fourth, Frank S. and Paul V. Aragona were involved in managing the day-to-day operations of the trust's various real-estate businesses.

We hold that the trust materially participated in real-property trades or businesses. For a taxpayer who has materially participated in real-property trades or businesses, the next steps in ascertaining whether the taxpayer benefits from the section 469(c)(7) exception are (1) to determine whether more than one-half of the personal services performed in trades or businesses by the taxpayer during the year are performed in real-property trades or businesses, and (2) to determine whether the taxpayer performed more than 750 hours of services during the year in the real-property trades or businesses. As to whether the trust qualifies for the section 469(c)(7) exception, however, the IRS has limited its arguments to the two arguments discussed above, namely (1) that trusts are categorically barred from qualifying under the section 469(c)(7) exception, and (2) that the trust did not materially participate in real-property trades or businesses. In the context of the arguments raised in this case, therefore, we hold the trust meets the section 469(c)(7) exception for the years at issue.

c. Conclusion

Once it is determined that the trust qualifies under the section 469(c)(7) exception, and that therefore the trust's rental real-estate activities are not per se passive activities, a theoretical next step is to determine whether the trust materially participated in its rental real-estate activities. If the trust materially participated in its rental real-estate activities, then its rental real-estate activities are not passive activities. If the trust did not materially participate in its rental real-estate activities, then its rental real-estate activities are passive activities. The IRS argues only that the trust is not excepted by section 469(c)(7). It does not argue that—in the event that we determine that the trust is excepted by section 469(c)(7)—the trust did not materially participate in its rental real-estate activities. We hold that, in the context of the arguments presented in this case, the trust's rental real-estate activities are not passive activities.

2. Are the fees that were paid by the trust to its trustees properly characterized as expenses of the trust's rental real-estate activities?

The notice of deficiency determined that the trust's rental real-estate activities were passive activities, a determination that if correct meant that all deductions related to the rental real-estate activities were passive-activity-loss deductions. The notice of deficiency treated the $302,400 in trustee fees as deductions other than passive-activity-loss deductions (and allowed the full deduction of $302,400).[32] The treatment of the $302,400 in trustee fees as deductions other than passive-activity-loss deductions assumes that the trustee fees were not expenses of the trust's rental real-estate activities. On brief, the IRS appears to defend this assumption: it apparently contends that the trustee fees were not the expenses of the trust's rental real-estate activities.[33] The trust appears to disagree with the assumption in the notice of deficiency: the trust apparently contends that the trustee fees were the expenses of the trust's rental real-estate activities.[34]

The question of whether the trustee fees were the expenses of the trust's rental real-estate activities is relevant only if the trust's rental real-estate activities are passive activities. Contrary to the notice of deficiency, we hold that the trust's rental real-estate activities were not passive activities. See supra part 1.c. Because of this holding, the losses associated with the trust's rental real-estate activities are not passive-activity-loss deductions. Therefore, it is unnecessary to decide whether the trustee fees were expenses of the trust's rental real-estate activity.[35]

---

32. In determining whether a taxpayer who qualifies for the sec. 469(c)(7) exception has materially participated in a rental real-estate activity, each interest in rental real estate is treated as a separate rental real-estate activity unless the taxpayer has made an election under section 469(c)(7)(A). If the taxpayer has made such an e lection, then all interests in rental real estate are treated as a single rental real-estate activity. Sec. 469(c)(7)(A). Before the years at issue, the trust made an election under sec. 469(c)(7)(A) — an election that was binding for subsequent tax years, absent changed circumstances — to treat all of its interests in rental real estate as a single activity.

33. A passive-activity loss is generally defined as the amount, if any, by which the passive-activity deductions for the year exceed the passive-activity gross income for the tax year. Sec. 1.469-2T(b)(1), Temporary Income Tax Regs., 53 Fed. Reg. 5711 (Feb. 25, 1988). Passive-activity gross income is generally all items of gross income from a passive activity. Sec. 1.469-2T(c), Temporary Income Tax Regs., supra. A passive-activity deduction is generally defined as a deduction arising in connection with the conduct of a passive activity. Sec. 1.469-2T(d)(1), Temporary Income Tax Regs., 53 Fed. Reg. 5716 (Feb. 25, 1988).

34. In its brief, the IRS frames the issue of proper characterization of the trustee fees as: "Whether petitioner should have reported trustee fee expenses on the front of its U.S. Income Tax Return for Estates and Trusts, Form 1041, or on the Schedule E, for the 2005 and 2006 years." It also frames the issue as: "Trustee fees are an expense of the trust and not [Holiday Enterprises, LLC]." Both phrasings appear to be an obscure reference to the notice of deficiency's assumption that the trustee fees are not the expenses of the trust's rental real-estate activity.

35. In its reply brief, the trust argues that the trustee fees are "properly included in the determination of the Trust's losses from its real estate activities." Strictly speaking, however, the computations in the notice of deficiency assumed that the trustee fees were not the expenses of the trust's rental real-estate activities.

3. Conclusion

We have considered all of the arguments the parties have made, and to the extent that we have not discussed them, we find them to be irrelevant, moot, or without merit.

To reflect the foregoing,

Decision will be entered under Tax Ct. R. Pract. & Proc. 155.

While the outcome in *Aragona Trust* helped answer many questions, there are several issues that remain open. In particular, for purposes of testing material participation, left undecided is whether a trustee's activities also include those performed in a nonfiduciary capacity and, furthermore, should the activities of non-trustee employees employed by the trust count towards determining material participation. Another "oddity" was footnote 16. Footnote 16 in *Aragona Trust* is important, and it reads as follows:

> We need not consider the effect of sec. 469(c)(7)(D)(ii), which provides that for purposes of sec. 469(c)(7)(B) personal services performed as an employee are generally not treated as performed in real-property trades or businesses. This rule has no application to the resolution of this case because, as we explain *infra*, the IRS has confined its challenges to the trust's qualification for sec. 469(c)(7) treatment to two challenges: (1) that trusts are categorically barred from sec. 469(c)(7) treatment, and (2) the trust did not materially participate in real-property trades or businesses. Thus, we need not, and do not, determine how many hours of personal services were performed by the trust in real-property trades or businesses. We also note that the IRS does not cite sec. 469(c)(7)(D)(ii) in its brief.

Given this footnote, one would have to anticipate that the next time the IRS contests the material participation of a trust, it will raise § 469(c)(7)(D)(ii) as part of its challenge. The Tax Court's ignoring § 469(c)(7)(D)(ii) is odd because, even if the IRS's challenge was confined to the arguments as stated in the footnote, statutes that specifically bear on such questions should be considered. Perhaps the Tax Court is signaling its intent to hold that the activities of trustee-employees are to be considered in determining material participation.

Over two decades have passed since the Treasury Department implicitly promised regulations to resolve these and other issues; this languishment on the Treasury's part does not bode well for taxpayer certainty.

Problem

A trustee of a testamentary trust owns title to an apartment complex. The trustee also owns title to nine other apartment complexes in his individual name, not the name of the trust. While the trustee devotes virtually every day to managing these ten properties, he has a staff of ten people who assist him. The apartment complex that the trust owns generates a $600,000 loss for the tax year in question. On the basis of these facts, would the loss generated be deemed active or passive?

B. The Overall Loss Limitation

Once taxpayers apply the three limitations cited above—the 165(c) limit, the Code § 465 at-risk limit, and the Code § 469 passive activity limit—there is a final limit which is found in Code § 461(l). Under this limitation, so-called "excess business losses" are disallowed and are treated as a net operating loss in the following tax year. Code § 461(l)(2).

The Code defines excess business losses as follows:

Taxpayer's aggregate deductions attributable to a trade or business

MINUS the Sum of:

(i) The aggregate gross income or gain attributable to such trades or business; plus

(ii) $250,000 (or, in the case of joint returns, $500,000), annually adjusted for inflation

A simple example illustrates this rule's application. Suppose a single taxpayer owns a business that experiences a $700,000 loss from inventory that is no longer marketable and also has $300,000 income from sales. In this case, the Code would disallow $150,000 of the taxpayer's losses computed as follows:

$700,000
($550,000) (i.e., $300,000 (gross income) + $250,000 (allowable losses))
$150,000

The Code would reclassify this disallowed loss as a net operating loss that could be carried forward indefinitely and used to offset up to 80% of the taxpayer's future income. Code § 172.

The Code does not specifically mention that Code § 461(l) applies to trusts and estates. Its heading, though, states that its application extends to all noncorporate taxpayers. That being the case, there is no reason to assume that trusts and estates are exempt from this limitation. To the contrary, as evidenced in the passive activity realm, trusts and estates can actively engage in trades and businesses and, like other noncorporate taxpayers, they are subject to the Code's entire gamut of loss limitation rules.

Problem

The trustee of a trust owns an operating cattle ranch that has 5,000 head of cattle. While the trustee is a full-time veterinarian, she regularly spends 15 to 20 hours weekly on the ranch and managing its cattle.

In the current year, the trust has income and losses from the following investments and activities:

- $20,000 interest income;
- ($500,000) loss from the sale of Apple stock;
- ($400,000) loss generated from an investment—purchased entirely from funds originating from a nonrecourse loan—in a limited partnership (not involved in a real estate enterprise);
- ($300,000) loss from ranch operations; and
- ($200,000) loss arising from amortization deductions in movie production enterprise in which the trust invested $1 million.

In light of the income earned and the losses incurred, identify which loss limitations rules will come into play.

V. Qualified Business Income Deduction

Internal Revenue Code: Section 199A(a)-(f)

Regulations: Section 1.199-5(e)(2)(i)

Embodied in Code § 199A is a unique deduction that permits taxpayers, including trusts and estates, to deduct up to 20% of their so-called qualified business income, at least until December 31, 2025, when this provision is scheduled to expire.[36] This deduction is taken below the line (i.e., after adjusted gross income is computed) and is in addition to the standard deduction. While the details of this deduction are complex and questions regarding its application remain, this Section's objective is fairly elementary: to permit business owners and entrepreneurs to bask in the glory

36. There is an additional 20% deduction for qualified REIT dividends and qualified publicly traded partnership income, and qualified cooperative dividends. Code §§ 199A(a)(2)(A), (b)(1)(B). Discussion of this element of the deduction is beyond the scope of this textbook.

of a low tax rate that is loosely comparable to the relatively low 21 percent corporate tax rate that C corporation taxpayers can capitalize upon. Code § 11. From a congressional perspective, trustees and executors can apparently function as full-fledged business owners and entrepreneurs and, as such, should be accorded the identical tax benefits as their corporate counterparts engaging in the same activities.

Mastering Code § 199A is not for the faint of heart, so students should brace themselves for an intense mental challenge. Here goes.

Before delving into the specifics of how Subchapter J and Code § 199A intersect, it is helpful to understand the structural framework and key terminology used by Code § 199A.

Qualified Trade or Business. For Code § 199A to apply, a taxpayer must own an interest in a "qualified trade or business" (QTB). The Code's definition of QTB starts off broadly to include any "trade or business," but excludes (A) a specified service trade or business (SSTB) for taxpayers above certain income levels and (B) the trade or business of performing services as an employee (regardless of the taxpayer's income level). Code § 199A(d)(1). But for the effect of these potentially significant exclusions, a trade or business activity conducted by an individual, trust, or estate—whether directly through a sole proprietorship or indirectly through a disregarded entity, partnership, LLC classified as a partnership, or S corporation—should constitute a QTB for purposes of Code § 199A.[37]

Definition of SSTB. Ascertaining the precise meaning of an SSTB excluded from QTB status requires a bit of statutory gymnastics. The term is defined, in part, by cross-reference from Code § 199A(d)(2)(A) to any trade or business described in Code § 1202(e)(3)(A), but without regard to the words "engineering" and "architecture" and substituting the words "owners or employees" for the word "employees." Once these word changes are taken into account, the SSTBs covered by Code § 199A(d)(2)(A) may be described as consisting of the following two discrete categories: (1) any trade or business involving the performance of services in the fields of health, law, accounting, actuarial science, performing arts, consulting, athletics, financial services, or brokerage services, and (2) any trade or business where the principal asset of such trade or business is the reputation or skill of one or more of its employees or owners. In addition, a third category of SSTB is set forth directly in the text of Code § 199A(d)(2)(B) (without cross-reference to Code § 1202), consisting of any trade or business which involves the performance of services that consist of investing and investment management, trading or dealing in securities, partnership interests, or commodities.

37. QTB status does not depend on whether the taxpayer's activity is "passive" or "active" within the meaning of the passive activity loss limitations of Section 469. Thus, for example, a taxpayer's interest in a trade or business may qualify as a QTB for purposes of the Section 199A deduction even if the income from such QTB is "passive" in nature and thereby potentially subject to the 3.8% tax on "net investment income" imposed by Section 1411.

There is a key exception to the SSTB exclusion for certain lower income taxpayers. If a taxpayer has taxable income less than the *threshold amount*, then the SSTB exclusion does not apply to such taxpayer (with the result that the business constitutes a QTB with respect to that particular taxpayer, even though it retains its definitional status as an SSTB for other owners whose taxable income exceeds the applicable threshold). Code § 199A(d)(3).

Definition of Threshold Amount. The phrase *threshold amount* is defined as $315,000 for married individuals filing jointly and $157,500 for all other taxpayers (including trusts, estates, and unmarried individuals), adjusted annually for inflation. Code § 199A(e)(2).

Definition of Qualified Business Income. Once it is determined that an eligible taxpayer owns an interest in a QTB, the taxpayer's qualified business income (QBI) from that business must be ascertained.[38] In general, this computation is determined by reference to the net amount of "items of income, gain, deduction and loss with respect to any qualified trade or business" to the extent that such items (i) are "effectively connected with the conduct of a trade or business" within the United States and (ii) are included or allowed in determining taxable income for the applicable year. Code § 199A(c).

The QBI definition, however, contains many exclusions. Such exclusions include (i) portfolio investment-type income, such as dividends, non-business interest income, annuities, short-term and long-term capital gains (and losses); (ii) reasonable compensation for services rendered by a taxpayer with respect to a QTB; (iii) Code § 707(c) guaranteed payments for services rendered by a partner with respect to the partnership's trade or business; and (iv) to the extent provided in regulations, Code § 707(a) payments for services rendered by a partner with respect to the partnership's trade or business. Code § 199A(c)(3)(B).

Cap Based on W-2 Wages and Qualified Property. To protect the tax base, Code § 199A's legislative history indicates that Congress sought to "deter high-income taxpayers from attempting to convert wages or other compensation for personal services to income eligible for the 20-percent deduction."[39] To achieve this objective, Congress instituted a cap on the amount of the allowable QBI deduction applicable to taxpayers who have taxable income above a threshold amount (identical to the aforementioned SSTB exclusion trigger). Specifically, a taxpayer's tentative deduction for each QTB is equal to the **lesser** of the following:

(A) 20% of the taxpayer's QBI with respect to the QTB; or

(B) The **greater** of—

 (i) 50% of the "W-2 wages" with respect to the QTB, or

---

38. Determining QBI must be done at the entity level.

39. Joint Explanatory Statement of the Committee of Conference submitted to the House and Senate on December 15, 2017 (H. Rept. 115-466) at p. 37.

(ii) The sum of 25% of the "W-2 wages" with respect to the QTB, plus 2.5% of the unadjusted basis immediately after acquisition of all "qualified property."

Code § 199A(b)(2). For ease of description, the amount set forth in clause (B), above (i.e., the greater of the two formulaic amounts listed in sub-clauses (i) and (ii) thereof) is referred to as the "wage/property cap."

Like the SSTB limitation rules, the wage/property cap does not apply if the taxpayer's taxable income does not exceed the designated threshold amounts ($315,000 for married individuals filing joint returns and $157,500 for all other taxpayers), but is gradually phased in for those taxpayers whose taxable incomes exceed the applicable threshold amounts. Code § 199A(b)(3).

The wage/property cap contains two terms of art which require further explication.

The first is *W-2 wages*. This term generally includes all wages paid by a business and certain deferred compensation arrangements, but not remuneration paid to independent contractors. Code § 199A(b)(4).

The second is *qualified property*. The Code defines this term to include depreciable tangible property that meets the following three conditions: (i) which is held by, and available for use in, the QTB at the close of the taxable year; (ii) which is used at any point during the taxable year in the production of QBI; and (iii) the "depreciable period" for which has not ended before the close of the taxable year. Code § 199A(b)(6)(A). Nestled in the definition of qualified property is yet another term of art—*depreciable period*—which requires further amplification. The Code defines "depreciable period" to be the period beginning on the date the taxpayer places the property into service and ending on the later of—"(i) the date that is 10 years after such date, or (ii) the last day of the last full year in the applicable recovery period that would apply to the property under § 168 (determined without regard to subsection (g) thereof)." Code § 199A(b)(6)(B).

Note that a taxpayer who has taxable income sufficiently high so that the wage/property cap applies and owns an interest in a QTB that pays no W-2 wages will have a § 199A deduction effectively limited to 2.5% of the taxpayer's allocable share of the QTB's unadjusted basis of qualified property.

Once taxpayers have mastered these definitions, limitations, and exceptions, they are poised to take advantage of the § 199A deduction. This deduction is somewhat unique: it reduces taxable income (i.e., it is to be taken "below the line"), not adjusted gross income,[40] but it is not treated as an itemized deduction and, as such, all taxpayers can use it, even if they take the standard deduction. Code § 63(b)(3).

Apportionment of § 199A Items Between Fiduciary and Beneficiary. To the extent that a trust or estate has QBI, a determination must be made regarding the availability

40. I.R.C. § 62(a) (new sentence at the end thereof added by Section 11011(b)(1) of the Act).

of a QBI deduction at the fiduciary level and beneficiary level. This determination requires the resolution of two separate and distinct apportionment questions: (i) first, how should the QBI initially recognized at the trust or estate level be apportioned between the fiduciary and the beneficiary; and (ii) second, for purposes of applying the wage/property cap, how should W-2 wages and the unadjusted basis of qualified property be apportioned between the fiduciary and the beneficiary? As with virtually everything related to trusts and estates, one would assume that DNI should play a pivotal role in both of these allocation determinations, but unfortunately the analysis is not that simple. As explained below, although the statutory language provides ample support for a DNI-driven allocation approach with respect to the apportionment of W-2 wages and the adjusted basis of qualified property, a similar conclusion with respect to apportionment of QBI can only be reached based on analogy to how other sections apply to trusts and estates and the determination of DNI.

Section 199A(f)(1)(B), under the heading "Application to Trusts and Estates," states that "[r]ules similar to the rules under § 199(d)(1)(B)(i) (as in effect on December 1, 2017) for the apportionment of W-2 wages shall apply to the apportionment of W-2 wages and the apportionment of unadjusted basis immediately after acquisition of qualified property under this section." In other words, the cross-reference from new § 199A(f)(1)(B) to former § 199(d)(1)(B)(i) was narrowly written so that it is limited in scope to the apportionment of W-2 wages and the adjusted basis of qualified property (and does not make any reference to the to-be-determined rules for apportioning QBI). Ascertaining the true meaning of this provision requires some background.

Section 199 (not to be confused with § 199A) — which was repealed by § 13305 of the 2017 Act, effective for taxable years beginning after December 31, 2017 — generally allowed a limited deduction for a taxpayer's (i) "qualified production activities income" (QPAI) or (ii) taxable income (determined without regard to the deduction allowed by § 199), subject to a cap based on the taxpayer's W-2 wages. Former § 199(d)(1)(B)(i) — i.e., the provision that is cross-referenced by new § 199A(f)(1)(B) — required apportionment between the fiduciary and beneficiary, in accordance with regulations prescribed by Treasury, with respect to the items entering into the calculation of the W-2 wages of the trust or estate. In fact, the Treasury did promulgate regulations under former § 199 generally providing for the apportionment of W-2 wages between fiduciary and beneficiary "in relative proportion of the trust's or estate's distributable net income (DNI), as defined by § 643(a), for the taxable year that is distributed or required to be distributed to the beneficiary or is retained by the trust or estate." Treas. Reg. § 1.199-5(e)(2)(i). In addition, "[t]o the extent that the trust or estate has no DNI for the taxable year, any QPAI and W-2 wages are allocated entirely to the trust or estate." *Id.* That being the case, DNI-driven rules for apportioning QBI between fiduciaries and beneficiaries appear apropos.

The example below illustrates how § 199A is expected to operate in the Subchapter J context. For purposes of simplicity, the example assumes that Treasury regulations will require the apportionment of QBI, W-2 wages, and unadjusted basis of qualified property between the fiduciary and the beneficiary in accordance with the same DNI-driven principles embedded in the regulations under former § 199.

Assumptions. Suppose Trust A (which is neither a grantor trust nor a so-called electing small business trust (both concepts are discussed in subsequent chapters of the textbook)) owns a 60% interest in a partnership (the Partnership). Suppose further that the terms of Trust A permit discretionary distributions and that the trustee distributes 10% of the trust's fiduciary accounting income (FAI) to Beneficiary X, one of the trust's named beneficiaries. Furthermore, assume the following:

- All allocations and distributions by the Partnership are made in accordance with the partners' respective percentage interests.
- The Partnership has $1 million of QBI for its taxable year ending December 31, 2023.
- The Partnership is not an SSTB.
- Beneficiary X is not married, so the threshold amount at the beneficiary level for purposes of § 199A is $157,500 (this dollar figure has not been adjusted for inflation), and Beneficiary X's taxable income, even after accounting for income received from this trust, is below the threshold amount.
- The Partnership has $300,000 of payroll expenses treated as W-2 wages (and taken into account as a deduction in arriving at the Partnership's QBI of $1 million).
- The Partnership owns qualified property with an unadjusted basis of $1,200,000.
- The Partnership makes cash distributions to its partners during 2023 exactly equal to its $1 million of QBI, so that Trust A receives a cash distribution of $600,000 (60% of $1 million).
- Trust A has no sources of QBI (or any other income or deductions) other than its share of QBI from the Partnership and its allowable distribution deduction. For simplicity, Trust A's personal exemption is not taken into account.
- Based on the foregoing oversimplified assumptions and assuming that the 199A deduction ultimately allowable to the trust will not reduce DNI; the DNI of Trust A is exactly equal to its FAI of $600,000.
- Trust A makes a cash distribution of $60,000 to Beneficiary X during 2023. Receipt of this distribution represents Beneficiary X's only potential source of QBI (or any other income or deductions) for 2023. For simplicity, Beneficiary X's standard deduction is not taken into account.
- Beneficiary X is the only beneficiary of Trust A who receives a distribution from Trust A with respect to calendar year 2023.

Under this set of assumptions, the QBI allocated by the Partnership to Trust A would be $600,000 (i.e., 60% × $1 million). However, because the trustee distributed 10% of FAI to Beneficiary X and retained 90% of FAI at the trust level and because Treasury promulgated regulations requiring QBI to be apportioned between fiduciary and beneficiary in proportion to the relative amounts of DNI retained or distributed,[41] Trust A would be apportioned $540,000 of QBI (i.e., $600,000 × 90%) and Beneficiary X would be apportioned $60,000 of QBI (i.e., $600,000 × 10%). As a result, Trust A would have a tentative QBI deduction of **$108,000** (20% × $540,000) and Beneficiary X would have a tentative QBI deduction of **$12,000** (20% × $60,000), in each case before taking into account the potential application of the wage/property cap and the limitation based on "ordinary" taxable income.

In this example, Trust A is subject to the wage/property cap,[42] whereas Beneficiary X is not.[43] For purposes of applying the wage/property cap, it is necessary to determine the apportionment of W-2 wages and the unadjusted basis of qualified property between Trust A and Beneficiary X. Based on the language of § 199A(f)(1)(B), it is reasonably clear that W-2 wages and the adjusted basis of qualified property should be allocated between a trust and its beneficiaries in proportion to the relative amounts of DNI retained or distributed. As a result, in the case of Trust A, the wage/property cap is the greater of the following:

(i) $81,000 (i.e., Trust A's allocable share of 50% of the Partnership's W-2 wages equals 60% × 50% × $300,000, or $90,000, which is then multiplied by the 90% portion of DNI retained at the trust level to arrive at $81,000).

(ii) $56,700 (i.e., the sum of the following amounts: (1) Trust A's allocable share of 25% of the Partnership's W-2 wages equals 60% × 25% × $300,000 or $45,000, which is then multiplied by the 90% portion of DNI retained at the trust level to arrive at $40,500; plus (2) Trust A's allocable share of 2.5% of the unadjusted basis of qualified property equals 60% × 2.5% of $1.2 million or $18,000, which is then multiplied by the 90% portion of DNI retained at the trust level to arrive at $16,200).

When all the dust settles, what this example denotes is that § 199A permits Trust A to be able to deduct $81,000 and Beneficiary X $12,000, in each case before applying the cap based on "ordinary" taxable income set forth in Code § 199A(a)(2).

There are many planning opportunities trustees and executors should consider. Among them are as follows: the risk of long-term planning in light of this provision's scheduled sunset, the incentive to own rather than lease qualified property, and the taxpayer's motivation to classify service-providers as employees rather than independent contractors.

---

41. Treas. Reg. § 1.199A-6(d).

42. Trust A is potentially subject to the wage/property cap because its taxable income, before subtracting the QBI deduction but after subtracting the allowable distribution deduction (on these facts, $60,000), exceeds the full phase-in amount of $207,500. (Note: the threshold amount is defined to be $157,500, but as a taxpayer's income increases beyond this amount, the Code gradually phases in a limitation as to availability of the Code § 199A deduction; at $207,500, the limitation is fully phased in.)

43. Beneficiary X is not subject to the wage/property cap because his or her taxable income, before subtracting the QBI deduction, does not exceed $157,500.

Problems

1. In the trust and estate context, what role, if any, would you anticipate the specified service trade or business limitation found in Code § 199A(d)(1)(A) plays regarding the qualified business income deduction?
2. Which Code § 199A limitation—(i) the 50% W-2 wage limitation or (ii) the 25% W-2 wage plus 2.5% of the unadjusted basis of qualified property limitation—would you anticipate more likely applying in the trust and estate context and why?
3. Between a trust that is required to distribute all of its income and a trust that has no requirement and does not distribute its income, in which would a qualified business income deduction most likely appear?
4. When could estate beneficiaries avail themselves of a qualified business income deduction?

VI. Charitable Contribution

Internal Revenue Code: Section 642(c)(1), (2)

Regulations: Sections 1.642(c)-1, -2(a), (d), -3(a), (b), 1.645-1(e)(2)(i), 1.645-1(e)(3)(i)

Just like individual taxpayers, the Code permits trusts and estates to deduct amounts that are donated to or used for charitable and public purposes. However, aside from the fact that individual taxpayers endure charitable deduction limitations equal to a percentage of their adjusted gross income (which vary depending upon the nature of the property given to charity and the nature of the charitable donee)[44] and trusts and estates do not (i.e., the charitable deduction amount is unlimited),[45] there are other salient differences as well. Enumerated below, these differences are grouped between those amounts which are destined for a charitable or public purpose that (1) immediately vest or (2) are permanently set aside.

A. Amounts That Immediately Vest

With respect to Subchapter J, to qualify for a charitable deduction, the following three conjunctive conditions must be met: the payment must be (i) made from gross income, (ii) pursuant to the terms of the governing instrument, and (iii) for a charitable or public purpose. Code § 642(c).

(i) Gross Income. Insofar as the concept of DNI is concerned (which is explored in the next chapter), with respect to principal and income distinctions, Congress

44. I.R.C. § 170(b).
45. I.R.C. § 642(c).

purposefully eschewed the notion of tracing.[46] However, with respect to distributions from trusts and estates made for charitable and public purposes, Congress mandated tracing: to qualify for a charitable deduction, distributions must be comprised of gross income, not principal. *See, e.g.*, Rev. Rul. 2003-123, 2003-50 I.R.B. 1200 (charitable deduction negated when a trustee donated a qualified conservation easement because the contribution was made from trust corpus, not gross income); Rev. Rul. 68-667, 1968-2 C.B. 289 (same). As expressed in Treasury regulations (Treas. Reg. § 1.642(c)-3(a)), gross income is broadly defined to include amounts received as income in respect of a decedent (see Chapter 8), but not tax-exempt income. Treas. Reg. § 1.642(c)-3(b)(1).

One other important point of clarification: gross income does not mean trust accounting income; instead, it means taxable income. *See* Code § 643(b) (which states that "the term 'income', when not preceded by the words 'taxable', 'distributable net', 'undistributed net', or 'gross', means the amount of income of the estate or trust for the taxable year determined under the terms of the governing instrument and applicable local law").

With this background in mind, consider the following three examples:

> **Example:** Suppose a trust receives $100,000 from an IRA and $50,000 of tax-exempt interest from a municipal bond and that same tax year donates $150,000 to the American Red Cross. The charitable amount deductible would be limited to $100,000.
>
> **Example:** Suppose a charity or governmental entity is entitled to a pecuniary bequest of $150,000. Its payment will not give rise to a charitable deduction, even if paid from gross income. *See, e.g., Wellman v. Welch*, 99 F.2d 75, 77 (1st Cir. 1938) ("There is no provision in the will authorizing the executor to pay from income as such any of the pecuniary legacies.").
>
> **Example:** In accordance with the terms of a decedent's will, her executor transfers a painting with a $150,000 fair market value in the decedent's estate to Harvard University. This bequest doesn't qualify for the § 642(c) deduction, because it is not made out of gross income.

(ii) Governing Instrument. Another sine qua non to securing a charitable deduction is that the governing instrument — whether the terms of the trust or the decedent's will — must specifically provide that income is to be contributed to or for the use of charitable organizations or governmental entities.

> **Example:** The terms of a decedent's will are silent about giving money to charity, but the decedent's heirs and beneficiaries instruct the executor to

46. H.R. Rep. No. 1337, 83rd Cong., 2d Sess. A199, 3 U.S.C. Cong. & Adm. News 4017, 4339 (1954); S. Rep. No. 1622, 83rd Cong., 2d Sess. 349, 3 U.S.C. Cong.& Adm. News 4621, 4990 (1954) (the concept of DNI seeks "to avoid the necessity for tracing of income").

give $5,000 to Yale University. The gift does not qualify for the § 642(c) deduction, because it was not made pursuant to the governing instrument.

In *Old Colony Trust Co. v. Commissioner*, 301 U.S. 379 (1937), the U.S. Supreme Court held that as long as the governing instrument *authorizes* such distributions to charities, an actual charitable distribution will qualify for the charitable deduction.

Note that the fact that a trustee or executor is magnanimous or the beneficiaries consent to a distribution will not substitute for explicit written instructions in the governing instrument itself. *See, e.g., Love Charitable Found v. U.S.*, 710 F.2d 1316 (8th Cir. 1983) (charitable deduction denied for charitable contributions which fulfilled settlor's wishes, but the trust instrument did not authorize); *Riggs Nat'l Bank v. U.S.*, 352 F.2d 812 (Ct. Cl. 1965) (same). *But see* Rev. Rul. 2004-5, 2004-3 I.R.B. 295 (although trust's governing instrument did not permit charitable deductions, it was nevertheless permitted a charitable deduction flowing from an investment it had made in a partnership that had made a charitable contribution). Furthermore, even if the terms of the trust instrument provide a beneficiary with a power of appointment and the beneficiary exercises such power in favor of a charity, distributions made pursuant to such exercise will not qualify for a charitable deduction unless the power extends specifically to charitable organizations. *Compare Estate of O'Connor v. Commissioner*, 69 T.C. 165 (1977) (surviving spouse was given a general power of appointment to appoint "to such persons and/or corporations" as she saw fit; however, because there was no mention in the power of appointment to "charitable corporations," the court denied a charitable deduction to the taxpayer), *with* Priv. Ltr. Rul. 2009-06-008 (a distribution of trust income made pursuant to a power of appointment in which a trust beneficiary was granted a limited power of appointment that could be exercised only in favor of charitable organizations was held to be deductible).

(iii) Charitable or Public Purpose. Deductions are permissible as long as the funds in question pass to a governmental entity of the United States exclusively for public purposes or, alternatively, to a "corporation, trust, or community chest, fund, or foundation . . . organized and operated exclusively for religious, charitable, scientific, literary, or educational purposes, or to foster national or international amateur sports competition . . . or for the prevention of cruelty to children or animals." Code § 170(c). In the context of trusts and estates, unlike for individuals, the fact that the charity is foreign does not negate eligibility for securing a charitable deduction. Code § 642(c)(1); *Tait Estate v. Commissioner*, 11 T.C. 731 (1948).

B. Amounts Permanently Set Aside for Charity

Estates and certain trusts can qualify for a charitable deduction if the amounts are permanently set aside for charitable and public purposes. Albeit a bit oversimplified, trusts that qualify for this deduction are those that are testamentary trusts that were established by a will executed on or before October 9, 1969, and inter vivos trusts that were created on or before October 9, 1969. Code § 642(c)(2)(A), (B). In addition, those revocable trusts that elect under Code § 645 to be treated as part of the taxpayer's estate can avail themselves of this deduction if they permanently set aside funds for charitable or public purposes. Treas. Reg. §§ 1.645-1(e)(2)(i), 1.645-1(e)(3)(i).

To qualify for a "set-aside" charitable deduction, the Treasury Department has ruled that the possibility of the funds not passing to a charitable or public purpose and instead to a nonqualified purpose or use must be "so remote as to be negligible." Treas. Reg. § 1.642(c)-2(d).[47] However, at least one court (*Hartwick College v. U.S.*, 801 F.2d 608 (2d Cir. 1986)) pioneered a meaningful exception to this rule when funds permanently set aside are used to meet the trust's income tax obligations; in such cases, a charitable deduction is permitted notwithstanding the fact that the charitable beneficiary may ultimately receive a lesser sum.

> **Example:** A taxpayer bequeaths his residuary estate to charity. During the tax year in question, the estate earns $2.4 million of income. The executor uses $1 million of this income to satisfy the estate's administrative expenses (e.g., fees for its lawyers, accountants, and appraisers) and deducts this amount on the taxpayer's estate return (i.e., Form 706), therefore precluding its deduction on the estate's income tax return (i.e., Form 1041). Code § 642(g). Albeit, the estate sought a $1.4 million charitable income tax deduction (i.e., $2.4 million income – $1 million of administration expenses), the estate nevertheless was obligated to pay approximately $370,000 of income tax ($1 million of nondeductible administration expenses × .37 assumed tax rate), resulting in $1,030,000 remaining ($2.4 million – $1 million in estate administration expenses – $370,000 in taxes). The IRS sought to deny the entirety of the deduction on the theory that the entire $1.4 million would not pass to the charity.[48] In *Hartwick*, the Eighth Circuit disagreed, positing that Congress could not have possibly intended such an outcome, allowing a full $1.4 million charitable deduction.

---

47. *Estate of Belmont*, 44 T.C. 84 (2015), illustrates the potential risk in claiming the set-aside deduction followed by unexpected litigation costs. The fiduciary had received a residence and had to pursue eviction of the decedent's brother, which action turned unexpectedly time-consuming and expensive, eventually consuming the moneys set-aside for charity. The Tax Court held that the possibility that litigation would continue at a steep expense was not "so remote as to be negligible."

48. The IRS position was that no charitable deduction should be permitted at all because, after the first $370,000 tax was imposed, only $1,030,000 (i.e., $1,400,000 – $370,000) remained to pass to the charity. However, the fact that the $370,000 which had to be paid to the government could not pass to charity created another tax and so on and so forth. Each successive round would preclude another dollar amount from passing to the charity. (In *Hartwick*, the then high marginal tax rate of 70% would have eliminated the charitable deduction in its entirety; in a lower tax rate environment, the charitable deduction would instead have become severely eroded.)

To augment the attractiveness of the charitable deduction under Subchapter J, the Code provides that trusts and estates may elect to treat a current year contribution as being made in the prior tax year. Code § 642(c) (last two sentences). What this means is that a trustee or executor who, pursuant to the terms of the governing instrument, contributes gross income for a charitable or public purpose can take a charitable deduction in the prior tax year if the detailed requirements for making this election are fulfilled. Treas. Reg. § 1.642(c)-1(b). This may require the filing of an amended return.

Problems

1. The terms of a decedent's will specify that $100,000 be paid to the Lutheran Church and the estate's residuary be paid to the decedent's sister, Jane. During the course of the year, on its $10 million corpus, the estate earns $200,000 of interest income and then distributes $100,000 to the Lutheran Church and $1.1 million to Jane. May the estate deduct the $100,000 passing to the Lutheran Church?
2. Suppose the terms of a trust permit discretionary distributions to be made to a charity, and the trustee exercises his prerogative and makes a $100,000 charitable contribution out of the trust's gross income. Will this donation qualify for a charitable deduction?
3. Suppose instead that the trust terms authorize this power upon trust termination, but the trustee nevertheless makes a $100,000 trust contribution from gross income to a charity prior to trust termination. Will this donation qualify for a charitable deduction?

Chapter 3

Distributable Net Income and Fiduciary Accounting Income[1]

Internal Revenue Code: Sections 643(a), 643(b)

Regulations: Sections 1.643(a)-0, 1.643(a)-3, 1.643(a)-5, 1.643(b)-1, 1.652(b)-1, 1.652(b)-2, 1.652(b)-3, 1.652(c)-4

The fundamental question concerning the income taxation of trusts and estates and their beneficiaries is how income should be divided between them. From the beginning, trusts and estates were treated to some extent as conduit vehicles insomuch that trusts and estates would be able to deduct the amount of income distributed to their beneficiaries. And, whatever income the trust or estate could deduct, the beneficiaries would include in their gross income.

Prior to the enactment of the 1954 Internal Revenue Code, the amount of income deemed distributed to beneficiaries was determined by tracing; that is, comparing the income received by the estate or trust with the amounts actually distributed to its beneficiaries and when such distributions were made. This led to taxpayer manipulation, because fiduciaries could segregate income in separate accounts and then determine when and to what extent they wanted to distribute such income during the year, or because documents could be drafted to effectively trap income in the trust for tax purposes while for all practical purposes distributing it out to the beneficiaries.

An example of taxpayer manipulation is found in *Commissioner v. Dean.*[2] In *Dean*, a trust provided for the payment of $10,000 out of income to be paid to each of two beneficiaries on January 3 of the succeeding year, if the beneficiaries were alive on that date. At the end of any year, neither beneficiary was entitled to the income for such year, because the beneficiary had to survive until January 3 of the following year. Thus, the money distributed was the income of the prior year and not of the current year. The consequence was that none of the income was taxable to the beneficiary, because it had already been taxed to the trust. The court, in affirming the order of the Board of Tax Appeals, stated, "Measured by the terms of the statute, respondent was liable for the tax only on that part, if any, of the income earned between January 1

1. Portions of this chapter have been excerpted from or are substantially similar to portions from Alan Acker, Bloomberg Tax Portfolio: Income Taxation of Trusts and Estates, No. 8524th T.M.

2. 102 F.2d 699 (10th Cir. 1939).

and 3, and distributable to him on January 4—during the calendar year. The income earned between January 4 and December 31 was taxable to the fiduciary."

The 1954 Internal Revenue Code completely overhauled how Subchapter J operated on the taxation of trusts and estates. First, when it came to determining how much income of a trust or estate was considered to have been distributed to the beneficiaries, Congress did away with tracing. Instead, Congress created the concept of distributable net income (DNI)—an amount equal to the trust's or estate's gross income with unique modifications—to be used to determine the amount and character of income included in a beneficiary's gross income. As explained below, DNI is computed at the end of the taxable year, and the timing of when an estate or trust received income or made a distribution to beneficiaries is irrelevant; thus, it eliminated the potential tax abuses associated with tracing.

By eliminating the need to trace actual income coming into and going out of the trust or estate for the purpose of determining the distribution deduction, it was necessary (i) to create a method of determining exactly what items of income were being distributed, and (ii) to treat all distributions as if they had occurred on the last day of the tax year. DNI was the method created for determining the income considered distributed by an estate or trust whenever the fiduciary makes distributions to beneficiaries.

Distributable net income (commonly referred to as DNI) is a number that represents the largest amount of income that can be treated as being (i) distributed and correspondingly deductible by a trust or estate and (ii) reportable as income by trust and estate beneficiaries. Any item of gross income of a trust or estate that is not a part of DNI cannot be taxed to a beneficiary. Think of DNI as a train that carries items of income from the trust or estate to the beneficiaries; if an item of income cannot get on the train, then it cannot be transported to the beneficiaries.

I. Determining DNI

The method of determining DNI is set forth in § 643(a) and amplified in the regulations. Section 643(a) defines DNI as the taxable income of the trust or estate with several modifications. Thus, determining DNI is simply a mathematical computation accomplished by following the directions of § 643(a) discussed below. For many domestic estates and trusts, DNI will equal the following:

> The taxable income determined before the distribution deduction and the personal exemption;
>
> less the net capital gains allocated to principal; and
>
> plus tax-exempt income reduced by expenses and any charitable deduction allocated to the tax-exempt income.

DNI often (but not always) approximates gross accounting income less allowed tax deductions. As a result, DNI often approximates the amount that a fiduciary would be required to distribute if the fiduciary was required to distribute all of the net accounting income (as defined in the Uniform Principal and Income Act).

DNI, as set forth in § 643(a), is determined by making the following modifications to taxable income:

A. No Distribution Deduction — § 643(a)(1)

The first modification to taxable income is to ignore the distribution deduction. This first "modification" to taxable income must occur by practical necessity, obviating the need for what otherwise would have been a complex circular computation. In computing taxable income, one must determine the distribution deduction which, in turn, hinges upon the trust's or estate's DNI. Given the interrelationship among these concepts, this requires that the identification of at least one element of the equation be temporarily ignored, which Congress chose to be the distribution deduction allowed under § 651 or § 661.

B. No Deduction for Personal Exemption — § 643(a)(2)

The second modification to taxable income is to ignore the deduction allowed in lieu of the personal exemption of $100, $300 or $600 allowed under § 642(b). To determine DNI, it must therefore be added back to taxable income.

C. Capital Gains and Losses — § 643(a)(3)

The third modification to taxable income is to sometimes ignore capital gains and losses. For DNI computation purposes, the Code bifurcates its treatment of capital gains and capital losses.

Capital gains are excluded from DNI to the extent such gains are allocated to principal for accounting purposes and are not:

(i) paid, credited, or required to be distributed to any beneficiary during the tax year; or

(ii) paid, permanently set aside, or to be used for charitable purposes.

Capital gains are a common item of gross income often excluded from DNI. Accordingly, to determine DNI of a trust or estate, capital gains often must be deducted from taxable income and, as a result, such gains are taxed to the trust or estate. Capital gains taxable to a trust or estate will be exposed to the unearned income Medicare contribution tax of § 1411.

However, capital gains will be a part of DNI whenever capital gains are (i) allocated to income, (ii) allocated to principal, and (a) treated consistently by the fiduciary on the books, records, and tax returns as part of a distribution to a beneficiary, (b) actually distributed to a beneficiary or (c) used by the fiduciary in determining the amount that is distributed or required to be distributed to a beneficiary, or

(iii) allocated to principal and paid, permanently set aside or to be used for charitable purposes so that a charitable deduction is allowed.[3]

In addition to the above requirements, Treasury Regulation § 1.643(a)-3(b) sets forth a prerequisite for capital gains to be a part of DNI: either (i) the distribution must be made pursuant to the terms of the governing instrument and applicable local law requirements[4] or (ii) the fiduciary (i.e., trustee or executor) exercises "reasonable and impartial" discretion "in accordance with a power granted to the fiduciary by applicable local law or by the governing instrument if not prohibited by applicable local law. . . ."

1. Directing That Capital Gains Be Allocated to Income (Treas. Reg. § 1.643(a)-3(b)(1)). Sometimes the terms of the governing instrument and applicable local law require that capital gains be allocated to income and, if so, they will then be added to DNI. As a practical matter, however, governing instruments rarely contain terms mandating that capital gains are to be allocated to income. This is because such terms would almost always run counter to the grantor's intentions.

> **Example:** John has established a trust for the benefit of his daughter, Jane. Under the terms of the trust, Jane is to receive all of the income annually and when Jane attains the age of 35 years, the trust is to terminate and all trust property is to be distributed to Jane. It is unlikely that John wants capital gains recognized by the trust before Jane is 35 years of age to be treated as accounting income and, thus, required to be distributed to Jane.

However, when dealing with an estate where income and principal distributions are always discretionary, or with a trust that provides for discretionary distributions of income and principal, such a provision would make it easier for an estate or trust to distribute such gains to its beneficiaries (but see the discussion below) and to make it easier for the estate or trust to avoid the net investment income tax imposed under § 1411.[5]

---

3. Treas. Reg. 1.643(a)-3(c). On the Form 1041, Schedule D, Part III there are places to allocate short-term and long-term capital gains between the beneficiaries and the entity. The fiduciary cannot allocate such amounts as desired; instead, capital gains not a part of DNI must be allocated to the trust or estate.

4. While this prerequisite is stated in the conjunction ("and"), the regulations seem to allow it if the terms of the governing instrument require it and local law does not prohibit it. *See* Example 4 of Treas. Reg. § 1.643(a)-3(e), which concludes that capital gain is included in DNI based on an explicit direction in the governing instrument that was not prohibited by local law

5. A provision in a trust or will directing that all capital gains be allocated to income may not be respected because of the unknown interplay between two regulations. Regulation § 1.643(b)-1, entitled "Definition of Income," states, in pertinent parts, that "trust provisions that depart fundamentally from traditional principles of income and principal will generally not be recognized," and "proceeds from the sale or exchange of trust assets are generally allocable to principal." Thus, a provision directing that capital gains be allocated to accounting income would seem to depart fundamentally from traditional principles of income and principal. However, Regulation § 1.643(a)-3(b) states that capital gains can be allocated to income if done so "pursuant to the terms of the governing instrument **and** applicable local law."

Example: Under the terms of a decedent's will, her estate is to be distributed to her children. During the tax year of the estate, the estate has ordinary income of $30,000 and capital gains of $5,000, and the executor has distributed $500,000 to the beneficiaries. It is not the estate's final year, and it still has assets in excess of $1,000,000. Under this set of facts, the estate will have taxable income of $5,000 represented by the capital gains. Had the capital gains been a part of DNI, such gains would have been distributed to the children who may be in lower tax brackets or, if the estate was on a fiscal year, then such tax may be deferred.

Aside from the governing instrument, sometimes state law provides that a fiduciary may make adjustments between principal and income if the fiduciary believes that such adjustment is needed to administer the trust or estate impartially, based on what is fair and reasonable to all of the beneficiaries.[6] Where state law permits a fiduciary to make adjustments, and the governing instrument authorizes the fiduciary to allocate capital gains to income, then a fiduciary could allocate some or all of the capital gains from principal to income under appropriate circumstances.

Example: The applicable state statute provides that a trustee may elect to pay an income beneficiary an amount equal to four percent of the fair market value of the trust assets, as determined at the beginning of each taxable year, in full satisfaction of that beneficiary's right to income. State statute also provides that this unitrust amount shall be considered paid first from ordinary and tax-exempt income, then from net short-term capital gain,

---

The question is then what does "applicable local law" mean in this context? The Uniform Principal and Income Act provides generally that the fiduciary must administer a trust or estate in accordance with the terms of the governing instrument even if there is a different provision in the principal and income act, and provides that capital gains are to be allocated to principal if the governing instrument is otherwise silent. Thus, if the phrase "applicable local law" in the above quoted regulation is understood to mean the law that directs the fiduciary to follow the terms of the governing instrument even if otherwise contrary to the principal and income act, then a provision in the governing instrument directing that capital gains be allocated to income should be respected and capital gains will be a part of DNI. However, if "applicable local law" in the regulation is understood to be how capital gains would be allocated between income and principal if the governing instrument was silent as to this point, then capital gains would be allocated to principal pursuant to the Uniform Principal and Income Act.

The better argument should be that such a provision in a governing instrument should be respected based on the facts that (1) Regulation § 1.643(a)-3(b)(1) appears to specifically allow such a provision, (2) principal and income acts are default provisions and governing instruments can override provisions of such acts so that applicable local law permits such a provision, and (3) if applicable local law is understood to never allow such a provision (absent a statute specifically allowing it), then Regulation § 1.643(a)-3(b)(1) becomes meaningless or illusory and we should not interpret statutes and regulations in a way that makes them meaningless or illusory.

Lastly, Example 4 under Regulation § 1.643(a)-3(e) seems to sanction such a provision, but the example appears to mashup Regulation § 1.643(a)-3(b) leaving doubt as to its conclusion.

6. If the trust or the will manifests an intention that the fiduciary should favor one or more beneficiaries relative to other beneficiaries, then the fiduciary can make an adjustment between principal and income to achieve the settlor's or decedent's intent.

> then from net long-term capital gain, and finally from return of principal. Trust's governing instrument provides that A is to receive each year income as defined under state statute. Trustee makes the unitrust election under state statute. At the beginning of the taxable year, Trust assets are valued at $500,000. During the year, Trust receives $5,000 of dividend income and realizes $80,000 of net long-term gain from the sale of capital assets. Trustee distributes to A $20,000 (4% of $500,000) in satisfaction of A's right to income. Net long-term capital gain in the amount of $15,000 is allocated to income pursuant to the ordering rule of the state statute and is included in distributable net income for the taxable year.

Treas. Reg. § 1.643(a)-3(e), Ex. 11.

2. Distributing Capital Gains by Consistent Treatment (Treas. Reg. § 1.643(a)-3(b)(2)). Capital gains will be part of DNI if such gains are allocated to principal but are treated consistently by the fiduciary on the trust's books, records, and tax returns as part of a distribution to a beneficiary.[7]

The regulations under § 643 provide guidance in determining whether capital gains will be treated as being distributed pursuant to consistent treatment and, thus, will be treated as a part of DNI. Examples 1-3 under Treas. Reg. § 1.643(a)-3(e) illustrate when capital gains are or are not distributed by consistent treatment and read as follows:

Example 1.

> Under the terms of Trust's governing instrument, all income is to be paid to A for life. Trustee is given discretionary powers to invade principal for A's benefit and to deem discretionary distributions to be made from capital gains realized during the year. During Trust's first taxable year, Trust has $5,000 of dividend income and $10,000 of capital gain from the sale of securities. Pursuant to the terms of the governing instrument and applicable local law, Trustee allocates the $10,000 capital gain to principal. During the year, Trustee distributes to A $5,000, representing A's right to trust income. In addition, Trustee distributes to A $12,000, pursuant to the discretionary power to distribute principal. Trustee does not exercise the discretionary power to deem the discretionary distributions of principal as being paid from capital gains realized during the year. Therefore, the capital gains realized during the year are not included in distributable net income and the $10,000 of capital gain is taxed to the Trust. In future years, Trustee must treat all discretionary distributions as not being made from any realized capital gains.

7. This is an advance from the test that previously existed. Previously, the test was whether the trustee followed a regular practice of distributing gains to the income beneficiary. This was less than satisfactory, because it was uncertain as to how many years the trustee had to follow such a practice to make it a regular practice. *See* Rev. Rul. 68-392, 1968-2 C.B. 284 and Priv. Ltr. Rul. 8429005.

Example 2.

> The facts are the same as in Example 1, except that Trustee intends to follow a regular practice of treating discretionary distributions of principal as being paid first from any net capital gains realized by Trust during the year. Trustee evidences this treatment by including the $10,000 capital gain in distributable net income on Trust's federal income tax return so that it is taxed to A. This treatment of the capital gains is a reasonable exercise of Trustee's discretion. In future years, Trustee must treat all discretionary distributions as being made first from any realized capital gains.

Example 3.

> The facts are the same as in Example 1, except that Trustee intends to follow a regular practice of treating discretionary distributions of principal as being paid from any net capital gains realized by Trust during the year from the sale of certain specified assets or a particular class of investments. This treatment of capital gains is a reasonable exercise of Trustee's discretion.

3. Actually Distributing Capital Gains to the Beneficiary (Treas. Reg. § 1.643(a)-3(b)(3)). Another way that capital gains will be a part of DNI is if such gains are actually distributed to the beneficiary or are used by the fiduciary in determining the amount that is distributed or required to be distributed to the beneficiary. Examples 5-9 under Treas. Reg. § 1.643(a)-3(e) illustrate when this rule will apply and read as follows:

Example 5.

> The facts are the same as in Example 1 [shown above], except that Trustee decides that discretionary distributions will be made only to the extent Trust has realized capital gains during the year and thus the discretionary distribution to A is $10,000, rather than $12,000. Because Trustee will use the amount of any realized capital gain to determine the amount of the discretionary distribution to the beneficiary, the $10,000 capital gain is included in Trust's distributable net income for the taxable year.

Example 6.

> Trust's assets consist of Blackacre and other property. Under the terms of Trust's governing instrument, Trustee is directed to hold Blackacre for ten years and then sell it and distribute all the sales proceeds to A. Because Trustee uses the amount of the sales proceeds that includes any realized capital gain to determine the amount required to be distributed to A, any capital gain realized from the sale of Blackacre is included in Trust's distributable net income for the taxable year.

Example 7.

> Under the terms of Trust's governing instrument, all income is to be paid to A during the Trust's term. When A reaches 35, Trust is to terminate and all the principal is to be distributed to A. Because all the assets of the trust,

including all capital gains, will be actually distributed to the beneficiary at the termination of Trust, all capital gains realized in the year of termination are included in distributable net income. See § 1.641(b)-3 for the determination of the year of final termination and the taxability of capital gains realized after the terminating event and before final distribution.

Example 8.

The facts are the same as Example 7, except Trustee is directed to pay B $10,000 before distributing the remainder of Trust assets to A. Because the distribution to B is a gift of a specific sum of money within the meaning of section 663(a)(1), none of Trust's distributable net income that includes all of the capital gains realized during the year of termination is allocated to B's distribution.

Example 9.

The facts are the same as Example 7, except Trustee is directed to distribute one-half of the principal to A when A reaches 35 and the balance to A when A reaches 45. Trust assets consist entirely of stock in corporation M with a fair market value of $1,000,000 and an adjusted basis of $300,000. When A reaches 35, Trustee sells one-half of the stock and distributes the sales proceeds to A. All the sales proceeds, including all the capital gain attributable to that sale, are actually distributed to A and therefore all the capital gain is included in distributable net income.

Also, if capital gains actually are paid, permanently set aside or to be used for charitable purposes so that a charitable deduction is allowed under § 642(c), then such gains will be included in DNI. This can only arise if the governing instrument directs or allows such action.[8]

Capital losses, like capital gains, are excluded from DNI. There is one important exception to the foregoing rule—at the trust or estate level, capital losses are first netted against capital gains, except for those capital gains used in determining the amount that is distributed or required to be distributed to a particular beneficiary.[9] Thus, if there is a net capital loss that decreases the taxable income of the trust or estate, such loss would be added to the taxable income in arriving at the DNI for such trust or estate. The general rule and its exception presuppose that in any instance in which capital gains are to be distributed, such gains should be offset first by any capital losses. Thus, the fiduciary cannot treat capital gains and losses independent of each other; for example, the fiduciary cannot distribute the gross amount of capital gains to beneficiaries while retaining the capital losses in the estate or trust.

---

8. An exception to the requirement that the governing instrument must direct charitable distributions is when a trust or estate is a partner in a partnership or a member in a limited liability company taxed as a partnership and the partnership or limited liability company made charitable distributions that are allocated to the partners or members for tax purposes.

9. Treas. Reg. § 1.643(a)-3(d).

Example: For the taxable year, a trust has $20,000 of interest income, dividend income of $50,000, capital gains of $5,000, and capital losses of $20,000. The trust also paid trustee fees of $16,000. In determining the DNI of the trust, the trust has tentative taxable income determined as follows:

Interest Income	$20,000
Dividend Income	50,000
Capital Gains	5,000
Capital Losses	–20,000
Trustee Fees	–16,000
Tentative Taxable Income	$39,000

The DNI for the trust is determined by offsetting the capital gains with the capital losses so that the above can be consolidated to the following:

Interest Income	$20,000
Dividend Income	50,000
Net Capital Losses	–15,000
Trustee Fees	–16,000
Tentative Taxable Income	$39,000

Thus, DNI will equal the tentative taxable income ($39,000), plus net capital losses ($15,000), or $54,000. This DNI equals the sum of the interest income and dividend income reduced by the trustee fees. The above ignores the fact that capital losses are limited to $3,000 (so that Tentative Taxable Income would be $51,000). Notwithstanding, DNI would still be $54,000. Do you know why?

D. Extraordinary Dividends and Taxable Stock Dividends — § 643(a)(4)

With respect to simple trusts (see Chapter 4), if under the terms of the governing instrument and applicable local law the fiduciary allocates extraordinary dividends and taxable stock dividends[10] to principal and does not pay them to any beneficiary, they are excluded from DNI. Remember that under a simple trust, the trustee is required to distribute all of the net accounting income at least annually. If the trustee allocates extraordinary and taxable stock dividends to principal, then such amounts are not accounting income and cannot be distributed to any income

10. Extraordinary dividends are defined in § 1059(c), and taxable stock dividends are defined in § 305(b).

beneficiary. By removing such items from DNI, the tax law aligns better with the actions and decisions of the trustee.[11]

> **Example:** A trust directs that all of its income is to be distributed annually and that the trustee has discretion to distribute principal. The trust receives a taxable stock dividend of $10,000. The trustee allocates such stock dividend to principal.
>
> The trustee does not make any discretionary distributions of principal so that the trust is a simple trust for the tax year. In determining the DNI for this trust, the trustee will exclude the taxable stock dividend. The DNI is then more likely to match with accounting income (although DNI and accounting income need not be the same). The taxable stock dividend will accordingly be taxed to the trust.
>
> Assume, on the other hand, that the trustee makes a modest discretionary distribution of principal during the year so that the trust is characterized as a complex trust for the tax year. As a result, the taxable stock dividend is a part of DNI and after applying deductions such stock dividend will be allocated to the beneficiaries in accordance with Code § 662.

E. Tax-Exempt Income — § 643(a)(5)

Tax-exempt income by its very nature is not included in gross income and, thus, is not a part of taxable income. Nevertheless, such interest income is included in DNI, reduced by those expenses allocable to such income under Code § 265 or deemed distributed to charity (see Chapter 2). The result is that tax-exempt income from state and local bonds, net of expenses and the amount deemed distributed to charity, is part of DNI and can be distributed to the beneficiaries. Just as with the prior adjustment, because tax-exempt income will be accounting income, by including tax-exempt income as part of DNI, this adjustment better aligns DNI with accounting income.

F. Income of Foreign Trusts — § 643(a)(6)

In computing DNI, foreign trusts are subject to a number of additional special rules that are beyond the scope of this textbook.

Summary: Distributable net income (DNI) establishes the greatest amount that a trust or estate may deduct for distributions made to beneficiaries and that

---

11. Note that with a complex trust extraordinary dividends and taxable stock dividends will both be a part of DNI whether or not the fiduciary allocates such items to income or principal. A by-product of the foregoing is that if a trust makes a charitable contribution deductible under § 642(c), it would be considered a complex trust and the extraordinary dividend or the taxable stock dividend, as the case may be, will be a part of DNI and charity will be considered to receive an appropriate part of it.

a beneficiary must include in gross income. DNI is equal to the taxable income of a trust or estate as modified as required by § 643(a). Any item of income not included in the DNI of a trust or estate cannot be passed to a beneficiary and must be taxed to the trust or estate.

Questions

1. During the first tax year, a trust has received $10,000 of interest income and $10,000 of qualified dividends, and paid trustee's commissions of $6,000. What is the DNI for this trust?
2. The same as above, except that the trust also recognized $8,000 of capital gains which it allocated to principal. The trustee did not make any distributions during the tax year. What is the DNI for this trust?
3. How might your answer to question 2 change if the trustee had made distributions of principal?

II. Determining the Specific Items of Income Comprising DNI

Section 643(a) informs how the gross amount of DNI is determined, but does not help in determining the amount of each item of income that is a part of DNI. Where a trust or estate is allowed a distribution deduction, the beneficiary is considered to receive, absent special provisions in the governing instrument, the same proportion of each item of income that is a part of DNI as the total of each item of income bears to the total DNI of the trust or estate.

> **Example:** A trust has interest income of $10,000, tax-exempt interest of $5,000, and dividends of $5,000. There are deductible expenses of $1,000, of which $250 are allocated to tax-exempt income and cannot be deducted. The tentative taxable income before the distribution deduction and the 642(b) deduction is $14,250. Applying the above rules, the DNI will be $19,000 (i.e., $14,250 tentative taxable income plus $4,750 net tax-exempt income). **But what is this $19,000 comprised of?** In other words, if the DNI is distributed to the beneficiaries, how much interest, tax-exempt interest, and dividends does each beneficiary receive?

The DNI will be comprised of the same classes of income received by the trust or estate. Thus, in the above example, the DNI will be comprised of income interest, tax-exempt interest, and dividends. We know the gross amounts for each of these classes ($10,000, $5,000, and $5,000, respectively), but we don't yet know how the $1,000 deduction should be charged against these items nor do we yet know how much of each item of income a beneficiary receives.

The regulations set forth the rules and provide guidance for how deductions are to be charged against the items of income that comprise DNI. This "roadmap" enables taxpayers to determine DNI particulars of a trust or estate.

A. Charging Tax Deductions Against Items of Income

To determine the specific items of DNI deemed distributed to the beneficiaries, one must determine how tax deductions are charged against the different items of income that comprise DNI.

> **Example:** A trust receives $10,000 of interest income and $6,000 of dividends, and distributes its net income equally to its two beneficiaries. If the trust has no expenses, each beneficiary is deemed to have received $5,000 of interest income and $3,000 of dividends.
>
> If the trust paid state and local taxes of $1,000, the amount of interest income and dividends deemed distributed to the two beneficiaries will depend on how such expense is charged against the items of income.

Tax deductions are charged against the items of income comprising DNI in accordance with the rules set forth in the regulations. In all events, deductions cannot reduce any item of income below zero, because a fiduciary cannot distribute a negative amount of income to a beneficiary. As enumerated below, deductions are classified either as (1) direct expenses or (2) indirect expenses.

1. Charging Direct Expenses against Items of Income. All deductible items directly attributable to one class of income must be charged against that class of income. For example, in determining the amount of rental income comprising DNI, an estate that incurred repairs, real estate taxes, and other deductible expenses directly attributable to rental property would charge these expenses against the rental income of that property.

If the deductions directly attributable to a particular class of income exceed the amount of that income, the excess generally is charged against other classes of income in the same manner as indirect expenses. However, if the expense is directly related to a class of ordinary income, then no portion of the expense needs to be charged against tax-exempt income; Treas. Reg. § 1.652(b)-3(d) provides that such excess can be charged against other items of taxable income, notwithstanding the general rule concerning indirect expenses. Similarly, excess deductions directly attributed to tax-exempt income cannot offset any other class of income.[12]

Based on the rules above, when determining the net amount of each class of income comprising DNI, it makes sense to deduct direct expenses before deducting indirect expenses.

2. Charging Indirect Expenses Against Items of Income. Tax deductions that are not directly attributable to a specific class of income may be charged against any item of income included in DNI, but a pro rata portion must be allocated against

---

12. The instructions to Schedule K-1 of Form 1041 provide that excess deductions from a passive activity cannot be allocated to income from a nonpassive activity or to portfolio income earned by the estate or trust (page 30 of Schedule K-1). Thus, excess deductions from a passive activity may be suspended.

tax-exempt income. If capital gains or qualified dividends are included in computing DNI, then indirect expenses may be charged against them.[13]

> **Example:** Referring to the previous example where a trust receives $10,000 of interest income and $6,000 of dividends, pays $1,000 of state and local taxes, and distributes its net income equally to its two beneficiaries, the above rules tell us that the trustee may charge the $1,000 against either the interest income or the dividends or some to each. If the dividends are qualified dividends and subject to a favorable income tax rate, then the trustee can charge all of the state and local taxes against the interest income to achieve the optimum tax result. If all the taxes are charged against the interest income, then each beneficiary is deemed to have received $4,500 of interest income and $3,000 of dividends.

3. Charging Indirect Expenses Against Tax-Exempt Income. Section 265 prohibits deductions for expenses allocated to tax-exempt income. This rule is easy to state, but determining how much of any expense should be allocated to tax-exempt income is not always easy. And, as noted above, Regulation § 1.652(b)-3(b) requires that a portion of indirect expenses incurred by a trust or estate must be charged against tax-exempt income.[14]

One method for allocating an appropriate portion of any deduction to tax-exempt income is to multiply the particular deduction by a fraction; the numerator being the amount of tax-exempt income and the denominator being all items of income that comprise gross income, plus the tax-exempt income.[15] For example, if tax-exempt income comprises 10% of the total of the gross income plus the tax-exempt income, then 10% of all deductions that are indirect expenses should be charged against the tax-exempt income. While this method for charging indirect expenses to tax-exempt income has not been accepted by the IRS or the courts, the following example demonstrates how it would work.

> **Example:** During the tax year, a trust has received $10,000 of capital gains, $8,000 of interest income and $2,000 of tax-exempt interest, and has paid trustee's commissions of $3,000. The amount of tax-exempt interest ($2,000) represents 10% of the total of (a) the gross income of the trust as represented by the capital gains and interest income, and (b) the tax-exempt interest of $2,000. Under this method of allocation, 10% of the trustee's commissions would be charged against the tax-exempt interest and not be deductible for income tax purposes.

---

13. *See* Treas. Reg. § 1.652(b)-3. Note that some computer tax-programs automatically may allocate indirect expenses proportionately so one must be alert to such default computations.

14. Also see the discussion in Chapter 2 discussing the receipt of tax-exempt income Section III. B.

15. Note that the smaller the fraction, the smaller the amount allocated to tax-exempt income. Thus, the taxpayer tries to increase the denominator, thereby maximizing the amount of the expense that is deductible.

The IRS has argued, and the courts have agreed, that the denominator of the fraction should equal the aggregate total of only those items of gross income that make up DNI (which includes tax-exempt income) and not the total gross income and tax-exempt income of the trust.[16] This holding is disadvantageous to taxpayers because, if the denominator is restricted to income that is a part of DNI, capital gains that are excluded from DNI do not enter into the equation. Thus, a reason to try to have capital gains be a part of DNI where there is tax-exempt income is that doing so will reduce the amount of indirect expenses that must be charged against tax-exempt income.

> **Example:** A simple trust recognizes ordinary income, tax-exempt interest, and capital gains, each in the amount of $10,000, and pays a deductible indirect expense of $3,000. Under the above rule, $1,500 of the expense will be charged against tax-exempt income and be nondeductible for income tax purposes. Had capital gains been a part of DNI or otherwise considered in determining the amount of the expense charged against tax-exempt interest, only $1,000 of the expense would have been so charged and, thus, nondeductible.[17]

But different methods of charging indirect expenses against tax-exempt income may be allowed if they reflect the circumstances of a particular situation. *See, e.g., Whittemore v. United States*,[18] where a trustee's termination fee was allocated based on the ratio of taxable to nontaxable income over the life of the trust. *Also see Fabens v. Commissioner.*[19] *Whittemore* and *Fabens* dealt with termination fees charged by the trustee in the final year of the trust. In *Whittemore*, the Eighth Circuit held that a reasonable basis for determining the deductible portion of the termination fee as it related to the municipal bonds in trust was the ratio of taxable to nontaxable income over the life of the trust. The Eighth Circuit stated, "While no formula can measure with exactness the value of a fiduciary's fees as they relate to taxable and nontaxable income, a ratio based on the earnings from each serves as a reasonably accurate measuring stick, particularly when the life of the trust extends, as here, over an extended period of years."

These cases indicate that one is not required to use the method of allocation found in the regulations where the fiduciary can show that a different method results in a fairer apportionment. Yet, as a practical matter, one suspects that trustees often make allocations based on the IRS formula.

---

16. *Manufacturer's Hanover Trust Co. v. United States*, 160 Ct. Cl. 582, 312 F.2d 785, *cert. den.* 375 U.S. 880 (1963); *Tucker v. Commissioner*, 322 F.2d 86 (2d Cir. 1963); Rev. Rul. 77-355, 1977-2 C.B. 82; Rev. Rul. 77-355.

17. Although one may argue that capital gains should be considered when determining that amount of an indirect expense chargeable against tax-exempt interest, and that only $1,000 of the indirect expense should be charged against the capital gains retained by the trust, such is not the law.

18. 383 F.2d 824 (8th Cir. 1967).

19. 519 F.2d 1310 (1st Cir. 1975).

Notwithstanding the above rules regarding the allocation of indirect expenses to tax-exempt income, pursuant to § 265(a)(1) and Rev. Rul. Rul. 61-86, set forth below, state income taxes allocable to exempt interest income remains fully deductible in accordance with § 164 for fiduciary income tax purposes regardless of the amount of tax-exempt interest. Such taxes are not deductible to the extent allocable to other tax-exempt income.

Rev. Rul. 61-86, 1961-1 C.B. 41

In the case of an estate or trust, only that portion of its State income taxes which is allocable to exempt income, other than exempt interest income, is nondeductible under section 26 USC 265 of the Internal Revenue Code of 1954. That portion of such taxes attributable to exempt interest income and to income subject to the Federal income tax is deductible under section 26 USC 164 of the Code.

(Also, Section 265; 26 CFR 1.265-1.)

Advice has been requested regarding the deductibility of state income taxes paid by a fiduciary of an estate or trust which receives taxable income, tax-exempt interest income, and other exempt income.

Section 26 USC 641(b) of the Internal Revenue Code of 1954 provides that the taxable income of an estate or trust shall be computed in the same manner as in the case of an individual, with certain exceptions not here material.

Section 26 USC 164 of the Code provides, in part, as follows:

(A) General Rule. Except as otherwise provided in this section, there shall be allowed as a deduction taxes paid or accrued within the taxable year.

Section 26 USC 212 of the Code provides, in part, that in the case of an individual, there shall be allowed as a deduction all the ordinary and necessary expenses paid or incurred during the taxable year for the production or collection of income.

State income tax imposed upon net income of estates and trusts is deductible from income under the provisions of section 26 USC 164 of the Code in the same manner as in the case of an individual. Since State income tax is not an expense relating to the production of income, its deductibility by an estate or trust is not controlled by section 26 USC 212 of the Code.

Section 26 USC 265 of the Code provides, in part, as follows:

No deduction shall be allowed for (1) Expenses. Any amount otherwise allowable as a deduction which is allocable to one or more classes of income other than interest (whether or not any amount of income of that class or classes is received or accrued) wholly exempt from the taxes imposed by this subtitle, or any amount otherwise allowable under section 26 USC

212 (relating to expenses for production of income) which is allowable to interest (whether or not any amount of such interest is received or accrued) wholly exempt from the taxes imposed by this subtitle.

From the foregoing, it is evident that section 26 USC 265 of the Code prohibits the deduction of an item otherwise allowable as a deduction, which is attributable to tax-exempt interest income only if such item is deductible under section 26 USC 212 of the Code as an expense related to the production of income. State income tax is not considered an expense for the production of income, deductible under section 26 USC 212 of the Code. However, the portion of such tax allocable to exempt interest income is deductible under section 26 USC 164 of the Code. State income tax attributable to the income of an estate or trust which is subject to the Federal income tax is also deductible under that section. However, any State income tax allocable to exempt income, other than exempt interest income, is nondeductible under section 26 USC 265 of the Code.

Accordingly, it is held that in the case of an estate or trust only that portion of its State income taxes which is allocable to exempt income, other than exempt income interest income, is nondeductible under section 26 USC 265 of the Code. That portion of such taxes attributable to exempt interest income and to income subject to the Federal income subject to the Federal income tax is deductible under section 26 USC 164 of the Code.

Example: A simple trust recognizes ordinary income, tax-exempt interest, and capital gains, each in the amount of $10,000, and pays trustee fees, a deductible indirect expense, of $3,000 and pays state income taxes of $6,000. As discussed above, the tax-exempt income represents one-half of the total DNI and, so, one-half of the trustee fees ($1,500) must be charged against tax-exempt income and, thus, is nondeductible for income tax purposes. However, because of the above Revenue Ruling, none of the state income taxes has to be charged against the tax-exempt income and, so, the entire $6,000 is deductible.

4. Charging Indirect Expenses Against Tax-Exempt Income When There Are Direct Expenses — Confusion in the Regulations. There is uncertainty within the regulations as to whether expenses directly attributable to classes of income should reduce such income prior to computing the proportionate amount of indirect expenses to be allocated to tax-exempt income. Treas. Reg. § 1.652(b)-3(b) discusses the rules for allocation of indirect expenses, and the second sentence in such regulation suggests that the allocation of indirect expenses to items of income is determined after items of income are reduced by direct expenses. (This regulation begins, "For example, if the income of a trust is $30,000 (after direct expenses). . . .") However, part (f) of the example found in Treas. Reg. § 1.652(c)-4 shows the allocation of indirect expenses without reducing income by direct expenses.

An example demonstrates the potential difference in the approaches.

Example: A trust has the following items of income and expenses:

Rents	$25,000
Dividends	50,000
Tax-exempt interest	25,000
Expenses directly related to rents	10,000
Trustee's commissions	4,000

In determining the amount of the trustee's commissions allocable to the tax-exempt income, should we first deduct from rental income its direct expenses? If we do so, the fraction applied against the commissions is $25,000 (the tax-exempt income), divided by $90,000 (the gross amount of items that comprises DNI, less direct expenses). As noted above, this approach is suggested in Treas. Reg. § 1.652(b)-3(b), second sentence ("For example, if the income of a trust is $30,000 (after direct expenses), . . .").

Or should we not reduce income by direct expenses? In this case, the fraction applied against the commissions is $25,000 (the tax-exempt income), divided by $100,000 (the gross amount of items that comprises DNI not reduced by direct expenses). This approach is set forth in the example under Treas. Reg. § 1.652(c)-4, part (f).

In the treatise entitled, *Federal Income Taxation of Estates and Beneficiaries,*[20] its authors address this conflict and write:

> It appears, however, that in this instance the Treasury may view simplicity as a greater virtue than verity, because the latter approach not only violates the express rule of the regulations but also fails to produce a sound result. A direct expense may equal or even exceed the DNI item to which it is attributable and, if so, that income item does not exist economically and should not affect the allocation base.

The above may highlight the limitation inherent in any allocation method, that is, we are trying to allocate by formula the efforts of the trustee over items of income without concern to the actual efforts expended. The method reflected in the example in the regulations perhaps only opts for simplicity over equity, and it is also the more taxpayer-friendly position.

Example: In the example immediately above, let us assume that the fiduciary owned marketable securities that generated the ordinary income and tax-exempt income and that the fiduciary expended little effort or time concerning these securities. Let us further assume that the fiduciary spent a

20. Ferguson & Ascher, Federal Income Taxation of Estates and Beneficiaries § 7.06[E] (Wolters Kluwer, 4th ed. 2022 update).

> great deal of effort and time with respect to the management of the rental property, and collecting the rents. Let us further assume that the rental property generated gross income of $25,000, but had direct expenses of $25,000, too.

Under the example in the regulations, the commissions to be allocated to tax-exempt income remains $1,000. Under the approach suggested in Treas. Reg. §1.652(b)-3(b), the commissions to be allocated to the tax-exempt income is $1,333. Under an approach that tries to weigh the fiduciary's time and effort spent with respect to each activity, arguably none of the commissions ought to be allocated to tax-exempt income. But this last approach would be subject to abuse and hard to enforce.

5. Charging the Charitable Deduction against Items of Income. The charitable deduction is not an expense, but, rather, is a distribution to a trust beneficiary that happens to be allowed as a charitable deduction. As a result, the rules mentioned above for direct expenses and indirect expenses do not apply when the fiduciary makes a distribution to charity. If a trust or estate makes a distribution to charity, the charity, absent specific provisions to the contrary, is deemed to receive a proportionate share of each class of income comprising DNI. Thus, if DNI includes tax-exempt income, then the charity will be considered to have received a proportionate share of such exempt income. Because the charitable deduction is allowed only for items of gross income paid, permanently set aside, or used for charitable purposes, amounts of tax-exempt income deemed paid to charity are not deductible for income tax purposes. In other words, the charitable deduction will be limited to those items of income comprising DNI that also are items of gross income for income tax purposes.

> **Example:** A trust has $10,000 of tax-exempt interest income, $5,000 of rental income, and $5,000 of taxable interest income. The trust distributes one-fourth of the accounting income, or $5,000, to charity in accordance with the terms of the governing instrument. The charity is considered to have received one-fourth of each item of income comprising DNI, i.e., $2,500 of the tax-exempt interest income, $1,250 of the rental income, and $1,250 of the taxable interest income. The trust will be entitled to a charitable deduction of $2,500, because no charitable deduction is allowed for the $2,500 of tax-exempt interest deemed distributed to the charity.

The regulations require that the items of income comprising DNI are to be first reduced by amounts deemed distributed to charity.[21] This general rule regarding the charging of any charitable deduction proportionately against the items of income comprising DNI will not apply if (a) the governing instrument or local law specifically mandates the income source out of which amounts are to be paid, permanently set aside or used for charity, but (b) only to the extent that provision or law

21. Treas. Reg. §1.662(b)-2.

has economic effect independent of income tax consequences.[22] For example, if the terms of a trust provide that the trustee is to distribute all dividends received by the trust to charity, then such a provision does have economic effect, and charity will be deemed to receive only dividend income and no other item of income. If, on the other hand, a trust provided that charity is to receive a specific amount, but the charity will be deemed to first receive such amount from dividends, then such a provision would not have economic effect because, in all cases, the charity receives the specific amount.[23]

As noted above, with respect to provisions of the governing instrument or local law allocating items of income to charity, such provisions will only be honored if they have an economic effect independent of the income tax consequences of such allocation. This independent economic effect rule also applies to income allocations to non-charitable beneficiaries.[24] With respect to non-charitable beneficiaries, the regulations speak of "specific allocations" of income to beneficiaries being recognized only if (a) the allocation is required in the trust instrument,[25] but (b) only to the extent that it has economic effect independent of the income tax consequences of the allocation.

The regulations do not define what is meant by a provision having an economic effect independent of the income tax consequences of such allocation. Presumably, independent economic effect means that the amount—actual dollars—that a beneficiary is to receive is impacted by the special allocation. To state this in a different way, if the beneficiary is to receive the same amount with or without the special allocation, then such special allocation would seem to have no economic impact independent of the income tax consequences. For example, in a charitable lead trust, if charity is to receive a specific amount whether or not there are special allocations directing that different classes of income be considered to be distributed in a particular order, then the ordering would seem to have no independent economic effect.

The regulations under Treas. Reg. § 1.652(b)-2(b) offer the following example of a special allocation that will not be recognized: an allocation pursuant to a trust provision directing the trustee to pay $10,000 to A and the balance, if any, to B, but directing the trustee first to allocate a specific class of income to A's share (to the

---

22. Treas. Reg. §§ 1.642(c)-3(b)(2), 1.643(a)-5(b), 1.652(b)-2(b), and 1.661(b)-2.

23. There was a time when not all the cited regulations contained the requirement that provisions in the governing instrument allocating specific items of income to charity needed to have an economic effect independent of income tax consequences. During that time, it was common for charitable lead trusts (see Chapter 7) to have provisions designed to preserve the most favorable tax benefits regarding payments to charity. However, pursuant to the regulations, Treasury has created an "independent economic effect" condition for ordering the types of income deemed allocated to charity and any other beneficiary. Only in the cases in which any special provision has independent economic effect will such provision be recognized.

24. Treas. Reg. § 1.652(b)-2(a) and (b).

25. The rule with respect to specific allocations of income to charity also references allocations required by local law. Treas. Reg. § 1.662(b)-2.

extent there is income of that class and to the extent it does not exceed A's share) is not a specific allocation by the terms of the trust. For income tax purposes, the result is that such special allocation will be ignored for determining the items of income allocated to A.[26]

Summary: While the Code sets forth how one determines the amount of DNI for a trust or estate, it is the regulations that provide the rules and guidance for determining the particulars of DNI. Thus, it is the regulations that set forth what charity is deemed to have received from DNI and how direct expenses and indirect expenses are to be charged against the different classes of income comprising DNI.

Questions

1. What is the general rule for determining how much charity has received from the various classes of income comprising DNI? When does the general rule not apply?
2. When direct expenses are more than the amount of the income to which they are directly related, how is such excess charged against the other classes of income comprising DNI?
3. What is the formula for allocating indirect expenses to tax-exempt income?

III. Method for Determining the Amount of Each Item of Income Comprising DNI

The following steps will help one determine the DNI for a trust or estate.

- First, set forth in a row all the items of income, including tax-exempt income, that comprise DNI. The only items of income that might not be a part of DNI will be capital gains because of § 643(a)(3), and extraordinary dividends and stock dividends because of § 643(a)(4). All other items of income will be a part of DNI.
- Second, if there is a charitable deduction, subtract from each item of income the proportionate share considered distributed to charity.

26. The regulations that pertain to the so-called separate share rule produce a different result. Example 9 under Treas. Reg. § 1.663(c) provides a residuary estate is to be divided equally between the testator's two children, but one child's share is to be funded first with the proceeds of the testator's IRA. (This allocation has no impact on the amount of the estate each child is to receive — each child receives one-half of the residuary estate in all events.) Notwithstanding, the example directs that for purposes of determining the DNI for each separate share, the proceeds of the IRA must be allocated to the child's share to which such proceeds are directed. This result is contrary to the requirement that special allocations have an economic effect independent of their income tax consequences. The reason for this difference may be because of the rule for items of income in respect of a decedent and the separate share rule where such income is allocated to the beneficiary entitled to it.

- Third, if there are any direct expenses, subtract those expenses from the items of income to which they relate. If any direct expenses are more than the item of income to which they relate (that is, there is a loss with respect to such type of income), then charge any excess[27] against any other item or items of income that yields the best tax outcome, without any need to charge part of the excess against tax-exempt income.
- Fourth, charge all indirect expenses among the items of income in any manner that is most-tax efficient (i.e., yields the best tax outcome), provided, however, that a proportionate share must be charged against tax-exempt income.

Example: During the tax year, a trust had the following receipts and expenses:

Receipts		Expenses	
Item	**Amount**	**Item**	**Amount**
Interest	$5,000	Interest Expense	$2,000
Dividends	10,000	Real Estate Taxes	3,000
Rents	20,000	Trustee Fees	5,000
Capital Gain	12,000		
Tax-Exempt Interest	15,000		

In addition to the above, the trustee distributed $5,000 of income to charity; the trustee allocated all capital gain to principal (i.e., no portion of such gains were a part of DNI); and the real estate taxes were directly related to the rents received by the trust.

Determining the total DNI, one needs to determine the taxable income before the distribution deduction (tentative taxable income), and then make the adjustments as directed by § 643(a). To determine the deductible portion of the charitable contribution[28] and indirect expenses, one must determine the amount of these items that must be charged against tax-exempt income. As discussed above, because tax-exempt interest ($15,000) represents 30% of the total DNI ($50,000), 30% of the charitable contribution and 30% of all indirect expenses must be charged against tax-exempt interest. Thus, only 70% of the charitable contribution and 70% of the indirect expenses are deductible. So, the deductible portion of the charitable contribution would

27. This assumes that the excess is deductible for income tax purposes. For example, if the loss is from a passive activity that is disallowed pursuant to § 469, there would be no "excess" to be deducted against other types of income.

28. Pursuant to § 642(c), only distributions of gross income to charity qualify for the charitable deduction. Thus, any deemed distributions of tax-exempt interest will not qualify for the charitable deduction.

be 70% of $5,000, or $3,500; the deductible portion of the interest expense would be 70% of $2,000, or $1,400; and the deductible portion of the trustee fees would be 70% of $5,000, or $3,500. Thus, the total amount charged against tax-exempt interest is $3,600. As a result, the tentative taxable income before the distribution deduction and DNI would look as follows:

Gross income	$47,000
Less charitable deduction	–3,500
Less real estate taxes	–3,000
Less interest expense	–1,400
Less trustee fees	–3,500
Less § 642(b) deduction	–100
Tentative taxable income	$35,500
Adjustments required under § 643(a):	
Ignore the § 642(b) deduction	+100
Remove capital gains	–12,000
Add tax-exempt interest	+15,000
Subtract charitable distribution and indirect expenses charged against tax-exempt interest	–3,600
Total DNI	$35,000

One can then follow the steps outlined above to compute the details of the DNI and this would look like the following:

	Interest	Dividends	Rents	Tax-Exempt Interest	Totals
Step 1: Gross Amount of Items of Income in DNI:	$5,000	$10,000	$20,000	$15,000	$50,000
Step 2: Less charitable deduction	–500	–1,000	–2,000	–1,500	–5,000
Step 3: Less direct expenses:					
Real estate taxes			–3,000		–3,000
Step 4: Less indirect expenses:					
Interest expense			–1,400	–600	–2,000
Trustee Fees			–3,500	–1,500	–5,000
Balance:	$4,500	$9,000	$10,100	$11,400	$35,000

Because the charitable deduction is 10% of the total gross amount of items of income in DNI, charity is considered to have received 10% of each item of income comprising DNI.

As discussed above, because tax-exempt interest is 30% of the total, 30% of each indirect expense must be charged against tax-exempt interest and, thus, is not deductible by the trust. The trustee charged the balance of the indirect expenses against the rents, but the trustee could have charged such balance among the items comprising DNI in any manner desired.

Based on the above, the DNI of the trust is $35,000, and it is comprised of interest income of $4,500, dividend income of $9,000, rental income of $10,100, and tax-exempt interest of $11,400.

Questions

1. An estate had the income and expenses shown below in its first tax year. Compute the total DNI and the particulars of the DNI for the estate. No distributions were made during the tax year.

Receipts		Expenses	
Item	**Amount**	**Item**	**Amount**
Interest	$15,000	Attorney Fees	$6,000
Dividends	10,000	Accounting Fees	3,000
		Probate Court Costs	300

2. The same as question 1, but the estate also recognized $8,000 of capital gains, all of which are allocated to principal.
3. The same as questions 1 and 2, but the estate also paid executor's commissions of $12,000.
4. The same as questions 1, 2, and 3, but the estate also received $5,000 of tax-exempt interest.

IV. DNI: Setting Deductibility and Inclusion Ceilings

A trust or estate is entitled to a deduction for certain distributions made to non-charitable beneficiaries (see Chapters 4 and 5). And the trust or estate will be entitled to this distribution deduction regardless of when distributions are made during the tax year.

The maximum amount of this deduction cannot be more than the total DNI of the trust or estate reduced by that portion, if any, of the DNI comprised of tax-exempt income. This amount sets the ceiling for the distribution deduction. While the distribution deduction may be less than this amount, it can never be more than this amount.

Similarly, the maximum amount that a beneficiary will include in gross income cannot be more than the DNI of the trust or estate reduced by that portion, if any, of the DNI comprised of tax-exempt income. In essence, there is balance; the maximum amount that a trust or estate may deduct as a distribution deduction also is the maximum amount that the beneficiaries, in the aggregate, must include in gross income. As a result, all taxable income of the trust or estate will be subject to tax, with the taxpayer being the trust or estate, the beneficiaries thereof, or a combination of both.

> **Example:** For the tax year, a simple trust has accounting income of $30,000 and has DNI of $27,000. The DNI includes $5,000 of tax-exempt interest. The distribution deduction allowed to this trust is $22,000 (its total DNI of $27,000 reduced by the $5,000 of tax-exempt interest).
>
> If there is one beneficiary, then such beneficiary will receive $30,000 but, for tax purposes, need only include $22,000 in his or her gross income.
>
> **Example:** The same as the preceding example except that there are two beneficiaries who are to receive the accounting income in equal shares. The distribution deduction allowable to the trust is the same as explained above—$22,000. As to the beneficiaries, each of them will receive $15,000, but, for tax purposes, need only include $11,000 in his or her gross income.
>
> **Example:** For the tax year, a simple trust has accounting income of $25,000 and has DNI of $30,000. The DNI includes $6,000 of tax-exempt interest. Because the trustee is required to distribute all of the accounting income and because the accounting income is less than the DNI, the trust is deemed to have distributed only $25,000 of its DNI, or five-sixths of the total DNI (i.e., $25,000 / $30,000). As a result, the trust is entitled to a distribution deduction of $20,000, which amount represents five-sixths of the total DNI ($30,000 × 5/6), less five-sixths of the tax-exempt interest ($6,000 × 5/6).
>
> If there is one beneficiary, then such beneficiary will only include $20,000 in his or her gross income.
>
> **Example:** For the tax year, an estate has DNI of $50,000, none of which is tax-exempt interest. The estate distributes $1,000,000 during the tax year. The estate is allowed a distribution deduction of $50,000, and each recipient beneficiary includes in his or her gross income only his or her portion of the $50,000 based on his or her proportionate share of the distributions. Thus, if one beneficiary received distributions totaling $800,000 (80% of the total distributed), then he will include $40,000 (80% of $50,000) in income.

Additionally, except as provided in § 663(a), amounts distributed to beneficiaries are considered to be distributions of DNI regardless of when the distributions occurred or the type of property distributed. For example, a distribution on the first day of the tax year will carry out DNI even though no DNI for that year had yet been earned.[29] Also, distributions made to persons who are not beneficiaries, regardless of the reason, will not carry out DNI.

> **Example:** A trust has interest of $10,000, dividends of $5,000, and tax-exempt income of $5,000. It has no expenses, so that its DNI is $20,000. The trustee has distributed $30,000 to the beneficiary during the year. The trust is entitled to a maximum distribution deduction of $15,000, because it cannot get a deduction for the $5,000 of tax-exempt income it is deemed to have distributed to the beneficiary. The beneficiary will report the interest of $10,000 and the dividends of $5,000 on his personal income tax return. The beneficiary will be deemed also to have received $5,000 of tax-exempt interest. The balance of the distribution ($10,000) is treated as a non-taxable distribution.

Summary: Distributable net income (DNI) establishes the greatest amount that a trust or estate may deduct for distributions made to beneficiaries and that a beneficiary must include in gross income. However, a trust or estate cannot deduct the amount of tax-exempt income comprising DNI and, correlatively, beneficiaries never need include the amount of tax-exempt income they are deemed to have received in federal gross income.

Questions

1. Continuing from the last question from the prior section, assume that the executor made a distribution of $100,000 during the tax year to the estate's sole beneficiary, Henry. How much can the estate deduct as a distribution deduction under § 661 and how much must Henry include in gross income?
2. The same as question 1 except that there are two beneficiaries, Henry and Anne, and the executor made a distribution of $100,000 to Henry and $200,000 to Anne. How much must Henry and Anne include in gross income?
3. How would your answer change if the executor had only distributed $5,000 to Anne during the tax year and made no distribution to Henry?

V. Amounts and Income Classes Received by Beneficiaries

Pursuant to Code § 651, a simple trust is entitled to a distribution deduction (see Chapter 4). The amount deductible is equal to its accounting income required to be distributed, but not more than the total DNI of the trust reduced by that portion, if any, of the DNI comprised of tax-exempt income. Similarly, pursuant to Code § 661,

---

29. *Harkness v. U.S.*, 199 Ct. Cl. 721, 469 F.2d 310 (1972), *cert. denied*, 414 U.S. 820 (1973).

a complex trust is entitled to a distribution deduction (see Chapter 5). The amount deductible is equal to all its accounting income required to be distributed and all other amounts properly paid, credited, or required to be distributed, but, again, not more than the total DNI of the trust or estate reduced by that portion, if any, of the DNI comprised of tax-exempt income.

And whatever deduction a trust or estate is entitled to pursuant to the distribution deduction, the recipient beneficiaries must include in gross income. Thus, all taxable income of a trust or estate will be subject to the income tax. This raises the obvious question of seeking to identify the type and amount of income that the beneficiaries are deemed to have received.

Treasury Regulation §1.662(b)-1 provides that answer. It states that amounts received "are treated as consisting of the same proportion of each class of items entering into the computation of distributable net income as the total of each class bears to the total distributable net income of the estate or trust unless the terms of the governing instrument specifically allocate different classes of income to different beneficiaries, or unless local law requires such an allocation." Mathematically, this looks like the following:

I = Amount of a class of income comprising DNI
DNI = Total amount of DNI
d = Total distribution to one beneficiary
D = Total of all distributions

$$\left[\left(\frac{D}{DNI}\text{ (but not greater than 1)}\right) \times I \times \frac{d}{D}\right] = \text{income received by a beneficiary for each class of income}$$

Examples can help demonstrate this principle and the application of this formula.

Example: For the tax year, a simple trust has accounting income of $30,000 and has DNI of $27,000. The DNI is comprised of $10,000 of interest income, $12,000 of dividend income, and $5,000 of tax-exempt interest. Because the trustee is required to distribute all of the accounting income and because the accounting income is more than the DNI, the trust is deemed to have distributed all of its DNI. Assuming one beneficiary and using the above formula, to compute the amount of interest income allocated to the beneficiary, we have the following:

I = $10,000 of interest income
DNI = $27,000
d = $30,000
D = $30,000

Using the above formula, the amount of interest income received by the beneficiary will equal:

$$\left[\left(\frac{\$30{,}000}{\$27{,}000 \text{ (but not more than 1)}} \times \$10{,}000 \times \frac{\$30{,}000}{\$30{,}000}\right)\right]$$
$$= \left(1 \times \frac{\$10{,}000}{\$27{,}000}\right) \times \$27{,}000 = \$10{,}000$$

This result is hardly surprising; when the amount distributed is more than DNI, then all DNI has been distributed to the beneficiaries; when there is only one beneficiary, she must receive the total amount of income from each class of income comprising DNI.

If there had been two beneficiaries who were to receive equal shares of the accounting income, then computing the amount of interest income that one of them received would be equal to the following:

$$\left[\left(\frac{\$30{,}000}{\$27{,}000 \text{ (but not more than 1)}} \times \$10{,}000 \times \frac{\$15{,}000}{\$30{,}000}\right)\right]$$
$$= \left(1 \times \$10{,}000 \times \frac{1}{2}\right) = \$5{,}000$$

Example: For the tax year, a simple trust has accounting income of $25,000 and has DNI of $30,000. The DNI is comprised of $12,000 of interest income, $12,000 of dividend income, and $6,000 of tax-exempt interest. Because the trustee is required to distribute all of the accounting income and because the accounting income is less than the DNI, the trust is deemed to have distributed only $25,000 of its DNI, or five-sixths of the DNI. Assuming one beneficiary and using the above formula, to compute the amount of interest income allocated to the beneficiary, we have the following:

I = $12,000 of interest income
DNI = $30,000
d = $25,000
D = $25,000

Using the above formula, the amount of interest income received by the beneficiary will equal:

$$\left[\left(\frac{\$25{,}000}{\$30{,}000 \text{ (but not more than 1)}} \times \$12{,}000 \times \frac{\$25{,}000}{\$25{,}000}\right)\right]$$
$$= \left(\frac{5}{6} \times \$12{,}000 \times 1\right) \$10{,}000$$

If there had been two beneficiaries who were to receive equal shares of the accounting income, then computing the amount of interest income that one of them received would be equal to the following:

$$\left[\left(\frac{\$25{,}000}{\$30{,}000\text{ (but not more than 1)}} \times \$12{,}000 \times \frac{\$12{,}500}{\$25{,}000}\right)\right]$$
$$= \left(\frac{5}{6} \times \$12{,}000 \times \frac{1}{2}\right) = \$5{,}000$$

Example: For the tax year, a trust has DNI of $40,000. The DNI is comprised of $20,000 of interest income, $15,000 of dividend income, and $5,000 of tax-exempt interest. During the tax year, the trustee distributes $30,000 to one beneficiary and $20,000 to another beneficiary. To compute the amount of interest income allocated to the beneficiary who received $30,000 and using the above formula, we have the following:

I = $20,000 of interest income
DNI = $40,000
d = $30,000
D = $50,000

Using the above formula, the amount of interest income received by this beneficiary will equal:

$$\left[\left(\frac{\$50{,}000}{\$40{,}000\text{ (but not more than 1)}} \times \$20{,}000 \times \frac{\$30{,}000}{\$50{,}000}\right)\right]$$
$$= \left(1 \times \$20{,}000 \times \frac{3}{5}\right) = \$12{,}000$$

This result should make sense, because total distributions were more than the DNI, so all income was distributed, and because this beneficiary received 60% of the distributions, she received 60% of the interest income.

Example: For the tax year, an estate has DNI of $100,000. The DNI is comprised of $60,000 of Income in Respect of a Decedent (IRD) arising from compensation,[30] $20,000 of interest income, $15,000 of dividend income, and $5,000 of tax-exempt interest. During the tax year, the trustee distributes $30,000 to one beneficiary and $20,000 to another beneficiary. To compute the amount of IRD allocated to the beneficiary who received $30,000 and using the above formula, we have the following:

I = $60,000 of IRD
DNI = $100,000
d = $30,000
D = $50,000

30. IRD is discussed in Chapter 8.

Using the above formula, the amount of interest income received by this beneficiary will equal:

$$\left[\left(\frac{\$50{,}000}{\$100{,}000} \times \$60{,}000 \times \frac{\$30{,}000}{\$50{,}000}\right)\right]$$
$$= \left(\frac{1}{2} \times \$60{,}000 \times \frac{3}{5}\right) = \$18{,}000$$

Example: In the example at the end of Section III, we had a trust that had the following receipts and expenses:

Receipts		Expenses	
Item	**Amount**	**Item**	**Amount**
Interest	$5,000	Interest Expense	$2,000
Dividends	10,000	Real Estate Taxes	3,000
Rents	20,000	Trustee Fees	5,000
Capital Gain	12,000		
Tax-Exempt Interest	15,000		

In addition to the above: the trustee distributed $5,000 of income to charity; the trustee allocated all capital gain to principal (i.e., no portion of such gains were a part of DNI); and the real estate taxes were directly related to the rents received by the trust. The details of the DNI of this trust is as follows:

	Interest	Dividends	Rents	Tax-Exempt Interest	Totals
Step 1: Gross Amount of Items of Income in DNI:	$5,000	$10,000	$20,000	$15,000	$50,000
Step 2: Less charitable deduction	−500	−1,000	−2,000	−1,500	−5,000
Step 3: Less direct expenses:					
Real estate taxes			−3,000		−3,000
Step 4: Less indirect expenses:					
Interest expense			−1,400	−600	−2,000
Trustee Fees			−3,500	−1,500	−5,000
Balance:	$4,500	$9,000	$10,100	$11,400	$35,000

During the tax year, the trustee made a discretionary distribution of $20,000 to a beneficiary. The beneficiary is deemed to have received $20,000/$35,000 of each item of income comprising DNI. As a result, the beneficiary will be deemed to have received $2,571 of interest, $5,143 of dividends, $5,771 of rent, and $6,514 of tax-exempt interest.

Example: An estate is distributable one-half to the surviving wife and one-half to the surviving children. The share passing to the children bears the burden of paying estate taxes. For convenience, whenever the executor pays estate taxes or makes a distribution to the children, she makes a corresponding distribution to the wife. In the current year, the executor has distributed $75 to the wife and $25 to the children, and has paid $50 in estate taxes. The DNI for the estate is $40 and is allocated 75% to the wife, or $30, and 25% to the children, or $10. Although the wife is entitled to only 50% of the estate, she received 75% of the distributions made to the beneficiaries in the current year, and, as a result, the wife is allocated 75% of the DNI.[31]

Summary: Beneficiaries of a trust or estate are deemed to receive the same classes of income that comprise DNI. Thus, the student must be able to determine the various classes of income and their respective amounts that comprise DNI. This determination is done by first determining all classes of income and their gross amounts comprising DNI and then following the rules and guidance set forth in the regulations on how the charitable deduction, direct expenses, and indirect expenses are allocated among the classes of income comprising DNI.

Questions

Fact Pattern: Assume that during the tax year, a trust has the following receipts, expenses, and distributions:

Receipts		Expenses		Distributions	
Item	**Amount**	**Item**	**Amount**	**Beneficiary**	**Amount**
Interest	$15,000	Interest Expense	$2,000	Jack	$20,000
Dividends	20,000	Real Estate Taxes	3,000	Jill	$10,000
Rents	20,000	Trustee Fees	5,000		
IRD	50,000	Legal Fees	10,000		
Capital Gain	12,000				

Assume further that the trustee distributed $5,000 of income to charity; the trustee allocated all capital gain to principal but the trustee has treated capital gains consistently on the trust's books, records, and tax returns as

31. *Harkness v. U.S.*, 199 Ct. Cl. 721, 469 F.2d 310 (1972), *cert. denied*, 414 U.S. 820 (1973).

part of a distribution to beneficiaries; and the real estate taxes are directly related to the rents received by the trust. There is no § 691(c) deduction available.

Based upon this fact pattern, determine (i) the total DNI for the trust, (ii) the particulars of the DNI, and (iii) the amount of each class of income that Jack and Jill are deemed to receive.

VI. No DNI Tracing

As noted above, trust and estate beneficiaries who receive distributions are considered to receive a proportionate share of each item of income comprising DNI, and this is so even if there are items of income that cannot be distributed or the fiduciary can prove were not actually distributed.

Example: A trust directs the trustee to pay all income equally to Tom and Jeff at least annually. During the year, the trustee receives dividends of $18,000. In addition, the trust's gross income includes $9,000 of original issue discount (OID) from a zero-coupon bond, so that, although this amount must be included in gross income for tax purposes, it is not income for accounting purposes. DNI will consist of the dividends and the OID income, and the distribution of accounting income to Tom and Jeff will be deemed to include both dividends and OID income.

Except as provided in Code § 663(a) (pertaining to specific bequests), amounts distributed to beneficiaries are considered to be distributions of DNI regardless of when the distribution occurred or the type of property distributed. For example, a distribution on the first day of the tax year will carry out DNI even though no DNI for that year had yet been earned.[32] Also, distributions made to persons who are not beneficiaries, regardless of the reason, will not carry out DNI.

Example: A simple trust receives a distribution of $200,000 from an estate, which distribution carries out estate DNI to the trust. The only income received by the estate for its tax year was $30,000 of dividend income. Thus, the recipient trust will be deemed to have received $30,000 of dividend income from the estate, which income it must report on its income tax return. However, for accounting purposes, the trustee of the recipient trust treats the estate distribution of $200,000 as principal and, so, such distribution (including the dividend income deemed distributed to the trust) cannot be distributed to the income beneficiaries of the trust. For the tax year of the simple trust, the trust had interest income of $6,000 and $9,000 of rental income and the trust had no expenses. The trustee distributes its accounting income of $15,000 to its beneficiaries as required by

32. *Harkness v. U.S.*, 199 Ct. Cl. 721, 469 F.2d 310 (1972), *cert. denied*, 414 U.S. 820 (1973).

the trust instrument. Such distribution carries out trust DNI, which DNI includes the dividend income deemed received from the estate. Thus, the $15,000 distribution of the accounting income represents one-third of the total DNI (interest income of $6,000, rental income of $9,000, and dividend income of $30,000). The trust beneficiaries will be deemed to receive a one-third share of each item of DNI, so that the beneficiaries will be deemed to receive $2,000 of interest income, $3,000 of rental income, and $10,000 of dividend income. Thus, the beneficiaries will report on their individual returns a total of $10,000 of dividend income notwithstanding the fact that the trustee could not have distributed such dividend income to them.

Example: During the tax year, a trustee makes distributions in January, April, July, and October. All distributions are deemed to carry out trust DNI determined as of the end of the year, and the recipient beneficiaries are deemed to receive DNI determined as of the end of the year notwithstanding that at the time of the actual distributions, some items of income had not yet been received and not all the other items of income had yet been received.

VII. Determining Fiduciary Accounting Income

By way of background, Code § 643(b) provides that the word "income" when standing alone and not preceded by an adjective, such as gross income, taxable income, distributed net income, etc., means the estate or trust income for the tax year determined for fiduciary accounting purposes. Code §§ 651 and 661, dealing with the distribution deduction allowed to trusts and estates refer to "income" (with no adjectives preceding its use). That being the case, fiduciary accounting income is an important metric for ascertaining distribution deductions. In other words, if you do not know the amount of fiduciary accounting income, you cannot determine the correct distribution deduction. Fiduciary accounting income is a state law concept; scouring the Code from cover to cover will not aid in its determination. In a nutshell, fiduciary accounting income will be determined in accordance with the terms of the governing instrument and the appropriate state Principal and Income Act.[33]

For example, all trust instruments will have provisions dealing with trust distributions of income and principal. Such a provision may read as follows:

33. Because states are free to enact their respective Principal and Income Act as each state considers best, references are made to the Uniform Principal and Income Act drafted by the National Conference of Commissioners on Uniform State Laws (now known as the Uniform Law Commission) as last amended or revised in 2008. In October 2018, the Uniform Law Commission issued the Uniform Fiduciary Income and Principal Act. The 2018 Act is available at the Uniform Law Commission website, www.uniformlaws.org.

> The trustee shall distribute all of the income to Jack at least annually. Upon Jack's death, the trustee shall distribute all accrued and undistributed income and all principal then comprising the trust to Jill.

The duties and the discretions of the trustee are clear—Jack is to receive all of the income, and Jill is to receive all that remains when Jack dies. But the trustee must determine which receipts are income for fiduciary accounting purposes and, thus, must be distributed to Jack, and which receipts are principal and, thus, held for ultimate distribution to Jill. Similarly, the trustee must determine which expenses are charged against income for fiduciary accounting purposes and, thus, reduce the income otherwise distributable to Jack, and which expenses are charged against principal and reduce the amount ultimately distributable to Jill.

In other words, whenever the trustee receives any money or property, the trustee must determine whether the money or property received is income, principal, or partly both. The same is true whenever the trustee pays any expense; the trustee must determine whether the money paid is charged against income, principal, or both; and if both, in what proportions. The answers to these questions are not found in the Code, but, rather, are found in the governing instrument and local law. Every state has enacted some variation of the Uniform Principal and Income Act. Its purposes are twofold: (1) to provide for a degree of national uniformity in how fiduciaries will determine whether receipts and expenses are income, principal, or partly both, and (2) to provide for a degree of equity and fairness in the determination of income and principal as between varying beneficial interests.

Under the Uniform Principal and Income Act, "income" means money or property that a fiduciary receives as a current return from a principal asset. So, from an accounting perspective, fiduciary accounting income will include interest, dividends, rents, and, generally, distributions from business entities. Fiduciary accounting income will not include capital gains, because such gains are not a current return from a principal asset, but, rather, the receipt of something (usually money) in exchange for an asset.

> **Example:** During the tax year, a trustee sold marketable securities and recognized capital gains of $50,000. For fiduciary accounting purposes, none of the recognized capital gains represents income; however, for income tax purposes, all of the recognized capital gains will be reportable as income.
>
> **Example:** A trust is a limited partner in a partnership. During the tax year, the trustee has received $5,000 from the partnership, but was allocated $10,000 of partnership income on the Schedule K-1 issued to the trust. Although for income tax purposes, the trust must report $10,000, for fiduciary accounting purposes, it has only $5,000 of accounting income.
>
> **Example:** A trust owns mortgaged real estate, and the trustee pays the monthly mortgage payment. A part of the payment represents an interest expense and is charged against the income of the trust. The balance of the

> payment represents a payment of the principal obligation and is charged against the principal of the trust.

Federal tax law is concerned with determining "income" subject to the income tax. Thus, the tax concept of income is broader than the fiduciary accounting concept of income under applicable principal and income acts. Under the Code, "gross income" means all income from whatever source derived, including gains derived from property and treasure trove. The policy objective is to impose an income tax whenever the taxpayer has experienced an accretion to wealth; it rightfully ignores equity concerns between or among trust and estate beneficiaries holding differing interests.

Treasury Regulation § 1.643(b)-1, aware of differences between gross income and fiduciary accounting income, in part, provides the following:

> *Trust provisions that depart fundamentally from traditional principles of income and principal will generally not be recognized.* For example, if a trust instrument directs that all the trust income shall be paid to the income beneficiary but defines ordinary dividends and interest as principal, the trust will not be considered one that under its governing instrument is required to distribute all its income currently for purposes of section 642(b) (relating to the personal exemption) and section 651 (relating to simple trusts). Thus, items such as dividends, interest, and rents are generally allocated to income, and proceeds from the sale or exchange of trust assets are generally allocated to principal.

> **Example:** A trust instrument provides that the entire mortgage payment paid by the trustee will be charged against income, including that portion of the mortgage payment that reduces the principal amount of the debt. While such a provision is valid and will be enforced under state law, it fundamentally departs from local law and will be disregarded for tax purposes by the IRS. The consequences of such can affect the deduction allowed under § 642(b) and the depreciation deduction, both of which are affected by the fiduciary accounting income retained by the trust.

But Treas. Reg. § 1.643(b)-1, acknowledges that complete reliance on fiduciary accounting income in some instances may be misplaced, particularly when the settlor's intent was to ensure that a minimum percentage of the trust assets inured to particular trust beneficiaries. That being the case, the Treasury regulation concedes the following:

> [A]n allocation of amounts between income and principal pursuant to applicable local law will be respected if local law provides for a reasonable apportionment between the income and remainder beneficiaries of the total return of the trust for the year, including ordinary and tax-exempt income, capital gains, and appreciation. For example, a state statute providing that income is a unitrust amount of no less than 3% and no more than 5% of the fair market value of the trust assets, whether determined annually or

averaged on a multiple year basis, is a reasonable apportionment of the total return of the trust.

> **Example:** State law allows a fiduciary to establish a "unitrust percentage" for the distribution of income.[34] Although state law suggests a unitrust percentage between 3% and 5%, the state law allows a fiduciary to use a different percentage if the governing instrument states that one or more beneficiaries are to be favored. Under a trust instrument, the trustee is directed to distribute all of the income at least annually, but the governing instrument states that the remainder beneficiaries are to be favored. The trustee, in good faith, decides upon a unitrust percentage of 2%. This trust will not be considered a trust required to distribute all of its income at least annually because of the above regulation. Notwithstanding, the trustee's decision is valid for state law, and its income for fiduciary accounting purposes will be 2% of the fair market value of the trust's assets.
>
> **Example:** Suppose instead in the example above, the trustee, in good faith, decides upon a unitrust percentage of 4%. This trust will be considered a trust required to distribute all of its income at least annually and its distributions will be considered fiduciary accounting income.

In a final concession, Treas. Reg. § 1.643(b)-1 admits that fiduciaries' scope of responsibilities is broad and, that being the case, they must be responsive to the legal needs of all involved parties:

> Similarly, a state statute that permits the trustee to make adjustments between income and principal to fulfill the trustee's duty of impartiality between the income and remainder beneficiaries is generally a reasonable apportionment of the total return of the trust.
>
> **Example:** A trust owns unimproved real estate for several years that the trustee recently sold. Because the real estate has been unproductive of income for several years, the trustee determines that a portion of the net sales proceeds should be allocated to accounting income in order to fulfill his fiduciary duty of impartiality between the income and remainder beneficiaries. As a result, although the net sales proceeds normally would be allocated entirely to accounting principal, the trustee adjusts a portion of the net sales proceeds from accounting principal to accounting income.

Evident in the tone of the Treasury Regulation is that the Treasury Department sought to be accommodating to taxpayers' needs and to recognize that there are many competing interests at stake. Furthermore, the regulations quell tax concerns that a switch between methods of determining fiduciary accounting income authorized by state statute will not constitute a recognition event for purposes of Code

34. A unitrust percentage means that the distribution for any year will be equal to a particular percentage (the unitrust percentage) multiplied by the fair market value of the trust assets, usually determined as of a particular date of the tax year.

§1001 and will not result in a taxable gift from the trust's grantor or any of the trust's beneficiaries.

A. Examples of Income and Principal for Accounting Purposes

Below are examples of **receipts** that will be treated as fiduciary accounting **income** under the Uniform Fiduciary Income and Principal Act that was issued in 2018 as drafted by the Uniform Law Commission (formerly known as the National Conference of Commissioners of Uniform State Laws):[35]

- Rents, including sums received for cancellation or renewal of a lease
- Interest income (including tax-exempt interest)
- Cash dividends
- Moneys received from a corporation, partnership, limited liability company, or other business entity that is not received in a liquidation or a partial liquidation
- A distribution of income from a trust or an estate
- Generally, three to five percent of the value of the liquidating asset or, if the value is unknown, 10 percent of the proceeds from a liquidating asset such as a leasehold, patent, copyright, royalty right, mineral rights, and timber
- Interest or other current return from asset-backed securities

Below are examples of **expenses** that will be charged against fiduciary accounting **income** under the Uniform Fiduciary Income and Principal Act:

- Ordinary expenses incurred in connection with trust administration and management, including real estate taxes
- Interest expense
- One-half of court costs and legal and other fees for accountings and judicial proceedings that involve both the income and remainder interests
- One-half of the fiduciary's regular compensation
- One-half of investment advisory or custodial service fees
- Income taxes based on receipts allocated to income

Below are examples of **receipts** that will be treated as **principal** under the Uniform Principal and Income Act:

- Assets received from a transferor or a decedent's estate
- Life insurance benefits and retirement benefits where the trust is named as the beneficiary

35. The Uniform Principal and Income Act may be found on the Uniform Law Commission website www.uniformlaws.org. As noted above, the Uniform Law Commission issued the Uniform Fiduciary Income and Principal Act in October, 2018.

- Capital gains
- Insurance proceeds on property comprising part of the principal
- Stock dividends
- Property received from a corporation, partnership, limited liability company or other business entity
- Proceeds from the disposition of bonds
- Proceeds of property taken by eminent domain
- Generally, the proceeds from a liquidating asset such as a leasehold, patent, copyright, royalty right, mineral rights, and timber not allocated to income
- Net income received in an accounting period during which there is no beneficiary to whom a trustee may or must distribute income

Below are examples of **expenses** that will be charged against fiduciary accounting **principal** under the Uniform Principal and Income Act:

- Principal payments on an indebtedness including a mortgage
- Cost of preparing property for rental or sale
- Cost of investing and reinvesting principal
- Capital gains tax for capital gains allocated to principal
- Estate or inheritance tax
- Expenses not charged against income

Where a trust is the owner of an IRA or other qualified retirement fund, the trustee is to determine the internal income of the IRA or fund and, with respect to any distribution received from such IRA or fund, the trustee allocates to income the amount up to the internal income of the IRA or fund and allocates the balance, if any, to principal.[36]

B. Special Tax Rules for Allocating the Depreciation Deduction between the Trust or Estate and the Beneficiaries

Rules regarding depreciation (and depletion) can illuminate differences between trust law and tax law.

1. Depreciation and Fiduciary Accounting. Under principles of trust law, the trustee owes duties to both income beneficiaries and remainder beneficiaries. As a result, when the trustee holds property that is depreciating in value, the trustee must be concerned about the decline in value of the principal to the detriment of the remainder beneficiaries. And the trustee may be required to make adjustments

36. Section 409(c) of the Uniform Fiduciary Income and Principal Act. *See*, Section 409(d) for special rules with respect to a marital trust.

to rectify any imbalance. The various principal and income acts try to resolve this potential conflict between income beneficiaries and remainder beneficiaries.

The Uniform Fiduciary Income and Principal Act addresses this potential conflict between the interests of the beneficiaries by allowing the trustee to make an allowance for depreciation as the trustee considers best by providing, in part, "A trustee may transfer to principal a reasonable amount of the net cash receipts from a principal asset that is subject to depreciation. . . ." Two items to note. First, the amount transferred need not be held in a separate fund. Second, the transfer to principal is to be made from the net proceeds received from the depreciating property; if the property is not earning income or insufficient income, the trustee cannot make a sufficient transfer.

But the depreciation allowance is not without its limitations. For example, no allowance is permitted for depreciation in the following four circumstances: (a) real property used by a beneficiary as a residence, (b) tangible personal property held or made available for the personal use or enjoyment of a beneficiary, (c) the asset is used in a business or activity that is being accounted for separately (e.g., the trust is operating a limited liability company that has depreciable property and such property is being depreciated under the books and records of the limited liability company), or (d) the asset is a liquidating asset and the fiduciary accounts for it as a liquidating asset.

> **Example:** Joe is the trustee of a trust which owns depreciable property. Pursuant to local law, Joe exercises his authority and charges against the income of the trust a $10,000 depreciation allowance. The depreciation allowed for income tax purposes is $25,000. The depreciation reserve determined for state law purposes does not need to equate to the depreciation allowed under the tax laws because their purposes are different (i.e., the Uniform Fiduciary Income and Principal Act and general fiduciary duties impose on a fiduciary the obligation to treat all beneficiaries fairly and, by way of contrast, the Code seeks to raise tax revenue).

2. Depreciation and Income Taxes. The tax rules regarding the depreciation deduction are unconcerned about any imbalance between income and remainder beneficiaries. And, as shown in the above example, the depreciation deduction allowed for tax purposes need not bear any relationship to any actual depreciation in value. For tax purposes, in the case of an estate, the depreciation deduction is apportioned between the estate and the heirs, legatees, and devisees based on the percentage of the **fiduciary accounting income** retained by the estate or distributed to the beneficiaries. The fiduciary accounting income is only used as the basis for determining the amount of the depreciation deduction to be allocated between the estate and beneficiaries. In the case of a trust, the depreciation deduction is allocated between the trust and the income beneficiaries in accordance with the pertinent provisions of the governing instrument or, in the absence of such provisions, based on the percentages of the accounting income kept by the trust and distributed to the beneficiaries. As discussed below, a depreciation reserve is the only "pertinent provisions of the governing instrument" allowed.

Code § 642(e) provides that a "trust shall be allowed the deduction for depreciation and depletion only to the extent allowable to beneficiaries under sections 167(d) and 611(b)." The cross-referenced Code sections read respectively (and virtually identically) as follows:

> Depreciation: In the case of property held in trust, the allowable deduction shall be apportioned between the income beneficiaries and the trustee in accordance with the pertinent provisions of the instrument creating the trust, or, in the absence of such provisions, on the basis of the trust income allocable to each. In the case of an estate, the allowable deduction shall be apportioned between the estate and the heirs, legatees, and devisees on the basis of the income of the estate allocable to each. [Code § 167(d).]
>
> Depletion: In the case of property held in trust, the deduction under this section shall be apportioned between the income beneficiaries and the trustee in accordance with the pertinent provisions of the instrument creating the trust, or, in the absence of such provisions, on the basis of the trust income allocable to each. [Code § 611(b)(3).]
>
> In the case of an estate, the deduction under this section shall be apportioned between the estate and the heirs, legatees, and devisees on the basis of the income of the estate allocable to each. [Code § 611(b)(4).]

With respect to trust instruments, the governing regulations limit the meaning of "in accordance with the pertinent provisions" of the trust instrument to only a provision concerning the requirement to establish a reserve for depreciation or depletion.[37] In other words, a provision in a trust that provides, for example, that the depreciation deduction will be allocated to a particular beneficiary or allocated among the beneficiaries as the trustee determines will not be recognized for income tax purposes. This interpretation was upheld in *Dusek v. Commissioner*,[38] where the Tenth Circuit held that a provision authorizing the trustee to apportion "all appropriate tax deductions for depletion and depreciation . . . in such manner as he may see fit" was not enforceable for income tax purposes.

> **Background:** *What Is a Depreciation or Depletion Reserve?* In fiduciary accounting, a depreciation or depletion reserve refers to the fiduciary converting a portion of the accounting income (usually the income generated by the property subject to depreciation or depletion) to accounting principal for the purpose of protecting the value of the underlying property. For example, assume that a trust owns commercial rental property. Over time, certain maintenance and repair costs can be anticipated, such as a new roof or HVAC, etc. To be able to pay for such costs without creating an undue financial burden on the trust, the trustee may establish a reserve to retain some portion of the rents to eventually pay for more significant repairs, maintenance, and improvements. Generally, the trustee need not physically

37. *See* Treas. Reg. §§ 1.167(h)-1(b) and 1.611-1(c)(4).

38. 376 F.2d 410 (10th Cir. 1967).

separate the amounts set aside in a reserve, but the books and records of the trustee should reflect accurately the amount of the reserve.

Because the person who gets the accounting income also gets the depreciation deduction (to the extent not first allocated to a depreciation reserve), the tax rules are grounded in practicality not equity (i.e., the persons to whom accounting income is allocated are always known, but the identity of the remainder beneficiaries may be uncertain or not in existence, or both). Thus, if all accounting income is to be distributed to a beneficiary, that beneficiary will receive the entire depreciation deduction in excess of any reserve established by the trustee. The deduction will be reflected on the Schedule K-1 for the beneficiary.

> **Example:** Under a trust, Jack receives all the income annually for his lifetime and, at his death, the trust will be distributed to his descendants or, if Jack has no descendants, to his sister, Jill. Jack currently is 21 years of age and has no children.
>
> The trust owns property that qualifies for the depreciation deduction. Logically, the depreciation deduction should inure to the persons whose interest is being lessened because of the depreciation—that is, Jack's descendants or Jill. But one can see the practical impossibility of this situation, because Jack does not yet have descendants and Jill's remainder interest may be negated. As a result, the tax rules allocate the depreciation deduction to Jack, because he received all the fiduciary accounting income.

Where a trustee sets up a reserve for depreciation, the trustee cannot distribute that portion of the income needed for the reserve, and the trust will receive the depreciation deduction to the extent of the reserve amount. Any excess depreciation deduction apportioned between the income beneficiaries and the trust will be based on the percentage of the fiduciary accounting income (in excess of the income set aside for the reserve or sinking fund) allocable to each.

> **Example:** In the above example, the trustee wishes to protect the interest of the remainder beneficiaries by establishing a reserve. To this end, the trustee establishes a reserve, the result of which is that a part of the income received by the trust is retained and allocated to the principal and not distributed to Jack. This is what is meant by charging the income with a depreciation reserve. As a result, the trust will receive the depreciation deduction allowed for income tax purposes up to the amount of the reserve. Jack will get the balance of the depreciation deduction, if any.

Note again that the amount of the reserve need not bear any relation to the amount of the depreciation deduction for tax purposes. In instances where it is intended or expected that the income beneficiary should have the benefit of the depreciation deduction, prudence dictates that in the governing instrument there be language that overrides any statutory provision that requires the trustee to establish a reserve. An example of such a provision is as follows: The Trustee will not establish out of income, or credit to principal, any allowance or reserve for depreciation on property subject to depreciation.

The tax law does not consider any allocation from income to principal of an estate as a depreciation reserve. Thus, with respect to an estate that is entitled to the depreciation deduction, the depreciation deduction allowable to the estate may be expressed formulaically as follows:

DD = the allowable depreciation deduction for tax purposes
AE = the fiduciary accounting income kept by the estate for the tax year
AI = the total fiduciary accounting income for the tax year

$$DD \times \frac{AE}{AI} = \text{depreciation deduction allowed to estate}$$

The depreciation deduction allowable to the beneficiaries will equal the allowable depreciation deduction not allowable to the estate, expressed formulaically as follows:

AB = the fiduciary accounting income received by a beneficiary for the tax year

$$DD \times \frac{AB}{AI} = \text{depreciation deduction allowed to an estate beneficiary}$$

With respect to a trust, the determination of the depreciation deduction allowable to a trust and its beneficiaries is the same as for an estate and its beneficiaries, **except that,** if a trust provides for a depreciation reserve, you first allocate the trust depreciation deduction up to the amount of the reserve, expressed formulaically as follows:

R = the depreciation reserve established by the trustee for the tax year
AT = the fiduciary accounting income kept by the trust for the tax year

$$R \text{ (but not more than DD)} + \left[(DD - R \text{ (but not less than zero)}) \times \frac{AT}{AI} \right]$$
$$= \text{depreciation deduction allowed to trust}$$

The depreciation deduction allowed to a trust beneficiary expressed formulaically is as follows:

$$\left[(DD - R \text{ (but not less than zero)}) \times \frac{AB}{AI} \right]$$
$$= \text{depreciation deduction allowed to a trust beneficiary}$$

Example: A trust is entitled to a $30,000 depreciation deduction for tax purposes. For the tax year, the trust created a depreciation reserve of $10,000, had fiduciary accounting income of $50,000, and distributed $5,000 of the accounting income to its beneficiary. Thus, the trust kept 90% of the accounting income and the beneficiary received 10% of the accounting income.

With respect to the $30,000 allowable depreciation deduction and using the formula above, the trust is entitled to a depreciation deduction of $28,000 in total determined as follows:

$$\text{R (but not more than DD)} + \left[(\text{DD} - \text{R (but not less than zero)}) \times \frac{\text{AT}}{\text{AI}} \right]$$
$$= \text{depreciation deduction allowed to trust}$$
$$\$10{,}000 + \left[(\$30{,}000 - \$10{,}000) \times \frac{\$45{,}000}{\$50{,}000} \right]$$
$$= \$10{,}000 + (\$20{,}000 \times 90\%) = \$28{,}000$$

The beneficiary is entitled to the depreciation deduction not allowed to the trust, or $2,000. Using the formula above, it would be determined as follows:

$$\left[(\text{DD} - \text{R (but not less than zero)}) \times \frac{\text{AB}}{\text{AI}} \right]$$
$$= \text{depreciation deduction allowed to a beneficiary}$$
$$(\$30{,}000 - \$10{,}000) \times \left(\frac{\$5{,}000}{\$50{,}000} \right)$$
$$= \$20{,}000 + 10\% = \$2{,}000$$

Example: The same as above, except that the trustee establishes a $35,000 depreciation reserve. Because the depreciation reserve is greater than the depreciation deduction allowable for tax purposes, the trust is allowed the entire $30,000 depreciation deduction. Using the formula above, it would look as follows:

$$\text{R (but not more than DD)} + \left[(\text{DD} - \text{R (but not less than zero)}) \times \frac{\text{AT}}{\text{AI}} \right]$$
$$= \text{depreciation deduction allowed to trust}$$
$$\$30{,}000 + \left[(\$30{,}000 - \$30{,}000) \times \frac{\$45{,}000}{\$50{,}000} \right]$$
$$= \$30{,}000 + (\$0 \times 90\%) = \$30{,}000$$

Example: The same as the first example, except that the trustee distributes all the accounting income to the beneficiary. The trust is allowed a depreciation deduction up to its reserve of $10,000, and the beneficiary is allowed a depreciation deduction for the remaining $20,000 because it received all the accounting income. Again, using the above formula, the depreciation deduction allowed to the trust would look as follows:

$$R \text{ (but not more than DD)} + \left[(\text{DD} - \text{R (but not less than zero)}) \times \frac{\text{AT}}{\text{AI}} \right]$$
$$= \text{depreciation deduction allowed to trust}$$
$$\$10{,}000 + \left[(\$30{,}000 - \$10{,}000) \times \frac{\$0}{\$50{,}000} \right]$$
$$= \$10{,}000 + (\$20{,}000 \times 0\%) = \$10{,}000$$

The depreciation deduction allowed to the beneficiary would look as follows:

$$\left[(\text{DD} - \text{R (but not less than zero)}) \times \frac{\text{AB}}{\text{AI}} \right]$$
$$= \text{depreciation deduction allowed to a beneficiary}$$
$$(\$30{,}000 - \$10{,}000) \times \left(\frac{\$50{,}000}{\$50{,}000} \right)$$
$$= \$20{,}000 \times 100\% = \$20{,}000$$

Example: A trust is entitled to a $30,000 depreciation deduction for tax purposes. For the tax year, the trust created a $9,000 depreciation reserve, had $15,000 of fiduciary accounting income, and distributed $5,000 of the accounting income to its beneficiary. Thus, the trust kept two-thirds of the accounting income, and the beneficiary received one-third of the accounting income. Using the formula from above, the trust is entitled to a depreciation deduction computed as follows:

$$R \text{ (but not more than DD)} + \left[(\text{DD} - \text{R (but not less than zero)}) \times \frac{\text{AT}}{\text{AI}} \right]$$
$$= \text{depreciation deduction allowed to trust}$$
$$\$9{,}000 + \left[(\$30{,}000 - \$9{,}000) \times \frac{\$10{,}000}{\$15{,}000} \right]$$
$$= \$9{,}000 + \left(\$21{,}000 \times \frac{2}{3} \right) = \$23{,}000$$

The beneficiary is entitled to the depreciation deduction not allowed to the trust, or $7,000. Using the formula above, it would be determined as follows:

$$\left[(\text{DD} - \text{R (but not less than zero)}) \times \frac{\text{AB}}{\text{AI}} \right]$$
$$= \text{depreciation deduction allowed to a beneficiary}$$
$$(\$30{,}000 - \$9{,}000) \times \left(\frac{\$5{,}000}{\$15{,}000} \right)$$
$$= \$21{,}000 \times \frac{1}{3} = \$7{,}000$$

Summary: Determining fiduciary accounting income is integral in determining taxable income of a trust or estate. Fiduciary accounting income is a state-law concept and is always determined by applying the applicable state law to the activities of the trust or estate. All states have some form of "principal and income act," which acts set forth the rules for how fiduciary accounting principal and income are to be determined.

With respect to the depreciation deduction, special rules apply to determine how much of this deduction a trust or estate and its beneficiaries are entitled to deduct. Generally, the depreciation deduction is allocated among the persons, including the trust or estate, based on the fiduciary accounting income retained by the trust or estate or distributed to beneficiaries. The only exception to applying this general rule is that, if a trust has established a depreciation reserve, the depreciation deduction is first allocated dollar for dollar to this reserve and the excess, if any, is allocated pro rata in accordance with the general rule.

Questions

1. A trust is entitled to a depreciation deduction of $5,000. The trust is required to distribute all its accounting income at least annually to Janet. The trust has accounting income of $25,000 and has DNI of $30,000. How is the depreciation deduction allocated between the trust and Janet?
2. The same as question 1, except that, the trust only has accounting income of $3,000 and DNI of $3,000.

Chapter 4

Simple Trusts

I. Introduction

Internal Revenue Code: Sections 643, 651, 652

Regulations: Sections 1.651(a)-1 through 1.651(a)-5; 1.651(b)-1; 1.652(a)-1 through 1.652(a)-2; 1.652(b)-1 through 1.652(b)-3; 1.652(c)-1 through 1.652(c)-4

The Code classifies a trust as a simple trust if it meets the following three criteria, namely:

1. The governing instrument requires that the trust distribute all of its fiduciary accounting income (sometimes referred to as trust accounting income) currently for the taxable year (Code § 651(a)(1));
2. The governing instrument does not provide for amounts to be paid, permanently set aside or used in the taxable year for charitable purposes as described in Code § 642(c) (as provided in Code § 651(a)(2)); and
3. The trust does not make any distribution during the year other than current income (Code § 651(a)(2); Treas. Reg. 1.651(a)-1).

> **Example:** Mary creates a trust for the benefit of John. The terms of the trust provide that all of the trust income must be distributed to John annually. The trustee is not permitted to distribute any corpus (principal) to John, and no amount of the trust income or principal may be paid, permanently set aside or used during the year for charitable purposes. This trust is a simple trust.

Note that the first two criteria must be met by the actual terms of the governing instrument, while the third criteria is determined by the trustee's actions during the year.

> **Example:** The terms of a trust instrument meet the first two criteria but also give the trustee discretion to distribute principal. Until the end of the tax year, it cannot be known if the trust will meet all criteria for a simple trust — if the trustee did not distribute any principal, the trust is a simple trust for that tax year; and if the trustee distributed any principal, the trust is not a simple trust for that tax year.

Code § 651 addresses the distribution deduction allowed to a trust that is characterized as a simple trust for the year. For purposes of Section 651, the income "required to be distributed currently" refers to the fiduciary accounting income for the taxable year, as determined under the governing instrument and applicable state laws. Code § 643(b).

Code § 652 addresses the inclusion of the income distributed from the trust in the gross income of the trust's beneficiaries.

Fiduciary accounting income is determined based on the governing instrument and applicable local laws that will apply to the extent the governing instrument is silent. Fiduciary accounting income is a net amount (i.e., receipts allocable to income minus expenditures chargeable against income). As more fully discussed below, it is to be distinguished from fiduciary accounting principal. Code § 643(b).

Whether income is required to be distributed currently depends on the terms of the trust instrument and applicable local laws. Treas. Reg. 1.651(a)-2(a). The regulations describe two situations in which, although a trustee is not distributing all of the trust income during the tax year, the terms of the trust are still deemed to require that all income be distributed currently, so that simple trust classification will nevertheless apply:

- A trust instrument provides for retaining a depreciation reserve or otherwise providing for an allowance to keep the trust principal intact by retaining a reasonable amount of current income for that purpose. Treas. Reg. 1.651(a)-2(a).
- Practical necessity requires a fiduciary to postpone mandatory trust income distributions until after the end of the trust's taxable year. Treas. Reg. 1.651(a)-2(a).

Consider two examples, the first describing a simple trust and the second a complex trust.

> **Example:** A calendar year trust is required to distribute all of its income currently, and distributes each quarter's income to its beneficiary on the 15th day of the month following the close of the calendar quarter. The distribution made on January 15 following the close of the trust's calendar year does not disqualify the trust from being classified as a simple trust.
>
> **Example:** The trust terms provide that no income be distributed until after the year of its receipt. Here, because the trust income is not required to be distributed currently, the trust will not be classified as a simple trust.

A trust will still be considered to be required to distribute all of its income if it converts the requirement to pay all fiduciary accounting income into a total return trust (providing for an annual payment to beneficiaries of a percentage of the value of the trust property—typically 3, 4, or 5 percent) as permitted by the state law or by a judicial reformation. Treas. Reg. 1.643(a)(1) and Treas. Reg. 1.643(b)(1). Thus, under a total return trust, the amount actually distributed may be less than or may be greater than the actual accounting income received by the trust. Note that the amounts paid from a total return trust (sometimes referred to as a "unitrust") may constitute fiduciary accounting income (see Chapter 3).

In determining if a trust is a simple trust, the amount of income to be distributed to a particular beneficiary is not material. So long as all of the income is to be distributed currently, simple trust classification will apply. More specifically, many trusts permit the trustee to "sprinkle" income in its discretion among multiple beneficiaries; if the amount to be distributed to a particular beneficiary is not known until the fiduciary acts, a trust will be a simple trust so long as all of the income must be distributed. Treas. Reg. 1.651(a)-2(b).

> **Example:** The Jones Family Trust provides that the trustee must distribute all of its fiduciary accounting income every year among the five Jones children but the trustee can distribute the income among any of the five Jones children in whatever proportions the trustee considers appropriate. Because all income must be distributed currently, the trust is a simple trust notwithstanding that the amount of income distributable to any one beneficiary is not known.

When considering whether "trust income" is required to be distributed, the Code refers to fiduciary accounting income. If the trust receives capital gains, taxable stock dividends, extraordinary dividends, or other items of gross income that the fiduciary properly allocates to trust principal, such receipts are not considered "income" that must be distributed. Code § 643(b).

In determining what is classified as "income," if a trust contains provisions that constitute a fundamental departure from local law concepts, those provisions will not be recognized in determining if a trust is a simple trust. For example, if the trust instrument directs that all trust income must be distributed currently, but defines interest and ordinary dividends as principal, the trust will not be recognized as a simple trust. Treas. Reg. 1.643(b)-1.

Even if the trust terms require principal to be distributed in a particular year, the trust is still considered a simple trust if all of the income but no principal distributions are actually made in that year. Treas. Reg. 1.651(a)-3(b). The same is also true for a trust that provides for amounts to be paid, permanently set aside, or used in the taxable year for charitable purposes but no charitable deduction is claimed. Treas. Reg. 1.651(a)-3(c). However, once a trust makes a distribution of principal rendering the trust complex, all other required distributions of principal must be included in the distribution deduction even if the amounts are not actually distributed.

> **Example:** Jack creates a trust for the benefit of Diane. The terms of the trust provide that all of the trust income is to be distributed to Diane annually. The trust also provides that the trustee has discretion to distribute up to five percent of the principal to Diane each year. In Year 1, Diane gets all the income, but no principal is distributed to Diane. For Year 1, the trust would be classified as a simple trust, despite the discretion to pay out principal—none was paid. In Year 2, the trustee pays Diane all the income, and makes a principal payment of $10,000—falling within the five percent limitation and the payment is made during the tax year. For Year 2, the trust would be a complex trust, because amounts of principal actually were paid during the tax year.

II. Simple Trust Versus a Complex Trust

The Code distinguishes between trusts classified as "simple trusts" and trusts classified as "complex trusts." A complex trust is any trust that does not meet the three aforementioned criteria to be characterized as a simple trust (i.e., governing instrument permits income accumulation, distributions are made to charity, or principal distributions are made). Treas. Reg. 1.651(a)-1.

Code § 661 addresses the distribution deduction allowed to a complex trust, and Code § 662 addresses the inclusion of the income distributed by a complex trust as income to the trust beneficiaries. (Complex trusts are discussed in Chapter 5.)

A decedent's estate is always taxed as a complex trust. If a decedent had a qualified revocable trust that made a Code § 645 election after the decedent's death so that the trust is considered to be a part of the decedent's estate, that trust will be taxed as an estate for the duration of the Section 645 election. Thereafter, the terms of the trust will determine whether the ongoing trust may be viewed as a simple trust.

III. Characterization as a Simple Trust May Vary from Year to Year

A trust may be considered "simple" for some years, and "complex" for other years.

A common situation in which this occurs involves trusts created for the benefit of a minor. While the beneficiary is a minor, the trust may give the trustee discretion to distribute income. For these years, the trust would be a complex trust, because it fails to require that the trust mandate current income distributions. However, if the trust provides that once the beneficiary attains a certain age, the trustee is then required to distribute all income to the beneficiary at least annually, the trust will be a simple trust—assuming the other criteria are met for characterization as a simple trust. Treas. Reg. 1.651(a)-2(c).

Aside from trusts established for the benefit of minors, there are other occasions when trusts can migrate between simple/complex classifications. *See, e.g., Steingold v. Commissioner*, T.C. Memo 2000-225, *aff'd per curiam*, 88 A.F.T.R.2d 5175 (4th Cir. 2001) (if a simple trust receives a court order directing the trustee to retain some or all of the trust income, the trust will be treated as a complex trust while such order remains in effect).

A trust may satisfy its obligation to pay out current income by making an in-kind distribution of trust property to a beneficiary. Because the obligation to pay all of the fiduciary accounting income is a pecuniary obligation, if the trustee satisfies this obligation with the distribution of appreciated property, the trust will be treated as having sold the property for its fair market value on the date of its distribution. *See* Treas. Reg. 1.661(a)-2(f); *Kenan v. Commissioner*, 114 F.2d 217 (2d Cir. 1940) (using appreciated securities to satisfy a pecuniary bequest was treated as a taxable exchange of the appreciated securities). Even if that distribution generates gain to the trust, if the amount distributed by the trust during the year does not exceed its fiduciary accounting income, it does not change the trust from being classified as a simple trust. Treas. Reg. 1.651(a)-2(d).

A trust may go through its entire existence as a simple trust. However, because all trusts in their final year distribute principal, they will always be classified as complex in the year of their termination. Treas. Reg. 1.651(a)-3(a).

IV. Taxation of Simple Trusts

While trusts are subject to many of the rules governing the income taxation of individuals, there are differences. The subsections below explore these differences from the vantage point of a simple trust, including (A) Income Determinations, (B) Allowable Deductions, and (C) Distribution Deductions.

A. Income Determinations

To determine a simple trust's taxable income, it is entitled to deduct all of its fiduciary accounting income not in excess of its distributable net income (DNI). To determine the amount of DNI that the trust may deduct, income items that are not included in the gross income of the trust (such as tax-exempt income) are excluded from the calculation — even if they may be allocated to fiduciary accounting income.

A trust that is required to distribute all of its income currently, such as a simple trust, is entitled to claim an annual deduction of $300. Code § 642(b). This deduction is in lieu of the personal exemption allowed individuals. It is not prorated for a short taxable year and is not affected by the amount of income taxable to the trust. High income, low income, or no income, the $300 exemption remains available. If it is not used in any tax year (that is, the trust's taxable income for any year is less than $300), it is not carried forward, and it is not part of a net operating loss. The use of this exemption does not reduce the DNI of a trust. The amount is not indexed to inflation.

> **Example:** A simple trust is created in September, and files as a calendar year taxpayer. The allowable deduction under Section 642(b) is $300, despite the tax year being less than twelve months. In the next year, a full twelve month year, the allowable deduction is again $300.

Since a simple trust is required to distribute all of its fiduciary accounting income and receives a distribution deduction under Section 651, when is this $300 deduction useful? The answer is that it will be useful in those years in which the simple trust has taxable income. There are four situations when a simple trust may have its own reportable taxable income, and where that is the case, the $300 deduction will offset otherwise taxable income.

(1) A simple trust will have taxable income whenever it receives money that is gross income for income tax purposes but that is allocated to principal for fiduciary accounting purposes. This may occur when the trust receives capital gains, taxable stock dividends, or extraordinary dividends which are allocated to principal under the governing instrument or state law. This also may occur where the trust recognizes income arising from depreciation recapture and such recapture is allocated to principal.

> **Example:** The trustee of a simple trust sells appreciated stock that was originally purchased for $10,000 and is sold for $110,000. The $100,000 gain (i.e., $110,000 – $10,000) is allocated to trust principal and thus taxable to the trust.

(2) A simple trust will have taxable income whenever (a) it receives distributions from other trusts or estates, (b) such distributions from such other trusts or estates carry out their own DNI to the simple trust, and (c) some or all of such distributions are allocated to the trust's principal. This particular event is known as a "trapping distribution," because gross income received from the distributing trust or estate is "trapped" in the principal of the receiving trust or estate. Where this occurs, the income is not part of the simple trust's fiduciary accounting income and is not distributable to the income beneficiaries. Accordingly, the simple trust becomes the taxpayer required to report this income.

> **Example:** A simple trust receives a pour-over distribution from an estate in the amount of $100,000. The estate provides a Schedule 1041 K-1 to the trust reporting the $100,000 payment as a taxable distribution. The estate claims a distribution deduction for the payment. Pursuant to the terms of the trust, the trustee is required to allocate the distribution to principal for fiduciary accounting purposes, even though it constitutes taxable income to the trust. None of the $100,000 may be distributed to the beneficiaries of the trust. The $100,000 distribution is "trapped" at the trust level, and the income is taxable to the trust.

(3) A simple trust will have taxable income whenever it is the recipient of so-called "phantom income." How does phantom income arise? A simple trust may be a partner in a partnership, a member of a limited liability company taxed as a partnership, or a shareholder in an S corporation. The partnership, limited liability company, or S corporation may have taxable income allocable to the simple trust as a partner, member, or shareholder that exceeds distributions. The excess of the reportable gross income over the amounts actually distributed is "phantom income." Where this occurs, such excess is treated as trust accounting principal and will remain with the trust, making it the reporting taxpayer. (In this situation the trust is *not* permitted to give a Form 1041 Schedule K-1 reporting the phantom income to the trust beneficiary.)

> **Example:** The Johnson Family Trust is a simple trust, required to distribute all of its income annually to the four Johnson adult children. During its

taxable year, the trust received $15,000 of taxable interest income from certificates of deposit and $25,000 of qualified stock dividends. The trust is also a limited partner in the JFP Partnership. The trust received a Schedule K-1 from the JFP Partnership reporting income allocable to the trust of $35,000. No payment was received from the Partnership. The reporting of the Johnson Family Trust would be addressed as follows:

Income Received:

Interest:	$15,000
Dividends	$25,000
Partnership Income	$35,000
Total Income:	$75,000 (assume no deductible expenses)

Distribution Deduction to Beneficiaries: $15,000 (interest) + $25,000 (dividends) = $40,000

Amount taxable to the Trust: $75,000 (total income) – $40,000 (distribution deduction) = $35,000 (partnership distribution) – $300 exemption = $34,700

Example: The trustee of a simple trust has interest income of $5,000 from original issue discount ("OID"). No interest is actually received or distributed to the beneficiary. The trust also receives $5,000 of rental income, which is income required to be distributed to the beneficiary. The trust will pay tax on the $5,000 of OID.

(4) Where a simple trust incurs an expense that reduces fiduciary accounting income but does not reduce taxable income, the trust will have DNI greater than accounting income and, thus, the trust will have taxable income.

Example: A simple trust earns $100,000 and pays $1,000 as an investment advisory fee which is not deductible due to its status as a miscellaneous itemized deduction. Code § 67(g). In such a case, DNI would be $100,000 and FAI would be $99,000. The distribution deduction would be $99,000. As such, $1,000 of taxable income would remain taxable to the trust.

B. Allowable Deductions

The most important deduction for a simple trust will typically be the distribution deduction allowed under Section 651. Before addressing the details of the distribution deduction, however, attention must be paid to other deductions allowed to simple trusts.

In general, trusts are permitted the same deductions afforded individual taxpayers. Code § 641(b). As enumerated in Chapter 2, however, the Code posits important variations between how trusts and individual taxpayers are taxed. The 2017 Tax Cuts and Jobs Act (the "2017 Act") raised issues involving miscellaneous itemized deductions.

The 2017 Act amended Code § 67 for tax years 2018 through 2025 to disallow the deduction of all miscellaneous itemized deductions. The law sunsets at the end of 2025 and reverts to the prior law, allowing these deductions once again, absent further developments in the law. Code § 67(g). This new rule requires a close examination of Code § 67, and a determination of which expenses are not miscellaneous itemized deductions and remain deductible by trusts and estates without any limitation, and which expenses are miscellaneous itemized deductions so that their deduction is now prohibited.

As a starting point, consider the fact that there are those deductions permitted as adjustments to gross income and listed in Code § 62 which are *not* miscellaneous itemized deductions and, as such, they are not limited by the new Code § 67(g). See Code § 63(d)(1). These include:

- Section 162 trade or business expenses;
- Losses from the sale or exchange of property (capital losses and Code § 1231 losses);
- Deductions attributable to rental property and royalties, allowed by Code §§ 161-199A,[1] Section 212, and Section 611, if the property is held for the production of income.
- Penalties for premature withdrawals from savings accounts and CDs; and
- Section 194 reforestation expenses.

If a deduction is allowable to a trust or estate that is not considered an adjustment to gross income as listed above, such deductions are itemized deductions and are potentially subject to the limitations of Code § 67(a). However, not all itemized deductions are miscellaneous itemized deductions. Code § 67(b) defines the term "miscellaneous itemized deductions" to mean itemized deductions *other than*:

- Interest (Section 163)
- State and local taxes (Section 164, subject to the $10,000 deduction limitation imposed by the 2017 Act)
- Charitable deductions (Sections 170 and 642(c))
- Medical expense deductions (Section 213) — these are not allowed to be claimed on a fiduciary income tax return
- Deductions claimed for federal estate taxes paid on items of income in respect of a decedent (Section 691)
- Deductions for repayment of amounts reported in income under a claim of right (Section 1341)

1. Note that the Section 199A qualified business income deduction created by the 2017 Act is a permitted deduction because it is not considered an itemized deduction. Code § 63(d)(3).

- Deductions allowed when annuity payments cease before an investment is recovered (Section 72(b)(3))
- Deductions for amortizable bond premiums (Section 171)
- Deductions related to cooperative housing corporations (Section 216)

In light of the foregoing discussion, what deductions remain available for trusts to claim and deduct? Those costs paid or incurred which meet the following two conditions: (i) incurred in connection with the administration of the trust or estate, and (ii) which would not have been incurred if the property were not held in a trust or estate. Code § 67(e)(1) and (2).

The Treasury regulations amplify the meaning of the statute. Treas. Reg. 1.67-4(a) provides that if an expense is incurred by a trust or estate, and commonly or customarily would be incurred by a hypothetical individual holding the same property, then such expense *is* considered a miscellaneous itemized deduction and its deduction is denied. Treas. Reg. 1.67-4(b)(1).

The regulations refer to "ownership costs," which are costs incurred by a property owner simply by reason of being the owner of the property. These costs are viewed as commonly and customarily incurred by an individual property owner. Ownership costs such as condominium fees, insurance costs, property maintenance, and lawn fees are deemed to be commonly and customarily incurred by individual owners and thus are miscellaneous itemized deductions subject to Section 67(g) disallowance. Treas. Reg. 1.67-4(b)(2). This limitation applies along with partnership or S corporation costs that pass through to partners or shareholders if such costs would be miscellaneous itemized deductions under Section 67(a). Treas. Reg. 1.67-2T(b).

The deductibility of fees paid by a trust or estate for preparing tax returns depends on the type of return being prepared. Fees paid for the preparation of fiduciary income tax returns as well as estate and generation-skipping transfer (GST) tax returns, and a decedent's final income tax return, are not miscellaneous itemized deductions subject to the section 67(a) limitation, but other returns that are prepared for individuals are so subject—for example, gift tax returns, which means that the cost incurred for preparing a decedent's unfiled gift tax returns is not deductible for income tax purposes. Treas. Reg. 1.67-4(b)(3).

The regulations generally conclude that investment advisory fees are miscellaneous itemized deductions subject to the Section 67(a) limitation. Treas. Reg. 1.67-4(b)(4). This conclusion takes into account the holding of the Supreme Court in *Knight v. Commissioner*, 552 U.S. 181 (2008), where it was held that investment advisory fees are commonly incurred by individuals and should be viewed as miscellaneous itemized deductions. However, the regulations address what the Court noted in *Knight*, that it is possible that "certain incremental costs of investment advice" might not be miscellaneous itemized deductions, to the extent charged in excess of the amount normally charged an individual. Treas. Reg. 1.67-4(b)(4).

The regulations also address appraisal fees. Some appraisal fees incurred by a trust or estate would not be commonly incurred by individuals, so would not be miscellaneous itemized deductions, such as appraisals used to determine the value of assets for purposes of filing tax returns or for determining distributions. Treas. Reg. 1.67-4(b)(5). However, it cannot be concluded that all appraisals avoid characterization as miscellaneous itemized deductions, since the regulations state that appraisals for other purposes such as for obtaining insurance are commonly obtained by individuals and are subject to the miscellaneous itemized deduction characterization. Treas. Reg. 1.67-4(b)(5).

The regulations acknowledge that certain fiduciary expenses are not commonly incurred by individuals. They cite a number of examples including probate court fees and costs; fiduciary bond premiums; legal publication costs of notices to creditors or heirs; the cost of certified copies of the decedent's death certificate; and costs related to fiduciary accountings. Treas. Reg. 1.67-4(b)(6). These expenses remain deductible without fear of characterization as miscellaneous itemized deductions.

The regulations address the payment of professional and fiduciary fees when such fees are for multiple services. If legal, accounting, fiduciary, or other fees are paid for multiple services rendered, fees attributable to certain services might be characterized as miscellaneous itemized deductions, while fees attributable to other services might not be so characterized. A single fee paid for multiple services is referred to as a "bundled fee" and must be "unbundled," i.e., allocated between costs that are considered miscellaneous itemized deductions and those that are not. Treas. Reg. 1.67-4(c)(1). If the bundled fee is not computed on an hourly basis, only the portion of that fee that is attributable to investment advice is considered a miscellaneous itemized deduction. Treas. Reg. 1.67-4(c)(2). The regulations allow any "reasonable method" to allocate a bundled fee between those costs that are miscellaneous itemized deductions and those that are not. Treas. Reg. 1.67-4(c)(4).

To the extent expenses of the trust are not miscellaneous itemized deductions, those expenses will be deductible and will reduce DNI; conversely, trust expenses that are miscellaneous itemized deductions will not be deductible by the trust and will not reduce DNI. Further, expenses that are not deductible for tax purposes but which reduce fiduciary accounting income will, all else being equal, result in DNI being more than fiduciary accounting income and will in turn result in a simple trust having taxable income. Thus, by eliminating miscellaneous itemized deductions, the 2017 Act will create tax liability at the trust level where no such liability had been imposed before.

> **Example:** The Watson Family Trust is a simple trust required to pay all of its income annually to Sarah Watson. In the current year, the Trust had ordinary interest income of $50,000. The Trust paid expenses for probate fees, a judicial accounting, and fiduciary income tax preparation in the total amount of $10,000, all charged against fiduciary accounting income. None of these fees would be classified as miscellaneous itemized

deductions. The fiduciary accounting income and the DNI of the Trust is $50,000 (income) – $10,000 (allowable deductions charged against fiduciary accounting income) = $40,000. The distribution to Sarah is $40,000. She pays tax on the $40,000 distribution, and the trust reports a distribution deduction of $40,000, leaving the trust with taxable income of (– $300). The exemption is available, but is not used.

Example: The Lewis Family Trust is a simple trust required to pay all of its income annually to Michael Lewis. In the current year, the Trust had ordinary interest income of $50,000. It had no other income. The Trust paid expenses for probate fees, a judicial accounting, and fiduciary income tax preparation in the total of $10,000, all charged against income. None of these fees would be classified as miscellaneous itemized deductions. The Trust also paid expenses to maintain a condominium owned by the trust, including insurance, all of which also were charged against fiduciary accounting income. These expenses amounted to $20,000. None of these expenses are deductible, since they constitute ownership costs, classified as nondeductible miscellaneous itemized deductions. The DNI of the Trust is $40,000 (i.e., $50,000 (income) – $10,000 (allowable deductions) = $40,000). However, after taking into account all of the expenses that were paid, the fiduciary accounting income of the trust is $20,000 (i.e., 50,000 ordinary income – $10,000 deductible expenses – $20,000 nondeductible expenses = $20,000). Accordingly, Michael receives the fiduciary accounting income of $20,000. The distribution deduction of the trust is the lesser of the DNI ($40,000) or the fiduciary accounting income required to be paid to Michael ($20,000), and the Lewis Family Trust is taxed on $19,700 of ordinary income (i.e., $50,000 income received – $10,000 allowable deductions – $20,000 distribution deduction to Michael – $300 deduction = $19,700).

C. Distribution Deductions (Code § 651)

To determine the taxable income of the trust, a simple trust may deduct all of its fiduciary accounting income in any tax year so long as the deduction is not in excess of the DNI of the trust, exclusive of tax-exempt income. Code §§ 651(a) and (b); Treas. Reg. 1.651(b)-1. Accordingly, the maximum distribution deduction for a simple trust is the lesser of its (i) fiduciary accounting income (excluding any tax-exempt income deemed distributed) or (ii) DNI (excluding any tax-exempt income). Code § 651(b). For example, if the trust received tax-exempt income, such income is removed from DNI in determining the available distribution deduction. Similarly, if expenses were incurred to produce tax-exempt income, such expenses would be non-deductible under Code § 265, and not taken into account in determining the DNI of the trust.

In order to properly understand how the trust and its beneficiaries will be taxed and what will be the available distribution deduction under Code § 651, the first step is to calculate the fiduciary accounting income and the DNI under the rules of Code § 643(a), which topics are covered in Chapter 3.

V. Taxation of Trust Beneficiaries (Code § 652)

The DNI of a trust and its fiduciary accounting income are entirely separate concepts. Accordingly, it is possible that the income required to be distributed to a beneficiary (fiduciary accounting income) is more than the amount actually taxable to the beneficiary (DNI). The regulations provide that if the amount of income required to be distributed currently exceeds the trust's DNI, each beneficiary includes in gross income an amount equivalent to the beneficiary's proportionate share of the DNI. In other words, the beneficiary of a simple trust includes in gross income the lesser of (i) the fiduciary accounting income of the trust or (ii) the DNI of the trust, reduced by any net tax-exempt income of the trust. Code § 652(a).

As a general rule, all of the allowable deductions of a simple trust (except a deduction for a capital loss) indirectly benefit the trust beneficiaries, since the deductions reduce the DNI of the trust, even if the deductions are allocated to principal by state law or the governing instrument. Where deductions are allocated to principal, the trust beneficiaries will receive some fiduciary accounting income without having to report it. Where the fiduciary accounting income exceeds DNI, the excess is treated as a non-taxable bequest or principal distribution to the beneficiary under Code § 102.

All taxable income of trusts and estates is subject to taxation — it is only a question of who must report such income: the trust / estate, the beneficiaries, or a combination thereof. To the extent that a simple trust is entitled to a distribution deduction resulting in income escaping taxation at the trust level, such income must be taxed at the beneficiary level. While Code § 651 addresses the distribution deduction for the trust, Code § 652 maintains balance and symmetry by requiring income avoiding taxation at the trust level to be taxed to the beneficiaries.

> **Example:** The Stevens Family Trust is a simple trust. It has two beneficiaries, Alan and Linda. Alan is entitled to receive two-thirds of the Trust income, and Linda is entitled to receive one-third. If the Trust has a total of $66,000 of fiduciary accounting income, Alan will receive $44,000 and Linda will receive $22,000. However, if DNI is $60,000, none of it consisting of tax-exempt income, Alan will include two-thirds of the DNI ($40,000) in his income, and Linda will include one-third of the DNI ($20,000) in her income.
>
> **Note:** In the above Example, suppose fiduciary accounting income was less than the DNI (e.g., the trust incurred a number of non-deductible trust expenses that did not reduce DNI, but did reduce the amount of fiduciary accounting income). Under this set of facts, the trust's deduction would be limited to the amount of fiduciary accounting income,

and, correspondingly, the beneficiaries' inclusion would be limited to the amount of fiduciary accounting income. The excess of DNI over the fiduciary accounting income would be taxable to the trust.

Example: The Wilson Family Trust is a simple trust with a single beneficiary. For its current year, the Trust received $80,000 of qualified dividends, $20,000 of taxable interest, and $40,000 of long-term capital gains. The Trust paid $16,000 of deductible trustee fees, which the Trust document charged $10,000 against fiduciary accounting income and $6,000 against fiduciary accounting principal.

The fiduciary accounting income of the Trust is $90,000 ($80,000 of qualified dividends + $20,000 of taxable interest less $10,000 of trustee fees charged against income). The DNI of the Trust is $84,000 ($80,000 of qualified dividends + $20,000 of taxable interest less $16,000 of trustee fees). The amount of income that the trustee must distribute to the Wilson Trust beneficiary is $90,000 (the fiduciary accounting income), but the beneficiary of the Trust is required to report for income tax purposes only the amount of the DNI of the Trust, $84,000.

In this example, the portion of the trustee fee allocated to principal inures to the benefit of the income beneficiary, since it entered into the calculation of DNI. The $40,000 long-term capital gain is taxable to the Trust, reduced only by the $300 exemption allowed to a simple trust, leaving the Trust with $39,700 of taxable income. The $6,000 trustee fee allocated to principal is not taken into account to reduce the amount of the long-term capital gain taxable to the trust, because it reduced the DNI.

A. Mandatory Income Inclusion

The key to taxation of a beneficiary of a simple trust is the *right* to receive the fiduciary accounting income under the terms of the trust irrespective of whether the trustee actually distributed the income. Code § 652(a).

The issue of a beneficiary not receiving the trust income but still being subjected to income tax as if the income has been received has arisen in a number of cases, and the courts have been consistent in holding that the beneficiary is taxable on the income, despite no receipt of it. Where a beneficiary's right to income was in dispute, it was held that the purported income beneficiary was required to report the trust income notwithstanding that the dispute had not yet been resolved. *Bruchman Estate v. Commissioner*, 53 T.C. 404 (1969).

Other disputes over other issues have not deterred the courts from finding that the trust beneficiary must report the income currently, including: a dispute over the validity of the trust (*United States v. Higginson*, 238 F.2d 439 (1st Cir. 1956)); the proper amount of income to be calculated under state law (*Debrabant v. Commissioner*, 90 F.2d 433 (2d Cir. 1937), Rev. Rul. 85-116, 1985-2 C.B. 174); a suspension of distributions pending the termination of a legal dispute as to whether items in the trust should be allocated to income or principal (Rev. Rul. 62-147, 1962-2 C.B. 151); and where the designated income beneficiary refused to accept distributions from the trust (*Seligson v. Commissioner*, T.C. Memo 1992-320). The phrase in Code § 652(a) requiring inclusion "in the gross income of the beneficiary to whom income is required to be distributed, whether distributed or not" has been the subject of consistent strict interpretations by the courts. *See Polt v. Commissioner*, 233 F.2d 893 (2d Cir. 1956) (income was found to be taxable to the trust beneficiary even where the trustee refused to distribute it pending a court determination of entitlement). In these cases, the courts have ignored the potentially harsh consequences of requiring taxable income to be reported where none was received and forcing amended personal income tax returns to be filed with possible interest and penalty charges.

> **Example:** The Wilson Family Trust is a simple trust requiring the trustee to distribute all of the trust income currently to its single beneficiary, Brenda Wilson. In the current year (Year 1), the trustee has been making quarterly distributions of income to Brenda, but made the last quarterly distribution to her for the current year on January 15 of the following year (Year 2). Since the trust is a simple trust required by its governing instrument to distribute all of its income currently, Code § 652(a) applies to require the Year 1 income to be deemed distributed in Year 1 whether it was distributed then or not. Accordingly, Brenda will be required to report all of the income in Year 1, and the Wilson Family Trust will be entitled to claim a distribution deduction for all of the Year 1 income as well.

For income tax planning purposes, this "deemed distribution" rule should generally be viewed favorably by taxpayers, at least from the perspective of minimizing overall tax liability between the trust and beneficiaries (if not timing), since the compressed income tax rates applied to trusts today would suggest that the government would collect more money by arguing for the trust to be the taxpayer, rather than the beneficiary. As seen from the case law, however, this has not been the case.

B. Dynamics of a Simple Trust with Multiple Beneficiaries

If the simple trust has more than one income beneficiary, the total amount of gross income included by all of the income beneficiaries is limited to the DNI of the trust (excluding tax-exempt income). The amount of DNI allocated to a beneficiary is a fraction of the trust's DNI equal to the amount of fiduciary accounting income distributable to a particular beneficiary, divided by the total amount of fiduciary accounting income required to be distributed currently. Code § 652(a); Treas. Reg. 1.652(a)-2.

> **Example:** The Spring Family Trust is a simple trust required to distribute all of its income currently. The fiduciary accounting income and the DNI for the current year are identical. The Trust has two equal beneficiaries, April and June. Each beneficiary will be considered to have received one-half of the trust's DNI.

Example: The Fisher Family Trust is a simple trust. The trust instrument requires one quarter of the trust income to be distributed to Scott Fisher and three quarters of the trust income to be distributed to Wendy Fisher. The fiduciary accounting income and DNI for the current year is $40,000, none of which is tax-exempt income. Scott must report $10,000 of income, and Wendy must report $30,000 of income for the year.

Example: In the prior Example, assume that the fiduciary accounting income is $40,000 but the DNI is $30,000, none of which is tax exempt income. Scott must report $7,500 of gross income (even though he received $10,000 of accounting income) and Wendy must report $22,500 of gross income (even though she received $30,000 of accounting income).

C. The Character of Income to Be Reported by the Beneficiaries

Items of income retain the same character in the hands of the beneficiary as they had in the hands of the trust. Code § 652(b). Classes of income are allocated to beneficiaries in proportion to their inclusion in DNI. The amounts are treated as consisting of the same proportion of each class of items entering into the computation of DNI of the trust as the total of each class bears to the total DNI of the trust, unless the terms of the trust specifically allocate different classes of income to different beneficiaries. Treas. Reg. 1.652(b)-2. This rule requires that the character of income at the trust level be preserved at the beneficiary level. Qualified dividends, rent, tax-exempt income, etc. all preserve their unique character as they move from trust to beneficiary.

Example: The Lincoln Family Trust is a simple trust. In the current year, it has DNI and fiduciary accounting income of $60,000 that consists of $20,000 of dividends, $30,000 of interest income and $10,000 of rental income. If the Trust has a single beneficiary, that beneficiary will receive $20,000 of dividends, $30,000 of interest income and $10,000 of rental income. In the alternative, if there were several beneficiaries, Alan, Bret and Carol, with Alan entitled to receive one-half of the trust income and Bret and Carol each entitled to receive one-fourth of the trust income, Alan will receive a Schedule K-1 indicating $10,000 of dividends, $15,000 of interest income and $5,000 of rental income allocated to him. Bret and Carol will each receive a Schedule K-1 allocating $5,000 of dividends, $7,500 of interest income and $2,500 of rental income to each of them.

Can the trustee exercise discretion to direct a particular category of income to one beneficiary or another, perhaps to pass taxable income to a beneficiary in a lower income tax bracket, and tax-exempt income or more favorably taxed income to a beneficiary in a higher income tax bracket? The regulations generally disallow such an outcome. If the trust instrument allows the trustee discretion to allocate different classes of income to different beneficiaries, or all the income of a particular class to a particular beneficiary, that will not be viewed as a permitted "specific allocation" by the terms of the trust. Treas. Reg. 1.652(b)-2(b)(1) and (2). However, an allocation made in accordance with a provision directing the trustee to pay half of some class of income to one beneficiary and the balance of the trust income to another beneficiary is viewed as an allowable specific allocation by the terms of the trust. Treas. Reg. 1.652(b)-2(b)(3). These latter allocations are respected, because they have independent economic effect.

D. Expense Allocations

If the trust has deductions that will offset the items of income being distributed, how are these deductions allocated? Code § 652(b) provides that items of deduction entering into the DNI computation shall be allocated in accordance with regulations. The regulations set forth several rules regarding how such deductions are to be allocated.

The Treasury Regulations divide deductions into two broad categories, namely direct expenses and indirect expenses. Deductible expenses directly attributable to a particular category of income must be allocated to that category of income, and offset that income. For example, expenses related to rental property such as repairs, maintenance, property taxes, etc. must be allocated against rental income. Similarly, expenditures directly attributable to a business conducted by a trust must be allocated to the income arising from the business. Treas. Reg. 1.652(b)-3(a).

The second category of expenses are the indirect expenses which are not directly attributable to a specific class of income. The rules are quite favorable here, as they provide that indirect expenses may be allocated to any item of income included in the DNI computation. Treas. Reg. 1.652(b)-3(b).[2] Examples of indirect expenses noted in the regulations include trustee's commissions, safe deposit box rental, and state income and personal property taxes. Treas. Reg. 1.652(b)-3(c).

From a planner's perspective, consider allocating indirect expenses to the most heavily taxed items of income, such as taxable interest income and ordinary dividends, and leave more favorably taxed items of income, such as qualified dividends, unreduced by expenses. Consider that the trust beneficiary may be taxed at a rate as high as 37 percent on some categories of income (such as taxable interest, and short term capital gains) and at a rate as high as 20 percent on other categories of income (such as long-term capital gains and qualified dividends). It may be advisable to not allocate indirect expenses to rental income, despite the relatively high tax rate to which rental income is subject, since rental income is passive activity income, and may be available to offset passive activity losses that the beneficiary might have. Where the beneficiary of a simple trust may be liable to pay the 3.8% net investment

---

2. Even if the governing instrument or applicable local law treats certain deduction items as attributable to income or principal which is not included in DNI, the rule addressing the allocation of indirect expenses is not affected (i.e., they can be allocated in ways that are tax favorable).

income tax, allocation of indirect expenses in the manner suggested here may also reduce the beneficiary's exposure to this tax as well, since the filing threshold for trusts subject to the net investment tax is so much lower than the threshold of this tax for individuals.

There is another rule that must be addressed with respect to indirect expenses, however. Where the trust has tax-exempt income, a portion of the indirect expenses of the trust must be allocated to it. Treas. Reg. 1.652(b)-3(b). This calculation is sometimes referred to as the "disallowance ratio." The amount of tax-exempt income is divided by the amount of income constituting the DNI of the trust to determine the percentage of the indirect expenses that must be allocated to tax-exempt income. More specifically, the disallowance ratio can be expressed in fractional form as follows:

$$\frac{\text{Tax-Exempt Income}}{\text{Gross Amount of Items Comprising DNI}} = \text{Disallowance Ratio}$$

If a simple trust has capital gain income that is allocated to principal, such gains may not be included in the formula for allocating indirect expenses to tax-exempt income (i.e., the denominator of the disallowance ratio does not include capital gains). Rev. Rul. 77-355, 1977-2 C.B. 82. Expenses directly attributable to tax-exempt income may not be offset against that income or any other class of income. Code § 265.

In the event that direct expenses allocable to a particular class of income exceed that class of income to which they relate, the excess deductions may be allocated to any other class of income included in the DNI of the trust, and unlike the rule for indirect expenses, no amount of the excess needs to be allocated to tax-exempt income. There is one exception: excess deductions allocated to tax-exempt income may not be allocated to any other class of income. Treas. Reg. 1.652(b)-3(d).

> **Example:** The Collins Family Trust is a simple trust. For its taxable year, it has $20,000 of dividend income, $10,000 of taxable interest income and $40,000 of rental income. The Trust incurred and paid $12,000 of rental expenses. It also paid a trustee fee of $6,000. The Trust did not receive any tax-exempt income. Since the rental expenses are directly related to the rental income, the entire amount of the rental expenses is allocated to the rental income, reducing the net rental income to $28,000 to be allocated to the beneficiaries. The trustee fee is an indirect expense of the Trust, and may be allocated against any category of income. Since there is no tax-exempt income present for this year of the trust, no allocation to tax-exempt income need be considered. The trustee may decide to allocate the trustee fee pro rata against all of the categories of the trust's income (indeed, many computer software programs make pro rata allocations). Is this the optimal decision? Arguably not. If the dividend income is constituted in whole or in part of qualified dividends, it is suggested that better planning would have

been to allocate none of the trustee fee against the qualified dividends and all of the fee against first the taxable interest and any balance against the rental income. Such a strategic allocation would permit the full amount of the lesser taxed category of income to pass to the Trust beneficiaries.

Example: A simple trust has $10,000 of tax-exempt interest along with $25,000 of dividends and $5,000 of taxable interest. The trust incurred a trustee's fee of $8,000. The amount of tax-exempt interest ($10,000) is divided by the items of income included in the DNI of the trust ($25,000 dividends + $5,000 taxable interest + $10,000 tax-exempt interest = $40,000). That yields a disallowance ratio of 1:4 ($10,000 divided by $40,000), so that one-fourth of the indirect expenses of the trust (here, the $8,000 trustee fee) must be allocated to tax-exempt income, making $2,000 of that trustee fee expense unavailable for allocation against taxable income.

As a general rule, trusts are required to be calendar year taxpayers. Code § 644. Estates and qualified revocable trusts making a Code § 645 election may select fiscal years for reporting their income. However, in the year that a trust terminates, it will have a short tax year (unless it terminates on December 31). If a trust beneficiary has a different tax year from the tax year of the trust, the amount of income to be included by the beneficiary in gross income is based on the income of the trust for the tax year of the trust ending with or within the year of the beneficiary. Treas. Reg. 1.652(c)-1.

Example: The Miller Family Trust is a trust reporting as a calendar year taxpayer and is for the benefit of Melissa Miller. The trust is to terminate when Melissa reaches age 25. Melissa turns age 25 on May 15 of the current year. On May 31, the trust distributes all of its income and assets to Melissa, and plans to file its final fiduciary income tax return as of its May 31 year end. Melissa will report the income she receives from the Trust in the tax year of the Trust's termination. The Trust's year ended within the taxable year of the beneficiary.

Example: The Brown Family Trust made a Code Section 645 election, and is permitted to file as a fiscal year taxpayer. A February 1–January 31 fiscal year is selected. Assume a distribution is made to Diane Brown on 2/28/23. That distribution will be taxable to Diane in the taxable year ending 1/31/24 — so that she will be able to defer paying the income tax on the distribution until she files her 2024 return — in April of 2025.

E. Death of a Beneficiary

Notwithstanding the general rule discussed above that a trust beneficiary includes in his or her income the income deemed distributed to him or her by a trust (or an estate) in the year in which or within which the taxable year of the trust (or an estate) ends, there is a special rule addressing how trust income is to be taxed in the year of the beneficiary's death. In the year of death (assuming the beneficiary is a cash basis reporting taxpayer), the beneficiary is subject to income tax only on the income the beneficiary actually received before his or her death. If income is required to be distributed to the beneficiary, but was not in fact distributed to the beneficiary prior to death, such income is distributed to the estate of the beneficiary or the beneficiary's successor, and must be included in the estate's or successor's gross income as income in respect of a decedent in accordance with the rules of Code § 691. Treas. Reg. 1.652(c)-2. (Income in respect of a decedent is discussed in Chapter 8 of this book.) The Treasury Regulation addressing the timing of the inclusion of income by a decedent and her estate was upheld in *Schimberg v. United States*, 245 F. Supp. 616 (N.D. Ill. 1965), *aff'd*, 365 F.2d 70 (7th Cir. 1966).

> **Example:** The Thomas Family Trust provides that all of the trust income is to be distributed annually or more frequently in equal shares to its two beneficiaries, Amy and Peter Thomas, both of whom are cash basis taxpayers. The Trust reports on a calendar year basis. The Trust typically has earned $80,000 of net fiduciary accounting income and DNI each year and distributed $40,000 each year to both Amy and Peter. In the prior calendar year, Peter died in August, having received income distributions from the Trust amounting to $15,000 by the time of his death. In preparing the fiduciary income tax return for the year of Peter's death, the income of the Trust (once again, a total of $80,000) was allocated as follows: Amy Thomas: $40,000; Peter Thomas: $15,000; the Estate of Peter Thomas: $25,000; The Thomas Family Trust: No taxable income—all was distributed.

The regulations do not address the (unlikely) event that a deceased beneficiary of a simple trust is an accrual basis taxpayer. The IRS, citing Code § 652 as authority, takes the position that if a deceased beneficiary is an accrual basis taxpayer, the income earned by the trust before the death of a taxpayer reporting income using the accrual method accrues on a daily basis, and is included in the final income tax return of that decedent, whether or not it was actually distributed to the beneficiary prior to death. Rev. Rul. 59-346, 1959-2 C.B. 165.

If the beneficiary of a simple trust is not an individual and if the existence of such a beneficiary terminates, the amount of income to be included in the gross income for such beneficiary for its last taxable year will be the sum of all income actually distributed prior to the beneficiary ceasing to exist (the same rule as if the beneficiary were a deceased individual), plus all income required to be distributed prior to the termination of the beneficiary's existence, but actually distributed to the beneficiary's successor in interest. Treas. Reg. 1.652(c)-3.

There is a planning opportunity to consider when the beneficiary of a simple trust is an individual who may be gravely ill. Since taxation turns on the actual distribution (or no distribution) of the income from the trust to the beneficiary in the year of the beneficiary's death, evaluate, if possible, the health and longevity of the beneficiary along with the income and expenses likely to be reported in the final year of the beneficiary's life. If, for example, there are large medical expenses being incurred and minimal income being received, consider accelerating the distribution of trust income so that it is received while the beneficiary is alive and its taxation will be offset by the medical expense deduction. Alternatively, if the trust beneficiary is a high income bracket taxpayer who may have already received significant income in what appears to be the final year of life, and the trust has a successor beneficiary who is a lower-bracket taxpayer, consider postponing distributions from the trust until after the beneficiary's death to possibly take advantage of a successor beneficiary's lower tax bracket.

VI. Common Planning Arrangements — Simple Trusts or Not?

Some commonly used estate planning arrangements may result in the formation of simple trusts. (*See* Chapter 1.) When a person creates a trust for purposes of the marital deduction, be it a qualified terminable interest property trust (QTIP trust) as described in Code § 2056(b)(7) or a general-power-of-appointment trust as described in Code § 2056(b)(5), such trust is potentially a simple trust in all years other than the year of termination (when the trust principal is distributed) because, by definition, these marital-deduction trusts require that the surviving spouse receive distributions at least annually of all of the trust income. If the trustee distributes principal to the surviving spouse in any year, for that year, the trust would be deemed a complex trust due to the principal distribution.

Trusts that are classified as "grantor trusts" (*see* Chapter 6) under Code §§ 671-678 are not considered simple trusts. Grantor trusts are viewed as the "alter egos" of the grantors and subjected to their own tax rules making the grantor of the trust responsible for the income tax. Various trusts used in gift and estate tax planning situations, such as Grantor Retained Annuity Trusts (GRATs), Grantor Retained Unitrusts (GRUTs), Qualified Personal Residence Trusts (QPRTs) and Intentionally Defective Grantor Trusts (IDGTs) are all classified as grantor trusts, and are not viewed as simple trusts.

Certain trusts are permitted to be shareholders of S corporation stock. A Qualified Subchapter S Trust (QSST) has a single beneficiary and is required to distribute all of its income currently to that beneficiary. Code § 1361(d). However, the beneficiary of the QSST is treated as the eligible S corporation shareholder, so that the QSST is viewed as a grantor trust, not as a simple trust.

Another form of trust, the Electing Small Business Trust (ESBT), is also a permitted S corporation shareholder. Code § 1361(e). An ESBT is not required to distribute all of its income currently, so it is not classified as a simple trust.

Questions

1. Once a trust is classified as a simple trust, can it ever be classified as a complex trust?

2. The trustee of a simple trust has declined to distribute the trust income for the current year to X, the named beneficiary of the trust, since Y and Z, the siblings of X, have threatened a lawsuit alleging that X is not the proper trust beneficiary. Is the trust, X, or someone else taxable on the trust income?

3. The Grant Family Trust is a simple trust. It was created September 1 of the prior year. It will file its initial fiduciary income tax return as a calendar year taxpayer. For the tax return being filed for the prior year, how much of the trust's deduction under Code § 642(b) may be claimed?

4. Fred creates a trust that is required to distribute all of its income currently to his adult daughter Wilma. The trustee is authorized to also distribute principal to Wilma for her health and support. No payments are provided for charity. Is the trust a simple trust in a year when no principal payments are made to Wilma?

5. Megan is the sole beneficiary of a simple trust. In the most recently concluded calendar year (Year 1), the trust received $80,000 of fiduciary accounting income, all distributable to Megan. However, she received $20,000 in March, $20,000 in July, $20,000 in October and a final payment of $20,000 on January 20 of the following tax year (Year 2). How much income should Megan report on her income tax return for Year 1? How much income may the trust deduct for Year 1?

6. Mark is the sole beneficiary of a simple trust. In the most recently concluded calendar year (Year 1), the trust received $60,000 of fiduciary accounting income, all distributable to Mark. Unfortunately, Mark died on August 13 of Year 1. As of the date of his death, Mark, a cash basis individual taxpayer, had received payments from the trust of $25,000. How much income must be reported on Mark's income tax return for Year 1? How much income may the trust deduct for Year 1?

7. The Hogan Family Trust is a simple trust. Siblings Nancy and Michael Hogan are equal beneficiaries of the trust income. The trust has DNI for the current year of $200,000, consisting of $100,000 of taxable interest income and $100,000 of qualified dividend income. Nancy and Michael would like all of the interest income to be allocated to Nancy and all of the qualified dividend income to be allocated to Michael, and ask the trustee if this may be done. How should the trustee respond to this inquiry?

8. The Hooper Family Trust is a simple trust. Ben Hooper is an 80% beneficiary of the trust. Pam Hooper and Josh Hooper are each 10% trust beneficiaries. The trust's income for the current year is $100,000, consisting of $60,000 rental income, $30,000 taxable interest income and $10,000 of qualified dividend income. How much income is deemed distributed to each beneficiary, and what is the character of the income to each?

9. A simple trust has $50,000 of taxable income for the current year, consisting of $25,000 of taxable interest income and $25,000 of qualified dividend income. The trust has a single beneficiary entitled to all of the income. The trust has allowable deductions of $20,000, consisting of $10,000 of state income tax, a $5,000 trustee fee, and a $5,000 professional fee. The trustee insists that the allowable fees must reduce each category of income proportionately, resulting in reporting to the beneficiary of $15,000 of taxable interest income and $15,000 of qualified dividend income. Do you agree?

10. Are the following statements True or False?

    a. A trust that is authorized to sprinkle its income among its beneficiaries cannot be a simple trust.

    b. A trust that realizes a capital gain on the sale of an appreciated asset may be a simple trust if the gain is allocated to fiduciary accounting principal and not distributed, and all of the fiduciary accounting income is currently required to be distributed to its beneficiaries.

    c. A trust that is authorized to make distributions to charity may not be considered a simple trust, even if no distributions are made to, used for, or permanently set aside for charity in the current tax year.

    d. A trust that is authorized to accumulate or distribute its income is not classified as a simple trust even if it distributes all of its income in the current year.

11. Alan Green created an irrevocable trust for the benefit of his adult daughter, Rita, and transferred various assets to the trust. In its most recently concluded taxable year (Year 1), the trust had the following items of income:

Interest from Morgan Stanley CD:	$10,000
Qualified dividends from Merck:	$20,000
Long-term capital gain from the sale of Apple stock:	$50,000
Income from State of Florida General Obligation Municipal Bonds:	$20,000

    The trust provides that Rita is to receive all of the trust income. It provides that capital gains are to be allocated to trust principal. There are no payments permitted to charities. The trust did not have any expenses in Year 1. The trust did not terminate in Year 1. For Year 1:

    a. What is the gross income of the trust?

    b. What is the tentative taxable income of the trust?

    c. What is the DNI of the trust?

    d. What is the fiduciary accounting income of the trust?

    e. What is the taxable income of the trust?

    f. How much taxable income must Rita report?

12. In the fact pattern of Question 11 above, assume all of the facts and information as stated above, except add the fact that the trust paid an annual trustee fee of $10,000.

    a. How much, if any, of the trustee fee would be deductible in Year 1?

    b. If deductible, would the deduction be claimed on the trust's return or Rita's return?

PROBLEM No. 4

Estate — Final Year

FEATURES

1. Interest and dividends are present
2. No tax-exempt income present
3. Long-term capital loss present
4. Short-term capital loss carryover present; long-term capital loss carryover present
5. Substantial fiduciary and professional fees present
6. Final year of the estate
7. Income and Losses:

Interest	4,000
Dividends (Qualified)	3,000
Long-Term Capital Loss	(23,000)
Short-Term Capital Loss Carryover	(15,000)
Long-Term Capital Loss Carryover	(25,000)

8. Expenses

Fiduciary Fees	20,000
Professional Fees	25,000

9. **Things to Note:**

    a. Carryover of capital losses to beneficiaries; these total $63,000 (see item 11 on Schedule K-1 reference Codes C and D)
    b. Excess deductions in year of termination (Schedule K-1) – What happens to them? See Internal Revenue Code Section 642(h). The $45,000 of expenses exceed the $7,000 items of income by $38,000 and such excess is carried out to the beneficiary (see item 11 on Schedule K-1 reference Code A)
    c. Estate's exemption is not allocated to beneficiaries
    d. Completion of Schedule B reflecting losses

Form **1041** Department of the Treasury—Internal Revenue Service
U.S. Income Tax Return for Estates and Trusts
Go to www.irs.gov/Form1041 for instructions and the latest information.
2022 OMB No. 1545-0092

A Check all that apply:
- [X] Decedent's estate
- [ ] Simple trust
- [ ] Complex trust
- [ ] Qualified disability trust
- [ ] ESBT (S portion only)
- [ ] Grantor type trust
- [ ] Bankruptcy estate—Ch. 7
- [ ] Bankruptcy estate—Ch. 11
- [ ] Pooled income fund

For calendar year 2022 or fiscal year beginning , 2022, and ending , 20

Name of estate or trust (If a grantor type trust, see the instructions.): PROBLEM 4

C Employer identification number: 22-2222222

Name and title of fiduciary

D Date entity created

Number, street, and room or suite no. (If a P.O. box, see the instructions.)

E Nonexempt charitable and split-interest trusts, check applicable box(es). See instructions.
- [ ] Described in sec. 4947(a)(1). Check here if not a private foundation . . . [ ]
- [ ] Described in sec. 4947(a)(2)

City or town, state or province, country, and ZIP or foreign postal code

B Number of Schedules K-1 attached (see instructions) 1

F Check applicable boxes: [ ] Initial return [X] Final return [ ] Amended return [ ] Net operating loss carryback [ ] Change in trust's name [ ] Change in fiduciary [ ] Change in fiduciary's name [ ] Change in fiduciary's address

G Check here if the estate or filing trust made a section 645 election . . . [ ] Trust TIN

Income	1	Interest income	1	4,000
	2a	Total ordinary dividends	2a	3,000
	b	Qualified dividends allocable to: (1) Beneficiaries ____ (2) Estate or trust 3,000		
	3	Business income or (loss). Attach Schedule C (Form 1040)	3	
	4	Capital gain or (loss). Attach Schedule D (Form 1041)	4	-3,000
	5	Rents, royalties, partnerships, other estates and trusts, etc. Attach Schedule E (Form 1040)	5	
	6	Farm income or (loss). Attach Schedule F (Form 1040)	6	
	7	Ordinary gain or (loss). Attach Form 4797	7	
	8	Other income. List type and amount	8	
	9	**Total income.** Combine lines 1, 2a, and 3 through 8	9	4,000
Deductions	10	Interest. Check if Form 4952 is attached [ ]	10	
	11	Taxes	11	
	12	Fiduciary fees. If only a portion is deductible under section 67(e), see instructions	12	20,000
	13	Charitable deduction (from Schedule A, line 7)	13	
	14	Attorney, accountant, and return preparer fees. If only a portion is deductible under section 67(e), see instructions	14	25,000
	15a	Other deductions (attach schedule). See instructions for deductions allowable under section 67(e)	15a	
	b	Net operating loss deduction. See instructions	15b	
	16	Add lines 10 through 15b	16	45,000
	17	Adjusted total income or (loss). Subtract line 16 from line 9 — 17: -41,000		
	18	Income distribution deduction (from Schedule B, line 15). Attach Schedules K-1 (Form 1041)	18	0
	19	Estate tax deduction including certain generation-skipping taxes (attach computation)	19	
	20	Qualified business income deduction. Attach Form 8995 or 8995-A	20	
	21	Exemption	21	
	22	Add lines 18 through 21	22	0
Tax and Payments	23	Taxable income. Subtract line 22 from line 17. If a loss, see instructions	23	-41,000
	24	**Total tax** (from Schedule G, Part I, line 9)	24	0
	25	Current year net 965 tax liability paid from Form 965-A, Part II, column (k) (see instructions)	25	
	26	**Total payments** (from Schedule G, Part II, line 19)	26	
	27	Estimated tax penalty. See instructions	27	
	28	**Tax due.** If line 26 is smaller than the total of lines 24, 25, and 27, enter amount owed	28	0
	29	**Overpayment.** If line 26 is larger than the total of lines 24, 25, and 27, enter amount overpaid	29	
	30	Amount of line 29 to be: a **Credited to 2023** ; b **Refunded**	30	

Sign Here Under penalties of perjury, I declare that I have examined this return, including accompanying schedules and statements, and to the best of my knowledge and belief, it is true, correct, and complete. Declaration of preparer (other than taxpayer) is based on all information of which preparer has any knowledge.

Signature of fiduciary or officer representing fiduciary | Date | EIN of fiduciary if a financial institution | May the IRS discuss this return with the preparer shown below? See instructions. [ ] Yes [ ] No

Paid Preparer Use Only Print/Type preparer's name | Preparer's signature | Date | Check [ ] if self-employed | PTIN
Firm's name | Firm's EIN
Firm's address | Phone no.

For Paperwork Reduction Act Notice, see the separate instructions. BAA REV 04/19/23 PRO Form **1041** (2022)

Form 1041 (2022) Page 2

Schedule A **Charitable Deduction.** Don't complete for a simple trust or a pooled income fund.

1	Amounts paid or permanently set aside for charitable purposes from gross income. See instructions	1	
2	Tax-exempt income allocable to charitable contributions. See instructions	2	
3	Subtract line 2 from line 1	3	
4	Capital gains for the tax year allocated to corpus and paid or permanently set aside for charitable purposes	4	
5	Add lines 3 and 4	5	
6	Section 1202 exclusion allocable to capital gains paid or permanently set aside for charitable purposes. See instructions	6	
7	**Charitable deduction.** Subtract line 6 from line 5. Enter here and on page 1, line 13	7	

Schedule B **Income Distribution Deduction**

1	Adjusted total income. See instructions	1	-3,000
2	Adjusted tax-exempt interest	2	
3	Total net gain from Schedule D (Form 1041), line 19, column (1). See instructions	3	0
4	Enter amount from Schedule A, line 4 (minus any allocable section 1202 exclusion)	4	
5	Capital gains for the tax year included on Schedule A, line 1. See instructions	5	
6	Enter any gain from page 1, line 4, as a negative number. If page 1, line 4, is a loss, enter the loss as a positive number	6	3,000
7	**Distributable net income.** Combine lines 1 through 6. If zero or less, enter -0-	7	0
8	If a complex trust, enter accounting income for the tax year as determined under the governing instrument and applicable local law 8		
9	Income required to be distributed currently	9	
10	Other amounts paid, credited, or otherwise required to be distributed	10	
11	Total distributions. Add lines 9 and 10. If greater than line 8, see instructions	11	
12	Enter the amount of tax-exempt income included on line 11	12	
13	Tentative income distribution deduction. Subtract line 12 from line 11	13	
14	Tentative income distribution deduction. Subtract line 2 from line 7. If zero or less, enter -0-	14	0
15	**Income distribution deduction.** Enter the smaller of line 13 or line 14 here and on page 1, line 18	15	0

Schedule G **Tax Computation and Payments** (see instructions)

Part I — Tax Computation

1	**Tax:**				
a	Tax on taxable income. See instructions	1a			
b	Tax on lump-sum distributions. Attach Form 4972	1b			
c	Alternative minimum tax (from Schedule I (Form 1041), line 54)	1c	0		
d	**Total.** Add lines 1a through 1c			1d	0
2a	Foreign tax credit. Attach Form 1116	2a			
b	General business credit. Attach Form 3800	2b			
c	Credit for prior year minimum tax. Attach Form 8801	2c			
d	Bond credits. Attach Form 8912	2d			
e	**Total credits.** Add lines 2a through 2d			2e	
3	Subtract line 2e from line 1d. If zero or less, enter -0-			3	0
4	Tax on the ESBT portion of the trust (from ESBT Tax Worksheet, line 17). See instructions			4	
5	Net investment income tax from Form 8960, line 21			5	0
6	Recapture taxes. Check if from: ☐ Form 4255 ☐ Form 8611			6	
7	Household employment taxes. Attach Schedule H (Form 1040)			7	
8	Other taxes and amounts due			8	
9	**Total tax.** Add lines 3 through 8. Enter here and on page 1, line 24			9	0

Part II — Payments

10	2022 estimated tax payments and amount applied from 2021 return	10	
11	Estimated tax payments allocated to beneficiaries (from Form 1041-T)	11	
12	Subtract line 11 from line 10	12	
13	Tax paid with Form 7004. See instructions	13	
14	Federal income tax withheld. If any is from Form(s) 1099, check here ☐	14	
15	Current year net 965 tax liability from Form 965-A, Part I, column (f) (see instructions)	15	
16	Other payments: **a** Form 2439 ______ ; **b** Form 4136 ______ ; **Total**	16c	
17	Credit for qualified sick and family leave wages for leave taken before April 1, 2021	17	
18	Credit for qualified sick and family leave wages for leave taken after March 31, 2021, and before October 1, 2021	18	
19	**Total payments.** Add lines 12 through 15 and 16c through 18. Enter here and on page 1, line 26	19	

REV 03/25/23 PRO Form **1041** (2022)

SCHEDULE D (Form 1041)

Department of the Treasury Internal Revenue Service

Capital Gains and Losses

Attach to Form 1041, Form 5227, or Form 990-T.
Use Form 8949 to list your transactions for lines 1b, 2, 3, 8b, 9, and 10.
Go to *www.irs.gov/F1041* for instructions and the latest information.

OMB No. 1545-0092

2022

Name of estate or trust: PROBLEM 2

Employer identification number: 11-1111111

Did you dispose of any investment(s) in a qualified opportunity fund during the tax year? . . . . ☐ Yes ☒ No
If "Yes," attach Form 8949 and see its instructions for additional requirements for reporting your gain or loss.

Note: *Form 5227 filers need to complete **only** Parts I and II.*

Part I Short-Term Capital Gains and Losses—Generally Assets Held 1 Year or Less (see instructions)

See instructions for how to figure the amounts to enter on the lines below. This form may be easier to complete if you round off cents to whole dollars.	(d) Proceeds (sales price)	(e) Cost (or other basis)	(g) Adjustments to gain or loss from Form(s) 8949, Part I, line 2, column (g)	(h) Gain or (loss) Subtract column (e) from column (d) and combine the result with column (g)
1a Totals for all short-term transactions reported on Form 1099-B for which basis was reported to the IRS and for which you have no adjustments (see instructions). However, if you choose to report all these transactions on Form 8949, leave this line blank and go to line 1b .				
1b Totals for all transactions reported on Form(s) 8949 with **Box A** checked				
2 Totals for all transactions reported on Form(s) 8949 with **Box B** checked				
3 Totals for all transactions reported on Form(s) 8949 with **Box C** checked				

4 Short-term capital gain or (loss) from Forms 4684, 6252, 6781, and 8824	4	
5 Net short-term gain or (loss) from partnerships, S corporations, and other estates or trusts	5	
6 Short-term capital loss carryover. Enter the amount, if any, from line 9 of the 2021 Capital Loss Carryover Worksheet	6	( )
7 **Net short-term capital gain or (loss).** Combine lines 1a through 6 in column (h). Enter here and on Part III, line 17, column (3)	7	

Part II Long-Term Capital Gains and Losses—Generally Assets Held More Than 1 Year (see instructions)

See instructions for how to figure the amounts to enter on the lines below. This form may be easier to complete if you round off cents to whole dollars.	(d) Proceeds (sales price)	(e) Cost (or other basis)	(g) Adjustments to gain or loss from Form(s) 8949, Part II, line 2, column (g)	(h) Gain or (loss) Subtract column (e) from column (d) and combine the result with column (g)
8a Totals for all long-term transactions reported on Form 1099-B for which basis was reported to the IRS and for which you have no adjustments (see instructions). However, if you choose to report all these transactions on Form 8949, leave this line blank and go to line 8b .	50,000.	0.		50,000.
8b Totals for all transactions reported on Form(s) 8949 with **Box D** checked				
9 Totals for all transactions reported on Form(s) 8949 with **Box E** checked				
10 Totals for all transactions reported on Form(s) 8949 with **Box F** checked.				

11 Long-term capital gain or (loss) from Forms 2439, 4684, 6252, 6781, and 8824	11	
12 Net long-term gain or (loss) from partnerships, S corporations, and other estates or trusts	12	
13 Capital gain distributions	13	
14 Gain from Form 4797, Part I	14	
15 Long-term capital loss carryover. Enter the amount, if any, from line 14 of the 2021 Capital Loss Carryover Worksheet	15	( )
16 **Net long-term capital gain or (loss).** Combine lines 8a through 15 in column (h). Enter here and on Part III, line 18a, column (3)	16	50,000.

For Paperwork Reduction Act Notice, see the Instructions for Form 1041. Cat. No. 11376V **Schedule D (Form 1041) 2022**

BAA REV 03/25/23 PRO

Schedule D (Form 1041) 2022 Page 2

Part III Summary of Parts I and II
Caution: *Read the instructions* ***before*** *completing this part.*

			(1) Beneficiaries' (see instr.)	(2) Estate's or trust's	(3) Total
17	**Net short-term gain or (loss)**	17	-12,000	-3,000	-15,000
18	**Net long-term gain or (loss):**				
a	Total for year	18a	-48,000	0	-48,000
b	Unrecaptured section 1250 gain (see line 18 of the worksheet)	18b			
c	28% rate gain	18c			
19	**Total net gain or (loss).** Combine lines 17 and 18a	19	-60,000	-3,000	-63,000

Note: *If line 19, column (3), is a net gain, enter the gain on Form 1041, line 4 (or Schedule A (Form 990-T), Part I, line 4a). If lines 18a and 19, column (2), are net gains, go to Part V, and* ***don't*** *complete Part IV. If line 19, column (3), is a net loss, complete Part IV and the* ***Capital Loss Carryover Worksheet****, as necessary.*

Part IV Capital Loss Limitation

20 Enter here and enter as a (loss) on Form 1041, line 4 (or Schedule A (Form 990-T), Part I, line 4c, if a trust), the **smaller** of:

a The loss on line 19, column (3) **or b** $3,000 . . . . . 20 (3,000)

Note: *If the loss on line 19, column (3), is more than $3,000,* ***or*** *if Form 1041, page 1, line 23 (or Form 990-T, Part I, line 11), is a loss, complete the* ***Capital Loss Carryover Worksheet*** *in the instructions to figure your capital loss carryover.*

Part V Tax Computation Using Maximum Capital Gains Rates

Form 1041 filers. Complete this part **only** if both lines 18a and 19 in column (2) are gains, or an amount is entered in Part I or Part II and there is an entry on Form 1041, line 2b(2), **and** Form 1041, line 23, is more than zero.

Caution: *Skip this part and complete the* ***Schedule D Tax Worksheet*** *in the instructions if:*

- *Either line 18b, col. (2), or line 18c, col. (2), is more than zero, or*
- *Both Form 1041, line 2b(1), and Form 4952, line 4g, are more than zero, or*
- *There are amounts on lines 4e and 4g of Form 4952.*

Form 990-T trusts. Complete this part **only** if both lines 18a and 19 are gains, or qualified dividends are included in income in Part I of Form 990-T, **and** Form 990-T, Part I, line 11, is more than zero. Skip this part and complete the **Schedule D Tax Worksheet** in the instructions if either line 18b, col. (2), or line 18c, col. (2), is more than zero.

21	Enter taxable income from Form 1041, line 23 (or Form 990-T, Part I, line 11)	21	
22	Enter the **smaller** of line 18a or 19 in column (2) but not less than zero	22	
23	Enter the estate's or trust's qualified dividends from Form 1041, line 2b(2) (or enter the qualified dividends included in income in Part I of Form 990-T)	23	
24	Add lines 22 and 23	24	
25	If the estate or trust is filing Form 4952, enter the amount from line 4g; otherwise, enter -0-	25	
26	Subtract line 25 from line 24. If zero or less, enter -0-	26	
27	Subtract line 26 from line 21. If zero or less, enter -0-	27	
28	Enter the **smaller** of the amount on line 21 or $2,800	28	
29	Enter the **smaller** of the amount on line 27 or line 28	29	
30	Subtract line 29 from line 28. If zero or less, enter -0-. This amount is taxed at 0%	30	
31	Enter the **smaller** of line 21 or line 26	31	
32	Subtract line 30 from line 26	32	
33	Enter the **smaller** of line 21 or $13,700	33	
34	Add lines 27 and 30	34	
35	Subtract line 34 from line 33. If zero or less, enter -0-	35	
36	Enter the **smaller** of line 32 or line 35	36	
37	Multiply line 36 by 15% (0.15)	37	
38	Enter the amount from line 31	38	
39	Add lines 30 and 36	39	
40	Subtract line 39 from line 38. If zero or less, enter -0-	40	
41	Multiply line 40 by 20% (0.20)	41	
42	Figure the tax on the amount on line 27. Use the 2022 Tax Rate Schedule for Estates and Trusts (see the Schedule G instructions in the Instructions for Form 1041)	42	
43	Add lines 37, 41, and 42	43	
44	Figure the tax on the amount on line 21. Use the 2022 Tax Rate Schedule for Estates and Trusts (see the Schedule G instructions in the Instructions for Form 1041)	44	
45	**Tax on all taxable income.** Enter the **smaller** of line 43 or line 44 here and on Form 1041, Schedule G, Part I, line 1a (or Form 990-T, Part II, line 2)	45	

REV 03/25/23 PRO **Schedule D (Form 1041) 2022**

661117

☒ Final K-1 ☐ Amended K-1 OMB No. 1545-0092

Schedule K-1 (Form 1041) **2022**

Department of the Treasury
Internal Revenue Service

For calendar year 2022, or tax year

beginning / / 2022 ending / /

Beneficiary's Share of Income, Deductions, Credits, etc.

See back of form and instructions.

Part I Information About the Estate or Trust

A Estate's or trust's employer identification number

B Estate's or trust's name

PROBLEM 4

C Fiduciary's name, address, city, state, and ZIP code

D ☐ Check if Form 1041-T was filed and enter the date it was filed

E ☒ Check if this is the final Form 1041 for the estate or trust

Part II Information About the Beneficiary

F Beneficiary's identifying number

123-45-6789

G Beneficiary's name, address, city, state, and ZIP code

Joe Doe
111 Main Street

Columbus OH 43212

H ☒ Domestic beneficiary ☐ Foreign beneficiary

Part III Beneficiary's Share of Current Year Income, Deductions, Credits, and Other Items

1	Interest income	11	Final year deductions	
			A	38,000.
2a	Ordinary dividends		B	0.
2b	Qualified dividends		C	15,000.
3	Net short-term capital gain		D	48,000.
4a	Net long-term capital gain			
4b	28% rate gain	12	Alternative minimum tax adjustment	
4c	Unrecaptured section 1250 gain			
5	Other portfolio and nonbusiness income			
6	Ordinary business income			
7	Net rental real estate income	13	Credits and credit recapture	
8	Other rental income			
9	Directly apportioned deductions	14	Other information	
10	Estate tax deduction			

*See attached statement for additional information.

Note: A statement must be attached showing the beneficiary's share of income and directly apportioned deductions from each business, rental real estate, and other rental activity.

For IRS Use Only

For Paperwork Reduction Act Notice, see the Instructions for Form 1041. www.irs.gov/Form1041 BAA REV 03/25/23 PRO Schedule K-1 (Form 1041) 2022

Schedule K-1 (Form 1041) 2022 Page **2**

This list identifies the codes used on Schedule K-1 for beneficiaries and provides summarized reporting information for beneficiaries who file Form 1040 or 1040-SR. For detailed reporting and filing information, see the Instructions for Schedule K-1 (Form 1041) for a Beneficiary Filing Form 1040 or 1040-SR and the instructions for your income tax return.

	Report on
1. Interest income	Form 1040 or 1040-SR, line 2b
2a. Ordinary dividends	Form 1040 or 1040-SR, line 3b
2b. Qualified dividends	Form 1040 or 1040-SR, line 3a
3. Net short-term capital gain	Schedule D, line 5
4a. Net long-term capital gain	Schedule D, line 12
4b. 28% rate gain	28% Rate Gain Worksheet, line 4 (Schedule D Instructions)
4c. Unrecaptured section 1250 gain	Unrecaptured Section 1250 Gain Worksheet, line 11 (Schedule D Instructions)
5. Other portfolio and nonbusiness income	Schedule E, line 33, column (f)
6. Ordinary business income	Schedule E, line 33, column (d) or (f)
7. Net rental real estate income	Schedule E, line 33, column (d) or (f)
8. Other rental income	Schedule E, line 33, column (d) or (f)
9. Directly apportioned deductions	
Code	
A Depreciation	Form 8582 or Schedule E, line 33, column (c) or (e)
B Depletion	Form 8582 or Schedule E, line 33, column (c) or (e)
C Amortization	Form 8582 or Schedule E, line 33, column (c) or (e)
10. Estate tax deduction	Schedule A, line 16
11. Final year deductions	
A Excess deductions – Section 67(e) expenses	Schedule 1 (Form 1040), line 24k (also see the beneficiary's instructions)
B Excess deductions – Non-miscellaneous itemized deductions	See the beneficiary's instructions
C Short-term capital loss carryover	Schedule D, line 5
D Long-term capital loss carryover	Schedule D, line 12; line 5 of the wksht. for Sch. D, line 18; and line 16 of the wksht. for Sch. D, line 19
E Net operating loss carryover — regular tax	Schedule 1 (Form 1040), line 8a
F Net operating loss carryover — minimum tax	Form 6251, line 2f
12. Alternative minimum tax (AMT) items	
A Adjustment for minimum tax purposes	Form 6251, line 2j
B AMT adjustment attributable to qualified dividends	See the beneficiary's instructions and the Instructions for Form 6251
C AMT adjustment attributable to net short-term capital gain	
D AMT adjustment attributable to net long-term capital gain	
E AMT adjustment attributable to unrecaptured section 1250 gain	
F AMT adjustment attributable to 28% rate gain	
G Accelerated depreciation	
H Depletion	
I Amortization	
J Exclusion items	2023 Form 8801

13. Credits and credit recapture	
Code	*Report on*
A Credit for estimated taxes	Form 1040 or 1040-SR, line 26
B Credit for backup withholding	Form 1040 or 1040-SR, line 25c
C Low-income housing credit	See the beneficiary's instructions
D Rehabilitation credit and energy credit	
E Other qualifying investment credit	
F Work opportunity credit	
G Credit for small employer health insurance premiums	
H Biofuel producer credit	
I Credit for increasing research activities	
J Renewable electricity, refined coal, and Indian coal production credit	
K Empowerment zone employment credit	
L Indian employment credit	
M Orphan drug credit	
N Credit for employer-provided child care and facilities	
O Biodiesel and renewable diesel fuels credit	
P Credit to holders of tax credit bonds	
Q Credit for employer differential wage payments	
R Recapture of credits	
Z Other credits	
14. Other information	
A Tax-exempt interest	Form 1040 or 1040-SR, line 2a
B Foreign taxes	Schedule 3 (Form 1040), line 1 or Schedule A, line 6
C Reserved for future use	
D Reserved for future use	
E Net investment income	Form 4952, line 4a
F Gross farm and fishing income	Schedule E, line 42
G Foreign trading gross receipts (IRC 942(a))	See the Instructions for Form 8873
H Adjustment for section 1411 net investment income or deductions	Form 8960, line 7 (also see the beneficiary's instructions)
I Section 199A information	See the beneficiary's instructions
Z Other information	See the beneficiary's instructions

Note: If you are a beneficiary who does not file a Form 1040 or 1040-SR, see instructions for the type of income tax return you are filing.

REV 03/25/23 PRO

Chapter 5

Complex Trusts and Estates

Internal Revenue Code: Sections 651, 652, 661, 662, 663(a)(1), 663(b), 643(e), 1361(d), 1361(e)

Regulations: Various regulations applicable to the above Code sections

I. Background

Subchapter J distinguishes among three types of trusts—simple trusts, complex trusts, and grantor trusts. Estates generally follow the same rules as those for complex trusts. This chapter focuses on the operation of complex trusts.

Identifying a trust as a simple or complex trust is important for one main reason: the rules governing the distribution deduction allowed a trust or estate and the amount that a beneficiary has to account for on his or her income tax return is different for complex trusts than for simple trusts. As indicated in Chapter 4, a "simple trust" is a trust that is required by its governing instrument to distribute its accounting income at least annually, does not provide for any charitable distributions, and no distributions of principal are actually made. A "complex trust" is a trust that does not meet the definition of a simple trust: it may accumulate income and make discretionary income distributions, corpus distributions, or charitable contributions.

Different Code sections govern the operations of simple and complex trusts. The distribution deduction allowed to simple trusts is determined under Code § 651 while the beneficiary income inclusion amount is determined under Code § 652. In contrast, the distribution deduction allowed to complex trusts is determined under Code § 661 while the beneficiary income inclusion amount is determined under Code § 662. These latter two Code sections are the focus of this chapter.

Section II discusses the distribution deduction that Code § 661 affords complex trusts. Section III then discusses the corresponding beneficiary income inclusion amount under Code § 662. Finally, Section IV concludes by examining special trusts that may hold S corporation stock, namely, (A) qualified Subchapter S trusts (QSSTs) and (B) electing small business trusts (ESBTs).

II. Distribution Deductions

When it comes to the distribution deduction, complex trusts adhere to the following rule: the Code permits a deduction for the sum of (i) trust accounting income required to be distributed currently (including any item—such as an annuity—payable out of income or corpus to the extent actually paid out of income) and (ii) any other amounts properly paid or credited or required to be distributed for the taxable year. Code § 661(a). However, the deduction otherwise permitted under Code § 661(a) cannot exceed DNI as computed under Code § 643(a).

Because complex trusts can be required to distribute accounting income as well as make discretionary distributions of income and principal, complex trust distributions are generally referred to as Tier 1 distributions and Tier 2 distributions, each of which are explored below.

A. Tier 1 Distributions

As determined under the terms of the will or trust instrument and applicable state law, a deduction is allowed for "income required to be distributed currently." Treas. Reg. 1.661(a)-2(b) and 1.651(a)-2. For these purposes, *income* means fiduciary accounting income or FAI (sometimes also referred to as "trust accounting income" or TAI) as opposed to gross income or taxable income. In general, the trustee must be under a duty to distribute income within the taxable year. If such a duty exists, the trust is allowed a deduction even if distributions are not made within the taxable year or are not made at all. Treas. Reg. 1.651(a)-2(a). By the same token, the trust beneficiary has income inclusion. This should be familiar, because it is the same rule that applies to simple trusts discussed in Chapter 4. DNI is deemed distributed first to the Tier 1 beneficiaries. Only if DNI remains is such DNI deemed distributed to the Tier 2 beneficiaries.

> **Example:** A trust requires all of its income be distributed to A. The trust's income for Year 1 is $10,000. The trustee makes $2,500 quarterly distributions of the trust's accounting income to A on March 15, June 15, September 15, and the following January 15. At the end of the year, the trustee informs A that he is required to report $10,000 of income on his income tax return. A disputes the trustee's conclusion that $10,000 must be included in his income, because he only received $7,500 during the year and received $2,500 in the following year. The trustee informs A that since the trust requires income to be distributed, he is taxable on the entire $10,000 trust accounting income regardless of whether A actually received it in Year 1 or not.

What does the term "income required to be distributed currently" mean? As already stated in Chapter 4, Treas. Reg. 1.651-2(a) provides that an amount of income is required to be distributed currently if the trustee is under an unconditional obligation to pay it out during the same taxable year in which it is received. Furthermore, Treasury Regulation 1.651(a)-2(b) states that, for the purposes of Sections 651, 652, 661, and 662, the income will be required to be distributed currently even though the trustee has discretion to pick and choose among a class of beneficiaries as to whom and how much each shall receive as long as the trustee is required to pay it all out before the end of the taxable year.

> **Example:** A trust has three beneficiaries—A, B, and C. The trust has $12,000 of trust accounting income. The trust instrument requires all the trust accounting income be distributed currently among the three beneficiaries as the trustee in his discretion determines. The trustee, in the exercise of discretion, distributes $3,000 to A, $9,000 to B, and nothing to C. Despite the fact that the trustee had discretion to distribute income among the three beneficiaries, the trust terms meet the definition of "income required to be distributed currently."

What if the trustee withholds income otherwise required to be distributed pending litigation? Is the income beneficiary still taxed on that income? Again, as was previously pointed out in Chapter 4, the answer is "Yes!"

> **Example:** A trust says the trustee is required to distribute all the income currently in equal shares to A and B, children of the grantor. The trust has $10,000 of income in the current year. The trustee doesn't distribute the income, because he is sued by another child, C, who hasn't been provided for in the trust and who claims that the trust is illegal. Pending the litigation to determine trust validity, the trustee decides to withhold the $10,000 payment. Despite this, A and B will nevertheless be taxed on the income. In Rev. Rul. 62-147, 1962-2 C.B. 151, the IRS ruled that even when the trustee in good faith withholds payment of income required to be distributed currently, the beneficiaries are still taxed on that income, regardless of the fact that the trustee in good faith withheld payment pending the outcome of litigation.

B. Tier 2 Distributions

In addition to receiving a deduction for income required to be distributed, a complex trust is also allowed a deduction for any "amounts properly paid or credited or required to be distributed." Code § 661(a)(2). The term "any other amounts properly paid or credited or required to be distributed" includes all amounts properly paid, credited, or required to be distributed by a trust or estate during the taxable year other than income required to be distributed currently. Such distributions often are referred to as Tier 2 distributions.

"Other amounts" properly paid, credited or required to be distributed refers to a discretionary distribution of income or a discretionary or mandatory distribution of principal. Distribution of these amounts will result in a deduction for the trust or estate under § 661(a)(2) and, correspondingly, income inclusion to the beneficiary under § 662(a)(2). The amount of this deduction cannot exceed the DNI of the trust reduced by the amount of the Tier 1 distribution. Said another way, if the Tier 1 distribution equaled or exceeded DNI, the trust receives no Tier 2 distribution, because the trust has no remaining DNI after the Tier 1 distribution.

Examples of amounts properly paid, credited or required to be distributed include the following:

- Discretionary income or principal payments. Treas. Reg. 1.661(a)-2(c).
- Annuity payments made from principal. Treas. Reg. 1.661(a)-2(c).
- Amounts used to discharge or satisfy a beneficiary's legal obligation. Treas. Reg. 1.661(a)-2(c).
- Amounts paid pursuant to court order or decree. Treas. Reg. 1.661(a)-2(e).
- Payments in kind, i.e., distributions of trust property other than cash. Treas. Reg. 1.661(a)-2(f).

An amount applied for a beneficiary, i.e., that is required to be used or is in fact used for the beneficiary's benefit, constitutes a distribution even though the beneficiary never acquires dominion and control over the payment in question.

> **Example:** A trust says that the trustee is authorized to pay funds to or for the benefit of a beneficiary. The trustee pays for the beneficiary's food, clothing, rent, and vacation bills. The payment of these expenses for the benefit of the beneficiary constitutes a distribution to the beneficiary. The trust is entitled to a distribution deduction, and the beneficiary is required to report the income on his income tax return computed in accordance with the rules of sections 661 and 662.

Note that Tier 2 distributions can be made in cash or in-kind. In the case of discretionary distributions, gains or losses are generally not recognized unless the trust elects to recognize gain under Code § 643(e)(3). Treas. Reg. 1.661(a)-2(f). However, in-kind distributions will result in gain realization automatically without the requirement of any election if the distribution consists of appreciated property made in satisfaction of a right to receive (i) a specific dollar amount, (ii) specific property other than that distributed, or (iii) income as defined in § 643(b) and the applicable regulations. Treas. Reg. 1.661(a)-2(f). The amount of any gain would be measured by the fair market value of the property distributed determined at the time of distribution, less its adjusted basis for tax purposes at the time of distribution. *Kenan v. Commissioner*, 114 F.2d 217 (2d Cir. 1940). Losses generally cannot be recognized because of the related party rules of Code § 267(b)(13).[1]

---

1. As discussed later in the chapter, note that with respect to in-kind distributions for which gain is not automatically recognized and no election must be made under section 643(e), the amount deductible is, generally, the lesser of (i) the basis of distributed property in the hands of the beneficiary or (ii) the fair market value of the property. Code § 643(e).

There are three limitations on distributions that otherwise might appear to constitute Tier 2 distributions. These limitations are found in Code § 663. This Code section provides that no deductions are allowed for the following:

- amounts properly paid or credited under the governing instrument as a gift or bequest of a specific sum of money or specific property payable in three or fewer installments are not allowed as a deduction under section 661;[2]
- "amounts properly paid or credited or required to be distributed" to a charitable beneficiary that qualifies for the charitable deduction under section 642(c) are not allowed as a deduction under section 661; and
- amounts paid, credited, or distributed in the taxable year but which were allowed as deductions under section 651 or 661 for a preceding taxable year are not allowed as a deduction under section 661 for the current taxable year.

Section 661 allows a deduction for amounts that are "properly credited" to a beneficiary. Transfers shown by book entries, on the annual work papers for the entity, and reflected on the tax return have been held not sufficient to treat funds as credited for purposes of § 661. For an amount to be credited to a beneficiary, such amount should be beyond recall by the fiduciary and be available for distribution upon demand by the beneficiary.

Estate of Johnson v. Commissioner

88 T.C. 225 (1987)

The Commissioner determined deficiencies in petitioner's Federal income tax for the taxable years 1980 and 1981 as follows:

Year	Deficiency
1980	$269,963
1981	109,165

Petitioner claims an overpayment in Federal income tax in the amounts of $712,045 for 1980 and $93,198 for 1981. The issues for decision are (1) whether petitioner correctly reported capital gains realized from its collection on certain notes in 1980 and 1981; and (2) whether petitioner properly deducted as income distributions in 1980 and 1981 amounts credited to the Estate of Willard T.C. Johnson.

Findings of Fact

Some of the facts have been stipulated and are so found. Petitioner is the Estate of Keith Wold Johnson (sometimes hereinafter referred to as "decedent's estate"). Petitioner's address was New York, New York, at the time its petition was filed. Petitioner timely filed fiduciary income tax returns for the taxable years 1980 and 1981.

2. However, a gift or bequest that can be paid only out of income would be deductible under Code § 661(a)(2). *See* Code § 663(a)(1).

Decedent, Keith Wold Johnson, was majority shareholder of American Video Corp. (AVC) at the time of his death. Toward the end of 1974, AVC required additional funding and sought a loan from the Union Commerce Bank of Cleveland (the bank). The bank agreed to loan the money to AVC only if decedent personally guaranteed the loan and assigned a life insurance policy on his life to the bank as collateral.

To induce decedent to enter into a guarantee agreement with the bank, AVC entered into an indemnity agreement with decedent on December 6, 1974. Decedent subsequently entered into a guarantee agreement with the bank. In accordance with the terms of the guarantee agreement, decedent purchased two adjustable term life insurance policies on his life from the Occidental Life Insurance Co. of California (Occidental) in the total amount of $7 million. Decedent designated the bank as beneficiary on the policies "as their interest may appear, balance, if any to the Estate of the insured." Both policies were issued on February 1, 1975, and assigned to the bank as collateral security for the loans to AVC. If decedent were to die before the AVC notes were repaid, the guarantee agreement provided that the bank would receive the proceeds from the insurance policies and assign its interest in the AVC notes to decedent's estate to the extent the proceeds satisfied the notes.

Decedent died on March 28, 1975, of acute cocaine poisoning. Because of the circumstances of his death, Occidental claimed that it had a complete defense to payment on the insurance policies and a dispute arose between Occidental on one side and the bank and petitioner on the other. On January 29, 1976, the bank and petitioner entered into an agreement under which the bank would release petitioner from liability on the loan to AVC and the parties would work together to collect the insurance proceeds. On June 14, 1976, Occidental and the bank settled their dispute. Pursuant to their agreement, Occidental paid the bank a net amount of $4,200,000. The bank then assigned to petitioner an interest in the AVC notes to the extent of $4,200,000.

Petitioner filed an estate tax return on or about June 17, 1976. On the return, petitioner attributed no value to the life insurance policies on decedent's life. In a statement attached to the return petitioner explained:

> Since the $4,200,000 of net insurance proceeds ultimately receivable was pledged as security for the AVC indebtedness to Union Commerce and was paid to the latter, the only right of the decedent or his estate at the date of death was a possible right to a subordinated participation in Union Commerce's loans to AVC.
>
> The value as of the date of decedent's death of a $4,200,000 subordinated participation in Union Commerce's loans to AVC under the terms of the Guarantee Agreement of December 6, 1974 has been appraised by Lehman Brothers, New York City, as having negligible value.

On October 10, 1978 respondent sent petitioner a Report of Estate Tax Audit Changes. The report proposed an increase in the value of petitioner's possible right to subordinated participation in the bank's loans to AVC from $0 to $2,100,000. On June 25, 1979, the parties entered into a closing agreement pursuant to section 7121.[3] The agreement established a value for estate tax purposes and an unadjusted basis for income tax purposes of $600,000 for petitioner's right to subordinated participation in the bank's loans to AVC.

AVC became financially solvent after substantial capital investment by a subsequent owner. In 1980 and 1981, AVC paid the balance of its debt to the bank and to petitioner. Petitioner received $3,699,526 from AVC in 1980 and $421,329 in 1981. On its fiduciary income tax return for 1980, petitioner reported a basis of $520,755 for its interest in the AVC notes. This amount represented the $600,000 unadjusted basis set in the closing agreement, less $79,245 received from AVC in 1979. Petitioner claimed a $0 basis in the notes on its fiduciary income tax return for 1981. Petitioner reported capital gains in the amount of $3,178,771 for 1980 and $421,329 for 1981.

Petitioner subsequently concluded that it was entitled to increase its basis in the AVC notes by the $4,200,000 that Occidental paid on the insurance policies. Petitioner filed amended returns claiming refunds of capital gains taxes paid in 1980 and 1981 on the repayment of the AVC notes. In his notice of deficiency dated March 21, 1985, respondent rejected petitioner's refund claims.

There are five residuary beneficiaries of decedent's estate: Willard T.C. Johnson (Willard), Elizabeth R. Johnson, Robert W. Johnson IV, Christopher Johnson, and Sheila Johnson Brutsch. Willard survived decedent but died soon after him, and Willard's estate was entitled to his distributive share of decedent's estate. The estates of decedent and Willard have the same executors and accountants.

The sole beneficiaries of Willard's estate are charitable organizations. In his will, Willard bequeathed $100,000 to the Lawrenceville School in Lawrenceville, N.J. The residue of his estate was to be transferred to a charitable foundation, the Willard T.C. Johnson Foundation, Inc. (the foundation), to be established by the executors of the estate. The estate transferred $100,000 to the Lawrenceville School on December 2, 1976, and organized the Foundation prior to 1980. The executors of Willard's estate were also the directors of the foundation.

The accounting firm of Main Hurdman or its predecessor has at all times served as accountant for both estates. Richard Stone, C.P.A., has been the partner charged with reviewing the estates' tax compliance. In this capacity he worked with Miles Rosenberg, C.P.A., a senior partner in Main Hurdman, and Samuel Klein, an executor of the two estates. Rosenberg is now deceased.

In the early part of 1976, Klein met with Rosenberg to discuss tax matters relating to petitioner, and particularly how to make annual distributions of income from petitioner to Willard's estate. On Rosenberg's advice, Klein instructed the accountants to transfer funds by making book entries on the records of each estate each

3. All section references are to the Internal Revenue Code of 1954 as amended and in effect during the years in issue.

year crediting a 20 percent share of petitioner's income to Willard's estate. The entries were characterized as deemed distributions from petitioner to Willard's estate. In the course of preparing fiduciary income tax returns for petitioner and for Willard's estate for each year, accountants at Main Hurdman prepared workpapers annually for each estate showing transfers of income from decedent's estate to Willard's estate. The workpapers are the only documentary evidence of income allocation from petitioner to Willard's estate.

Petitioner elected to credit Willard's account through entries on the workpapers rather than actually transferring funds because of the significant contingent liabilities and other contingencies that prevented it from settling the estate. Klein testified that the executors would not make any cash distributions until they had collected all of petitioner's assets and settled its liabilities. There had been no cash transferred between the estates as of the end of 1981 and Willard's estate had not transferred any funds to the foundation. As of the close of 1981 petitioner had not made distributions of income to any of its other beneficiaries.

For each of the years 1976 through 1981 petitioner deducted as a distribution the amount of book entry credited to Willard's estate. Willard's estate included the distributions in gross income but because all of its income was irrevocably vested in a charitable foundation, it had no income tax liability.

The workpaper showing petitioner's transfer of income to Willard's estate for 1981 was prepared in March 1982. The practice of the accounting firm was to prepare tax workpapers after the close of the taxable year.

There is no date on the workpaper for 1980 and no indication of who prepared it, but Stone testified that workpapers were prepared by his staff members in the ordinary course of business. The workpaper for petitioner for 1980 was prepared on a copy of the workpaper for 1979. The year 1979 and the name of the preparer were crossed out, and the year 1980 and new information were inserted. The entries on the work paper were made in pencil and, in some places, numbers had been erased. Stone did not know who had made the erasures or what had been erased but stated that entries on workpapers were always made in pencil. The workpaper was found in petitioner's file with other 1980 work papers.

At the time of his death, decedent had amassed significant contingent assets and liabilities. Numerous disputes arose concerning decedent's liabilities and, as a result, petitioner had not been able to make principal distributions to any of its beneficiaries by the end of 1981. The many outstanding contingent liabilities and other contingencies made it reasonable for decedent's estate to be kept open through 1981.

The executors also kept Willard's estate open through 1981. There were no unsettled claims to which Willard's estate was subject in 1980 or 1981, and 100 percent of the income and corpus of the estate was irrevocably vested in the foundation. The executors, however, had yet to collect the interest of Willard's estate in petitioner, which was a substantial asset of perhaps $2 million. The executors determined that they could not close Willard's estate and make a final accounting until decedent's estate had settled all of the disputes concerning its liabilities and was prepared to distribute its assets.

In his notice of deficiency dated March 21, 1985, respondent disallowed petitioner's income-distributions deductions for 1980 and 1981.

Opinion

The first issue we must decide is whether petitioner correctly reported its capital gain on the disposition of the AVC notes in 1980 and 1981. After recovering the $600,000 unadjusted basis in the notes set by the 1979 closing agreement, petitioner reported as capital gain for each year, the amounts paid by AVC. Subsequently, petitioner concluded that it had been entitled to adjust basis by the $4,200,000 of insurance proceeds that Occidental paid to the bank and that as a result it realized no gain when AVC repaid its $4,200,000 indebtedness.[4] Respondent rejected petitioner's claims for refunds for 1980 and 1981 as a breach of the closing agreement. A closing agreement, once approved by the Secretary, is a final and conclusive agreement between the parties as to all matters contained therein. The agreement may not be annulled, modified, set aside, or disregarded except "upon a showing of fraud, malfeasance or misrepresentation of a material fact." Sec. 7121(b)(2); see *Cramp Shipbuilding Co. v. Commissioner*, 14 T.C. 33, 37 (1950), affd. per curiam sub nom. *Commissioner v. Harriman Ripley & Co.*, 202 F.2d 280 (3d Cir. 1953). Petitioner contends that it is not attempting to disregard or set aside the closing agreement, but seeks only to adjust its basis in the notes to reflect events that occurred subsequent to decedent's death, the date for which the agreement set the basis.

The basis of an asset set by a closing agreement is subject to adjustment by subsequent events. Basis is set as of a particular date, and events occurring after that date, as for example depreciation of, or improvements to, property can necessitate adjustments to that basis. The closing agreement, in this case, set petitioner's unadjusted basis in its right to subordinated participation in the AVC notes, as of the date of decedent's death, at $600,000. After decedent's death but before the parties entered into the closing agreement, Occidental paid $4,200,000 on its insurance policies on decedent's life to the bank, and the bank transferred $4,200,000 worth of AVC notes to petitioner pursuant to the guarantee agreement. Petitioner contends that it constructively received the insurance proceeds and transferred them to the bank in exchange for the AVC notes.[5]

---

4. Petitioner recognizes that if its position is correct, Occidental's payment on the insurance policies increased its basis to $4,800,000 ($4,200,000 plus $600,000), resulting in a capital loss when AVC repaid the notes. Petitioner chose not to claim a capital loss on its amended returns for 1980 and 1981.

5. If these were the facts, petitioner would acquire a cost basis in the notes equal to the $4,200,000 that the bank was paid for them. Petitioner would not realize any gain on the payment of those notes by AVC. Moreover, the insurance proceeds would be excluded from income. Sec. 101(a).

Respondent concedes that the basis of an asset set in a closing agreement may be adjusted to reflect subsequent events, but contends that petitioner cannot adjust its basis in the notes in this case because to do so would contradict the position that petitioner took, and respondent accepted, in entering into the closing agreement. We agree. Petitioner reported on its estate tax return and represented in the closing agreement that it had no right to the life insurance proceeds because it had assigned that right to the bank as collateral security for the bank's loans to AVC, and had retained only a subordinated participation right in the notes.[6] In agreeing to enter into a closing agreement setting the value (and consequent income tax basis) of petitioner's subordinated participation right in the notes at $600,000, respondent relied on petitioner's representation. Petitioner now attempts to change that representation and contends that it should be deemed to have received the insurance proceeds under the doctrine of subrogation and the terms of the guarantee agreement and to have transferred the proceeds to the bank in exchange for the AVC notes.

Petitioner does not suggest that there was any fraud, malfeasance, or misrepresentation of a material fact by respondent that would allow this Court to disregard the closing agreement. See sec. 7121(b). Moreover, petitioner's current argument is not based on any facts that petitioner could not have known or anticipated at the time it entered into the closing agreement. Indeed the insurance proceeds had already been paid to the bank. In setting petitioner's basis in its right to payment on the notes, the parties knew about the very transaction that petitioner now seeks to characterize as a subsequent event that requires an adjustment to basis. Payment of the insurance proceeds was the heart of the controversy settled by the closing agreement. The bank had been paid; petitioner held the AVC notes and was no longer liable to the bank; and the only remaining issue was the value of petitioner's prospect of recovering on the notes. Thus, regardless of whether petitioner's current position is correct,[7] it contradicts the position petitioner agreed to in entering into the closing agreement and, having entered into that agreement, petitioner is bound by it. See *Cramp Shipbuilding Co. v. Commissioner*, 14 T.C. at 37. Petitioner, therefore, correctly reported its capital gain on the repayment of the AVC notes on its 1980 and 1981 income tax returns.

The next issue for decision is whether petitioner was entitled to deductions pursuant to section 661(a)(2) for income it claims to have distributed to the Estate of Willard T.C. Johnson in 1980 and 1981. The resolution of this issue depends on

6. Petitioner states on its estate tax return the following:

> Since the $4,200,000 of net insurance proceeds ultimately receivable was pledged as security for the AVC indebtedness to Union Commerce and was paid to the latter, the only right of the decedent or his estate at the date of death was a possible right to a subordinated participation in Union Commerce's loans to AVC.

7. Because of our agreement with respondent on this issue, we do not express any view on the merits of whether Occidental's payment to the bank is a constructive receipt of insurance proceeds by petitioner.

our resolution of three sub-issues: (1) Whether the administration of the Estate of Willard T.C. Johnson was unduly prolonged; (2) whether the crediting and debiting of income on the accounting workpapers relating to the 1980 and 1981 fiduciary income tax returns of each estate constituted distributions; and (3) if the credits and debits were distributions, whether they were made in the years for which petitioner claimed distribution deductions.

Whether the administration of an estate has been unduly prolonged is a question of fact. *Stewart v. Commissioner*, 196 F.2d 397, 398 (5th Cir. 1952); *Estate of Farrier v. Commissioner*, 15 T.C. 277, 282 (1950). If the administration of an estate is unduly prolonged beyond a reasonable time for the performance of all administrative duties, the estate will be deemed to be closed for Federal tax purposes. Sec. 1.641(b)-3(a), Income Tax Regs.; *Stewart v. Commissioner, supra*. Where an executor is also named trustee of a trust created under a will, the period of administration continues until the executor completes his administrative duties and assumes his duties as trustee. Sec. 1.641(b)-3(a), Income Tax Regs. The administration of an estate will not be considered to be unduly prolonged if, upon diligent effort, the executor has not completed the ordinary duties of administration such as the collection of assets and the payment of debts, taxes, legacies and bequests.[8]

Respondent contends that the administration of Willard's estate was unduly prolonged and that the estate should be deemed terminated as of the beginning of 1980. Termination would have the effect of treating any amount credited to Willard's estate in 1980 and 1981 as if it had been credited to the foundation, the sole remaining residuary beneficiary under Willard's will. Consequently, petitioner could not deduct any amount credited to the foundation because such an amount would not be distributed to a beneficiary, sec. 1.661(a)-2, Income Tax Regs., and because decedent's will did not specifically provide for any distribution to a charity. Sec. 642(c); sec. 1.663(a)-2, Income Tax Regs.; *United States Trust Co. v. Internal Revenue Service*, 803 F.2d 1363 (5th Cir. 1986); *Estate of O'Connor v. Commissioner*, 69 T.C. 165 (1977). Petitioner argues that because Willard's estate was entitled to receive a 20 percent share in decedent's estate, the executors could not close Willard's estate until decedent's estate was prepared to distribute its assets. The parties have stipulated that decedent's estate was not prepared to distribute its assets in 1980 or 1981.

The burden of proving entitlement to a deduction generally rests on petitioner. *Welch v. Helvering*, 290 U.S. 111, 115 (1933); Rule 142(a), Tax Court Rules of Practice and Procedure. If respondent introduces a new issue, however, he bears the burden of proof as to that issue. *Achiro v. Commissioner*, 77 T.C. 881, 890 (1981). Respondent first argued that Willard's estate had been unduly prolonged at trial, prejudicing petitioner's opportunity to prepare for trial. As to this issue, therefore, respondent bears the burden of proof. He has not met that burden.

---

8. See *Maresca Trust v. Commissioner*, T.C. Memo. 1983-501.

By the end of 1981, due to no fault of theirs, the executors of Willard's estate had not yet performed one of their principal functions as executors, the collection of all of the assets of the estate. See sec. 1.641(b)-3(a), Income Tax Regs.; cf. *Old Virginia Brick Co. v. Commissioner*, 44 T.C. 724, 730 (1965). In addition, the executors, who also served as directors of the foundation, had not assumed their duties as directors by the end of 1981. See sec. 1.641(b)-3(a), Income Tax Regs. (administration of estate continues until executors who are also trustees actually assume duties as trustees). The administration of Willard's estate was, therefore, not unduly prolonged as of the close of 1981.

Next we must determine whether the crediting of income on the accountant's workpapers and the reporting of income on the fiduciary income tax returns of petitioner and of Willard's estate in 1980 and 1981 can be considered to be distributions within the meaning of section 661. Section 661(a) provides:

> SEC. 661(a). Deduction.—In any taxable year there shall be allowed as a deduction in computing the taxable income of any estate or trust (other than a trust to which subpart B applies), the sum of—
>
> (1) any amount of income for such taxable year required to be distributed currently * * * and
>
> (2) any other amounts properly paid or credited or required to be distributed for such taxable year;
>
> but such deduction shall not exceed the distributable net income of the estate or trust.

The Second Circuit has interpreted the requirement that amounts be "properly credited" as follows:

> *The income must be so definitively allocated to the legatee as to be beyond recall*; "credit" for practical purposes is the equivalent of "payment." Therefore, a mere entry on the books of the fiduciary will not serve unless made in such circumstances that it cannot be recalled. If the fiduciary's account be stated inter partes, that would probably be enough * * * But the unilateral act of entering items in the account is not conclusive. * * * [*Commissioner v. Stearns*, 65 F.2d 371, 373 (2d Cir. 1933), cert. denied sub nom. *Stearns v. Burnet*, 290 U.S. 670 (1933). Emphasis added.][9]

Harris v. United States, 370 F.2d 887, 892 (4th Cir. 1966); see *Igoe v. Commissioner*, 19 T.C. 913, 923–924 (1953).

Petitioner and Willard's estate have the same executors and accountants. In 1976 Klein, one of the executors, met with Rosenberg, a senior partner of Main

---

9. In *Commissioner v. Stearns*, the Second Circuit interpreted section 162(c) of the Revenue Act of 1928, which provided a deduction for an estate for amounts "properly paid or credited during such year to any legatee, heir, or beneficiary." 65 F.2d at 373. The Internal Revenue Code of 1954 did not materially change the relevant language.

Hurdman, and instructed him to make the appropriate entries each year to credit 20 percent of petitioner's income to Willard's estate. Since 1976, under the direction of Richard Stone, who was the accountant charged with reviewing tax compliance for both estates, staff members of Main Hurdman have prepared annual work papers for both estates showing the distributions. The workpapers were prepared in the ordinary course of business. The entries on the work papers do not reflect any actual exchange of money, but Willard's estate treated the amounts credited as income on its 1980 and 1981 income tax returns pursuant to section 662(a), and petitioner claimed distributions deductions for the same amounts on its 1980 and 1981 returns. See sec. 661(a)(2).

Petitioner contends that because of the identity of executors and accountants, neither formal bookkeeping entries nor actual separation of funds was necessary to credit income from petitioner to Willard's estate within the meaning of section 661(a)(2). In petitioner's view, the informal workpapers, prepared in the ordinary course of business, were sufficient to evidence a commitment to set aside funds beyond the recall of petitioner, its creditors, and its other beneficiaries. Petitioner also argues that the consistent reporting of the transfers on the income tax returns for both estates is further evidence of its intent to permanently set aside the funds for Willard's estate. Respondent contends that the workpapers did not place the amounts transferred beyond petitioner's recall and that the amounts were, therefore, not properly credited within the meaning of section 661(a)(2).

We agree with respondent. The workpapers, which were informal documents prepared in pencil, are the only records showing the transfers of funds between the estates. Stone testified that workpapers were prepared in the ordinary course of business after the close of each taxable year, always in pencil, and kept in the files for each estate. We nonetheless cannot find that the workpapers were sufficiently permanent documents to function as the books of the estate. We are convinced that, were petitioner to make a bad investment or incur unexpected indebtedness on its large contingent liabilities, the funds credited on the workpapers to Willard's estate would not be insulated from the claims of petitioner's creditors or other beneficiaries.

Petitioner chose to credit Willard's account through entries on the work papers rather than actually transferring cash specifically because of the numerous contingent liabilities and other contingencies preventing it from settling the estate. Although the consistent income tax reporting of the transfers by both estates is evidence that the amounts were intended to be permanently set aside for Willard's estate (cf. *In re Estate of O'Neil*, 68 Misc. 2d 634, 327 N.Y.S.2d 725, 732 (Surr. Ct. 1972)), it is not enough to meet petitioner's burden of proof. Willard's estate, as a residuary beneficiary, can receive only the residue of petitioner's assets. Thus, it was prudent for the executors not to make cash distributions until they had collected all of petitioner's assets and settled its liabilities. As one of the executors testified, "we did not make any distributions to any of the beneficiaries * * * we felt it would be prejudicial to them to divide the thing in five places, we felt it was our duty to stay there and settle all claims, negotiate the claims, pay our taxes, collect all the assets and dispose of the liabilities."[10]

We do not hold that, where the representatives or accountants for estate and beneficiary are the same, funds must be physically segregated to satisfy the "properly credited" standard of section 661(a)(2). Entries on the books of the estate may be sufficient in such cases, but we do not believe that workpapers such as those prepared in this case can achieve an allocation beyond the recall of the executors, and petitioner has not shown us that New York law is otherwise. The amounts credited to Willard's estate in 1980 and 1981 were not, for Federal income tax purposes, distributions within the meaning of section 661, and petitioner is not entitled to deductions for them.

Because we hold that petitioner is not entitled to deductions for the amounts credited to Willard's estate in 1980 and 1981, we need not decide whether the amounts were actually credited in the years for which petitioner claimed deductions.

To reflect the foregoing,

Decision will be entered for the respondent.

While section 661(a)(2) states that "any other amounts properly paid or credited or required to be distributed" are allowed in determining the amount of the distribution deduction, assignments of items of income in respect of a decedent have been held in the following case and in the Revenue Ruling that follows it not to be "other amounts properly paid" and, thus, outside the reach of section 661.

Rollert Residuary Trust v. Commissioner

80 T.C. 619 (1983), *aff'd*, 752 F.2d 1128 (6th Cir. 1985)

WHITAKER, Judge:

Respondent determined deficiencies in petitioner's Federal income taxes in the amounts of $83,795 for 1973; $68,686 for 1974; and $2,675 for 1975.

This case was submitted fully stipulated under Rule 122, Tax Court Rules of Practice and Procedure. The primary issues for decision are: (1) Whether rights to receive bonus payments under the General Motors bonus plan, which were attributable to an individual's employment with General Motors before his death but which were not formally awarded until several months after his death, are rights to income in respect of a decedent; and (2) whether rights to income in respect of a decedent which were distributed by the decedent's estate to petitioner in prior years acquired a basis in the hands of petitioner equal to their fair market value on the date of distribution. With respect to this second issue, we must specifically decide whether the rights to income in respect of a decedent were amounts "properly paid or credited"

---

10. Transcript of trial, June 27, 1986, at 169.

for purposes of sections 661(a)(2)[11] and 662(a)(2). The second issue applies to post-death installments of bonus awards made prior to death, concededly income in respect of a decedent, as well as the postmortem bonus awards (issue 1), if we determine issue (1) in respondent's favor.

On December 31, 1960, Edward D. Rollert, as Settlor, and Genesee Merchants Bank & Trust Co., as trustee, executed a revocable trust agreement (hereinafter trust agreement). This trust agreement provided for the establishment of two separate trusts — a marital trust and a residuary trust — to administer assets owned by Mr. Rollert at death. The residuary trust is the petitioner herein. When the petition was filed, the principal place of business of the trustee was Flint, Mich.

For several years prior to his death on November 27, 1969, Edward D. Rollert had been employed as an executive vice president of General Motors Corp. and had participated in the corporation's Stock Option Plan and its bonus plan. These plans were designed to compensate corporate executives and other employees by providing cash and stock bonuses payable in installments in subsequent years. Amounts awarded under the plans were interrelated: if an employee was awarded a stock option bonus, any award under the bonus plan was reduced. All awards under the bonus plan for more than $2,000 were to be paid in cash or stock in annual installments over a 5-year period following the year of award. Bonuses under the stock option plan were in the form of contingent credits for General Motors stock. After the termination of stock options concurrently awarded to the executive, the contingent credits would entitle the executive to receive the stock. Like the bonuses under the Bonus Plan, the contingent credits under the Stock Option Plan were credited in installments over a five-year period. However, the period for applying the contingent credits started running from the date the options were terminated. Mr. Rollert's options terminated within 12 months after his death.

During the period between the award of bonus rights under either of these plans and the employee's receipt of the final installment payment attributable to such rights, the employee had to "earn out" his or her right to the award by continuing to be employed by the corporation and not committing acts inimical to the best interests of the corporation. Death relieved an employee from the duty of earning out a bonus; thus, upon an employee's death, his or her estate, or the party entitled to the right, possessed a nonforfeitable right to subsequent installments of the bonus award.

General Motors made awards to Mr. Rollert under both the bonus plan and the stock option plan for each of the years 1964 through 1968. These awards, which exceeded $300,000 for each of these years, are referred to collectively as the "lifetime bonus awards." When Mr. Rollert died on November 27, 1969, the remaining installment payments of these bonuses became nonforfeitable and payable to Mr. Rollert's estate.

11. Unless otherwise indicated, all statutory references are to the Internal Revenue Code of 1954 as amended.

Shown on page 623 is a copy of Joint Exhibit 6-F listing the following information with respect to lifetime bonus awards made to Mr. Rollert:

- (A) Year of award determination.—This shows the year in which the lifetime awards were determined.
- (B) Year of receipt.—This shows the year in which installments of lifetime bonus awards were paid by General Motors and received by the Estate of Edward D. Rollert (hereinafter the estate) or petitioner. Lifetime bonus awards received in cash are so recorded; those received in stock are shown with the number of shares and the fair market value at delivery indicated.
- (C) Year of final installment.—This shows the year in which the final installment of each lifetime bonus award was paid or delivered.

On March 2, 1970, decedent was awarded a bonus under the bonus plan of 1,786 shares of General Motors common stock and $285,763 cash with respect to his almost 11-months employment with the corporation in 1969. This is referred to hereafter as the "postmortem bonus award." The parties have stipulated that decedent "had no rights to the post-mortem bonus award during his lifetime." This bonus was to be paid in five annual installments, with the first installment in March 1970, and the subsequent installments on January 10 of the next 4 years. The installments for 1970, 1971, 1972, and 1973 each consisted of $57,168 cash and 357 shares of General Motors stock.[12] For 1974, the installment consisted of $57,090 cash and 358 shares of stock. No award was made to Mr. Rollert under the stock option plan with respect to his employment in 1969.

The procedures for awarding bonuses under the bonus plan to an executive vice president, such as Mr. Rollert, were the same as those with respect to other employees. The bonus plan stated that it was contemplated that bonuses would be awarded annually but that the committee had the right from time to time to modify or suspend the plan. Bonuses were awarded under the bonus plan in all the years 1956 through 1969, and it was the practice during this period to grant awards to all executive vice presidents.

Installments of Bonus Awarded During Lifetime but Paid after Death

Year of award determination	Year final installment paid		Year of receipt 1970		
	Stock	Cash	Stock# Shs.	F.M.V.	Cash
1964	1974		222		
1965	1975	1970			$ 61,500

12. The fair market values of the stock when distributed were $25,258 for 1970; $29,408 for 1971; $27,935 for 1972; $29,497 for 1973; and $16,738 for 1974.

Year of award determination	Year final installment paid		Year of receipt 1970		
	Stock	Cash	Stock# Shs.	F.M.V.	Cash
1966	1975	1971			69,000
1967	1974	1972			66,750
1968	1975	1973			73,500
1969	1975		298		
Totals			520	$45,250	270,750

[Discrepancies in the above Joint Exhibit were not addressed by the parties.]

Year of award determination	Year of receipt 1971			Year of receipt 1972		
	Stock# Sh.	F.M.V.	Cash	Stock# Sh.	F.M.V.	Cash
1964	223			222		
1965	183			184		
1966	202		$69,000	202		
1967	260		66,750	260		$66,750
1968	278		73,500	278		73,500
1969	299			298		
Totals	1445	$113,071.25	209,250	1444	$118,949	140,250

[Discrepancies in the above Joint Exhibit were not addressed by the parties.]

Year of award determination	Year of receipt 1973			Year of receipt 1974	
	Stock # Sh.	F.M.V.	Cash	Stock # Sh.	F.M.V.
1964	223			223	
1965	184			184	
1966	203			203	
1967	259			259	
1968	278		$73,500	278	
1969	299			299	
Totals	1446	$119,476	73,500	446	$67,601

[Discrepancies in the above Joint Exhibit were not addressed by the parties.]

Year of award determination	Year of receipt 1975		Total installments paid after death	
	Stock # Sh.	F.M.V.	Stock (#)	Cash
1964			1112	
1965	184		919	$61,500
1966	203		1010	138,000
1967	260		1298	200,050
1968	278		1390	294,000
1969			7223	
Totals	925	$33,878	7223	693,750

[Discrepancies in the above Joint Exhibit were not addressed by the parties.]

The first step to be taken in each year in deciding whether to award bonuses under the bonus plan was for the corporation's independent public accountants to determine an amount to be set aside in a reserve to be used to pay any bonuses that might be awarded under the two plans. The amount set aside was computed under a formula based generally on the corporation's net earnings, but the corporation's bonus and salary committee (hereinafter the committee) had discretion to direct that a lesser amount be credited. For the year 1969, an initial determination of the amount available for payment of bonuses was made on October 6, 1969, approximately 1½ months prior to Mr. Rollert's death. This determination was reviewed monthly until February 2, 1970, when it was accepted as final.

The second step in awarding bonuses was the selection of eligible employees for awards under the bonus plan. To do this, the committee designated a monthly salary rate, and with a few exceptions, all employees earning in excess of that rate were considered for bonuses in that year. On November 3, 1969 (again prior to the date of death), the committee made a tentative determination of awards for all executive vice presidents, including Mr. Rollert. This determination was reviewed monthly until finalized on March 2, 1970. During the review on January 5, 1970, the committee decided to make an award on account of Mr. Rollert's service despite his death but reduced it to an amount roughly equivalent to 11/12ths of the amount originally determined. This accorded with the committee's practice of prorating awards on the basis of the amount of actual service during the year. On March 2, 1970, the award for Mr. Rollert's 1969 service was formally made. It was for the amount determined on January 5, 1970.

The provisions of the bonus plan stated that an employee would be eligible for consideration for a bonus in the year his or her employment terminated, at the discretion of the committee and under such rules as the committee might prescribe. As of the date of decedent's death, the committee had prescribed no rules dealing with the awarding of bonuses to employees who had died during the award year; but it had been the committee's practice, generally, to treat eligible employees who had at least 2-months active service in the award year the same as employees not terminating their service. Thus, the committee would deny a postmortem award to an employee with at least 2-months service in the award year only if his performance had declined to the extent that he would not have been given an award if he had lived, or if he had acted or conducted himself in a manner inimical or in any way contrary to the best interests of the corporation. None of these exceptions applied to Mr. Rollert.

Mr. Rollert did not report on his pre-death income tax returns any of the bonus awards at issue here. Nor were any of these amounts reported in Mr. Rollert's final individual income tax returns.

Mr. Rollert executed his last will and testament on March 14, 1961. After he died, this will was admitted to probate. The executor of the estate, Genesee Merchants Bank & Trust Co. performed the administration of the estate and filed the U.S. Estate Tax Return, Form 706, for the estate. This return included in the gross estate the date-of-death values of the installments of the lifetime bonus awards that had not been paid or delivered to Mr. Rollert as of the date of death, but it did not include the postmortem awards. The date-of-death values for both the stock and cash portions of the lifetime bonus awards were discounted values, reflecting the fact that the amounts were not to be delivered until future years.

The will made certain specific bequests of property, and devised the residue to the marital and residuary trusts created under the trust agreement. None of the rights to receive future installments of lifetime or postmortem bonus awards were subject to distribution as a specific bequest. All these rights to installments of bonus awards were administered as part of the residue of the estate and were subject to distribution to petitioner under the residuary clause of the will. The bonus plan and the stock option Plan did not permit the assignment by a deceased employee's estate of the rights to receive future bonus installments except that the estate could transfer such rights to the party entitled to them as testamentary beneficiary or heir.

During the administration of the estate, the executor made five separate distributions to petitioner of certain of the rights to receive cash or stock due in subsequent years as installments of lifetime bonus awards, and a distribution of the right to the final installment due under the postmortem bonus award. These six distributions included a December 30, 1970, distribution of the right to receive 1,446 shares of General Motors stock on January 10, 1973; a December 30, 1970, distribution of the right to receive $73,500 on January 10, 1973; a December 21, 1971, distribution of the right to receive 1,446 shares of General Motors stock on January 10, 1974; a December 22, 1972, distribution of the right to receive 925 shares of General Motors stock on January 10, 1975; a December 22, 1972, distribution of the right to receive $57,090 on January 10, 1974; and a December 31, 1973, distribution of the right to receive 358 shares of General Motors stock on January 10, 1974. Each distribution of a right to receive future bonus installments was made prior to the year in which payment or delivery of the installment was due.

To record these six distributions of the rights to receive bonus installments, the estate and petitioner each made book entries for deliveries or receipts of "accounts receivable." No other act of transfer occurred between the estate and petitioner.

Each of the distributions of the rights to future bonus installments was treated by the estate and petitioner in essentially the following manner. With respect to each right that was distributed, the present value of the right was determined as of the date of distribution. The estate claimed a distribution deduction for this amount on its U.S. Fiduciary Income Tax Return, Form 1041. Petitioner reported on its U.S. Fiduciary Income Tax Return, Form 1041, for the year of distribution the same value as gross income received from the estate. In each of the years in which rights to bonus installments were distributed, the estate had distributable net income, as defined in section 643, consisting primarily of bonus installments actually received by the estate in that year.[13] For each year, the amount of distributable net income exceeded the total of the correct date-of-distribution value of rights to future bonus installments plus the amount of cash distributions which were made in each of these years to the marital trust.

In the subsequent years, when the bonus installments were due, General Motors paid them directly to petitioner. Petitioner reported on its income tax return as ordinary income only the amount, if any, by which the bonus installment paid to it by General Motors exceeded the corrected value of the right to the bonus installment as of the date the right was distributed to it.[14] Due to fluctuations in stock prices, two of the bonus installments had values lower than the bases previously assigned to the rights to these installments. Petitioner claimed no losses in these instances. The estate did not include in income any portion of the bonus installments that were paid directly to petitioner.

The following description of the treatment by the estate and petitioner of the stock portion of the distribution on December 30, 1970, illustrates how the distributions of the rights were treated. On December 30, 1970, the executor distributed to petitioner the right to receive future payment and delivery of the bonus installment of 1,446 shares of General Motors common stock which was payable and deliverable

13. The estate reported distributable net income on its income tax returns in the amounts of $450,562 for 1970; $420,915 for 1971; $376,895 for 1972; and $107,247 for 1973.

14. For three of the rights to bonus installments, petitioner used a different value than the amount it had reported on its income tax return in the year the right was distributed. This difference is due to the fact that the values initially determined and used on its returns were incorrect and were subsequently adjusted on petitioner's books to the corrected amounts. There is nothing in the record, however, to indicate that petitioner filed amended returns to correct its initial use on its Forms 1041 of incorrect values for the rights to future bonus installments that it received and treated as income.

by General Motors to the estate on January 10, 1973. Both the estate and petitioner used $92,941 as the value as of December 30, 1970, of this bonus right. The estate claimed a distribution deduction of $92,941 on its income tax return, and petitioner reported $92,941 on its income tax return. The trustee subsequently made an adjustment on the books of petitioner to increase the reported present value of the right distributed to it as of December 30, 1970, from $92,941 to $108,242, which was the correct present value of the right as of December 30, 1970. On January 10, 1973, General Motors paid the installment due on that date by delivery of the 1,446 shares of common stock to petitioner. As of this date, the total fair market value of the 1,446 shares was $119,476. Petitioner reported on its 1973 income tax return $11,234 as a receipt of ordinary income. This amount represented the difference between the fair market value of the stock on January 10, 1973 ($119,476), and the corrected December 30, 1970, present value of the right to receive the stock ($108,242). The estate reported no gain or income with respect to this payment either in 1973, when the installment of the bonus award was paid to petitioner, or in any other year.

Respondent examined petitioner's income tax returns for the years 1973, 1974, and 1975, and determined deficiencies in each of these years. When the notice of deficiency was issued to petitioner on September 6, 1979, petitioner had no right to file for refund with respect to the years 1970, 1971, and 1972. It has been respondent's position that the distribution of the rights to the lifetime and postmortem bonus installments were income in respect of a decedent, that receipt of these installments did not give petitioner any basis in these rights, and that petitioner therefore had to include as income the entire amount of each bonus installment when paid to it. In computing the amounts of deficiencies, respondent did not allow any deductions under section 691(c) for estate taxes paid with respect to the lifetime bonus awards. On brief, respondent concedes that to the extent petitioner must include in its gross income items of income in respect of a decedent, a deduction under section 691(c) should be allowed for the Federal estate tax paid with respect to such income. Respondent also states on brief that if the Court finds that the contested bonus installments were income in respect of a decedent, then the maximum tax rates under section 1348 will apply in computing the amounts of deficiencies owed by the petitioner.

Characterization of the Bonus Payments as Income in Respect of a Decedent

The first question we must resolve is whether the bonus payments were income in respect of a decedent under section 691.

In its answering brief, petitioner for the first time suggests that installment payments of the contingent credits awarded under the stock option plan might not constitute income in respect of a decedent. However, in paragraph 6(L) of its amended petition, petitioner conceded that the rights to the installment payments of the lifetime bonus awards were rights to income in respect of a decedent, and the case was initially briefed by both parties on this basis. Petitioner cannot now raise a new issue by arguing contrary to the conceded facts. See, e.g., *Sicanoff Vegetable Oil Corp. v.*

Commissioner, 27 T.C. 1056, 1065–1066 (1957), revd. on another issue 251 F.2d 764 (7th Cir. 1958).

We are, however, squarely faced with the issue whether payments of the post-mortem bonus award were income in respect of a decedent. Petitioner argues that Mr. Rollert had no right or entitlement to a bonus award with respect to his employment in 1969 since the bonus was not formally awarded by General Motors until March 2, 1970—over 3 months after his death. We disagree. For purposes of section 691, we believe that as of the date of his death, Mr. Rollert had a right to a bonus award for 1969, in view of General Motors' established practices in awarding bonuses and its tentative decisions to assign substantial funds to the bonus pool for 1969 and to award bonuses to all executive vice presidents.

Section 691(a) provides that gross income of an estate shall include all income in respect of a decedent, but nowhere in the Code is this phrase defined. The only definition appears in section 1.691(a)-1(b), Income Tax Regs.,[15] but this definition does little to clarify the meaning of the term. Thus, the courts have frequently been called upon to establish the dimensions of the term. *Estate of Peterson v. Commissioner*, 74 T.C. 630, 638 (1980), affd. 667 F.2d 675 (8th Cir. 1981).

In determining whether particular receipts should be treated as income in respect of a decedent, courts have focused on whether the decedent had a right or entitlement to receive income as of the date of his death. *Estate of Peterson v. Commissioner*, 667 F.2d at 679, and cases cited therein. The parties have stipulated in this case that Mr. Rollert "had no rights to the post-mortem bonus award during his lifetime." Respondent takes the position that for purposes of the stipulation, the term "rights" should be read as referring to contract rights or other legally enforceable rights, and that the stipulation establishes only that the decedent had during his lifetime no legally enforceable right to an award not yet made. Petitioner contends, however, that the stipulation establishes that decedent had no right or entitlement to the postmortem bonus and that the installment payments of this bonus were therefore not income in respect of a decedent. We do not accept petitioner's view. Whether decedent had a right or entitlement to a bonus award for 1969 is a

---

15. Sec. 1.691(a)-1(b), Income Tax Regs., provides:

(b) General definition. In general, the term "income in respect of a decedent" refers to those amounts to which a decedent was entitled as gross income but which were not properly includible in computing his taxable income for the taxable year ending with the date of his death or for a previous taxable year under the method of accounting employed by the decedent. See the regulations under section 451. Thus, the term includes:

(1) All accrued income of a decedent who reported his income by use of the cash receipts and disbursements method;

(2) Income accrued solely by reason of the decedent's death in case of a decedent who reports his income by use of an accrual method of accounting; and

(3) Income to which the decedent had a contingent claim at the time of his death.

See secs. 736 and 753 and the regulations thereunder for "income in respect of a decedent" in the case of a deceased partner.

question of law, and it is well established that this Court may disregard a stipulation of law. *Mead's Bakery, Inc. v. Commissioner*, 364 F.2d 101, 106 (5th Cir. 1966), affg. on this point a Memorandum Opinion of this Court. This is particularly so when facts are presented, as they have been in this case, that conflict with the suggested interpretation of the stipulation. *Mead's Bakery, Inc. v. Commissioner, supra* at 106; *Jasionowski v. Commissioner*, 66 T.C. 312, 318 (1976).

Petitioner relies on several cases that have applied the "right-to-income" or "entitlement" test in determining whether post-death payments constitute income in respect of a decedent. *Estate of Peterson v. Commissioner, supra*; *Halliday v. United States*, 655 F.2d 68 (5th Cir. 1981); *Claiborne v. United States*, 648 F.2d 448 (6th Cir. 1981); *Keck v. Commissioner*, 415 F.2d 531 (6th Cir. 1969), revg. 49 T.C. 313 (1968); and *Trust Co. of Georgia v. Ross*, 392 F.2d 694 (5th Cir. 1967). We agree with petitioner that this test should be applied but find on the facts of this case that as of the date of his death, Mr. Rollert had a right or entitlement to a bonus for 1969.

Keck v. Commissioner, supra, and *Trust Co. of Georgia v. Ross, supra*, were the first cases to squarely reject reliance on the "economic activity" test under which the inquiry had been limited to consideration of whether the significant economic activity giving rise to income received after death had been performed prior to death. These two opinions indicated that all facts should be examined to determine whether at the date of death the decedent had the right to the post-death payments. *Trust Co. of Georgia* involved proceeds from the sale of property pursuant to a binding contract which decedent had executed prior to death. Although there were a few aspects of the transaction not completed by the date of death, the court found that these were not of such a scope as would negate the right possessed by decedent under the contract. In contrast, the *Keck* court was presented with a situation in which the occurrence of post-death contingencies would defeat the existence of a right to income. The particular fact situation before the court in the *Keck* case involved the treatment of liquidation distributions from corporations in which decedent had owned stock. Prior to decedent's death, the corporations had agreed to sell their assets in pursuance of a contemplated liquidation, but the sale was not consummated until after the decedent's death. The Court of Appeals stressed that the sale of the stock was subject to a number of contingencies, such as prior Interstate Commerce Commission approval and the continued agreement of the majority shareholder. On these facts, the court found that decedent had neither the right nor the power to require the corporations to liquidate and thus did not possess, prior to his death, the right to receive any proceeds from the contemplated liquidation.

In *Claiborne v. United States, supra*, the right-to-income or entitlement test was applied in the context of the sale of property on which the decedent had granted an option prior to her death. Because the decedent had died before the optionee paid her the purchase price, the court recognized that she was not entitled as a strict matter of law to the full purchase price as of the date of her death. However, the court found that under State law the decedent had the right in equity to specific performance of the land purchase agreement at the full purchase price because the optionee had already taken full possession of the realty prior to the decedent's death. The *Claiborne* opinion holds that the right-to-income or entitlement test is satisfied when a decedent possesses as of the date of death a legal or equitable entitlement to income. It does not state, however, that the existence of a right enforceable at law or in equity is an absolute prerequisite to finding a pre-death entitlement to income.

These three appellate opinions left considerable room for disagreement over exactly what constitutes a right or entitlement to income. However, *Halliday v. United States, supra*, and *Estate of Peterson v. Commissioner, supra*, have clarified this test.

In *Halliday* the Fifth Circuit rejected the view that a legally enforceable right was necessary in order for income to be taxed under section 691. The court characterized the right-to-income test as simply a "more precise" definition of income in respect of a decedent, rather than as a repudiation of the line of cases that had found the existence of income in respect of a decedent in the absence of a legally enforceable right. It elaborated on the right-to-income test as follows:

> We find that for purposes of Section 691, a right to income arises where the evidence shows a substantial certainty that benefits directly related to the decedent's past economic activities will be paid to his heirs or estate upon his death, notwithstanding the absence of a legally enforceable obligation. * * * [655 F.2d at 72.]

The fact situation in *Halliday* was quite similar to that now presented to us. The *Halliday* court was asked to decide whether section 691 applied to life insurance renewal commissions received by the estate of an insurance agent after his death. The agent had no contractual right to the payment of these renewal commissions. Nevertheless, the insurance company had a longstanding policy of paying benefits at a set rate to the beneficiaries of a deceased agent, and this policy had been embodied in corporate resolutions. On the basis of these facts, the court found that the decedent had a right, albeit not necessarily a legally enforceable one, to post-death renewal commissions, and therefore that the benefits paid to his estate by the insurance company constituted income in respect of a decedent.

The "substantial certainty" approach adopted in the *Halliday* opinion is consistent with the approach we took in *Estate of Peterson v. Commissioner, supra*. That case involved the tax treatment of sales proceeds under a contract for the sale of calves, which had been entered into by the decedent prior to his death. Based on our review of the case law and regulations, we found in *Estate of Peterson* that the following four requirements have been applied to test whether a decedent possessed the requisite right to sales proceeds at the time of death: (1) Whether the decedent entered into a legally significant arrangement regarding the subject matter of the sale; (2) whether the decedent performed the substantive acts required as preconditions to the sale; (3) whether there existed at the time of decedent's death any economically material contingencies which might have disrupted the sale; and (4) whether the decedent would have eventually received the sales proceeds if he or she had lived.[16] We found that the proceeds from the contract for the sale of the calves satisfied three of these four requirements but did not satisfy the second requirement. Substantial and essential acts that the decedent had been required to perform under the contract had not been completed as of the date of his death since one-third of the calves were too young to be deliverable as of that date and had to be raised by the estate for more than 1 month thereafter. We therefore held that the sales proceeds were not income in respect of a decedent.

We now apply to the facts of this case the right-to-income test as elaborated in *Halliday v. United States, supra*, and *Estate of Peterson v. Commissioner, supra*.

General Motors had no contractual obligation as of the date of decedent's death to pay him a bonus with respect to 1969. However, the decedent had a longstanding contractual employment relationship with General Motors, and under the terms of his employment, he was eligible to participate in the bonus plan, which was a formalized deferred compensation arrangement and under which bonuses had been paid consistently in preceding years. In this factual context, it is apparent that the bonus payments were made in relation to "a legally significant arrangement" between the decedent and General Motors. See *Estate of Peterson v. Commissioner*, 74 T.C. at 639. It is also clear that decedent's 11-months employment with General Motors in 1969 and his refraining from taking any actions that would have disqualified him from bonus eligibility for that year constituted his performance of all the substantive acts required as a precondition of his being awarded a bonus for 1969. Cf. *Estate of Peterson v. Commissioner, supra*.

When Mr. Rollert died, he had no legally enforceable right to a bonus for 1969 since the bonuses for that year had not yet been declared, and General Motors had reserved the right to modify or suspend the bonus plan. However, as a practical matter, by the date of Mr. Rollert's death, and barring some unforeseen and unpredictable change in corporate plans, bonuses would be awarded for 1969. In each of the 13 years preceding 1969, General Motors had awarded bonuses. Prior to the date of decedent's death, it was anticipated that under the net earnings formula set forth in the plan, substantial funds would be added to the bonus pool for 1969. There is no evidence to suggest the committee ever considered exercising its discretion to modify or suspend the plan in 1969 or to reduce the amount added for 1969 below the amount computed under the net earnings formula. To the contrary, over 7 weeks before Mr. Rollert's death, the committee had made an initial determination of the amount available for bonuses for 1969.

It is also clear that Mr. Rollert was assured prior to his death of being one of the individuals to whom awards would be made for 1969. The committee had never denied an award to an executive vice president, and Mr. Rollert had received bonuses

16. In *Estate of Peterson v. Commissioner*, 74 T.C. 630, 639 n.9 (1980), affd. 667 F.2d 675 (8th Cir. 1981), we cautioned that the four factors were not meant to be an ironclad formula but might change based on the type of transaction to be analyzed.

in excess of $300,000 for each of the 5 years preceding 1969. More importantly, over 3 weeks before Mr. Rollert's death, the committee had made a determination (albeit a tentative one) to grant bonus awards for 1969 to all executive vice presidents. The parties agree that during 1969, Mr. Rollert committed no act that would have disqualified him from receipt of an award for that year. At least implicitly, the committee recognized this fact by failing to exclude him from the executive vice president group and the possibility of forfeiture died with the decedent. Although the tentative bonus determinations were subject to monthly reviews until March 2, 1970, in point of fact, the amount formally awarded on March 2, 1970, with respect to Mr. Rollert's employment during 1969 was substantially the same as the initially determined amount, except that it was reduced by 1/12th to reflect the fact that he performed no services for General Motors in December 1969.

The bonus plan provided the committee with discretion in determining the eligibility of employees for consideration for bonuses in the year their employment terminated, but the existence of this discretion did not significantly affect Mr. Rollert's chances of receiving a bonus for 1969. The committee had no written rules or guidelines circumscribing their discretion with respect to terminated employees. However, the committee's established practice had been to make awards to terminated employees who were otherwise qualified so long as they had at least 2 months active service in the year for which the award was being granted. *Halliday v. United States, supra* at 72, paid particular attention to the fact that the corporation had consistently followed its established policy of paying post-death benefits even absent a contractual obligation. Here, it is equally clear that under established practices, the bonus award with respect to Mr. Rollert's service in 1969 would not have been denied on the basis of his cessation of employment in that year.[17] Thus, as of the date of Mr. Rollert's death, there was no material contingency comparable to that in *Keck v. Commissioner, supra*, that might have resulted in denial of a bonus award for 1969.[18] On these facts, it is established that Mr. Rollert had a substantial certainty as of the date of his death of receiving a bonus award for 1969.

---

17. We note that had General Motors deviated from its established policy of treating terminated employees with at least 2-months service in the award year, in the same manner as continuing employees, and thereby denied decedent's bonus award for 1969, it may be that the estate could have sued to obtain the award. Compare *Hainline v. General Motors Corp.*, 444 F.2d 1250 (6th Cir. 1971), in which the court found that the bonus committee's discretion to allow terminated employees to receive accrued bonus awards was restricted by its past decisions, and for that reason, the committee could not arbitrarily deny the right to receive such accrued bonuses but must examine the facts of the particular case, with *Parrish v. General Motors Corp.*, 137 So. 2d 255 (Fla. App. 1962), in which the court held that General Motors had discretion under the bonus plan in granting or withholding bonus awards to its employee.

18. We note that although the Sixth Circuit did not use the term "substantial certainty" in *Keck v. Commissioner*, 415 F.2d 531 (6th Cir. 1969), revg. 49 T.C. 313 (1968), the effect of the court's stressing the contingencies affecting the sale of the stock which gave rise to the liquidation proceeds shows that it took the same practical approach as the Fifth Circuit did in *Halliday v. United States*, 655 F.2d 68 (5th Cir. 1981).

Thus, the analyses in the *Halliday* and *Estate of Peterson* opinions lead us to the conclusion that as of the date of his death, Mr. Rollert had a right or entitlement to a bonus for 1969. Accordingly, the payments under the portmortem bonus award were income in respect of a decedent when received by the estate or petitioner.

Distribution of Rights to Income in Respect of a Decedent

We must determine now whether the estate's distribution to petitioner of the rights to receive bonus installments in subsequent years gave petitioner a basis in these rights equal to their fair market values when distributed, and whether such basis could be used by petitioner to reduce the income it received when the bonus installments were actually paid to it. This is a question of first impression.

As a preliminary matter, we address petitioner's claim that respondent is estopped from contesting its treatment of the bonus rights because of his failure to question such treatment in earlier years. Petitioner points out that respondent failed to challenge the treatment by both the estate and petitioner of the transfers of the rights to bonus installments as distributions of the estate's distributable net income in the years the rights were transferred. This argument must be rejected, first of all, because it was raised for the first time on brief. Time and again this Court has reiterated that we will not consider issues not raised in the pleadings. See, e.g., *Markwardt v. Commissioner*, 64 T.C. 989, 997 (1975); *Estate of Mandels v. Commissioner*, 64 T.C. 61, 73 (1975); *Frentz v. Commissioner*, 44 T.C. 485, 491 (1965), affd. without discussion of this issue 375 F.2d 662 (6th Cir. 1967). Furthermore, even if the issue were properly before us, it is clear there is no basis for finding estoppel against respondent, here. There is no indication that respondent ever examined the estate tax return or petitioner's returns for the prior years. Also, it is a well-established principle that the Commissioner's failure to challenge erroneous treatment of an item in earlier years does not preclude an examination of the correctness of the treatment of such item for the tax years in issue. *Automobile Club of Michigan v. Commissioner*, 353 U.S. 180, 183 (1957); *DuPont Testamentary Trust v. Commissioner*, 66 T.C. 761, 765 (1976), affd. per curiam 574 F.2d 1332 (5th Cir. 1978).

In resolving this case, we must analyze the relationship between the rules of section 691 for the taxation of income in respect of a decedent and those of subchapter J, part I, governing the income taxation of estates. In general, the provisions of subchapter J, part I, are designed to allocate between the estate and its beneficiaries taxable income received by the estate, so that income will be taxed at only one level. For an estate that may accumulate income, such as Mr. Rollert's estate, this general allocation scheme is accomplished through the distribution rules of sections 661 through 663. Section 691 serves a totally different purpose. It is designed to deal with the problem of how to tax income that has been earned but not received by an individual as of the date of his or her death. Under section 691, income that has accrued to a decedent prior to death but has not yet been received is not included in the decedent's final income tax return, even though the right to such income may be included on the estate's estate tax return. Instead, the income is reported when received by the person who actually receives the income. See *Estate of Sidles v.*

Commissioner, 65 T.C. 873, 879 (1976), affd. without published opinion 553 F.2d 102 (8th Cir. 1977).

Here, petitioner used the distribution rules of section 662 in an attempt to reduce the income taxed to it under section 691. In effect, what petitioner did here was to report part of the payments of income in respect of a decedent as income under section 662, even before the payments were made by General Motors. When the payments were actually made in subsequent years, petitioner excluded the previously reported amounts from its section 691 income. Because the treatment of payments of income in respect of a decedent in this manner would completely undermine the mandate of section 691 that the recipient of such income report it for the year when received, we agree with respondent that petitioner had no right to reduce its income in respect of a decedent in the year it received the bonus payments by the amounts it had previously reported as income under section 662.

Section 691(a)(1)[19] provides that the amount of all items of income in respect of a decedent shall be included in gross income, for the taxable year when received. This rule applies to income in respect of a decedent received by (A) the decedent's estate if it has acquired from the decedent the right to receive such income; (B) a person who has acquired, by reason of the decedent's death, the right to receive such income if the right to receive such income was not acquired by the decedent's estate from decedent; and (C) a person who has acquired the right to receive the amount by bequest, devise, or inheritance from the decedent, after a distribution by the decedent's estate of such right. See also sec. 1.691(a)-2(a), Income Tax Regs. In this case, subparagraph (A) required Mr. Rollert's estate to include in income amounts received with respect to those rights to bonus installments that it did not distribute to petitioner, and subparagraph (C) required petitioner to include those bonus installments that it received with respect to rights the estate had distributed to it.[20]

---

19. Sec. 691(a)(1) provides:

(a) Inclusion in Gross Income.—

(1) General rule.—The amount of all items of gross income in respect of a decedent which are not properly includible in respect of the taxable period in which falls the date of his death or a prior period (including the amount of all items of gross income in respect of a prior decedent, if the right to receive such amount was acquired by reason of the death of the prior decedent or by bequest, devise, or inheritance from the prior decedent) shall be included in the gross income, for the taxable year when received, of:

(A) the estate of the decedent, if the right to receive the amount is acquired by the decedent's estate from the decedent;

(B) the person who, by reason of the death of the decedent, acquires the right to receive the amount, if the right to receive the amount is not acquired by the decedent's estate from the decedent; or

(C) the person who acquires from the decedent the right to receive the amount by bequest, devise, or inheritance, if the amount is received after a distribution by the decedent's estate of such right.

20. Sec. 691(a)(2), which requires income to be recognized upon the "transfer" of a right to receive income in respect of a decedent, does not apply to this case since "transfer" is defined specifically to exclude transfers, such as those involved in this case, to a person entitled to receive the

Under section 661(a), an estate deducts in computing its taxable income (1) any amount of income required to be distributed currently and (2) "any other amounts properly paid or credited or required to be distributed for such taxable year." However, the total amount of these deductions may not exceed the estate's distributable net income.[21] Under section 662, the beneficiary to whom these distributions are made must include in gross income a corresponding amount.[22] Sections 661(b) and 662(b) are designed to assure that the character of the amounts deducted by the estate and taken into income by the beneficiary is proportionate to the character of items entering into the computation of distributable net income.

Petitioner and the estate applied the distribution rules of sections 661 and 662 to the distribution of the rights to receive subsequent bonus installments. With respect to each bonus right it distributed, the estate deducted the entire fair market value of the right as a distribution of its distributable net income. Petitioner took this same amount into income and used it as its basis in the right to the bonus installment. The character of petitioner's income was determined under sections 661(b) and 662(b) by reference to the character of the estate's distributable net income rather than by reference to the character of the bonus, itself.

Petitioner treated section 691 as coming into play only when the actual payments of the bonus installments were made. It treated each bonus payment as income when received but only to the extent, if any, that the amount paid to it exceeded the basis it had previously assigned the bonus right.

Petitioner claims that the distribution to it of the rights to the bonus installments falls squarely within the literal language of sections 661(a)(2) and 662(a)(2) as "amounts properly paid or credited." Since the rights were irrevocably transferred to petitioner and had an acknowledged value to it at the time of distribution, which was taken into income as a distribution from the estate, the distribution appears on its face to fall within the ambit of these provisions. However, the terms "amounts properly paid or credited" would be excessively broad if read literally. Thus, these words must be interpreted in the light of the statutory framework and overall legislative objectives of subchapter J. *Mott v. United States*, 199 Ct. Cl. 127, 462 F.2d 512, 517 (1972); *Estate of O'Connor v. Commissioner*, 69 T.C. 165, 178 (1977).

In characterizing the distribution of the rights to the bonus installments as amounts properly paid or credited, petitioner placed particular reliance upon

---

right to income in respect of the decedent by reason of the death of the decedent or by bequest, devise, or inheritance from the decedent.

21. Distributable net income is computed under sec. 643 by making specified adjustments to the estate's taxable income. Respondent does not challenge the correctness of the particular amounts of distributable net income reported by the estate in 1970, 1971, 1972, and 1973, the years in which rights to bonus installments were distributed.

22. Sec. 663 lists various types of distributions that are not considered distributions subject to secs. 661 and 662, but none of the sec. 663 exclusions apply here.

sections 1.661(a)-2(c) and (f), Income Tax Regs.[23] Section 1.661(a)-2(c) specifies that the term "any other amounts properly paid or credited or required to be distributed" includes a distribution of property in kind, which petitioner believes includes the distribution here of the rights to the bonus installments. Section 1.661(a)-2(f)(2), Income Tax Regs., states that, in determining the amount deductible by the estate and includable in gross income of the beneficiary, the property distributed in kind is taken into account at its fair market value at the time it was distributed, credited, or required to be distributed.[24] There is no dispute in this case as to the fair market values of the rights on the dates of distribution. Section 1.661(a)-2(f)(3) provides that to the extent the fair market value of the property is included in a beneficiary's gross income, the beneficiary takes such amount as its basis for the property.

Respondent points out that the assigning of tax basis to the rights to income in respect of a decedent has enabled petitioner to escape income taxation on much of

---

23. Sec. 1.661(a)-2(c), Income Tax Regs., provides in pertinent part:

> (c) The term "any other amounts properly paid or credited or required to be distributed" includes all amounts properly paid, credited, or required to be distributed by an estate or trust during the taxable year other than income required to be distributed currently. Thus, the term includes the payment of an annuity to the extent it is not paid out of income for the taxable year, and a distribution of property in kind (see paragraph (f) of this section). * * *

Sec. 1.661(a)-2(f), Income Tax Regs., provides:

> (f) If property is paid, credited, or required to be distributed in kind:
>
> (1) No gain or loss is realized by the trust or estate (or the other beneficiaries) by reason of the distribution, unless the distribution is in satisfaction of a right to receive a distribution in a specific dollar amount or in specific property other than that distributed.
>
> (2) In determining the amount deductible by the trust or estate and includible in the gross income of the beneficiary the property distributed in kind is taken into account at its fair market value at the time it was distributed, credited, or required to be distributed.
>
> (3) The basis of the property in the hands of the beneficiary is its fair market value at the time it was paid, credited, or required to be distributed, to the extent such value is included in the gross income of the beneficiary. To the extent that the value of property distributed in kind is not included in the gross income of the beneficiary, its basis in the hands of the beneficiary is governed by the rules in sections 1014 and 1015 and the regulations thereunder. * * *

24. In his answer to par. 6(1) of the amended petition, respondent admitted lifetime bonus installments were "property rights to income in respect of the decedent." Petitioner suggests that this is a concession by respondent that the bonus rights were "property" and thus subject to sec. 1.661(a)-2(f), Income Tax Regs. However, respondent specifically denied in the same paragraph that the transfer from the estate to petitioner resulted in an income tax basis in the bonus rights. In view of respondent's consistent argument that these rights are not subject to the distribution rules of secs. 661 and 662, because sec. 691 governs, it is clear respondent did not concede that sec. 1.661(a)-2(f), Income Tax Regs., applied to these bonus rights. We note that we are not concerned here with a dispute as to whether rights to income in respect of a decedent constitute property for sec. 661 purposes. At least in some contexts, rights to income in respect of a decedent are property for tax purposes. Indeed, sec. 1014(c) refers to "property which constitutes a right to receive an item of income in respect of a decedent," and the congressional report relating to the predecessor of sec. 691 distinguishes between the decedent's right to income and his "other property." S. Rept. 1631, 77th Cong., 2d Sess. (1942), 1942-2 C.B. 504, 580. We simply do not reach this issue in view of our holding that sec. 691 takes precedence over secs. 661 and 662.

the income payable under those rights. In each year in which the rights to the bonus installments were distributed, the estate had distributable net income consisting primarily of bonus payments actually received by it in that year. The estate retained part of this income, but offset this action by distributing to petitioner rights to bonus installments that had not yet been paid to the estate. Because it treated the transfers of the rights as distributions of distributable net income, the estate's deduction for distributions of distributable net income included the date-of-distribution values of the bonus rights. The estate thereby reduced its taxable income by carrying its distributable net income out to petitioner,[25] even though it retained much of the income it had received. Petitioner increased its income in the years of distribution by taking into income the date-of-distribution values of the bonus rights, in other words, the discounted value of the future installments of income. However, by assigning basis under section 1.661(a)-2(f)(3), Income Tax Regs., to these rights, its income was reduced by the same amounts in the later years when the bonus installments were actually paid, except with respect to two installments of stock which had declined in value between the date the rights were awarded and the dates the installments were paid, in which case the reduction in income was limited by the value of the stock when the installments were paid. Thus, for the bonus rights that increased in value between the dates of distribution and receipt, the net effect of the treatment of the bonus rights by petitioner and the estate was to reduce the aggregate taxable income of the estate and petitioner by the fair market values of the bonus rights as of the dates of distribution.[26] For the two stock installments that declined in value during

---

25. During 1970 through 1973, the distributions of the bonus rights were used to carry out over $ 400,000 of the estate's distributable net income.

26. The following examples illustrate the escape from taxation caused by petitioner's treating the distribution of a right to income in respect of a decedent (IRD) as a distribution of distributable net income (DNI).

EXAMPLE A (right to IRD not distributed):

Fact — Year 1: Estate has DNI of $50,000. No DNI distributed.
Year 2: Estate has no DNI except for IRD of $30,000. After receiving the $30,000, estate distributed it to legatee.

Tax treatment —
Year 1: $50,000 income to estate; no income to legatee.
Year 2: $30,000 income to legatee; no income to estate.

EXAMPLE B (right to IRD distributed in year 1 and treated as DNI distribution):

Facts — Year 1: Estate has DNI of $50,000. No DNI distributed except that right to IRD payable in year 2 is distributed to legatee. Present value of this right to IRD is $28,000.
Year 2: Estate has no DNI. The $30,000 of IRD is paid directly to legatee.

Tax treatment —
Year 1: $22,000 income to estate; $28,000 income to legatee.
Year 2: No income to estate; $2,000 income to legatee (i.e., $30,000 IRD minus basis of $28,000).

this period, aggregate taxable income was reduced by the values of the stock when paid to petitioner.

We therefore agree with respondent that the approach taken by petitioner and the estate allowed substantial sums of income to escape taxation.[27] Section 691 and its legislative history evince a clear purpose to tax income in respect of a decedent in the same manner as if it had been received by the decedent. Allowing the escape from taxation suggested by petitioner would undermine this purpose. In this respect, we believe the following language from *Commissioner v. Linde*, 213 F.2d 1, 5-6 (9th Cir. 1954), which we quoted with approval in *Estate of Sidles v. Commissioner*, 65 T.C. 873, 879 (1976), affd. without opinion 553 F.2d 102 (8th Cir. 1977), is instructive:

> there is nothing in the legislative history or in the text of Sec. 126 [the 1939 I.R.C. predecessor to section 691] to indicate that it was intended to be anything other than an improved device to accomplish the general purpose of the internal revenue code that all income should pay a tax and that death should not rob the United States of the revenue which otherwise it would have had. * * * [Fn. ref. omitted.]
>
> * * *
>
> It is our view that section 126 was but an improved method adopted by Congress in aid of its continuing effort to avoid the loss of tax upon income

---

COMPARISON:

	Income to estate	Income to legatee	Aggregate income to estate and legatee
Example A	$50,000	$30,000	$80,000
Example B	22,000	30,000	52,000
			$28,000 (Amount escaping taxation)

27. Commentators who have examined the tax consequences of an estate's distribution of rights to income in respect of a decedent have generally recognized that application of the distribution rules of secs. 661 and 662 would allow substantial sums to escape taxation. But they also recognize that a literal reading of secs. 661 and 662 and the regulations thereunder would allow this result. Some of the commentators believe these provisions of the Code and regulations must be interpreted as inapplicable to the distribution of rights to income in respect of a decedent. See 2 A. Casner, Estate Planning 804–805 (1980); M. Ferguson, J. Freeland & R. Stephens, Federal Income Taxation of Estates and Beneficiaries 533–534 (1970); Rammel, "'Income in Respect of Decedent' Provisions Lend Themselves to Postmortem Estate Planning," 7 Tax'n for Acct. 358, 361 (1971). Others have concluded, however, that the distribution of the rights to income in respect of a decedent should be accepted as "amounts distributed" for purposes of secs. 661 and 662. See Quigley, "The IRS's Position on Income in Respect of a Decedent," 121 Tr. & Est. 15 (1982); Wilf, "Planning for Distributions of Property-in-Kind After the Tax Reform Act," 12 Inst. on Est. Plan., sec. 1612(1978); "Income in Respect of a Decedent," 5 Real Prop. Prob. & Tr. J. 307, 309 (1970).

merely because of the death of the decedent who would have paid a tax upon the same economic returns had he lived to receive them.

Petitioner would have us accept its taking into income under section 662(a) the value of the bonus rights when distributed as satisfying the objective of section 691 to tax all income in respect of a decedent to the actual recipient of the income. Petitioner is correct that the overall amount of income reported by it under either section 662(a) or section 691 was similar to the amount it would have reported had it not treated the receipt of the rights to future bonus installments as distributions of the estate's distributable net income. However, as we have explained above, the aggregate amount of income reported by the estate and petitioner was substantially reduced by petitioner's approach since the distributions of the rights to future bonus installments were treated as carrying out to petitioner the estate's distributable net income. The estate thereby reduced its reported income and was able to accumulate funds which could subsequently be paid out, tax-free, to petitioner, the residuary legatee.

For this reason, we do not believe that petitioner's reporting income under section 662 when it received the rights to subsequent bonus installments should be treated as satisfying the requirement that the recipient report all income in respect of a decedent. Furthermore, even if we were to assume that petitioner's treatment of the bonus rights and installments satisfied the requirement of section 691 that income in respect of a decedent be taxed to the recipient of such income, we see no way that it could also satisfy the timing and characterization rules of that section.

Section 691(a)(1) requires income in respect of a decedent to be included in income "for the taxable year when received." It is designed to defer taxation of these amounts until actual receipt. Were we to accept petitioner's view that its reporting income when the rights to bonus installments were distributed satisfied the objective that it be taxed on the income in respect of a decedent, it would be apparent that the timing rule had been violated. Under petitioner's approach, the only income deferred until actual receipt would be the excess of the amount received over the amount reported in the year the right was distributed.

Section 691(a)(3) requires the character of income in respect of a decedent to be the same as it would have been in the hands of the decedent if the decedent had lived and received such income. Here, however, only that income actually reported in the year of receipt as income in respect of a decedent took its character under section 691(a)(3). The character of the rights to income in respect of a decedent that were distributed was determined under section 662(b) by reference to the character of the estate's distributable net income. Thus, it is apparent that petitioner's approach would also cripple the characterization rule for income in respect of a decedent.

It is a well-accepted principle of law that a specific statute controls over a general one, even if the latter might otherwise appear to govern. *Bulova Watch Co. v. United States*, 365 U.S. 753, 758 (1961); *Estate of O'Connor v. Commissioner, supra* at 178; *Essenfeld v. Commissioner*, 37 T.C. 117, 122–123 (1961), affd. 311 F.2d 208 (2d Cir. 1962).

As we have explained, there is an apparent conflict between section 691 and the distribution rules of sections 661 and 662. In view of the nature of section 691 as a specific statutory scheme for the taxation of income in respect of a decedent, which would be largely defeated were rights to income in respect of a decedent allowed to acquire basis under the distribution rules, we believe section 691 must take precedence, here.

Although the legislative history of section 691 and the regulations under that section do not specifically address the issue presented in this case, they do tend to support our conclusion that sections 661 and 662 should not be applied to an estate's distribution of rights to income in respect of a decedent. Example 1 of section 1.691(a)-2(b), Income Tax Regs., which illustrates the application of the general principle of taxing income in respect of decedent, when received, involves a fact situation quite similar to that now before us. A decedent was entitled to salary payments in five annual installments after his death. The estate collected the first two payments and then distributed to the residuary legatee the right to the remaining three installments. The example states that the estate must include the first two installments in its gross income and the legatee must include the subsequent three installments in his gross income. This example does not even refer to the possibility of the right to the final three installments being treated as a distribution governed by sections 661 and 662. If the distribution rules were meant to apply to distributions of rights to income in respect of a decedent, the absence of any reference to this effect in the regulation is incomprehensible.

The current rules in section 691 for the taxation of income in respect of a decedent are derived primarily from section 126, I.R.C. 1939, which was added by section 134 of the Revenue Act of 1942, 56 Stat. 831. The legislative history of that provision clearly states Congress' intent that amounts of income in respect of a decedent—

> be treated, in the hands of the persons receiving them, as income of the same nature and to the same extent as such amounts would be income if the decedent remained alive and received such amounts. [S. Rept. 1631, 77th Cong., 2d Sess. (1942), 1942-2 C.B. 504, 580.]

At several points, the Senate report indicates the provision was designed to place the recipient of the income in respect of a decedent in the same position as the decedent with respect to both the amount and character of income. Nothing in the legislative history of the Internal Revenue Code of 1954, which introduced the distribution rules of sections 661 and 662, indicates any congressional desire to change the requirement that income in respect of a decedent be taxed in the same manner as it would have been treated if it had been received by the decedent, himself. The decedent would normally report for tax purposes each installment as received, with the full installment being included as income. The provisions of the legislative history cited by petitioner[28] do not indicate otherwise. All that

28. H. Rept. 1337, 83d Cong., 2d Sess. 60, A198 (1954); S. Rept. 1622, 83d Cong., 2d Sess. 84, 348 (1954).

these provisions are concerned with is the general rule of sections 661 and 662 that all distributions are deductible by the estate and includable by the beneficiary when distributed. They do not deal, however, with the question before us now of whether a distribution of rights to income in respect of a decedent is a distribution subject to sections 661 and 662.

Contrary to petitioner's contention, the changes made when the Internal Revenue Code of 1954, was enacted actually support respondent. H. Rept. 1337, 83d Cong., 2d Sess. 64, A218-A219 (1954); S. Rept. 1622, 83d Cong., 2d Sess. 87-88, 373–374 (1954). Congress extended section 691(a)(1) so that it applies to rights to income in respect of a prior decedent that are acquired by a beneficiary from a second decedent. As an example of how this provision works, the committee reports mention a widow who was entitled to receive insurance renewal commissions but who died before receiving such commission income. Under the pre-1954 law, the fair market value of the right to receive the commissions had to be included in the widow's final income tax return, even though she left to her son the right to receive the commissions. Congress explained that section 691 was being expanded so that no income would be realized on the transfer to the widow's estate of the right to income from the prior decedent. The commissions earned by the prior decedent should be taxed to the recipient upon receipt and their character determined by reference to the prior decedent. These results outlined in the reports under the post-1954 law could not be obtained if petitioner's theory were accepted, since petitioner would treat the distribution from the estate of the prior decedent to the widow as a distribution of a right to income in respect of a decedent, which would require the widow to recognize income and would create a basis in the right to receive future commissions. The rights to the commission income had necessarily been distributed from the estate of the prior decedent to the widow, and under petitioner's theory, the widow would have reported the fair market value of such rights when they were distributed to her and taken such value as her basis in the rights. Nowhere do the committee reports even intimate that this might be the proper treatment.

We address finally petitioner's contention that its treatment of the bonus rights did not defeat the overall scheme of section 691, since section 1.661(a)-2(f), Income Tax Regs., forgives any income tax on the appreciation in value of property in kind distributed by an estate or trust.[29] It is apparent that this regulation does cause the nonrecognition of some unrealized appreciation. However, there are several key distinctions between the nonrecognition sanctioned by this regulation and the situation before us now. First of all, petitioner has assumed that the difference between the value of a right to income in respect of a decedent and its basis can properly be labeled as appreciation. However, the right to income in respect of a decedent is the right to compensation income, which was already earned by the decedent and became nonforfeitable upon his death. This is simply income that has been earned

29. See generally M. Ferguson, J. Freeland & R. Stephens, Federal Income Taxation of Estates and Beneficiaries 525–533 (1970).

but not yet reported, and thus cannot be seen as constituting appreciation in the value of property. Any increase in the value of bonus rights resulted from the fact that they were initially discounted because of the delay that had to be borne until the recipient could actually enjoy receipt of the income.

More importantly, petitioner's analogy to appreciated property is misplaced because it fails to consider that section 1014(a) generally allows a step-up in basis to the date-of-death valuation for property acquired from a decedent, while section 1014(c) denies a basis step-up for rights to income in respect of a decedent. Petitioner's approach would allow an escape from income taxation for all income in respect of a decedent represented by the value of the right to such income when distributed. This would have the effect of allowing a step-up in basis for increases in value of rights to income in respect of a decedent occurring before the decedent's death, as well as those occurring between the date of death and the date of distribution. Thus, petitioner's interpretation of section 1.661(a)-2(f), Income Tax Regs., sees respondent as having allowed by regulation what was specifically denied by statute under section 1014(c), i.e., a step-up basis to the date-of-death value for rights to income in respect of a decedent.

We hold as a general principle that section 691 overrides sections 661 and 662 and precludes the assignment of a basis to a right to income in respect of a decedent when that right is transferred by an estate to a legatee. Therefore, we find in this case that petitioner improperly offset against its income in respect of a decedent, basis previously assigned to the rights to the bonus installments. Because the lifetime bonus installments were included in the gross estate, in computing petitioner's income tax liability relative to the contested bonus installments, a deduction under section 691(c) should be allowed for the Federal estate tax the estate paid with respect to the rights to these installments.

Decision will be entered under Rule 155.

Rev. Rul. 68-195, 1968-1 CB 305 — IRC Sec. 661

The distribution to a sole beneficiary by an estate of the right to receive future payments under section 736(a) of the Internal Revenue Code of 1954, is not property distributed in kind for purposes of the deduction provisions of section 661(a) of the Code and the regulations thereunder. If in lieu of distribution of this right to receive future section 736(a) payments, the estate distributes cash proceeds from a loan, the result is the same as to the availability of a deduction under section 661(a) of the Code.

Advice has been requested whether, under the circumstances described below, the distribution by a decedent's estate to a sole beneficiary of its right under a partnership agreement, to receive payments measured by a share of future partnership earnings, represents an amount properly paid or credited or required to be distributed for such taxable year, for purposes of a deduction by the estate under section 661(a) of the Internal Revenue Code of 1954.

Prior to his death, the decedent filed Federal income tax returns on a calendar year accounting period and was a member of a partnership that also filed returns on a calendar year accounting period. The decedent's distributive share of partnership net income for 1964 was 50x dollars which had been withdrawn by him before his death on December 30, 1964.

The decedent's return filed for the period ending with his death did not include any of his share of partnership net income for 1964, all of which was properly included in the income of the estate for its first taxable year.

The decedent's probate estate consisted only of the right to receive amounts estimated at 40x dollars, payable under the partnership agreement as a share of future partnership earnings for the three years following the year in which the decedent died.

In its first taxable year, the estate distributed the right to receive such payments to the beneficiary.

Section 736(a)(1) of the Code provides that payments in liquidation of the interest of a deceased partner shall be considered as a distributive share to the recipient of partnership income if the amount thereof is determined with regard to the income of the partnership.

Section 661(a) of the Code provides in part that in any taxable year there shall be allowed as a deduction in computing the taxable income of an estate, any amounts properly paid or credited or required to be distributed for such taxable year to the extent of the distributable net income of the estate. Section 1.661(a)-2(c) of the Income Tax Regulations provides, in pertinent part, that the term "any other amounts properly paid or credited or required to be distributed" includes a distribution of property in kind. Section 1.661(a)-2(f)(2) of the regulations provides that in determining the amount deductible by the estate, the property distributed in kind is taken into account at its fair market value.

The estate's right to receive payments estimated at 40x dollars, payable under the partnership agreement as a share of future partnership earnings for the three years following the year in which the decedent died represents a right to receive partnership income for such years within the meaning of section 736(a)(1) of the Code. This right to receive income is not within the term "any other amounts properly paid or credited or required to be distributed" for purposes of section 661(a) of the Code and the regulations thereunder.

Accordingly, in the instant case, the distribution to the sole beneficiary by the decedent's estate of its right to receive future payments under section 736(a) of the Code is not property distributed in kind for purposes of the deduction provisions of section 661(a) of the Code and the regulations thereunder.

Under the same general facts, if in lieu of a distribution of the right to receive section 736(a) payments, the estate distributes cash of 40x dollars representing proceeds of a loan, the result is the same as to the availability of a deduction under section 661(a) of the Code. The effect of such a transaction will be treated the same as though the estate had distributed the right to receive section 736(a) payments to the beneficiary and then with the proceeds of the loan had purchased the right to receive the payments from the beneficiary for 40x dollars. Under the provisions of section 691(a)(2) of the Code, the beneficiary has ordinary income of 40x dollars. The estate has purchased an asset in which it has a basis of 40x dollars as provided by section 1012 of the Code. No deduction to the estate under section 661(a) of the Code results.

III. Income Inclusion

As with simple trusts, complex trust and estate beneficiaries include in gross income the amount for which the entity has received a distribution deduction under § 661. Code § 662.

The key to understanding the distribution rules for complex trusts and estates and the DNI allocations requires mastering the following important concepts: (A) the "tier system" of distributions; (B) the separate share rule, (C) the 65-day rule under § 663(b), (D) specific bequest rules under § 663(a)(1), and (E) in-kind distributions. These topics are discussed in the material that follows.

A. The "Tier System"

Akin to simple trusts, complex trust and estate distributions are generally considered to carry out a pro rata part of each item of DNI. Code § 662(b). In other words, complex trust or estate distributions are deemed to consist of the same proportion of each class of items entering into the DNI computation as the total of each class bears to overall DNI. Treas. Reg. 1.662(b)-1. However, section 661 makes a distinction between beneficiaries who are entitled to accounting income and beneficiaries who are recipients of discretionary distributions. This allocation is controlled by the "tier system" contained in § 662(a).

With respect to the tier system, the following nine points are important to keep in mind:

1. The tier system is applied in determining the tax effects of distributions on the trust and estate beneficiaries. It has no independent tax effect on the trust or estate itself.

2. The tier system does not apply to simple trusts.

3. The purpose of the tier system is to adjust the tax effects of distributions between and among first and second tier beneficiaries.

4. When all beneficiaries who have received distributions are in the same tier, the tier system has no practical application due to the general rule that DNI is allocated pro rata based on distribution amounts received by each beneficiary.

5. A first tier beneficiary is one to whom an amount of income is required to be distributed currently.

6. A second tier beneficiary is one who receives a distribution of income that is not required to be distributed currently, i.e., a discretionary distribution, or, receives a mandatory or discretionary distribution of corpus.[30]

7. For tax purposes, but not for distribution purposes, a second tier beneficiary is favored. For distribution purposes, but not for tax purposes, a first tier beneficiary is favored. The reasoning is flushed out in the paragraphs that follow.

8. The separate share rule (discussed below) insulates beneficiaries of one share from being taxed upon the income belonging to another share.

9. The separate share rule applies to estates.

With these nine points in mind, consider how the tier system operates.

First-tier beneficiaries include in gross income all income required to be distributed but not in excess of DNI (excluding, for this purpose, any tax exempt interest included in DNI). If the amount required to be distributed currently to all first-tier beneficiaries exceeds DNI, then each first-tier beneficiary is required to include in gross income only that beneficiary's proportionate share of DNI.[31] Code § 662(a)(1). This is the same result that would apply effectively to a simple trust.

Second-tier beneficiaries include in gross income all amounts properly paid, credited, or required to be distributed, but not greater than the amount, if any, by which DNI exceeds all first-tier distributions. If second-tier distributions are greater than the amount by which DNI exceeds first-tier distributions, second tier beneficiaries include in gross income a proportionate share of such excess based on the ratio of the amount distributed to each second-tier beneficiary to the amount distributed to all second-tier beneficiaries. Section 662(a)(2).

Two formulae portray how DNI is allocated under the tier regime:

$$\frac{\text{Tier-one distributions to the beneficiary}}{\text{Tier-one distributions to all beneficiaries of DNI}} \times \text{DNI} = \text{Beneficiary's Share}$$

$$\frac{\text{Tier-two distributions to the beneficiary}}{\text{Tier-two distributions to all beneficiaries of remaining DNI}} \times \text{Remaining DNI} = \text{Beneficiary's Share}$$

Example: A trust instrument requires the trustee to distribute the first $30,000 of income to A and gives the trustee to discretion the distribute income and principal to B. The trust has $40,000 of DNI. The trustee

30. The terms of most wills do not require current income distributions. That being the case, the vast majority of estate distributions constitute second-tier distributions.

31. DNI is modified for first tier beneficiaries if the trust or estate is entitled to a charitable deduction. See the example below.

distributes $30,000 to A and $20,000 to B. If the normal pro rata rules were applied to the distributions, A would report 60% of the DNI, or $24,000 of the DNI ($30,000/$50,000 × $40,000) and B would report 40% of DNI, or $16,000 of the DNI ($20,000/$50,000 × $40,000). The DNI would be allocated pro rata to each beneficiary based on distributions to each. The tier system, however, requires a different result. Because the trust is required to distribute $30,000 of income to A, A is a first-tier beneficiary. B, whose distribution is discretionary with the trustee, is a second-tier beneficiary. Under the tier system, DNI would be allocated first to A (the first-tier beneficiary) to the extent of the income required to be distributed to A ($30,000), and the balance of the DNI after taking into consideration the distribution to A ($40,000 DNI less 30,000 DNI allocated to A or $10,000) would be allocated to B (the second-tier beneficiary). Although B received a distribution of $20,000 equal to 40% of the total distributions, there is only $10,000 of DNI remaining to be allocated to his distribution after allocating $30,000 of DNI to the first-tier beneficiary, namely, A. The $10,000 balance of the $20,000 distributed to B is treated as a tax-free distribution to B.

Example: A trust has $40,000 of DNI and accounting income. The trust is required to distribute 1/2 of the income annually to A, with the balance being distributable in the trustee's discretion. The trustee distributes $20,000 to A and makes discretionary distributions of $20,000 to each of B and C. A must include $20,000 in his gross income, while B and C each include $10,000 in their gross income. Since A is a first-tier beneficiary, 1/2 of the $40,000 DNI is allocable to A. The $20,000 balance of the DNI remaining after distributions to the first-tier beneficiary ($40,000 less $20,000 allocated to A) is allocated equally between B and C, both second-tier beneficiaries. Note that although all of the beneficiaries received the same amount ($20,000), the amount included in their gross income is different based upon their status as first- or second-tier beneficiaries. Although they all received $20,000, the tier system causes $20,000 of the total $40,000 of DNI to be allocated to A; furthermore, B and C, who are second-tier beneficiaries, split the remaining $20,000 of DNI between themselves, each reporting $10,000 of DNI.

A beneficiary may be both a first and second-tier beneficiary.

Example: Under the terms of Trust X, A and B are each required to be paid 25 percent of net income quarterly. The trustee has discretion to pay other amounts of income and principal to A, B, and C. For the trust's taxable year, accounting income is $100,000, DNI is $90,000, and, in addition to TAI required to be distributed to A and B, the trustee made discretionary payments of $10,000 to A and $90,000 to C. The table below illustrates the allocation of DNI among A, B, and C under the tier system.

	A	B	C	DNI
First-tier	$25,000	$25,000	$ 0	$50,000
Second-tier	4,000	0	36,000	40,000
Total	$29,000	$25,000	$36,000	$90,000

Fifty percent of the accounting income is required to be distributed currently to A and B. These are first-tier amounts, and A and B are first-tier beneficiaries. Thus, A and B are each allocated $25,000 of DNI. Next, any remaining DNI—$40,000 in the example—is allocated to second-tier beneficiaries, namely, A, B, and C. A received 10 percent of second-tier distributions ($10,000/$100,000) and is thus allocated $4,000 of the remaining DNI (10% of $40,000 remaining DNI). C received 90 percent of second-tier distributions ($90,000/$100,000), and thus $36,000 of the remaining DNI (90% of $40,000 remaining DNI) is allocated to him. B, also a potential second-tier beneficiary, did not receive any discretionary distribution, so none of the remaining $40,000 of DNI is allocated to him. Note that A is both a first and second tier beneficiary.

As is also true for simple trusts, the amounts distributed and deducted by the trust or estate are treated as consisting of the same proportion of each class of items entering into the DNI computation as the total of each class bears to the total DNI, unless the governing instrument specifically allocates different classes of income to different beneficiaries. Code § 662(b).

Deductions entering into the DNI computation are allocated between and among the income items comprising DNI in accordance with the same principles that govern simple trusts. There is one exception to the foregoing rule: charitable distributions are first ratably apportioned among each class of items of income entering into the DNI computation, including tax-exempt income. Treas. Reg. 1.661(b)-2.[32]

Two of those nuances—the rules that relate to the charitable deduction and the timing of inclusion—are explained below. The third—the death of a beneficiary—is left for a more advanced course on fiduciary income taxation.

1. Charitable Deductions

If trust or estate is entitled to a charitable deduction, special rules apply for determining the amount taxable to first-tier beneficiaries and the character of such amounts.

32. This rule does not apply to simple trusts, because a simple trust, by definition, cannot have a charitable deduction.

The second sentence of Code § 662(a)(1) and the last two sentences of § 662(b) provide that if the amount of income required to be distributed exceeds DNI computed without the charitable deduction, then the first-tier beneficiaries take into income a higher, modified, DNI. More specifically, the DNI for first-tier beneficiaries is modified by not taking the charitable deduction into account. Such modified DNI sets the ceiling for taxing first-tier beneficiaries. As a result, first-tier beneficiaries never receive any advantage from the charitable deduction. The language of § 662(a) requires that the income required to be distributed be considered as distributed first to the individual beneficiaries and then to charities.

Treas. Reg. 1.662(b)-2 explains that the charitable deduction is disregarded "to the extent that it exceeds the [accounting] income of the trust for the taxable year reduced by the amounts for the taxable year required to be distributed currently." In essence, the regulation is treating all required distributions as being first from gross income before any distribution to charity. The regulations have the following example.

> A trust instrument provides that $30,000 of its income must be distributed currently to A, and the balance may either be distributed to B, distributed to a designated charity, or accumulated. Accumulated income may be distributed to B and to the charity. The trust for its taxable year has $40,000 of taxable interest and $10,000 of tax-exempt income, with no expenses. The trustee distributed $30,000 to A, $50,000 to charity X, and $10,000 to B.
>
> Distributable net income for the purpose of determining the character of the distribution to A is $30,000 (the charitable contributions deduction, for this purpose, being taken into account only to the extent of $20,000, the difference between the income of the trust for the taxable year, $50,000, and the amount required to be distributed currently, $30,000).
>
> The charitable contributions deduction taken into account, $20,000, is allocated proportionately to the items of income of the trust, $16,000 to taxable interest and $4,000 to tax-exempt income.
>
> Under section 662(a)(1), the amount of income required to be distributed currently to A is $30,000, which consists of the balance of these items, $24,000 of taxable interest and $6,000 of tax-exempt income.
>
> In determining the amount to be included in the gross income of B under section 662 for the taxable year, however, the entire charitable contributions deduction is taken into account, with the result that there is no distributable net income and therefore no amount to be included in gross income.

In determining the character of the amounts distributed to first-tier beneficiaries, the last sentence of § 662(b) provides that DNI is computed without regard to any portion of the charitable deduction that is not attributable to income of the taxable year (e.g., income paid in one year but elected to be treated as paid in the prior year).

2. *Timing of Inclusion*

If a trust or estate and a beneficiary have the same taxable year, distributions are included in the beneficiary's income in the year distributed. If a beneficiary and a trust or estate have different taxable years, the beneficiary will report the distribution for the taxable year that includes the last day of the taxable year of the trust or estate. § 662(c). This is the same rule that applies to simple trusts. As shown below, this rule provides the tax benefit of deferral.

> **Example:** An estate has a January 31 fiscal year-end. The trustee makes a distribution to the beneficiary on June 30, 2019. The beneficiary reports the distribution for the taxable year that includes the last day of the taxable year of the trust or estate. The last day of taxable year of the estate is January 31, 2020, which falls into the beneficiary's 2020 tax year. Thus, the beneficiary reports (and pays tax on) the distribution on his 2020 tax year (he or she doesn't have to pay until April 15, 2021) even though he received the distribution on June 30, 2019. The use of a fiscal year by an estate thus enables beneficiaries to defer income recognition.

B. Separate Share Rule and Unequal Distributions

The general rule is that DNI is allocated proportionately to beneficiaries based on distributions made to each. However, where separate shares exist for beneficiaries, applying the rules of sections 661 and 662 can lead to illogical and unfair results. The separate share rule is designed to address this inequity.

The separate share rule is set forth in § 663(c). It provides as follows: "For the sole purpose of determining the amount of distributable net income in the application of sections 661 and 662, in the case of a single trust having more than one beneficiary, substantially separate and independent shares of different beneficiaries in the trust shall be treated as separate trusts." The identical rule applies to estates. *Id.* ("Rules similar to the rules of the preceding provisions of this subsection shall apply to treat substantially separate and independent shares of different beneficiaries in an estate having more than 1 beneficiary as separate estates.").

The separate share rule allocates DNI among multiple beneficiaries based on their "share" of the trust. § 663(c). Note that, like the tier system, the separate share rule only applies if there is more than one beneficiary; furthermore, distributions to beneficiaries who do not have separate shares are allocated DNI based on the distributions made to them over the total distributions made to all the beneficiaries in a particular year, namely, a proportionate share of DNI.

The effect of the separate share rule is to limit a trust beneficiary's potential tax liability to the amount of the DNI attributable to such beneficiary's share of the trust.

Harkness v. United States

469 F.2d 310 (Ct. Cl. 1972)

PER CURIAM:[33]

In her 1955 federal income tax return, plaintiff included in her gross income $413,379.04 as income received during that year from her husband's estate. In 1961, the District Director of Internal Revenue for the Manhattan District, New York, took the position that, instead of such sum, plaintiff should have included the amount of $630,740.04, i.e., an additional $217,361. The inclusion of such larger amount in plaintiff's gross income resulted (after the making of various adjustments) in plaintiff's allegedly owing an additional $188,153.35 in income tax for such year, and the Director at that time assessed plaintiff in such amount, plus interest thereon in the amount of $60,103.40, or a total of $248,256.75. Plaintiff paid the additional tax and interest so assessed, and then filed a timely claim for refund therefor. Having received neither a notice of disallowance nor any refund, plaintiff instituted the instant suit to recover such assessed amount, plus interest.

Plaintiff's husband died on August 12, 1954. By his will, he gave plaintiff one-half of his residuary estate. The remaining half was, after the deduction therefrom of any "legacy, succession, transfer, estate or inheritance taxes payable by [the] estate with respect to any property disposed of by [the] Will or payable by any recipient of any such property," given, in equal shares, to the trustees of four testamentary trusts for the children of plaintiff and the decedent (i.e., the issue of their or prior marriages). The will provided that such taxes "shall be paid by [the] Executors out of [the] estate as part of the expenses of administration thereof," with the proviso that "no part of such taxes shall be deducted from or payable out of the one-half (½) of [the] residuary estate" which the decedent bequeathed to plaintiff.

During 1955, and prior to the ultimate distribution of the residuary estate, the executors made distributions to the five beneficiaries thereof in the total sum of $36,004,082.23. Of this amount plaintiff, by eleven payments, received $27,467,768.51. The four trusts, by ten payments to each, received the balance of $8,436,295.75 (in equal shares of approximately $2,134,000). All the distributions were in the form of cash, stocks and bonds. None of the distributions were required by the will to be made prior to the ultimate distribution of the residuary estate.

The federal fiduciary income tax return filed by the executors on behalf of the estate showed distributable net income[34] for 1955 in the amount of $1,005,682.94. A deduction of $826,758.68 was shown on the return for distributions of such income

33. This opinion incorporates the opinion of Trial Commissioner Saul Richard Gamer (now Chief Commissioner), with modifications and additions made in the light of the presentation by the parties to the judges which, in the case of the Government, differed in substantial part from the presentation to the Trial Commissioner.

34. Section 643 of Part I, "Estates, Trusts and Beneficiaries," of Subchapter J, "Estates, Trusts, Beneficiaries, and Decedents" of the Internal Revenue Code of 1954 (26 U.S.C. § 643 (1958)) defines

to the five residuary estate beneficiaries, the difference of $178,924.26 between such two figures consisting of tax-exempt income (and expenses allocable thereto).

Section 662(a)(2)(B) of the Internal Revenue Code of 1954 (26 U.S.C. § 662(a)(2)(B) (1958)) provides that, where the amounts distributed to all beneficiaries of an estate accumulating income or distributing corpus exceed the distributable net income of the estate, each beneficiary shall include in his gross income an amount which bears the same ratio to distributable net income as the total amount distributed to him bears to the total of the amounts distributed to all the beneficiaries.[35]

The amount of $27,467,768.51 which plaintiff received in 1955 from the residuary estate equaled 76.2907 percent of the total amount of $36,004,082.23 distributed to all beneficiaries during such taxable year. Since such total amount distributed exceeded the distributable net income, the District Director concluded that the provisions of Section 662(a)(2)(B) were applicable and accordingly applied the same percentage to the taxable distributable net income of the estate, the resulting

---

the term "distributable net income" as "the taxable income of the estate or trust" with certain modifications set forth therein.

35. Section 662 provides as follows:

§ 662. INCLUSION OF AMOUNTS IN GROSS INCOME OF BENEFICIARIES OF ESTATES AND TRUSTS ACCUMULATING INCOME OR DISTRIBUTING CORPUS.

(a) Inclusion.

Subject to subsection (b), there shall be included in the gross income of a beneficiary to whom an amount specified in section 661(a) is paid, credited, or required to be distributed (by an estate or trust described in section 661), the sum of the following amounts:

(1) Amounts required to be distributed currently.

The amount of income for the taxable year required to be distributed currently to such beneficiary, whether distributed or not. If the amount of income required to be distributed currently to all beneficiaries exceeds the distributable net income (computed without the deduction allowed by section 642(c), relating to deduction for charitable, etc., purposes) of the estate or trust, then, in lieu of the amount provided in the preceding sentence, there shall be included in the gross income of the beneficiary an amount which bears the same ratio to distributable net income (as so computed) as the amount of income required to be distributed currently to such beneficiary bears to the amount required to be distributed currently to all beneficiaries. For purposes of this section, the phrase "the amount of income for the taxable year required to be distributed currently" includes any amount required to be paid out of income or corpus to the extent such amount is paid out of income for such taxable year.

(2) Other amounts distributed.

All other amounts properly paid, credited, or required to be distributed to such beneficiary for the taxable year. If the sum of—

(A) the amount of income for the taxable year required to be distributed currently to all beneficiaries, and

(B) all other amounts properly paid, credited, or required to be distributed to all beneficiaries exceeds the distributable net income of the estate or trust, then, in lieu of the amount provided in the preceding sentence, there shall be included in the gross income of the beneficiary an amount which bears the same ratio to distributable net income (reduced by the amounts specified in (A)) as the other amounts properly paid, credited or required to be distributed to the beneficiary bear to the other amounts properly paid, credited, or required to be distributed to all beneficiaries.

figure being regarded as the amount which plaintiff should have included in her gross income. Application of such 76.2907 percent to the taxable distributable net income figure of $826,758.68 produces the aforementioned figure of $630,740.04 as the amount the District Director concluded plaintiff was required by the statute to have included in her gross income. The inclusion of such amount in plaintiff's gross income produced the additional income tax which is the subject of this suit.

Plaintiff contends that, pursuant to accurate accounting by the executors in calculating the amount of the estate corpus and income which they distributed to the five beneficiaries in 1955, she in fact actually received during the year only the taxable amount of $413,379.34, which amount was but one-half of the taxable distributable net income, and not 76.2907 percent thereof, the figure that the statutory formula produces. Such accounting in the administration of the estate was, plaintiff says, in no way tax motivated, but was in accordance with common practices followed at that time by executors in New York in the administration of estates, and was permitted by the terms of the will and applicable local law. Furthermore, she points out, the accounts of the executors for the year 1955, which set forth the income distributions to plaintiff and the four trusts on a basis of one-half to plaintiff and the other half to the trusts, were judicially settled and allowed by the Surrogate Court of New York County, New York.[36]

Although the approximately $27,500,000 paid to plaintiff during the year greatly exceeded the aggregate amount of approximately $8,500,000 paid to the four trusts, each of such total payments concededly consisting of both corpus and income, plaintiff says that such unequal amounts nevertheless included the equal amounts of $413,379.34 of taxable net income. For this result, plaintiff relies upon the manner in which the executors made their distributions of what they designated as "corpus." The executors, in accordance with a common New York practice, made simultaneous distributions of "principal" and "income" among all the residuary legatees on a basis proportionate to their respective interests in the residuary estate. Further, since here the will directed that all legacy, succession, transfer, estate, or inheritance taxes (sometimes collectively referred to as "death taxes") were to be paid as administration expenses of the estate, but with plaintiff's share of the residuary estate to be undiminished thereby, whenever the executors made any such tax payments (which were, according to their accounting, entirely out of corpus), they also made, again following a common New York practice where wills provided for payment of death taxes out of one or more shares of the residue but not out of one or more other shares, "corpus" distributions to the plaintiff simultaneously with and in the same amounts as such tax payments. Thus, these simultaneous distributions to plaintiff always served, says plaintiff, to keep the remaining corpus interests of the plaintiff and the four trusts in the residuary estate in equal balance, with such equal corpus

36. Three of the four children were minors and a special guardian appointed by the court to represent them reported that, insofar as their interests were concerned, the executors' accounts were correct.

shares therefore always generating equal amounts of income. The result of adopting these simultaneous distributions practices was the avoidance of complicated calculations of shares of income earned, over varying periods of time, by unequal shares of principal (or by undistributed income). (In this case the decedent's will specifically provided that the income should be distributed proportionately to the residuary legatees, and that if distribution of the residuary estate was not made simultaneously, "an adjustment of the income shall be made by my Executors.") To illustrate, when, on January 1, 1955, the executors distributed $1,125,000 to each of the trusts—amounts which the executors designated as coming entirely from corpus[37]—they simultaneously paid plaintiff $4,500,000, also designated as a corpus distribution. And when, on February 8, 1955, they paid $4,310,000 on account of the New York estate tax, they distributed the identical amount (again designated as principal on their accounts) to plaintiff. Similarly, when, on November 14, 1955, they paid $14,621,454.81 on account of the federal estate tax, plus an amount aggregating $3,524,558.49 to the four trusts, such sums totaling $18,146,013.29, they distributed the identical total sum to plaintiff (all amounts again being designated as coming entirely out of principal). In accordance with the will, the New York and federal estate tax payments were deducted from the trusts' aggregate one-half interest in the residuary estate. The several 1955 distributions to plaintiff and the four trusts which the executors designated as distributions of estate income were so calculated by the executors that the amount of such income distributed to plaintiff on any date equaled the aggregate amount distributed to the trusts on the same date.

It is on the above basis that plaintiff argues she actually received only one-half of the distributable net income of the estate in 1955, and not 76 percent.

In a situation such as the instant one, plaintiff contends, Section 662(a)(2)(B) was not intended to be applicable for the formula there prescribed would attribute to plaintiff income which she in fact did not receive. She should not, she argues, have attributed to her more than her actual share of estate income simply because the executors, in their authorized discretion, made principal distributions to her in order to balance the death tax payments and other principal distributions to the trusts. The purpose of the statutory provision here involved was, she contends, to prevent fiduciaries, where the estate had principal, current income, and accumulated income, from controlling tax consequences by manipulating distributions, as, for instance, making distributions designated as coming from "income" to beneficiaries in low income tax brackets, while distributions designated as coming from "principal" are made to beneficiaries in high brackets, and therefore not taxable at all.[38] There was no intent here on the part of the executors, she argues, to gain any kind of income tax advantage for plaintiff.

37. As of that date, the executors' accounts showed $1,155.42 of undistributed 1954 estate income.

38. Under 26 U.S.C. § 102 (1970), the value of property acquired by bequest is not taxable income to the distributee. However, income from bequeathed property, as well as a gift composed of income

These contentions cannot be accepted as justifying recovery. There can be no doubt but that plaintiff's situation falls squarely within the literal provisions of Section 662(a)(2)(B), and plaintiff is not understood to contend otherwise. The nub of her contention is that the payments here involved should not be treated as being covered by the statute because the executors' actions were not tax motivated. Even so, the section applies. Clear statutory coverage of this kind, based upon a presumption that any distribution is deemed to be a distribution of the estate's income to the extent of its income for the year, does not and cannot be made to depend on such intangible factors as the subjective intent of executors.

Section 662(a)(2)(B) was specifically intended, for the purposes of that section, "to avoid the necessity for tracing of income."[39] Such tracing was required by the 1939 Code, which provided that distributions by an estate or trust to its beneficiaries were taxed to the beneficiaries for the taxable year in which they received the distributions only if the distributions were made from the current income of the estate or trust.[40] As shown, this lent itself to various kinds of manipulations by executors in the labeling of estate moneys as "income" or "principal." To eliminate such manipulations and tax consequences based upon such estate tax accounting designations of what was "principal" and "income" and from which source a distribution had been made, the "tracing" requirement was, for such distribution purposes, eliminated. Instead, "[t]he beneficiary's proportionate share of the distributable net income * * * is determined by taking the same fractional part of [the] distributable net income as the * * * amounts * * * distributed to him * * * bear to the total of [the] amounts * * * distributed to all beneficiaries."[41] In short, Congress wished to establish an easily

---

from property, must be included in the legatee's gross income. The section goes on to provide, however, in subsection (b), that amounts included in the gross income of a beneficiary under Subchapter J, pertaining to "Estates, Trusts, Beneficiaries, and Decedents," and which contains Section 662, shall be treated as a bequest of income from property. Section 663(a)(1) of Subchapter J excludes from amounts falling within Section 662(a) any amount which, under the terms of the governing instrument, is paid as a gift or bequest of a specific sum of money or of specific property, provided it is paid all at once or in not more than three installments. It further provides, however, that "an amount which can be paid * * * only from the income of the estate shall not be considered as a gift or bequest of a specific sum of money."

39. H.R. Rep. No. 1337, 83d Cong., 2d Sess. A199, 3 U.S.C. Cong. & Adm. News 4017, 4339 (1954); S. Rep. No. 1622, 83d Cong., 2d Sess. 349, 3 U.S.C. Cong. & Adm. News 4621, 4990 (1954).

40. For instance, under Section 162(d) of the 1939 Code, as amended, a distribution, in the first 65 days of a taxable year, of income of the preceding taxable year, was treated as having been made in such preceding year. In addition, if there also was current year income, tracing was necessary to determine which year's income had been distributed. And, in addition to the current-accumulated interest problem, tracing would, of course, be required to determine whether the distribution contained corpus. 26 U.S.C. § 162(d) (1946).

41. 3 U.S.C. Cong. & Adm. News, *supra* n. 6, at 4340, 4990. The portions of the House and Senate Reports here involved are identical. *Id.*, at 4339-40, 4989-90. In pertinent part, they stated:

> Subsection (a) provides that the beneficiary of an estate or trust * * * must include in gross income any amounts paid, credited, or required to be distributed to him for the taxable year of the estate or trust; however, the amount so includible may not exceed the

useable formula, and to avoid both the necessity of "tracing" and an inquiry into the subjective intention of executors or trustees. As was pointed out in *Manufacturers Hanover Trust Co. v. United States*, 160 Ct Cl. 582, 596, 312 F.2d 785, 793, [11 AFTR 2d 785] cert. denied, 375 U.S. 880 (1963):

> * * * Around this concept of "distributable net income" the Code builds its provisions for (a) the deduction allowed the trust for its current distributions to the beneficiaries, and (b) the distributions which the beneficiaries must include in their own gross incomes. "Thus, distributable net income has been termed the measuring rod or yardstick to be employed in determining, on the one hand, the maximum deduction for distributions which may be allowed to the estate or trust and for gauging, on the other hand, the extent to which beneficiaries may be taxable on the distributions." 6 Mertens "Law of Federal Income Taxation" § 36.04.

We accept plaintiff's contention that there were no tax motivations on the part of the executors in making the distributions at the times and in the amounts they did, and that they made the "balancing" corpus distributions to plaintiff only to avoid complicated calculations of estate income due to the beneficiaries which would result from their having disproportionate interests in the residuary estate.[42] The fact nevertheless remains that, by making the discretionary "balancing" distributions as they did—required neither by the will nor state law—plaintiff received, under their estate accounting, less of the distributable net income than she probably

---

> beneficiary's proportionate share of the distributable net income. The effect of limiting the taxation of a beneficiary to his proportionate share of the distributable net income is to preserve the conduit principle by providing that all distributions * * * from an estate or trust will be taxable but not to an extent in excess of the taxable income of the estate or trust * * *. It is thus possible largely to avoid the necessity of tracing income which exists generally under existing law. Instead of determining whether a particular distribution represents amounts of current or accumulated trust income, this revision, broadly speaking, provides that any distribution is considered a distribution of the trust or estate's current income to the extent of its taxable income for the year. This principle is similar to the determination of whether a dividend has been distributed, i.e., that every distribution made by a corporation is deemed to be out of earnings and profits to the extent thereof and from the most recently accumulated earnings and profits.
>
> * * *
>
> If the estate or trust pays * * * to beneficiaries amounts other than income which is required to be distributed currently, paragraph (2) provides that these other amounts * * * are includible in the gross income of the recipient beneficiaries but only to the extent of each beneficiary's proportionate share of the distributable net income * * *. * * * The beneficiary's proportionate share of the distributable net income * * * is determined by taking the same fractional part of such distributable net income * * * as the other amounts paid * * * bear to the total of other amounts paid * * * to all beneficiaries. * * *

42. Such as would occur after the death taxes were paid and deducted from the shares of the trusts, thereby diminishing the interests of the trusts in the residuary estate from the dates of such payments, with proportionate diminutions in the income which would be produced after such dates from such diminished shares.

otherwise would have.[43] There is no showing that—either by not making distributions until the estate was wound up finally, or otherwise—the residuary estate could not have been so managed as to produce the same result as the statutory formula. Thus, in that sense (and not in the sense of tax avoidance), the distributions were "manipulated" so that plaintiff, who received over 75 percent of the 1955 payments, is nevertheless said to have received in that year only 50 percent of the taxable distributable net income. On its face and as its purpose is shown by its development and legislative history, the statute was designed to prevent such a result for tax purposes. Indeed, the statutory formula could be considered as providing the more natural and logical result—income earned during the administration of the residuary estate is allocated to the beneficiaries in the same ratio as their interests in the corpus of such estate. Generally, of course, various percentages of corpus will produce like percentages of income. It is thus plain that plaintiff's situation is, by the unambiguous provisions thereof, covered by the statute[44] and although recognizing, of course, the difficulties involved in envisaging every specific situation that could arise under general statutory language, it would nevertheless appear to constitute the type of situation that Congress intended should be covered.[45]

---

43. Defendant, apparently attempting to minimize the complications were the balancing distributions not made, cites *In re Shubert's Will*, 10 N.Y. 2d 461, 180 N.E. 2d 410, 225 N.Y.S. 2d 13 (1962), which it construes as holding that, under Section 17-b of Personal Property Law, N.Y. Consol. Laws Ann. (McKinney 1962), as it existed at the time of the administration of the estate herein, the shares of income to be received by the four trusts would not have been reduced as a result of the payment of the death taxes. It seems clear that defendant errs. In that case, the statute provided that "Unless otherwise expressly provided by the will of a person dying after this act takes effect, all income from real and personal property earned during the period of administration of the estate of such testator and not payable to others or otherwise disposed of by the will shall be distributed pro rata as income among the beneficiaries of any trusts created out of the residuary estate of such testator and the other persons entitled to such residuary estate." The court held that where, in accordance with the direction of the testator, payment of the death taxes was made out of the residuary estate, the net income earned by the estate during administration was to be divided pro rata among the income beneficiaries in proportion to the division of the residuary estate set up in the will before consideration of the effect of the tax payments. However, the court specifically pointed out that the will did not provide for the payment of the taxes prior to distributions to the beneficiaries or that the taxes were to be treated as administration expenses to be subtracted initially. Thus there was no provision in the will "otherwise expressly" providing differently from the Section 17-b formula. The court held that a general direction that death taxes be paid out of the residuary estate was not equivalent to a direction that the taxes be treated as administration expenses.

In the instant case, however, the will expressly provided (1) that an adjustment of the income should be made in the event simultaneous distribution of the residuary estate was not made to the beneficiaries, and (2) that the trusts' one-half share was to be calculated "after the deduction therefrom of" the death taxes, with the taxes to be considered as part of the estate's administration expenses.

44. In their fiduciary income tax return for 1955, in which they took a deduction of $826,758.68 for distributions to the five estate beneficiaries, the executors attached an explanatory statement setting forth the "allocations of shares of income and credits" to such beneficiaries which "may result" from the "[a]pplication of the formula for determining inclusions in gross income of beneficiaries prescribed in Section 662(b) of the Internal Revenue Code, if proper in this case * * *."

45. It is felt by some that the present Section 662(a) provisions lead to inequitable results in certain situations, and proposals have been made which would reinstitute, at least to a limited extent,

Plaintiff further contends that, even if Section 662(a) is applicable, its formula was erroneously applied because the death taxes should be included in the "amounts properly paid, credited, or required to be distributed to * * * beneficiaries." Crediting the trusts with such taxes as if they constituted distributions to the trusts would result in plaintiff and the trusts receiving equal total amounts. Accordingly, they would, under the statutory formula, be considered as having received equal amounts of the taxable distributable net income.

Plaintiff's basis for treating the payment of the death taxes as distributions to the trusts is based upon the provisions of Regulations §1.662(a)-4 (26 C.F.R.) that "[a]ny amount which, pursuant to the terms of a will * * * is used in full or partial discharge or satisfaction of a legal obligation of any person is included in the gross income of such person under section 662(a) * * * (2) * * * as though directly distributed to him as a beneficiary, * * *." Since the taxes were not deductible from or payable out of plaintiff's one-half of the residuary estate, they therefore were, argues plaintiff, a charge upon, or obligation of, the remaining one-half passing to the trusts. As such an obligation, they should, plaintiff says, be considered, under the Regulations, as expenditures made on behalf of the trusts.

This contention too cannot be sustained. The death tax moneys never constituted a part of, nor were they ever incorporated in, the trusts. The will bequeathed one-half of the residuary estate to the trusts "*after* the deduction therefrom of all of the [death] taxes * * *." (Emphasis supplied.) There is, therefore, no warrant for adding to the amounts paid to the trusts the amount of the death taxes, an amount which was never paid or payable to the trusts and which the trusts were, under the will, never to receive. Furthermore, these taxes were the legal obligations of the estate, and not of the trusts, the will specifically so recognizing and providing that such taxes, "payable by my estate * * * shall be paid * * * out of my estate as part of the expenses of administration thereof * * *." The taxes were a "charge" upon, or an "obligation" of, the trusts only in the loose sense that, in calculating the net amount of the residuary estate which the trusts were to receive, the amount of the taxes was to be deducted from the share left to the trusts. They were not a "legal obligation" of the trusts in the sense used by the regulation upon which plaintiff relies.

---

the prior "tracing" concepts and practices. See, *Final Report of the Advisory Group on Subchapter J of the Internal Revenue Code of 1954*, dated December 30, 1958, in *Hearings on Advisory Group Recommendations on Subchapters C, J and K of the Internal Revenue Code before the House Committee on Ways and Means*, 86th Cong., 1st Sess. 257, 286-92. Among the proposals of the Advisory Group was the exclusion from Section 662(a) of amounts properly paid, during the first three years of the estate, out of the corpus of the estate in full or partial satisfaction of a bequest. Effect would be given to a fiduciary's identification of the source of a distribution, as was permitted under the 1939 Code. During the hearings held in the course of consideration of proposed amendatory legislation, various examples were cited of alleged inequities under the 1954 Code provisions, including one which, on the facts, was substantially identical with the instant case. *3 Hearings on Topics Pertaining to the General Revision of the Internal Revenue Code Before the House Committee on Ways and Means*, 85th Cong., 2d Sess. 2801-2802. (The same factual situation is also discussed in Fillman, *Selections From Subchapter J*, 10 Tax Law Rev. 453, 471 (1955).) However, no such legislation has been enacted.

The trusts received $8,536,313.72 from the estate in 1955. It is such amount that is properly to be considered as the amount "properly paid, credited, or required to be distributed to" them under the statute. The $18,931,454.81 in death taxes paid during the year by the executors, described by the will as part of the administration expenses of the estate, were not "amounts properly paid, credited, or required to be distributed * * * beneficiaries" within the meaning of the statute or the regulation.

Finally, plaintiff contends that if Section 662(a), properly construed, does cover the instant situation, it is unconstitutional as applied to her because it would impose an unapportioned direct tax on principal or capital in violation of Article I of the Constitution. Section 2, clause 3 of the Article provides that direct taxes shall be apportioned among the several states according to their respective numbers, and section 9, clause 4 provides that no direct tax shall be laid unless in proportion to the census or enumeration directed by the Constitution to be taken. Plaintiff relies on the cases of *Pollock v. Farmers' Loan & Trust Co.*, 158 U.S. 601 [3 AFTR 2602] (1895), *Eisner v. Macomber*, 252 U.S. 189 [3 AFTR 3020] (1920), and *Taft v. Bowers*, 278 U.S. 470 [7 AFTR 8852] (1929), among others, for the proposition that a tax on principal or capital is a direct tax which must be apportioned among the states in proportion to the census.

Although Section 662(a)(2)(B) purports to be an income tax, nevertheless, plaintiff contends, the section, as here applied, actually imposes a tax on the principal or capital distributions received by plaintiff from the estate of her deceased husband. The Sixteenth Amendment, plaintiff points out, empowers only the levying of taxes "on *incomes* * * * without apportionment among the several States, and without regard to any census or enumeration." (Emphasis supplied.)[46]

Additionally, plaintiff argues that Section 662(a)(2)(B) deprives her of property without due process of law because, although she actually received only 50 percent of the taxable income which the estate distributed to the beneficiaries in 1955, she has been taxed on an additional 26.2907 percent of such income. That part of the income, she says, was in fact received by the trusts and not by her, and to attempt to measure her tax by reference to the income of others, i.e., the four trusts, would, she argues, conflict with the due process clause of the Fifth Amendment.[47]

In upholding constitutionality, defendant urges the broad proposition that, even though the disputed amount ($217,361) which taxpayer received in 1955 may have constituted corpus, still the challenged sections (as applied here) are valid on two

46. In addition to Section 662(a)(2)(B), plaintiff also attacks, for the same reasons, the constitutionality of that part of Section 102(b) which provides that any amount included in the gross income of a beneficiary under Subchapter J shall be treated as a gift, bequest, or inheritance of income from property, such gifts, bequests, or inheritances being, as hereinabove set forth, excluded from the provision of Section 102(a) that "Gross income does not include the value of property acquired by gift, bequest, devise, or inheritance." See n. 5.

47. In support, plaintiff cites *Hoeper v. Tax Commission*, 284 U.S. 206 (1931), and *Lewis v. White*, 56 F.2d 390 (D. Mass.), appeal dismissed, 61 F.2d 1046 (1st Cir. 1932).

alternative grounds, first, that the receipt of a bequest, devise or inheritance (whether or not it be from corpus) properly falls within the Sixteenth Amendment as "income" to the recipient, and, second, that in any event the sections impose an indirect tax upon the receipt of property which under the Constitution need not be apportioned. On either of these views, plaintiff's invocation of the Fifth Amendment would also fail because the taxpayer would clearly not be taxed on the income of property of others.

We do not have to delve into the difficult issues of large scope which the Government presents because, as we see it, there is a much narrower ground upon which to sustain the statute as applied to plaintiff's case. That more limited approach stresses the factor (which plaintiff underplays) that the executors did have a choice in 1955 whether to make the distributions in the form they did or, instead, so to manage distributions, to the extent governed by Section 662(a), that the several beneficiaries would not be taxable under Section 662(a) on more than their share of the estate's income. Plaintiff has failed to show that this could not be done.[48] There was no legal compulsion, in the will or in New York law, to make the "balancing" distributions of corpus and income which were made. That course was selected because the other would have been much more burdensome, requiring over the years complicated calculations of shares of income, earned either by principal or by undistributed income, which were due to the various residuary legatees. But the choice was not a forced one, and the other route could have been picked (though at the cost of more work and trouble).[49] If the application of Section 662(a)(2)(B) was deemed unfair to plaintiff taxwise, when such "balancing" distributions were made, the presumed inequity could be avoided by not making "balancing" distributions but employing the other methods of distribution which were available.

That these other methods would have occasioned more trouble (and possibly some more expense) does not invalidate the statutory formula. As we have already indicated, Congress could properly assume, as it did, that in the generality of instances the formula would correspond to reality and not be unfair to any beneficiary. At least where an option is open to avoid an unfair and unrealistic result, use of the formula is not prohibited in the minority of instances in which it may be thought harsh or inequitable. In view of the broad Congressional power in taxation (cf. *Fernandez v. Wiener*, 326 U.S. 340, 351-53 [34 AFTR 276] (1945); *A. Magnano Co. v. Hamilton*, 292 U.S. 40, 44 (1934)), Congress is not required by the Constitution to assure that the way of the option be just as easy as the way of the formula; added work and some added expense, if the option is selected, are permissible accompaniments of that choice. Taxation is not a field in which Congress must use a watchmaker's refinement and instruments, or a jeweler's balance, to achieve precise equality in treatment.

---

48. At the oral argument plaintiff's counsel admitted that this could be done, albeit with substantial trouble, under the will and the law.

49. It is absolutely plain on this record that the executors deliberately chose to make the distributions in the form they did, and that they were under no compulsion of law. Taxpayer so concedes. See also *infra*.

The use of formulas which can be avoided if the taxpayer considers them unfair or not to reflect reality in his particular case is, of course, no stranger to the federal income tax system. The best-known is the standard formula for deductions on the individual income tax form; if the standard deduction is thought to be unfair or inadequate, the deductions can be itemized—sometimes at the cost of considerable extra work and some expense. Although the parallel is not exact (particularly since the standard deduction involves deductions, not income), the option available in plaintiff's case is roughly comparable to this common choice open each year to millions of individual taxpayers. We cite this example to show that formula solutions are not uncommon, and are invulnerable to attack where an escape-hatch is available if the formula proves unjust in a particular instance.

It may be said that Mrs. Harkness, the taxpayer, did not have or make the choice here—the executors did. Technically that is the situation, but there is no hint that plaintiff objected in any way to the estate's course of action, or suggested the other course, or was compelled to accept the large distributions of principal in 1955. It is unrealistic to suppose that, if she had objected on the ground that the estate's mode of distribution increased her own taxes, the executors would nevertheless have forced her to accept those large payments. Indeed, there is no reason to believe that under the will the executors could lawfully compel her to accept the large corpus distributions in 1955, if she was unwilling to do so because of the tax consequences to her.[50] Plaintiff's reply brief to the court makes it clear that plaintiff was not so compelled, and suggests that a deliberate chance was taken as to how the law would be applied. The brief indicates that the executors (and probably plaintiff's own counsel) believed that § 662(a)(2)(B) should not be interpreted (in this type of case) as the Internal Revenue Service and we have construed it—and they acted accordingly.[51]

Without intimating in any way that the statute would be invalid if applied where there was no such option as in this case, we hold that the existence of the choice removes whatever defect there might otherwise be. At least where the option is present, Congress can reasonably and validly forbid "tracing" and presume that its formula in § 662(a)(2)(B) gives an accurate reflection of the division of the estate's "distributable net income" among the beneficiaries. Cf. *Smith v. Westover*, 191 F.2d 1003 [41 AFTR 2d 192] (9th Cir. 1951), aff'g 89 F.Supp. 432 [39 AFTR 2d 293] (S.D. Cal. 1950). Normally, use of the formula would be fair and accurate enough. If discretionary "balancing" payments which include large amounts of corpus are made and accepted, as here, the necessary consequence is to invoke the formula nonetheless, and the taxpayer will not be allowed to "trace" in order to show that the source of part of his receipts was in fact not "distributable net income" but corpus. If the tax consequences of this approach are deemed sufficiently undesirable, there is the

50. Article ELEVENTH of the will would not seem to contemplate such a forced distribution of principal.

51. The 1954 Internal Revenue Code, which first contained § 662(a)(2)(B), became law on August 16, 1954, and the first full calendar year of its effectiveness was 1955, the year involved here.

other route which can and should be taken. In these circumstances, there is no compulsion to accept an unfair or unrealistic division of "distributable net income."

For these reasons, we hold that the tax was lawfully imposed and that plaintiff is not entitled to recover.

SKELTON, Judge, dissenting:

I respectfully dissent. In my opinion, the majority opinion by failing to hold that Section 662(a)(2)(B) of the Internal Revenue Code of 1954 (26 U.S.C. § 662(a)(2)(B) (1958)) and the related Treasury Regulations 1.662(a)-3 are unconstitutional and invalid, has placed a stamp of approval upon the acts of the Internal Revenue Service in collecting income taxes from the plaintiff that she did not owe and in exempting the trusts from income taxes that they owed. This has caused an unconscionable result to be reached in this case.

Regardless of the elaborate and complicated provisions of the statute and regulations and the involved and sophisticated reasoning of the government, we end up with the following undisputed facts:

(1) The plaintiff has been required to pay income taxes on $217,361 of the income of the decedent's estate that she never received.

(2) The trusts were exempted from the payment of income taxes on the $217,361 income of the estate which they received and which taxes they owed.

(3) The tax on the $217,361 was levied upon the property of the plaintiff and collected from her under the guise of an income tax, but was actually a direct tax on the corpus of the decedent's estate that she inherited from him (her husband) under the terms of his will.

(4) The direct taxes levied upon and collected from the corpus of the decedent's estate received by the plaintiff was not a tax that had been apportioned among the several states according to their respective numbers and in proportion to their population as required by the United States Constitution.

(5) All indirect taxes (estate and inheritance taxes) had already been paid on the transfer of decedent's estate ($14,500,000 Federal and $4,300,000 to the State of New York).

With these well-established and admitted facts in mind, I will proceed to show that the statute and related regulations, as well as the acts of the Internal Revenue Service, were unconstitutional and invalid, which is the main thrust of plaintiff's appeal. The majority chose to sidestep this question and refused to decide it. Instead, they decided the case on the narrow basis that the executors of the estate had an option to distribute the corpus and income as they did which resulted in the tax on plaintiff, or to effect distribution a different way without such resulting tax on plaintiff. There is no showing that plaintiff had any control over the executors or that she had anything whatever to do with what they did. It seems unjust to me to place a beneficiary of an estate in a position of owing or not owing an income tax according to the whim and actions of the executors of the estate. It also appears that this is an unrealistic solution of the problem because ordinarily a person either owes an income tax or he does not owe it according to law and not according to what someone else over whom he has no control does with respect to his property. The court cites *Smith v. Westover*, 191 F.2d 1003 [41 AFTR 2d 192] (9th Cir. 1951), aff'g 89 F.Supp. 432 [39 AFTR 2d 293] (S.D. Cal. 1950). That case does not appear to be applicable because it involved the division of trust income for income tax purposes between a trust and a beneficiary of a trust. Whereas, here we are concerned with a formula to allocate estate income among various estate beneficiaries for income tax purposes. Furthermore, in that case, there was an attempt at tax avoidance when the testator tried in his will to convert income to principal by saying such income was principal. None of these facts are present here. Also, the statute in that case did not involve the allocation formula that we have here. The cases are clearly distinguishable.

In my opinion, the court should have decided the constitutional question instead of avoiding it. When it appears that a provision of the Internal Revenue Code is clearly contrary to the Constitution, it is the duty of a court to declare it unconstitutional. *Nicol v. Ames*, 173 U.S. 509, 515 [3 AFTR 2661] (1899). I cannot accept the solution of the majority of the problem involved because it avoids the constitutional questions that should decide the case. All that the majority really decides is that the government wins and the plaintiff loses.

The statute and related regulations involved in this case are contrary to and violate Article I (Section 2, Clause 3) (Section 8, Clause 1) (Section 9, Clause 4), and the Fifth and Sixteenth Amendments of the United States Constitution, as will be clearly shown below.

Section 662(a)(2)(B) and Related Treasury Regulations Violate the Fifth Amendment by Depriving Plaintiff of Property Without Due Process of Law

The relationship of the Fifth Amendment of the Constitution will be considered first because its violation by the statute and regulations is so clearly apparent and obvious. The tax collected from plaintiff was collected as an income tax in connection with her income tax returns. Section 662(a)(2)(B) is an income tax statute and is found in the income tax section of the Code (subchapter J of Subtitle A) and was used by the District Director in taxing plaintiff on the $217,361 income of the estate that she never received. He simply added that amount to her gross income. There was no doubt that the IRS considered the tax exacted of the plaintiff to be a tax on income at the time it was collected. In fact, when the case was before our trial judge, the defendant so contended by saying in its brief presented to him:

> * * * [I]t is quite clear that Section 662(a) has not imposed a tax upon a distribution of corpus of the estate, but rather *the tax has been imposed on the income of the estate.* [Emphasis supplied.] [*Id.* at 29.][52]

52. As will be discussed later, defendant now admits the tax was upon the *corpus* and not on *income.*

In fact, the tax exacted of plaintiff was figured and calculated according to the rates applicable to income taxes.

On appeal before us the defendant admits in its brief that plaintiff never received the $217,361 of estate income on which she was taxed when it stated:

> * * * [T]axpayer repeatedly states * * * she was entitled to income from only one-half of the corpus of the estate, that *she received only this portion* of the estate's income, * * *. *The Government here concedes these facts.* [Emphasis supplied.] [*Id.* at 15.][53]

Having conceded that plaintiff did not receive the $217,361 on which she paid an income tax, the act of the government in taxing her on such income flies squarely in the face of the Fifth Amendment as the taking of property without due process of law.

The cases are legion that prohibit the taking of one's property without due process of law. It hardly seems necessary to cite any of such authorities here because the case is so plain and conclusive that such a taking occurred in this case. Simply stated, plaintiff's property was taken for an income tax on income she did not receive and applied to the payment of the income tax owned by the trusts which received the income but who were not required to pay the tax. This appears to be a classic example of the taking of one's property without due process of law. This amounts to a confiscation of plaintiff's property and is forbidden by the Fifth Amendment to the Constitution. See also, *Nichols v. Coolidge*, 274 U.S. 531, 542 [6 AFTR 6758] (1927); *Hoeper v. Tax Comm'n of Wisconsin*, 284 U.S. 206 [10 AFTR 468] (1931) (decided under the Fourteenth Amendment, but *Heiner v. Donnan*, 285 U.S. 312, 326 [10 AFTR 1609] (1932) and *Coolidge v. Long*, 282 U.S. 582 [9 AFTR 1394] (1931) hold that legislative restraint imposed by the due process clause of the Fifth and Fourteenth Amendments is the same). See also, *Lewis v. White*, 56 F.2d 390, 391 [10 AFTR 1311] (D. Mass. 1932), appeal dismissed, 61 F.2d 1046 [11 AFTR 1043] (1st Cir. 1932); and *A. Magnano Co. v. Hamilton*, 292 U.S. 40, 44 (1934).

Section 662(a)(2)(B) and Related Treasury Regulations Violate Article 1 of the Constitution

The government now says in its brief in this court that the tax imposed on plaintiff on the $217,361 of income of the estate was a tax upon the corpus of the estate distributed to the plaintiff. In this connection, it says:

> * * * [T]he allocation of distributable net income is a measure of a tax upon all distributions *including distributions of corpus.* [Emphasis supplied.] [*Id.* at 38.]

In conceding that the tax imposed on plaintiff was a tax on corpus or principal, the defendant runs afoul of Article I of the Constitution by imposing on plaintiff an unapportioned direct tax on principal or capital.

53. The $217,361 on which plaintiff was taxed was not a portion of the one-half of the income plaintiff received, but was a portion of the one-half the trusts received.

Article I, Section 2, clause 3, provides in part:

> * * * [D]irect Taxes shall be apportioned among the several States which may be included within this Union, according to their respective Numbers, * * *.

Article I, Section 8, clause 1, provides:

> The Congress shall have Power to lay and collect Taxes, Duties, Imposts and Excises, to pay the Debts and provide for the common Defense and general Welfare of the United States; but all Duties, Imposts and Excises shall be uniform throughout the United States;

Article I, Section 9, clause 4, provides:

> No Capitation, or other direct, Tax shall be laid, unless in Proportion to the Census or Enumeration herein before directed to be taken. [Footnote omitted.]

The Supreme Court held in the early case of *Pollock v. Farmers' Loan & Trust Co.*, 158 U.S. 601, 634, 637 [3 AFTR 2602] (1895), that a tax on capital or principal is a direct tax which must be apportioned among the states in proportion to the population as shown by the census, because of the requirements of the above provisions of Article I.

A direct tax on corpus or principal without such apportionment is unconstitutional, and this cannot be avoided by merely calling it a tax on income. See *Richardson v. United States*, 294 F.2d 593, 596 [8 AFTR 2d 5465] (6th Cir. 1961), cert. denied, 369 U.S. 802 (1962); *Commissioner v. Obear-Nester Glass Co.*, 217 F.2d 56, 58 [46 AFTR 1122] (7th Cir. 1954), cert. denied, 348 U.S. 982 (1955), rehearing denied, 349 U.S. 948.

The defendant makes no claim or pretense that the tax imposed on plaintiff as a direct tax on principal or capital had been uniformly apportioned among the states according to the census as required by Article I of the Constitution. Accordingly, Section 662(a)(2)(B) and related regulations are unconstitutional and the levying and collection of such taxes from the plaintiff was invalid. In further support of this proposition, it should be pointed out that it is the universal practice of the IRS in all of the states not to tax beneficiaries of estates on the corpus of such estates when received by them where there has been no income earned by the estate, but in the case before us a beneficiary has been taxed on the corpus of an estate which she received pursuant to the terms of her husband's will. This has been done despite the requirement of Article I, Section 8, clause 1, that provides in part:

> * * * [A]ll Duties, Imposts and Excises *shall be uniform throughout the United States*; [Emphasis supplied.]

Section 662(a)(2)(B) and Related Treasury Regulations Violate the Sixteenth Amendment to the Constitution

The defendant makes the further argument that even if the tax imposed on the plaintiff is a direct tax on the corpus or principal that she received to the extent of a tax on the $217,361, nevertheless, it is a legal tax because such corpus or principal that she received is income and taxable. This is indeed a novel and unreasonable contention. Here again defendant's argument is contrary to another provision of the Constitution, namely, the Sixteenth Amendment.

Prior to the adoption of the Sixteenth Amendment, the Supreme Court held in *Pollock v. Farmers' Loan & Trust Co., supra*, that Congress did not have the power to impose an income tax. In that case the Court held invalid the Act of August 15, 1894 [August 27, 1894], c. 349, § 28, 28 Stat. 509, 553, which included in income subject to tax of "money and the value of all personal property acquired by gift or inheritance." The Sixteenth Amendment was adopted in 1913. The very first income tax law enacted by Congress after the adoption of the Amendment, provided that the value of property acquired by "gift, bequest, devise or descent" was excluded from net income. Act of 1913, c. 16, § IIB, 38 Stat. 114, 167. The same exclusions have existed ever since. For instance, Section 102 of the Internal Revenue Code of 1954 provides:

> § 102. Gifts and inheritances.
>
> (a) General rule.
>
> Gross income does not include the value of property acquired by gift, bequest, devise, or inheritance. [26 U.S.C. § 102 (1954)]

The attempt of defendant to include the inheritance (corpus or principal) of the plaintiff in her gross income is directly contrary to such section of the Code. The defendant seeks to avoid this provision of Section 102(a) by pointing to Section 102(b)(2), added in 1954, which provides in part:

> (b) Income.
>
> Subsection (a) shall not exclude from gross income—
>
> (2) where the gift, bequest, devise, or inheritance is of income from property, the amount of such income.
>
> * * * Any amount included in the *gross income* of a beneficiary under subchapter J shall be treated for purposes of paragraph (2) as a gift, bequest, devise, or inheritance of income from property. [Emphasis supplied.]

The defendant relies especially on the last paragraph quoted above by arguing that since the corpus of the estate was included by the IRS in the gross income of the plaintiff, at least to the extent of the $217,361, such corpus to that extent became *income*. I do not agree. The above section of the Code refers to gross income. As will be pointed out below, income is income and not corpus. Income is completely separate and distinct from principal, corpus, or capital. Even if Congress intended the section to have the meaning defendant attributes to it, Congress had no power to convert corpus into income by merely calling it income. I do not think that Congress intended any such meaning. The section refers to income and not to corpus or principal. If it does mean corpus or principal, then it is unconstitutional as a direct unapportioned tax on principal or capital. Furthermore, it violates the Sixteenth Amendment to the Constitution which authorizes an income tax only on income.

The Sixteenth Amendment did not define "income," but as has been pointed out by the courts, the term had a well-defined meaning at the time the Amendment was adopted. This meaning was separate, apart, and different from capital, corpus, or principal. In *Eisner v. Macomber*, 252 U.S. 189 [3 AFTR 3020] (1920), Mr. Justice Holmes stated:

> * * * I think that the word "incomes" in the Sixteenth Amendment should be read in "a sense most obvious to the common understanding at the time of its adoption." * * * [*Id.* at 219-20.]

In *United States v. Safety Car Heating & Lighting Co.*, 297 U.S. 88 [16 AFTR 1311] (1936), Mr. Justice Cardozo said:

> Income within the meaning of the Sixteenth Amendment is the fruit that is born of capital, not the potency of fruition. With few exceptions, if any, it is income as the word is known in the common speech of men. [*Id.* at 99.]

It is clear that when the Sixteenth Amendment was adopted, the term "income" had a well-defined meaning that was distinguished from principal or capital.

The Supreme Court has held that the meaning of the Sixteenth Amendment cannot "be extended beyond the meaning clearly indicated by the language used." *James v. United States*, 366 U.S. 213 [7 AFTR 2d 1361] (1961). In that case, Mr. Justice Whittaker said:

> * * * Equally well settled is the principle that the Sixteenth Amendment "is to be taken as written and is not to be extended beyond the meaning clearly indicated by the language used." *Edwards v. Cuba R. Co.*, 268 U.S. 628, 631.[54] [5 AFTR 5398] * * *

The Sixteenth Amendment authorized Congress to lay and collect taxes on incomes. As shown by the above decisions, income was not and is not the same as principal or capital. Consequently, the attempt of defendant in this case to convert principal or corpus of the estate of the deceased into income of the plaintiff is clearly contrary to the Sixteenth Amendment and to Section 102 of the Internal Revenue Code of 1954.

The Tax Imposed on Plaintiffs not an Indirect Tax on the Receipt of Property that need not be Apportioned

Defendant makes one last argument which in my opinion has no validity and is completely unrealistic. It argues that in any event the tax imposed on plaintiff is an *indirect tax on the receipt of property* and it need not be apportioned. This appears to

54. "A proper regard for its genesis, as well as its very clear language, requires also that [the Sixteenth] Amendment shall not be extended by loose construction.... Congress cannot by any definition [of income] it may adopt conclude the matter, since it cannot by legislation alter the Constitution, from which alone it derives its power to legislate, and within whose limitations alone that power can be lawfully exercised." *Eisner v. Macomber*, 252 U.S. 189, 206, 40 S.Ct. 189, 64 L.Ed. 521. [*Id.* at 248, 81 S.Ct. at 193.]

be an exercise in semantics. It is just another way of describing a tax on the *transfer* of property. An indirect tax is a tax imposed on the transfer of property. The estate or inheritance tax is a good example. The receipt of the corpus of an estate by a beneficiary is an integral part of the transfer of such corpus from the estate. The transfer (estate) taxes had already been paid on the estate of the decedent in the total sum of $18,800,000 before the tax involved here was collected from the plaintiff. If carried to its logical conclusion, defendant's argument would lead to double taxation on the transfer of the estate. There is no authority in law that authorizes the government to impose any kind of tax, direct or indirect, on the receipt of the corpus of an estate by a beneficiary without apportionment as required by Article I of the Constitution. The argument of defendant to the contrary is purely theoretical and without support in the Constitution, the Internal Revenue Code, or the decisions of the courts.

Defendant's theory of an indirect tax on the receipt of property would have one of two results, namely (1) a double tax on the transfer of property, or (2) a tax on the ownership of property, which is a direct tax on the principal or corpus and is invalid unless apportioned as required by the Constitution.

Furthermore, Section 1(a) of the Internal Revenue Code of 1954 imposes a tax "*on the taxable income*" of every individual. It does not impose a tax on the *transfer* or *receipt* of property. The tax here was imposed on the $217,361 included in plaintiff's *taxable income.*

Conclusion

The defendant argues that Congress enacted Section 662(a)(2)(B) in order to eliminate the necessity of "tracing" the source of distributed property and to facilitate bookkeeping and auditing by executors and the IRS. Even though this may be a laudable intent, such purpose does not allow the Congress to circumvent or override the provisions of the Constitution. The Constitution is the source of the powers of the Congress and it defines the boundaries within which Congress can function. In the case before us, Congress has exceeded its powers and gone beyond the boundaries established for its operation by the Constitution. There can be no doubt that there is a limitation on the taxing power conferred upon Congress by the Constitution. When the enforcement and application of a taxing statute is so arbitrary as to amount to the confiscation of a taxpayer's property, as is the case here, both the statute and the action should be held to be unconstitutional and invalid. See *Nichols v. Coolidge*, 274 U.S. 531 [6 AFTR 6758] (1927) and *Heiner v. Donnan*, 285 U.S. 312 [10 AFTR 1609] (1932).

The majority opinion states:

> * * * [T]he taxpayer will not be allowed to "trace" in order to show that the source of part of his receipts was in fact not "distributable net income" but corpus.

This is directly contrary to the decision of the Supreme Court in *Heiner v. Donnan, supra*, when the court said in commenting upon the statute, involved in *Schlesinger v. Wisconsin*, 270 U.S. 230 [7 AFTR 8833] (1926):

> * * * a statute which imposes a tax upon an assumption of fact *which the taxpayer is forbidden to controvert, is so arbitrary and unreasonable that it cannot stand under the Fourteenth Amendment.* [Emphasis supplied.] [*Id.* at 325.]

The court stated further in that case:

> Nor is it material that the Fourteenth Amendment was involved in the *Schlesinger* case, instead of the Fifth Amendment, as here. The restraint imposed upon legislation by the due process clauses of the two amendments is the same. *Coolidge v. Long*, 282 U.S. 582, 596 [9 AFTR 1394]. That a federal statute passed under the taxing power may be so arbitrary and capricious as to cause it to fall before the due process of law clause of the Fifth Amendment is settled. *Nichols v. Coolidge*, 274 U.S. 531, 542 [6 AFTR 6758]; *Brushaber v. Union Pac. R. Co.*, 240 U.S. 1, 24-25 [3 AFTR 2926]; *Tyler v. United States, supra*, p. 504. [*Id.* at 326.]

It appears that the majority opinion, contrary to the above decision of the Supreme Court, is upholding a statute which "assumes as a fact which the taxpayer is forbidden to controvert" that the $217,361 was "income" and not "corpus." The statute, given this meaning, clearly violates the due process clause of the Fifth Amendment to the Constitution.[55]

The majority opinion holds, in effect, that Section 662(a)(2)(B) creates a conclusive presumption that distributions subject to the operation of that section are distributions of income, and, consequently cannot be rebutted by the taxpayer. We held otherwise in the case of *Mott v. United States*, 199 Ct. Cl. __, 462 F. 2d 512 [30 AFTR 2d 72-5193] (July 14, 1972) when we ruled that such a presumption was not conclusive with respect to charitable distributions, and we held that tracing should be allowed to show that the distributions were from corpus and not from income. It is of particular significance that the government in that case argued that such tracing should be allowed notwithstanding the statute, in order to defeat a charitable deduction, which is exactly contrary to the position it takes in the present case. We agreed with the government in that case that tracing should be allowed in order to prevent injustice and inequity toward the government. Here, equity and justice is on the side of the taxpayer, especially since it is conceded that there was no manipulation of the distribution by the executors to avoid taxes. Yet the majority refuses to make an exception for the taxpayer in this case as we did for the government in the Mott case. As tracing was allowed as an exception in that case, it should be allowed here, although admittedly the facts are different.

---

55. See George Craven, *Taxation of Estate and Trust Income Under the 1954 Code*, 103 Univ. of Pa.L.Rev., 602, 614 (1954-1955), where it is stated: "* * * There is a serious question about the constitutionality of an income tax statute which taxes to a beneficiary receiving principal an amount of income in excess of an amount which may inure to his benefit. This provision requires prompt remedial action by Congress in order to eliminate any requirement that amounts of principal distributed by an estate in process of administration shall be treated as distributions of income."

Since the majority refuses to face the constitutional issue, an equitable solution of the whole problem would be to interpret the statute in such a way as to hold that it creates a rebuttable presumption that such distributions as we have here are from income, which may be overcome by evidence of the taxpayer.[56] On that basis, the plaintiff would prevail in this case because it is admitted by the government that the distribution of $217,361 to the plaintiff on which she was taxed was to that extent corpus and not income of the estate received by plaintiff during the taxable year in question. Such an interpretation of the statute would remove the constitutional question from the case.

A solution to this whole problem would be for Congress to amend Section 663(c) of the Internal Revenue Code so as to make it apply to estates. As now written, it only applies to trusts and is known as the "separate share" rule. In other words, where a trust has more than one beneficiary, the separate shares of the beneficiaries are treated as separate trusts. This prevents a beneficiary who receives corpus from being taxed on an amount in excess of the distributable net income of the trust of his share. If the separate share rule were extended to estates, the problem we have in the present case would not arise.[57] There is no logical reason why Section 663(c) should not apply to estates as well as to trusts. This was no doubt an oversight when the statute was drafted.

When the facts and the arguments of the parties are carefully considered and one arrives at the moment of decision in this case, it is clear that the IRS either taxed the plaintiff on the $217,361 of the income of the estate that she did not receive, or it levied and collected such tax on the corpus of the estate which she did receive under the guise of an income tax. In either case, the tax was unconstitutional and invalid.

For all of the foregoing reasons, I would hold that Section 662(a)(2)(B) and Section 1.662(a)-3 of the Treasury Regulations as applied to plaintiff in this case are unconstitutional and the collection of the tax from the plaintiff was invalid. Alternatively, I would hold that the statute and the regulations create a rebuttable presumption that distributions such as we have here are from income which might be overcome by the taxpayer by credible evidence, and that the taxpayer has overcome such presumption in this case. In either case, I would enter judgment for the plaintiff for the sum of $248,256.75, plus interest from the date of payment as authorized by law.

Comment: *Harkness* dealt with distributions from an estate prior to when the Code made the application of the separate share rule applicable to estates. It

56. This would be similar to the practice in tax cases of allowing a taxpayer to overcome the presumption of correctness of a determination by the Commissioner of Internal Revenue Service with reference to income taxes.

57. For a discussion of the separate share rule, see George Craven, *Taxation of Estate and Trust Income Under the 1954 Code, supra*, at 616; and Kamin, Surrey Warren, *The Internal Revenue Code of 1954, Trusts, Estates and Beneficiaries*, 54 Colum.L.Rev. 1237, 1257-59 (1954).

illustrates that disproportionate distributions to multiple beneficiaries can lead to a beneficiary being allocated more DNI than his share of the estate. When this case was adjudicated, the separate share rule did not apply to estates. If the separate share rule had applied, then the taxpayer, being entitled to only one-half of the estate, would have been taxed only on the DNI allocated to her one-half share. Absent the separate share rule, the distributions resulted in the taxpayer being taxed on three-fourths of the estate's DNI.

> **Example:** A trust provides for separate shares to be established for its two beneficiaries, A and B. The trustee has discretion to distribute income and principal to A or B from her share. For the current tax year, the trust has \$20,000 of DNI (none of which is tax-exempt interest). The trustee distributes \$30,000 to A from A's share and \$10,000 to B from B's share. Under the normal pro-rata rules of sections 661 and 662, A would be allocated \$15,000 of DNI (\$30,000/\$40,000 × \$20,000 DNI) and B would be allocated \$5,000 of DNI (\$10,000/\$40,000 × \$20,000 DNI). However, if A's share and B's share of the trust each independently earned \$10,000 of the total DNI of \$20,000, under the separate share rule, A is deemed to receive only his \$10,000 share of the DNI and B is deemed to receive only his \$10,000 share of the DNI.

In order for the separate share rule of § 663(c) to apply, there must be identifiable shares.[58]

> **Example:** The terms of a trust require the trustee to distribute one-half of the income to A and one-half of the income to B. The trust also gives the trustee the authority to invade corpus for the benefit of either A or B as the trustee determines. There are no substantially separate and independent shares if the trustee has the power to invade corpus for the benefit of one beneficiary to the detriment of the other beneficiary. Neither A nor B have an identifiable share of the trust.

Generally, the separate share rule will apply if "the governing instrument and the applicable local law create separate economic interests in one beneficiary or class of beneficiaries of [an] estate or trust. Ordinarily, a separate share exists if the economic interests of the beneficiary or class of beneficiaries neither affect nor are affected by the economic interests accruing to another beneficiary or class of beneficiaries." Treas. Reg. 1.663(c)-4(a). The separate share rule governs DNI allocation among distributees. However, in recognition of the separate share rule's apparent complexity, the Treasury Regulations state that a fiduciary is instructed to use "a reasonable and equitable method to make the allocations, calculations, and valuations. . . ." Treas. Reg. 1.663(c)-2(c).

58. A common provision in many inter vivos and testamentary trusts contains language such as the following: "upon my death, the trustee will establish as many shares, equal in value, as is necessary to create one share for each child of mine who survives me and one share for each child who does not survive me, but has descendants who do survive me."

Bequests of specific property and sums of money under section 663(a)(1) are not separate shares because the satisfaction of such specific bequests does not carry out DNI. Treas. Reg. 1.663(c)-4(a). However, the income on bequeathed property is a separate share if the recipient of the specific bequest is entitled to such income. *Id.* This makes sense, because the income should be taxable to the person entitled to receive it.

> **Example:** D's will directs the executor to distribute X stock and all the dividends thereon to child A and the residue of the estate to child B. The estate has two separate shares — the income on the X stock bequeathed to A and the residue of the estate bequeathed to B. The bequest of the X stock is a specific bequest and therefore is not a separate share. If any distributions other than the shares of X stock are made during the year to either A or B, gross income attributable to dividends on the X stock must be allocated to A's separate share, and any other income must be allocated to B's separate share. *See* Treas. Reg. 1.663(c)-5, Example 8.

> **Example:** A will bequeaths XYZ stock to A and the residue of the estate to B. In year 1, the only income earned in the trust is a $10,000 dividend on XYZ stock to which A is entitled to under the applicable state law. The executor distributes $15,000 to each of A and B. Without the application of the separate share rule, each beneficiary would have reported $5,000 of income based on his pro-rata share of DNI ($10,000 DNI × $15,000/$30,000). Under the separate share rule, however, the $10,000 of dividends are allocable to A's separate share, and A is taxed on $10,000, the DNI allocable to his share. B's share earned no DNI in year 1, so the distribution to B is tax-free.

Separate shares come into existence at the earliest moment that the fiduciary can determine — based on the known facts — that a separate share exists. Treas. Reg. 1.663(c)-2(a). In the case of an estate, this determination is usually made at the moment of a taxpayer's death; in the case of a trust, this determination is usually made at the moment the trust is established.

An easy way to think about the separate share rule is to think of two siblings who go out trick or treating together. Each has their own trick or treat bag in which they collect candy. When they get home, their parents tell them to take the candy to their respective bedrooms and one sibling is not permitted to take any candy from the other sibling's bag. They each have separate shares. One child, per their parents' instructions, has no rights to take candy from the other child's bag. The candy represents the DNI. If one sibling collected more candy than the other and the candy was considered to be owned separately by each of them, it would be unfair to treat one sibling as being the owner of more than his share. The separate share rule caps the DNI allocated to them to the actual "candy" each collected. Now suppose, instead, when the siblings got home, their parents tell them to dump all the candy they both collected on the kitchen table and that each child could help himself to the candy. They no longer have separate shares: each child can take "candy" that the other child collected. In that case, DNI would be allocated to the child based on the relative candy distributions.

The gross income allocation is made according to the amount of income to which the separate share is entitled under the governing instrument and local law; by the same token, the trust's distribution deduction is allocated on a per share basis. DNI is then allocated based upon this net amount, capping the dollar figure upon which each beneficiary may be taxed. Furthermore, if separate shares exist, DNI is computed separately for each share. Deductions or losses solely attributable to one share are not available to any other share. Treas. Reg. 1.663(c)-2(b)(5).

> **Example:** A discretionary trust has $20,000 of DNI. The trustee distributes $30,000 to A and $10,000 to B. Under the normal pro-rata distribution rules, A would include $15,000 of DNI ($30,000 distribution/$40,000 total distribution × $20,000 DNI). Under normal pro-rata rules, B would include $5,000 of DNI ($10,000 distribution/$40,000 total distribution × $20,000 DNI). Now suppose the trust, instead of being a discretionary trust, says A and B have separate shares. Suppose the distributions are the same, but that A's trust earned $2,000 of interest and $6,000 of dividends for a total of $8,000 of DNI. Although A received a $30,000 distribution, he would be taxed on only $8,000, the DNI earned by his share of the trust. Suppose B's share of the trust earned $4,000 of interest and $8,000 of dividends for a total of $12,000 of DNI. B received a distribution of $10,000 and would be taxed on the entire $10,000 distribution, as that is less than the $12,000 of DNI earned by his share of the trust. The remaining $2,000 of B's DNI, since it was not distributed to B, would be taxed to the trust. The trust consists of two separate shares and has $20,000 of DNI — $8,000 from A's share and $12,000 from B's share. The trust receives a distribution deduction of $18,000 based on the $8,000 of DNI deemed distributed to A and the $10,000 of DNI deemed distributed to B. The income taxed to the trust is $2,000, which constitutes the DNI amount from B's share that was not distributed to him. The income tax payable by the trust will be charged against B's share. Note that the trust is treated as having separate shares *solely* for purposes of allocating DNI between A and B. It does not mean that the trust must file two tax returns or that the trust is allowed two $100 exemptions.

The separate share rule will not apply where a single trust is split into several separate trusts, as opposed to separate shares of the same trust. Treas. Reg. 1.663(c)-1(a).

The separate share rule strictly affects DNI determinations. It does not permit the treatment of separate shares as separate trusts for any other purposes, such as filing separate returns, claiming multiple exemptions, or allowing the separate shares to have a separate "run up the brackets" for purposes of calculating the trust's income tax liability. Thus, a trust or estate with separate shares will be treated as one trust for all other purposes such as for tax identification number purposes, for tax return filing requirements, for estimated tax purposes, and for personal exemptions.

Note that the application of the separate share rule can be intentionally avoided by drafting the trust in such a way that separate and independent shares do not exist. For example, a trust may be drafted as a "spray" or discretionary trust. Alternatively, a trust document may subdivide the trust into separate trusts. Each trust, being a separate trust, would file its own tax return.

The separate share rule can be summarized as follows:

1. The separate share rule applies to both trust and estates.

2. Under the separate share rule, DNI is computed separately for each share.

3. Beneficiaries of a separate share can only receive the DNI determined for such share.

4. For the separate share rule to apply, a trustee or executor is not required to maintain separate accountings for each share. Thus, the separate share rule may apply even though separate and independent accounts are not required or maintained and even though no physical segregation of assets is required or made. Treas. Reg. 1.663(c)-1(c).

5. The separate share rule is not elective. If its requirements are met, the rule must be applied. Treas. Reg. 1.663(c)-1(d).

The separate share rule may apply to concurrent interests (that is, two or more beneficiaries have interests in a trust at the same time). However, the separate share rule does not apply to successive interests in point of time. Treas. Reg. 1.663(c)-3(e). For example, when a particular beneficiary's interest ends and a successor beneficiary's interest begins (e.g., such as the year in which the income beneficiary dies and the successor beneficiary becomes entitled to distributions), the separate share rule does not apply to each beneficiary's interest in that year or at any other time.

> **Example:** Trust X provides that trust income be paid quarterly to A, remainder to B. A dies July 1. Separate share treatment is not available for pre-death and post-death shares of A and B.

C. The 65-Day Rule and the § 663(b) Election

In general, absent any special rule, for a complex trust or estate to take a tier-two distribution deduction, the distribution must be paid or credited to the beneficiary during the trust's or estate's taxable year. Treas. Reg. 1.661(a)-1. However, a problem may arise for a trustee or executor who has not distributed all of the trust's or estate's DNI in a particular year due to the inability to compute DNI until after year-end when the trust's or estate's books are closed. To alleviate this problem, § 663(b) allows a trustee or executor, subject to limitations in the regulations, to elect to treat any portion of a distribution to a beneficiary made within the first 65 days of the trust's or estate's subsequent tax year as if it had been paid or credited to the beneficiary on the last day of the preceding tax year.

Although the distribution must be made within 65 days of the new year, the election must be made no later than the fiduciary income tax return due date (including extensions). The election is made on an annual basis and is irrevocable after the last day prescribed for making it. Treas. Reg. 1.663(b)-2(a)(1), (2). The election is made by checking the appropriate box on page 3, line 6 of Form 1041 (2022 version). A late election (or revocation) is possible under Treas. Reg. 1.9100-1 if the trustee can demonstrate that it acted reasonably and acted promptly to request an extension once it discovered the error. Priv. Ltr. Ruls. 200834006, 200617004, and 200250003. If no return is due, the election is made by filing a statement to that effect with the IRS office where the return would have been filed and within the time such return would have been due. Treas. Reg. 1.663(b)-2(a)(2). The election does not need to be made for all the distributions made in the first 65 days — the fiduciary may designate the distributions that he or she wants to subject to the 65-day-rule election. Treas. Reg. 1.663(b)-1(a).

For tax purposes, the 65-day-rule election (also known as the § 663(b) election) provides flexibility in distribution timing, permitting a fiduciary to make a decision based on actual income for the year. This allows a fiduciary to better coordinate the income tax planning for a trust and estate and its beneficiaries.

Example: A trust has $10,000 of DNI for the year. In the trustee's discretion, it may distribute income and principal. During the year, the trustee distributes $6,000 to the beneficiaries. If the trustee makes no further distributions, the trust will (i) receive a $6,000 distribution deduction (and the beneficiary will report that income on his own tax return) and (ii) pay tax on the remaining $4,000 of DNI. On the other hand, the trustee could exercise his discretion and make an additional distribution of up to $4,000 to the beneficiary on or before March 6 the following year. (Caution: February has 29 days in a leap year, so a distribution would have to be made by March 5 in a leap year.) If the trustee makes the § 663(b) election for $4,000, the $4,000 distribution will be treated as if it were made on December 31 of the prior year. The trust would thus be entitled to an income distribution deduction of $10,000, and the beneficiary would report $10,000 on his tax return. The amount paid pursuant to a § 663(b) election is not deductible again for the trust year in which the payment is actually made — it is deductible in the year to which the § 663(b) election applies (namely, the prior tax year).

If an election is made, the deduction is limited to the greater of (i) DNI or (ii) trust accounting income, reduced by amounts paid, credited, or required to be distributed in such taxable year (other than amounts treated as being distributed in the prior year because of the 65-day election). Treas. Reg. 1.663(b)-1(a)(2).

Example: In year 2 of its existence, X Trust, a calendar year trust, has $1,000 of trust accounting income and $800 of DNI. On January 15 of year 2, the trust pays $550 to A, a beneficiary, which the trustee elects to treat under § 663(b) as paid on December 31 of year 1. Furthermore, in year 2, the trust pays $600 on July 19 and, in year 3 on January 17, $450 to A. For year 2, the maximum amount that may be elected under § 663(b) to be treated as property paid or credited on the last day of that year is $400 (i.e., $1,000 – $600). The $550 paid on January 15 of year 2 does not reduce the maximum amount to which the election may apply, because that amount is treated as paid on December 31 of year 1.

In sum, the 65-day-rule election is a valuable tool for trustees and executors. It can be used to have income taxed to the beneficiaries rather than being subject to the compressed income tax brackets of trusts and estates. In addition, it may prove useful to potentially avoid having net investment income earned and retained by a trust or estate subject to the 3.8% surtax. See Code § 1411(a).

D. Distributions That Are Not Subject to the Distribution Deduction Rules

Section 663(a)(1) is an exception to the § 661 and § 662 rules governing distributions from trusts and estates. If a distribution meets the requirements of § 663(a)(1), the trust or estate is not entitled to a distribution deduction under § 661, and the beneficiary is not treated as receiving any DNI under § 662.

To qualify under § 663(a)(1), the following three requirements must be met:

(1) First, the distribution must be of specific property or a specific, pecuniary sum of money. The regulations indicate that a gift or bequest is "specific" if the amount of money or the identity of the property is ascertainable under the terms of the testator's will as of the date of death or under the terms of an inter vivos trust instrument as of the date of the inception of the trust. Treas. Reg. 1.663(a)-1(b)(1).

(2) Second, the distribution must be paid either all at once or in not more than three installments. However, Treas. Reg. 1.663(a)-1(c) contains four modifications to the three-installment rule:

a. First, gifts of items of personal or household use are disregarded, even when the will requires that they be distributed in more than three installments.

b. Second, real estate that vests in the devisee at the testator's death is not taken into account — it does not constitute an amount paid, credited, or required to be distributed under § 661. Treas. Reg. 1.663(a)-1(c)(1)(ii); Treas. Reg. 1.661(a)-2(e); Rev. Rul. 68-49, 1968-1 C.B. 304.

c. Third, gifts and bequests under a decedent's will for which no time of payment or crediting is specified, and which are to be paid or credited in the ordinary course of administration of the decedent's estate, are considered as required to be paid or credited in a single installment. Treas. Reg. 1.663(a)-(c)(1)(iii).

d. Fourth, all gifts and bequests payable at any one specified time under the terms of the governing instrument are deemed paid in a single installment. Treas. Reg. 1.663(a)-1(c)(1)(iv).

Example: A decedent's will makes a specific bequest to a beneficiary of $40,000. Although not required by the will, the personal representative makes partial distributions of the bequest over four installments. As long as the distributions are accomplished within the ordinary course of administration and the will does not specify the time for payment, the distributions are considered to be paid in a single installment and will qualify as a specific bequest.

(3) Third, no portion of the gift or bequest of a specific sum of money can be paid only from income of the estate or trust. § 663(a)(1), last sentence.

Example: Decedent leaves $10,000 in her will to her nephew, Thaddeus. Since the bequest is ascertainable at the date of the decedent's death, Thaddeus is not treated as receiving any of the DNI from the $10,000 received, and the estate does not get a corresponding distribution deduction.

Example: Decedent's will declares, "I leave my grand piano to my niece, Mildred." The bequest of the grand piano is a bequest of specific property under § 663(a)(1). As a result, the distribution of the piano to Mildred will not be deemed to carry out any DNI to Mildred, and the estate is not entitled to a distribution deduction.

Pursuant to the regulations, the following amounts are not considered gifts or bequests of a sum of money or of specific property:

- An amount which can be paid or credited only from the income of an estate or trust, whether from the income for the year of payment or crediting, or from the income accumulated from a prior year;
- An annuity, or periodic gifts of specific property in lieu of or having the effect of an annuity;
- A residuary estate or the corpus of a trust; or
- A gift or bequest paid in a lump sum or in not more than three installments, if the gift or bequest is required to be paid in more than three installments under the terms of the governing instrument.

A bequest of a specific amount that is permitted to be satisfied in cash or in kind, is a bequest of a specific sum of money, even though it may be satisfied by an in-kind distribution. Rev. Rul. 86-105, 1986-2 C.B. 82; Rev. Rul. 66-207, 1966-2 C.B. 243.

To qualify as a bequest of specific property, at the time of death, the identity of the property must be ascertainable.

Example: A bequest of a specific dollar amount of XYZ stock, but not more than all of the XYZ stock, where the value of the stock was to be determined as of the date of distribution is not a bequest of specific property or of a specific sum. Rev. Rul. 72-295, 1972-1 C.B. 197. The amount of stock to be distributed could only be determined as of the date of distribution. Thus, only the type of property could be ascertained as of the date of death, but not the specific amount of the property bequeathed.

For purposes of § 663(a)(1), a formula marital or credit shelter bequest (*see* Chapter 1) is not a bequest of a specific sum of money even though it is treated as fixed and ascertainable for other purposes. Treas. Reg. 1.663(a)-1(b)(1); Rev. Rul. 60-87, 1960-1 C.B. 286. The identity of the property and the amount of money are dependent both on the exercise of the executor's discretion and on the payment of administration expenses and other charges, neither one of which are facts existing as of the decedent's death.

> **Example:** Decedent's will leaves Jasper a sum of money equal to 10% of his gross estate less deductions allowed under § 2053 and § 2054. The amount Jasper will receive is not ascertainable as of the decedent's death. This is due to the fact that, for example, the executor may elect to claim administration expenses either as an estate tax deduction or a fiduciary income tax deduction. If the executor elects to deduct administration expenses on the estate's income tax return, the amount of the formula bequest will be higher than if those expenses were deducted on the estate tax return. Thus, the amount of the adjusted gross estate is not ascertainable until that election is made at some point after the decedent's death, i.e., the amount is not ascertainable as of the date of the decedent's death. The distribution thus carries out DNI to Jasper, and the estate will receive a corresponding distribution deduction.

If a bequest of a specific sum of money is satisfied with appreciated or depreciated property or if a bequest of specific property is satisfied with different property, the distribution will result in a gain or loss. Treas. Reg. 1.661(a)-2(f).[59]

> **Example:** The terms of a trust declare that Jackie, upon attaining age 50, is to receive the sum of $50,000. In satisfaction with this instruction, the trustee distributes stock with a fair market value of $50,000 but a cost basis of $20,000 to Jackie. The bequest of $50,000 is a specific bequest under § 663(a)(1). As such, the trust is not entitled to a distribution deduction, and Jackie is not required to include the $50,000 worth of stock in her income. However, since the specific bequest of $50,000 is satisfied with a distribution of appreciated property, the trust must recognize a gain of $30,000, the difference between the $50,000 fair market value of the stock and cost basis of $20,000. Treas. Reg. 1.661(a)-2(f); *Kenan v. Commissioner*, 114 F.2d 217 (2d Cir. 1940).

The beneficiary who receives a § 663(a)(1) distribution of property that was included in the decedent's gross estate will receive a basis in the asset equal to the date of death (or alternate valuation) value. Section 1014(a). A beneficiary who

59. Although the regulation references the recognition of loss, losses are not allowed in transactions between related parties pursuant to Code § 267. Pursuant to § 267(b)(6), trustees and trust beneficiaries are related parties; pursuant to § 267(b)(13), executors and beneficiaries of the estate are related parties, except in the case of a sale or exchange in satisfaction of a pecuniary bequest.

receives a § 663(a)(1) distribution of property from an irrevocable trust that was not included in the decedent's estate will receive a carryover tax basis. Code § 1015(a).[60]

A distribution of the income earned by a specific bequest is not exempt under § 663(a)(1). It will qualify for a distribution deduction under § 661 and be includible in the beneficiary's income under § 662.

> **Example:** A will leaves a specific bequest of XYZ stock to B. State law requires that the income earned on the specific bequest be distributed to the beneficiary of the specific bequest. The bequest of the stock qualifies as a specific bequest under § 663(a)(1). The dividends on the stock do not meet the requirements of § 663(a)(1). When the dividends are distributed to B, they will be taxable to B and deductible by the estate.

A draftsperson should structure a distribution as a specific bequest under § 663(a)(1) whenever it is desirable to avoid having the beneficiary pay income tax on a distribution. For example, a bequest leaving all of a person's tangible personal property qualifies under § 663(a)(1) so that the beneficiary does not have to pay income tax on the value of the tangibles when distributed. Such bequests are intentionally used in a will or trust to avoid income tax consequences to the distributee.

> **Example:** Decedent's will states, "I give my entire estate to my wife, Lillian." A distribution of tangible personal property (e.g., an automobile) will result in a distribution deduction to the estate and taxable income, limited to DNI, to Lillian. The decedent could have avoided this result if the will contained two separate clauses: "First, I give my tangible personal property to my wife, Lillian. Second, I give the residue of my estate to my wife, Lillian." The clause leaving Lillian the tangible personal property qualifies as a specific bequest under § 663(a)(1).

E. In-Kind Distributions and the § 643(e) Election

Code § 643(e) discusses tax consequences associated with in-kind property distributions made from trusts and estates when such distributions do not automatically result in realized gain or loss. The two most salient are the tax basis of the distributed property in the beneficiary's hands and the amount deemed distributed for purposes of the distribution deduction. Below, part 1 discusses the tax basis and holding period in property that a beneficiary receives; part 2 explores the amount that is deemed distributed; and, finally, part 3 investigates an election the Code offers trusts and estates to voluntarily recognize gain.[61]

---

60. For purposes of computing losses, the Code requires that the taxpayer use the lesser of (i) carryover tax basis or (ii) fair market value on the date of gift. Code § 1015(a).

61. Note that Code § 643(e) only applies to residuary dispositions, not specific bequests.

1. Tax Basis and Holding Period in Property Received by a Beneficiary

When a beneficiary receives a property distribution from a trust or estate, the Code provides that the beneficiary's tax basis in the property will be a carryover tax basis, adjusted for any gain or loss recognized. Code § 643(e)(1). Because such distributions do not ordinarily give rise to any gain or loss, absent an election to recognize gain or loss, there will be no adjustment. If, however, the entity makes a recognition election (see below), there may be an upward or downward tax basis adjustment.

In the absence of a recognition election, the holding period of the distributed property carries over to the distributee and, as such, the holding period tacks under § 1223(2), which applies if the tax basis of the distributed asset is determined in whole or in part with reference to the asset's basis in the hands of the transferor. Note that if the asset was held at the date of death and was included in the decedent's gross estate for federal estate tax purposes, the holding period of the transferor will be an automatic long-term holding period under § 1223(9).

2. Amount Deemed Distributed

When a beneficiary receives a property distribution from a trust or estate, the Code also determines the amount deemed distributed. It provides this amount shall be equal to the **lesser** of (i) the tax basis of such property in the recipient's hands or (ii) the property's fair market value. Code § 643(e)(2).[62]

Under the general rule and absent a recognition election, a distribution will carry out DNI equal to the lesser of the property's tax basis or its fair market value on the date of distribution. Code § 643(e)(2). Accordingly, the amount treated as a distribution deduction under § 661(a)(2) and included in the beneficiary's income under § 662(a)(2) is the lower of the tax basis or fair market value of the distributed property.

> **Example:** A trust has DNI of $50,000. The trustee funds a residuary bequest by transferring stock with a fair market value of $50,000 and a basis of $20,000. The trustee does not makes a § 643(e) election. The stock distribution carries out $20,000 of DNI (the lower of the cost basis or fair market value of the stock). Since the trustee did not make a § 643(e) election, the trust doesn't recognize any gain. The beneficiary takes a $20,000 basis in the distributed stock (the trust's $20,000 basis plus zero gain recognized by the trust). Since the beneficiary's basis is determined in whole or in part by reference to the trust's basis in the stock, the trust's holding period of

62. In those instances when a 643(e) election is made (see below), these dollar amounts should be the same and will result in a greater amount of DNI being deemed distributed out of the entity and into the beneficiary's hands.

the stock is tacked onto the beneficiary's holding period for purposes of determining if the gain is long-term or short-term.

3. *Section 643(e) Election*

A Code § 643(e) election provides an opportunity to fiduciaries to shift tax consequences between a trust or estate and its beneficiaries. For example, if an election is made, gains and losses can be absorbed by the entity; in contrast, in the absence of an election, such gains and losses will be preserved for recognition by the beneficiary upon a future realization event. If the trust or estate makes a recognition election, a distribution will carry out DNI equal to the property's fair market value. Code § 643(e)(3). Accordingly, to the extent of DNI available, the amount treated as a distribution deduction under § 661(a)(2) and included in the beneficiary's income under § 662(a)(2) is the fair market value of the distributed property.

> **Example:** A trust has DNI of $50,000. The trustee funds a residuary bequest by transferring stock with a fair market value of $50,000 and a basis of $20,000. The trustee makes a § 643(e) election. The distribution of stock carries out $50,000 of DNI (the fair market value of the stock). The § 643(e) election causes the trust to recognize gain of $30,000 ($50,000 FMV less $20,000 basis). The beneficiary takes a $50,000 basis in the distributed stock (the trust's $20,000 basis plus the $30,000 of gain recognized by the trust), and a new holding period commences.

A Code § 643(e) election is made by the trust or estate on its income tax return for the taxable year for which the distribution was made. The election is made by checking a box on page 3, line 7 of the Form 1041 (2022 version). The election applies to all property distributions made during the year with the exception of § 663(a) property distributions. Code § 643(e)(3)(B), (e)(4). In other words, fiduciaries may not make a Code § 643(e) election in a particular year for some property distributions, but not for others. Once made, the election may only be revoked with the consent of the Secretary of the Treasury. Code § 643(e)(3)(B), last sentence. The election is made on a year-by-year basis, i.e., it can be made for property distributions in one year, but not the next. The revocation of a § 643(e) election may be accomplished through a Treas. Reg. 301.9100 relief request. Priv. Ltr. Rul. 9641018.

IV. Special Subchapter S Trusts

The Code severely limits those taxpayers who can be "S corporation shareholders" (i.e., those shareholders who own corporate shares in which an "S election" has been made). These limitations are found in Code § 1361. In particular, an S corporation cannot "have as a shareholder a person (other than an estate [or] a trust described in subsection (c)(2) . . .) who is not an individual." Code § 1361(b)(1)(B). Code § 1361(c)(2) and (d) lists those trusts that constitute eligible shareholders, including (A) qualified subchapter S trusts and (B) electing small business trusts.

A. Qualified Subchapter S Trust (QSST)

Special rules are provided under §1361(d) for "Qualified Subchapter S Trusts" (QSST). A QSST is an eligible shareholder of S corporation stock provided that the benefits of the S corporation stock are largely dedicated to one individual beneficiary and that the beneficiary agrees to be treated as the deemed owner of the trust.[63]

Under Code §1361(d)(3) the five requirements of a QSST are as follows:

(i) The trust distributes or is required to distribute all of its accounting income annually to one U.S. citizen or resident;

(ii) The trust distributes no principal other than to the income beneficiary;

(iii) The income beneficiary's interest terminates at death or when the trust terminates, whichever occurs first;

(iv) If the trust terminates when the income beneficiary is alive, the trust assets must be distributed to the income beneficiary; and

(v) The income beneficiary must elect to be treated as the owner of that portion of the trust consisting of the S corporation stock.

A trust becomes a QSST only upon an affirmative election by the income beneficiary. This election causes the income beneficiary to be treated as the owner of that portion of the trust consisting of the S corporation stock, as if the beneficiary owned that portion under §678. Code §1361(d)(1)(B). Thus, all of the income, deductions, and credits attributable to the QSST flow through and are taxed to the beneficiary. Treas. Reg. 1.1361-1(j)(7). An exception to this rule is when a disposition of the S stock occurs. In that case, the beneficiary is not treated as the owner, and any resulting gain or loss that is recognized will be reported by the trust. Treas. Reg. 1.1361-1(j)(8).

The election must be filed within the time described by Treas. Reg. 1.1361-1(j)(6)(iii), although relief is available for the inadvertent failure to file a timely election. Rev. Proc. 2013-30, 2013-36 I.R.B. 173.[64] Generally, the election must be made within two months and 16 days after S corporation stock is transferred to the trust (Code §1361(d)(2)(D)) or, if the trust holds stock of a corporation that makes an S election, after the S election is effective. The election is irrevocable. Code §1361(d)(2)(C).

Once the election is in effect, it is treated as being made for successive beneficiaries unless a successor beneficiary affirmatively refuses to consent to the election

63. Section 1361(d)(3) (flush language) permits a *share* of a trust to be treated as a separate trust for QSST purposes if the share qualifies as a "substantially separate and independent share of a trust within the meaning of §663(c)." This provision permits a trust to have multiple beneficiaries and still be eligible to be treated as a QSST without requiring separate trusts for each beneficiary. Each separate share counts as one shareholder, because each share is considered to be a separate trust for QSST purposes. The separate share rule may be applied even though separate and independent accounts are not maintained or required and no physical segregation of assets is maintained or required. A separate QSST election must be made for each of the separate shares.

64. A special QSST election procedure is available for an ESBT that converts to a QSST. Treas. Reg. 1.1361-1(m)(7).

within two months and 15 days of becoming the current income beneficiary. Code § 1361(d)(2)(B)(ii); Treas. Reg. 1.1361-1(j)(9), (10). As a practical matter, unlike direct S corporate shareholders, a QSST beneficiary may unilaterally terminate an S election.

A trust ceases to be a QSST as of the date it no longer satisfies any of the QSST requirements. Code § 1361(d)(4)(A); Treas. Reg. 1.1361-1(j)(5).

B. Electing Small Business Trust (ESBT)

An ESBT is another type of trust that is an eligible S corporation shareholder.

Where a trust holds S corporation stock in which the trustee makes an election to have the trust treated as an ESBT, all the income from the S corporation is taxed to the trust at the highest income tax bracket, regardless of whether any income is distributed to a beneficiary. Code § 641(c). The portion of the trust that holds the S corporation stock is treated as if it is a separate trust. The trust will not receive a distribution deduction for any distributions made from the ESBT to the trust beneficiaries.

An ESBT is any trust all the beneficiaries of which are U.S. individuals, estates, or certain charitable organizations eligible to be S corporation shareholders, no interest of which is acquired by purchase or other taxable transfer. Code § 1361(e)(1)(A). Ineligible trusts include QSSTs, tax-exempt trusts, and charitable remainder annuity or unitrusts. Code § 1361(e)(1)(B).

A trust is an ESBT only if the *trustee* elects to have it so treated by filing a statement with the IRS Service Center where the S corporation files its income tax return. Once made, the election applies for the year it is made and all future years, unless revoked with IRS consent. Code § 1361(e)(3). The election is made by the trustee; the consent of the beneficiaries is not needed. Guidance on making the election is outlined in Treas. Reg. 1.1361-1(m)(2).

Unlike a QSST, an ESBT may have two or more beneficiaries, accumulate income, and distribute both income and principal among the beneficiaries. Each potential current beneficiary of an ESBT is counted as a shareholder for purposes of the 100 shareholder S corporation limitation. Code § 1361(b)(1)(A). A "potential current beneficiary" is defined as any person who is currently entitled to receive or may, in the discretion of the trustee, receive a distribution from the income or principal of the trust. Code § 1361(e)(2).[65] Furthermore, the Code provides that a potential current beneficiary is determined without regard to any power of appointment to the extent such power remains unexercised at the end of the period. *Id.*

The law, anticipating that a trust may accumulate income, provides for the ESBT itself to be treated as the shareholder for purposes of the 100 shareholder limitation. Code § 1361(c)(2)(A)(v).

---

65. Nonresident aliens are permitted to be potential current beneficiaries of an electing small business trust. Code § 1361(c)(2)(B)(v).

For income tax purposes, the portion of an ESBT that consists of stock of an S corporation to which the ESBT election applies is treated as a separate trust. Treas. Reg. 1.641(c)-1(a), (b)(2). The trust is taxable on its share of S corporation income, i.e., Subchapter J rules governing the income taxation of trusts and estates are ignored. The income an ESBT earns is taxed at the highest trust income tax rate, which is currently 37% on ordinary income and 20% on long-term gains. Code § 641(c)(2)(A). The separate tax calculation applies not only to the items of S corporation income, but also to all gains and losses from the sale of S corporation stock.

The tax imposed on the income earned by an ESBT is computed with limited deductions. Permitted deductions include administrative expenses and state taxes attributable to income taxable as an ESBT. Code § 641(c)(2)(C). Section 641(c)(2)(C) lists the deductions available to ESBTs, and that list does not include the § 199A deduction. However, one of the few items allowed under § 641(c)(2(C) includes "[t]he items required to be taken into account under Section 1366." Section 1366 describes the pass-through of items to S corporation shareholders, which seems to include the § 199A deduction. The final § 199A regulations clarify any confusion by specifically allowing the § 199A deduction to reduce the ESBT income.

An ESBT does not receive an income distribution deduction as would a normal trust or estate; correspondingly, the income of an ESBT is not included in the trust's DNI or in a beneficiary's gross income. Code § 641(c)(3). Thus, the non-ESBT share of a trust does not include the ESBT's income in calculating the non-ESBT's DNI or distribution deduction. The normal fiduciary income tax rules apply to the non-ESBT share. Thus, normally two shares are present—an ESBT share and a non-ESBT share. The regular Subchapter J rules for the taxation of trusts apply to the non-ESBT share while the special ESBT rules apply to the ESBT share.

In sum, ESBTs allow trusts which make discretionary distributions or accumulate income to hold S corporation stock. The cost of this flexibility is often a higher tax burden on the S corporation's net income.

Example of a 2022 Fiduciary Income Tax Return for a Complex Trust

Below is a comprehensive example of the application of the rules discussed in this chapter applicable to complex trusts. The example incorporates the following concepts:

1. The calculation of trust accounting income (TAI).
2. The allocation of the TAI among the various beneficiaries.
3. The calculation of taxable income which is the starting point for the calculation of distributable net income (DNI).
4. The allocation of administration expenses and the charitable deduction to tax-exempt income.
5. The allocation of the depreciation deduction between the trust and the beneficiaries.

6. The calculation of DNI.
7. The allocation of direct expenses to the income that generates those expenses, and the allocation of indirect expenses to various classes of income.
8. Calculation of the distribution deduction and the application of the tier system.
9. Calculation of the taxable income of the trust and the allocation of the amount and character of income to the various beneficiaries based on the distributions made to each.
10. An indication of where all this information is reported on the fiduciary income tax return, Form 1041.

Assume that a trust provides that 50% of the income must be paid currently to Will. In 2022, the trustee also makes the following discretionary distributions of income: 25% to Cam and 25% to charity. No reserve for depreciation is required. The following income and expenses occurred in 2022:

Income

Rents	$40,000
Taxable interest	30,000
Tax-exempt interest	15,000
Long-term capital gain	8,000

Expenses

Depreciation of rental property	6,000
Real estate rental expenses	14,000
Trustee expenses — Principal	1,000
Trustee expenses — Income	2,000

Distributions

Required:	50% to Will
Discretionary:	25% to Cam
	25% to charity

1. Computation of Trust Accounting Income:

Rents	$40,000
Taxable interest	30,000
Tax-exempt interest	15,000
Gross trust accounting income	85,000
Less: Rental real estate expenses	(14,000)
Trustee expenses — income	(2,000)
Trust accounting income	69,000
(Enter on Form 1041, Sch. B, Line 8)	

Note: Tax-exempt interest is an item of trust accounting income. Its tax character is irrelevant. Capital gains are usually allocated to principal and are not part of trust accounting income.

2. Amount of trust accounting income received by each beneficiary:

Will	50% × 69,000 TAI =	$34,500
Cam	25% × 69,000 TAI =	17,250
Charity	25% × 69,000 TAI =	17,250
Total		69,000

3. Taxable income (before income distribution deduction):

Rental income	$40,000
Taxable interest	30,000
Tax-exempt interest ($15,000)	0
Long-term capital gains	8,000
Gross income	78,000
Less: rental real estate expenses	(14,000)
Less: Trustees' compensation	(2,471)*
Less: Charitable deduction	(14,206)**
Less: 642(b) deduction	(100)
Taxable income before distribution deduction	47,223

Note: The expenses must be allocated to the various items of income. The real estate rental expenses are allocated against rental income, because such expenses are attributable directly to rental income. However, a portion of the trustee's compensation and the charitable deduction must be allocated against tax-exempt interest and, as a result, such portion is not deductible. The portion is proportionate to the total of the tax-exempt interest ($15,000) divided by the gross amount of the items of income comprising DNI ($85,000). Thus, the portion of the commissions and charitable distribution that is not deductible is computed as follows:

* Trustee's commissions attributable to tax-exempt interest:

$3,000 × 15,000/85,000 = 529

$3,000 – 529 = 2,471

** Charitable deduction attributable to tax-exempt interest:

$17,250 × 15,000/85,000 = 3,044

$17,250 – 3,044 = 14,206

Note: If the trustee does not establish a reserve for depreciation, the depreciation deduction is apportioned between the income beneficiaries and the trust on the basis of the trust accounting income allocable to each. Here, since all of the trust accounting income is allocated to the beneficiaries, the trust is not entitled to deduct any depreciation.

4. Calculation of DNI:

Taxable income before distribution deduction			47,223
Add: 642(b) deduction	100		
Add: Tax-exempt interest (§ 643(a)(5))	15,000		
Less: trustee comp allocable		(529)	
Less: charitable deduction allocable		(3,044)	11,427
Less: Long-term capital gain			(8,000)
DNI—Put on Form 1041, Sch. B, Line 7			50,750

The items of DNI can be broken down into the following categories of income:

GI as % of TI	47.06%	35.29%	17.65%	100%
	Rental Income	Taxable Interest	Tax-exempt Interest	Total
Gross accounting income	40,000	30,000	15,000	85,000
Less:				
Rental expenses	(14,000)			(14,000)
Commissions *	(1,412)	(1,059)	(529)	(3,000)
Charitable deduction**	(8,118)	(6,088)	(3,044)	(17,250)
Totals	16,470	22,853	11,427	50,750

* The commissions can be allocated against any class of income. Treas. Reg. 1.652(b)-3.

** Charitable distributions must be apportioned ratably among each class of items of income. Treas. Reg. 1.661(b)-2.

5. Distributions deduction:

Income required to be distributed currently—tier-one distribution	34,500
All other amounts properly paid—tier-two distributions	17,250
Total	51,750
Limited to DNI	50,750

Note: The difference between the income required to be distributed and properly paid and DNI is the trustee's compensation of $1,000 allocated to principal.

§ 661(b): Character of amount deductible under § 661(a) is same as character of DNI:

Taxable character of DNI	$39,323
Tax-exempt character of DNI	11,427*
Distribution deduction	39,323

* The trust does not get a distribution deduction for the tax-exempt income. § 661(c); Treas. Reg. 1.661(c)-1.

6. Taxable income of the trust:

Taxable income before distribution deduction	47,223
Distribution deduction	(39,323)
Taxable income	7,900

Note: The taxable income equals the long-term capital gains less the exemption. This is correct, because all of the trust accounting income was distributed.

7. Tax consequences to beneficiaries:

Will—first tier beneficiary	34,500
(Received $34,500; limited to DNI of 50,750)	
Cam—second tier beneficiary	16,250
(Received $17,250; limited to remaining DNI: 50,750–34,500)	
Total (equal to DNI)	50,750

8. Character of DNI:

Taxable character: 39,323/50,750 = 77.48%

Exempt character: 11,427/50,750 = 22.52%

Will: Taxable 34,500 × 77.48% =	26,731
Less: 50% share of depreciation	(3,000)
Net taxable:	23,731

Cam: taxable 16,250 × 77.48%	12,592
Less: 25% share of depreciation	(1,500)
Net taxable:	11,092

The individual items of income that comprise Will and Cam's respective distributions also can be illustrated. Will receives 34,500/50,750 of each item, and Cam receives 16,250/50,750 of each item.

	Rental Income	Taxable Interest	Tax-exempt Interest	Total
Will (.679803)	11,196	15,536	7,768	34,500
Cam (.320197)	5,274	7,317	3,659	16,250
Total	16,470	22,853	11,427	50,750

9. Who gets taxed on what:

Taxable income before distribution deduction	47,223
Depreciation deductible by beneficiaries	(4,500)
Income which is taxed	42,723

Taxed to trust	7,900
Taxed to Will	23,731
Taxed to Cam	11,092
Total	42,723

Questions

1. What is a complex trust? What distinguishes it from a simple trust?
2. During a trust's existence, in what year will it always be a complex trust?
3. (a) A dies and bequeaths $10,000 to B and the residue of his estate to C. In the current year, B receives $10,000 and C receives $40,000 in distributions from the estate (during which it has $10,000 of DNI). How much of the estate's DNI are B and C deemed to receive?

   (b) If B and C are each 50% residuary beneficiaries?
4. (a) Trust T, a complex trust, has a calendar tax year. In year 1, suppose T has $10,000 of DNI and $20,000 of accounting income. On March 1 of year 2, suppose T distributes $15,000 to its beneficiaries. To what tax year does the distribution relate if T made no other distributions during year 1?

   (b) Suppose T was a simple trust?
5. In question 4, suppose T was instead an estate?
6. The Holt Trust has $50,000 of trust accounting income (TAI) and distributable net income (DNI) for the current year. The trust has three beneficiaries: Arthur, Betty and Carol. Under the terms of the trust instrument, Arthur is required to receive 20% of the trust accounting income. The trust instrument allows the trustee, in his discretion, to make additional distributions to all three beneficiaries. During the taxable year in question, the trustee makes discretionary distributions of $10,000 to Arthur, $60,000 to Betty and $30,000 to Carol. What is the total amount of taxable income taxable to each beneficiary? Please show your calculations and the reasoning for your answer.
7. (a) What is the separate share rule?

   (b) A creates a trust for the benefit of B, C, and D, equally. The trust provides that income is to be paid to the beneficiaries equally, and corpus may be distributed to any of the beneficiaries at the sole discretion of the Trustee. For tax purposes, must the trustee treat the interests of B, C, and D as separate shares?

   (c) Is there a separate share rule for estates?
8. Under the terms of a trust, one half of the income is paid to A, and the other half is paid out at the discretion of the trustee to B, C, and D, or accumulated. For the current tax year, the trust reported the following:

Rents	$130,000
Dividends	$20,000

Interest	$10,000
Tax Exempt Interest	$40,000
Capital Gains	$50,000
Capital Losses	$10,000
Direct Rental Expenses	$40,000
Trustee's Commissions (not allocated)	$10,000
Depreciation	$10,000

In addition to the required distribution to A, the trustee distributes $10,000 of trust accounting income to each of B, C, and D. Compute trust accounting income, taxable income, DNI, the trust's distribution deduction, and the character and amount of the beneficiaries' inclusion.

9. Suppose in question 8, the discretionary distributions to B, C, and D had been $50,000 each?

10. Suppose in question 8, the capital losses had been $60,000?

11. A dies on March 31 of the current year and bequeaths 20% of his $25 million residuary estate to his private foundation. The bequest qualifies for the charitable contribution deduction under Code § 2055. Between A's death and the distribution to the foundation on December 31, the estate earns $2 million of income. The $5 million distributed to the foundation is the estate's only distribution for the year. You are asked if the estate can take a deduction under Code § 661 for the distribution.

12. The Betts Trust has two beneficiaries: Marcus and Lynn. Pursuant to the trust instrument, the trustee split the trust into two equal shares, one for Marcus and one for Lynn. Marcus and Lynn are entitled to discretionary distributions only from their share of the trust. For the current year, Marcus' share of the trust earns $10,000 of qualified dividends and $30,000 of taxable interest, while Lynn's share of the trust earns $12,000 of qualified dividends and $18,000 of taxable interest. During the taxable year, the trustee makes a discretionary distribution of $25,000 to Marcus and $40,000 to Lynn. (1) What is the amount of distributable net income (DNI) of the trust, (2) how much DNI is reportable by each beneficiary, (3) what is the distribution deduction allowed to the trust and (4) how much, if any, income is taxable to the trust?

13. (a) Trust has DNI and trust accounting income of $50,000 and distributes the entire amount to A, who is required under the trust instrument to receive all income annually (i.e., A is a first tier beneficiary). Trust makes a $40,000 charitable contribution. How much does A report as income?

    (b) Facts are the same as above except that the mandatory distribution to A is only $20,000, and the trustee makes $25,000 of distributions to other beneficiaries (second tier beneficiaries).

PROBLEM No. 2

Complex Trust — Capital Gain Distributed

FEATURES

1. Interest and dividends present
2. No tax-exempt income present
3. Long-term capital gain present — and distributed to beneficiary
4. Fiduciary and professional fees present
5. Income:

Interest	6,000
Dividends (Qualified)	5,000
Long-term Capital Gain	50,000

6. Expenses:

Fiduciary fees	5,000
Accounting fees	5,000

7. **Thing to Note:**

    a. Effect of the long-term capital gain and its distribution to the beneficiary on the completion of Schedule D (Part III) on DNI (Schedule B) and as distributed (Schedule K-1)

Form **1041** Department of the Treasury—Internal Revenue Service
U.S. Income Tax Return for Estates and Trusts
Go to www.irs.gov/Form1041 for instructions and the latest information.
2022 OMB No. 1545-0092

A Check all that apply:
- [ ] Decedent's estate
- [ ] Simple trust
- [X] Complex trust
- [ ] Qualified disability trust
- [ ] ESBT (S portion only)
- [ ] Grantor type trust
- [ ] Bankruptcy estate—Ch. 7
- [ ] Bankruptcy estate—Ch. 11
- [ ] Pooled income fund

For calendar year 2022 or fiscal year beginning , 2022, and ending , 20

Name of estate or trust (If a grantor type trust, see the instructions.): PROBLEM 2

Name and title of fiduciary:

Number, street, and room or suite no. (If a P.O. box, see the instructions.):

City or town, state or province, country, and ZIP or foreign postal code: Columbus OH

C Employer identification number: 11-1111111

D Date entity created:

E Nonexempt charitable and split-interest trusts, check applicable box(es). See instructions.
- [ ] Described in sec. 4947(a)(1). Check here if not a private foundation . . . [ ]
- [ ] Described in sec. 4947(a)(2)

B Number of Schedules K-1 attached (see instructions): 1

F Check applicable boxes: [ ] Initial return [ ] Final return [ ] Amended return [ ] Net operating loss carryback [ ] Change in trust's name [ ] Change in fiduciary [ ] Change in fiduciary's name [ ] Change in fiduciary's address

G Check here if the estate or filing trust made a section 645 election . . . [ ] Trust TIN

Income	1	Interest income	1	6,000
	2a	Total ordinary dividends	2a	5,000
	b	Qualified dividends allocable to: (1) Beneficiaries ____ (2) Estate or trust 5,000		
	3	Business income or (loss). Attach Schedule C (Form 1040)	3	
	4	Capital gain or (loss). Attach Schedule D (Form 1041)	4	50,000
	5	Rents, royalties, partnerships, other estates and trusts, etc. Attach Schedule E (Form 1040)	5	
	6	Farm income or (loss). Attach Schedule F (Form 1040)	6	
	7	Ordinary gain or (loss). Attach Form 4797	7	
	8	Other income. List type and amount	8	
	9	**Total income.** Combine lines 1, 2a, and 3 through 8	9	61,000
Deductions	10	Interest. Check if Form 4952 is attached [ ]	10	
	11	Taxes	11	
	12	Fiduciary fees. If only a portion is deductible under section 67(e), see instructions	12	5,000
	13	Charitable deduction (from Schedule A, line 7)	13	
	14	Attorney, accountant, and return preparer fees. If only a portion is deductible under section 67(e), see instructions	14	5,000
	15a	Other deductions (attach schedule). See instructions for deductions allowable under section 67(e)	15a	
	b	Net operating loss deduction. See instructions	15b	
	16	Add lines 10 through 15b	16	10,000
	17	Adjusted total income or (loss). Subtract line 16 from line 9 — 17: 51,000		
	18	Income distribution deduction (from Schedule B, line 15). Attach Schedules K-1 (Form 1041)	18	51,000
	19	Estate tax deduction including certain generation-skipping taxes (attach computation)	19	
	20	Qualified business income deduction. Attach Form 8995 or 8995-A	20	
	21	Exemption	21	100
	22	Add lines 18 through 21	22	51,100
Tax and Payments	23	Taxable income. Subtract line 22 from line 17. If a loss, see instructions	23	-100
	24	**Total tax** (from Schedule G, Part I, line 9)	24	0
	25	Current year net 965 tax liability paid from Form 965-A, Part II, column (k) (see instructions)	25	
	26	**Total payments** (from Schedule G, Part II, line 19)	26	
	27	Estimated tax penalty. See instructions	27	
	28	**Tax due.** If line 26 is smaller than the total of lines 24, 25, and 27, enter amount owed	28	0
	29	**Overpayment.** If line 26 is larger than the total of lines 24, 25, and 27, enter amount overpaid	29	
	30	Amount of line 29 to be: **a Credited to 2023** ; **b Refunded**	30	

Sign Here Under penalties of perjury, I declare that I have examined this return, including accompanying schedules and statements, and to the best of my knowledge and belief, it is true, correct, and complete. Declaration of preparer (other than taxpayer) is based on all information of which preparer has any knowledge.

Signature of fiduciary or officer representing fiduciary | Date | EIN of fiduciary if a financial institution | May the IRS discuss this return with the preparer shown below? See instructions. [ ] Yes [ ] No

Paid Preparer Use Only

Print/Type preparer's name	Preparer's signature	Date	Check [ ] if self-employed	PTIN
Firm's name			Firm's EIN	
Firm's address			Phone no. ( )	

For Paperwork Reduction Act Notice, see the separate instructions. BAA REV 04/19/23 PRO Form **1041** (2022)

Form 1041 (2022) Page 2

Schedule A **Charitable Deduction.** Don't complete for a simple trust or a pooled income fund.

1	Amounts paid or permanently set aside for charitable purposes from gross income. See instructions	1	
2	Tax-exempt income allocable to charitable contributions. See instructions	2	
3	Subtract line 2 from line 1	3	
4	Capital gains for the tax year allocated to corpus and paid or permanently set aside for charitable purposes	4	
5	Add lines 3 and 4	5	
6	Section 1202 exclusion allocable to capital gains paid or permanently set aside for charitable purposes. See instructions	6	
7	**Charitable deduction.** Subtract line 6 from line 5. Enter here and on page 1, line 13	7	

Schedule B **Income Distribution Deduction**

1	Adjusted total income. See instructions	1	51,000
2	Adjusted tax-exempt interest	2	
3	Total net gain from Schedule D (Form 1041), line 19, column (1). See instructions	3	50,000
4	Enter amount from Schedule A, line 4 (minus any allocable section 1202 exclusion)	4	
5	Capital gains for the tax year included on Schedule A, line 1. See instructions	5	
6	Enter any gain from page 1, line 4, as a negative number. If page 1, line 4, is a loss, enter the loss as a positive number	6	-50,000
7	**Distributable net income.** Combine lines 1 through 6. If zero or less, enter -0-	7	51,000
8	If a complex trust, enter accounting income for the tax year as determined under the governing instrument and applicable local law — 8: 51,000		
9	Income required to be distributed currently	9	61,000
10	Other amounts paid, credited, or otherwise required to be distributed	10	
11	Total distributions. Add lines 9 and 10. If greater than line 8, see instructions	11	61,000
12	Enter the amount of tax-exempt income included on line 11	12	
13	Tentative income distribution deduction. Subtract line 12 from line 11	13	61,000
14	Tentative income distribution deduction. Subtract line 2 from line 7. If zero or less, enter -0-	14	51,000
15	**Income distribution deduction.** Enter the smaller of line 13 or line 14 here and on page 1, line 18	15	51,000

Schedule G **Tax Computation and Payments** (see instructions)

Part I — Tax Computation

1	**Tax:**				
a	Tax on taxable income. See instructions	1a			
b	Tax on lump-sum distributions. Attach Form 4972	1b			
c	Alternative minimum tax (from Schedule I (Form 1041), line 54)	1c	0		
d	**Total.** Add lines 1a through 1c			1d	0
2a	Foreign tax credit. Attach Form 1116	2a			
b	General business credit. Attach Form 3800	2b			
c	Credit for prior year minimum tax. Attach Form 8801	2c			
d	Bond credits. Attach Form 8912	2d			
e	**Total credits.** Add lines 2a through 2d			2e	
3	Subtract line 2e from line 1d. If zero or less, enter -0-			3	0
4	Tax on the ESBT portion of the trust (from ESBT Tax Worksheet, line 17). See instructions			4	
5	Net investment income tax from Form 8960, line 21			5	0
6	Recapture taxes. Check if from: ☐ Form 4255 ☐ Form 8611			6	
7	Household employment taxes. Attach Schedule H (Form 1040)			7	
8	Other taxes and amounts due			8	
9	**Total tax.** Add lines 3 through 8. Enter here and on page 1, line 24			9	0

Part II — Payments

10	2022 estimated tax payments and amount applied from 2021 return	10	
11	Estimated tax payments allocated to beneficiaries (from Form 1041-T)	11	
12	Subtract line 11 from line 10	12	
13	Tax paid with Form 7004. See instructions	13	
14	Federal income tax withheld. If any is from Form(s) 1099, check here ☐	14	
15	Current year net 965 tax liability from Form 965-A, Part I, column (f) (see instructions)	15	
16	Other payments: **a** Form 2439 ____; **b** Form 4136 ____; **Total**	16c	
17	Credit for qualified sick and family leave wages for leave taken before April 1, 2021	17	
18	Credit for qualified sick and family leave wages for leave taken after March 31, 2021, and before October 1, 2021	18	
19	**Total payments.** Add lines 12 through 15 and 16c through 18. Enter here and on page 1, line 26	19	

SCHEDULE D (Form 1041)

Department of the Treasury Internal Revenue Service

Capital Gains and Losses

Attach to Form 1041, Form 5227, or Form 990-T.
Use Form 8949 to list your transactions for lines 1b, 2, 3, 8b, 9, and 10.
Go to *www.irs.gov/F1041* for instructions and the latest information.

OMB No. 1545-0092

2022

Name of estate or trust: PROBLEM 2

Employer identification number: 11-1111111

Did you dispose of any investment(s) in a qualified opportunity fund during the tax year? . . . . ☐ **Yes** ☒ **No**
If "Yes," attach Form 8949 and see its instructions for additional requirements for reporting your gain or loss.

Note: *Form 5227 filers need to complete only Parts I and II.*

Part I — Short-Term Capital Gains and Losses—Generally Assets Held 1 Year or Less (see instructions)

See instructions for how to figure the amounts to enter on the lines below. This form may be easier to complete if you round off cents to whole dollars.	**(d)** Proceeds (sales price)	**(e)** Cost (or other basis)	**(g)** Adjustments to gain or loss from Form(s) 8949, Part I, line 2, column (g)	**(h) Gain or (loss)** Subtract column (e) from column (d) and combine the result with column (g)
1a Totals for all short-term transactions reported on Form 1099-B for which basis was reported to the IRS and for which you have no adjustments (see instructions). However, if you choose to report all these transactions on Form 8949, leave this line blank and go to line 1b .				
1b Totals for all transactions reported on Form(s) 8949 with **Box A** checked				
2 Totals for all transactions reported on Form(s) 8949 with **Box B** checked				
3 Totals for all transactions reported on Form(s) 8949 with **Box C** checked				

4	Short-term capital gain or (loss) from Forms 4684, 6252, 6781, and 8824	**4**	
5	Net short-term gain or (loss) from partnerships, S corporations, and other estates or trusts	**5**	
6	Short-term capital loss carryover. Enter the amount, if any, from line 9 of the 2021 Capital Loss Carryover Worksheet	**6**	( )
7	**Net short-term capital gain or (loss).** Combine lines 1a through 6 in column (h). Enter here and on Part III, line 17, column (3)	**7**	

Part II — Long-Term Capital Gains and Losses—Generally Assets Held More Than 1 Year (see instructions)

See instructions for how to figure the amounts to enter on the lines below. This form may be easier to complete if you round off cents to whole dollars.	**(d)** Proceeds (sales price)	**(e)** Cost (or other basis)	**(g)** Adjustments to gain or loss from Form(s) 8949, Part II, line 2, column (g)	**(h) Gain or (loss)** Subtract column (e) from column (d) and combine the result with column (g)
8a Totals for all long-term transactions reported on Form 1099-B for which basis was reported to the IRS and for which you have no adjustments (see instructions). However, if you choose to report all these transactions on Form 8949, leave this line blank and go to line 8b .	50,000.	0.		50,000.
8b Totals for all transactions reported on Form(s) 8949 with **Box D** checked				
9 Totals for all transactions reported on Form(s) 8949 with **Box E** checked				
10 Totals for all transactions reported on Form(s) 8949 with **Box F** checked.				

11	Long-term capital gain or (loss) from Forms 2439, 4684, 6252, 6781, and 8824	**11**	
12	Net long-term gain or (loss) from partnerships, S corporations, and other estates or trusts	**12**	
13	Capital gain distributions	**13**	
14	Gain from Form 4797, Part I	**14**	
15	Long-term capital loss carryover. Enter the amount, if any, from line 14 of the 2021 Capital Loss Carryover Worksheet	**15**	( )
16	**Net long-term capital gain or (loss).** Combine lines 8a through 15 in column (h). Enter here and on Part III, line 18a, column (3)	**16**	50,000.

For Paperwork Reduction Act Notice, see the Instructions for Form 1041. Cat. No. 11376V **Schedule D (Form 1041) 2022**

BAA REV 03/25/23 PRO

Schedule D (Form 1041) 2022 Page **2**

Part III Summary of Parts I and II
Caution: *Read the instructions* ***before*** *completing this part.*

			(1) Beneficiaries' (see instr.)	(2) Estate's or trust's	(3) Total
17	**Net short-term gain or (loss)**	17			
18	**Net long-term gain or (loss):**				
a	Total for year	18a	50,000	0	50,000
b	Unrecaptured section 1250 gain (see line 18 of the worksheet)	18b			
c	28% rate gain	18c			
19	**Total net gain or (loss).** Combine lines 17 and 18a	19	50,000	0	50,000

Note: *If line 19, column (3), is a net gain, enter the gain on Form 1041, line 4 (or Schedule A (Form 990-T), Part I, line 4a). If lines 18a and 19, column (2), are net gains, go to Part V, and* ***don't*** *complete Part IV. If line 19, column (3), is a net loss, complete Part IV and the* ***Capital Loss Carryover Worksheet****, as necessary.*

Part IV Capital Loss Limitation

20 Enter here and enter as a (loss) on Form 1041, line 4 (or Schedule A (Form 990-T), Part I, line 4c, if a trust), the **smaller** of:

a The loss on line 19, column (3) **or b** $3,000 . . . 20 ( )

Note: *If the loss on line 19, column (3), is more than $3,000,* ***or*** *if Form 1041, page 1, line 23 (or Form 990-T, Part I, line 11), is a loss, complete the* ***Capital Loss Carryover Worksheet*** *in the instructions to figure your capital loss carryover.*

Part V Tax Computation Using Maximum Capital Gains Rates

Form 1041 filers. Complete this part **only** if both lines 18a and 19 in column (2) are gains, or an amount is entered in Part I or Part II and there is an entry on Form 1041, line 2b(2), **and** Form 1041, line 23, is more than zero.

Caution: *Skip this part and complete the* ***Schedule D Tax Worksheet*** *in the instructions if:*

- *Either line 18b, col. (2), or line 18c, col. (2), is more than zero, or*
- *Both Form 1041, line 2b(1), and Form 4952, line 4g, are more than zero, or*
- *There are amounts on lines 4e and 4g of Form 4952.*

Form 990-T trusts. Complete this part **only** if both lines 18a and 19 are gains, or qualified dividends are included in income in Part I of Form 990-T, **and** Form 990-T, Part I, line 11, is more than zero. Skip this part and complete the **Schedule D Tax Worksheet** in the instructions if either line 18b, col. (2), or line 18c, col. (2), is more than zero.

21	Enter taxable income from Form 1041, line 23 (or Form 990-T, Part I, line 11)	21	
22	Enter the **smaller** of line 18a or 19 in column (2) but not less than zero	22	
23	Enter the estate's or trust's qualified dividends from Form 1041, line 2b(2) (or enter the qualified dividends included in income in Part I of Form 990-T)	23	
24	Add lines 22 and 23	24	
25	If the estate or trust is filing Form 4952, enter the amount from line 4g; otherwise, enter -0-	25	
26	Subtract line 25 from line 24. If zero or less, enter -0-	26	
27	Subtract line 26 from line 21. If zero or less, enter -0-	27	
28	Enter the **smaller** of the amount on line 21 or $2,800	28	
29	Enter the **smaller** of the amount on line 27 or line 28	29	
30	Subtract line 29 from line 28. If zero or less, enter -0-. This amount is taxed at 0%	30	
31	Enter the **smaller** of line 21 or line 26	31	
32	Subtract line 30 from line 26	32	
33	Enter the **smaller** of line 21 or $13,700	33	
34	Add lines 27 and 30	34	
35	Subtract line 34 from line 33. If zero or less, enter -0-	35	
36	Enter the **smaller** of line 32 or line 35	36	
37	Multiply line 36 by 15% (0.15)	37	
38	Enter the amount from line 31	38	
39	Add lines 30 and 36	39	
40	Subtract line 39 from line 38. If zero or less, enter -0-	40	
41	Multiply line 40 by 20% (0.20)	41	
42	Figure the tax on the amount on line 27. Use the 2022 Tax Rate Schedule for Estates and Trusts (see the Schedule G instructions in the Instructions for Form 1041)	42	
43	Add lines 37, 41, and 42	43	
44	Figure the tax on the amount on line 21. Use the 2022 Tax Rate Schedule for Estates and Trusts (see the Schedule G instructions in the Instructions for Form 1041)	44	
45	**Tax on all taxable income.** Enter the **smaller** of line 43 or line 44 here and on Form 1041, Schedule G, Part I, line 1a (or Form 990-T, Part II, line 2)	45	

REV 03/25/23 PRO **Schedule D (Form 1041) 2022**

661117

☐ Final K-1 ☐ Amended K-1 OMB No. 1545-0092

Schedule K-1 (Form 1041) **2022**

Department of the Treasury Internal Revenue Service

For calendar year 2022, or tax year

beginning / / 2022 ending / /

Beneficiary's Share of Income, Deductions, Credits, etc.

See back of form and instructions.

Part I Information About the Estate or Trust

A Estate's or trust's employer identification number

11-1111111

B Estate's or trust's name

PROBLEM 2

C Fiduciary's name, address, city, state, and ZIP code

John Doe
111 Main Street
Columbus OH 43212

D ☐ Check if Form 1041-T was filed and enter the date it was filed

E ☐ Check if this is the final Form 1041 for the estate or trust

Part II Information About the Beneficiary

F Beneficiary's identifying number

111-11-1111

G Beneficiary's name, address, city, state, and ZIP code

Beneficiary
111 Main Street

Delaware OH 43015

H ☒ Domestic beneficiary ☐ Foreign beneficiary

Part III Beneficiary's Share of Current Year Income, Deductions, Credits, and Other Items

1	Interest income	0.
2a	Ordinary dividends	1,000.
2b	Qualified dividends	1,000.
3	Net short-term capital gain	0.
4a	Net long-term capital gain	50,000.
4b	28% rate gain	
4c	Unrecaptured section 1250 gain	
5	Other portfolio and nonbusiness income	
6	Ordinary business income	
7	Net rental real estate income	
8	Other rental income	
9	Directly apportioned deductions	
10	Estate tax deduction	
11	Final year deductions	
12	Alternative minimum tax adjustment	A 0.
13	Credits and credit recapture	
14	Other information	E 1,000.

*See attached statement for additional information.

Note: A statement must be attached showing the beneficiary's share of income and directly apportioned deductions from each business, rental real estate, and other rental activity.

For IRS Use Only

Schedule K-1 (Form 1041) 2022 Page **2**

This list identifies the codes used on Schedule K-1 for beneficiaries and provides summarized reporting information for beneficiaries who file Form 1040 or 1040-SR. For detailed reporting and filing information, see the Instructions for Schedule K-1 (Form 1041) for a Beneficiary Filing Form 1040 or 1040-SR and the instructions for your income tax return.

	Report on
1. Interest income	Form 1040 or 1040-SR, line 2b
2a. Ordinary dividends	Form 1040 or 1040-SR, line 3b
2b. Qualified dividends	Form 1040 or 1040-SR, line 3a
3. Net short-term capital gain	Schedule D, line 5
4a. Net long-term capital gain	Schedule D, line 12
4b. 28% rate gain	28% Rate Gain Worksheet, line 4 (Schedule D Instructions)
4c. Unrecaptured section 1250 gain	Unrecaptured Section 1250 Gain Worksheet, line 11 (Schedule D Instructions)
5. Other portfolio and nonbusiness income	Schedule E, line 33, column (f)
6. Ordinary business income	Schedule E, line 33, column (d) or (f)
7. Net rental real estate income	Schedule E, line 33, column (d) or (f)
8. Other rental income	Schedule E, line 33, column (d) or (f)
9. Directly apportioned deductions	
Code	
A Depreciation	Form 8582 or Schedule E, line 33, column (c) or (e)
B Depletion	Form 8582 or Schedule E, line 33, column (c) or (e)
C Amortization	Form 8582 or Schedule E, line 33, column (c) or (e)
10. Estate tax deduction	Schedule A, line 16
11. Final year deductions	
A Excess deductions – Section 67(e) expenses	Schedule 1 (Form 1040), line 24k (also see the beneficiary's instructions)
B Excess deductions – Non-miscellaneous itemized deductions	See the beneficiary's instructions
C Short-term capital loss carryover	Schedule D, line 5
D Long-term capital loss carryover	Schedule D, line 12; line 5 of the wksht. for Sch. D, line 18; and line 16 of the wksht. for Sch. D, line 19
E Net operating loss carryover — regular tax	Schedule 1 (Form 1040), line 8a
F Net operating loss carryover — minimum tax	Form 6251, line 2f
12. Alternative minimum tax (AMT) items	
A Adjustment for minimum tax purposes	Form 6251, line 2j
B AMT adjustment attributable to qualified dividends	See the beneficiary's instructions and the Instructions for Form 6251
C AMT adjustment attributable to net short-term capital gain	See the beneficiary's instructions and the Instructions for Form 6251
D AMT adjustment attributable to net long-term capital gain	See the beneficiary's instructions and the Instructions for Form 6251
E AMT adjustment attributable to unrecaptured section 1250 gain	See the beneficiary's instructions and the Instructions for Form 6251
F AMT adjustment attributable to 28% rate gain	See the beneficiary's instructions and the Instructions for Form 6251
G Accelerated depreciation	See the beneficiary's instructions and the Instructions for Form 6251
H Depletion	See the beneficiary's instructions and the Instructions for Form 6251
I Amortization	See the beneficiary's instructions and the Instructions for Form 6251
J Exclusion items	2023 Form 8801

13. Credits and credit recapture	
Code	*Report on*
A Credit for estimated taxes	Form 1040 or 1040-SR, line 26
B Credit for backup withholding	Form 1040 or 1040-SR, line 25c
C Low-income housing credit	See the beneficiary's instructions
D Rehabilitation credit and energy credit	See the beneficiary's instructions
E Other qualifying investment credit	See the beneficiary's instructions
F Work opportunity credit	See the beneficiary's instructions
G Credit for small employer health insurance premiums	See the beneficiary's instructions
H Biofuel producer credit	See the beneficiary's instructions
I Credit for increasing research activities	See the beneficiary's instructions
J Renewable electricity, refined coal, and Indian coal production credit	See the beneficiary's instructions
K Empowerment zone employment credit	See the beneficiary's instructions
L Indian employment credit	See the beneficiary's instructions
M Orphan drug credit	See the beneficiary's instructions
N Credit for employer-provided child care and facilities	See the beneficiary's instructions
O Biodiesel and renewable diesel fuels credit	See the beneficiary's instructions
P Credit to holders of tax credit bonds	See the beneficiary's instructions
Q Credit for employer differential wage payments	See the beneficiary's instructions
R Recapture of credits	See the beneficiary's instructions
Z Other credits	See the beneficiary's instructions
14. Other information	
A Tax-exempt interest	Form 1040 or 1040-SR, line 2a
B Foreign taxes	Schedule 3 (Form 1040), line 1 or Schedule A, line 6
C Reserved for future use	
D Reserved for future use	
E Net investment income	Form 4952, line 4a
F Gross farm and fishing income	Schedule E, line 42
G Foreign trading gross receipts (IRC 942(a))	See the Instructions for Form 8873
H Adjustment for section 1411 net investment income or deductions	Form 8960, line 7 (also see the beneficiary's instructions)
I Section 199A information	See the beneficiary's instructions
Z Other information	See the beneficiary's instructions

Note: If you are a beneficiary who does not file a Form 1040 or 1040-SR, see instructions for the type of income tax return you are filing.

REV 03/25/23 PRO

PROBLEM No. 3

Complex Trust with Capital Gains Not Distributed

FEATURES

1. Dividends are present
2. Tax-exempt income is present
3. Short and long-term capital gains are present—and not distributed
4. Taxes, fiduciary fees, legal fees and investment advisory fees present
5. Income distribution to the beneficiary
6. Income:

Tax-exempt interest	13,000
Dividends	19,000 (Qualified = 18,000)
Short-term capital gain	6,000
Long-term capital gain	29,000

7. Expenses:

State taxes from a prior year	600
Fiduciary Fees	9,000
Legal Fees	1,000
Investment Advisor Fees	10,000

8. **Things to Note:**

   a. Reduction of expenses due to presence of tax-exempt income
   b. The trust pays tax on the capital gain
   c. Tax is calculated on Schedule D
   d. The net investment income tax (Code Section 1411) is computed on Form 8960
   e. Under Code Section 67(g), the deduction for the investment advisor fee (i.e., a miscellaneous expense) is not deductible. This limitation sunsets at the end of until 2025

Form **1041** Department of the Treasury—Internal Revenue Service
U.S. Income Tax Return for Estates and Trusts
Go to www.irs.gov/Form1041 for instructions and the latest information.
2022 OMB No. 1545-0092

A Check all that apply: For calendar year 2022 or fiscal year beginning , 2022, and ending , 20

☐ Decedent's estate
☐ Simple trust
☒ Complex trust
☐ Qualified disability trust
☐ ESBT (S portion only)
☐ Grantor type trust
☐ Bankruptcy estate—Ch. 7
☐ Bankruptcy estate—Ch. 11
☐ Pooled income fund

Name of estate or trust (If a grantor type trust, see the instructions.): PROBLEM 3
C Employer identification number: 11-1111111
Name and title of fiduciary:
D Date entity created:
Number, street, and room or suite no. (If a P.O. box, see the instructions.)
E Nonexempt charitable and split-interest trusts, check applicable box(es). See instructions.
☐ Described in sec. 4947(a)(1). Check here if not a private foundation . . . ☐
☐ Described in sec. 4947(a)(2)
City or town, state or province, country, and ZIP or foreign postal code

B Number of Schedules K-1 attached (see instructions) 1
F Check applicable boxes: ☐ Initial return ☐ Final return ☐ Amended return ☐ Net operating loss carryback ☐ Change in trust's name ☐ Change in fiduciary ☐ Change in fiduciary's name ☐ Change in fiduciary's address
G Check here if the estate or filing trust made a section 645 election . . . . ☐ Trust TIN

Income	1	Interest income	1	
	2a	Total ordinary dividends	2a	19,000
	b	Qualified dividends allocable to: (1) Beneficiaries 18,000 (2) Estate or trust 0		
	3	Business income or (loss). Attach Schedule C (Form 1040)	3	
	4	Capital gain or (loss). Attach Schedule D (Form 1041)	4	35,000
	5	Rents, royalties, partnerships, other estates and trusts, etc. Attach Schedule E (Form 1040)	5	
	6	Farm income or (loss). Attach Schedule F (Form 1040)	6	
	7	Ordinary gain or (loss). Attach Form 4797	7	
	8	Other income. List type and amount	8	
	9	**Total income.** Combine lines 1, 2a, and 3 through 8	9	54,000
Deductions	10	Interest. Check if Form 4952 is attached ☐	10	
	11	Taxes	11	600
	12	Fiduciary fees. If only a portion is deductible under section 67(e), see instructions	12	5,344
	13	Charitable deduction (from Schedule A, line 7)	13	
	14	Attorney, accountant, and return preparer fees. If only a portion is deductible under section 67(e), see instructions	14	594
	15a	Other deductions (attach schedule). See instructions for deductions allowable under section 67(e)	15a	
	b	Net operating loss deduction. See instructions	15b	
	16	Add lines 10 through 15b	16	6,538
	17	Adjusted total income or (loss). Subtract line 16 from line 9 — 17: 47,462		
	18	Income distribution deduction (from Schedule B, line 15). Attach Schedules K-1 (Form 1041)	18	12,462
	19	Estate tax deduction including certain generation-skipping taxes (attach computation)	19	
	20	Qualified business income deduction. Attach Form 8995 or 8995-A	20	
	21	Exemption	21	100
	22	Add lines 18 through 21	22	12,562
Tax and Payments	23	Taxable income. Subtract line 22 from line 17. If a loss, see instructions	23	34,900
	24	**Total tax** (from Schedule G, Part I, line 9)	24	7,279
	25	Current year net 965 tax liability paid from Form 965-A, Part II, column (k) (see instructions)	25	
	26	**Total payments** (from Schedule G, Part II, line 19)	26	
	27	Estimated tax penalty. See instructions	27	0
	28	**Tax due.** If line 26 is smaller than the total of lines 24, 25, and 27, enter amount owed	28	7,279
	29	**Overpayment.** If line 26 is larger than the total of lines 24, 25, and 27, enter amount overpaid	29	
	30	Amount of line 29 to be: **a Credited to 2023** ; **b Refunded**	30	

Sign Here Under penalties of perjury, I declare that I have examined this return, including accompanying schedules and statements, and to the best of my knowledge and belief, it is true, correct, and complete. Declaration of preparer (other than taxpayer) is based on all information of which preparer has any knowledge.

Signature of fiduciary or officer representing fiduciary | Date | EIN of fiduciary if a financial institution | May the IRS discuss this return with the preparer shown below? See instructions. ☐ Yes ☐ No

Paid Preparer Use Only Print/Type preparer's name | Preparer's signature | Date | Check ☐ if self-employed | PTIN
Firm's name | Firm's EIN
Firm's address | Phone no.

For Paperwork Reduction Act Notice, see the separate instructions. BAA REV 04/19/23 PRO Form **1041** (2022)

Form 1041 (2022) Page 2

Schedule A — Charitable Deduction. Don't complete for a simple trust or a pooled income fund.

1	Amounts paid or permanently set aside for charitable purposes from gross income. See instructions	1	
2	Tax-exempt income allocable to charitable contributions. See instructions	2	
3	Subtract line 2 from line 1	3	
4	Capital gains for the tax year allocated to corpus and paid or permanently set aside for charitable purposes	4	
5	Add lines 3 and 4	5	
6	Section 1202 exclusion allocable to capital gains paid or permanently set aside for charitable purposes. See instructions	6	
7	**Charitable deduction.** Subtract line 6 from line 5. Enter here and on page 1, line 13	7	

Schedule B — Income Distribution Deduction

1	Adjusted total income. See instructions	1	47,462
2	Adjusted tax-exempt interest	2	8,938
3	Total net gain from Schedule D (Form 1041), line 19, column (1). See instructions	3	
4	Enter amount from Schedule A, line 4 (minus any allocable section 1202 exclusion)	4	
5	Capital gains for the tax year included on Schedule A, line 1. See instructions	5	
6	Enter any gain from page 1, line 4, as a negative number. If page 1, line 4, is a loss, enter the loss as a positive number	6	-35,000
7	**Distributable net income.** Combine lines 1 through 6. If zero or less, enter -0-	7	21,400
8	If a complex trust, enter accounting income for the tax year as determined under the governing instrument and applicable local law — 8: 21,400		
9	Income required to be distributed currently	9	21,400
10	Other amounts paid, credited, or otherwise required to be distributed	10	
11	Total distributions. Add lines 9 and 10. If greater than line 8, see instructions	11	21,400
12	Enter the amount of tax-exempt income included on line 11	12	8,938
13	Tentative income distribution deduction. Subtract line 12 from line 11	13	12,462
14	Tentative income distribution deduction. Subtract line 2 from line 7. If zero or less, enter -0-	14	12,462
15	**Income distribution deduction.** Enter the smaller of line 13 or line 14 here and on page 1, line 18	15	12,462

Schedule G — Tax Computation and Payments (see instructions)

Part I — Tax Computation

1	**Tax:**				
a	Tax on taxable income. See instructions	1a	6,441		
b	Tax on lump-sum distributions. Attach Form 4972	1b			
c	Alternative minimum tax (from Schedule I (Form 1041), line 54)	1c	0		
d	**Total.** Add lines 1a through 1c			1d	6,441
2a	Foreign tax credit. Attach Form 1116	2a			
b	General business credit. Attach Form 3800	2b			
c	Credit for prior year minimum tax. Attach Form 8801	2c			
d	Bond credits. Attach Form 8912	2d			
e	**Total credits.** Add lines 2a through 2d			2e	
3	Subtract line 2e from line 1d. If zero or less, enter -0-			3	6,441
4	Tax on the ESBT portion of the trust (from ESBT Tax Worksheet, line 17). See instructions			4	
5	Net investment income tax from Form 8960, line 21			5	838
6	Recapture taxes. Check if from: ☐ Form 4255 ☐ Form 8611			6	
7	Household employment taxes. Attach Schedule H (Form 1040)			7	
8	Other taxes and amounts due			8	
9	**Total tax.** Add lines 3 through 8. Enter here and on page 1, line 24			9	7,279

Part II — Payments

10	2022 estimated tax payments and amount applied from 2021 return	10	
11	Estimated tax payments allocated to beneficiaries (from Form 1041-T)	11	
12	Subtract line 11 from line 10	12	
13	Tax paid with Form 7004. See instructions	13	
14	Federal income tax withheld. If any is from Form(s) 1099, check here ☐	14	
15	Current year net 965 tax liability from Form 965-A, Part I, column (f) (see instructions)	15	
16	Other payments: **a** Form 2439 ________ ; **b** Form 4136 ________ ; **Total**	16c	
17	Credit for qualified sick and family leave wages for leave taken before April 1, 2021	17	
18	Credit for qualified sick and family leave wages for leave taken after March 31, 2021, and before October 1, 2021	18	
19	**Total payments.** Add lines 12 through 15 and 16c through 18. Enter here and on page 1, line 26	19	

REV 04/19/23 PRO Form **1041** (2022)

Form 1041 (2022) Page 3

	Other Information	Yes	No
1	Did the estate or trust receive tax-exempt income? If "Yes," attach a computation of the allocation of expenses.	×	
	Enter the amount of tax-exempt interest income and exempt-interest dividends . . . . . $ 13,000		
2	Did the estate or trust receive all or any part of the earnings (salary, wages, and other compensation) of any individual by reason of a contract assignment or similar arrangement?		×
3	At any time during calendar year 2022, did the estate or trust have an interest in or a signature or other authority over a bank, securities, or other financial account in a foreign country?		×
	See the instructions for exceptions and filing requirements for FinCEN Form 114. If "Yes," enter the name of the foreign country		
4	During the tax year, did the estate or trust receive a distribution from, or was it the grantor of, or transferor to, a foreign trust? If "Yes," the estate or trust may have to file Form 3520. See instructions		×
5	Did the estate or trust receive, or pay, any qualified residence interest on seller-provided financing? If "Yes," see the instructions for the required attachment		×
6	If this is an estate or a complex trust making the section 663(b) election, check here. See instructions . . . ☐		
7	To make a section 643(e)(3) election, attach Schedule D (Form 1041), and check here. See instructions . . . ☐		
8	If the decedent's estate has been open for more than 2 years, attach an explanation for the delay in closing the estate, and check here . . . . ☐		
9	Are any present or future trust beneficiaries skip persons? See instructions		×
10	Was the trust a specified domestic entity required to file Form 8938 for the tax year? See the Instructions for Form 8938		×
11a	Did the estate or trust distribute S corporation stock for which it made a section 965(i) election?		×
b	If "Yes," did each beneficiary enter into an agreement to be liable for the net tax liability? See instructions . . .		
12	Did the estate or trust either make a section 965(i) election or enter into a transfer agreement as an eligible 965(i) transferee for S corporation stock held on the last day of the tax year? See instructions		×
13	**ESBTs only.** Does the ESBT have a nonresident alien grantor? If "Yes," see instructions		
14	**ESBTs only.** Did the S portion of the trust claim a qualified business income deduction? If "Yes," see instructions		

REV 04/19/23 PRO Form **1041** (2022)

SCHEDULE D (Form 1041)

Department of the Treasury Internal Revenue Service

Capital Gains and Losses

Attach to Form 1041, Form 5227, or Form 990-T.

Use Form 8949 to list your transactions for lines 1b, 2, 3, 8b, 9, and 10.

Go to *www.irs.gov/F1041* for instructions and the latest information.

OMB No. 1545-0092

2022

Name of estate or trust: PROBLEM 3

Employer identification number: 11-1111111

Did you dispose of any investment(s) in a qualified opportunity fund during the tax year? . . . . ☐ Yes ☒ No

If "Yes," attach Form 8949 and see its instructions for additional requirements for reporting your gain or loss.

Note: *Form 5227 filers need to complete only Parts I and II.*

Part I Short-Term Capital Gains and Losses—Generally Assets Held 1 Year or Less (see instructions)

See instructions for how to figure the amounts to enter on the lines below. This form may be easier to complete if you round off cents to whole dollars.	(d) Proceeds (sales price)	(e) Cost (or other basis)	(g) Adjustments to gain or loss from Form(s) 8949, Part I, line 2, column (g)	(h) Gain or (loss) Subtract column (e) from column (d) and combine the result with column (g)
1a Totals for all short-term transactions reported on Form 1099-B for which basis was reported to the IRS and for which you have no adjustments (see instructions). However, if you choose to report all these transactions on Form 8949, leave this line blank and go to line 1b .	6,000.	0.		6,000.
1b Totals for all transactions reported on Form(s) 8949 with **Box A** checked				
2 Totals for all transactions reported on Form(s) 8949 with **Box B** checked				
3 Totals for all transactions reported on Form(s) 8949 with **Box C** checked				

4	Short-term capital gain or (loss) from Forms 4684, 6252, 6781, and 8824	4	
5	Net short-term gain or (loss) from partnerships, S corporations, and other estates or trusts	5	
6	Short-term capital loss carryover. Enter the amount, if any, from line 9 of the 2021 Capital Loss Carryover Worksheet	6	( )
7	**Net short-term capital gain or (loss).** Combine lines 1a through 6 in column (h). Enter here and on Part III, line 17, column (3)	7	6,000.

Part II Long-Term Capital Gains and Losses—Generally Assets Held More Than 1 Year (see instructions)

See instructions for how to figure the amounts to enter on the lines below. This form may be easier to complete if you round off cents to whole dollars.	(d) Proceeds (sales price)	(e) Cost (or other basis)	(g) Adjustments to gain or loss from Form(s) 8949, Part II, line 2, column (g)	(h) Gain or (loss) Subtract column (e) from column (d) and combine the result with column (g)
8a Totals for all long-term transactions reported on Form 1099-B for which basis was reported to the IRS and for which you have no adjustments (see instructions). However, if you choose to report all these transactions on Form 8949, leave this line blank and go to line 8b .	29,000.	0.		29,000.
8b Totals for all transactions reported on Form(s) 8949 with **Box D** checked				
9 Totals for all transactions reported on Form(s) 8949 with **Box E** checked				
10 Totals for all transactions reported on Form(s) 8949 with **Box F** checked.				

11	Long-term capital gain or (loss) from Forms 2439, 4684, 6252, 6781, and 8824	11	
12	Net long-term gain or (loss) from partnerships, S corporations, and other estates or trusts	12	
13	Capital gain distributions	13	
14	Gain from Form 4797, Part I	14	
15	Long-term capital loss carryover. Enter the amount, if any, from line 14 of the 2021 Capital Loss Carryover Worksheet	15	( )
16	**Net long-term capital gain or (loss).** Combine lines 8a through 15 in column (h). Enter here and on Part III, line 18a, column (3)	16	29,000.

For Paperwork Reduction Act Notice, see the Instructions for Form 1041. Cat. No. 11376V **Schedule D (Form 1041) 2022**

BAA REV 04/19/23 PRO

Schedule D (Form 1041) 2022 Page 2

Part III	**Summary of Parts I and II** *Caution: Read the instructions **before** completing this part.*		(1) Beneficiaries' (see instr.)	(2) Estate's or trust's	(3) Total
17	**Net short-term gain or (loss)**	17		6,000	6,000
18	**Net long-term gain or (loss):**				
a	Total for year	18a		29,000	29,000
b	Unrecaptured section 1250 gain (see line 18 of the worksheet)	18b			
c	28% rate gain	18c			
19	**Total net gain or (loss).** Combine lines 17 and 18a	19		35,000	35,000

Note: *If line 19, column (3), is a net gain, enter the gain on Form 1041, line 4 (or Schedule A (Form 990-T), Part I, line 4a). If lines 18a and 19, column (2), are net gains, go to Part V, and **don't** complete Part IV. If line 19, column (3), is a net loss, complete Part IV and the **Capital Loss Carryover Worksheet**, as necessary.*

Part IV Capital Loss Limitation

20 Enter here and enter as a (loss) on Form 1041, line 4 (or Schedule A (Form 990-T), Part I, line 4c, if a trust), the **smaller** of:

a The loss on line 19, column (3) **or b** $3,000 . . . 20 ( )

Note: *If the loss on line 19, column (3), is more than $3,000, or if Form 1041, page 1, line 23 (or Form 990-T, Part I, line 11), is a loss, complete the **Capital Loss Carryover Worksheet** in the instructions to figure your capital loss carryover.*

Part V Tax Computation Using Maximum Capital Gains Rates

Form 1041 filers. Complete this part **only** if both lines 18a and 19 in column (2) are gains, or an amount is entered in Part I or Part II and there is an entry on Form 1041, line 2b(2), **and** Form 1041, line 23, is more than zero.

Caution: *Skip this part and complete the **Schedule D Tax Worksheet** in the instructions if:*

- *Either line 18b, col. (2), or line 18c, col. (2), is more than zero, or*
- *Both Form 1041, line 2b(1), and Form 4952, line 4g, are more than zero, or*
- *There are amounts on lines 4e and 4g of Form 4952.*

Form 990-T trusts. Complete this part **only** if both lines 18a and 19 are gains, or qualified dividends are included in income in Part I of Form 990-T, **and** Form 990-T, Part I, line 11, is more than zero. Skip this part and complete the **Schedule D Tax Worksheet** in the instructions if either line 18b, col. (2), or line 18c, col. (2), is more than zero.

21	Enter taxable income from Form 1041, line 23 (or Form 990-T, Part I, line 11)			21	34,900		
22	Enter the **smaller** of line 18a or 19 in column (2) but not less than zero	22	29,000				
23	Enter the estate's or trust's qualified dividends from Form 1041, line 2b(2) (or enter the qualified dividends included in income in Part I of Form 990-T)	23	0				
24	Add lines 22 and 23	24	29,000				
25	If the estate or trust is filing Form 4952, enter the amount from line 4g; otherwise, enter -0-	25	0				
26	Subtract line 25 from line 24. If zero or less, enter -0-			26	29,000		
27	Subtract line 26 from line 21. If zero or less, enter -0-			27	5,900		
28	Enter the **smaller** of the amount on line 21 or $2,800			28	2,800		
29	Enter the **smaller** of the amount on line 27 or line 28			29	2,800		
30	Subtract line 29 from line 28. If zero or less, enter -0-. This amount is taxed at 0%					30	0
31	Enter the **smaller** of line 21 or line 26			31	29,000		
32	Subtract line 30 from line 26			32	29,000		
33	Enter the **smaller** of line 21 or $13,700			33	13,700		
34	Add lines 27 and 30			34	5,900		
35	Subtract line 34 from line 33. If zero or less, enter -0-			35	7,800		
36	Enter the **smaller** of line 32 or line 35			36	7,800		
37	Multiply line 36 by 15% (0.15)					37	1,170
38	Enter the amount from line 31			38	29,000		
39	Add lines 30 and 36			39	7,800		
40	Subtract line 39 from line 38. If zero or less, enter -0-			40	21,200		
41	Multiply line 40 by 20% (0.20)					41	4,240
42	Figure the tax on the amount on line 27. Use the 2022 Tax Rate Schedule for Estates and Trusts (see the Schedule G instructions in the Instructions for Form 1041)			42	1,031		
43	Add lines 37, 41, and 42			43	6,441		
44	Figure the tax on the amount on line 21. Use the 2022 Tax Rate Schedule for Estates and Trusts (see the Schedule G instructions in the Instructions for Form 1041)			44	11,176		
45	**Tax on all taxable income.** Enter the **smaller** of line 43 or line 44 here and on Form 1041, Schedule G, Part I, line 1a (or Form 990-T, Part II, line 2)					45	6,441

REV 04/19/23 PRO **Schedule D (Form 1041) 2022**

Form **8960** Department of the Treasury Internal Revenue Service

Net Investment Income Tax— Individuals, Estates, and Trusts

Attach to your tax return.
Go to www.irs.gov/Form8960 for instructions and the latest information.

OMB No. 1545-2227 **2022** Attachment Sequence No. **72**

Name(s) shown on your tax return: PROBLEM 3 | Your social security number or EIN: 11-1111111

Part I Investment Income ☐ Section 6013(g) election (see instructions) ☐ Section 6013(h) election (see instructions) ☐ Regulations section 1.1411-10(g) election (see instructions)

1	Taxable interest (see instructions)			1	
2	Ordinary dividends (see instructions)			2	19,000.
3	Annuities (see instructions)			3	
4a	Rental real estate, royalties, partnerships, S corporations, trusts, etc. (see instructions)	4a			
b	Adjustment for net income or loss derived in the ordinary course of a non-section 1411 trade or business (see instructions)	4b			
c	Combine lines 4a and 4b			4c	
5a	Net gain or loss from disposition of property (see instructions)	5a	35,000.		
b	Net gain or loss from disposition of property that is not subject to net investment income tax (see instructions)	5b			
c	Adjustment from disposition of partnership interest or S corporation stock (see instructions)	5c			
d	Combine lines 5a through 5c			5d	35,000.
6	Adjustments to investment income for certain CFCs and PFICs (see instructions)			6	
7	Other modifications to investment income (see instructions)			7	
8	Total investment income. Combine lines 1, 2, 3, 4c, 5d, 6, and 7			8	54,000.
Part II	**Investment Expenses Allocable to Investment Income and Modifications**				
9a	Investment interest expenses (see instructions)	9a			
b	State, local, and foreign income tax (see instructions)	9b	600.		
c	Miscellaneous investment expenses (see instructions)	9c			
d	Add lines 9a, 9b, and 9c			9d	600.
10	Additional modifications (see instructions)			10	5,938.
11	Total deductions and modifications. Add lines 9d and 10			11	6,538.
Part III	**Tax Computation**				
12	Net investment income. Subtract Part II, line 11, from Part I, line 8. Individuals, complete lines 13–17. Estates and trusts, complete lines 18a–21. If zero or less, enter -0-			12	47,462.
	Individuals:				
13	Modified adjusted gross income (see instructions)	13			
14	Threshold based on filing status (see instructions)	14			
15	Subtract line 14 from line 13. If zero or less, enter -0-	15			
16	Enter the smaller of line 12 or line 15			16	
17	Net investment income tax for individuals. Multiply line 16 by 3.8% (0.038). **Enter here and include on your tax return** (see instructions)			17	
	Estates and Trusts:				
18a	Net investment income (line 12 above)	18a	47,462.		
b	Deductions for distributions of net investment income and deductions under section 642(c) (see instructions)	18b	12,462.		
c	Undistributed net investment income. Subtract line 18b from line 18a (see instructions). If zero or less, enter -0-	18c	35,000.		
19a	Adjusted gross income (see instructions)	19a	35,500.		
b	Highest tax bracket for estates and trusts for the year (see instructions)	19b	13,450.		
c	Subtract line 19b from line 19a. If zero or less, enter -0-	19c	22,050.		
20	Enter the smaller of line 18c or line 19c			20	22,050.
21	Net investment income tax for estates and trusts. Multiply line 20 by 3.8% (0.038). **Enter here and include on your tax return** (see instructions)			21	838.

For Paperwork Reduction Act Notice, see your tax return instructions. BAA REV 04/19/23 PRO Form **8960** (2022)

661117

☐ Final K-1 ☐ Amended K-1 OMB No. 1545-0092

Schedule K-1 (Form 1041) **2022**

Department of the Treasury
Internal Revenue Service

For calendar year 2022, or tax year

beginning / / 2022 ending / /

Beneficiary's Share of Income, Deductions, Credits, etc.

See back of form and instructions.

Part I Information About the Estate or Trust

A Estate's or trust's employer identification number
11-1111111

B Estate's or trust's name
PROBLEM 3

C Fiduciary's name, address, city, state, and ZIP code

D ☐ Check if Form 1041-T was filed and enter the date it was filed

E ☐ Check if this is the final Form 1041 for the estate or trust

Part II Information About the Beneficiary

F Beneficiary's identifying number
111-11-1111

G Beneficiary's name, address, city, state, and ZIP code
Beneficiary #1
111 Main Street

Delaware OH 43015

H ☒ Domestic beneficiary ☐ Foreign beneficiary

Part III Beneficiary's Share of Current Year Income, Deductions, Credits, and Other Items

1	Interest income	
2a	Ordinary dividends	12,462.
2b	Qualified dividends	12,462.
3	Net short-term capital gain	
4a	Net long-term capital gain	
4b	28% rate gain	
4c	Unrecaptured section 1250 gain	
5	Other portfolio and nonbusiness income	
6	Ordinary business income	
7	Net rental real estate income	
8	Other rental income	
9	Directly apportioned deductions	
10	Estate tax deduction	
11	Final year deductions	
12	Alternative minimum tax adjustment	A 0.
13	Credits and credit recapture	
14	Other information	A 8,938. E 12,462.

*See attached statement for additional information.

Note: A statement must be attached showing the beneficiary's share of income and directly apportioned deductions from each business, rental real estate, and other rental activity.

For IRS Use Only

For Paperwork Reduction Act Notice, see the Instructions for Form 1041. www.irs.gov/Form1041 BAA REV 04/19/23 PRO Schedule K-1 (Form 1041) 2022

Allocation of Deductions for Tax-Exempt Income 2022

Name	Employer Identification Number
PROBLEM 3	11-1111111

1041 Line #	Type of Income	(a) Total	(b) Tax-exempt Income	(c) Taxable Income
1	Interest income	13,000.	13,000.	
2	Dividends	19,000.		19,000.
3	Gross income from Schedule C			
4	Total net gain from Schedule D, line 19, col. (1)			
5 a	Gross rents/royalties from Schedule E			
5 b	Income/loss Sch E, pg 2, lines 32, 37 and 39			
6	Gross income from Schedule F			
7	Ordinary gain or loss			
8	Other income — Direct Entry / From K-1s			
	Totals	32,000.	13,000.	19,000.
		100.0000 %	40.6250 %	59.3750 %

1041 Line #	Type of Deduction	(a) Amounts totally allocable to taxable income	(b) Amounts totally allocable to tax exempt income	(c) Amts to be allocated between exempt and taxable income	(d) Amounts allocable to taxable income col (c) x 0.5938	(e) Deductible amounts (a + d)
10	Interest					
10 a	Investment interest Form 4952					
11	Taxes	600.				600.
12	Fiduciary fees			9,000.	5,344.	5,344.
14	Attorney, accountant, return preparation fees			1,000.	594.	594.
15 a	Other deductions					
	Totals	600.		10,000.	5,938.	6,538.

Total allocated amounts from column (c) not deductible . . . . . . 4,062.

FIFW0501.SCR 01/20/20

11-1111111 1

Additional Information From 2022 Federal Fiduciary Tax Return

SMART WORKSHEET FOR: Form 1041: U.S. Income Tax Return for Estates and Trusts
State inc taxes, col a **Itemization Statement**

Description	Amount
State taxes prior year	600.
Total	**600.**

SMART WORKSHEET FOR: Form 1041: U.S. Income Tax Return for Estates and Trusts
Line 12, col c **Itemization Statement**

Description	Amount
Fiduciary fee	9,000.
Total	**9,000.**

SMART WORKSHEET FOR: Form 1041: U.S. Income Tax Return for Estates and Trusts
Line 14, col c **Itemization Statement**

Description	Amount
Legal Fees	1,000.
Total	**1,000.**

PROBLEM No. 4

Estate — Final Year

FEATURES

1. Interest and dividends are present
2. No tax-exempt income present
3. Long-term capital loss present
4. Short-term capital loss carryover present; long-term capital loss carryover present
5. Substantial fiduciary and professional fees present
6. Final year of the estate
7. Income and Losses:

Interest	4,000
Dividends (Qualified)	3,000
Long-Term Capital Loss	(23,000)
Short-Term Capital Loss Carryover	(15,000)
Long-Term Capital Loss Carryover	(25,000)

8. Expenses

Fiduciary Fees	20,000
Professional Fees	25,000

9. **Things to Note:**

    a. Carryover of capital losses to beneficiaries; these total $63,000 (see item 11 on Schedule K-1 reference Codes C and D)
    b. Excess deductions in year of termination (Schedule K-1) – What happens to them? See Internal Revenue Code Section 642(h). The $45,000 of expenses exceed the $7,000 items of income by $38,000 and such excess is carried out to the beneficiary (see item 11 on Schedule K-1 reference Code A)
    c. Estate's exemption is not allocated to beneficiaries
    d. Completion of Schedule B reflecting losses

Form 1041 Department of the Treasury—Internal Revenue Service
U.S. Income Tax Return for Estates and Trusts **2022** OMB No. 1545-0092
Go to www.irs.gov/Form1041 for instructions and the latest information.

A Check all that apply: For calendar year 2022 or fiscal year beginning , 2022, and ending , 20

- [X] Decedent's estate
- [ ] Simple trust
- [ ] Complex trust
- [ ] Qualified disability trust
- [ ] ESBT (S portion only)
- [ ] Grantor type trust
- [ ] Bankruptcy estate—Ch. 7
- [ ] Bankruptcy estate—Ch. 11
- [ ] Pooled income fund

Name of estate or trust (If a grantor type trust, see the instructions.): PROBLEM 4
C Employer identification number: 22-2222222
Name and title of fiduciary:
D Date entity created:
Number, street, and room or suite no. (If a P.O. box, see the instructions.):
E Nonexempt charitable and split-interest trusts, check applicable box(es). See instructions.
[ ] Described in sec. 4947(a)(1). Check here if not a private foundation . . . [ ]
[ ] Described in sec. 4947(a)(2)
City or town, state or province, country, and ZIP or foreign postal code:

B Number of Schedules K-1 attached (see instructions) 1
F Check applicable boxes: [ ] Initial return [X] Final return [ ] Amended return [ ] Net operating loss carryback [ ] Change in trust's name [ ] Change in fiduciary [ ] Change in fiduciary's name [ ] Change in fiduciary's address
G Check here if the estate or filing trust made a section 645 election . . . [ ] Trust TIN

Income	1	Interest income	1	4,000
	2a	Total ordinary dividends	2a	3,000
	b	Qualified dividends allocable to: (1) Beneficiaries ______ (2) Estate or trust 3,000		
	3	Business income or (loss). Attach Schedule C (Form 1040)	3	
	4	Capital gain or (loss). Attach Schedule D (Form 1041)	4	-3,000
	5	Rents, royalties, partnerships, other estates and trusts, etc. Attach Schedule E (Form 1040)	5	
	6	Farm income or (loss). Attach Schedule F (Form 1040)	6	
	7	Ordinary gain or (loss). Attach Form 4797	7	
	8	Other income. List type and amount	8	
	9	**Total income.** Combine lines 1, 2a, and 3 through 8	9	4,000
Deductions	10	Interest. Check if Form 4952 is attached [ ]	10	
	11	Taxes	11	
	12	Fiduciary fees. If only a portion is deductible under section 67(e), see instructions	12	20,000
	13	Charitable deduction (from Schedule A, line 7)	13	
	14	Attorney, accountant, and return preparer fees. If only a portion is deductible under section 67(e), see instructions	14	25,000
	15a	Other deductions (attach schedule). See instructions for deductions allowable under section 67(e)	15a	
	b	Net operating loss deduction. See instructions	15b	
	16	Add lines 10 through 15b	16	45,000
	17	Adjusted total income or (loss). Subtract line 16 from line 9 — 17: -41,000		
	18	Income distribution deduction (from Schedule B, line 15). Attach Schedules K-1 (Form 1041)	18	0
	19	Estate tax deduction including certain generation-skipping taxes (attach computation)	19	
	20	Qualified business income deduction. Attach Form 8995 or 8995-A	20	
	21	Exemption	21	
	22	Add lines 18 through 21	22	0
Tax and Payments	23	Taxable income. Subtract line 22 from line 17. If a loss, see instructions	23	-41,000
	24	**Total tax** (from Schedule G, Part I, line 9)	24	0
	25	Current year net 965 tax liability paid from Form 965-A, Part II, column (k) (see instructions)	25	
	26	**Total payments** (from Schedule G, Part II, line 19)	26	
	27	Estimated tax penalty. See instructions	27	
	28	**Tax due.** If line 26 is smaller than the total of lines 24, 25, and 27, enter amount owed	28	0
	29	**Overpayment.** If line 26 is larger than the total of lines 24, 25, and 27, enter amount overpaid	29	
	30	Amount of line 29 to be: **a Credited to 2023** ; **b Refunded**	30	

Sign Here Under penalties of perjury, I declare that I have examined this return, including accompanying schedules and statements, and to the best of my knowledge and belief, it is true, correct, and complete. Declaration of preparer (other than taxpayer) is based on all information of which preparer has any knowledge.

Signature of fiduciary or officer representing fiduciary | Date | EIN of fiduciary if a financial institution | May the IRS discuss this return with the preparer shown below? See instructions. [ ] Yes [ ] No

Paid Preparer Use Only Print/Type preparer's name | Preparer's signature | Date | Check [ ] if self-employed | PTIN
Firm's name | Firm's EIN
Firm's address | Phone no.

For Paperwork Reduction Act Notice, see the separate instructions. BAA REV 04/19/23 PRO Form **1041** (2022)

Form 1041 (2022) Page 2

Schedule A — Charitable Deduction. Don't complete for a simple trust or a pooled income fund.

1	Amounts paid or permanently set aside for charitable purposes from gross income. See instructions	1	
2	Tax-exempt income allocable to charitable contributions. See instructions	2	
3	Subtract line 2 from line 1	3	
4	Capital gains for the tax year allocated to corpus and paid or permanently set aside for charitable purposes	4	
5	Add lines 3 and 4	5	
6	Section 1202 exclusion allocable to capital gains paid or permanently set aside for charitable purposes. See instructions	6	
7	**Charitable deduction.** Subtract line 6 from line 5. Enter here and on page 1, line 13	7	

Schedule B — Income Distribution Deduction

1	Adjusted total income. See instructions	1	-3,000
2	Adjusted tax-exempt interest	2	
3	Total net gain from Schedule D (Form 1041), line 19, column (1). See instructions	3	0
4	Enter amount from Schedule A, line 4 (minus any allocable section 1202 exclusion)	4	
5	Capital gains for the tax year included on Schedule A, line 1. See instructions	5	
6	Enter any gain from page 1, line 4, as a negative number. If page 1, line 4, is a loss, enter the loss as a positive number	6	3,000
7	**Distributable net income.** Combine lines 1 through 6. If zero or less, enter -0-	7	0
8	If a complex trust, enter accounting income for the tax year as determined under the governing instrument and applicable local law — 8		
9	Income required to be distributed currently	9	
10	Other amounts paid, credited, or otherwise required to be distributed	10	
11	Total distributions. Add lines 9 and 10. If greater than line 8, see instructions	11	
12	Enter the amount of tax-exempt income included on line 11	12	
13	Tentative income distribution deduction. Subtract line 12 from line 11	13	
14	Tentative income distribution deduction. Subtract line 2 from line 7. If zero or less, enter -0-	14	0
15	**Income distribution deduction.** Enter the smaller of line 13 or line 14 here and on page 1, line 18	15	0

Schedule G — Tax Computation and Payments (see instructions)

Part I — Tax Computation

1	**Tax:**				
a	Tax on taxable income. See instructions	1a			
b	Tax on lump-sum distributions. Attach Form 4972	1b			
c	Alternative minimum tax (from Schedule I (Form 1041), line 54)	1c	0		
d	**Total.** Add lines 1a through 1c			1d	0
2a	Foreign tax credit. Attach Form 1116	2a			
b	General business credit. Attach Form 3800	2b			
c	Credit for prior year minimum tax. Attach Form 8801	2c			
d	Bond credits. Attach Form 8912	2d			
e	**Total credits.** Add lines 2a through 2d			2e	
3	Subtract line 2e from line 1d. If zero or less, enter -0-			3	0
4	Tax on the ESBT portion of the trust (from ESBT Tax Worksheet, line 17). See instructions			4	
5	Net investment income tax from Form 8960, line 21			5	0
6	Recapture taxes. Check if from: ☐ Form 4255 ☐ Form 8611			6	
7	Household employment taxes. Attach Schedule H (Form 1040)			7	
8	Other taxes and amounts due			8	
9	**Total tax.** Add lines 3 through 8. Enter here and on page 1, line 24			9	0

Part II — Payments

10	2022 estimated tax payments and amount applied from 2021 return	10	
11	Estimated tax payments allocated to beneficiaries (from Form 1041-T)	11	
12	Subtract line 11 from line 10	12	
13	Tax paid with Form 7004. See instructions	13	
14	Federal income tax withheld. If any is from Form(s) 1099, check here ☐	14	
15	Current year net 965 tax liability from Form 965-A, Part I, column (f) (see instructions)	15	
16	Other payments: **a** Form 2439 ________ ; **b** Form 4136 ________ ; **Total**	16c	
17	Credit for qualified sick and family leave wages for leave taken before April 1, 2021	17	
18	Credit for qualified sick and family leave wages for leave taken after March 31, 2021, and before October 1, 2021	18	
19	**Total payments.** Add lines 12 through 15 and 16c through 18. Enter here and on page 1, line 26	19	

REV 03/25/23 PRO Form **1041** (2022)

SCHEDULE D (Form 1041)

Department of the Treasury
Internal Revenue Service

Capital Gains and Losses

Attach to Form 1041, Form 5227, or Form 990-T.
Use Form 8949 to list your transactions for lines 1b, 2, 3, 8b, 9, and 10.
Go to *www.irs.gov/F1041* for instructions and the latest information.

OMB No. 1545-0092

2022

Name of estate or trust: PROBLEM 4

Employer identification number

Did you dispose of any investment(s) in a qualified opportunity fund during the tax year? . . . . ☐ Yes ☒ No
If "Yes," attach Form 8949 and see its instructions for additional requirements for reporting your gain or loss.

Note: *Form 5227 filers need to complete only Parts I and II.*

Part I Short-Term Capital Gains and Losses—Generally Assets Held 1 Year or Less (see instructions)

See instructions for how to figure the amounts to enter on the lines below. This form may be easier to complete if you round off cents to whole dollars.	(d) Proceeds (sales price)	(e) Cost (or other basis)	(g) Adjustments to gain or loss from Form(s) 8949, Part I, line 2, column (g)	(h) Gain or (loss) Subtract column (e) from column (d) and combine the result with column (g)
1a Totals for all short-term transactions reported on Form 1099-B for which basis was reported to the IRS and for which you have no adjustments (see instructions). However, if you choose to report all these transactions on Form 8949, leave this line blank and go to line 1b .				
1b Totals for all transactions reported on Form(s) 8949 with **Box A** checked				
2 Totals for all transactions reported on Form(s) 8949 with **Box B** checked				
3 Totals for all transactions reported on Form(s) 8949 with **Box C** checked				

		Line	(h)
4	Short-term capital gain or (loss) from Forms 4684, 6252, 6781, and 8824	4	
5	Net short-term gain or (loss) from partnerships, S corporations, and other estates or trusts	5	
6	Short-term capital loss carryover. Enter the amount, if any, from line 9 of the 2021 Capital Loss Carryover Worksheet	6	(15,000.)
7	**Net short-term capital gain or (loss).** Combine lines 1a through 6 in column (h). Enter here and on Part III, line 17, column (3)	7	-15,000.

Part II Long-Term Capital Gains and Losses—Generally Assets Held More Than 1 Year (see instructions)

See instructions for how to figure the amounts to enter on the lines below. This form may be easier to complete if you round off cents to whole dollars.	(d) Proceeds (sales price)	(e) Cost (or other basis)	(g) Adjustments to gain or loss from Form(s) 8949, Part II, line 2, column (g)	(h) Gain or (loss) Subtract column (e) from column (d) and combine the result with column (g)
8a Totals for all long-term transactions reported on Form 1099-B for which basis was reported to the IRS and for which you have no adjustments (see instructions). However, if you choose to report all these transactions on Form 8949, leave this line blank and go to line 8b .	23,000.	46,000.		-23,000.
8b Totals for all transactions reported on Form(s) 8949 with **Box D** checked				
9 Totals for all transactions reported on Form(s) 8949 with **Box E** checked				
10 Totals for all transactions reported on Form(s) 8949 with **Box F** checked				

		Line	(h)
11	Long-term capital gain or (loss) from Forms 2439, 4684, 6252, 6781, and 8824	11	
12	Net long-term gain or (loss) from partnerships, S corporations, and other estates or trusts	12	
13	Capital gain distributions	13	
14	Gain from Form 4797, Part I	14	
15	Long-term capital loss carryover. Enter the amount, if any, from line 14 of the 2021 Capital Loss Carryover Worksheet	15	(25,000.)
16	**Net long-term capital gain or (loss).** Combine lines 8a through 15 in column (h). Enter here and on Part III, line 18a, column (3)	16	-48,000.

For Paperwork Reduction Act Notice, see the Instructions for Form 1041. Cat. No. 11376V **Schedule D (Form 1041) 2022**

BAA REV 03/25/23 PRO

Schedule D (Form 1041) 2022 Page **2**

Part III **Summary of Parts I and II**
Caution: *Read the instructions* ***before*** *completing this part.*

			(1) Beneficiaries' (see instr.)	(2) Estate's or trust's	(3) Total
17	**Net short-term gain or (loss)**	17	-12,000	-3,000	-15,000
18	**Net long-term gain or (loss):**				
a	Total for year	18a	-48,000	0	-48,000
b	Unrecaptured section 1250 gain (see line 18 of the worksheet)	18b			
c	28% rate gain	18c			
19	**Total net gain or (loss).** Combine lines 17 and 18a	19	-60,000	-3,000	-63,000

Note: *If line 19, column (3), is a net gain, enter the gain on Form 1041, line 4 (or Schedule A (Form 990-T), Part I, line 4a). If lines 18a and 19, column (2), are net gains, go to Part V, and* ***don't*** *complete Part IV. If line 19, column (3), is a net loss, complete Part IV and the* ***Capital Loss Carryover Worksheet****, as necessary.*

Part IV **Capital Loss Limitation**

20 Enter here and enter as a (loss) on Form 1041, line 4 (or Schedule A (Form 990-T), Part I, line 4c, if a trust), the **smaller** of:

a The loss on line 19, column (3) **or b** $3,000 . . . 20 (3,000)

Note: *If the loss on line 19, column (3), is more than $3,000,* ***or*** *if Form 1041, page 1, line 23 (or Form 990-T, Part I, line 11), is a loss, complete the* ***Capital Loss Carryover Worksheet*** *in the instructions to figure your capital loss carryover.*

Part V **Tax Computation Using Maximum Capital Gains Rates**

Form 1041 filers. Complete this part **only** if both lines 18a and 19 in column (2) are gains, or an amount is entered in Part I or Part II and there is an entry on Form 1041, line 2b(2), **and** Form 1041, line 23, is more than zero.

Caution: *Skip this part and complete the* ***Schedule D Tax Worksheet*** *in the instructions if:*

- *Either line 18b, col. (2), or line 18c, col. (2), is more than zero, or*
- *Both Form 1041, line 2b(1), and Form 4952, line 4g, are more than zero, or*
- *There are amounts on lines 4e and 4g of Form 4952.*

Form 990-T trusts. Complete this part **only** if both lines 18a and 19 are gains, or qualified dividends are included in income in Part I of Form 990-T, **and** Form 990-T, Part I, line 11, is more than zero. Skip this part and complete the **Schedule D Tax Worksheet** in the instructions if either line 18b, col. (2), or line 18c, col. (2), is more than zero.

21	Enter taxable income from Form 1041, line 23 (or Form 990-T, Part I, line 11)			21			
22	Enter the **smaller** of line 18a or 19 in column (2) but not less than zero	22					
23	Enter the estate's or trust's qualified dividends from Form 1041, line 2b(2) (or enter the qualified dividends included in income in Part I of Form 990-T)	23					
24	Add lines 22 and 23	24					
25	If the estate or trust is filing Form 4952, enter the amount from line 4g; otherwise, enter -0-	25					
26	Subtract line 25 from line 24. If zero or less, enter -0-			26			
27	Subtract line 26 from line 21. If zero or less, enter -0-			27			
28	Enter the **smaller** of the amount on line 21 or $2,800			28			
29	Enter the **smaller** of the amount on line 27 or line 28			29			
30	Subtract line 29 from line 28. If zero or less, enter -0-. This amount is taxed at 0%					30	
31	Enter the **smaller** of line 21 or line 26			31			
32	Subtract line 30 from line 26			32			
33	Enter the **smaller** of line 21 or $13,700			33			
34	Add lines 27 and 30			34			
35	Subtract line 34 from line 33. If zero or less, enter -0-			35			
36	Enter the **smaller** of line 32 or line 35			36			
37	Multiply line 36 by 15% (0.15)					37	
38	Enter the amount from line 31			38			
39	Add lines 30 and 36			39			
40	Subtract line 39 from line 38. If zero or less, enter -0-			40			
41	Multiply line 40 by 20% (0.20)					41	
42	Figure the tax on the amount on line 27. Use the 2022 Tax Rate Schedule for Estates and Trusts (see the Schedule G instructions in the Instructions for Form 1041)			42			
43	Add lines 37, 41, and 42			43			
44	Figure the tax on the amount on line 21. Use the 2022 Tax Rate Schedule for Estates and Trusts (see the Schedule G instructions in the Instructions for Form 1041)			44			
45	**Tax on all taxable income.** Enter the **smaller** of line 43 or line 44 here and on Form 1041, Schedule G, Part I, line 1a (or Form 990-T, Part II, line 2)					45	

REV 03/25/23 PRO **Schedule D (Form 1041) 2022**

661117

[X] Final K-1 [ ] Amended K-1 OMB No. 1545-0092

Schedule K-1 (Form 1041) **2022**

Department of the Treasury
Internal Revenue Service

For calendar year 2022, or tax year

beginning / / 2022 ending / /

Beneficiary's Share of Income, Deductions, Credits, etc.

See back of form and instructions.

Part I Information About the Estate or Trust

A Estate's or trust's employer identification number

B Estate's or trust's name

PROBLEM 4

C Fiduciary's name, address, city, state, and ZIP code

D [ ] Check if Form 1041-T was filed and enter the date it was filed

E [X] Check if this is the final Form 1041 for the estate or trust

Part II Information About the Beneficiary

F Beneficiary's identifying number

123-45-6789

G Beneficiary's name, address, city, state, and ZIP code

Joe Doe
111 Main Street

Columbus OH 43212

H [X] Domestic beneficiary [ ] Foreign beneficiary

Part III Beneficiary's Share of Current Year Income, Deductions, Credits, and Other Items

1	Interest income	11	Final year deductions	
		A		38,000.
2a	Ordinary dividends	B		0.
2b	Qualified dividends	C		15,000.
3	Net short-term capital gain	D		48,000.
4a	Net long-term capital gain			
4b	28% rate gain	12	Alternative minimum tax adjustment	
4c	Unrecaptured section 1250 gain			
5	Other portfolio and nonbusiness income			
6	Ordinary business income			
7	Net rental real estate income	13	Credits and credit recapture	
8	Other rental income			
9	Directly apportioned deductions			
		14	Other information	
10	Estate tax deduction			

*See attached statement for additional information.

Note: A statement must be attached showing the beneficiary's share of income and directly apportioned deductions from each business, rental real estate, and other rental activity.

For IRS Use Only

Schedule K-1 (Form 1041) 2022 Page **2**

This list identifies the codes used on Schedule K-1 for beneficiaries and provides summarized reporting information for beneficiaries who file Form 1040 or 1040-SR. For detailed reporting and filing information, see the Instructions for Schedule K-1 (Form 1041) for a Beneficiary Filing Form 1040 or 1040-SR and the instructions for your income tax return.

	Report on
1. Interest income	Form 1040 or 1040-SR, line 2b
2a. Ordinary dividends	Form 1040 or 1040-SR, line 3b
2b. Qualified dividends	Form 1040 or 1040-SR, line 3a
3. Net short-term capital gain	Schedule D, line 5
4a. Net long-term capital gain	Schedule D, line 12
4b. 28% rate gain	28% Rate Gain Worksheet, line 4 (Schedule D Instructions)
4c. Unrecaptured section 1250 gain	Unrecaptured Section 1250 Gain Worksheet, line 11 (Schedule D Instructions)
5. Other portfolio and nonbusiness income	Schedule E, line 33, column (f)
6. Ordinary business income	Schedule E, line 33, column (d) or (f)
7. Net rental real estate income	Schedule E, line 33, column (d) or (f)
8. Other rental income	Schedule E, line 33, column (d) or (f)
9. Directly apportioned deductions	
Code	
A Depreciation	Form 8582 or Schedule E, line 33, column (c) or (e)
B Depletion	Form 8582 or Schedule E, line 33, column (c) or (e)
C Amortization	Form 8582 or Schedule E, line 33, column (c) or (e)
10. Estate tax deduction	Schedule A, line 16
11. Final year deductions	
A Excess deductions – Section 67(e) expenses	Schedule 1 (Form 1040), line 24k (also see the beneficiary's instructions)
B Excess deductions – Non-miscellaneous itemized deductions	See the beneficiary's instructions
C Short-term capital loss carryover	Schedule D, line 5
D Long-term capital loss carryover	Schedule D, line 12; line 5 of the wksht. for Sch. D, line 18; and line 16 of the wksht. for Sch. D, line 19
E Net operating loss carryover — regular tax	Schedule 1 (Form 1040), line 8a
F Net operating loss carryover — minimum tax	Form 6251, line 2f
12. Alternative minimum tax (AMT) items	
A Adjustment for minimum tax purposes	Form 6251, line 2j
B AMT adjustment attributable to qualified dividends	See the beneficiary's instructions and the Instructions for Form 6251
C AMT adjustment attributable to net short-term capital gain	
D AMT adjustment attributable to net long-term capital gain	
E AMT adjustment attributable to unrecaptured section 1250 gain	
F AMT adjustment attributable to 28% rate gain	
G Accelerated depreciation	
H Depletion	
I Amortization	
J Exclusion items	2023 Form 8801

13. Credits and credit recapture	
Code	*Report on*
A Credit for estimated taxes	Form 1040 or 1040-SR, line 26
B Credit for backup withholding	Form 1040 or 1040-SR, line 25c
C Low-income housing credit	See the beneficiary's instructions
D Rehabilitation credit and energy credit	
E Other qualifying investment credit	
F Work opportunity credit	
G Credit for small employer health insurance premiums	
H Biofuel producer credit	
I Credit for increasing research activities	
J Renewable electricity, refined coal, and Indian coal production credit	
K Empowerment zone employment credit	
L Indian employment credit	
M Orphan drug credit	
N Credit for employer-provided child care and facilities	
O Biodiesel and renewable diesel fuels credit	
P Credit to holders of tax credit bonds	
Q Credit for employer differential wage payments	
R Recapture of credits	
Z Other credits	
14. Other information	
A Tax-exempt interest	Form 1040 or 1040-SR, line 2a
B Foreign taxes	Schedule 3 (Form 1040), line 1 or Schedule A, line 6
C Reserved for future use	
D Reserved for future use	
E Net investment income	Form 4952, line 4a
F Gross farm and fishing income	Schedule E, line 42
G Foreign trading gross receipts (IRC 942(a))	See the Instructions for Form 8873
H Adjustment for section 1411 net investment income or deductions	Form 8960, line 7 (also see the beneficiary's instructions)
I Section 199A information	See the beneficiary's instructions
Z Other information	See the beneficiary's instructions

Note: If you are a beneficiary who does not file a Form 1040 or 1040-SR, see instructions for the type of income tax return you are filing.

REV 03/25/23 PRO

Chapter 6

Grantor Trusts

Internal Revenue Code: Sections 671 through 678

Regulations: (As indicated in each section of this Chapter)

Rev. Rul. 85-13, 1985-1 C.B. 184, 1985-7 I.R.B. 28

A grantor who acquires the corpus of a trust in exchange for the grantor's unsecured promissory note will be considered to have indirectly borrowed the trust corpus. As a result, the grantor will be treated as the owner of the trust and the grantor's acquisition of the trust corpus will not be viewed as a sale for federal income tax purpose. The Service will not follow the Rothstein decision.

Issues

(1) Whether a grantor's receipt of the entire corpus of an irrevocable trust in exchange for an unsecured promissory note given to the trustee, the grantor's spouse, constituted an indirect borrowing of the trust corpus which caused the grantor to be the owner of the entire trust under section 675(3) of the Internal Revenue Code.

(2) To the extent that a grantor is treated as the owner of a trust, whether the trust will be recognized as a separate taxpayer capable of entering into a sales transaction with the grantor.

Facts

In 1980, A, an individual, created an irrevocable trust, T. W, A's spouse, is the trustee of T. The trust instrument of T provides that all income of T is to be paid semiannually to C, A's child, for a term of 15 years. Upon expiration of the trust term, or if C dies before the trust term expires, the corpus of T will be distributed to C's child or to the estate of C's child. Neither A nor any other person has a power over or an interest in T that would cause A to be treated as the owner of T under the grantor trust provisions of the Code, section 671 and following.

A funded T with a contribution of 100 shares of stock in Corporation Z. The 100 shares represented all of the outstanding stock of Corporation Z. When A funded T, A's basis in the shares was $20x.

On December 27, 1981, when the fair market value of the Corporation Z shares was $40x, W, as trustee, transferred the 100 shares to A. In exchange, A gave W A's unsecured promissory note with a face amount of $40x, bearing an adequate annual rate of interest, payable semiannually, beginning six months following the date on which the shares were transferred to A. Principal payments on the note were scheduled to be paid in 10 equal annual installments, the first installment being due 3 years following the date on which the 100 shares were transferred to A, December 27, 1984.

On January 20, 1984, A sold the 100 shares to an unrelated party for $50x. Corporation Z did not make any distributions with respect to the 100 shares at any time before the sale of those shares to the unrelated party.

Law and Analysis

Under section 675(3) of the Code, a grantor will be treated as the owner of any portion of a trust in respect of which the grantor has directly or indirectly borrowed the trust corpus or income and has not completely repaid the loan, including any interest, before the beginning of the taxable year, unless the loan (1) provides for adequate interest, (2) is adequately secured, and (3) is not made by the grantor or by a related or subordinate trustee who is subservient to the grantor.

Section 1.675-1 of the Income Tax Regulations explains that, in effect, section 675 of the Code treats the grantor as the owner of a trust if under the terms of the trust instrument, or the circumstances attendant to its operation, administrative control is exercisable primarily for the benefit of the grantor rather than the beneficiaries of the trust. Section 675(3) differs from the other provisions of section 675 which provide rules for determining grantor ownership of a trust, because it requires an affirmative act (borrowing) rather than a retained power, before it applies. Nevertheless, the same theme underlies section 675(3) as underlies the other provisions of section 675 which treat the grantor as owning the trust. In all of these cases the justification for treating the grantor as owner is evidence of substantial grantor dominion and control over the trust.

Section 1.671-3(a)(1) of the regulations states that if a grantor is treated as the owner of an entire trust, the grantor takes into account in computing the grantor's income tax liability all items of income, deduction, and credit to which the grantor would have been entitled had the trust not been in existence during the period the grantor is treated as the owner. If the grantor is treated as the owner of a portion of a trust and that portion consists of specific trust property and its income, section 1.671-3(a)(2) provides that all items directly related to that property are to be taken into account in computing the grantor's income tax liability.

In this case, A has acquired control over and use of the entire trust corpus, the 100 shares of Corporation Z stock, in exchange for A's unsecured note. If A, instead of giving W a note in exchange for the 100 shares, had made a cash payment of $40x to W and subsequently borrowed that cash, giving W the unsecured note to evidence the borrowing, section 675(3) of the Code would be applicable and A would be the owner of T. Although A did not engage in this kind of direct borrowing, A's acquisition of the entire corpus of T in exchange for an unsecured note was, in substance, the economic equivalent of borrowing trust corpus. Accordingly, under section 675(3), A is treated as the owner of the portion of T represented by A's promissory note. Further, because the promissory note is T's only asset, A is treated as the owner of the entire trust.

Because A is treated as the owner of the entire trust, A is considered to be the owner of the trust assets for federal income tax purposes. See Ringwalt v. United States, 549 F.2d 89 (8th Cir. 1977), cert. denied, 432 U.S. 906 (1977); Estate of O'Connor v. Commissioner, 69 T.C. 165 (1977); Example 5, section 1.1001-2(c) of the regulations; Rev. Rul. 81-98, 1981-1 C.B. 40; Rev. Rul. 78- 175, 1978-1 C.B. 144; Rev. Rul. 77-402, 1977-2 C.B. 222; Rev. Rul. 74-613, 1974-2 C.B. 153; Rev. Rul. 72- 471, 1972-2 C.B. 201; Rev. Rul. 70-376, 1970-2 C.B. 164; Rev. Rul. 66-159, 1966-1 C.B. 162; but cf. Rev. Rul. 74-243, 1974-1 C.B. 106. In this case, A is considered to be the owner of the promissory note held by the trust. Therefore, the transfer of the Corporation Z shares by T to A is not recognized as a sale for federal income tax purposes because A is both the maker and the owner of the promissory note. A transaction cannot be recognized as a sale for federal income tax purposes if the same person is treated as owning the purported consideration both before and after the transaction. See Dobson v. Commissioner, 1 B.T.A. 1082 (1925).

A's basis in the shares received from T will be equal to A's basis in the shares at the time he funded T because the basis of the shares was not adjusted during the period that T held them. See Rev. Rul. 72-406, 1972-2 C.B. 462, a ruling involving the determination of a grantor's basis in property upon reversion of that property to the grantor at the expiration of a trust's term.

In Rothstein v. United States, 735 F.2d 704 (2d Cir. 1984), the court considered a transaction that is in substance identical to the facts described in this ruling. The court held that the grantor was the owner of a trust under section 675(3) of the Code because by exchanging an unsecured note for the entire trust corpus, the grantor had indirectly borrowed the trust corpus. The court held further, however, that although the grantor must be treated as the owner of the trust, this means only that the grantor must include items of income, deduction, and credit attributable to the trust in computing the grantor's taxable income and credits, and that the trust must continue to be viewed as a separate taxpayer. The court held, therefore, that the transfer of trust corpus to the grantor in exchange for an unsecured promissory note was a sale and that the taxpayer acquired a cost basis in the assets.

In Rothstein, as in this case, section 671 of the Code requires that the grantor includes in computing the grantor's tax liability all items of income, deduction, and credit of the trust as though the trust were not in existence during the period the grantor is treated as the owner. Section 1.671-3(a)(1) of the regulations. It is anomalous to suggest that Congress, in enacting the grantor trust provisions of the Code, intended that the existence of a trust would be ignored for purposes of attribution of income, deduction, and credit, and yet, retain its vitality as a separate entity capable of entering into a sales transaction with the grantor. The reason for attributing items of income, deduction, and credit to the grantor under section 671 is that, by exercising dominion and control over a trust, either by retaining a power over or an interest in the trust, or, as in this case, by dealing with the trust property for the grantor's benefit, the grantor has treated the trust property as though it were the grantor's property. The Service position of treating the owner of an entire trust as the owner of the trust's assets is, therefore, consistent with and supported by the rationale for attributing items of income, deduction, and credit to the grantor.

The court's decision in Rothstein, insofar as it holds that a trust owned by a grantor must be regarded as a separate taxpayer capable of engaging in sales transactions with the grantor, is not in accord with the views of the Service. Accordingly, the Service will not follow Rothstein.

Holdings

(1) A's receipt of the entire corpus of the trust in exchange for A's unsecured promissory note constituted an indirect borrowing of the trust corpus which caused A to be the owner of the entire trust under section 675(3) of the Code.

(2) At the time A became the owner of the trust, A became the owner of the trust property. As a result, the transfer of trust assets to A was not a sale for federal income tax purposes and A did not acquire a cost basis in those assets. Accordingly, when A sold the shares of Corporation Z stock on January 20, 1984, A recognized gain of $30x (amount realized of $50x less adjusted basis of $20x). Further, this holding would apply even if the trust held other assets in addition to A's promissory note if A, under any of the grantor trust provisions, was treated as the owner of the portion of the trust represented by the promissory note because A would be treated as the owner of the purported consideration (the promissory note) both before and after the transaction. See section 1.671-3(a)(2) of the regulations. Rev. Rul. 85-13, 1985-1 C.B. 184, 1985-7 I.R.B. 28.

I. Introduction

This Chapter explores grantor trusts and the role they play in Subchapter J. Notwithstanding the fact that these trusts are "ignored" for income tax purposes and thus their tax treatment is theoretically easily addressed, they present their own challenges. The material which follows explores the contours of grantor trust status, its history, and the tax consequences surrounding this status.

A. General Overview of Grantor Trust Status

A grantor trust is a trust in which either the grantor or another person possessing sufficient specifically enumerated rights or interests in or over the trust is considered to be the "owner" of the trust. The retention or possession of these rights gives the person identified as the grantor dominion and control over the trust property, the trust income, or both.

The basic issue in the grantor trust area is who should be taxed when the grantor has retained a certain degree of control—the trust, the beneficiary, or the grantor. Once a trust is characterized as a grantor trust, the grantor includes in his or her taxable income all of the income, deductions, and credits available at the trust level.

In order to determine whether a grantor possesses the specifically enumerated rights and interests as described in the governing trust instrument to require classification of the trust as a grantor trust, Code §§ 673 through 677 must be examined, as they define the circumstances under which income of a trust is taxed to the grantor. Treas. Reg. 1.671-1(a). In addition, a person who is not a transferor of property to the trust, but who, as a beneficiary of the trust possesses certain rights, such as a power of withdrawal over the trust income or principal, may be deemed a grantor of the trust and considered to be an owner of the entire trust or a portion of the trust for income tax purposes. Code § 678.

To the extent that the grantor or another person retains certain benefits or control over the trust, the normal rules governing taxation of nongrantor trusts contained in Subparts A–D of Part I of Subchapter J (i.e., primarily the discussion of simple trusts and complex trusts) do not apply. Instead, the trust income is taxed to the grantor or other person with control over the trust under the rules set forth in Subpart E of Subchapter J, Code §§ 671–678 and their regulations.

B. Historical Background into Grantor Trust Status

When the federal income tax was enacted in 1913, it did not require the grantor of a trust to be taxed on income generated by the trust assets even if the grantor retained control of those assets. Changes made to the Internal Revenue Code in 1924 required the income of a revocable trust to be taxed to the grantor. The next thirty years saw inventive taxpayers try myriad planning techniques using trusts designed to shift income to persons in lower tax brackets and the government trying to thwart such attempts.

The early cases had a common theme. They all involved efforts by the grantor of a trust to keep varying degrees of control over trust principal or income, or both, but to have the trust treated as the taxpayer in order to take advantage of the lower income tax rates then in effect for trusts. In *Corliss v. Bowers*, 281 U.S. 376 (1930), for example, Mr. Corliss created a revocable trust for the benefit of his wife and children. The trust paid income to his wife, but the IRS assessed income tax against Mr. Corliss. The couple had filed separate income tax returns. Justice Holmes had no problem finding for the government, as he wrote, "[If] a man disposes of a fund in such a way that another is allowed to enjoy the income which it is in the power of the first to appropriate it does not matter whether the permission is given by assent or by failure to express dissent. The income that is subject to a man's unfettered command and that he is free to enjoy at his own option may be taxed to him as income, whether he sees fit to enjoy it or not."

In these cases, taxpayers' strategy amounted to anticipatory assignments of income to shift the tax consequences of income receipts to the lowest-bracket taxpayer. However, in *Lucas v. Earl*, 281 U.S. 111 (1930), the Supreme Court had already held that income must be taxed to the one who earns it, a theme later echoed in the grantor trust rules. The Supreme Court affirmed this position in *Helvering v. Horst*, 311 U.S. 112 (1940). In *Horst*, the passage of bond interest coupons from donor to donee was held ineffective to give away the right to income since the donor still controlled the bonds from which the interest coupons were derived: since the taxpayer retained the "tree" (i.e., the bonds), he remained taxable on its "fruit" (i.e., the interest coupons).[1]

The current grantor trust rules are an extension of the foregoing Supreme Court jurisprudence. Congress enacted these rules as part of the 1954 Internal Revenue Code. At that time, individual taxpayers were faced with extremely progressive and high tax rates. Under the 1939 Code, there were twenty separate tax brackets, reaching from 19.2 percent on the first $2,000 to 89 percent on taxable income over $200,000. After 1953, the lowest bracket was due to decline to 17 percent, and the top bracket to 88 percent. The 50 percent tax rate was reached at $20,000. As a planning technique, wealthy taxpayers did whatever they could to shift income to persons, typically family members, in lower income tax brackets. Multiple trusts were created for these persons with the intent that each trust would be recognized as an independent taxpayer to be taxed beginning at the lower end of the progressive rate structure. However, the creators of these trusts tried to maintain as much control over them as they possibly could.

Enter the grantor trust rules. By including §§ 671–678 in the 1954 Internal Revenue Code, Congress forced trust grantors to make a choice — either transfer property into a trust for another person and relinquish control over the income and principal of the trust, and over much of the administration of the trust, and shift the income tax obligation to the trust and its beneficiaries — or retain one or more elements of control or administrative power, and be taxed on the trust income despite having created the trust arrangement for the benefit of another person.

The regulations provide that since the principle underlying Subpart E is generally that income of a trust over which the grantor or another person has retained substantial dominion and control should be taxed to the grantor or other person rather than to the trust which receives the income or to the beneficiary to whom the income may be distributed, it is ordinarily immaterial whether the income involved constitutes income or principal for fiduciary accounting purposes.

1. *Compare Blair v. Commissioner*, 300 U.S. 5 (1937) (where property rights were transferred and the donor gave his entire interest, the property assignees were recognized as valid donees, and the income was taxed to them), *with Harrison v. Schaffner*, 312 U.S. 579 (1941) (a trust beneficiary assigned specified amounts of trust income for a limited term and, as such, did not part with a substantial interest in property).

Accordingly, the references in Subpart E to "income" attributed to the grantor or another person, unless specifically limited, are references to income determined for tax purposes and not to income for fiduciary accounting purposes. If there is an intent to refer to fiduciary accounting income (as described in Treas. Reg. 1.643(b)-1), the Subpart E regulations use the phrase "ordinary income." Treas. Reg. 1.671-2(b).

II. Grantor Trust Status — The "Ground Rules"

Internal Revenue Code: Section 671

Regulations: 1.671-1, 1.671-2, 1.671-3

Like any other tax issue in the Code, identification is pivotal. Subpart E is no exception and identification issues will soon be addressed. But Subpart E puts the proverbial cart before the horse: via Code § 671, it first enumerates the tax consequences associated with grantor trust status.

A. General Rules

Code § 671 provides generally that a grantor of a trust will be taxed on all of the income, deductions, and credits of a trust when such person retains certain powers over or interests in the trust. Code § 672 provides a series of definitions, and Code §§ 673–678 (all discussed below) detail what powers will — and will not — cause a trust grantor to be subject to the grantor trust rules. A grantor can be taxable on the income or principal of a trust, or both. If the grantor is treated as the owner of only part of the trust, the grantor will be taxed on the income from that part of the trust, and the rest of the income will be taxed according to the regular rules regarding the income taxation of trusts and estates. Treas. Reg. 1.671-2(d).

Even if the grantor avoids being taxed on the trust income under the grantor trust rules, it is still possible for the grantor to be taxed under another rule of income taxation, such as the assignment of income doctrine. Code § 671; Rev. Rul. 58-337, 1958-2 C.B. 13.

Under the grantor trust rules a "grantor" includes "any person to the extent such person either creates a trust, or directly or indirectly makes a gratuitous transfer of property to a trust." Treas. Reg. 1.671-2(e)(1). A gratuitous transfer is any transfer of property (including cash) to a trust for other than fair market value. Treas. Reg. 1.671-2(e)(2). A person who creates a trust but makes no gratuitous transfers to the trust is not treated as an owner of any portion of the trust under Code §§ 671–677. Treas. Reg. 1.671-2(e)(1).

A trust can have multiple grantors. For example, suppose Susan creates and funds a trust for the benefit of her children, Paula and Julian. Thereafter, Matthew makes a gift to the same trust. Both Susan and Matthew will be considered grantors of this trust. Treas. Reg. 1.671-2(e)(6), Ex.1

A grantor trust is a trust under which the grantor (or a person other than the grantor who has been granted the power to vest income or principal in himself or herself) has retained substantial benefits or control of the trust so that the grantor (or other person) is treated as the "owner" of the trust assets for income tax purposes. If grantor trust status is met, Code § 671 essentially declares that the grantor or such other person must include in his or her own computation of income taxes all items of income, deductions, and credits against tax attributable to the portion of the trust of which the grantor or such other person is deemed to be the owner. A person will be treated as a grantor or owner of a trust if "certain circumstances" are present. These "circumstances" refer to the retention of broad powers over and interests in a trust that constitute the basis of the remaining provisions of the grantor trust rules, Treas. Reg. 1.671-1(a):

- If the grantor has retained a reversionary interest in the trust of a certain value, within specified time limits. Code § 673 (*see* Section IV, below);
- If the grantor or a nonadverse party has certain powers over the beneficial interests in the trust. Code § 674 (*see* Section V, below);
- If certain administrative powers over the trust exist under which the grantor can or does benefit. Code § 675 (*see* Section VI, below);
- If the grantor or a nonadverse party has a power to revoke the trust or return the trust principal to the grantor. Code § 676 (*see* Section VII, below);
- If the grantor or a nonadverse party has the power to distribute income to or for the benefit of the grantor or the grantor's spouse. Code § 677 (*see* Section VIII, below); and
- If a person other than the grantor has the sole power to vest income or principal in himself or herself so as to be treated in the same manner as would be a grantor of the trust. Code § 678 (*see* Section IX, below).

The operative theory of the grantor trust rules is that the trust is not a separate taxpayer with respect to the various items of income, deductions, and credits which the trust itself may generate. Instead, those items must be taxed directly to the grantor or some other person with a grantor-like power over the trust. An item of income, deduction, or credit included in computing the taxable income and credits of a grantor or another person under Code § 671 is treated as if it had been received or paid directly by the grantor or other person, whether or not an individual. Treas. Reg. 1.671-2(c). In applying the grantor trust rules, a grantor will be treated as holding any power held by an individual who was the spouse of the grantor at the time the power or interest was created, or an individual who became the spouse of the grantor after the power or interest was created (but, in the latter case, only for periods after the individual became the grantor's spouse). Code § 672(e).

As a result of these rules, since an item of income, deduction, or credit attributed to a grantor must be treated as if it had been received or paid directly by the grantor, the character of that item passes through to the grantor. The existence of the trust does not "filter" or otherwise alter the character of an item. For example, items of tax-exempt income pass through the trust to the grantor (Rev. Rul. 60-370, 1960-2 C.B. 203), as do capital gain items. *Scheft v. Commissioner*, 59 T.C. 428 (1972).

B. Compliance Issues: Tax Reporting Requirements for Grantor Trusts

Insofar as securing a taxpayer identification number for a grantor trust is concerned, the rules are bifurcated. In some situations, no separate taxpayer identification number is necessary; in other situations, the Code requires that such number be secured.

Consider first the situation in which no separate taxpayer identification number is necessary. When a trust is treated as a grantor trust due to the fact that the grantor retains a power to revoke the trust under Code § 676 (see Section VII below) and the grantor is a trustee, the grantor should not obtain a separate taxpayer identification number. Instead, such trusts should use the grantor's social security number. Treas. Reg. 301.6109-1(a)(2); 1.671-4(b)(1). Similarly, no separate taxpayer identification number is required for a trust if spouses are the sole grantors, one or both spouses serve as trustees or co-trustees, one or both spouses are the owner(s) of the trust and they file a joint return for the year. Treas. Reg. 1.671-4(b)(2). If any of these situations apply, the grantor does not file a separate income tax return for the trust, and reports the trust income on his or her Form 1040.

In all other situations, the trustee should secure a taxpayer identification for the trust. Additionally, when a reason that would exempt the trust from not requiring a tax-identification number ceases to apply (e.g., the grantor resigns as trustee), the trust should obtain a tax ID number.

The Treasury regulations provide three permissible grantor trust reporting methods. There is the "traditional" reporting method of using Form 1041, or one of two optional Form 1099 reporting methods. Each of these options is described below.

1. The 1041 Alternative — Treas. Reg. 1.671-4(a)

The trustee applies for a taxpayer identification number for the trust. The trustee files a Form 1041 information return, checks the "Grantor Trust" box, does not complete the separate lines on the return, and instead attaches to the return a statement of items of income, deductions, and credits for the year in question. The statement (usually a Schedule K-1 or a plain paper schedule) indicates that the reportable items of the trust are being reported by the grantor under the grantor's social security number, and is furnished to the grantor for use in preparing the grantor's income tax return. This method is the one that has traditionally been used by most fiduciaries and tax preparers.

2. The 1099 Grantor-TIN alternative — Treas. Reg. 1.671-4(b)(2)(i)(A)

The trustee need not obtain its own taxpayer identification number if the trustee provides all payors of reportable income with the name and tax identification number of the grantor and the address of the trustee. The trustee is not required to file either a Form 1041 or Form 1099 with the IRS. Income payers must send Form 1099s to the trust showing the reportable income as taxable to the grantor. The trustee delivers all the Form 1099s it receives to the grantor; in addition the trustee must (i) secure a completed Form W-9 from the grantor and (ii) furnish the grantor with a detailed statement of the applicable items of income, deductions, and credits by the due date (including extensions) of the Form 1041. (Note: if the grantor is the trustee or a co-trustee of the trust, the statement need not be furnished to the grantor.) The trustee will need to obtain a taxpayer identification number for the trust for either (1) the first taxable year in which the trust, or any part of the trust is no longer a grantor trust, or (2) the first taxable year of the trust in which the trustee does not report using the grantor's social security number alternative.

3. The 1099 Trust-TIN alternative — Treas. Reg. 1.671-4(b)(2)(i)(B)

The trustee applies for a tax identification number for the trust. The trustee provides all payors of reportable income with the name, tax identification number, and address of the trust. The trustee is not required to file Form 1041, but income payers must send Form 1099s to the trust reflecting taxable income, and the trustee is required to file the Form 1099s with the IRS by the end of February, reporting the total interest, dividends, and gains and losses received on a Form 1099-INT or 1099-DIV, whichever are applicable. The applicable Form 1099 shows the trust as the payor and the grantor as both the owner of the trust and as payee. Gross proceeds of sales are reported separately for each sale on a 1099-B. Copies of the Form 1099 are not sent to the grantor. Instead, the trustee sends a statement summarizing this information to the grantor by the due date of the Form 1041. If the grantor is a trustee or co-trustee of the trust, the statement need not be furnished to the grantor. This alternative involves an extra layer of administrative duties i.e., issuance of Form 1099s from the trust to the IRS.

III. Section 672 — Grantor Trust Definitions and Rules

Internal Revenue Code : Section 672

Regulations: 1.672(a)-1; 1.672(b)-1; 1.672(c)-1

In the grantor trust context, the purpose of Code § 672 is to describe relevant rules and definitions. Code §§ 672(a) through (c) define key terms such as "adverse party," "nonadverse party" and "related or subordinate party." The rules describing when conditions precedent must be satisfied to exercise a grantor power are found in Code § 672(d). Next, important rules addressing the role of the grantor's spouse are described in Code § 672(e). Finally, rules addressing grantor trusts with domestic beneficiaries and foreign grantors are found in Code § 672(f).

A. Adverse Party

Throughout the grantor trust rules, distinctions are made between an "adverse party" and a "nonadverse party." Often, the presence of an adverse party is significant because the grantor may be protected from a finding of grantor trust treatment (and required income taxation of the grantor) if a particular power of the grantor may only be exercised with the consent of or in conjunction with an adverse party. Conversely, under the various grantor trust provisions of Code §§ 673 through 678, if a nonadverse party holds a power over a trust, even if the grantor does not hold that power, the grantor may be treated as the owner of the trust; furthermore, if only the consent of a nonadverse party to a particular action of the grantor is required, the grantor may also be treated as the owner of the trust. Clearly, then, the distinction between an adverse party and a nonadverse party is significant.

The term "adverse party" requires a person to have a beneficial interest in the trust. It is defined to mean "any person having a substantial beneficial interest in the trust which would be adversely affected by the exercise or non-exercise of the power which he possesses respecting the trust." Code § 672(a). A "nonadverse party" is defined broadly as any person who is not an adverse party. Code § 672(b).

As the definition of adverse party indicates, the presence of a beneficial interest for such party is an essential element of the definition. Accordingly, a trust beneficiary will be an adverse party, if the beneficiary holds a general power of appointment over the trust. The interest of the beneficiary may be adverse with respect to the entire trust or be limited to either the income or principal portion of the trust, depending on whether the beneficiary is an income or a remainder beneficiary. If the beneficiary holds its partial interest in a trust (such as an interest in the income only, or in the principal only, or in a contingent remainder interest only), the beneficiary may be an adverse party only with respect to that part of the trust. Treas. Reg. 1.672(a)-1(a), 1.672(a)-1(b.) A remainderman may have an interest adverse to the exercise of a power over the trust principal, but not adverse to the exercise of a power over an income interest that precedes his or her remainder interest. Treas. Reg. 1.672(a)-1(d).

The cases recognize a presumption that any adverse party will act in his or her own best interests, independent of the wishes or desires of the grantor, regardless of the identity of the adverse party or the relationship between the adverse party and the grantor. Members of the grantor's family and the grantor's close friends can be considered adverse parties when they have substantial interests in a trust that are adverse to the exercise or non-exercise of a power held by the grantor or by an adverse party. *Savage v. Comm'r*, 82 F.2d 92 (3d Cir.1936).

In order for an interest to be considered adverse to the grantor's interest, it must be adverse to the exercise or non-exercise of the power held by the grantor or by a nonadverse party over the income or principal of the trust. It is not enough for just a relationship to be adverse — it is the actual interest in the trust that must be adverse. It is certainly possible for a party with a partial share in a trust to be adverse to the grantor only as to that partial share of the trust. Treas. Reg. 1.672(a)-1(b); 1.672(a)-1(d). A "beneficial interest" requires the adverse interest to be economically adverse.[2]

> **Example:** Alice, Brenda, Carrie, and Donna are equal income beneficiaries of a trust. Sam is the grantor of the trust and has the right to revoke the trust with the consent of Alice. In this situation, Sam is treated as the owner of three-fourths of the trust since only Alice is an adverse party with respect to Sam. Accordingly, the items of income, deduction, and credit attributable to the three-fourths interest in the trust are included in determining Sam's income tax liability. Treas. Reg. 1.672(a)-1(b).

A trustee is not an adverse party merely because of having an interest as trustee. Being a trustee in and of itself does not convey a beneficial interest in the trust. Having a right to fees and commissions as a fiduciary does not convey a beneficial interest in the trust. Treas. Reg. 1.672(a)-1(a); *Reinecke v. Smith*, 289 U.S. 172 (1933); *Duffy v. United States*, 487 F.2d 282 (6th Cir. 1973), *cert. denied,* 416 U.S. 938 (1974). For a trustee to be considered as an adverse party, the trustee must also possess a substantial beneficial interest in the trust that would be adversely affected by the exercise or non-exercise of one or more of the powers granted to the trustee.

> **Example:** Grantor creates a trust that provides the trustee with the power to distribute all of the income and principal of the trust to himself or herself. The trustee will be considered to be an adverse party to the grantor. *Estate of Paxton v. Commissioner*, 44 T.C.M. 771 (1982). Alternatively, if the trustee occupies merely an administrative role, and lacks discretion with respect to the beneficial interests in the trust, the trustee will not be considered an adverse party even if the trustee is also a beneficiary of the trust.

Another important component of the definition of an adverse party is the requirement that the interest of the person holding the beneficial interest must be "substantial." An interest is a substantial interest if its value in relation to the total value of the property subject to the power held by the adverse party is not insignificant. Treas. Reg. 1.672(a)-1(a). This limited guidance offered by the regulations has led to a number of cases attempting to define the meaning of a "substantial" beneficial interest. The cases typically depend on an analysis of the particular facts and circumstances. Where the interest of the beneficiary is wholly discretionary in the judgment of the trustee, the beneficiary does not have a substantial beneficial interest; however, where persons were both beneficiaries and also members of a

2. Attribution rules, such as those found in Code § 318, are not applied to determine if a beneficiary has an interest in a trust.

distribution committee, they were found to have adverse interests in the trust. Priv. Ltr. Ruls. 200731019 (May 1, 2007), 200729025 (April 10, 2007), 200247013 (Aug. 14, 2002) and 200148028 (Aug. 27, 2001). Where the interest of the potential adverse party is remote and contingent, the cases indicate that the interest of such party is not "substantial." *Holt v. United States*, 669 F. Supp. 751 (W.D. Va. 1987), *aff'd*, 842 F.2d 1291 (4th Cir. 1988); *Barker v. Comm'r*, 25 T.C. 1230 (1956); *Chase National Bank v. Comm'r*, 225 F.2d 621 (8th Cir. 1955), *cert. denied*, 350 U.S. 965 (1956). However, an interest that is contingent as opposed to immediately vested is not automatically considered an "insignificant" interest. Actuarial calculations may be necessary in order to determine the potential significance of a contingent interest. Treas. Reg. 1.672(a)-1(c). Where an apparent adverse interest proves to be a sham (such as when the apparently adverse party has agreed in advance that the adverse interest will not be exercised) such an interest will be disregarded for purposes of the grantor trust rules. *Wesenberg v. Comm'r*, 69 T.C. 1005 (1978).

B. Related or Subordinate Party

There are situations arising under the grantor trust rules where so-called "independent trustees" are permitted to exercise certain powers without causing the grantor to be taxed as the owner of the trust. To be an "independent trustee," the trustee cannot be an adverse party and cannot be considered a related or subordinate party to the grantor.

Defined in Code § 672(c), the phrase "related or subordinate party" means any nonadverse party who is either the grantor's spouse if living with the grantor; the grantor's father, mother, issue, brother or sister (including brothers and sisters of the half-blood, see Rev. Rul. 58-19, 1958-1 C.B. 251); an employee of the grantor; a corporation or any employee of a corporation in which the stockholdings of the grantor and the trust are significant from the viewpoint of voting control; or a subordinate employee of a corporation in which the grantor is an executive. All of these persons are presumed to be subservient to the grantor with respect to the exercise or non-exercise of the powers conferred on them unless shown to not be subservient by a preponderance of the evidence. Code § 672(c); Treas. Reg. 1.672(c)-1. Other relatives, such as step-brothers and step-sisters, nieces, nephews, cousins, grandparents, grandchildren and in-laws are not included in the definition of related or subordinate parties.[3]

3. If the grantor possesses a power to remove a trustee and appoint a successor trustee who is not considered "related or subordinate" to the grantor within the meaning of Code § 672(c), the grantor will not be considered to have retained a power to affect the beneficial enjoyment of the trust property that will result in estate tax inclusion under Code § 2036 or 2038. It is essential here that the grantor does not retain a power to appoint him or herself as a successor trustee. Rev. Rul. 95-58, 1995-2 C.B. 191; *Estate of Wall v. Commissioner*, 101 T.C. 300 (1993).

In order to rebut the presumption that a related or subordinate party acting as trustee is subservient to the grantor, the person making such a claim has the burden of proving that the trustee was not acting in accordance with the grantor's wishes. S. Rep. No. 1622, 83d Cong. 2d Sess. 87 (1954). A person who is serving as a corporate director is not, absent other evidence, considered an employee of the corporation, even where the holdings of the grantor and the trust are significant in terms of voting control. Rev. Rul. 66-160, 1966-1 C.B. 164. Nor does a partner of the grantor automatically fall within the definition of related or subordinate party. Similarly, persons who serve the grantor in the roles of accountant or attorney are generally independent contractors, not employees, so such persons should not be considered related or subordinate parties, even in situations where such "independent" persons allow the grantor to make virtually all of the decisions involving the trust. *Goodwyn Estate v. Comm'r*, 35 T.C.M. 1026 (1976).

There have been a number of rulings issued addressing the question of whether a family-owned private trust company is a related or subordinate party. The rulings address situations where the families involved have been careful to require a separation between the ownership of interests in property and acting on discretionary distribution committees where those property interests are involved. Where this separation is successfully accomplished, grantor trust characterization is avoided. In the fact patterns of the rulings, various trust grantors did not own any (or a significant amount of) interests in the stock of the private trust company. Only truly independent persons served on the distribution committees. In some situations, the members of the distribution committees had substantial beneficial interests in the income and corpus of the trusts, making them adverse parties. While the rulings are conditioned on the usual "particular facts and circumstances" limitations, they do provide guidance for persons wishing to use a private trust company as trustee and avoid attribution of the ownership of the trust to the grantor. Notice 2008-63, 2008-2 C.B. 261; Priv. Ltr. Ruls. 200637025 (June 5, 2006), 200546052 (Aug. 2, 2005), 200546053 (Aug. 2, 2005), 200546054 (Aug. 2, 2005), 200546055 (Aug. 2, 2005).

C. Grantor Power Limited by a Condition Precedent

A person is considered to have a power as the grantor of a trust even if this power is subject to limitations. The Code specifies two limitations which are ineffectual to preclude grantor trust status: (i) a condition precedent of the giving of notice or (ii) where an interest takes effect only after a certain time after the exercise of the power. Code § 672(d). These provisions are designed to reduce or eliminate any opportunity for a grantor to attempt to manipulate the rules by distinguishing a presently exercisable power from a contingent power.

> **Example:** Kelly is the grantor of a trust for the benefit of her daughter Carol. Kelly retains the power to revoke the trust, but provides that the revocation is effective only after the expiration of three years from the date she

exercises the power. Kelly will be treated as the owner of the trust from the date of its inception. Treas. Reg. 1.672(d)-1.

D. Powers and Interests Held by the Grantor's Spouse

For purposes of the grantor trust rules, the grantor is treated as holding any power or interest held by any individual who was the spouse of the grantor at the time of the creation of such power or interest, or any individual who became the spouse of the grantor after the creation of such power or interest, but only with respect to those time periods after such individual became the grantor's spouse. Code § 672(e)(1).

An individual legally separated from a spouse under a decree of divorce or separate maintenance when the power or interest in the trust is created shall not be considered as married. Code § 672(e)(2). Accordingly, it is not necessary to have terminated the marriage by a formal divorce decree to prevent the application of the grantor trust rules.

It is important to note here that a person who is married at the time the transfer in trust occurs is deemed to hold the powers and interests in the trust held by his or her spouse, even if the parties later divorce. Priv. Ltr. Rul. 9625021 (March, 20, 1996). Code § 672(e)'s test for marital status is applied when the trust is created. There is nothing in the law to allow a later retest if there is a change in marital status. If the transfer in trust is made after marital dissolution, then the parties are considered not married for purposes of the application of the grantor trust rules.

As part of the 1986 Tax Reform Act, Congress added Code § 672(e). There was a concern that a grantor could circumvent the application of the grantor trust rules by giving his or her spouse powers or interests in the trust that the grantor could not hold directly. The legislative history of Code § 672(e) indicates that it is applicable only in cases where the spouse is living with the grantor and able to file a joint income tax return with the grantor for the relevant period.

One of the principal effects of the enactment of the spousal attribution rules is to prevent the grantor's spouse from ever being treated as an adverse party, since any power or interest which might otherwise make the spouse an adverse party is directly imputed to the grantor.

Questions

1. John owns 100 shares of IBM stock that pays an annual dividend of $800. John directs IBM to pay the dividend to his daughter, Mary, for the next five years. Who is taxed on the dividend income?

2. Laverne creates a trust and names her brother, Lewis as trustee. Is he considered a related or subordinate party? What if the trust provides all income is to be paid annually to Laverne's daughter, Jasmine, with principal payable to Jasmine when she turns age 25? Is Lewis an adverse party in this situation?

3. Evan creates a trust for the benefit of his two children, Ann and Bill. The trust provides that the trustee has discretion to distribute the income to either Ann or Bill, or both. Evan names his office manager, Fran, as the trustee. Is Fran a related or subordinate party? Is Fran an adverse party? What if instead of Fran, Evan named his attorney, Nancy, as the trustee. Is Nancy related or subordinate? Is she adverse?

IV. Section 673—Retention of a Reversionary Interest

Internal Revenue Code: Section 673

Regulation: 1.673(a)-1

Section 673 provides that the grantor is treated as the owner of any portion of a trust in which the grantor has a reversionary interest in the trust income or principal that has a value, determined at the inception of the trust, *i.e.*, the date of transfer of property to the trust, in excess of five percent of the value of the trust property. Code § 673(a). The same rule applies to a reversionary interest held by the grantor's spouse, since the grantor is treated as the owner of any interest his or her spouse owns. Code § 672(e). If the grantor is treated as the owner of a portion of the trust, all of the trust's income, attributes, etc. would be treated as belonging to the grantor or to the grantor's spouse, as if no trust had been created. Code § 673.

A. Background on How Code § 673 Evolved

The "old" Code § 673 was the Code Section that provided the "roadmap" for the preparation of what was known for many years as a "Clifford Trust," *i.e.*, a trust by which the grantor transferred property for the benefit of a beneficiary for a period of at least ten years, the beneficiary became the taxpayer, after which period the trust property could then revert to the grantor. This was the response of Congress to the decision of the Supreme Court in *Clifford v. Helvering*, 309 U.S. 331 (1940), which held the grantor taxable on the income of an irrevocable trust in which the grantor retained significant control and which was to terminate in the grantor's favor after a five-year term. Congress allowed a transferred interest of ten years to counter the Court's holding. If the ten-year test of delaying the reversion was satisfied, the grantor was *not* taxed on the trust income under the old grantor trust rules, and had effectively shifted the taxation of the trust income to the beneficiary, a person presumably in a lower income tax bracket. The "old" Code § 673 and the use of the ten-year Clifford Trust was a legislative guideline to a very popular acceptable avoidance of the assignment of income doctrine.

As written, the "old" Code § 673(c) provided that the grantor would be treated as the owner of any portion of a trust in which he or she had a reversionary interest in either the trust corpus or the income therefrom if, as of the inception of that portion of the trust, the interest will or may reasonably be expected to take effect in possession or enjoyment within ten years commencing with the date of the transfer of that portion of the trust. "Old" Code § 673 also included an exception to the effect that if the reversion to the grantor only occurred as the result of the death of the income beneficiary (regardless of the actuarial life expectancy of the income beneficiary), such reversion would not make the grantor the owner of the trust for income tax purposes. Every addition to the trust and/or extension of the trust term was treated as a new transfer that had to meet the tests of "old" Code § 673(a). The repeal of "old" Code § 673 and its replacement by current Code § 673 was a repudiation of the "permitted" assignment of income exception, and the institution of a rule causing the grantor to be treated as the owner of a trust for income tax purposes if almost any reversionary interest is retained.

When the current Code § 673 was adopted, it became effective only with respect to trusts created after March 1, 1986. The previous version of Code § 673 continues to apply to trusts created on and before March 1, 1986. Many, if not all of those trusts (especially if designed as limited to ten-year trusts) have now terminated, but if a grantor opted for a delayed reversion term well in excess of the ten year minimum statutory period, it is possible that the "old" version of Code § 673 is still applicable to these trusts.

Despite possible distinctions between the "old" rules and the new rules of Code § 673, and the outcome of the actuarial calculations to be performed, if a grantor retains a reversionary interest in the principal of a trust, the grantor will be treated as the owner of the principal of such trust, even if the five percent reversion rule of Code § 673 is not violated. A grantor will be treated as the owner of any portion of a trust the income of which is or may be held or accumulated for future distribution to the grantor or the grantor's spouse. Where such items as capital gains are allocated to the trust principal under the trust instrument or local law, they are being held or accumulated for future distribution to the grantor as holder of the reversionary interest in the trust principal. Code § 677(a)(2); Treas. Regs. 1.673(a)-1(a); 1.677(a)-1(g), Ex. 2. Accordingly, while Code § 673 determines whether the retention of a reversionary interest alone makes a trust a grantor trust, Code § 677(a)(2) is a broader inclusion provision that may require a finding of grantor trust status even if Code § 673 does not. This suggests a note of caution to be raised for persons drafting trusts designed to minimize a reversionary interest so as to avoid Code § 673, since Code § 677 may cast a broader net. *See* the discussion of Code § 677 in Section VIII, below.

B. The Reversionary Interest

A reversionary interest is an interest retained by the grantor in the trust property that will allow the grantor to recover either the principal of the trust or the income arising therefrom. For example, if a grantor creates a trust, transfers property to the trust for the benefit of a beneficiary, and provides that upon the death of the beneficiary or upon the expiration of a fixed number of years, the transferred property returns to the grantor, the grantor has retained a reversionary interest. If the actuarial value of the reversionary exceeds five percent, a grantor retaining such a reversionary interest will be treated as the owner of the entire trust from its inception. Treas. Reg. 1.671-3(b)(3); Priv. Ltr. Rul. 9519029 (Feb. 10, 1995).

C. Determining the 5 Percent Interest

The five percent reversionary interest is computed in accordance with standard actuarial principles. It is calculated by considering the maximum amount that the grantor could receive upon the termination of the trust. Code § 673(c). Code § 7520 and the regulations thereunder include actuarial tables that apply to reversionary interests that become possessory upon the expiration of a fixed period of time or at the death of a specified person or persons. The actuarial tables are based on the prevailing interest rates at the time the transfer occurs, using the monthly updated applicable federal rate (AFR) issued by the IRS. As a general rule, when interest rates are low, a longer term of the trust will be necessary to fall below the five percent reversionary interest threshold; conversely, in a higher interest rate environment, a shorter term of the trust will yield a reversionary interest that falls below the five percent interest threshold. The actuarial tables are also influenced by mortality rates. While variations will occur depending upon the fluctuations in the applicable interest rate, it presently appears that even using the highest AFRs in the IRS tables, a reversionary interest must be delayed in the range of 28 to 32 years if it is to be worth five percent or less of the value of the transferred property. Treas. Reg. 20.2031-7(d)(6), Table B.

When determining the value of the grantor's reversionary interest, it is to be assumed that if there is any discretion exercisable in favor of the grantor, such discretion will be exercised in the grantor's favor to the maximum possible extent. Code § 673(c).

> **Example:** The grantor creates and funds a trust with a duration of 20 years for the benefit of the grantor's children with distributions to be made in the discretion of the trustee, after which time the trust property will revert to the grantor or the grantor's estate. In determining the value of the grantor's interest under Code § 673, it must be assumed that no distributions are made to the grantor's children during the 20-year term of the trust. Assume when the trust is created, the prevailing Code § 7520 rate is 6.2 percent. The value of the reversionary interest would be approximately 30 percent, clearly greater than five percent, and the trust would be a grantor trust. If instead, the term of the trust was 50 years, the value of the reversionary interest would have been approximately 4.9 percent, clearly less than five percent, and the trust would not be a grantor trust. Alternatively, when using a 4.0 percent interest rate instead of a 6.2 percent rate, the actuarial

value of a remainder interest is 5.0754 percent following a term certain of 76 years; the actuarial value of a remainder interest is 4.8801 percent following a term certain of 77 years. Rev. Rul. 76-178, 1976-1 C.B. 273.

As a general rule, the grantor's health is irrelevant in applying the rules of the actuarial tables indicated above. There is, however, an exception for situations when the grantor is terminally ill. A person suffering from an incurable disease or other deteriorating physical condition is considered terminally ill if there is at least a 50 percent probability that the individual will die within one year. Actual physical condition *is* relevant in determining the value of an interest for income tax purposes. Treas. Reg. 1.7520-3(b)(3). In such a case, the IRS can ignore the results of the actuarial tables. This exception is modified by an additional rule providing that an individual who survives 18 months or longer after the date of the property transfer is presumed not to have been terminally ill, absent clear and convincing evidence to the contrary. Where this exception applies, the IRS is required to use the actuarial tables to value the interest contingent upon the individual's life expectancy. Treas. Reg. 1.7520(b)(3); *Miami Beach First National Bank v. United States*, 443 F.2d 116 (5th Cir. 1971); Priv. Ltr. Rul. 9402011 (October 8, 1993). In these circumstances, it is worthwhile to obtain a physician's certification addressing the probability of death. *Fabric Estate v. Comm'r*, 83 T.C. 932 (1984).

A difficult valuation problem may arise where the trust beneficiary possesses a power of appointment over the trust property. Must (or should) the possibility that the beneficiary could affirmatively exercise that power in favor of the grantor be taken into account in determining the value of a reversionary interest of the grantor? Arguably, yes. Code § 673(c) provides that the value of the grantor's reversionary interest shall be determined by assuming the maximum exercise of discretion by the power holder in favor of the grantor.

D. Exception for Lineal Descendants Who Die Before Age 21

A possible reversionary interest in the grantor or the grantor's spouse that follows the death of a lineal descendant of the grantor or the grantor's spouse prior to such descendant attaining age 21 will not be counted to attribute grantor trust status provided the lineal descendant holds all of the present interests in any portion of the trust, unless and until the reversion actually occurs. Code § 673(b). This exception enables income earned by a Code § 2503(c) trust, an irrevocable trust created for the benefit of a minor the proceeds of which must be held or used for the minor until attaining age 21 and then distributed to the minor. to be taxed to the minor beneficiary of the trust rather than to the grantor. Thus, a traditional Code § 2503(c) trust should not be a grantor trust merely because the grantor or the grantor's spouse will receive the trust funds back if the income beneficiary dies before attaining 21—assuming the reversion was not the result of the exercise of a general power of appointment contained in the trust document.

Questions

1. Grantor created a trust in 1980, providing that all of the trust income would be payable to Grantor's daughter for 10 years and one month, and thereafter the trust was to terminate and the property returned to Grantor. Who was taxable on the income of this trust?
2. In Question 1, assume the facts are identical, with the exception that Grantor created the trust in 1990. Who was taxable on the income of this trust?
3. Grantor creates a trust in the current year for S, Grantor's son. S is age 7. All of the trust income is to be paid to S for his lifetime. In the event of S's death, the trust is directed to terminate. If S dies before attaining age 21, the trust property is to be paid to Grantor, if then living, or to Grantor's spouse if then living. Otherwise, the trust property is payable to S's estate. Does Grantor have a reversionary interest in this trust under Code § 673?

V. Section 674—Power to Control Beneficial Enjoyment

Internal Revenue Code: Section 674

Regulations: 1.674(a)-1 through 1.674(d)-2

Code § 674 provides a broad general rule making a trust a grantor trust where the grantor has the power to dispose of or affect the beneficial enjoyment of the trust for himself or herself or others, without prevention by an adverse party.

The broad general rule is then subjected to a series of exceptions that modify the general rule by enumerating circumstances allowing the grantor, independent trustees, or certain others to exercise specific powers over the trust that do not confer grantor trust status on the grantor.

A. The General Rule of Code § 674(a)

Code § 674(a) provides that the grantor is treated as the owner of any portion of a trust in respect of which the beneficial enjoyment of the trust, *i.e.*, the principal or income therefrom, is subject to a "power of disposition," exercisable by the grantor, the grantor's spouse, or a nonadverse party, without the approval or consent of any adverse party. The adverse party is an important consideration here. If, for example, a co-trustee is also a beneficiary who is adverse to the exercise of a power by the grantor over the trust, and if the trust requires the trustees to act unanimously, Code § 674(a) would not be applicable.

A "power of disposition" requires further explication. The Treasury Regulations and IRS view it to include a fiduciary power, a power of appointment, and any other power to direct the enjoyment of the benefits of the trust, regardless of the capacity in which the power is held, and regardless of whether the power holder can personally benefit. Treas. Reg. 1.674(a)-1; Priv. Ltr. Ruls. 200730011 (July 27, 2007) and 9625021 (March 20, 1996).

A power to affect the beneficial enjoyment of a trust has been broadly interpreted by case law. Several cases and a revenue ruling illustrate this point:

- The grantor's retained right to alter or amend the trust documents was sufficient to treat the grantor as the trust owner under Code § 674 even though such a right could only be exercised in the capacity of a trustee, with no personal benefit possible for the grantor. *Swanson v. Commissioner*, 518 F.2d 59 (8th Cir. 1975).
- A power to allocate income between or among trust beneficiaries is a power of disposition over beneficial enjoyment regardless of whether the grantor is a permissible recipient. Rev. Rul. 54-41, 1954-1 C.B. 22.
- The grantor's retaining a direct or indirect power to "sprinkle" income and principal of a trust will result in the finding of grantor trust status. *Carson v. Commissioner*, 92 T.C. 1134 (1989).
- The right to use the property of the trust without paying adequate compensation for it is a power of disposition over the beneficial enjoyment of the trust, classifying the trust as a grantor trust. *Wesenberg v. Commissioner*, 69 T.C. 1005 (1978), *nonacq*. 1978-2 C.B. 4.
- The power to determine which beneficiary would be the recipient of income is a power to affect beneficial enjoyment. *Laganas v. Commissioner*, 281 F.2d 731 (1st Cir. 1960).
- When a grantor borrowed money from a bank and loaned the borrowed funds to a trust, with the funds repayable to the grantor on demand, the court found the grantor taxable on the trust's income under Code § 674(a) because the demand power gave the grantor the power to control the beneficial enjoyment of the trust corpus at any time. *Wysong v. Commissioner*, T.C. Memo 1988-344.

Example: Greg creates a trust for the benefit of Ann and Bart. The remainder will pass to Bart on Ann's death. Greg names his wife, Wendy, as the trustee and gives her the power to distribute income and principal to Ann or Bart for any purpose. This is a power to alter or control the beneficial enjoyment of both the income and principal of the trust. While Wendy cannot exercise the power in favor of Greg, under Code § 672(e) all powers held by Greg's wife are deemed to be held by Greg. As a result, he is treated as having the power to alter or control the beneficial enjoyment of the trust and, therefore, for income tax purposes, the trust is treated as a grantor trust even though Greg personally has not retained any direct right to alter or control the beneficial enjoyment of the trust.

Example: Assume the same facts as above except that the trust now provides that Wendy and Ann serve as co-trustees, and that the trustees, acting jointly, have the power to distribute *income* to Ann or Bart, or both, but may not exercise this power in favor of Greg. The trust is not treated as a grantor trust with respect to the fiduciary accounting income because the power to alter or control the beneficial enjoyment of the income interest is exercisable only with the consent of an adverse party (Ann). However, with respect to principal, the trust is treated as a grantor trust because the power to alter or control the beneficial enjoyment of the principal is not subject to the consent or approval of an adverse party.

The breadth of Code § 674(a) is so broad that if standing alone it would require almost every trust involving any grantor rights or powers to be treated as a grantor trust. However, exceptions to the general rule of Code § 674(a) are found in §§ 674(b), (c), and (d). More specifically, there are exceptions from the general rule for certain powers which the grantor or any other person may hold set forth in Code § 674(b); there are exceptions for powers which a nonadverse, independent trustee may exercise as set forth in Code § 674(c), and there is an exception for a power which a non-independent, non-adverse trustee (other than the grantor or the grantor's spouse) may exercise as indicated in Code § 674(d). All of these exceptions allow actions that affect the beneficial enjoyment of the trust without causing the grantor to be treated as the owner of the trust.

B. Exceptions to the General Rule of Code § 674(a) Under Code § 674(b)

Internal Revenue Code: Section 674(b)

Regulations: 1.674(b)-1(b)(1), 1.674(d)-2

Code § 674(b) contains eight exceptions to the general rule. The exceptions describe powers that can be held by any person, including the grantor, without causing the grantor to be taxable as the owner of the trust.

1. Power to Apply Income to Discharge a Legal Support Obligation

A grantor is not taxable as the owner of a trust just because another person, the trustee or the grantor acting as trustee or co-trustee possesses a power to use trust income to discharge a legal support obligation of the grantor. Instead, the grantor is taxable as the trust's owner only to the extent the trust income is actually used to discharge a support obligation as described in Code § 677(b). Treas. Reg. 1.677(b)-1. State law determines the extent of the grantor's support obligation. Rev. Rul. 56-484, 1956-2 C.B. 23. If the distribution that satisfies the grantor's support obligation is made from principal, the tax consequences of the distribution are governed by the normal rules of Subchapter J, i.e., Code §§ 661 and 662.

If the grantor possesses this power in a nonfiduciary capacity, mere possession of the power alone will cause the grantor to be taxed on the trust income whether or not the trust income is used to support the grantor's dependents. Code § 674(b)(1) only protects the grantor when serving as a trustee of the trust.

> **Example:** Gary is the grantor of his trust and retains the right to require the trustee to distribute income for the health, education, maintenance, and support of his children. Gary is not a trustee of the trust. No distributions are made to Gary's children during the year. The trust is a grantor trust. The Code § 674(b) exception does not apply because the power to distribute income can be exercised by Gary in a nonfiduciary capacity.

2. Power Affecting Beneficial Enjoyment Only After the Occurrence of an Event

A postponed power to affect a trust's beneficial enjoyment creates a grantor trust unless it is postponed for a period which, were it a reversionary interest, would be protected from grantor trust status because the reversionary interest is 5% or less. Unless the power is relinquished, the grantor will be taxed on the income after the occurrence of the event. Code § 674(b)(2); Treas. Reg. 1.674(b)-1(b)(2).

> **Example:** Linda creates a trust at a time when the Code § 7520 rate is four percent. Income is to be paid to Ryan for 20 years. At the expiration of the 20-year period, Linda will have discretion to determine who receives the income of the trust. Under Code § 674(b)(2), although Linda can only exercise her power after 20 years have elapsed from the date of the trust's creation, Linda is still deemed to own the entire trust from its inception since the value of her reversionary interest in the trust is greater than five percent.

3. Power Exercisable Only by Will

A power exercisable only by a person's will is another exception to the general rule of Code § 674(a). This exception applies regardless of the nature of the power and applies even in the case where the grantor or a nonadverse party, or both, hold the power and such power may be exercised without the approval or consent of an adverse party.

> **Example:** Paul creates an irrevocable trust and names his friend, Larry, as the trustee. The trust provides that Paul, by his will, may appoint the principal of the trust among his children. Paul will not be taxed as the owner of this trust.

This exception, however, is subject to the following limitations (which constitute exceptions to the exception and thus result in grantor trust status):

(1) This exception does not apply to income accumulated for testamentary disposition by the grantor;

(2) This exception does not apply to income that may be accumulated for testamentary disposition by the grantor in the discretion of the grantor or a nonadverse party, or both, without the approval or consent of an adverse party; and

(3) If a trust instrument provides that the income (referring to taxable income here, not fiduciary accounting income) is payable to another person for life, but the grantor (or the grantor's spouse) retains a testamentary power of appointment (general or limited) over the remainder, and under the trust instrument and local law capital gains are added to principal, the grantor is treated as the owner of a portion of the trust and capital gains and losses are included in that portion. Treas. Reg. 1.674(b)-1(b)(3); 1.671-3.

> **Example:** Gina creates a trust during her lifetime. The trustee is given discretion to pay the income to Brian or accumulate it during Brian's lifetime. Gina retains the power to appoint the trust principal and any accumulated income by her will. The trust is a grantor trust. The Code § 674(b)(3) exception would not apply and Gina's retained power to control the trust property would subject Gina to taxation under the general rule of Code § 674(a).

4. Power to Allocate Among Charitable Beneficiaries

The general rule of Code § 674(a) will not apply if any person has a power to allocate the beneficial enjoyment of the trust principal or income among charitable beneficiaries where the trust is irrevocably designated for charitable purposes specified in Code § 170(c) (relating to the definition of charitable contributions). Thus, a grantor can create a trust with an irrevocable gift of the income or principal to charity and retain a power to designate which charities will receive distributions from the trust and how much they will receive. For example, a grantor can retain the right to designate the remainder beneficiaries of a charitable remainder trust and the trust will not be treated as a grantor trust. Grantor trust status will also not be found if the grantor has retained the discretion to "sprinkle" the trust income or principal among the charities described in Code § 170. If the grantor also retained the power to designate noncharitable beneficiaries of the same funds, this exception to the general rule of Code § 674(a) would not apply and grantor status would be found.

> **Example:** Norman creates a trust which provides that the trust income and principal are irrevocably payable solely to religious or educational institutions that are qualified charitable organizations under Code § 170(c). Norman is not treated as the owner of the trust under Code § 674(a) even though he retains the power to allocate the income and principal among such organizations in his discretion.

> **Example:** Norman creates a second trust which is designed and qualifies as a charitable lead annuity trust. He names his friend, Lon, as the trustee of this trust. Lon is given full discretion to determine the charitable beneficiaries of this trust. Although Lon is a nonadverse trustee, since the trust beneficiaries are charitable organizations, the power of allocation given to Lon does not cause grantor trust status to be applied to Norman. Priv. Ltr. Ruls. 9604015 (Oct. 27, 1995) and 9604016 (Oct. 27, 1995).

5. Power to Distribute Principal

Code § 674(b)(5) provides two additional exceptions to the general rule of Code § 674(a) with respect to the power to distribute the principal of a trust. The first provides that grantor trust treatment will not apply to a power to distribute principal either to or for a beneficiary or class of beneficiaries whether or not they are income beneficiaries or remaindermen, provided that the power is limited by a reasonably definite standard which is set forth in the trust instrument. Code § 674(b)(5)(A). The second applies when principal distributions may be made solely in favor of current income beneficiaries, provided that the principal distributions are required to be charged against those beneficiaries' proportionate shares of the trust principal held in trust for payment of income to that beneficiary, as if the principal constituted a separate trust whether or not it was physically segregated. Code § 674(b)(5)(B); Treas. Reg. 1.674(b)-1(b)(5).

> **Example:** Karen creates a trust providing for the payment of income to her adult children in equal shares for 10 years, after which the principal is to be distributed to her grandchildren in equal shares. Karen reserves the power to pay each child up to one-half of the trust principal during the 10-year period, but if such payments are made, they will proportionately reduce subsequent income and principal payments made to the child receiving the principal. If one-half of the principal is paid to one child, all of the income from the remaining half is thereafter payable to the other child. In this situation, Karen is not treated as the owner of the trust since it qualifies under the Code § 674(b)(5)(B) exception. Treas. Reg. 1.674 (b)-1(b)(5)(iii), Ex. 3.

Note that these two exceptions apply to the enumerated powers regardless of by whom they are held, meaning that the grantor or a nonadverse party or both may hold these powers without requiring the approval or consent of an adverse party, and still avoid incurring grantor trust status. If a trust has only one beneficiary, then the grantor, or the grantor's spouse, or a nonadverse party can have complete discretion to distribute principal to a current income beneficiary without having the trust declared a grantor trust. If a trust has but a single beneficiary, principal distributions will necessarily be charged against such beneficiary's share of trust principal. The permissible distributees must be either income beneficiaries or remaindermen. The exception does not apply if the power could be exercised in favor of a person who was not otherwise a beneficiary of the trust. Treas. Reg. 1.674(b)-1(b)(5)(iii), Ex. 1.

The "reasonably definite standard" exception will not apply, however, if any person has a right or power to add to the named beneficiaries or to a class of beneficiaries designated to receive the trust income or principal, except in the case where the additions are only to provide for after-born or after-adopted children as beneficiaries. The regulations clarify this point by indicating that in order to trigger grantor trust status, this power (to add beneficiaries) must be held by a non-adverse party.

If a non-adverse party has the power to add beneficiaries, other than after-born or after-adopted children, the trust will be treated as owned by the grantor of the trust. Treas. Reg. 1.674(d)-(2)(b).

The regulations do offer some guidance as to what is meant by a "reasonably definite standard." Treas. Reg. 1.674(b)-1(b)(5). The entire context and intent of a provision of a trust instrument creating a power must be considered in determining whether the power is limited by a reasonably definite standard. It is not required that the standard consist of the needs and circumstances of the beneficiary. A clearly measurable standard under which the holder of a power is legally accountable is deemed a reasonably definite standard for these purposes. A power to distribute trust principal for the education, support, maintenance, or health of the beneficiary, for the reasonable support and comfort of the beneficiary, or to enable the beneficiary to maintain an accustomed standard of living or to meet an emergency would all be considered limited by a reasonably definite standard. However, a power to distribute principal for the pleasure, desire or happiness of a beneficiary is not limited by a reasonably definite standard. There is no reasonably definite standard if the exercise or non-exercise of the power is left entirely to the conclusive discretion of the trustee.[4] But if the trustee has discretion to act within the defined standard, that may be satisfactory. Treas. Reg. 1.674(b)-1(b)(5)(i); *see also United States v. DeBonchamps*, 278 F.2d 127 (9th Cir. 1960) (standard referring to "needs, maintenance and comfort" was found to be a reasonably definite standard).

> **Example:** Howard creates a trust that provides for the payment of income to his adult children for life with the principal payable to his grandchildren in equal shares. Howard reserves the power to distribute trust principal to pay medical expenses and education expenses that may be incurred by his children or his grandchildren. Howard will not be treated as the owner of this trust by reason of the reserved power to pay medical or educational expenses since it is limited by a reasonably definite standard. Alternatively, if the power reserved by Howard was the power to distribute the trust principal to his children and grandchildren for their general happiness, Howard would be treated as the owner of the trust since the power would not then be limited by a reasonably definite standard. Treas. Reg. 1.674(b)-1(b)(5)(iii), Examples 1 and 2.
>
> **Example:** If, in the above example, Howard also retained the power to add the spouses of his children as additional trust beneficiaries, the trust would be considered a grantor trust with respect to Howard. If the power was limited to add as additional beneficiaries only after-born or after-adopted children of his children, the trust would not be a grantor trust as to Howard.

4. All acts of a trustee are subject to court review so, arguably, a provision stating that a trustee's determination is to be conclusive does not necessarily make it so.

6. Power to Withhold Income Temporarily

A grantor will not be treated as the owner of a trust if any person has the power:

- To distribute fiduciary accounting income to or for any current income beneficiary; or
- To accumulate such income for such beneficiary so long as the accumulated income is distributed either (a) to the beneficiary from whom it was withheld, to the beneficiary's estate or to the beneficiary's appointees if the beneficiary possesses a power of appointment that does not exclude from the class of permissible appointees anyone other than the beneficiary, the estate of the beneficiary, the creditors of the beneficiary, and the creditors of the beneficiary's estate, or (b) on termination of the trust, or in conjunction with a distribution of principal that is augmented by such accumulated income to the current income beneficiaries in shares irrevocably specified in the trust instrument.

Example: Robert creates a trust and names his wife Joanne as the trustee. The trust provides that Joanne can pay the trust income to Robert's two adult children, or accumulate the income until each child reaches age 40, at which time all accumulated income must be paid to Robert's children. The trustee's power does not cause Robert to be treated as the owner of the trust because the accumulated income must be distributed to the beneficiaries when age 40 is attained.

The grantor or any other person is therefore permitted to divert current income from one beneficiary or class of beneficiaries to another, provided that the secondary beneficiaries are current beneficiaries of the trust and the trust clearly defines their shares. However, this exception will not apply if the power is in substance one to shift ordinary income from one beneficiary to another. Treas. Reg. 1.674(b)-1(b)(6)(i)(c). Furthermore, the exception under Code § 674(b)(6) will not apply if anyone has the power to add trust beneficiaries, other than beneficiaries who are after-born or after-adopted children.

Achieving the protection of the Code § 674(b)(6) exception from grantor trust status can thus be accomplished by providing that accumulated income will be paid to the current income beneficiary from whom it was withheld so long as the beneficiary survives to the distribution date designated by the trust. The trust must, in turn, provide for a distribution date that is reasonably expected to occur within the lifetime of such income beneficiary. The trust must also provide that should the income beneficiary die before the designated distribution date, the share allocated to the income beneficiary must pass to the estate of such beneficiary or to the appointees of the beneficiary or, in the absence of such appointees, to the takers in default of appointment, or to other beneficiaries specified irrevocably in the trust, but not to the grantor or the grantor's estate.

Example: David created a trust providing for payment of income to his adult son, Alex, with David retaining the power to accumulate the income until

David's death, at which time all accumulated income is to be paid to Alex. If Alex predeceases David, all accumulations are, at David's death, to be paid to David's son, Matthew, or if he is not living, to alternate beneficiaries (which do not include David's estate) in specified shares. The power retained by David is covered by the exception to Code § 674(a) because the date of distribution (the date of David's death) should reasonably be expected to occur during Alex's lifetime. It is not necessary for this exception to apply that the accumulations be payable to the estate of Alex or to his appointees should Alex predecease David. Treas. Reg. 1.674(b)-1(b)(6)(ii), Ex. 3.

Example: A trust provides that the income shall be payable in equal shares to George's two adult daughters, but George reserves the power to withhold from either daughter any part of that daughter's share of the income and add it to principal of the trust until the younger daughter reaches age 30. When the younger daughter reaches age 30, the trust is to terminate and the principal is to be divided equally between the two daughters or their estates. Although the exercise of the power may permit the shifting of accumulated income from one beneficiary to the other, because the principal plus all accumulated income will be divided equally, the power is excepted by Code § 674(b)(6)(B) because the shares passing to the two daughters at the termination of the trust are irrevocably set forth in the trust agreement. Thus, the grantor is not treated as owner of the trust.

Example: Assume the facts are the same as in the previous example except that George reserves the power to distribute accumulated income to the beneficiaries in such shares as he chooses. In this situation the power would not come within the exception of Code § 674(b)(6)(A) (since the income is not payable to his daughter, her estate, her appointees or takers in default set forth in the trust instrument) nor Code § 674(b)(6)(B) (since the income which may be accumulated pursuant to the power is neither required to be payable only in conjunction with the principal distribution nor is it required to be paid on shares which have been irrevocably specified in the trust instrument).

7. Power to Withhold Income During Disability of a Beneficiary

A grantor will not be treated as the owner of a trust over which any person holds a power to distribute or apply fiduciary accounting income to or for a beneficiary or to accumulate and add the income to the principal of the trust during the legal disability of any current income beneficiary or while any income beneficiary is under age 21. This exception is applicable even if the income is not ultimately distributed to the beneficiary from whom it is withheld, or to the estate or appointees of such beneficiary. Instead, the accumulated income can be added to principal and ultimately distributed to others with the exception of the grantor or the grantor's spouse. Treas. Reg. 1.674(b)-1(b)(7)(A) and (B). The term "legal disability" is not defined in the Code or in the regulations.

Query: Would delayed distributions due to substance abuse, gambling addiction, or cult membership qualify as a "legal disability"?

A power will not qualify for this exception if any person has a power to add beneficiaries or a class of beneficiaries designated to receive the income or principal of the trust, except where such action is taken to provide for beneficiaries who are after-born or after-adopted children.

> **Example:** Bill creates an irrevocable trust for the benefit of his minor daughter, Laura, to pay her the income of the trust for her lifetime, remainder to his grandchildren. If Bill reserves the power to accumulate income and add it to the principal of the trust while Laura is under age 21, he will not be treated as the owner of the trust. The trust may further provide that upon reaching age 21, the accumulated income may be paid to Laura or accumulated and added to principal so that it may never inure to her benefit but may pass to others (e.g., her children) instead. The power to accumulate income prior to the time Laura is age 21 is a power to affect the beneficial enjoyment of the trust property, but Bill is not taxed on the trust income under Code § 674(a) because of the exception of Code § 674(b)(7).

8. Power to Allocate Between Principal and Income

The general rule of Code § 674(a) does not apply to a power held by any person to allocate receipts and disbursements between principal and income, even though expressed in broad language. The Service has ruled that the power of a trustee to make a reasonable allocation to income from capital gains realized on assets that had produced limited or no income for the trust qualified for this exception and did not cause grantor trust status where state law authorized inclusion of such a power in the governing instrument. Priv. Ltr. Rul. 9442017 (July 19, 1994). This power can be significant where the income and principal beneficiaries are different persons and allocations of income and expense can benefit one interest to the detriment of the other.

> **Example:** Glen creates a trust, income to Amy for life, remainder to Bob. Glen has the power to allocate receipts and disbursements between income and principal. When an item is received by the trust, Glen exercises his power and allocates the receipt to principal meaning that, at trust termination, Bob will benefit. Glen pays a trustee's fee and charges it to income thereby reducing the income to be received by Amy for that year. The power to allocate receipts and disbursements between income and principal is a power to affect beneficial enjoyment, but Glen will not be taxed on the trust income as the result of possessing that power. The reason is Code § 674(b)(8) provides that no matter how broad the power to allocate trust receipts and disbursements between income and principal, the grantor will not be taxable on the trust's income.

C. Exceptions to the General Rule of Code § 674(a) Under Code § 674(c)

Internal Revenue Code: Section 674(c)

Regulation: 1.674(c)-1

The general rule of Code § 674(a) will not be applied in the case of certain powers that are solely exercisable without the approval or consent by any other person by trustees, none of whom is the grantor or the grantor's spouse and no more than half of whom are related or subordinate parties who are subservient to the wishes of the grantor. The powers falling within this exception include (1) the power to distribute, apportion or accumulate income to or for a beneficiary or beneficiaries, or to, for, or within a class of beneficiaries, or (2) the power to pay out principal to or for a beneficiary or beneficiaries or to or for a class of beneficiaries, whether or not they are income beneficiaries.

This is clearly a powerful exception to the general rule of Code § 674(a). Note that these are reasonably broad discretionary powers that may be exercised by a non-adverse person without the consent of an adverse person, and still avoid the grantor trust rules.

The exception provided in Code § 674(c) will not apply if any person has a power to add a beneficiary or beneficiaries to a class of beneficiaries designated to receive the income or principal of the trust, with the exception of actions taken to provide for after-born and/or after-adopted children as beneficiaries.

> **Example:** Paula creates an irrevocable trust for the benefit of her three adult children. Paula names an independent trustee and gives the trustee the power to allocate without any restrictions the amount of income to be paid to each child each year. This power will not cause Paula to be treated as the owner of the trust. Alternatively, if Paula had named herself the trustee, or one of several co-trustees and retained this power, Paula would be treated as the owner of the trust. If Paula refrained from naming herself as a trustee or as a co-trustee, but named as trustees her spouse or her sister, Paula would be taxed as the owner of the trust.

D. Exceptions to the General Rule of Code § 674(a) Under Code § 674(d)

Internal Revenue Code: Section 674(d)

Regulation: 1.674(d)-1

The general rule of Code § 674(a), which taxes the grantor as the owner of a trust to which he or she controls the beneficial enjoyment, is subject to another exception in Code § 674(d). In this case, the general rule will not apply to a power to distribute, apportion or accumulate income to or for a beneficiary or beneficiaries, or to, for, or within a class of beneficiaries if the power is limited by a "reasonably definite external standard" set forth in the trust instrument.[5] This exception is available if the power is solely exercisable without the approval or consent of any other person by a trustee or trustees, none of whom is the grantor or the grantor's spouse living with the grantor.[6] Note also that there is no prohibition under Code § 674(d) for the trustee being related or subordinate to the grantor as there is with respect to the independent trustee exception provided by Code § 674(c) discussed above.

This exception is available whether or not the conditions discussed above of Code §§ 674(b)(6) and 674(b)(7) are satisfied. However, this exception is not available if any person has a power to add to the beneficiary or beneficiaries or to a class of beneficiaries designated to receive the income or principal of the trust except where such action is to provide for after born and/or after-adopted children as beneficiaries.[7]

E. The Power to Remove a Trustee

Internal Revenue Code: Section 674(d)

Regulation: 1.674(d)-2(a)

A grantor must be careful if he or she wishes to retain a power to remove or replace a trustee. Such a power in the grantor's hands could prevent the trust from qualifying for the exceptions provided by Code §§ 674(c) and (d). If the grantor possesses a power to remove an independent trustee and substitute any person, including the grantor or the grantor's spouse as trustee, the trust will not qualify under these exceptions. Conversely, if the power of the grantor to remove, substitute or add a trustee is limited so that the exercise of this power could not alter the trust in any manner that would disqualify it under Code §§ 674(c) or (d), the existence of the power itself will not disqualify the trust from the exceptions to grantor trust status provided under these sections. Treas. Reg. 1.674(d)-2(a).

> **Example:** Ben creates a trust and names Dan, an unrelated party, as the sole trustee. Ben retains the power to remove Dan as the trustee and substitute

---

5. Note that there may be a distinction between a "reasonably definite external standard" and an "ascertainable standard." Case law and guidance from the IRS are divided as to whether provisions for an "emergency" constitute an ascertainable standard. *Compare Martin v. United States*, 780 F.2d 1147 (4th Cir. 1986), *and Estate of Sowell v. Commissioner*, 708 F.2d 1564 (10th Cir. 1983) (both finding an "emergency" acceptable as part of an ascertainable standard), *with* TAMs 8606002 (October 31, 1985); 8304009 (October 25, 1982) (both finding references to an "emergency" not part of an ascertainable standard). The distinction may turn on the totality of the words used to fashion the desired standard—but the takeaway by the student should be to be careful of the wording of a standard.

6. Note that Code § 674(d) refers to the spouse as one "living with the grantor," while Code § 674(c) does not add this "living with" requirement. Code § 674(d); Treas. Reg. 1.674(d)-1.

7. Note that there is no prohibition under Code § 674(d) for the trustee being related or subordinate to the grantor as there is with respect to the independent trustee exception provided by Code § 674(c) discussed above.

any other person, including himself, as the successor trustee. In this situation, Ben's power is too broad to permit the exceptions of Code §§ 674(c) and (d) to apply. *See Corning v. Commissioner*, 24 T.C. 907 (1955), *aff'd*, 239 F.2d 646 (6th Cir. 1956) (grantor's power to substitute trustees without cause required that the powers of the trustee be attributed to the grantor). Alternatively, suppose Ben retained the power to remove Dan as the trustee and substitute another independent trustee in Dan's place, which trustee could not be Ben or Ben's spouse. In this latter case, such a power should not affect the availability of any of the exceptions allowed under Code § 674. Similarly, if Ben named First Bank as the trustee and he retained the power to replace First Bank with another corporate trustee, such a retained power would not affect the availability of any of the exceptions allowed under Code § 674.

F. The Power to Add Beneficiaries

Regulation: 1.674(d)-2

As discussed above with respect to the various exceptions to the general rule of Code § 674(a) described in Code §§ 674(b)(5), (6) and (7) and Code §§ 674(c) and (d), these exceptions are not available if any person, whether independent or adverse, has a power to add one or more beneficiaries or to a class of beneficiaries to receive trust income or principal, except where the action is to provide for after-born and/or after-adopted children. However, this limitation does not apply to a power held by a beneficiary to substitute other beneficiaries to succeed to his or her own interest in the trust; in such a case, the beneficiary holding such a power would then become an adverse party as to the exercise or non-exercise of that power.[8]

Example: Carol is a beneficiary of a trust created by her sister, Anne. The trust is not a spendthrift trust. Carol has the right to assign her interest in the trust to her children. This right of assignment is not considered to be a power to add to the group of beneficiaries (since Carol would be an adverse party as to the exercise or non-exercise of her power), so it does not threaten to trigger grantor trust status for Anne, the grantor. Similarly, if Carol had a testamentary power of appointment to name one or more additional beneficiaries by her will, that would not be considered a power to add to the group of beneficiaries and would not trigger grantor trust status for the grantor because it is allowed under Code § 674(b)(3). Treas. Reg. 1.674(d)-2(b).

Sometimes grantors seek grantor trust status for the trusts they establish. One way to accomplish this would be to give a non-adverse party the power to add

8. Another way to establish grantor trust status would be to give a third party who is not a trustee and not a beneficiary (such as a trust protector) a presently exercisable power of appointment over the trust.

charitable beneficiaries as additional beneficiaries of the trust. If the power to add beneficiaries is the only trust power causing characterization as a grantor trust, the grantor or the designated power holder can release this power to terminate grantor trust status if that should become desirable or necessary.

Questions

1. Grantor creates an irrevocable trust and declares herself trustee. The trust provides that the trustee may distribute income or principal or both to D, Grantor's adult daughter, in the trustee's discretion for D's health, education, maintenance and support. The trust terminates at D's death, and the remaining trust property will pass to D's estate. If there is any trust income not distributed to D before her death, it is to be paid to her estate. Is Grantor the owner of any part of this trust under the rules of Code § 674?
2. Assume the same facts as described in Question 1, except that instead of Grantor serving as the sole trustee, D's adult child, S, is named as a co-trustee with Grantor. Is Grantor the owner of any part of this trust under Code § 674?
3. Grantor creates an irrevocable trust giving the trustee discretion to distribute income to his brother, B, with no standard for distributions described. When B dies, if there is any income left in the trust, it is to pass to B's issue, per stirpes. Grantor names Local Bank as the trustee. Is Grantor the owner of any part of this trust under the rules of Code § 674?

VI. Section 675 — Administrative Powers Retained by the Grantor

Internal Revenue Code: Section 675

Regulation: 1.675-1

Code § 675 provides that certain administrative powers held by the grantor, the grantor's spouse or others will cause the trust to be characterized as a grantor trust. Code § 675 addresses situations where administrative controls are exercisable primarily for the benefit of the grantor rather than for the trust beneficiaries. If the grantor or the grantor's spouse has a power to amend the administrative provisions of the trust that is broad enough to permit an amendment that would cause Code § 675 to apply to at least a portion of the trust, then the grantor will be treated as the owner of that portion from trust inception.

There are four categories of administrative powers and controls that make a grantor the owner of the portion of the trust to which they apply: (A) Power to Deal for Less than Adequate and Full Consideration; (B) Power to Borrow without Adequate Interest or Security; (C) Borrowing of Trust Funds; and (D) General Powers of Administration. Each of these four categories is described below.

A. The Power to Deal for Less than Adequate and Full Consideration

Internal Revenue Code: Section 675(1)

Regulation: 1.675-1(b)(1)

The grantor will be treated as the owner of a trust, or portion of a trust, if the grantor or a non-adverse party, or both, without the approval or consent of any adverse party, holds a power that enables the grantor or any person to purchase, exchange, or otherwise deal with or dispose of the trust principal or the income therefrom for less than an adequate consideration in money or money's worth. Code § 675(1).

If a power exercisable by a trustee is described in broad terms, that does not necessarily mean that the trustee has the authority to purchase, exchange, or otherwise deal with or dispose of the trust property for less than adequate and full consideration. However, examination of the actual administration of the trust may lead to the conclusion that such authority exists. Treas. Reg. 1.675-1(c).

Nothing in Code § 675(1) prohibits the grantor or a non-adverse party from dealing with trust assets for adequate consideration in money or money's worth. Transactions such as entering into a purchase of the trust assets for their fair market value or entering into a lease at a fair rental price should not trigger Code § 675(1). However, before concluding that the presence of fair and adequate consideration automatically removes the possibility of grantor trust status, one must consider the other administrative provisions of Code § 675 discussed below, in particular the power to reacquire trust assets by substituting assets of equal value set forth in Code § 675(4)(C). For example, a sale and leaseback to a trust by the grantor has been held to result in grantor trust status. Rev. Rul. 54-9, 1954-1 C.B. 20.

B. The Power to Borrow without Providing Adequate Interest or Security

Internal Revenue Code: Section 675(2)

Regulation: 1.675-1(b)(2)

The grantor will be treated as the owner of any portion of a trust where the grantor or a non-adverse party may exercise a power which enables the grantor to borrow the principal or income of the trust directly or indirectly, without providing both adequate interest and adequate security. An example of indirect borrowing is sale of the assets of the trust to the grantor on credit (in exchange for the promissory note of the grantor). This is considered an indirect borrowing by the grantor. If the grantor's power extends to borrowing the principal or income of the trust, the grantor trust status will extend over the entire trust. See Priv. Ltr. Rul. 200840025 (June 13, 2008) (the power held by a non-adverse trustee to lend to the grantor a portion of the trust property that was not limited to any particular portion of the trust caused the grantor to be treated as the owner of the entire trust for income tax purposes).

There is an exception to the foregoing rule. A loan can be made without adequate interest or security when a trustee (other than the grantor or the grantor's spouse acting alone as trustee), is authorized under a general lending power to make loans to any person without regard to interest or security. Should the grantor possess a general lending power, acting alone as trustee, under which the grantor has the power to determine interest rates and the adequacy of security, such power does not in itself indicate that the grantor in fact has the power to borrow the principal or income of the trust without adequate interest or adequate security. Treas. Reg. 1.675-1(b)(2).[9]

Allowing the grantor to have the power to borrow funds from the trust without providing *either* adequate interest or adequate security is sufficient to cause the trust to be treated as a grantor trust. If a trustee is given the power to make an unsecured loan to the grantor, the trust will be treated as a grantor trust even if the loan provides for adequate interest. Priv. Ltr. Ruls. 199942017 (July 22, 1999), 9645013 (Aug. 9, 1996) and 9525032 (March 22, 1995).

C. Borrowing of the Trust Funds

Internal Revenue Code: Section 675(3)

Regulation: 1.675-1(b)(3)

Section 675(3) provides a broad general rule that the grantor will be treated as the owner of any portion of a trust where the grantor has borrowed, directly or indirectly, principal or income of the trust and has not completely repaid the loan, including any interest, before the beginning of the taxable year. That being the case, if a loan to the grantor has been outstanding at any time during the year, grantor trust status will apply for the entire year, even if the loan is repaid, with interest, before the end of the taxable year. Rev. Rul. 86-82, 1986-1 C.B. 253; *Mau v. United States*, 355 F. Supp. 909 (D. HI. 1973). A loan made on December 31 of Year 1 and repaid on January 2 of Year 2 would cause a trust to be treated as a grantor trust for all of Year 1 and Year 2.

Section 675(3) provides an important exception to the foregoing rule. It states that grantor trust status will not result if the loan to the grantor or the grantor's spouse provides (i) adequate interest and adequate security and (ii) the loan is made by a trustee other than the grantor, the grantor's spouse, or a related or subordinate

9. Note that the mere existence of the power to borrow without adequate interest or adequate security held by the grantor or the grantor's spouse will cause grantor trust status to be recognized, regardless of whether the power is actually exercised. Treas. Reg. 1.675-1(b)(2); Priv. Ltr. Ruls. 200840025 (October 3, 2008), 199942017 (October 22, 1999), 9645013 (November 8, 1996) and 9525032 (June 23, 1995).

party. See *Zand v. Commissioner*, 71 T.C.M. 1758 (1996), *aff'd on other grounds*, 143 F.3d 1393 (11th Cir. 1998) (loans made to a grantor that provided for adequate interest and adequate security by trustees who were the grantor's attorneys and not considered related or subordinate parties were found to qualify under this exception and to not trigger grantor trust status).

D. General Powers of Administration

Internal Revenue Code: Section 675(4)

Regulation: 1.675-1

There are three general powers of administration over a trust which, if held by any person in a nonfiduciary capacity without the approval or consent of any person in a fiduciary capacity, will cause the trust to be characterized as a grantor trust. If a power is exercisable by a trustee, it is presumed to be exercisable in a fiduciary capacity primarily in the interests of the beneficiaries. If the power is not exercisable by a trustee, the determination of whether the power is exercisable in a fiduciary capacity depends on the terms of the trust and all the facts and circumstances surrounding its creation and administration.[10]

The three powers of administration set forth under Code § 675(4) are:

1. A power to vote or direct the voting of the trust's stock or other securities of a corporation in which the holdings of the trust and the grantor are significant from the viewpoint of voting control, without the approval of any person in a fiduciary capacity. No guidance is offered as to the meaning of "significant."[11]

2. A power to control the trust's investments in stock or securities of a corporation in which the holdings of the trust and the grantor are significant from the viewpoint of voting control, either by directing or vetoing the trust's investments or reinvestments. Again, no guidance is offered as to the meaning of "significant."

3. A power to reacquire the assets of the trust by substituting other property of an equivalent value. The power to reacquire trust assets need not be expressly stated in the trust instrument to create a grantor trust. A grantor who retained a lien on property transferred to a trust was held to have a power to reacquire the trust assets by substituting assets of equal value. *Barber v. United States*, 251 F.2d 436 (5th Cir. 1948).

10. The IRS will typically not rule on whether a power is exercisable in a fiduciary or in a nonfiduciary capacity. The IRS has called this a question of fact that may only be resolved after the tax returns have been filed. Priv. Ltr. Ruls. 200731019 (August 3, 2007), 199942017 (October 22, 1999), and 9645013 (June 8, 1996).

11. Code § 2036(b)(2) refers to the requirement of having the right to vote stock possessing at least 20 percent of the total combined voting power of all classes of stock before Code § 2036 will apply.

Modification of an irrevocable trust (through decanting or court order, for example) in accordance with state law provisions giving the donor a power of substitution in a non-fiduciary capacity without requiring the approval of anyone in a fiduciary capacity is the creation or affirmation of a grantor trust. Priv. Ltr. Ruls. 200848006 (November 27, 2008), 200848015, 200848016, 200848017 (November 28, 2008).

Possession of one or more of these powers in a nonfiduciary capacity results in grantor trust status regardless of the identity of the person (adverse, non-adverse, independent, etc.).

Planning Opportunity

A grantor may keep a right to substitute assets of equivalent value so as to be treated as the grantor of the trust for income tax purposes, without having the trust property included in his or her estate for estate tax purposes. This power has been a "favorite" of planners seeking to leave the grantor taxable on the income of a trust while alive, but keep the trust property from being taxed in the grantor's estate. The estate inclusion issue was addressed in Rev. Rul. 2008-22, 2008-1 C.B. 796 (April 17, 2008). The ruling concluded that a grantor's retained power, exercisable in a nonfiduciary capacity, to acquire property held in trust by substituting property of equivalent value will not, by itself, cause the value of the trust corpus to be includible in the grantor's gross estate under Code § 2036 or Code § 2038, provided an independent trustee has a fiduciary obligation (under local law or the trust instrument) to ensure the grantor's compliance with the terms of this power by satisfying itself that the properties acquired and substituted by the grantor are in fact of equivalent value, and further provided that the substitution power cannot be exercised in a manner that can shift benefits among the trust beneficiaries. The key factor seems to be the affirmation by the independent trustee of the equivalency of value with respect to the substitution of properties. This is the essence of the trustee's fiduciary obligation in these situations. *See* the discussion in Section X of this Chapter.

While the statute states that administrative powers may be held by any person in a nonfiduciary capacity, the regulations refer to powers of administration held in a nonfiduciary capacity "by any non-adverse party." Treas. Reg. 1.675-1(b)(4). Accordingly, giving the power of substitution to anyone who could be deemed an adverse party or requiring approval of an adverse party would create a problem for the grantor who desired to be treated as the grantor of the trust.

With the high federal transfer tax exemption enacted by the 2017 Tax Cuts and Jobs Act, planning for most taxpayers shifts to income tax planning. Securing stepped-up basis adjustments is a centerpiece for income tax planning. An advantage of the substitution power is the flexibility of exchanging low basis assets held by a grantor trust with higher basis assets owned by the grantor individually, without requiring recognition of gain or income. Rev. Rul. 85-13, 1985-1 C.B. 184. If the grantor holds the low basis assets returned to the grantor in the exchange until death, they will receive a fair market value basis at that time. Code § 1014.

Questions

1. Which of the following administrative powers included in a trust would **not** cause the grantor of the trust to be considered the owner of the trust under Code § 675?

   a. The power to deal with the principal and income for less than full and adequate consideration.

   b. The power held by a trustee other than the grantor and other than a related or subordinate trustee subservient to the grantor to make loans to the grantor for adequate interest and adequate security.

   c. The power exercisable in a non-fiduciary capacity by any person without the approval or consent of any person in a fiduciary capacity to vote or direct the voting of stock or other securities of a corporation in which the holdings of the grantor and the trust are significant from the viewpoint of voting control.

   d. The power to control the investment of the trust funds either by directing investments in a non-fiduciary capacity by any person without the approval or consent of any person in a fiduciary capacity.

2. Grantor creates an irrevocable trust and funds it by transferring real property (Blackacre) to the trust. Grantor includes a provision in the trust stating that Grantor's spouse, W, has the right, acting in a nonfiduciary capacity, to substitute other property for Blackacre provided that such other property has a value equivalent to Blackacre. First Bank is named trustee of the trust. Is Grantor the owner of this trust under Code § 675?

3. Grantor created an irrevocable trust and declared that she retains the right to borrow the trust property without providing adequate interest or adequate security. The trust has been in existence for twenty years, and Grantor has never borrowed the trust property for any reason. Is the Grantor the owner of the trust under Code § 675?

VII. Section 676 — The Power to Revoke a Trust

Internal Revenue Code : Section 676

Regulations : 1.676(a)-1, 1.676(b)-1

Section 676 provides the general rule that the grantor is treated as the owner of any portion of a trust as to which any one or more of the grantor, the grantor's spouse, or a non-adverse party can exercise the power to revoke or revest title to any portion of the trust in the grantor. (The power need not be actually exercised for these rules to apply.) A typical inter vivos trust over which the grantor retains the right to revoke the trust is thus a grantor trust; the same is true if a trustee has discretion to distribute trust principal to the grantor, and the trustee is a non-adverse party, Code § 676 will apply. Rev. Rul. 57-8, 1957-1 C.B. 204.[12]

The power to revest is broadly defined to include not only the power to revoke the trust, but also the power to terminate, alter, or amend the trust, or to appoint the trust property, so long as the trust property will return to the grantor. The grantor's (or the grantor's spouse's) power to purchase trust assets for less than full and adequate consideration will likewise trigger Code § 676 (as well as Code § 675(1)), as will powers to invade, withdraw, alter (depending on particular facts) or amend the trust. See, e.g., Rev. Rul. 71-548, 1971-2 C.B 250 (the transfer of stock to a trust and the retained power to direct the sale of that stock, terminate the trust, and receive the trust property was held to be the power to revoke the trust).

> **Example:** Christine creates a trust, funds it with her personal assets, names herself the beneficiary and trustee, and retains the right to revoke the trust. During Christine's lifetime, she is the trust income and principal beneficiary. This trust is an example of a typical so-called "living trust" used by many persons throughout the United States. It is a grantor trust for a number of reasons, not the least of which is the retained right to revoke the trust per Code § 676. As such, all of the trust income will be taxed to Christine.
>
> **Example:** Fred creates an irrevocable trust for the benefit of his adult child, Dean, naming his spouse, Wilma, as the trustee. Wilma has the right, in her sole discretion, to return the trust property to Fred at any time. Since Wilma is Fred's spouse, her power to revest title to the trust property to Fred, the grantor, is attributable to Fred and therefore this is a grantor trust.
>
> Alternatively, if Fred named the First Trust Company as the trustee and not Wilma, while the First Trust Company is obviously not a spouse, it is a non-adverse trustee. Therefore, if the First Trust Company has the same discretion to distribute the trust property to Fred, Fred will be taxable as the owner of the trust even though he cannot directly or indirectly compel the actions of the trustee. Compare these alternatives with a third alternative in which Fred names his child, Dean, as the trustee of the trust. Here, since Dean is also the trust beneficiary, his discretionary power to return the trust property to Fred is adverse to his own interests as a beneficiary. Accordingly, in this situation, the trust would not be considered a grantor trust because the only way Fred can receive a return of the trust property

12. A grantor will also be treated as the owner of a trust which could be revoked only upon receiving the unanimous consent of the grantor and a trustee which was not adverse to the grantor. Rev. Rul. 75-257, 1975-2 C.B. 251. Conversely, if the power to revoke retained by the grantor is made conditional on receiving the consent of an adverse party, it will not be viewed as a power to revest the trust property in the grantor, and Code § 676 will not apply. Priv. Ltr. Ruls. 200731019 (May 1, 2007) and 200729025 (April 10, 2007).

is by the action of an adverse party. *See Goldsmith v. Starr*, 241 F.2d 797 (2d Cir. 1957); Rev. Rul. 66-72, 1966-1 C.B. 58.

To create a revocation power in its simplest, most obvious form, the grantor states in the trust instrument that the grantor has reserved the power to revoke the trust. It is possible, however, that a trust may be deemed to be revocable by state law presumptions where, for example, a state law provides that any trust not made explicitly irrevocable is deemed to be revocable. Such a situation could result in an unanticipated (and possibly unwanted) grantor trust characterization. *Gaylord v. Commissioner*, 153 F.2d 408 (9th Cir. 1946); *United States v. Pierce*, 137 F. 2d 428 (8th Cir. 1943). It may be possible to retroactively amend or reform a trust (or possibly to decant it) to avoid the state law presumption and obtain the desired characterization. *Flitcroft v. Commissioner*, 328 F. 2d 449 (9th Cir. 1964); *Heintz v. Commissioner*, T.C.M. 1980-524.

A Totten trust is an arrangement whereby a person deposits funds in his or her own name in a savings or similar account for a chosen beneficiary, naming himself or herself as the designated "trustee" for such beneficiary. These accounts are sometimes designated as "ITF" trusts (in trust for) or P.O.D. (payable on death) accounts. The depositor/trustee generally has the unlimited right to withdraw the assets from the account while living and revest the property in himself or herself; accordingly, the depositor/trustee is treated as establishing the equivalent of a revocable trust and, as such, is taxable on all trust income. Rev. Rul. 62-148, 1962-2 C.B. 153. Whether or not the depositor/trustee actually withdrew funds from the trust is irrelevant; the right to withdraw is the determinative factor. *Oppenheimer v. Commissioner*, 52 T.C.M. 980 (1986).

Note that to be considered an "adverse interest," the interest of the adverse party must be a substantial beneficial interest that would be adversely affected by the distribution of trust income or principal. If the allegedly adverse interest is remote or contingent, whether it is truly "adverse" or not may be challenged by the IRS. In such cases, the question becomes an issue that turns on the facts and circumstances of the particular trust. *Holt v. United States*, 669 F. Supp. 751 (W.D. Va. 1987) (where the likelihood of the trustees ever becoming beneficiaries was after a chain of deaths of younger beneficiaries and highly unlikely, so no adverse interest was found); *Moore v. Commissioner*, 3 T.C. 1205 (1944), *acq.*, 1944 C.B. 20 (trust property could be recovered only with the approval of all corporate directors and shareholders, which was unlikely, so no adverse interest was found).

In the typical living trust, the grantor retains the right to revoke the entire trust, so, where that is the case, it follows that the grantor is treated as the owner of the entire trust. If, however, the grantor's power of revocation extends over only a portion of the trust, only that portion will be considered as owned by the grantor under Code § 676. How the power to retain an interest in the trust is described in the trust document may be a key determining factor as to whether the grantor has retained a full or partial right to revest title in himself or herself.

If the grantor's spouse, but not the grantor, possesses the power to revoke the trust and revest title in the grantor, grantor trust status will apply.

> **Example:** Craig creates a trust for the benefit of his children and retains the right to revoke the trust and revest the property in himself. The trust is a grantor trust as to Craig. Assume further that Craig is married to Ariel. If Craig relinquishes the power to revoke the trust and gives the exclusive power of revocation to Ariel, so long as title to the trust property can still be revested in Craig if the trust is revoked, grantor trust status will apply.

The Code provides an exception to grantor trust status if the right to revoke is not immediate and commences after an event or period of time. However, this exception only applies in those situations when, had the power been a reversionary interest, the grantor would not have been taxed as trust owner under Code § 673. (Recall that Code § 673 causes the grantor to be taxed as owner of a trust where the grantor possesses a more than five percent reversionary interest in the trust property. *See* Section IV, above.) Once the deferral period ends, the grantor will be treated as the owner of the entire trust by virtue of the power to revoke, unless the grantor relinquishes that power.

> **Example:** Bob creates a trust for the lifetime benefit of his son, remainder to his son's children, and provides that, in the event his son remarries, Bob has the right to revoke the trust. Assuming that Bob's interest in this trust is valued at less than five percent, this trust would not be treated as a grantor trust. If Bob's son does remarry, then Bob's right to revoke would cause him to be treated as the owner of the trust, unless he relinquishes the power of revocation.

Questions

1. Gary creates a trust during his lifetime. The trust provides that all of the income is to be paid to Gary's child, Laura, for her lifetime. Upon the death of Laura, the trust is to terminate, and the remaining property is to be paid to Laura's issue, per stirpes. Gary names the Central Trust Company as the sole trustee.

    a. Gary retains the right to revoke the trust in his own discretion. Is he treated as the owner of the trust?

    b. Alternatively, Gary retains the right to revoke the trust if Central Trust Company consents to the revocation. Is Gary treated as the owner of the trust?

    c. Alternatively, Gary retains the right to revoke the trust if Laura consents to the revocation. Is Gary treated as the owner of the trust?

    d. Alternatively, Gary retains the right to revoke the trust if Gary's wife, Toni, consents to the revocation. Is Gary treated as the owner of the trust?

VIII. Section 677: Income for the Benefit of the Grantor

Internal Revenue Code: Section 677

Regsulations: 1.677(a)-1, 1.677(b)-1

Section 677(a) treats the grantor as the owner of any portion or all of a trust as to which the grantor or any non-adverse party (or both) may use the trust income for the benefit of the grantor or the grantor's spouse without requiring the approval or consent of an adverse party. "Income" here means income in a tax sense and not fiduciary accounting income. As described below, Code § 677 covers a wide variety of situations where the grantor is benefitted by the trust income.

Just the possibility of payments to or accumulations for the grantor or the grantor's spouse is enough to trigger Code § 677(a), assuming no approval or consent of an adverse party is needed. It is not necessary to demonstrate that actual distributions were received from the trust. Code § 677(a) applies both to actual distributions and constructive distributions from a trust. Constructive distributions to the grantor or to the grantor's spouse include distributions on behalf of the grantor or the grantor's spouse or payments made to others at the direction of the grantor or the grantor's spouse.

> **Example:** Joe creates a trust for the benefit of himself and his wife, Betty. First Bank is named the trustee. The trustee is authorized to accumulate the income and only pay it to Joe or Betty in the event of an emergency. Code § 677 applies; the trust is a thus a grantor trust.

As a general rule, the grantor is treated as the owner of a portion of a trust the income of which is, or in the discretion of the grantor or a non-adverse party, or both, may be applied to discharge a legal obligation of the grantor or the grantor's spouse. The "legal obligations" of a person are generally determined by the rules of local law. Obligations include not only support, but also debts, tax obligations, and general claims of creditors.

A. Specific Situations Described in Code § 677(a)

Section 677(a) will cause a trust to be characterized as a grantor trust when the trust income, without the approval or consent of any adverse party is, or, in the discretion of the grantor or a non-adverse person, or both, may be used in one or more of the following situations:

- Distributed to the grantor or to the grantor's spouse. Code § 677(a)(1);
- Held or accumulated for future distribution to the grantor or the grantor's spouse. Code Section 677(a)(2); or
- Applied to the payment of premiums on life insurance policies on the life of the grantor or the grantor's spouse, other than life insurance policies which are irrevocably payable for charitable purposes. Code § 677(a)(3).

Each of these situations is discussed below.

1. *Possible or Actual Income Distributions to the Grantor or to the Grantor's Spouse*

Where a trust requires or permits the income to be distributed to the grantor or to the grantor's spouse, the grantor will be treated as the owner of the income portion of the trust, so long as such distributions may be made without the approval or consent of any adverse party.

CCA 200445025 (Nov. 5, 2004). Where the grantor's spouse is a discretionary income beneficiary, and the trustee holds no beneficial interest and so is not an adverse party, the grantor will be treated as the owner of the trust. *Amabile v. Commissioner*, 51 T.C.M. 963 (1986).[13]

> **Example:** Grantor creates a trust with First Bank as trustee, providing that income may be paid to Grantor or Grantor's adult children as the trustee determines in the trustee's sole discretion. All income is paid to the Grantor's adult children during the year in question. Since the income could have been paid to the Grantor in the discretion of a non-adverse party (i.e., First Bank), the Grantor is taxable on all of the trust income.

Furthermore, a grantor will be treated as the owner of a portion of a trust the income of which is, or in the discretion of the grantor or a non-adverse party, or both, may be paid, applied or accumulated to discharge the personal legal obligations of the grantor (or the grantor's spouse in the case of property transferred in trust by the grantor after October 9, 1969). Code § 677(a); Treas. Reg. 1.677(a)-1(d).[14]

References to a "portion" of a trust may result in part or all of the trust being treated as owned by the grantor. For example, if capital gains can be distributed to or used for the benefit of the grantor, but not ordinary income, the grantor is taxed only

---

13. The distinction between the presence of adverse parties or non-adverse parties is important. In a situation where the grantor was not entitled to receive the trust income under the terms of the trust agreement, but received it anyway based on the consent of all of the beneficiaries, Code § 677(a) was held inapplicable because the beneficiaries were adverse parties, and, but for their approval, no trust income would have been payable to the grantor. *Commissioner v. Makransky*, 321 F. 2d 598 (3d Cir. 1963). Likewise, when a power of appointment is involved, if the grantor can only receive distributions from the trust with the consent of the other potential appointees, they will be considered adverse parties, and the grantor will not be considered the owner of the trust. Priv. Ltr. Ruls. 200731019 (May 1, 2007), 200729025 (April 10, 2007) and 200148028 (August 27, 2001). However, where all of the discretion to make distributions to the grantor or the grantor's spouse is in the hands of a non-adverse trustee, even if the grantor and the grantor's spouse have the right to veto a distribution, that is not viewed as a sufficient power to make the spouses adverse as to each other. Consequently, the grantor will be treated as the owner of the trust. Treas. Reg. 1.677(a)-1(b)(2); Priv. Ltr. Rul. 9536002 (May 12, 1995).

14. Under the discharge of indebtedness rule, a grantor will be taxable as the owner of a trust where the trust income could have been used to pay the grantor's mortgage obligation, rent or other household expenses. Rev. Rul. 54-516, 1954-2 C.B. 54; *Wiles v. Commissioner*, 59 T.C. 289 (1972), *acq.*, 1973-2 C.B. 4, *aff'd*, 491 F.2d 1406 (5th Cir. 1974); C.C.A. 200628026 (July 14, 2006).

on the capital gains of the trust; conversely, if only ordinary income and not capital gains can be distributed to or for the benefit of the grantor, then the grantor is taxed only on the trust's ordinary income. Treas. Reg. 1.677(a)-1(g) Examples 1 and 2.

2. Trust Income Being Held or Accumulated for Future Distribution to the Grantor

Grantor trust treatment will result if the income of the trust may be accumulated without the consent of an adverse party for future distribution to the grantor or to the grantor's spouse. Code § 677(a)(2).

It is not unusual for a trust to exist where the grantor has retained some form of a reversionary interest and income arises (typically capital gains allocable to the principal of the trust) throughout the duration of the trust. Since trust principal is being held for future distribution to the grantor, whatever income that accrues to principal, whether under the governing trust instrument or under local law, is treated as being accumulated for future distribution to the grantor, even if no other interest or power would cause grantor trust exposure. In such a case, even though the grantor may not be considered the owner of the income portion of the trust (perhaps because the value of the grantor's reversionary interest falls below the five percent threshold set forth in Code § 673), the grantor will be taxed on the trust income being accumulated for the grantor's benefit. *Duffy v. United States*, 487 F.2d 282 (6th Cir. 1973); *cert. denied*, 416 U.S. 938 (1974); Treas. Reg. 1.677(a)-1(g), Ex. 2; Rev. Rul. 79-223, 1979-2 C.B. 254; Rev. Rul. 75-267, 1975-2 C.B. 225. This, in turn, may cause a cash flow hardship to the grantor, since this income may not be currently available for distribution to the grantor.

3. Trust Income Used to Pay Life Insurance Premiums on the Life of the Grantor or the Grantor's Spouse

The grantor of a trust is treated as the owner of any trust or portion of a trust the income from which can be used, without the consent of an adverse party, to pay life insurance premiums on the life of the grantor or the grantor's spouse, unless the insurance proceeds are irrevocably payable for a charitable purpose specified in Code § 170(c). Code § 677(a)(3). The trust does not have to direct that the trust income be used to pay life insurance premiums. The fact that trust income is (or may be) actually used for this purpose is sufficient to make the grantor the owner of the portion of the trust allowing income to be so used. Treas. Reg. 1.677(a)-1(b)(2).[15]

15. The present status of the law is unclear here: on the one hand, A series of older decisions took the view that the trust must actually own policies for Code § 677(a)(3) to be applicable. According to these cases, the amount of income on which the grantor may be taxed is limited to the income actually used by the trustee to pay premiums on the policies held by the trust. *See, e.g., Commissioner v. Mott*, 85 F.2d 315 (6th Cir. 1936). On the other hand, in a series of private letter rulings, the IRS has suggested that a mere premium payment power would be sufficient to cause a trust to be a wholly owned grantor trust. *See* Priv. Ltr. Ruls. 8852003 (Aug. 31, 1988) (holding that a power to pay

Example: George owns a $500,000 life insurance policy on his life. He transfers it into an irrevocable trust for the benefit of his two children. He also transfers income producing property to the trust so that the trustee (Second National Bank) can use the income to pay the premiums on the life insurance policy. In addition, George's spouse, Denise, also transfers income producing property to the trust. George will be taxed on the income generated by the property that he transferred to the trust because that income is being used to pay premiums on his life insurance. Denise will be taxed on the balance of the income (the trust income generated by the portion of the property Denise transferred to the trust). Because Denise transferred property to the trust, the income from which is being used to pay premiums on the life insurance on the life of her spouse, Denise is treated as the grantor of that portion of the trust to the extent of the property she contributed to the trust.

B. Using Trust Income to Satisfy the Grantor's Obligation of Support

The possibility that trust income may be used to discharge the grantor's or grantor spouse's obligations for support and maintenance of a trust beneficiary is not sufficient to cause the income of the trust to be taxed to the grantor. Instead, Code § 677(b) provides a rather broad exception to the general rule of Code § 677(a) discussed above. Trust income will not be considered taxable to the grantor, in the discretion of another person, or the trustee, or the grantor acting as trustee or co-trustee, merely because such income *may* be applied or distributed for the support or maintenance of a beneficiary (other than the grantor's spouse) whom the grantor is legally obligated to support or maintain — *except* to the extent that such income is so applied or distributed. Accordingly, in the absence of the grantor's legal support obligation and in the absence of the grantor's nonfiduciary power to direct discretionary distributions, simply distributing trust income to a relative of the grantor (such as a child who the grantor is not obligated to support) will not trigger grantor trust status under Code § 677(a).

The general rule of Code § 677(a) (taxing the grantor on the trust income) and not the exception of Code § 677(b) will apply if the discretion to apply or distribute trust income rests solely in the grantor (or in the grantor acting in conjunction with other persons), unless the grantor's discretion must be exercised as a trustee or as a co-trustee. Treas. Reg. 1.677(b)-1(e). Moreover, the general rule of Code § 677(a) and not the exception of Code § 677(b) will apply to the extent that the trust income is required, without any discretionary determination being made, to be applied

premiums alone causes the entire trust to be a grantor trust) and 8839008 (June 23, 1988) (the IRS determined that it is immaterial whether the premium payments come from the income or principal of the trust for fiduciary accounting purposes).

to support a beneficiary whom the grantor is legally obligated to support. Treas. Reg. 1.677-1(b)-1(f). In that case, the grantor will be taxable on that part of the trust income required to be paid and applied, as well as any additional amounts that were actually paid and applied in discharge of the grantor's support obligation.

> **Example:** Hugh creates a trust for the benefit of his minor daughter, Sharon. The trust provides that the trustee may pay income to or for the benefit of Sharon for her health, education, maintenance, and support. Hugh's brother, Paul, is named trustee of the trust. In the first five years of the trust's operation, no income is paid to Sharon and the income is accumulated in the trust. The income is taxable to the trust, not to Hugh, as the exception contained in Code § 677(b) applies. In year 6, Paul distributes all of the trust income for Sharon's benefit (assume she is still a minor) to pay for her medical expenses. The year 6 income is taxed to Hugh, since it has been used to discharge his obligation to support his daughter. At the end of year 6, Hugh removes Paul as the trustee of the trust, and names himself as the trustee. In years 7 and 8, no distributions are made from the trust as the income is again accumulated. Even though Hugh is the trustee, he is not taxed on the income because he is acting in a fiduciary capacity, and no distributions were made to satisfy his support obligation. In years 9 and 10 (assume Sharon is still a minor), Hugh uses the trust income to pay for a variety of Sharon's basic living expenses. Here, Hugh is taxed on the trust income, even though he is acting in a fiduciary capacity, since he is using the income of the trust to satisfy his obligation of support, so that the exception of Code § 677(b) is inapplicable, and the general rule of Code § 677(a) now applies.

There are no rules in the Internal Revenue Code and no federal standard that defines what is meant by a legal obligation of support. The regulations only provide that the grantor's legal obligation of support is to be determined under local law. Treas. Reg. 1.662(a)-4. State laws vary widely in determining when a support obligation arises, and will be determinative of the extent of a parent's obligation. Rev. Rul. 56-484, 1956-2 C.B. 23. In most states, parents have an obligation to provide support for children until age eighteen is attained, regardless of the resources of the child, but some states extend the support obligation to age twenty-one.[16]

---

16. Payments of income received under statutes such as the Uniform Transfers to Minor's Act are taxable to the grantor when deemed to satisfy a support obligation. Rev. Rul. 59-357, 1959-2 C.B. 212; Rev. Rul. 56-484, 1956-2 C.B. 23. With little statutory guidance from the states, most of the law made in this area arises in the context of matrimonial law cases where one spouse tries to require the other to pay for a variety of expenses, generally including higher education of children, based on the argument that payment of such expenses constitutes "necessary support." The cases addressing the support issue have not been uniformly decided. *Compare, e.g., Wyche v. United States*, 36 A.F.T.R.2d 75-5816 (Ct. Cl. Tr. J. 1974) (private school tuition, music and dancing lessons were not support obligations under South Carolina law, so the grantor was not taxable on the income of a trust created to provide for these items), *with Braun v. Commissioner*, 48 T.C.M. 210 (1984) (college education expenses for emancipated children and private school expenses for minor children were found to be within the scope of a parental support obligation of a financially capable parent

Questions:

1. Megan creates an irrevocable trust for the benefit of her adult son, Ben. The trust provides that Ben is entitled to all the income of the trust for his lifetime and such part of the principal as the trustee determines to pay Ben for his general happiness, remainder to his descendants, per stirpes. Megan names Local Bank as trustee. Is Megan the owner of this trust under Code § 677?

2. Mark creates an irrevocable trust for the benefit of his daughter, Dara, age 11. The trust provides that the income and principal can be used to provide for the health, education, maintenance and support of Dara until she turns age 25, at which time the remaining trust principal and any undistributed income is to be paid to her. If Dara is not then living, the trust property is payable to her issue, per stirpes, and if none, to her estate. No distributions are made to Dara or for her benefit during the tax year.

   a. Mark is the trustee of this trust. Is Mark the owner of this trust under Code § 677?

   b. Alternatively, assume Local Bank is the trustee of this trust instead of Mark. Is Mark the trust owner under Code § 677?

   c. Alternatively, assume Mark's business partner is named the trustee of this trust, not Mark or Local Bank. Is Mark the owner of the trust under Code § 677?

3. Assume the facts of Question 1 above as to the terms of the trust, but now assume that Dara is now age 18, and the trust income and principal are used to pay for her college education. How might your answers change, if at all?

IX. Section 678 — A Person Other than the Grantor Treated as Substantial Owner of the Trust

Internal Revenue Code: Section 678

Regsulations: 1.678(a)-1, 1.678(b)-1, 1.678(c)-1. 1.678(d)-1

A. General Rules and Background of Code § 678

A person other than the grantor may be treated as the owner of any portion of a trust if such person has a power exercisable solely by himself or herself to vest the principal or the income of the trust in himself or herself. The rule applies whether or not the power is exercised. Rev. Rul. 67-241, 1967-2 C.B. 225.

---

under New Jersey law so that the income of trusts used to provide for these expenses was taxed to the grantor).

Section 678(a) will not apply if consent is needed from any third party regardless of whether the third party is adverse or not. Accordingly, if a trust provides that a beneficiary may direct the trustee to distribute the trust principal or income to himself or herself only with the consent of a third party, such beneficiary is not treated as the owner of the trust under Code § 678(a). Priv. Ltr. Rul. 8926032 (March 31, 1989). If an actual distribution of trust income is made to such person, that person will be treated as a beneficiary of the trust under the standard beneficiary rules of Subchapter J, Code §§ 661 and 662, but not as the owner of the trust within the rules of Code § 678(a). Priv. Ltr. Rul. 8213140 (Dec. 31, 1981).

In addition, a person other than the grantor will be treated as the owner of any portion of a trust as to which the person has previously partially released or otherwise modified a power to vest the trust principal or income in himself or herself and has retained such control over the trust that would, had the power been retained by the grantor of the trust, cause the grantor trust rules as set forth in Code §§ 671 through 677 to apply. The effect of Code § 678(a)(2) is to treat a person who has modified or released a Code § 678 power as though that person is the creator of the continuing trust. Powers that lapse may also be included within the reach of Code § 678(a)(2).

A person with the power to vest in himself or herself only the fiduciary accounting income of a trust will be treated as the owner of only the ordinary income portion of the trust. If a person has the power to vest in himself or herself all of the trust principal, that person will be treated as the owner of the entire trust. Treas. Regs. 1.671-3(b)(1) and 1.671-3(b)(3).

The genesis behind the establishment of the Code § 678 rules was *Mallinckrodt v. Nunan*, 146 F.2d 1 (8th Cir. 1945), *cert. denied*, 324 U.S. 871 (1945). The case held that the beneficiary's unrestricted access to the trust property was the trigger for finding grantor trust status for the beneficiary. The case involved a trust beneficiary who was entitled to receive whatever portion of the trust income that he might request. The beneficiary was also a co-trustee with broad management powers, and had the right to terminate the trust at any time and receive the entire trust estate. The court found that the possession of the demand power over the income of the trust was so extensive that the possessor of the power should be considered the taxpayer. This was the result, even if the income not demanded by the beneficiary during the year was added to trust principal at the end of the year, thereby putting the foregone income out of the beneficiary's control.

> **Example:** Joanne created an irrevocable trust which provided that Bill was the income beneficiary for his lifetime, remainder to Cheryl in the event of Bill's death. The trust gave Bill a general power to appoint the trust income or principal to himself or his estate at any time during his lifetime or by his will. As the result of this power, under Code § 678(a), Bill will be treated as the owner of the trust. Rev. Rul. 67-241, 1967-2 C.B. 225.

> **Example:** Terry created an irrevocable trust with separate shares for each designated trust beneficiary. The trust provided that any beneficiary who

had attained age 30 had the right to withdraw some or all of the trust principal, but those beneficiaries who had not yet attained age 30 did not possess this right. Those beneficiaries over age 30 would be taxed as owners of the trust income and principal under Code § 678(a), but those beneficiaries under age 30 would not be taxed as owners of the trust. *See* Priv. Ltr. Rul. 8545076 (Aug. 14, 1985).

A person will be treated as the owner of a trust under Code § 678(a) if that person has a power exercisable solely by himself or herself to apply the trust income or principal in satisfaction of his or her legal obligations, other than the obligation to support a dependent. Treas. Reg. 1.678(a)-1(b). (Regarding obligations of support, see the discussion immediately below.)

There are two common situations in which the general rule of Code § 678(a) apples, namely, with respect to so-called five-and-five powers and Crummey withdrawal rights.

1. Five and Five Powers

Trust beneficiaries are often granted withdrawal rights from trusts that are designed to fall within the scope of an exception to the estate tax and gift tax inclusion rules. More specifically, if a beneficiary is given the power to withdraw from the trust on an annual, non-cumulative basis, an amount limited to the greater of $5,000 or five percent of the value of the trust property out of which the power could be satisfied, the lapse of such withdrawal right is excluded from the definition of "release" for estate tax purposes under Code § 2041(b)(2) and for gift tax purposes under Code § 2514(e).

However, for income tax purposes, the holder of so-called "five and five" withdrawal rights which lapse if not exercised in any given year is treated as an owner of that portion of the trust principal to which the power applies, regardless of whether or not the power of withdrawal is exercised, provided the holder of the power has retained such other control over the trust as would, if retained by the grantor of the trust, subject the grantor to being treated as the owner of the trust under Code §§ 671 through 677. Treas. Reg. 1.678 (a)-1(a); Rev. Rul. 67-241,1967-2 C.B. 225; Priv. Ltr. Rul. 200022035 (March 3, 2000).

2. Crummey Powers

A "Crummey power" is used in trust drafting to give a trust beneficiary a limited power of withdrawal over property contributed to the trust (*i.e.*, additions made to the trust) for a limited period of time (often 30 days). This withdrawal window period is done in an effort to qualify the beneficiary's right of withdrawal as a present interest gift. As such, the donor of the addition to the trust does not have to use his or her lifetime gift tax exclusion for the transfer, or, if the donor's lifetime gift exclusion has already been exhausted, so that the donor does not have to pay any gift tax.

As a general rule, the IRS will treat the holder of a Crummey power as the owner of that portion of the trust as to which the withdrawal power applies while the power exists under Code § 678(a)(1), and as the owner of a portion of the trust after the power lapses, if the power holder is also a beneficiary of the trust under Code § 678(a)(2). This rule will even extend to the case of a minor beneficiary with a Crummey power even though local law legally prevents the minor from exercising the power absent the appointment of a legal guardian. The existence of the withdrawal power, and not the legal ability of the minor beneficiary to exercise it, is viewed by the Service as the determinative factor. Rev. Rul. 81-6, 1981-1, C.B. 385; Priv. Ltr. Rul. 200011058 (Dec. 15, 1999). The withdrawal powers make the beneficiaries taxable as the owners of both the income and principal of their portion of the trust under Code § 678(a). Rev. Rul. 67-241, 1967-2 C.B. 225.[17]

B. Obligations of Support

A person will not be taxable as the owner of a trust under the general rules of Code § 678(a) merely because that person, acting in the capacity as trustee or co-trustee, may apply trust income for the support and maintenance of another person whom the holder of the power is legally obligated to support or maintain except to the extent the income is so applied. Code § 678(c). Where amounts are so applied or distributed from principal or from other than income of the taxable year, such amounts will be treated as an amount paid or credited under Code § 661(a)(2) and taxed to the holder of the power under Code § 662.[18]

Section 678 does not make any reference to an ascertainable standard. However, many planners take the position that a person acting in the capacity of a trustee will not be taxed on the income of the trust under Code § 678 if the discretion of the trustee is limited by an ascertainable standard. This position is based on the fact that the language of Code § 678 requires that the trustee be able to vest income or principal in himself or herself "solely by himself," and if a decision as to distributions must be made in accordance with whether an ascertainable standard has been satisfied, the trustee is not making the determination "solely by himself."[19]

---

17. Technically, each beneficiary may be required to report a portion of the trust income. In Private Letter Ruling 9541029, (July 14, 1995), the IRS ruled that each of seven beneficiaries who had a Crummey power over one-seventh of the contributions to the trust must each include those items of income, deduction and credit against tax attributable to or included in the portion of trust principal over which each beneficiary had a right of withdrawal during that calendar year.

18. Note the parallel here with Code § 677(b), which provides that a grantor of a trust will not be treated as the owner of the trust merely because the grantor, acting as a trustee or as a co-trustee, *may* apply the trust income for the support and maintenance of a beneficiary whom the grantor is legally obligated to support and maintain — except to the extent the income is *in fact* so applied or distributed. In Private Letter Ruling 8939012 (June 29, 1989), the IRS held that a sole trustee was not taxable as a grantor under Code § 678 where the beneficiaries of the trust were the adult children and descendants of the trustee to whom no legal obligation of support was owed.

19. There is some support for this position in the legislative history of Code § 678 which provides that a person would be treated as the owner of a trust if the person had an "unrestricted power

If a person, acting in any capacity *other than* as a trustee or as a co-trustee, holds a power exercisable solely by himself or herself to apply trust income to discharge an obligation of support and maintenance for someone such person is legally obligated to support, such person will be treated as the owner of the trust, regardless of whether or not the income of the trust is so applied. In this situation, the general rule of Code § 678(a) and not the protective exception of Code § 678(c) is applied. Treas. Reg. 1.678(c)-1(b). If a person does not hold such power solely by himself or herself, Code § 678(a) does not apply. *See Mesker v. United States*, 261 F. Supp. 817 (E.D. Mo 1966) (a husband was found to not be taxable on the income of a trust over which he had the power to direct the trustees to pay the trust income to his wife, since he did not have the power exercisable solely by himself to apply the trust income to discharge his legal obligation to support his wife under state law). Likewise, a power to vest income in oneself as a co-trustee will not be treated as a power "exercisable solely" by oneself. Priv. Ltr. Rul. 200901030 (Sept. 29, 2008).

Example: Anthony creates a trust for the benefit of his minor grandchild, Jane. Anthony names his daughter, Doris, the mother of Jane, as the trustee of this trust. Doris has the power under the trust document to use the trust income for the support and maintenance of Jane. If Doris does not distribute any of the trust income to or for the support and maintenance of Jane, Doris will not be treated as the owner of the trust. However, if Doris distributes trust income to or for the support and maintenance of Jane, Doris will be treated as the owner of the trust — to the extent of the distributions made for the support and maintenance of Jane.

Example: Assume in the example above that instead of naming Doris as the trustee of the trust, Anthony named First Bank, a corporate trustee, as the sole trustee of the trust, but gave Doris the power to direct that the income of the trust could be used or applied for the support and maintenance of Jane. In such a case, since Doris is not acting in a fiduciary capacity, she would be treated as the owner of the trust and all of the trust income would be taxable to Doris, whether or not she directed that the income of the trust be used for the support and maintenance of Jane.

A power of withdrawal over a trust held by a minor may qualify as a Code § 678(a) power resulting in the taxation of the minor even if the minor is legally prohibited from exercising that power. A minor beneficiary of a trust was treated as the owner of the portion of the trust with respect to which the beneficiary had the power to vest the principal or income in himself, even though no guardian had yet been appointed for the minor. The IRS position is that it is the existence of a power rather

to take the trust principal or income." S. Rep. No. 1622, 83d Cong., 2d Sess. 87 (1954). The obligation to apply an ascertainable standard has been viewed as a limitation on the "unrestricted power" referred to in the legislative history. Where there is an objective standard limiting the discretion of the beneficiary, ownership of the trust by the beneficiary has not been found. *United States v. DeBonchamps*, 278 F.2d 127 (9th Cir. 1960); *Funk v. Commissioner*, 185 F. 2d 127 (3d Cir. 1950).

than the capacity to exercise it that determines whether a person other than the grantor shall be treated as the owner of any part of a trust. The minor may not know of his or her rights or have any way of exercising such rights absent the appointment of a legal guardian. Rev. Rul. 81-6, 1981-1 C.B. 385; Priv. Ltr. Rul. 9535047 (June 6, 1995).[20]

C. Renunciation or Disclaimer of a Power

Section 678(a) does not apply with respect to a power which has been renounced or disclaimed within a reasonable time after the holder of the power first became aware of its existence. Code § 678(d); Treas. Reg. 1.678(d)-1. What constitutes a "reasonable time" or a valid disclaimer is a matter for determination by state law, since neither Code § 678 nor its regulations provide any guidelines as to what will constitute a valid disclaimer for these purposes. While Code §§ 2518(a) and 2046 provide substantial guidance with respect to what constitutes a "qualified disclaimer" for federal gift and estate tax purposes (and set a nine-month period commencing at the time of the transfer for qualified disclaimers), they do not apply for income tax purposes. The IRS has taken the position that a trust beneficiary who disclaims trust income remains taxable on the trust income realized prior to the disclaimer. See Rev. Rul. 64-62, 1964-1 C.B. 221 (the disclaimer of a Code § 678 power did not allow the disclaimant to avoid income taxation on the income earned by the trust prior to the disclaimer).

D. Conflicting Powers of Grantor and Power Holder

The general rule of Code § 678 does not apply with respect to a power over income whether originally granted or subsequently modified if the original trust grantor is otherwise treated as trust owner under Code §§ 671 through 677. In effect, the presence of a "true" grantor "trumps" the status of a power holder as a potential grantor. There is not a shared grantor status in these situations. Code § 678(b); Treas. Reg. 1.678(b)-1.[21]

Section 678(b) is necessary to prohibit a trust grantor who retains one or more grantor trust powers from allowing another person to have a power described in Code § 678(a) and thereby shift the tax consequences of the trust to such person. If

---

20. Persons subject to the so-called kiddie tax (applicable to most of the unearned income of children under age 19 or children who are full-time students under age 24) will result in much of the child's income being taxed at the tax rates applicable to their parents' tax rates. Code § 1(g).

21. For example, the IRS has issued a number of private letter rulings holding that the grantor trust provisions will "trump" a Code § 678(a) power attributable to a person holding a Crummey withdrawal right that lapses. The original grantor of the trust has been held to continue to be treated as the "owner" of all of the trust income and principal despite the existence of a Crummey clause in the trust giving other persons rights over the trust. Priv. Ltr. Ruls. 200729016 (March 27, 2007), 200603040 (October 24, 2005) and 200011054 (December 15, 1999).

this could be done, grantors could create appropriate powers in low-bracket taxpayers which would most likely never be exercised, but would have the effect of allocating some of the trust's taxable income to such low-bracket persons. This would obviously undermine the intent of the grantor trust rules.

> **Example:** Gina creates a revocable trust and gives Betty, the trust beneficiary, the power to demand annual distributions of the income of the trust. Since the trust is revocable, causing Gina to be treated as the trust grantor under Code § 676, all of the trust income is taxable to Gina, even if Betty exercises her power of withdrawal and receives the trust income.

The literal language of Code § 678(b) and Treas. Reg. 1.678(b)-1 does not end the discussion of this issue, however, since it addresses only a power over *income*, and many withdrawal powers over a trust, including Crummey powers, may also address powers over the trust principal. There is some useful guidance in the legislative history of these provisions where it is stated, "A person other than the grantor may be treated as a substantial owner of a trust if he has an unrestricted power to take the trust principal or income . . . unless the grantor himself is deemed taxable because of such a power." H.R. Rep. No. 1337, 83d Cong., 2d Sess. 63 (1954); S. Rep. No. 1622, 83d Cong. 2d Sess. 87 (1954).

Numerous commentators have cited this language and suggested that the power "over income" reference was a drafting error and should be disregarded, since Code § 678(a) applies to powers over income and principal, or that the reference to "income" is broadly meant to refer to "taxable income," and not narrowly to fiduciary accounting income. In its Private Letter Rulings, the IRS has not made a distinction between the power over income and the power over principal. Priv. Ltr. Ruls. 200840025 (June 13, 2008), 200732010 (May 1, 2007). In these rulings, the IRS often cites Treas. Reg. 1.671-2(b) referring to "income" as taxable income, not fiduciary accounting income, without making any distinction between the ordinary income and capital gains of the trust. If different persons (the grantor and the beneficiaries) had specific and possibly separate rights in fiduciary accounting income and/or fiduciary accounting principal, a "shared" trust ownership may be a reasonable conclusion here. Without such clear distinctions, the "power over income" language is likely to continue to be interpreted to refer to a power over income and principal.

Questions

1. Michelle is the grantor of an inter vivos trust for the benefit of her adult son, Paul. Michelle will make annual contributions to the trust, and grants Paul the right to withdraw an amount annually not to exceed the amount of the annual present interest gift tax exclusion. Michelle retains the right to revoke the trust. Local Bank is named the trustee. Under Code § 678, who will be treated as the owner of this trust?

2. John is the grantor of a trust. He funds the trust and provides that his daughter, Eleanor, has the right to use the trust income as desired to support her minor

daughter, Lucy. John names Eleanor as trustee of the trust. Eleanor does not use any of the trust income for the support of Lucy. Will Eleanor be treated as the owner of this trust? What if the Diamond Sky Bank is named the trustee instead of Eleanor? Will that make Eleanor the owner of the trust?

3. Sherry is the grantor of an inter vivos trust for the benefit of her adult daughter Dawn. The trust provides that one-half of the trust income and principal is required to be distributed to Dawn upon attaining age 30, and the balance to be paid to Dawn upon reaching age 40. The trust receives income each year. Upon turning age 30, Dawn is aware of her interest in the trust, but takes no action to seek a distribution. The trust continues to earn income. How should the trust income be taxed?

X. Using Grantor Trusts in Tax Planning Situations

In many different contexts, grantor trusts have become an especially useful and popular device for tax planning. Although a non-grantor trust that does not distribute its income is subject to the highly compressed income tax rates imposed on trusts and estates, the income of a grantor trust is taxed at the tax rate of the individual grantor, which is typically much more favorable.

Some of the planning techniques that feature grantor trusts are discussed briefly below.

A. The Revocable Trust

A revocable trust is the most commonly used form of grantor trust. Often called a "living trust," the revocable trust allows the grantor to transfer assets to a trust while retaining the right to income from the trust and control over the trust assets. The revocable trust is a grantor trust under the rules of Code § 676 (*see* Section VII, above). In those states where probate is cumbersome or expensive, the revocable trust is often the centerpiece of an estate plan, as it allows the grantor to control assets while living and pass assets at death to heirs through the trust without being subjected to probate administration. Most states treat a will as a public document, and some state laws make public an inventory of a decedent's assets that pass through probate. The use of the revocable trust in these jurisdictions allows a grantor and the grantor's family to maintain privacy after the grantor's passing with respect to the grantor's assets.

Even where probate administration and privacy are not serious issues, a revocable trust is often used as a management vehicle for the grantor's assets. Perhaps the grantor is aging, and becoming less comfortable or capable of managing his or her assets. Placing those assets in a revocable trust allows the grantor not only to remain in control of those assets as the trustee of the trust for as long as possible, but also to name a co-trustee or successor trustee to assist in management or to take over management, as the case may be. This planning may allow for an easy transition of control should the grantor become incapacitated without the need to have conservators or guardians appointed to manage the grantor's property. When the grantor dies, the fiduciaries are in place, the assets titled in the name of the trust are well-organized and easily identifiable, so that management of the grantor's estate can proceed efficiently.

If a person has real estate holdings in more than one state, a revocable trust is often a good way to hold title to those properties. If the grantor dies, instead of having to address ancillary probate proceedings in each state to transfer title from the grantor's name to the names of the grantor's heirs, the title in the name of the revocable trust is undisturbed and the trust beneficiaries can enjoy the property without the requirement of potentially cumbersome and expensive ancillary probate administrative proceedings.

From a tax perspective, the revocable trust is generally treated as the alter ego of the grantor. The taxable year of the trust and method of accounting used must follow those used by the grantor. Rev. Rul. 57-390, 1957-2 C.B. 326. All of the income of the trust is taxable to the grantor. There is no gain or loss recognized and no change to the income tax basis of the grantor's assets when those assets are placed in the trust. If a transfer is made by the grantor to the trust, it is not a taxable gift, since the grantor retains the right to revoke the trust. If the trust makes a gift to a third party, it is treated as a gift from the grantor individually to such third party. If the grantor of a revocable trust dies, all of the trust property is included in the grantor's taxable estate by reason of the grantor's right to revoke the trust. Code § 2038.

When the grantor dies, the trust will cease to be characterized as a grantor trust. It will then be subjected to the general rules of trust income taxation as provided by Subchapter J of the Internal Revenue Code. However, a revocable trust is eligible to make an election under Code § 645 to be taxed as if it were part of the grantor's estate for two years from the grantor's date of death if no estate tax return is required or the date which is six months after the date of the final determination of estate tax liability if an estate tax return is required. The election is made by filing a Form 8855 by the due date of the estate's first fiduciary income tax return. The laws addressing estate income tax administration are somewhat more favorable than those available in the case of a trust's income tax administration.

Other income tax rules that apply to the grantor as an individual remain applicable even though the grantor's property has been transferred to a revocable trust. The grantor can continue to claim itemized income tax deductions for home mortgage interest (Code § 163) and real property taxes (Code § 164), even though the property is titled in the name of the revocable trust. Priv. Ltr. Rul. 9516026 (Jan. 19, 1995). The exclusion of gain from the sale of a principal residence available under Code § 121 remains available to the grantor and the grantor's spouse even if the residence is held in a revocable trust at the time of the sale, assuming, of course, that the ownership and use requirements of Code § 121 are satisfied. Priv. Ltr. Rul. 199912026 (Dec. 23, 1998).

Transferring Series E or Series EE U.S. Savings Bonds with untaxed interest to a revocable trust does not accelerate taxation of the deferred income on the bonds. Rev. Rul. 58-2, 1958-1 C.B. 236; Priv. Ltr. Rul. 9009053 (Dec. 6, 1989). A grantor who suffers an involuntary conversion of real property can use the deferral of gain provisions of Code § 1033 even if the property is titled in the name of a revocable trust. Rev. Rul. 66-159, 1966-1 C.B. 162. Similarly, where a grantor owned property individually that was the subject of an involuntary conversion and later made the qualifying replacement property acquisition by using a grantor trust, the Service concluded that the trust's status would be disregarded for income tax purposes, and the grantor was considered to have purchased the property, thereby satisfying the requirements of Code § 1033. The trust was viewed as the purchasing and entitling agent of the grantor. Rev. Rul. 88-103, 1988-2 C.B. 304.

A decedent spouse may transfer his or her qualified retirement plan benefits to a grantor trust of the surviving spouse where the surviving spouse is the sole trustee and the current income beneficiary. If the surviving spouse then rolls over the plan benefits to the survivor's own IRA, the transaction will be viewed as a proper tax-free rollover by the surviving spouse. The fact that the plan benefits went from the decedent to the grantor trust to the spouse does not disqualify the transfer from tax-free rollover treatment. Had the trust been a trust other than a grantor trust, the spouse would not have been eligible for tax-free rollover treatment, unless the spouse could show he or she was the sole trustee and sole trust beneficiary with complete discretion over the trust property. Priv. Ltr. Ruls. 9813018 (Dec. 30, 1997) and 9820020 (Feb. 18, 1998).

A grantor may transfer an installment obligation to a revocable trust or may receive an installment obligation from a revocable trust. Neither of such transfers will be treated as a disposition of an installment obligation which would have the effect of accelerating deferred gain. Rev. Rul. 74-613, 1974-2 C.B. 153; Rev. Rul. 73-584, 1973-2 C.B.162; Rev. Rul. 76-100, 1976-1 C.B 123. However, the transfer of an installment obligation to an irrevocable trust of which the grantor is not treated as the owner ordinarily triggers the recognition of gain by the grantor. Rev. Rul. 67-167, 1967-1 C.B. 107; Rev. Rul. 76-530, 1976-2 C.B. 132.

For purposes of the net investment income tax under Code § 1411, a grantor trust is not subjected to the trust's threshold for imposition of the tax, but rather the individual grantor is subject to the thresholds applicable to individual taxpayers which depend upon one's filing status.

A potential drawback to revocable trust use is the requirement that the grantor's assets must be titled in trustee name to be effective. Clients must consider the cost and complexity of undertaking and monitoring this complexity versus the probate avoidance, management advantages, and privacy protection offered by revocable trust use.

B. The Grantor Trust as a Permitted Shareholder of an S Corporation

Grantor trusts are often used in the context of planning with S corporations because grantor trusts are qualified S corporation shareholders, provided the grantor (or deemed owner of the trust under Code § 678, if applicable) is an individual who is a citizen or resident of the United States. Code § 1361(c)(2)(A)(i). The entire trust must be owned by an individual meeting these criteria. If a grantor (or deemed trust owner) dies, and the trust met this test immediately before the grantor's death, the trust may continue to be a qualified S corporation shareholder, but only for the two-year period beginning on the date of the grantor's (or deemed owner's) death. Code § 1361(c)(2)(A)(ii); Treas. Reg. 1.1361-1(h).

The grantor trust is often a far more flexible planning vehicle for owning S corporation stock in a trust than the other trusts permitted to hold S corporation stock, namely the qualified subchapter S trust ("QSST") and the electing small business trust ("ESBT"), which require election notification to the IRS and specific (and in the case of the ESBT, unfavorable) income tax reporting and payment rules.

C. The Grantor Retained Annuity Trust (GRAT)

A Grantor Retained Annuity Trust (GRAT) is an irrevocable trust designed to meet the requirements for retaining a "qualified interest" in the trust. The grantor creates the trust and funds it with whatever property the grantor desires to use, including cash, stocks, bonds, mutual funds, real estate, business interests, etc. Generally, the intent of the GRAT is for the grantor to contribute property to the trust that has meaningful appreciation potential. The grantor of the GRAT retains the right to receive an annuity from the trust. The right to receive trust income makes the trust a grantor trust. Code § 677. The annuity may take the form of either a fixed dollar amount or a fixed percentage of the initial fair market value of the trust property. Code § 2702; Treas. Reg. 25. 2702-1.

The grantor is making a taxable gift for gift tax purposes of the remainder interest in the property transferred, i.e., the fair market value of the property less the value of the grantor's retained interest. This is not a gift eligible for the present interest gift tax exclusion. It is possible that the value of the gift to the remainder beneficiaries is zero, eliminating all gift tax liability, if the retained interest by the grantor is substantial enough to equal the value of the property used to fund the trust. This "zeroed-out GRAT" has been approved by the Tax Court and accepted by the IRS. *Walton v. Commissioner*, 115 T.C. 289 (2000); *acq.* Notice 2003-72, 2003-44 I.R.B. 964 (November 3, 2003); Treas. Reg. 25.2702-2(a)(5). The goal is to have the transferred property appreciate to an extent beyond what must be returned to the grantor, resulting in a transfer tax-free benefit to the remainder beneficiaries.

The annuity is created for a fixed period of years as selected by the grantor. Generally, the selected term is at least two years, and not more than twenty years. Since there are adverse federal estate tax consequences associated with the grantor of the GRAT dying before the end of the GRAT term (i.e., an estate inclusion of an amount necessary to produce the remaining annuity due to the grantor), it is advisable to select a term based on the age and health of the grantor that gives the grantor a reasonable likelihood of surviving the chosen retained interest term. Attention must be given to this "mortality risk." The annuity payments may be made to the grantor monthly, quarterly, semiannually, or annually, as desired by the grantor, but in any event, the annuity must be payable at least annually.

Since the grantor will be receiving an annuity, it is generally advisable, but not required, that the property selected to fund the GRAT be property that is income producing. Otherwise, principal is returned to the grantor to satisfy the required annual payments, defeating the goal of leaving more appreciated property to the remainder beneficiaries. During the annuity term of the trust, a GRAT is a grantor trust, so that the grantor is taxed on all of the income of the GRAT, whether or not such income is actually received by the grantor. Note that a GRAT is considered to be a 100% grantor trust so long as trust principal can be used to make the required GRAT annuity payments. Most GRATs are drafted to provide this.

At the termination of the annuity period, the trust property passes to the beneficiaries selected by the grantor, thus avoiding probate issues as well as further transfer taxation (assuming the grantor survived the term of the trust), and ensuring a measure of succession planning desired by the grantor.

The basic "theory" of how the GRAT works and why it may be desirable is that property is transferred to fund a trust and the grantor retains an annuity interest that is calculated based on both the selected qualified retained interest of the grantor and an interest rate prescribed monthly by the IRS (the Code § 7520 rate), with a remainder interest to pass to designated beneficiaries. The assumption by the government in permitting this planning is that the transferred property will generate a cash flow consistent with the prescribed interest rate, and that the value of the property will not fluctuate. If the property generates a return that exceeds the applicable Code § 7520 interest rate (sometimes referred to as the "hurdle rate"), either attributable to increased cash flow or capital appreciation, the remainder interest will have been undervalued at the date of creation of the trust, and the remainder beneficiaries will acquire property without additional transfer tax being imposed on the grantor (beyond the original gift tax — or use of the applicable gift tax exclusion — when the trust was created). It is this expectation of future appreciation beyond the gift tax value that was used at the inception of the trust that makes the GRAT a popular planning technique.

D. The Qualified Personal Residence Trust (QPRT)

A Qualified Personal Residence Trust (QPRT) is an irrevocable trust under which the grantor retains the right to use and enjoy a residence for a term of years. The Code treats a grantor as the owner of the trust property under Code § 677 (by virtue of a retained right to the trust income), under Code § 675 (by virtue of a retained administrative power over the trust) and under Code § 673 (by virtue of a possible reversion to the grantor's estate); thus, the QPRT will be treated as a grantor trust for federal income tax purposes. Once grantor trust status has been determined, the grantor will be able to claim the allowable deductions for taxes, mortgage interest and any other deductions or exclusions arising from the residential property that may be properly chargeable to or excluded from income. Code § 2702; Treas. Reg. 25.2702-5.

> **Example:** In a typical personal residence trust, the grantor creates an irrevocable trust for the benefit of family members. The grantor transfers her personal residence to the trust, retaining the right to use and occupy the residence for a number of years, which number of years she reasonably expects to survive. If she survives the retained interest term, the residence is then owned by the remainder beneficiaries of the trust (the family members). The grantor is treated as having made a gift of the fair market value of the residence on the date of the transfer, less the value of her retained interest, i.e., a gift of the present value of the remainder interest. Determining these values requires an actuarial calculation. Since the gift to the remainder beneficiaries will only benefit them in the future, when the retained interest term expires, the gift to the remainder beneficiaries is a gift of a future interest, and the grantor may not use her present interest gift tax exclusion to offset any portion of the value of the gift. To report the QPRT, a gift tax return (Form 709) must be filed for the year the residence is transferred. The goal that underlies QPRT use is that the personal residence appreciates beyond its value upon transfer, so that the grantor has made a gift of property "frozen" at the date of gift value less the grantor's retained interest, and worth substantially more when the beneficiaries receive it, with no further transfer tax being due.

If the grantor dies before her retained interest term is exhausted, her death occurred while she retained the right to use and occupy the transferred personal residence property. Accordingly, the fair market value of the transferred property as of her date of death is included in her gross estate for federal estate tax purposes. Code § 2036. In that case, the basis of the residence to the heirs is the fair market value of the property as of the deceased grantor's date of death. Code § 1014(a).[22]

E. The Intentionally Defective Grantor Trust

The term "intentionally defective grantor trust" refers to an irrevocable trust that intentionally "violates" one or more of the grantor trust rules. As a result, trust income remains taxable to the grantor. When working with the intentionally

22. If the grantor outlives the retained interest term, and later dies, the value of the residence is not included in her gross estate for federal estate tax purposes, as she did not retain any interest in the transferred property at the time of her death, and the basis of the property to heirs is the grantor's basis in the property.

defective grantor trust as a planning technique, the general objective is to leave the grantor taxable on the trust income, but make certain that the trust property will not be included in the taxable estate of the grantor.

The rules relating to the taxation of trusts for income tax purposes and for transfer tax purposes are not necessarily consistent. Differences between the transfer tax rules and the income tax rules thus allow a discrepancy to exist—a trust grantor may be treated as the owner of the trust for income tax purposes, but the trust property may be excluded from the grantor's estate for estate tax purposes. This "asymmetrical" tax treatment allows the intentionally defective grantor trust to exist.

Where these circumstances are present, the trust is considered "defective" for income tax purposes (the grantor's transfer failed to relieve the grantor of the income tax obligations of the transferred property). Where the grantor created the trust specifically to achieve this result, the grantor trust is said to be "intentionally defective."

The intentionally defective grantor trust ("IDGT") has a number of desirable tax and estate planning uses. It can be used as an estate freezing technique whereby the value of property transferred by the grantor to the trust is "frozen" as of the date of transfer so that all future appreciation may benefit the trust beneficiaries. Gifts or sales to an intentionally defective grantor trust may be used to accomplish this goal. Depending on the assets used to fund the trust, valuation discounts for minority interest and lack of marketability may be available for transfers of partnership, LLC, real estate, and closely-held corporate business interests.

IDGTs may also be used as an income tax planning technique. The grantor will transfer property with the intention of removing such property from the grantor's taxable estate. However, the grantor still wishes to be taxed on the income from the trust property for income tax purposes. Having the grantor remain subject to income tax, rather than the trust, serves three purposes. First, it leaves the income taxable to an individual who may be in a lower income tax bracket than the trust. Second, by having the grantor pay the income tax on the trust's income, the trust itself is allowed to grow in value because the trust is not obligated to pay the tax. Accordingly, more funds remain in the trust to pass to the trust beneficiaries. Third, by having the grantor pay the income tax on the trust's income, the grantor's estate is reduced by the amount of income taxes paid by the grantor over the duration of the trust. This is sometimes referred to as "burning" off assets from the grantor's potential estate, a desirable result if the grantor's eventual estate will be large enough to be taxable.

Consider using an IDGT in any situation where the planning goal is to move family wealth from the grantor to the trust and its beneficiaries, including even a simple annual exclusion gift trust for the benefit of children or grandchildren. Leaving the grantor taxable on the trust income is a powerful estate reduction planning tool for the grantor. The former planning "mantra" of shifting taxation of income to persons in lower tax brackets has changed to retaining the income tax burden in the hands of the wealthy senior family member as an effective estate planning strategy.

An IDGT may be used to implement a sale of assets between the grantor and the trust. The grantor may sell assets to the trust in exchange for a long-term interest-bearing installment note. If the transaction is structured properly, the trust grantor has converted an appreciating asset (the asset sold) into an asset with a fixed value (the promissory installment note); hence the "freeze". The sale transaction is entered into at fair market value, so the sale by the grantor does not result in it being treated as a gift or bargain sale to the trust beneficiaries. The grantor will not be subject to income tax on the sale of the assets to the trust. Why? Because, for income tax purposes, the grantor is treated as the trust owner. See Rev. Rul. 85-13, 1985-1 C.B. 184 (transactions between the grantor and the grantor trust will not have any income tax consequences, since the grantor and the trust are treated as one taxpayer). This allows the sale of assets by the grantor to the trust to avoid capital gains taxes, and the note interest received by the grantor to avoid being subjected to income taxes. Appreciation on the assets sold to the trust grows outside of the grantor's estate. If the grantor dies before the note has been paid in full, only the unpaid note balance is included in the grantor's estate, not the date of death value of the transferred property.

The grantor of an IDGT will not retain any voting, economic, or reversionary rights in the assets transferred to the trust. The grantor should not be the trustee.

The only gift tax element of this transaction arises from the belief that the trust must be capitalized ("seeded") with sufficient assets (aside from the property being transferred to the trust in exchange for the trust's note) to establish the independence of the trust from the assets to be sold by the grantor to the trust. This gift is considered to be a contribution of equity to the trust to be distinguished from the debt represented by the note arising from the sale of the property to the trust. The capitalization by gift is generally recommended to be at least 10% of the value of the installment note, so that there is a debt (*i.e.*, the amount of the note) to equity (*i.e.*, the amount of the gift) ratio of not more than 10:1. It is important that the trust have independent equity, so that the note owed to the grantor is not recharacterized as an equity interest, which could, in turn, result in the inclusion of the transferred property in the grantor's estate on the theory that an equity interest has been retained in the property sold to the trust by the grantor.

It is crucial to the success of this planning technique that the grantor power be retained by the grantor be a power that will trigger application of the grantor trust rules, but not trigger any of the Code sections that will result in estate tax inclusion. In other words, the power must be one "big enough" to leave the grantor taxable on the trust income, but not "so big" as to require inclusion in the grantor's estate.

Planners typically favor several of the grantor powers discussed earlier in this Chapter to accomplish this goal.

First, drafters may give the trustee or a non-adverse third party (perhaps a "trust protector") the right to add a charitable beneficiary. Code § 674. The grantor should not be the person allowed to possess the power to add beneficiaries. Retaining such a power in the hands of the grantor could cause an inclusion in the grantor's estate under Code §§ 2036 or 2038. Where this is the power used by the grantor, it is recommended that the power granted to the non-adverse party to add potential additional beneficiaries be limited to charitable beneficiaries.

Second, there are several powers set forth in Code § 675 that are administrative powers which the grantor may retain and thereby be taxed on the income of the trust, but retaining such administrative powers does not rise to the level of requiring inclusion of the trust property in the estate of the grantor. A power of administration is exercisable in a nonfiduciary capacity by any person without the approval or consent of any person in a fiduciary capacity. Code § 675(4). Among the administrative powers satisfying these criteria are the following:

1. The power to borrow the income or principal of the trust, directly or indirectly, without providing adequate interest or without providing adequate security exercisable by the grantor or a non-adverse party will cause the grantor to be treated as the owner of the trust property for income tax purposes. Code § 675(2). Properly created, this power should not be viewed as creating a threat that the trust property will be included in the grantor's estate. As a practical suggestion, it may not be advisable to allow the grantor to have the power to borrow without adequate interest, since that may cause the imputed interest rules and Code § 7872 to apply, resulting in an unwanted complication for the trust. Allowing the grantor to borrow the trust income or principal without providing adequate security will provide the desired grantor trust status and avoid the unwanted estate tax inclusion.

2. The power most often used in the creation of the IDGT is the power of substitution held in a non-fiduciary capacity under Code § 675(4)(C) as described above. This power causes the grantor to be taxed on the trust income, but does not result in the inclusion of the trust property in the grantor's estate.[23] Using this power can give the grantor the opportunity to allow the trust property to appreciate in the trust, then substitute high basis assets for the property in the trust, recovering the appreciated low basis assets sold to the trust for the grantor, and then holding the

23. Rev. Rul. 2008-22, 2008-16 I.R.B. 796 (April 17, 2008), indicates that this result will apply *provided* the trustee has a fiduciary obligation (either under local law or required by the terms of the governing instrument) to ensure that the properties acquired and substituted by the grantor are, in fact, of equivalent value, and *further provided* that the power of substitution cannot be exercised by the grantor in a manner to allow the shifting of interests among the beneficiaries of the trust. The trustee must have a duty of impartiality toward the beneficiaries. Where the power of substitution is used as the "defective" retained interest, the grantor should *not* be permitted to act as the trustee. Subsequent to the issuance of Rev. Rul. 2008-22, the IRS issued Private Letter Ruling 200944002 (July 15, 2009) which follows Revenue Ruling 2008-22, providing a "roadmap" as to how to proceed using a power of substitution.

recovered assets until death and leaving them to heirs in order to gain a fair market value at death income tax basis to heirs.

Taxpayers who created grantor trusts in the years prior to the passage of the 2017 Tax Cuts and Jobs Act may now find, due to the significant increase in the lifetime exemption amount, that they have little estate tax exposure but substantial income tax exposure. That being the case, they may wish to relinquish the powers that made the trust a grantor trust and allow the trust (or more likely the trust beneficiaries) to become the taxpayer. Furthermore, there may be a rush to establish non-grantor trusts for families with multiple members to create eligibility for the Code § 199A deduction where that opportunity was not available to the grantor acting alone as the only taxpayer. As with so many tax planning issues, the circumstances of each taxpayer must be evaluated separately. No advisor should ever assume that "one size fits all" is a correct view of tax planning.

Chapter 7

Charitable Trusts

Internal Revenue Code: Sections: 664(a)-(f) & 170(f)(2)(B)

Regulations: 664-1, -2, -3, -4 & 1.170A-6(c)

I. Introduction

This chapter is designed to provide a basic understanding of charitable remainder trusts (sometimes referred to as CRTs) and charitable lead trusts (sometimes referred to as CLTs) and how they are treated for income tax purposes. We begin with an overview of how each work and then explore how they are treated for income tax purposes. This chapter will give you the background needed to gain a basic understanding of charitable remainder trusts and charitable lead trusts. If you can master this material, you will know more about these trusts than many professional advisors.

Charitable remainder trusts and charitable lead trusts each have their own unique taxation rules. This chapter discusses the income taxation of both types of trusts. The regulations governing each type of trust contain much more detail than is covered in this chapter.

II. Income Taxation of Charitable Remainder Trusts

The name itself of a charitable remainder trust indicates its purpose — a remainder interest passing to charity. These trusts often appeal to taxpayers who are charitably-minded, but who want or need to keep a right to receive annual payments for themselves or their loved ones.

A. Introduction and Background

Charitable remainder trusts ("CRTs") are frequently used for estate planning and planned-giving purposes. However, before we dive into the income taxation of CRTs, it is important to provide some background.

A CRT is a trust that meets the following four requirements from section 664:

1. It provides for a distribution of a specified sum (an annuity trust) or a fixed percentage (a unitrust) at least annually to one or more persons, at least one of whom must be a non-charitable beneficiary. The annuity amount cannot be less than 5 percent and not more than 50 percent of the initial fair market value of all property placed in the trust; the unitrust percentage cannot be less than 5 percent and not more than 50 percent of the net fair market value of the assets, valued annually.
2. The payments must be for the life or lives of the individual beneficiaries (all of whom must be living at the time the trust is created) or for a term of years not in excess of 20 years.
3. Upon the termination of the non-charitable interest, the remainder must either be held in a continuing trust for charitable purposes or paid to or for the use of one or more charitable organizations described in Code § 170(c).
4. The present value of the remainder interest (i.e., the amount of the donor's charitable deduction) must be equal to at least 10% of the initial value of the assets contributed to the trust.

There are two basic types of charitable remainder trusts under § 664—a charitable remainder annuity trust (CRAT) and a charitable remainder unitrust (CRUT).

In addition to the four requirements listed above, regarding a CRAT, the IRS takes the position that a charitable deduction is not allowed for a gift of a remainder interest in trust where there is more than a five percent probability that the charitable remainder beneficiaries will not receive any trust corpus. Rev. Rul. 77-374, 1977-2 C.B. 329. This is known as the 5% exhaustion test. The rationale for this rule is found in both the estate and gift tax regulations. Those regulations provide that no deduction is allowable if a charitable transfer is subject to a condition "unless the possibility that the charitable transfer will not become effective is so remote as to be negligible." Treas. Reg. 20.2055-2(b)(1), 25.2522(c)-3(b)(1).[1]

While the annual amount paid by a CRAT will be the same each year, the amount paid by a CRUT will fluctuate each year, because its annual payments are a percentage of the fair market value of the trust assets valued each year.

There are four types of charitable remainder unitrusts (CRUTs) allowed under section 664:

---

1. In a low interest rate environment, the application of the 5% exhaustion test makes it difficult for younger individuals to be able to establish a charitable remainder annuity trust with lifetime payouts. That is due to the fact that there would be more than a 5% probability that the trust corpus would be exhausted during the individual's lifetime. As a result, the IRS has issued Rev. Proc. 2016-42, 2016-34 IRB 1, to provide relief from the 5% exhaustion test. Rev. Proc. 2016-42 effectively allows the 5% exhaustion test to be disregarded if language is provided in the CRT stating that the trust will terminate if, in the future, it fails the requirements that the charity receive at least 10% of the CRT's initial value as its remainder interest. Sample language to satisfy this requirement is included in the revenue procedure.

1. A standard charitable remainder unitrust. The standard CRUT pays a fixed percentage of the net fair market value, valued annually, to one or more beneficiaries.
2. A net income charitable remainder unitrust (NICRUT). A NICRUT provide for the payment of the lesser of the fixed percentage or the net income of the trust.
3. A net income charitable remainder unitrust with a make-up provision (NIM-CRUT). A net income unitrust may have what is commonly referred to as a "makeup" provision. A makeup provision provides that whenever the net income is less than the amount determined by the fixed percentage, such shortfall can be paid in any subsequent year when the net income is more than the amount determined by the fixed percentage. This is referred to as a net income with make-up CRUT (or NIMCRUT).
4. A "flip" charitable remainder unitrust. A CRUT may begin as a NICRUT or a NIMCRUT and later convert to a standard CRUT. Treas. Reg. 1.664-3(a)(1)(c). These types of CRUTs are referred to as "flip" CRUTs, because they "flip" from a NICRUT or NIMCRUT to a standard CRUT.

Taxpayers who establish charitable remainder trusts during their lifetimes may, for income and gift tax purposes, deduct the actuarial value of the charitable remainder interest; taxpayers who establish charitable remainder trusts upon death may, for estate tax purposes, deduct the actuarial value of the charitable remainder interest. However, our focus is on how a charitable remainder trust, as an entity, is taxed for income tax purposes.

One more thing before we review the income taxation of CRTs. Certain rules applicable to private foundations also apply to CRTs. Code § 4947(a)(2). The private foundation rules that relate to CRTs could be an entire course by themselves, but they are reviewed here only summarily. The private foundation rules that deal with excise taxes are found in §§ 4940 to 4948. Those rules impose an excise tax on investment income under § 4940, self-dealing under § 4941, failure to distribute income under § 4942, excess business holdings under § 4943, jeopardy investments under § 4944, and taxable expenditures under § 4945. Excise taxes are imposed for violation of these rules. The CRT governing instrument must contain provisions prohibiting a CRT from violating these rules. Treas. Reg. 1.664-1(b); 1.508-2(b)(1)(vi); Rev. Rul. 72-395, 1972-2 C.B. 340.

B. Income Taxation of Charitable Remainder Trusts

A CRT is exempt from income tax unless it has unrelated business taxable income (UBTI). Code § 664(c). Thus, none of the income or capital gains of a CRT are subject to tax at the trust level unless those items constitute UBTI. In simple terms, UBTI is income generated from an activity of a commercial nature unrelated to a charity's tax-exempt function. The UBTI rules are contained in Code §§ 511-514.

The tax exempt status of a CRT allows, for example, a CRT to sell appreciated property contributed by the grantor without paying any tax on the gain. However, the payments of the annuity or unitrust interest to the non-charitable beneficiary are not necessarily income tax-free to the beneficiary. The distributions from a CRT to the non-charitable beneficiary are taxed under a tier system of taxation. The tier system of taxation applicable to CRTs is not to be confused with the tier system governing the distributions from a complex trust under §§ 661 and 662; instead, the tier system for CRTs is governed by § 664(b).

1. *Taxation of the Income a CRT Generates*

The tier system of taxation of a CRT is based generally on a worst-in, first-out system of taxation. In other words, a non-charitable beneficiary is deemed to first receive items of gross income taxed at higher income tax rates before being deemed to receive items of gross income taxed at lower rates. This general rule and applicable exceptions are discussed below.

The distributions to a non-charitable beneficiary from a CRT are deemed to come from the following four income categories, in the order set forth below:

Tier 1—ordinary income to the extent of the trust's ordinary income for the current year and undistributed ordinary income for prior years;

Tier 2—capital gain, first as short-term capital gain to the extent of the trust's net short-term capital gain for the current year and undistributed net short-term capital gain for prior years, and then as long-term capital gain to the extent of the trust's net long-term capital gain for the taxable year and undistributed net long-term capital gain for prior years;

Tier 3— other income, generally tax-exempt income, to the extent of the trust's other income for the current year and for undistributed other income for prior years; and

Tier 4—trust principal.

Distributions to a beneficiary are deemed to originate first from the highest tier (i.e., Tier 1) and then cascade down to the lowest tier (i.e., Tier 4). Once all of the income in a particular tier is exhausted, the beneficiary's distribution is deemed to come from the next tier of income until all of the income in that tier is exhausted. The progression continues down the tiers. Thus, distributions are deemed to come from the ordinary income tier, before the capital gain tier, and from the capital gain tier before the tax-exempt tier.

> **Example:** A CRT is required to pay an annuity of $50,000 per year to a non-charitable beneficiary. In its initial year, the CRT has $10,000 of ordinary income, $25,000 of long-term capital gain, and $20,000 of tax-exempt income. The $50,000 distribution to the non-charitable beneficiary is deemed to consist of, in this order: (1) $10,000 of ordinary income, (2) $25,000 of long-term capital gain, and (3) $15,000 of tax-exempt income.

The remaining $5,000 of undistributed tax-exempt income is carried forward to the next year as Tier 3 income to be taken into account as distributions are made in future years.

Current income from each tier is deemed distributed first before undistributed income from prior years. Distributions to non-charitable beneficiaries consist first of ordinary income to the extent of the trust's ordinary income for the taxable year of the distribution and then the trust's ordinary income from prior years not deemed to have been previously distributed. After all of the current year and prior years' undistributed ordinary income has been exhausted, the distribution to non-charitable beneficiaries is deemed to consist of capital gain income to the extent of the trust's capital gain for the year and then undistributed capital gain income from previous years. Once the capital gain tier is exhausted, the distribution is deemed to consist of, first, current year and then previous year tax-exempt income, until that tier of income is exhausted. If the income in Tiers 1-3 is exhausted, then, and only then, will the distribution be deemed to be a non-taxable return of the trust's principal.

Example: A CRAT is required to pay a $50,000 annuity per year to a non-charitable beneficiary. In the year the CRAT was established, suppose it had $10,000 of undistributed ordinary income and $10,000 of undistributed net long-term capital gain. In year 2, suppose the trust earned $20,000 of ordinary income, $10,000 of net long-term capital gain, and $10,000 of tax-exempt income. In year 2, the $50,000 distribution to the non-charitable beneficiary will be deemed to consist of, in this order: (1) $20,000 of ordinary income earned in year 2, (2) $10,000 of undistributed ordinary income earned in year 1, (3) $10,000 of net long-term capital gain earned in year 2 and (4) $10,000 of undistributed net long-term capital gain earned in year 1. None of the tax-exempt income will be deemed to have been distributed to the non-charitable beneficiary.

Notice how distributions are not deemed to consist of income assigned to a lower tier until all of the current and accumulated income in the higher tiers has been exhausted. That is why the tier system of taxation of a CRT is referred to a worst-in, first out system of taxation — the worst, or income taxed at highest rate of tax, is deemed distributed to a beneficiary before income taxed at a lower rate.

But we are not quite done with the complexities. There are different items of gross income within Tier 1 and Tier 2 as follows:

- Tier 1 has two classes of income:
  - Items of ordinary income potentially subject to the highest income tax rates (currently 37%), and
  - Qualified dividends potentially subject to a 20% maximum tax rate.
- Tier 2 has four classes of income:
  - Short-term capital gains potentially subject to the highest income tax rates (currently 37%);

- Long-term capital gains on collectibles potentially subject to a 28% maximum tax rate;
- Unrecaptured §1250 gain potentially subject to a 25% maximum tax rate; and
- Other long-term capital gains potentially subject to a maximum tax rate of 20%.

Treas. Reg. 1.664(d).

> **Example.** A CRT requires an annual distribution of $50,000. During the year in question the CRT has ordinary income of $5,000 (tier 1), qualified dividends of $10,000 (tier 1), short-term capital gain of $8,000 (tier 2), long-term capital gain from collectibles of $7,500 (tier 2), long term capital gain of $15,000 (tier 2), and tax-exempt income of $12,000 (tier 3). The distribution to the beneficiary is deemed to consist of tier 1 income first, and within the tier 1 income, of ordinary income of $5,000 first and then qualified dividends of $10,000. Once the items in tier 1 are exhausted, the distribution is deemed to consist of tier 2 income in the order of highest to lowest taxed tier 2 income, i.e., first $8,000 of short-term capital gain (potential 37% tax rate), next $7,500 long-term collectible gains (potential 28% tax rate), and finally long-term capital gain of $15,000 (potential tax rate of 20%). Once the income in tier 1 and tier 2 has been exhausted, we drop down to tier 3. Of the tier 3 tax-exempt income of $12,000, only $4,500 of tier 3 income is needed to cover the $50,000 distribution to the non-charitable beneficiary. The remaining $7,500 of tier 3 tax-exempt income is carried forward as tier 3 income to the subsequent years. Thus, the beneficiary will report on his income tax return the following income: $5,000 of ordinary income, $10,000 of qualified dividends, $8,000 of short-term capital gains, $7,500 of long-term capital gains from collectibles, $15,000 of long-term capital gain, and $4,500 of tax-exempt income.

Note that the above example demonstrates an exception to the worst-in, first-out system of taxation, because qualified dividends taxed at a maximum rate of 20% are deemed distributed before short-term capital gains potentially taxable at a 37% tax rate and long-term collectible gains potentially taxable at a 28% tax rate.[2] Within each tier, distributions are treated as coming first from the class of assets with the highest marginal rate of tax until the income from that class is exhausted, and then from the next class of assets within that tier until all types of income within that tier are exhausted. Treas. Reg. 1.664-1(d)(1)(ii)(b). Then distributions are treated as coming from the next tier, and within that tier, from the class of income within that

2. Prior to 2001, dividends were taxed at the same rate as other items of ordinary gross income. When the law was changed to tax qualified dividends at a preferential maximum tax rate of 20%, regulations still treated qualified dividends as Tier 1 income.

tier that is taxed at the highest marginal rate of tax. For example, distributions from Tier 2 are deemed to come first from short-term gains, then from collectibles, if any, taxed at a maximum rate of 28%, then from §1250 unrecaptured gain taxed at a rate of 25%, and finally from long-term capital gains taxed at a maximum rate of 20%.

The chart on page 343 illustrates how the distributions are treated when there is both income from the current year and accumulated but undistributed income from prior years. Although we refer to the tier system as a "worst-in, first-out" type of distribution system, this is not always the case, especially when there is also accumulated but undistributed income from prior years.

> **Example:** A charitable remainder trust has investment income of $500, qualified dividend income of $200 and qualified REIT dividends of $1,000. The trust distributes $1,000 to the CRT beneficiary. The CRT has two classes of income within the ordinary income tier: (1) ordinary income consisting of the investment income of $500 and the qualified REIT dividends of $1,000 and (2) qualified dividend income of $200. The $1,000 distribution to the CRT beneficiary consists of $333 of investment income ($500 investment income/$1,500 total ordinary income × $1,000 distribution) and $667 of qualified REIT dividends ($1,000 qualified REIT dividends/$1,500 total ordinary income × $1,000 distribution). Notice that none of the qualified dividends is deemed distributed. Although all the income is allocated to Tier 1, the investment income and qualified REIT dividends are taxed at the same rate within the same class which is higher than the rate of tax for the qualified dividends which is in a separate class within Tier 1.

The following diagrams illustrate the tier system, the categories of tiers and the classes of income within those tiers and the order in which income in the various categories and classes are deemed distributed to the non-charitable beneficiary.

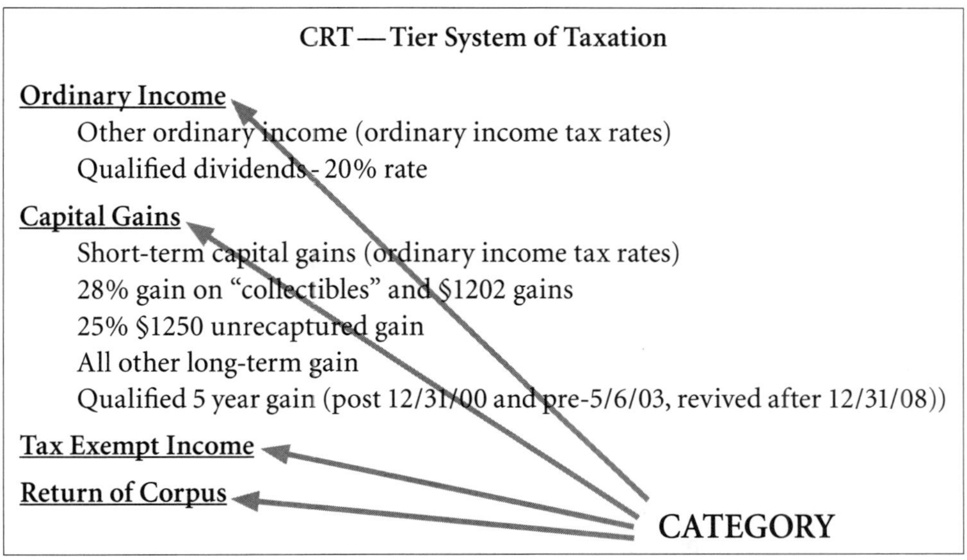

CRT—Tier System of Taxation

<u>Ordinary Income</u>

- Other ordinary income (ordinary income tax rates)
- Qualified dividends—20% rate

<u>Capital Gains</u>

- Short-term capital gains (ordinary income tax rates)
- 28% gain on "collectibles" and §1202 gains
- 25% §1250 unrecaptured gain
- All other long-term gain
- Qualified 5 year gain (post 12/31/00 and pre-5/6/03, revived after 12/31/08))

<u>Tax Exempt Income</u>

<u>Return of Corpus</u>

CLASS

CRT—Tier System of Taxation

<u>Ordinary Income</u>*

- Other ordinary income (ordinary income tax rates)
- Qualified dividends—20% rate

<u>Capital Gains</u>*

- Short-term capital gains (ordinary income tax rates)
- 28% long-term gain on "collectibles" and §1202 (qualified small business) gains
- 25% §1250 unrecaptured gain
- All other long-term gain—taxed at 20%
- Qualified 5 year gain (post 12/31/00 and pre-5/6/03, revived after 12/31/12))

<u>Tax Exempt Income*</u>

<u>Return of Corpus</u>

* Current year income *in each class* deemed distributed first, followed by *each class* of income accumulated in a previous year. In other words, distributions are deemed eat through all classes of current year income before they are deemed distributed from any class of accumulated income e.g. current year ordinary income, then current year qualified dividends, then accumulated current income, then accumulated qualified dividends.

In determining the amount of capital gain distributed, long-term gains are netted against long-term losses, and short-term gains are netted against short-term losses. The short-term capital gains are deemed distributed before long-term gains. Special carryover rules apply to both ordinary and capital losses. Thus, if losses are not all used in a given year, they may be carried forward, within the specific tiers to offset ordinary income or capital gains incurred in future years. Treas. Reg. 1.664-1(d)(1)(iii). Losses are never carried back.

Tier System — Order of Distribution

Tier I	**Current Year**	**Prior Year**
Ordinary Income	1	2
Qualified Dividends	3	4
Tier II		
STCG	5	6
28% Gain	7	8
25% Gain	9	10
Other LTCG	11	12
§1202 Gain	13	14
Tier III — T/E	15	16
Tier IV — Corpus	17	

Treas. Reg. 1.664-1(d) sets forth the ordering rules

The income that CRTs generate is not subject to the 3.8% net investment income tax imposed under §1411. Instead, in the hands of CRT beneficiaries, such income is subject to the tax to the extent that CRT distributions include items that constitute net investment income.[3]

2. Allocation of Deductions

Deductions that are directly attributable to one or more classes of items within a tier are allocated to the items to which they relate. Treas. Reg. 1.664-1(d)(2). For example, rental expenses would be allocated to rental income. All other deductions are allocated among the items in a given tier in the proportion that the gross income of each class of items included in the tier, reduced by the deductions attributed to that class under the first allocation, bears to all income in the tier. Said more simply, they are allocated pro-rata among the classes of income within the tier. *Id.* However, the allocation cannot create or increase a net loss within a class. Any deductions that are not allocable under either of the first two provisions can be allocated in any manner. *Id.*

3. Unrelated Business Taxable Income (UBTI)

Currently, if a CRT receives unrelated business taxable income, a 100% excise tax is imposed on the UBTI.[4] Code §664(c)(2)(A). Other income earned by the CRT remains tax exempt.

---

3. For students wishing to learn more about this area, the Treasury Regulations contain much more detail and examples. *See generally* Treas. Reg. 1.1411-3(d).

4. Prior to 2007, if a CRT had even one dollar of UBTI, the CRT lost its exemption from income tax. In other words, all of the income for the year the trust had UBTI, including any gain on the

Even though the UBTI is subject to a 100% excise tax, depending on the type of income, the UBTI is assigned to one of the four tiers. The trust's UBTI constitutes trust income for purposes of determining the character of a distribution made to a beneficiary; furthermore, the trust income is allocated among the tiers without regard to whether part of the income is UBTI. Treas. Reg. 1.664-1(c)(1). The tax on UBTI is allocated to corpus and is not deductible in determining the taxable income to the beneficiary. Treas. Reg. 1.664-1(c)(1) and (2) and (d)(2). As a result, UBTI earned by a CRT is potentially subject to double taxation—the 100% excise tax and to the beneficiary when distributed.

> **Example:** A CRT is required to make a $50,000 distribution to the non-charitable beneficiary. The trust has $25,000 of ordinary income that constitutes UBTI and $30,000 of long-term capital gain. The trust is liable for a 100% excise tax on its $25,000 of UBTI and does not receive a deduction for this payment. In addition, the UBTI, as ordinary income, is tier 1 income. Thus, the $50,000 distribution to the beneficiary is deemed to consist of $25,000 of ordinary income and $25,000 of long-term capital gain. The remaining $5,000 of long-term capital gain is carried over as tier 2 income to subsequent years. Notice how the UBTI is double taxed—once as a 100% excise tax and then to the beneficiary as a distribution of tier 1 income.

4. *Year of Inclusion*

Charitable remainder trusts are required to adopt a calendar year. Code § 644.

Distributions from a CRT are deemed made on the last day of the trust's taxable year in which the amount is required to be distributed, even if the annuity or unitrust amount is not actually distributed until after the close of the trust's taxable year. Treas. Reg. 1.664-1(d)(4)(i). Akin to simple and complex trusts, a CRT beneficiary reports distributions in the taxable year in which the trust's year ends.

> **Example:** A CRT (which is required to be on a calendar year) makes a $50,000 distribution to the non-charitable beneficiary on September 15 of Year 1. The beneficiary, who is an individual also on a calendar year, must account for the distribution on his Year 1 income tax return.

5. *Planning with Charitable Remainder Trusts*

Although the tier system of taxation provides opportunities for valuable tax planning, it has led to some misconceptions. For example, those not familiar with the income tax rules governing CRTs sometimes assume that CRTs funded with

---

sale of appreciated assets contributed to the CRT during the year, was subject to income tax as if the trust was a complex trust. *Leila G. Newhall Unitrust v. Commissioner*, 104 T.C. 236 (1995). This was a harsh result for a CRT earning UBTI.

appreciated assets that are sold and immediately invested in tax-exempt bonds will yield tax-exempt income to the noncharitable beneficiary.[5] However, the tier system prevents this result.

> **Example:** A CRT is funded with $500,000 of publicly traded stock purchased more than a year ago for $100,000. The trustee sells the appreciated stock and immediately invests the entire proceeds in tax-exempt municipal bonds. The CRT calls for annual distributions of $25,000 to the noncharitable beneficiary. The $400,000 capital gain realized upon the sale of stock is assigned to Tier 2. The tax-exempt income earned by the CRT is assigned to Tier 3. The $25,000 annual distributions to the noncharitable beneficiary are deemed to consist of capital gain income until the entire Tier 2 capital gain is exhausted. Only after the entire $400,000 capital gain and other Tier 1 or Tier 2 income is exhausted will the distribution have the potential to be characterized as tax-exempt income. In fact, the only possible way for the CRT to be able to have 100% of the distributions to the noncharitable beneficiary deemed to consist of tax-exempt income is to fund the CRT in cash and immediately invest 100% of the cash in tax-exempt municipal bonds. Investing in assets yielding Tier 1 (ordinary income) or Tier 2 (capital gain) income will cause that income to be deemed distributed before tax-exempt income.

Careful investment of the CRT assets can yield favorable income tax results to the noncharitable beneficiary. As a general rule, investments in equities (stocks) are favored over taxable fixed income (bonds) due to the difference in income tax rates applicable to qualified dividends (maximum of 20% rate) versus interest income (up to 37% rate).

> **Example:** Same facts as the preceding example except that the trustee invests in growth stocks and stocks paying qualified dividends. Thus, the only income that can be distributed to the noncharitable beneficiary is Tier 1 qualified dividends taxed at a maximum rate of 20% or long-term capital gain also taxed at a 20% maximum rate of tax. Thus, by careful selection of investments and avoiding investments yielding ordinary income, the trustee can ensure that distributions to the noncharitable beneficiary are taxed at a favorable maximum tax rate of 20%.

---

5. Treas. Reg. 1.664-1(a)(3) provides that a trust is not a CRT if its terms include a provision which restricts the trustee from investing the trust assets in a manner which could result in the annual realization of a reasonable amount of income or gain from the sale or disposition of trust assets. Thus, a provision in a trust mandating the trustee to invest only in tax-exempt securities would result in the trust not being characterized as a CRT.

6. *Reporting Requirements*

CRTs never file a Form 1041. Rather, CRTs must file Form 5227 annually. For the trust's first taxable year, a copy of the governing instrument, certified by the fiduciary under penalties of perjury to be true and complete, must be attached to Form 5227. If the CRT is liable for the UBTI tax (or private foundation excise tax, which can also apply to a CRT), the tax is reported on Form 4720. Any distributions to the noncharitable beneficiary are reported on a Form 1041 Schedule K-1.

The Forms 5227 and 4720, if applicable, are filed annually on or before the 15th day of the fourth month following the close of the trust's taxable year, i.e., April 15th. An automatic six month filing extension for both Form 5227 and Form 4720 can be obtained by filing a Form 8868 prior to the due date of the return.

Questions

1. Prior to 1969, a charitable deduction was allowed with respect to trust contributions as long as the chance that the charity would receive nothing was "so remote as to be negligible." Why do you think Congress changed the law by requiring that charitable interests in a trust be in the form of an annuity or unitrust?
2. A charitable remainder trust is required to distribute $30,000 annually to a non-charitable beneficiary. For the year in question, the trust has corporate bond interest of $3,000, qualified dividend income of $5,000, short-term capital gain of $14,000, long-term capital gain of $6,000, and tax-exempt income of $6,000. How much income must the non-charitable beneficiary report and what is its character?
3. A charitable remainder annuity trust (CRAT) is required to make a $20,000 payment to individual beneficiary A. The trust has the following income: Qualified dividends of $30,000 and short-term capital gains of $20,000. How much income must A report and what is its character?
4. In the above example, what happens to the income not deemed distributed?
5. Donor funds a charitable remainder trust with $500,000 of stock which has a cost basis of $100,000. In the year of funding, the trustee sells the stock. Does the trust pay tax on the gain?
6. A charitable remainder trust has UBTI consisting of business income from a partnership that it owns. What are the tax consequences to the trust of having UBTI?
7. Your client comes to you and says he wants to establish a charitable remainder trust with himself as the individual beneficiary and fund it with appreciated property. Once the trustee sells the appreciated property and re-invests the proceeds, he wants to make sure that he will not have to recognize any ordinary income (taxed up to a maximum tax rate of 37%) on the distributions he will receive. Explain how you could achieve this result for your client.

III. Income Taxation of Charitable Lead Trusts

Like charitable remainder trusts, names speak loudly and here, too, this axiom is true—in the case of charitable lead trusts (CLTs), the charity gets the annuity or unitrust payments (hence the moniker "lead"). Once again, CLTs are designed to appeal to those taxpayers who are charitably-minded, but who want to keep a delayed financial hand in the game for themselves or their loved ones.

A. Introduction and Background

A CLT is an irrevocable trust, established during life or at death, which provides for the upfront or "lead" interest being paid to charity in the form of a guaranteed annuity or unitrust payment and the remainder interest passing to or continuing in trust for non-charitable beneficiaries. It is the exact mirror image of a CRT.

The Code does not specifically refer to CLTs by name. The CLT rules are contained in §§170(f)(2)(B) (income tax), 2055(e)(2)(B) (estate tax), and 2522(c)(2)(B) (gift tax). Treasury regulations that amplify the statutory rules are found in Treas. Reg. 1.170A-6(c)(2)(i), (ii); 20.2055-2(e)(2)(vi), and (vii); 25.2522(c)-3(c)(2)(vi) and (vii).

At the time of the creation of a CLT, two gifts are made by the donor: (1) a gift of the annuity or unitrust interest to charity and (2) a gift of the remainder interest to the non-charitable beneficiaries.

A qualified CLT provides for a payment, at least annually, to one or more qualified charitable organizations in the form of either an annuity (a fixed dollar amount—a CLAT) or a unitrust (a fixed percentage of the fair market value of the trust property, valued annually—a CLUT).[6] It may be created either during the donor's lifetime[7] or under the donor's will (testamentary). A CLT established while the grantor is living provides the donor with a gift tax charitable deduction in an amount equal to the present value of the annuity or unitrust interest payable to charity (Code §2522(c)(2)) and, in certain cases, may provide income tax benefits to the grantor (e.g., an immediate tax deduction). A testamentary CLT provides an estate tax charitable deduction for the present value of the annuity or unitrust interest payable to charity. Code §2055(e)(2).

Depending on a CLT's terms (i.e., the lead interest payable to charity), it is possible to produce a charitable gift or estate tax deduction that equals the amount transferred to the trust resulting in a gift and estate tax-free transfer; in other words, it is possible to zero out the value of the remainder interest so there is no gift or estate tax payable on the remainder interest payable to the non-charitable beneficiary.

---

6. A non-qualified CLT is one that does not have the requisite annuity or unitrust interest. Such a trust does not entitle the donor to an income tax charitable deduction upon transfer of property to the CLT and is taxed under the normal rules of trust taxation.

7. Trusts established during the grantor's life sometimes are called *inter vivos* (Latin for "during life") trusts.

In general, a donor is not entitled to an income tax charitable deduction for transfers made to a CLT. An income tax charitable deduction is only available if the CLT is structured as a grantor trust, i.e., a trust in which the donor retains a power under §§ 673-677 that causes the income of the trust to be taxed to the donor. Code § 170(f)(2)(B).

A CLT can benefit the charity, the donor, and the donor's heirs.

- Charity. A CLT provides an immediate stream of payments to charity for the term of the lead interest.
- Donor. The CLT also provides the donor with a gift or estate tax charitable deduction for the actuarial value of the lead interest payable to charity. If the CLT is structured as a grantor CLT, it will provide an income tax charitable deduction to the donor in the year of funding for the actuarial value of the lead interest payable to charity. Code § 170(f)(2)(B). The benefit of the income tax deduction may be offset by two factors. First, the donor of a grantor CLT is taxable on all the CLT income during the charitable term (without an offsetting charitable deduction, § 170(f)(2)(C); Treas. Reg. § 1.671-1(d)). Second, during the charitable term, if the donor dies or the CLT otherwise ceases to be a grantor trust, the income tax deduction is "recaptured" and must be reported as income by the donor. Code § 170(f)(2)(B).
- Remainder Beneficiaries. If the CLT assets outperform the assumed rate of return (the § 7520 rate) used to value the charity's lead interest, the remaindermen will receive an amount in excess of the amount reported to the IRS as a tax-free gift. Thus, the primary use of a CLT for gift and estate tax planning purposes is its potential to transfer wealth on a deferred basis to children or grandchildren at a reduced or no gift or estate tax cost and, at the same time, further the donor's charitable goals.

A non-grantor trust is one over which the donor has not retained any power specified in §§ 673-677. If the CLT is treated as a non-grantor trust, the CLT is taxed under normal rules that apply to a complex trust, meaning that the CLT is taxed on all its undistributed income and capital gains. A non-grantor CLT will receive a fiduciary income tax charitable deduction under § 642(c) for distributions made to the charitable lead beneficiary. Unlike a CRT, a CLT is not exempt from income tax.

The salient attributes of grantor CLTs and non-grantor CLTs are set forth in a chart at the end of this chapter, but Subsection B immediately below outlines how grantor CLTs operate, and Subsection C further below details how non-grantor CLTs operate.

B. Grantor Charitable Lead Trust

Due to its grantor trust status, a grantor CLT necessitates that the donor pays tax on the current income and gains accumulated for future distribution to the non-charitable remainder beneficiaries. The donor's payment of the income tax on income earned by the CLT, however, is not considered a taxable gift to the ultimate trust beneficiaries. Rev. Rul. 2004-64, 2004-27 IRB 7. As a result, the CLT may more readily accumulate wealth — wealth that may ultimately inure to the non-charitable remainder beneficiaries.

Furthermore, at the creation of the CLT, the donor will receive a one-time income tax charitable deduction for the actuarial value of the lead interest. 26 U.S.C. § 170(f)(2)(B). Depending upon the nature of the charitable recipient, the donor's deductible amount may be limited.[8]

The income earned by a grantor CLT is fully taxable to the donor during the term of the trust with no offsetting income tax charitable deduction for the annual payments from the trust to charity. The trust receives no further charitable deductions because, as a grantor trust, it has received no gross income for the year, and under § 642(c), the trust is allowed a charitable deduction only for the amount paid out of its gross income. The donor is denied a deduction for the annual payments from the trust. Code § 170(f)(2)(C); Treas. Reg. § 1.671-1(d). This is so despite the fact that all or a significant portion of the income will be paid to charity and none of the income is paid to the donor.

The donor is, in effect, trading an income tax deduction at the time the CLT is established for the future imputation and taxation on the trust income. The net effect to CLT donors is that their income tax is deferred via the upfront charitable deduction at the time the trust is funded rather than tax liability elimination. Donors may find that the present value of the upfront income tax charitable deduction will be greater than the present value of the future tax burden on the trust income, especially if tax rates decline in the future. If donors are able to use the income tax deduction at a higher income tax rate than the rate at which they will be taxed on the trust income in later years, they may be economically better off structuring the CLT as a grantor trust for income tax purposes.

> **Example:** Donor sets up a grantor CLT and gets an income tax charitable deduction in the year he funds the trust. However, in return for receiving an income tax charitable deduction, he must report the income from the trust for each year that the CLT remains a grantor trust. This would work in his favor if the income tax deduction he gets in the year of funding outweighs the present value of the aggregate taxes paid on the CLT's income that he must report. The donor can, to some extent, control the tax he has to pay on the CLT income. For example, if the CLT is invested in tax-free municipal bonds (ignoring, for the moment, the trustee's fiduciary duty to

8. In general, if the lead interest is held by a public charity, the deduction limitation is normally limited to 50% of the donor's contribution base. Code § 170(b)(1)(A). Section 170(b)(2)(H) defines "contribution base" as the taxpayer's adjusted gross income (AGI) computed without regard to any net operating loss carryback to the taxable year. In contrast, when the lead interest is not held by a public charity, the deduction limitation is normally limited to 30% of the donor's contribution base. Code § 170(b)(1)(B).

> diversify), the donor will not have an income tax liability. Alternatively, if the CLT is invested in growth stocks or in stocks paying qualified dividends, under current law, the long-term capital gains or qualified dividends would be taxed to the donor at a maximum income tax rate of 20%. Because the trust is a grantor trust, the trust will not receive an income tax deduction; instead, all of the trust's income, deductions, and credits will be reported on the donor's individual income tax return.

Note that if the donor dies during the lead term of the trust or otherwise ceases to be treated as the owner of the trust for income tax purposes, all or part of the income tax charitable deduction will be recaptured and taxed as ordinary income. Code § 170(f)(2)(B); Treas. Reg. 1.170A-6(c)(4). More specifically, the donor must recognize as income an amount equal to the amount of the deduction the donor received when the trust was funded, reduced by the present value on the date of the trust's creation of all amounts that were required to be, and actually were, paid to the lead charitable beneficiaries before the donor's grantor trust status ceased. Code § 170(f)(2)(B); Treas. Reg. 1.170A-6(c)(4) and (5), Example 3.[9] Furthermore, if the CLT ceases to be a grantor trust, the trust continues and is taxed as a complex trust.

> **Example:** Donor transfer $100,000 to a grantor CLT in 2015, paying a charity an annuity of $5,000 per year for 9 years and receives, in return, an income tax charitable deduction of $34,000.[10] On December 31, 2017, the donor dies, and the CLT ceases to be the owner of the CLT. The discounted value as of 2015 of the amount paid to charity ($5,000 per year for 3 years) is $13,365. The calculation of the discounted value is set forth in Treas. Reg. 1.170A-6(c)(4). The amount of the income tax charitable deduction that the donor took in 2015 that must be recaptured and reported on the donor's final income tax return is $20,635 ($34,000 donor's initial income tax charitable deduction less the discounted value of the $15,000 earned by the trust and taxed to the donor, i.e., $13,365). For years after 2017, the CLT is treated as a non-grantor trust and the trust will then be allowed an income tax charitable deduction each year under § 642(c) of $5,000, the amount paid to charity each year.

The extent to which the donor is taxed on the ordinary income or capital gains of a grantor CLT depends upon the specific grantor trust powers retained by the donor. Under the grantor trust rules, the donor is taxed on the portion of the trust income over which he is considered to be the owner. If the donor is treated as the owner of the entire trust (corpus and income), he must report both the trust's income and capital gains on his individual income tax return. On the other hand, if the donor

---

9. If the recapture occurs because of the donor's death, the income is included on the donor's final income tax return.

10. During the intervening years, suppose the CLT earns $6,000 in 2015, $4,000 in 2016 and $5,000 in 2017, all of which is taxable to the donor under the grantor trust rules. These earnings do not affect computation of the recapture amount.

is treated as the owner of a specific fraction or portion of the trust, only the ordinary income and capital gains allocable to that fraction or portion are taxed to the donor—the balance is taxed to the trust. If the donor's power is only over ordinary income, the donor is taxed on the ordinary income and not the capital gains. See the chapter on Grantor Trusts for a detailed discussion of the operation of the grantor trust rules.

There are at least three common methods to have a CLT qualify as a grantor trust:

1. Reversionary Right. One way to make a CLT a grantor trust is to have the donor or the donor's spouse retain a reversion (right to get the trust property back at the end of the lead interest) having a value greater than 5% of the value of the trust at the inception of the trust. Code § 673(a). However, if the trust property reverts to the donor or his or her spouse, the CLT will be included in the donor's gross estate for estate tax purposes.
2. Another way to make the CLT a grantor trust but at the same time avoid estate tax inclusion is to have the remainder pass into a trust from which the trustee (someone other than the donor or his or her spouse) can pay the entire corpus to the donor's spouse. Because the maximum exercise in favor of the donor's spouse (or the donor) is presumed (Code § 673(c)), the reversion to a trust for the spouse's benefit would be valued at more than 5% of the trust value.
3. Substitution Power. Theoretically, one way to make a trust a grantor trust is to give the donor the power to substitute property of equivalent value under Code § 675(4)(C) or a power to loan trust property to the donor without adequate interest or security under § 675(2). However, such methods are not available for a CLT, because if the donor has either of these powers, the trust will fail to be a qualified CLT, because it cannot engage in any act of self-dealing described in § 4941. Code § 4947(a)(2). An act of self-dealing is any economic transaction between the trust and any person who is a "disqualified person" as defined in § 4946, and the grantor of a charitable split-interest trust is always a disqualified person. The exercise and probably the mere existence of these powers is most likely self-dealing. Nevertheless, a person who is not a disqualified person may hold the power to substitute property of equivalent value under § 675(4)(C), and this should result in the trust being treated as a grantor trust. Priv. Ltr. Rul. 9224029.[11]

A grantor lead trust files tax returns as any other grantor trust would and provides the grantor with a statement of items of income, deduction and credit which will be included in the grantor's individual income tax return.

---

11. Proposed sample language: An individual other than the donor, the trustee, or other disqualified person as defined in § 4946(a)(1), namely, XXX, shall have the right, exercisable only in a nonfiduciary capacity and without the consent or approval of any person acting in a fiduciary capacity, to acquire any property held in the trust by substituting other property of equivalent value.

C. Non-Grantor Charitable Lead Trust

The rules for non-grantor CLTs are completely different from the rules for grantor CLTs.

The donor of a lifetime non-grantor CLT does not receive an income tax charitable deduction for the value of the lead interest. Code § 170(f)(2)(B); Treas. Reg. 1.170A-6(c). Instead, the non-grantor CLT is taxed as a complex trust and gets an unlimited fiduciary income tax charitable deduction under § 642(c) for the gross income paid annually to the charitable lead beneficiary. By the same token, unlike a charitable remainder trust (CRT), a non-grantor CLT is not exempt from income tax and is also subject to the § 1411 3.8% surtax on undistributed net investment income.

Although contributors into a nongrantor CLT do not receive an income tax charitable deduction, they are not required to include any of the taxable income earned by the trust. To be entitled to an income tax charitable deduction under § 642(c), the payments must be made (1) pursuant to the terms of the governing instrument and (2) paid out of gross income (in the tax sense). Thus, if the lead payment is not made out of gross income, it is not deductible. Furthermore, if the trust income exceeds the amount of the charitable deduction (and all other allowable deductions, such as trustee fees), the excess income will be taxed to the trust under Subchapter J.

> **Example:** A non-grantor CLT requires an annual payment to the charity (the lead interest) of $10,000. During the year, the trust earns $25,000 of ordinary income. The trust will receive a charitable deduction of $10,000 under § 642(c) for the $10,000 paid to charity. Assuming no other deductions, the taxable income of the trust is $15,000 ($25,000 income less the $10,000 charitable deduction).

There is one important benefit of a non-grantor CLT that distinguishes it from a grantor CLT. Non-grantor CLTs avoid the income tax charitable deduction limitations applicable to individuals. This is especially beneficial if the donor's charitable contributions are so large that they would preclude part or all of other charitable deductions.[12]

---

12. As previously noted, a CLT is entitled to an unlimited income tax charitable deduction for the amounts of gross income paid from the CLT to the charitable lead beneficiary. Code § 642(c); Treas. Reg. 1.642(c)-1(a)(1). However, Code § 681 limits the income tax charitable deduction to the extent the payment to charity consists of UBTI. Treas. Reg. 1.642(c)-3(d). Despite this disallowance, Code § 512(b)(11) offers partial relief. Specifically, if the lead interest of a CLT is held by a domestic charity and the payment to charity consists of UBTI for the year in question, the income tax charitable deduction for the amount of the UBTI payable to charity is subject to the percentage limitations applicable to individuals. Code § 681(a); Treas. Reg. 1.681(a)-2(a). The deductibility ceilings are applied against the UBTI, not the trust's entire income. Code § 512(b)(11). If the CLT has UBTI, the benefits of a CLT are diminished, because the charitable deduction for the UBTI is limited. Thus, the trust income (including the UBTI) is paid to charity, but to the extent the fiduciary's income tax charitable deduction is denied for part of the UBTI, the trust will be exposed to additional income tax on the non-deductible portion of the UBTI paid to charity. For example, suppose a charitable

If a non-grantor CLT distributes appreciated property to satisfy the lead payout, the distribution is treated as if the CLT sold the appreciated property and distributed cash. Rev. Rul. 83-75, 1983-1 C.B. 114; Treas. Reg. 1.661(a)-2(f); *Kenan v. Commissioner*, 114 F.2d 217 (2d Cir. 1940). This will trigger recognition of the gain by the CLT. Priv. Ltr. Rul. 200920031. The gain, however, will be treated as having been paid to charity so that the CLT will be entitled to a fair-market value income tax charitable deduction under § 642(c). Rev. Rul. 83-75, 1983-1 C.B. 114.

A CLT may take an income tax charitable deduction for the current year as long as the amount is paid to the charity in the current year or before the last day of the subsequent year. Code § 642(c)(1); Treas. Reg. 1.642(c)-(1)(b). Thus, if the lead payment is paid after the close of the taxable year and before the last day of the following year, the trustee may elect to treat the charitable payments as being made in the preceding year. The trustee makes the election by filing a statement with the return for the year in which the contribution is considered paid.

> **Example:** A trust files its 2020 income tax return. It did not make a distribution to charity in 2020. Prior to December 31, 2021, the trust makes a charitable contribution which satisfies the requirements of § 642(c) for an income tax charitable deduction. The trust can make an election to have the amount distributed to charity in 2021 as paid in 2020 and deducted on its 2020 income tax return. An amended return would be required to take such a charitable deduction if the prior year return has already been filed.

Unless the trust document specifically states otherwise, amounts paid from the trust to charity are deemed to consist of a proportionate amount of each class of income earned by the trust. Treas. Reg. 1.642(c)-3(b)(2). The regulations provide an exception if the trust document states the source of the amounts paid to charity and such allocations have "independent economic effect." Treas. Reg. 1.642(c)-3(b)(2) and 1.643(a)-5(b).

Section 4947(a)(2) governs the applicability of the private foundation rules. It provides that the private foundation rules are applicable to CLTs because, according to the statute, (1) they are not exempt from tax under § 501(a); (2) not all of their unexpired interests (i.e., the remainder interest) are devoted to "charitable" (Code § 170(c)(2)(B)) purposes; and (3) they have amounts in trust for which a deduction was allowed under §§ 170, 2055 and/or 2522. Violations of the private foundation rules result in a two-tier excise tax payable by the CLT. These rules include a prohibition of (1) self-dealing between the CLT and a "disqualified person" as defined in § 4946, (2) excess business holdings, (3) jeopardy investments and (4) taxable expenditures. CLTs are exempt from the excess business holdings and jeopardy investment excise

---

lead annuity trust has as its sole source of income $10,000 of UBTI. The trust requires $10,000 annually be paid to a public charity. The trust pays $10,000 in cash to the charity, but Code § 681 disallows a corresponding deduction. However, § 512(b)(11) allows a partial income tax charitable deduction equal to 50% (30% if appreciated property was transferred to the charity) of the $10,000 UBTI or $5,000.

taxes if (1) the value of the charitable deduction for the lead interest does not exceed 60% of the total fair market value of all the interests held by the trust and (2) the entire income interest of the trust and none of the remainder interest is devoted exclusively to charitable purposes. § 4947(b)(3)(A).

A non-grantor CLT trustee must prepare and file an income tax return each year by filing Form 1041. Any trust that claims a charitable deduction under § 642(c) or any split-interest trust described in § 4947(a)(2) that is not exempt from tax must also file an annual information return, Form 5227. A CLT reports excise tax required to be paid for a breach of the private foundation rules on Form 4720. All forms must be filed on or before the 15th day of the fourth month following the end of the taxable year of the trust, i.e., April 15th. An automatic six-month extension to file the Form 5227 or Form 4720 is available by filing an extension request on Form 8868 before the normal filing date. A five-and-one-half month extension for filing a Form 1041 is available by filing a Form 7004 before the normal filing date.

IV. Conclusion

You have hopefully mastered the salient features regarding charitable trusts. Having said this, you should know that when it comes to drafting such trusts, you do not have to start from scratch. To the contrary, the IRS has put together a number of pro forma documents that practitioners regularly use. The location of these pro forma documents are set forth below along with a short description of each. Note that the use of these forms assures compliance with both the Code and Regulations, albeit, the IRS permits variations from these documents, but taxpayers do so at their own risk and peril.

Pro Forma Charitable Trust Documents

Types of Charitable Remainder Annuity Trusts for Which Sample Forms for Declarations of Trust Have Been Provided by Revenue Procedures

Rev. Proc. 2003-53, 2003-2 C.B. 230

- Inter vivos charitable remainder annuity trust: one life

Rev. Proc. 2003-54, 2003-2 C.B. 236

- Inter vivos charitable remainder annuity trust: term of years

Rev. Proc. 2003-55, 2003-2 C.B. 242

- Inter vivos charitable remainder annuity trust: two lives, consecutive interests

Rev. Proc. 2003-56, 2003-2 C.B. 249

- Inter vivos charitable remainder annuity trust: two lives, concurrent and consecutive interests

Rev. Proc. 2003-57, 2003-2 C.B. 257

- Testamentary charitable remainder trust: one life

Rev. Proc. 2003-58, 2003-2 C.B. 262
- Testamentary charitable remainder annuity trust: term of years

Rev. Proc. 2003-59, 2003-2 C.B. 268
- Testamentary charitable remainder annuity trust: two lives, consecutive interests

Rev. Proc. 2003-60, 2003-2 C.B. 274
- Testamentary charitable remainder annuity trust: two lives, concurrent and consecutive interests

Types of Charitable Remainder Unitrusts for Which Sample Forms for Declarations of Trust Have Been Provided by Revenue Procedures

Rev. Proc. 2005-52, 2005-2 C.B. 326
- Inter vivos charitable remainder unitrust: one life

Rev. Proc. 2005-53, 2005-2 C.B. 339
- Inter vivos charitable remainder unitrust: term of years

Rev. Proc. 2005-54, 2005-2 C.B. 353
- Inter vivos charitable remainder unitrust: two lives, consecutive interests

Rev. Proc. 2005-55, 2005-2 C.B. 367
- Inter vivos charitable remainder unitrust: two lives, concurrent and consecutive interests

Rev. Proc. 2005-56, 2005-2 C.B. 383
- Testamentary charitable remainder unitrust: one life

Rev. Proc. 2005-57, 2005-2 C.B. 392
- Testamentary charitable remainder unitrust: term of years

Rev. Proc. 2005-58, 2005-2 C.B. 402
- Testamentary charitable remainder unitrust: two lives, consecutive interests

Rev. Proc. 2005-59, 2005-2 C.B. 412
- Testamentary charitable remainder unitrust: two lives, concurrent and consecutive interests

Types of Inter Vivos Charitable Lead Trusts for Which Sample Forms for Declarations of Trust Have Been Provided by Revenue Procedures

Rev. Proc. 2007-45, 2007-2 C.B. 89
- Inter vivos charitable lead non-grantor annuity trust
- Inter vivos charitable lead grantor annuity trust

Rev. Proc. 2008-45, 2008-2 C.B. 224
- Inter vivos charitable lead non-grantor unitrust trust
- Inter vivos charitable lead grantor unitrust trust

Types of Testamentary Charitable Lead Trusts for Which Sample Forms for Declarations of Trust Have Been Provided by Revenue Procedures

Rev. Proc. 2007-46, 2007-2 C.B. 102
- Testamentary charitable lead annuity trust

Rev. Proc. 2008-45, 2008-2 C.B. 238

- Testamentary charitable lead unitrust trust

Questions

1. A non-grantor charitable lead annuity trust requires an annual payment of $30,000 to the charitable lead beneficiary. The trustee, not having cash to make the payment, transfers appreciated stock having a fair market value of $30,000 and a cost basis of $10,000 from the trust to the charity to satisfy its payment obligation. What, if any, are the income tax consequences to the trust?
2. A grantor charitable lead annuity trust allows a donor to obtain an individual income tax charitable deduction but also requires a donor to report the income earned by the trust on his individual income tax return for the year in which the trust is classified as a grantor trust. Can you think of reasons why a donor would want to establish a grantor charitable lead annuity trust?

Additional Questions

1. Briefly describe and explain why a person would set up or contribute to any of the trusts below:
   (a) A Charitable Remainder Annuity Trust (CRAT).
   (b) A Charitable Remainder Unitrust (CRUT).
   (c) A Charitable Lead Annuity Trust (CLAT).
   (d) A Charitable Lead Unitrust (CLUT).
2. When designing the trusts listed in question 1, are any pro forma IRS forms available?
3. (a) Why were limitations placed in the 1969 Tax Reform Act regarding charitable trusts?
   (b) May a CRAT or CRUT have more than one non-charitable beneficiary?
   (c) May a CRAT or CRUT have more than one charitable beneficiary?
4. (a) How often must payments be made from a CRAT or CRUT?
   (b) How long may the payments be made for?
   (c) What are the limitations on the type of investments that a CRAT or CRUT can make?
   (d) How are payments determined under a CRAT?
   (e) A creates a CRAT in 2020 by transferring $100,000 to a trust and reserving a fixed payment of $5,000 per year for life. In 2023, he desires to add $50,000 to this amount and reserve $7,500 per year. May he do so?
   (f) (1) A creates a CRAT. He transfers $100,000 and reserves a payment for life or 20 years, whichever is *longer*, of $5,000 per annum. A is

55 years of age. Will A receive a charitable contribution deduction for the remainder?

(2) Suppose the term was for A's life and then to B (a lineal descendent) for 20 years or his life, whichever is *longer*, then to the Red Cross.

(3) Same as (2), except the annuity is to B for his life or 20 years from the date of creation, whichever is *shorter*.

(4) Suppose in (3), the term was for the *longer* of B's life or 20 years from the date of creation.

(5) Suppose in (2), A created the trust for the *shorter* of 21 years or B's life.

(g) (1) What is the 5% probability test discussed in Rev. Rul. 77-374?

(2) Does this rule apply to CRUTs?

5. (a) How are payments from a CRUT determined? Is there a minimum payment amount?

(b) May a CRUT be limited to income only?

(c) May a CRUT have a "make-up" provision?

(d) A establishes a CRUT by transferring $100,000 to the trust and reserves a 5% interest for life. The trust provides for a full make-up provision. The trust reports the following:

Year	Value of Principal	Trust Income
2019	100,000	4,000
2020	130,000	6,000
2021	150,000	8,500
2022	140,000	12,000

Determine the distributions to A.

(e) What is *income* for CRUT purposes for determining if it is less than the required payment?

(f) (1) A contributed Blackacre, a real estate income producing property, with a basis of $100,000 and a fair market value of $500,000, to a CRUT. If the CRUT sells Blackacre for $600,000, can any of the gain be allocated to income?

(2) Suppose in (1), Blackacre was subject to a $200,000 mortgage for which A is personally liable. The trust agrees to pay off the mortgage with the income that it receives. How is this treated for federal income tax purposes?

(g) May additions to corpus be made in a CRUT?

(h) (1) What is a "flip" unitrust, and when may it be used?

(2) What are the requirements of a flip unitrust?

6. (a) How are CRATs and CRUTs taxed?

   (b) What is unrelated business taxable income?

   (c) (1) May a CRAT or CRUT distribute property in kind to satisfy the annuity or unitrust amount?

   (2) What is the distributee's basis for property distributed?

   (d) Are CRATs or CRUTs subject to excise taxes similar to private foundations?

   (e) A sets up a CRUT by transferring $100,000 to the trust. Two years later, he sells Blackacre, worth $50,000, to the trust for $5,000. Are there any problems?

7. (a) What is the "tier system" under CRTs?

   (b) A CRAT has $3,000 of ordinary income for the year and accumulated ordinary income of $15,000. It is required to pay $5,000 to Pete. The CRAT has short term capital gains of $4,000 for the year. What is the character of the income to Pete that is distributed?

   (c) Suppose in (b) there was $1,000 of accumulated ordinary income, $2,000 of net short term capital gains, and $2,000 of net long term capital gains?

   (d) A CRAT has the following results:

	Ordinary Income	Short-Term C/G	Long-Term C/G
2020	$ 8,000	$ 6,000	$ 3,000
2021	$ 6,000	$ 7,000	$(4,000)
2022	$ 7,000	$(5,000)	$ 3,000

   The CRAT is required to distribute $10,000 per year to non-charitable beneficiary A. Describe how A will be taxed on the amounts distributed to him each year.

   (e) In the foregoing problem, assume that the trust reports income on the calendar year and that distributions are made $6,000 in July of 2020 and $8,000 in February 2021. Pete is also a calendar year taxpayer. In what year is Pete taxable on these distributions?

8. (a) Briefly explain the estate and gift tax aspects of charitable remainder trusts.

   (b) What are the consequences of transferring encumbered property?

9. (a) What is a charitable lead trust (CLT)?

   (b) When are CLTs most used?

   (c) (1) Who are permissible charitable beneficiaries?

   (2) Who are permissible non-charitable beneficiaries?

(d) In a CLT:

(1) What is the maximum number of years?

(2) What is the minimum payout?

(3) What is the difference between a CLAT and a CLUT?

(4) Can a CLUT be "income only"?

(5) Is a current income tax deduction allowed for an inter vivos CLT?

(6) Is a CLT a taxable entity?

(7) During the period that a non-grantor CLT is paying income to the charitable beneficiary, how is the trust taxed?

(8) During Roger's life, he creates a 10-year CLAT and is permitted a current income tax deduction (i.e., it's a grantor trust). In years 1-5, Roger includes the CLAT's income in his gross income. In year 6, Roger unexpectedly dies. What are the consequences?

(9) In 8, suppose Roger wanted the CLAT trustee to invest in tax-free municipal bonds. Is this permissible?

(10) What is a "zero out" CLT?

(11) Does the IRS prescribe sample forms for CLTs as it does for CRTs?

(12) Can a CLT allow trustees to choose the charitable beneficiaries on an annual basis?

(13) A creates a CLAT reserving a 20% charitable payout during C's life. Thereafter, the trust's assets pass to C's children. C is A's friend who is 45 years old, but who has a debilitating disease that makes it unlikely that he will live beyond 10 more years. Is C an acceptable measuring life?

(14) Suppose in (13), the measuring life is A. Assume A is in the same condition as C in (13).

(15) Suppose A in (14) has a terminal disease and has only about 6 months to live.

Summary of Taxation of Charitable Lead Trusts

	Grantor CLT	Nongrantor CLT
Exempt from income tax	No	No
Individual income tax charitable deduction	Yes — allowed at time of funding for actuarial value of lead interest. Subject to recapture if trust ceases to be grantor trust.	None allowed.
Income taxation	All trust income, deductions, gains and credits reported by grantor on his individual income tax return.	Taxed as a complex trust.
Annual distribution of lead interest to charity	No income tax deduction.	Fiduciary income tax charitable deduction under § 642(c).
Estate tax/gift tax charitable deduction	Deduction allowed for actuarial value of income interest.	Deduction allowed for actuarial value of income interest

Chapter 8

Income in Respect of a Decedent[1]

Internal Revenue Code: Section 691

Regulations: 1.691(a)-1, 1.691(a)-2, 1.691(a)-4(b), 1.691(c)-1(a)

Income in respect of a decedent (or more commonly referred to by its acronym, IRD) relates, broadly speaking, to moneys owed to a decedent at the time of his or her death that, had the decedent lived to collect such moneys, the decedent would have reported some or all of the amount collected as gross income on his or her income tax return. Thus, there are two parts to the concept of IRD: (1) the right to receive the item of IRD, e.g., the right to receive compensation owing at the taxpayer's death; and (2) the recognition of such IRD as income, e.g., collecting the compensation. The concept of IRD is not unique to trusts or estates, but, because IRD only arises after a taxpayer's death, trusts and estates often recognize items of IRD. Thus, an understanding of the workings of IRD is necessary if one is to have a complete understanding of how trusts and estates are taxed.

The tax statute governing the taxation of IRD is Code § 691 and this "modern" version has been in the law since the early 1940s. After more than 70 years, one might think that the courts or the IRS would have addressed all outstanding issues. But this is not the case, and there are several issues for which no guidance exists.

This chapter will discuss the following five topics:

- Congressional Motivation to Enact an IRD Regime;
- Defining IRD;
- IRD Taxation;
- The § 691(c) Deduction; and
- Open IRD Issues.

---

1. Portions of this chapter have been excerpted from or are substantially similar to portions from Bloomberg BNA Tax Management Portfolio 862 T.M., Income in Respect of a Decedent, © Tax Management, Inc., a Bloomberg BNA company. Reprinted with permission.

I. Congressional Motivation to Enact an IRD Regime

Broadly speaking, the general underpinning of the income tax law is that all gross income should be subject to income tax when recognized. This principle is embodied in Code § 61, which states, "gross income means all income from whatever source derived." This broad definition includes wealth accretions resulting from the investment or use of property (e.g., interest), labor (e.g., wages), and capital appreciation (modified by a realization principle expressed in Code § 1001). Although Code § 61 includes IRD as an example of gross income, it makes no attempt to define IRD.

Several important exceptions to Code § 61 exist. For example, capital gains are generally not recognized until there is a realization event.[2] However, such exceptions often merely postpone, rather than eliminate, recognition based on the proposition that the taxpayer has not sufficiently changed his economic position; such capital gains will be recognized, if at all, only when subsequent events occur, i.e., the sale or exchange of the capital asset. In other instances, gross income is not recognized based upon countervailing policy considerations.[3]

Death is among the events that can remove potential income from being taxed. Code § 1014 provides generally that property received from a decedent will receive a new basis for income tax purposes equal to the fair market value of the property determined as of the date of death (or alternate valuation date, if applicable).

> **Example:** When Joe died, he owned 1,000 shares of XYZ Company stock. When acquired, the price that Joe paid to purchase these shares was $400,000. At Joe's death, these 1,000 shares of XYZ Company stock were worth $1,300,000. Two months after his death, Joe's executor sells all 1,000 shares for $1,350,000. Because of Code § 1014, Joe's estate recognizes capital gains of $50,000 ($1,350,000 – $1,300,000). Had Joe lived and sold these shares for $1,350,000, he would have recognized capital gains of $950,000 ($1,350,000 – $400,000). Joe's death thus allowed his estate to eliminate $900,000 of capital gains ($950,000 – $50,000).

> **Example:** When Joe died, he also was owed $100,000 in deferred compensation from his employer. Under the general rules of Code § 1014, Joe's estate would theoretically have an income tax basis equal to the fair market value of this receivable — $100,000 — and upon collecting the compensation, Joe's estate would not recognize any income. However, the general rules of Code § 1014 don't apply to this case (Code § 1014 does not apply to items of IRD), and Joe's estate will thus recognize $100,000 of income upon receipt of the compensation.

---

2. *See, e.g.*, Code §§ 351, 721, 1001, 1014, 1031–1045.
3. *See, e.g.*, Code §§ 101–139, entitled, "Items Specifically Excluded from Gross Income."

The idea of IRD was created to address situations exactly like Joe's deferred compensation—to prevent a person's death from sheltering income from taxation. Loosely stated, this goal is accomplished by providing that the basis "equal to fair market value" rule of § 1014 does not apply to income owed to a decedent if the decedent would have received such income had he or she continued to live.

Code § 1014(c) expresses this rule. It provides that the basis "equal to fair market value" rule "shall not apply to property which constitutes a right to receive an item of income in respect of a decedent under section 691."[4]

A defining characteristic of IRD is that it must be a receivable, in the broadest sense of the term. Found in the first sentence of § 691(a)(1), it declares that IRD is "the **right to receive** such amount . . . acquired by reason of the death. . . ." Thus, there is a distinction between having actual money and property and having a right to receive money and property. All money and property actually owned by a decedent will be entitled to a new basis under Code § 1014; conversely, all rights to receive money or property, if such receivable is an item of IRD, will not be entitled to a new basis under Code § 1014.

There is a related concept of "deductions in respect of a decedent" (DRD) for obligations owed by the decedent that had the decedent lived to pay such obligations, such payments would have been deductible for income tax purposes. However, § 691(b) limits items of DRD to trade or business expenses deductible under § 162, interest deductible under § 163, taxes deductible under § 164, expenses for the production of income deductible under § 212, and depletion deductible under § 611.

Summary: With few exceptions, the Code seeks to impose tax at least once on all wealth accretions. The taxation of IRD items furthers this objective, eliminating death as an event that would safeguard wealth accretions from taxation.

Questions

1. A taxpayer owns Apple stock that has appreciated from $100 per share to $1,000 per share. If the taxpayer dies owning this stock, will the taxpayer's estate recognize any income if it sells the Apple stock for $1,000 per share?
2. A taxpayer has an IRA that is worth $1,000,000 and his estate is named as the primary beneficiary. The taxpayer dies testate, and his executor withdraws $50,000 to pay estate expenses. Is this $50,000 taxable?
3. What justification, if any, is there for the different results in questions 1 and 2?

---

4. Although § 1014(c) uses the phrase "right to receive," such right need not be a legally enforceable right in all situations. *See, e.g., O'Daniel Est. v. Comr.*, 173 F.2d 966 (2d Cir. 1949) (after taxpayer's death, company awarded a bonus that the court found to be IRD notwithstanding that the bonus did not exist at the date of taxpayer's death and, thus, taxpayer could not have had a legal right to the bonus at the time of death).

II. Defining IRD

There is no definition of "income in respect of a decedent." Not in the Code, not in the regulations, not in public or private rulings, and not in court decisions. At first blush, this may seem odd. But the phrase, "income in respect of a decedent" defies being easily defined, and this makes sense if one remembers that IRD must be elastic enough to encompass all situations where it ought to be applied. Thus, whether a receivable will be an item of IRD will depend on the context in which it arises.

Treasury Regulation 1.691(a)-1(b) sets forth a general guide to the meaning of IRD. This regulation reads as follows:

> In general, the term "income in respect of a decedent" refers to those amounts to which a decedent was entitled as gross income but which were not properly includible in computing his taxable income for the tax year ending with the date of his death or for a previous tax year under the method of accounting employed by the decedent.

Although this general reference may express the intent of the IRD regime, that is, items of gross income not reportable by the decedent should not escape income taxation, it provides little help in identifying items of IRD.

Because no definition of IRD appears in the Code or the regulations, courts have been pressed to establish the breadth and scope of IRD under various circumstances. However, the courts have not tried to define IRD beyond the situation before them, narrowly crafting opinions that serve limited utility.

What may a student glean from all this? That, depending on the circumstances, the IRD definition changes. Does this mean that any attempt at defining IRD is meaningless? Not at all. To the contrary, attempts at defining IRD can prove productive in the identification process.

We will look at how the IRD regime applies with respect to (A) compensation (i.e., where the decedent is owed compensation at death), (B) investment income (i.e., where the decedent is owed income in the nature of accrued interest, rents, or declared, but not yet paid, dividends), (C) sales (i.e., where the decedent has sold an asset and sales proceeds are owed at death), and (D) miscellaneous situations (i.e., where the decedent is owed income at death that does not fall into one of the other areas, but should be encompassed by the IRD regime).

A. Compensation

The compensation area, as the name suggests, refers to amounts due the decedent that are compensatory in nature, that is, amounts due the decedent because of his or her labors or services. Such amounts would include salary, wages, bonuses, vacation pay, and the like.

1. Court Decisions

Compensation was the initial catalyst behind the IRD regime. Before the enactment of the IRD regime, where a decedent was owed compensation, his or her estate received a basis in such compensation equal to the amount owed the decedent. Thus, when the estate collected the compensation, it was not required to report its collection as income. In terms of policy, allowing compensation owed at death to escape the income tax violated the fundamental tenet that all income should be taxed at least once, and Congress eventually sought to address this inequity.

In this area of the law, the leading case is *O'Daniel's Estate v. Commissioner*, 173 F.2d 966 (2d Cir. 1949).[5] The facts of *O'Daniel's Estate* are straightforward: a discretionary bonus for 1943 (the year of death) was fixed and paid to the decedent's estate in 1944. The Second Circuit held that the payment gave rise to IRD, stating in part:

> It is true that the decedent would not have had a legally enforceable right to receive the foregoing amount . . . , but the payment clearly represented compensation for his services and any right to receive it that was realized by his estate was acquired through him and never arose in any other way or through any other source. . . . We believe it is not disputed that if the decedent had lived and received the bonus in the year 1944, it would have been reportable and taxable in that year as income for services. . . . The bonus was derived through rights he had acquired, which even if not fixed at the time of his death were then expectancies which later bore fruit. It seems apparent from what we have already said that "the right . . . acquired by the decedent's estate from the decedent" which is referred to in § 126(a)(1)(A) [the predecessor to § 691(a)] *is not necessarily a legally enforceable right but merely any right derived through his services rendered while living.* Such a right as we have mentioned passes to his executors under his will and moneys received by virtue of it became taxable in the year when the payments were received. (Emphasis added.)

The impact of this case cannot be overstated. The court ignored the fact that the taxpayer did not have an enforceable right to the bonus as of his death. In reaching its holding that the bonus constituted IRD and its collection was taxable to the estate, the court relied exclusively on Code § 126 of the 1939 Code (the predecessor of Code § 691), never mentioning (a) the catch-all provision of § 22(a) of the 1939 Code

5. *See also Bausch's Estate v. Comr.*, 186 F.2d 313 (2d Cir. 1951). In *Rollert Residuary Trust v. Comr.*, 80 T.C. 619 (1983), *aff'd*, 752 F.2d 1128 (6th Cir. 1985), an employment bonus awarded more than three months after the decedent's death was determined to be an item of IRD. Although the decedent had no legally enforceable right to receive the bonus at the time of his death, the court concluded that his longstanding relationship with his employer, his consistent receipt of bonuses in prior years pursuant to a formalized deferred compensation arrangement, and the absence of any material contingency that may have resulted in the denial of the bonus, established to a "substantial certainty" the decedent's "right or entitlement" to the bonus payment as of the date of death.

(the predecessor of Code § 61), under which the payment was clearly includible in the recipient's gross income, or (b) any possible basis step-up under the predecessor of § 1014(a). Not only did the court rely exclusively on the IRD regime (§ 126 of the 1939 Code), its interpretation of the word "right" was expansive: it construed it to mean a mere hope or expectancy at death that later bears fruit rather than a legally enforceable right existing at death. The decision makes more sense (but does not justify its reasoning or conclusion) when one realizes that the court recognized that the estate incorrectly included the bonus in its gross estate and claimed a basis step-up. As the court itself said, "Matters are of course vastly complicated where there has been erroneous estate inclusion." The court could have held that, at the decedent's death, this item did not yet exist and could not be included in the decedent's gross estate and therefore could not receive a basis in the hands of the decedent. Further, that payment of the bonus was income to the recipient under the general rules of income taxation.

Because of the approach taken by the court, it was forced to interpret the word "right" as including an expectancy, and this is the interpretation in the compensation area.

The *O'Daniel's Estate* decision was relied upon in *Halliday v. U.S.*, 655 F.2d 68 (5th Cir. 1981), for the proposition that IRD includes *substantial certainty* of a post-death payment. In *Halliday*, the court found compelling evidence that reflected "a substantial certainty that benefits directly related to the decedent's economic activities [would] be paid to his heirs or estate upon his death, notwithstanding the absence of a legally enforceable obligation" (this became known as the substantial certainty test).[6] Akin to a bonus payment, this expectancy should be taxed in a similar manner.

Rollert Residuary Trust v. Commissioner, 752 F.2d 1128 (6th Cir. 1985), *aff'g* 80 T.C. 619 (1983), synthesized the *O'Daniel's Estate* and *Halliday* holdings. Edward Rollert was an executive vice president of General Motors at the time of his death on November 27, 1969. Edward Rollert had participated in General Motors' executive bonus plan. On March 2, 1970, General Motors awarded its bonuses for 1969. Thus, at the time of his death, all parties agreed that the decedent had no right to the 1969 bonus. The taxpayer's estate argued that the bonus was not an IRD item because the decedent did not have a legally enforceable right at the time of his death to receive the bonus. The court, however, rejected this argument, stating its express support for *O'Daniel's Estate* and *Halliday* as follows:

> The Second Circuit held, in *O'Daniel's Estate v. Commissioner*, . . . , a case factually identical to the instant case, that as long as the decedent had provided services from which he had a reasonable expectation that he would be rewarded, any bonuses awarded subsequent to his death for those prior services would constitute income in respect of the decedent, notwithstanding

---

6. *Id.* at 72. This "substantial certainty" test was followed in *Rollert Residuary Trust v. Comr.*, 80 T.C. 619 (1983), *aff'd*, 752 F.2d 1128 (6th Cir. 1985).

> that he did not have a legally enforceable right to the bonus. Other circuits have expressed their approval of this holding. [Citations omitted.]
>
> *O'Daniel's Estate* should be followed in this case. The key test for determining whether the decedent had a "right" or was "entitled" to the post-mortem bonus should be based on the likelihood, at the time of his death, that he would receive the bonus, *not* on his legal rights to it. The alternative interpretation "would permit parties to avoid taxation simply by failing to embody obligations incurred by reason of decedent's services into a binding contract even in situations where benefits were otherwise paid to discharge these obligations." *Halliday v. United States*, 655 F.2d 68, 71 (5th Cir. 1981). If Congress had intended such result, it could have expressly adopted the legal enforceability test. Similarly, the Service could have done the same, through its regulatory powers, if it had believed that this was Congress' intent. Given their failure to do so, we believe it is unwise for the courts to impose such a requirement.
>
> There was substantial certainty, at the time of decedent's death, that he would be awarded a bonus for his work for G.M. in 1969. G.M. had consistently awarded bonuses to its executive vice-presidents and it had already made a tentative decision, even prior to his death, to award bonuses to decedent and its other vice-presidents for their 1969 labors. Accordingly, the decedent had a "right" to the post-mortem bonus, within the meaning of § 691, and the bonus, therefore, constituted income in respect of a decedent. Since the bonus is such income, § 691 mandates that Taxpayer report it as income when it was received, not when the rights to it were received.

As enunciated in the court's holding, the "substantial certainty" test is the metric by which to determine a decedent's "right" to a post-mortem bonus. If no post-death bonus had been paid to Mr. O'Daniel or to Mr. Rollert, there would have been no IRD notwithstanding how substantial the receipt expectation was, and these cases would never have occurred. Thus, this raises the question as to how substantial the certainty must be for the post-death bonus to constitute IRD. In practical terms, it may be a self-answering question: one may conclude that whenever a post-death payment is actually paid by a decedent's employer as part of a formal bonus plan or as part of a pattern, any expectation to the post-death payment is always substantial and, thus, IRD.

Where no bonus plan exists and where there has been no history of bonuses or, perhaps, a sporadic or inconsistent payment of bonuses, and where there is no certainty of any post-death bonus, any bonus paid after death in recognition of the decedent's services and labors should not be IRD. Because of the broad scope of Code § 61, however, such payment will not be exempt from taxation.

Collins v. U.S.[7] potentially extended the reach of *O'Daniel's Estate* to payments that the decedent could never receive. In *Collins*, the decedent and his employer had

---

7. 318 F. Supp. 382 (C.D. Cal. 1970), *aff'd per curiam*, 448 F.2d 787 (9th Cir. 1971).

an agreement under which payments would be made after the decedent's death to his wife. The court noted that the decedent had the right to select the recipient of these post-death payments and no payments could ever be made to the decedent while living. The court found that the wife did not acquire the right from the decedent as defined under § 1014(b) and, thus, there was no basis step-up under § 1014(a). The court should have stopped at this point in its decision, but the opinion states, "There is a separate and alternative ground for granting judgment to the government, i.e., that the income in question is income in respect of a decedent under IRC Section 691 . . . ." This conclusion was based on the economic activities of the decedent, and the court concluded its opinion with the following paragraph:

> It is submitted that where one is dealing with post-death payments attributable to the personal services of a decedent and payable upon his death, the right to receive the money has certainly matured and the decedent's entitlement to the payments is simply not relevant. If, however, decedent's entitlement is a *sine qua non* of income in respect of a decedent, I submit that such entitlement could be found under the facts of the case at bar. The decedent here bargained for these payments in return for his personal services and for his remaining employed up to the date of his death. The consideration for those payments flowed entirely from him. He could have directed the payments to any person or entity he chose. He directed that they be paid to his widow, the contract being in essence a third-party beneficiary contract. Under the circumstances, with the decedent having furnished all of the consideration and economic benefit, it would be unrealistic in the extreme to hold that the income in question is not income in respect of a decedent, because the decedent chose to have it payable to someone other than himself or his estate. In every economic sense the decedent was the person "entitled" to the income. I conclude that the payments in question are income in respect of a decedent and, by virtue of Section 1014(c), are ineligible for a stepped-up basis.

Collins demonstrates the courts' continuing lack of IRD understanding. The court held, on the one hand, that the item was not acquired from the decedent and, thus, not entitled to a step up in basis, and, yet, on the other hand, that the wife did acquire the item from the decedent because the decedent directed payments to her. Put somewhat differently, because of the court's initial finding that the post-death payments were not entitled to a basis step up under Code § 1014, the income in question would not have escaped taxation — the central catalyst that was the genesis behind the IRD regime.

2. Definition of IRD in the Compensation Area

With the above cases as background, one may find helpful the following suggested definition of IRD in the compensation area.

Items of IRD will encompass the following in the compensation area:

- wages, compensation, and other benefits payable to the decedent attributable to his or her services and labor ("economic activities" in the words of *O'Daniel's Estate*) over which the decedent has a legal right to enforce such payments;
- post-death bonuses or other payments payable to the decedent attributable to his or her services and labor and in which there was a "substantial certainty" existing at the date of the decedent's death that such bonuses or other payments would be awarded to the decedent, even though the decedent had no legally enforceable right to such bonuses or payments; and
- post-death payments payable to a third party attributable to a decedent's services and labor in which there was a substantial certainty existing at the date of the decedent's death that such payments would be made to the third party, even though the decedent had no legally enforceable right to such bonuses or payments.

The characterization of compensatory items as IRD is independent of their inclusion in the decedent's gross estate for estate tax purposes. Also, based on *Collins*, the decedent's entitlement to such payments is irrelevant as long as the decedent can direct the recipient of such payments.

B. Investment Income

In the IRD context, the scope of investment income is broad. It encompasses the right to receive income in the nature of interest, dividends, rents, and royalties (i.e., income resulting from the mere ownership of property). However, despite its breadth, its scope does not include capital appreciation.

Unlike the compensation area, with respect to investment income, the activities of the decedent are irrelevant. Instead, the salient consideration is whether the decedent owned the property that gave rise to the income. Thus, IRD investment income will exist if the following three conditions are met:

(1) at death, the decedent owned the income-producing investment;

(2) the decedent was legally entitled to such income so that, had the decedent lived, he or she would have collected such income; and

(3) such accrued income is not includable in the decedent's final or earlier income tax return.

Because the decedent could never have been entitled to income earned that is attributable to a period after the decedent's death, such investment income will not be IRD, but rather ordinary income to its recipient by virtue of Code § 61.[8]

Example: When Adam died, he owned various corporate and government bonds and stock in several publicly-traded companies. On the date of

8. *See, e.g.*, Rev. Rul. 79-340, 1979-2 C.B. 320; Rev. Rul. 76-153, 1976-1 C.B. 180.

Adam's death, all his bonds had accrued interest. In addition, Adam died owning stock in several publicly-traded corporations. Several of the corporations had declared, but had not yet paid, dividends, and Adam died after the record date for such declared dividends. The accrued interest and declared dividends are estate receivables that are also IRD items.

C. Sales

The sales area refers to amounts owed a decedent when he has entered into a contract to sell property but dies before the actual sale is consummated. The sales area does not refer to sales designed to be consummated after death, such as is often the situation with buy-sell agreements.

Example: Sidney owns 10,000 shares of X Corporation. Sidney and X Corporation enter into an agreement whereby X Corporation agrees to buy and Sidney agrees that his estate will sell his 10,000 shares at book value determined as of the date of Sidney's death. Upon Sidney's death, his stock of X Corporation is purchased by X Corporation in accordance with their agreement. Because the sale of the stock must be consummated after Sidney's death, there is no IRD with respect to the appreciation in the value of X Corporation stock owned by Sidney at his death.[9]

Case law helps illustrates the application of when sale proceeds will and will not be considered IRD.

Emblematic of the confusion sown in this area of the law is the case of *Trust Company of Georgia v. Ross.*[10] In this case, Carling Dinkler, Sr. sought to sell the Dinkler Hotel chain,[11] but died before the sale was complete, tasking the court to determine whether the anticipated sale proceeds were an IRD item. The court focused intently on the fact that Mr. Dinkler was instrumental in the negotiations and in procuring a contract (i.e., whether the decedent's "economic activities" in negotiating and obtaining the contract were decisive, the same as the court had done in the *O'Daniel's Estate* case dealing with post-death bonuses). As a result of the decedent's activities, the court found that IRD existed.

On appeal, the Fifth Circuit Court of Appeals affirmed the decision, but not the lower court's reasoning.[12] For the appellate court, the decedent's economic activities in procuring the sale were irrelevant to the issue of IRD. Instead, the sole determinative factor was whether the decedent had the legal right to the sale proceeds. If yes, then IRD existed; if no, then IRD did not exist. In this case, since the decedent

9. Treas. Reg. 1.691(a)-2(b), Ex. 4.

10. 262 F. Supp. 900 (N.D. Ga. 1966), *aff'd*, 392 F.2d 694 (5th Cir. 1967).

11. The hotel chain was actually owned by several corporations in which Carlilng Dinkler, Sr. had a controlling interest.

12. 392 F.2d 694 (5th Cir. 1967).

had entered into a binding contract and only ministerial tasks remained to be done, the sale proceeds constituted IRD.

> **Example:** Jack negotiated the sale of commercial property that he owned. He has spent many hours with the prospective buyers discussing sale details, ultimately reaching an understanding regarding price and payment terms and having an appropriate contract drawn for execution. Prior to the contract signing, Jack suffers a heart attack and dies. His estate completes the sale on the same terms and provisions that Jack had negotiated. The sale proceeds are not an item of IRD, and the commercial property is entitled to a step-up in basis upon Jack's death, because there was no binding contract at Jack's death. Notwithstanding Jack's "economic activities" to reach a deal, at his death, Jack was not legally entitled to any sale proceeds. Hence, there is no IRD. Thus, pre-death negotiations without a binding contract can never give rise to IRD.

In *Estate of Peterson v. Commissioner*,[13] the Tax Court listed the following four requirements for determining whether post-death sales proceeds are IRD:

(1) the decedent entered into a legally significant arrangement, e.g., a contract, regarding property disposition;

(2) as precondition to the sale, the decedent performed required substantive acts, and thus, the property in question was in a deliverable state at the decedent's death;

(3) at the time of the decedent's death, there were no economically material contingencies which might have disrupted the sale; and

(4) if the decedent had lived, he or she would have received, actually or constructively, the sale proceeds.

Determining whether an item of IRD exists often depends upon determining whether substantial conditions remain to be performed after the decedent's death or whether the executor has only a passive or ministerial role to play in completing the sale. The outcome of such determinations will depend upon the facts and circumstances of each case.

Relative to other IRD areas of the law, the sales area is sometimes beset by uncertainty. In the areas of compensation, investment income, and miscellaneous receipts, either the amounts due the decedent are collected or they are not. If the money is collected,[14] income is recognized and Code § 691 applies; conversely, if the money is not collected, no income is recognized and the receivable, in effect, disappears. In the sales area, if the money is collected, gain is recognized and Code § 691 applies. If the money is not collected, the receivable may no longer exist, but the property that

---

13. 74 T.C. 630 (1980), *aff'd*, 667 F.2d 675 (8th Cir. 1981).

14. Property also could be collected, for example, if crop rents were due the decedent at the time of the decedent's death.

was the subject of the sale still exists. And how Code § 691 applies, if at all, to the property if the sale is not completed has never been addressed.

> **Example:** John takes all steps to liquidate his wholly-owned corporation. All material terms have been complied with and material actions have been performed; the only remaining item is the liquidation of the corporation and the distribution of corporate assets to John. John dies before this occurs. In these circumstances, an unanswered question is whether Code § 691 applies if John's estate revokes the liquidation.

The stated dilemma is whether post-death events can negate IRD status. Based on seminal cases addressing IRD in the sale area,[15] whether a receivable is an item of IRD should be determined as of the date of the decedent's death—period. This provides certainty; that is, one looks at the facts and circumstances that exist at the decedent's death to determine whether a right to receive contract proceeds is an item of IRD. Bearing this precept in mind, IRD in the sales area should exist whenever the following exists: The decedent has so changed his or her position with respect to property that it may be said that he or she no longer owns the property in question, but rather owns the right to proceeds arising from the disposition of such property. This can be said to have happened when a binding contract—not merely substantial certainty—for the sale of an item exists and all material matters concerning that sale have occurred prior to the decedent's death. At the decedent's death, there were no economically material contingencies, and the object of the sale was in a deliverable state.

Once the sale proceeds are determined to be an IRD item, even if the parties subsequently abandon the transaction, the Code should not accord the property in question (which remains in the estate's hands) a step up in basis under Code § 1014, but any subsequent sale should no longer relate back to the decedent. The latter part is a practical answer.[16] It would be helpful for the IRS to address this issue.

D. IRD Miscellaneous Items

IRD items are not confined to compensation, investment income, and sales. Whenever the decedent has taken some action or events have developed that, without more than the mere passage of time, the decedent would have received income or gain had the decedent survived, then such income or gain ought to be IRD. Examples of IRD items that fall within the miscellaneous category can include trust

15. *Trust Co. of Georgia v. Ross*, 392 F.2d 694 (5th Cir. 1967), *cert. denied*, 393 U.S. 830 (1968); *Keck v. Comr.*, 415 F.2d 531 (6th Cir. 1969); *Sidles Est. v Comr.*, 65 T.C. 873 (1976), *aff'd by unpub. opin.*, 553 F.2d 102 (8th Cir. 1977), *acq.*, 1976-2 C.B. 2.

16. A key aspect of the Code § 691 is that the recognition of the IRD is to be treated as if the decedent had completed his or her transaction. This makes sense when the contract that gives rise to IRD in the sales area is consummated. It does not make sense if the contract is not carried out. Any subsequent sale or exchange of the property bears no relationship to the decedent.

or estate income distributed to a beneficiary after his or her death, rights to damage claims, and alimony arrears. Such items are best identified by reference to the purpose and intent of the IRD regime.

Summary: The term IRD is not prone to an easy definition. Rather, any definition must be elastic enough to permit the purpose of the IRD regime to accomplish its goal of precluding wealth accretions from escaping taxation. Identifying IRD items is easier if one understands its purpose and examines the broad areas where IRD income commonly arises, including the areas of compensation, investment income, and sales. Broadly, IRD may be said to exist if at a person's death, had he lived, he would have received something of value without any further action and such receipt would have been gross income.

Questions

1. Give a general definition of IRD.
2. Name at least four examples of IRD.
3. What makes post-death bonus awards different from other types of IRD?
4. At his death, James had a binding contract to sell a building for $1,000,000, and at the date of his death, all material actions had been taken other than the closing. What tax uncertainties might arise if the buyer and James' estate terminate the contract?
5. Mark is the sole shareholder of his successful corporation. Mark, as the sole shareholder, adopts a plan of liquidation and files with the State's Secretary of State an intention to dissolve, thereby obligating the corporation to cease doing business and to distribute its assets to its shareholder. Mark dies before his corporation is liquidated. Is the stock of Mark's corporation an item of IRD? Why or why not?

III. IRD Taxation

Once taxpayers have identified IRD items, their responsibilities do not end. To the contrary, several distinct tasks remain. More specifically, the following determinations must be made: (A) who is taxed, (B) when is the IRD taxed, and (C) what amount is reportable as gross income.

A. Who Is Taxed

Once a particular receivable is determined to be an IRD item, the statute limits the persons who can recognize IRD to the following:

1. **The Decedent's Estate:** the decedent's estate, if the right to receive the amount is acquired by the decedent's estate from the decedent (Code § 691(a)(1)(A));

2. **An Estate Distributee:** the person who acquires from the decedent the right to receive the amount by bequest, devise, or inheritance, as a result of a distribution by the decedent's estate of such right (i.e., passing vis-à-vis the probate or administration process) (Code § 691(a)(1)(B)); and
3. **Non-Probate Distributee:** the person who, by reason of the death of the decedent, acquires the right to receive the amount, if it is not acquired from the decedent's estate (i.e., passing vis-à-vis a non-probate process) (Code § 691(a)(1)(C)).

The importance of the limiting provisions found in Code § 691(a)(1)(A), (B), and (C), cannot be overstated, because any person who is not described in one of these three categories cannot recognize IRD, and any transfer of an item of IRD to a person not described in one of these categories results in the transferor immediately recognizing the IRD.

1. The Decedent's Estate

A decedent's estate can recognize IRD if the right to receive the amount is acquired by the estate from the decedent. The estate often recognizes IRD because a decedent's receivables frequently are collected by the estate.

> **Example:** At John's death, he was owed vacation time and 17 days of salary, aggregating $7,235. John also had accrued bond interest of $2,000 and accrued interest on his savings account at his local bank of $37.82. Shortly after John's death, his employer paid to the personal representative of John's estate all amounts owed. Also, John's estate collected the accrued interest on the bonds, and the local bank posted the accrued interest. All these items are items of IRD and John's estate acquired the rights to these items because of John's death. As a result, the estate recognizes these IRD items as each receivable is collected.

2. An Estate Distributee

A person who acquires from the decedent the right to receive an item of IRD by bequest, devise, or inheritance will recognize the IRD if the estate assigns such item of IRD to such person and such person then collects the IRD or otherwise engages in a transaction that triggers recognition of the IRD.

Note that if the estate collects the IRD item, it recognizes the IRD. But when the IRD item is distributed before its collection to a person who acquires the right to receive that item of IRD by bequest, devise or inheritance, the distributee will recognize the IRD when the distributee collects the IRD or transfers the IRD item.[17] More specifically, Treas. Reg. 1.691(a)-4(b)(2) provides that if a right to IRD is transferred by an estate to a specific or residuary legatee, only this distributee taxpayer can include such income in gross income.

17. *See* Treas. Reg. 1.691(a)-4(b)(2).

Example: At Robert's death, he is entitled to deferred compensation that has a $50,000 fair market value. Robert bequeaths his deferred compensation to his wife, Mary. An assignment of the right to receive the deferred compensation from Robert's estate to Mary will not trigger IRD recognition by Robert's estate, because Mary acquired the right to receive the deferred compensation by bequest. As Mary collects the deferred compensation, she will recognize the IRD items as gross income.

Example: Gail bequeaths her entire estate to her daughter, Grace. Gail's estate includes IRD items, which items her executor assigned to Grace. The assignment of IRD items to Grace will not trigger IRD recognition because she acquired the right to the IRD items by bequest. As Grace collects the IRD, she will recognize the IRD items as gross income.

When there are two or more residuary beneficiaries and the executor is permitted to make distributions in cash or in kind, including non-pro-rata distributions of undivided interests in property, can it be said that the residuary beneficiary in question acquired the legal right to a particular asset, let alone an IRD item by bequest, devise, or inheritance? In other words, where the executor, through the exercise of its discretion, assigns an item of IRD to one residuary beneficiary as opposed to another residuary beneficiary, will such transfer cause the estate to recognize the IRD? With respect to this query, Treas. Reg. 1.691(a)-4(b)(2) responds in a pro-taxpayer manner, holding that all residuary beneficiaries who receive IRD items acquire the right to receive such items by bequest or devise.

Example: Jack named his estate as the beneficiary of his IRA accounts. Jack left a certain percentage of his estate to named charities and the remaining percentage of his estate to named individuals. The will permitted the executor to make distributions in cash or in kind, including non-pro-rata distributions of undivided interests in property. Pursuant to the authority granted, the executor assigned the IRA accounts to the charities in satisfaction of their percentage share of the estate. Who should recognize the IRD—the estate or the charities upon receipt of the IRA funds? Pursuant to Treas. Reg. 1.691(a)-4(b)(2), the charities that received the IRA accounts must ultimately recognize the IRD.[18]

Observation: Where an item of IRD is specifically bequeathed to an individual and the estate collects the IRD and distributes the proceeds in satisfaction of the bequest, the income recognized for such IRD will be allocated to the recipient of the IRD proceeds.[19] The beneficiary entitled to the item of IRD will be considered to have a separate share and as such all income related to such share will be allocated to such beneficiary.[20]

---

18. Priv. Ltr. Rul. 200234019.

19. Treas. Reg. 1.663(c)-2(b)(3).

20. But for the rule set forth in Treas. Reg. 1.663(c)-2(b)(3), the distribution of IRD in satisfaction of a specific bequest will not carry out any DNI (§ 663(a)) and, thus, without the rule, the

Any transfer—broadly defined to include a sale, exchange, or other disposition—of an IRD right results in a recognition event to the transferor; the income recognition amount is equal to the fair market value of the IRD right "at the time of such transfer plus the amount by which any consideration for the transfer exceeds such fair market value." Code § 691(a)(2). In the estate administration process, application of the foregoing recognition principles commonly arises with respect to transfers (a) to satisfy pecuniary bequests and (b) to fund pecuniary trusts.

a. Pecuniary Bequests

By way of background, in *Kenan v. Commissioner*,[21] an estate recognized gain for using appreciated securities to satisfy a pecuniary bequest, that is, a bequest of a specific dollar amount. The rationale was that there was a taxable exchange of the appreciated securities in satisfaction of a fixed obligation. Treasury Regulation 1.1014-4(a)(3), succinctly states the rule as follows: "gain or loss must be recognized by the transferor to the extent required by the revenue laws, and the transferee acquires a basis equal to the fair market value of the property on the date of the transfer." The Treasury Regulation adds this example:

> [I]f the trustee of a trust created by will transfers to a beneficiary, in satisfaction of a specific bequest of $10,000, securities which had a fair market value of $9,000 on the date of the decedent's death (the applicable valuation date) and $10,000 on the date of the transfer, the trust realizes a taxable gain of $1,000 and the basis of the securities in the hands of the beneficiary would be $10,000.

Application of the foregoing logic has been used with respect to the transfer of an item of IRD in satisfaction of a pecuniary bequest. Reliance on *Kenan* and Treas. Reg. 1.1014-4(a)(3) is understandable, but nevertheless misguided. When dealing with transfers of IRD items, the Service, courts, and practitioners would be better served by reaching conclusions based on an analysis of Code § 691. More specifically, a distribution of an IRD item that is made to one who is not permitted to recognize IRD causes the transferor to recognize the IRD under § 691(a)(2).

> **Example:** At Robert's death, he is entitled to deferred compensation that has a fair market value of $50,000. Robert's will provides for a specific bequest of $50,000 to his son William. The executor assigns the right to receive the deferred compensation to William in satisfaction of his specific bequest. William is not a person who acquires from the decedent the right to receive the deferred compensation by bequest, devise, or inheritance. Because William is not a person who can recognize this particular item of IRD, the assignment of the right to receive the deferred compensation results in the estate recognizing the $50,000 of deferred compensation as IRD because

---

beneficiary would receive the income, but the tax consequence would be borne by the trust or the other beneficiaries receiving other distributions.

21. 114 F.2d 217 (2d Cir. 1940).

of § 691(a)(2). William will not recognize income when he collects the first $50,000 of deferred compensation, because such income already has been recognized by Robert's estate.[22]

Consider the situation when an estate has insufficient assets to meet a pecuniary bequest and therefore must resort to the use of IRD items. In such a situation, one ought to be able to avoid IRD recognition up to the amount needed to satisfy the bequest, because the legatee would have the right to receive some portion of the IRD items.

The above analysis recognizes that determining the tax consequences affecting IRD items should be the exclusive province of Code § 691 unless it can be demonstrated that another Code section should be given primacy over Code § 691 (such as Code § 401(a)(9) or § 408 governing distributions from qualified retirement plans and IRAs).

b. Pecuniary Trusts

Funding pecuniary formula trusts in part or in whole with IRD items raises the IRD recognition issue discussed in the preceding section, and also whether the distributing trust or estate is entitled to a distribution deduction under Code § 661.

Example: Carl has a living trust that provides for a so-called marital deduction trust to be established upon his death (see Chapter 1). The amount of Carl's trust to be allocated to the marital deduction trust is determined by a pecuniary formula. After Carl's death, the trustee assigns account receivables with a $300,000 fair market value to the marital deduction trust in partial satisfaction of the bequest. The account receivables were owed to Carl from his professional practice and are IRD items. The trustee could have used other assets that were not items of IRD to satisfy the marital bequest and, as a result, whether under an analysis under Code § 691 or reliance on *Kenan* and Treas. Reg. 1.1014-4(a)(3), the trust recognizes the IRD of $300,000. Note that the trust recognizes the entire $300,000 even though the marital deduction trust may not, actually, collect all $300,000.[23]

The distributing trust recognizes the IRD income, and this amount will be a part of its DNI. In a nutshell, however, pursuant to *Rollert Residuary Trust v. Commissioner*,[24] Rev. Rul. 68-195,[25] and Priv. Ltr. Rul. 8943058, the prevailing rule is that the distribution, itself, is not deductible under Code § 661.

---

22. *See also* C.C.A. 200644020 (trust had gross income under § 691(a)(2) when it assigned portion of decedent's IRA to charities in satisfaction of pecuniary legacies).

23. Barnett, Bernard, *IRD—The Atomic Bomb in the Estate of the Professional Partner*, 18 U. Miami Inst. Est. Plan. 18 (1984).

24. 80 T.C. 619 (1983).

25. 1968-1 C.B. 305.

3. Non-Probate Recipient of IRD Item

By reason of the decedent's death, a person who acquires a right to receive IRD will recognize it as long as it was not acquired from the decedent's estate.[26] In the commonplace situation, IRD does not pass to or through a decedent's estate, but, rather, passes directly to a person by operation of law or otherwise.[27] Ways in which an IRD right passes directly include the following:

- owning an asset as joint tenants with right of survivorship or by tenants in the entirety;
- having the title to an asset reflect a "payable on death" or "transfer on death" beneficiary;
- bank accounts that are designated as "in trust for" a third party, sometimes known as Totten trusts;
- assets owned by a trust;
- rights that pass by contract such as beneficiary designations under retirement plans or insurance policies; and
- rights that pass by contract as may be found under partnership agreements or operating agreements for partnerships and limited liability companies.

Aside from these commonplace scenarios, there are a few other situations in which IRD items pass to transferees who are not beneficiaries of a decedent's probate estate. Such scenarios include IRD recipients in the community property context, holders of completed gifts (e.g., father made a gift to his son of the right of income and the father died before the son received the income),[28] and successive decedents.[29]

---

26. Code § 691(a)(1)(B). *See, e.g.*, Priv. Ltr. Rul. 9132021 (distributions made from decedent's individual retirement account (IRA) to estate to pay estate tax attributable to IRA is IRD to IRA beneficiaries; this is because executor could recover estate taxes directly from IRA beneficiaries who were liable for such payment).

27. Examples include a bank account payable on death to a third person, so that any accrued interest will give rise to IRD when paid. Similarly, a co-owner or beneficiary of a Series E savings bond will have IRD for all accrued interest on the bond not taxable to the decedent in his or her lifetime. Treas. Reg. 1.691(a)-2(b), Ex. (3).

28. Carr Ferguson, James G. Freeland & Mark L. Ascher, Federal Income Taxation of Estates, Trusts & Beneficiaries pp. 3:20-21 (2d ed. 1993).

29. Code § 691(a)(1); Treas. Reg. 1.691(a)-1(c), -2(b), Ex. (2), -4(b)(1). *See* Treas. Reg. 1.691(a)-2(b), Ex. (2) ("Linda acquired by bequest from her husband the right to receive renewal commissions on life insurance sold by him in his lifetime, which commissions were payable over a period of years. Linda died before having received all of the commissions, and her son Mark inherited the right to receive the rest of the commissions. The commissions received by Linda were includible in her gross income. The commissions received by Mark were not includible in Linda's gross income but are included in Mark's gross income.").

Questions

1. Who are the only persons allowed under § 691 to recognize IRD?
2. John has a deferred compensation agreement with his employer that provides for John to receive $50,000 if he is still employed at the time of his retirement. It also provides that if he dies before his retirement, his employer will pay $50,000 to his surviving spouse or, if he does not have a surviving spouse, to his estate. John dies prior to retirement. In the following situations, who reports the IRD as gross income?
   a. John has no surviving spouse, and his employer pays the $50,000 to the personal representative of his estate.
   b. John has no surviving spouse, and the personal representative assigns the right to receive this compensation to the residuary beneficiary. The company pays the $50,000 to John's residuary beneficiary.
   c. John is survived by his wife, Jane, and his employer pays $50,000 to Jane.
   d. John is survived by his wife, Jane. Jane assigns the right to $17,000 of this compensation to her son, Tom, and assigns the right to $17,000 to her daughter-in-law, Mary. John's employer pays $16,000 to Jane, $17,000 to Tom, and $17,000 to Mary.

B. When Is IRD Taxable?

One should never forget that a critical aspect of taxation is timing. It dictates the applicable law, tax rates, and liquidity issues. In general, taxpayers seek to defer the receipt of taxable income and hence the need to pay taxes; conversely, the IRS typically views that income is taxable at the earliest point in time, with the goal of income acceleration. With IRD, the stances of the taxpayers and IRS follow this traditional pattern.

1. Necessity of an Event

The mere existence of an item of IRD does not itself generate income.

> **Example:** Adam was employed by Fly By Night, Inc., and at his death, he was owed $10,000 in wages. Fly By Night, Inc. had filed for bankruptcy, and no payment to Adam's estate was ever made. Although Adam's estate had an item of IRD (the right to wages of $10,000), no income will ever be recognized, because Fly By Night, Inc. went bankrupt and couldn't pay.

There is no IRD until one of two events occur: (a) the IRD item is collected or (b) the IRD item is transferred to a person who cannot recognize the IRD.

a. Collection of the IRD Receivable

The most obvious and the most common triggering event is collecting the IRD.[30]

30. Code § 691(a)(1); Treas. Reg. 1.691(a)-2(a), -2(b), Exs. (1) and (2).

b. Transfers of Items of IRD

i. Non-Taxable Transfers

A transfer to one entitled to receive the item of IRD by reason of the decedent's death or by bequest, devise, or inheritance from the decedent, or the transmission of the IRD item to the decedent's estate is not a transfer that triggers IRD recognition, and the transferee steps into the shoes of the transferor. These non-taxable transfers can continue indefinitely, e.g., the estate of a decedent can transfer the item of IRD to a testamentary trust which can transfer it to the trust remainder beneficiary who can bequeath it to his or her testamentary trust, etc., all without tax.[31]

ii. Taxable Transfers

If any person makes a taxable transfer of an item of IRD, then the transferor recognizes gross income for the tax year in which the transfer occurs.[32] The term "transfer" includes sale, exchange or other disposition, or the satisfaction of an installment obligation at other than face value.[33] Examples of taxable transfers include a gift of IRD[34] and the use of an IRD item to satisfy a pecuniary legacy.[35]

iii. Transfers of IRD Items in Otherwise Nontaxable Transactions

Does a disposition of IRD result in income recognition when the transaction, by reason of another Code section, would shield such income from taxation? For example, Code §§ 351 and 721 provide that a person who exchanges property for a stock interest that meets the conditions of Code § 351 or exchanges property for a partnership interest that meets the conditions of Code § 721 will not recognize gain or loss because of the exchange. These sections are in direct conflict with Code § 691(a)(2).

If Code § 351, § 721, and other nonrecognition of gain or loss statutes were to take precedence over § 691, at first blush it would seem that no harm to the underlying philosophy of IRD occurs. However, the taxpayer who recognized the IRD, its timing, and its character may be different than if Code § 691 applied, and this is easily manipulated. That being the case, Code § 691 is the exclusive section for IRD taxation, and Code § 691 sets forth who can recognize IRD and those few transfers that will not give rise to IRD taxation. Thus, a transfer of an IRD item that otherwise triggers recognition under Code § 691(a)(2) should still trigger recognition even in transactions that qualify under the Code's nonrecognition provisions.[36]

31. Treas. Reg. 1.691(a)-4(b). This assumes that the item of IRD is not collected during this time.

32. Code § 691(a)(2).

33. *Id.*

34. Treas. Reg. 1.691(a)-4(a).

35. *Noel Est. v. Comr.*, 50 T.C. 702 (1968); *Findlay v. Comr.*, 332 F.2d 620 (2d Cir. 1964).

36. Carr Ferguson, James G. Freeland & Mark L. Ascher, Federal Income Taxation of Estates, Trusts & Beneficiaries pp. 3:24-25 (2d ed. 1993), concludes that Code § 691 takes precedence and gain is recognized.

Example: Joe has received an item of IRD and would like to give this item to his children. Joe knows that giving the item of IRD to his children will result in his recognizing the IRD. Joe and his children establish a partnership, and Joe transfers his item of IRD in exchange for his partnership interest. Afterwards, Joe gives his partnership interest to his children, who then liquidate the partnership and take the item of IRD. If Joe is successful in this ruse, then everyone could use this device to transfer items of IRD in contravention of the rules of Code § 691.

iv. Transfers of Installment Obligations

Installment obligations[37] are items of IRD, and special rules apply to them. Section 453B(c) mandates that the general rule concerning gain or loss recognition on installment obligation transmission at death is inapplicable in favor of Code § 691. Thus, an installment obligation is an item of IRD by statute.

The general IRD recognition rule will happen when the installment obligation is collected[38] and, likewise, will apply if transferred.[39] In the installment note context where the installment obligation was reportable by the decedent on the installment method under § 453, a transfer to the obligor will be considered a taxable transfer, any cancellation of the obligation will be treated as a transfer, and any cancellation of the obligation occurring at the death of the decedent will be treated as a transfer by the estate of the decedent (or, if the obligation is held by a person other than the decedent before the death of the decedent, by such person).[40]

(a) Transfer to Obligor

A transfer of an installment obligation to its obligor will result in IRD recognition, notwithstanding that the obligor also is the person to whom the transfer of other IRD receivables would not trigger recognition of IRD.[41] This special rule is needed to prevent the income from being avoided. Installment obligations held by an estate and bequeathed to the obligors are not considered transferred until the notes are distributed or canceled pursuant to state law.[42]

Example: Jane sold property to her daughter Cathy in exchange for Cathy's promissory note. Jane specifically bequeathed such note to Cathy in her will and after Jane's death, Jane's executor delivers Cathy's promissory note to her. The transfer is a taxable transfer pursuant to Code § 691(a)(5). As noted

---

37. Installment obligations are obligations reportable by the decedent under the installment method under § 453.

38. Treas. Reg. 1.691(a)-5(a).

39. Treas. Reg. 1.691(a)-5(b).

40. Code § 691(a)(5)(A).

41. Code § 691(a)(5)(A).

42. T.A.M. 8552007.

above, because of Treas. Reg. 1.663(c)-2(b)(3), the income recognized will be allocated to Cathy.

(b) Value of Obligation

If the decedent and obligor were related persons within the meaning of Code § 318(a) or § 267(b), then, for any taxable transfer, the fair market value of the obligation will not be less than its face value; conversely, if the decedent and the obligor are not related, then the obligation will be valued at its fair market value in the same manner as any other asset, applying the traditional willing buyer-willing seller test.[43]

(c) Cancellation of Obligation

Any cancellation of an installment obligation is treated as a transfer.[44] Where the cancellation occurs at the decedent's death, it is treated as a transfer by the estate or by the obligation's holder if the holder is not the decedent.[45]

2. Transfers of Items of IRD and the § 643(e) Election

When a trust or estate transfers property in kind that is not in satisfaction of a specific bequest or of a pecuniary bequest, such distribution generally will qualify for the distribution deduction under Code § 661. When property is so distributed, Code § 643(e) sets forth rules dictating the amount deemed distributed for purposes of Code § 661 — whether (i) the property's basis or (ii) its fair market value — which depends on whether the fiduciary elects to treat such transfer as a sale or exchange. However, *Rollert Residuary Trust v. Commissioner*[46] and Rev. Rul. 68-195[47] both hold that distributions of IRD items do not constitute in-kind property distributions for purposes of Code § 661(a). And if distributions of IRD items are not subject to Code § 661, this would preclude application of Code § 643(e).[48]

Questions

1. What two events will trigger IRD recognition?
2. Assuming there is IRD recognition, when is it recognized?

---

43. Code § 691(a)(5)(B).

44. Code § 691(a)(5)(A)(ii). *See, e.g.*, Priv. Ltr. Rul. 9108027 (testamentary cancellation of note for which decedent elected Code § 453 installment treatment was a transfer under Code § 691(a)(5)(A) which accelerated the estate's gain recognition on the note). For this purpose, an installment obligation that becomes unenforceable (e.g., where the debtor can successfully plead the statute of limitations) is treated as if it were canceled. Code § 691(a)(5)(C).

45. Code § 691(a)(5)(A)(iii).

46. 80 T.C. 619 (1983), *aff'd*, 752 F.2d 1128 (6th Cir. 1985).

47. 1968-1 C.B. 305.

48. The holdings in *Rollert Residuary Trust* and Rev. Rul. 68-195 were necessary to prevent IRD items escaping taxation and both occurred prior to the enactment of Code § 643(e). Had Code § 643(e) existed, the *Rollert Residuary Trust* case would not have happened, and Rev. Rul. 68-195 would not have been issued. To date, the question has never been answered whether the enactment of Code § 643(e) now allows transfers of IRD items to be subject to Code § 661.

C. The IRD Amount Recognized

Depending upon circumstances, the amount of IRD recognized will vary.

In most situations, the IRD recognized is equal to the amount received, less any offset available. The amount received is the cash and fair market value of the property paid in respect to the IRD receivable. In most instances, this amount equals the face amount of the IRD item.

Under Code § 691(a)(2), where an IRD receivable is transferred (e.g., sold, exchanged, or disposed of (including by gift)), that gives rise to a recognition event, the IRD amount recognized will be the greater of the consideration received or the fair market value of the IRD item at the time of the transfer.[49]

Special rules apply to installment sales. If the IRD item is an installment obligation, and if the obligor and obligee of the installment obligation are related persons, the obligation's fair market value is treated as not less than its face amount.[50] In addition, under Code § 453B, with respect to installment obligations, the law specifically states that the amount includible in gross income is reduced by an amount equal to the decedent's basis in the obligation.[51]

> **Example:** Before a cash method taxpayer's death, he sold property for a $100 installment note, to be paid in $10 cash increments over a ten-year period, beginning the following year. The taxpayer's basis in the property was $90, and upon his death, neither the $100 receivable had been received nor was recognition required. Under the literal language of Code § 691(a)(2), if the taxpayer's estate sells the installment note for $98, the estate would have $98 of income. This result is unsupportable, and the IRD amount recognized should be $8.

In determining the amount of IRD recognized, accounting for the decedent's basis in the installment note is in keeping with the IRD regime: taxing the recipient on that amount which would have been income to the decedent had he or she lived to receive it.

Finally, amounts spent to preserve or collect an IRD receivable offset the recognized income.[52]

Summary: Only certain persons can recognize IRD — the decedent's estate; one who is entitled to receive the item of IRD by bequest, devise, or inheritance; and one who is entitled to receive the item of IRD directly from the decedent. IRD will

---

49. Treas. Reg. 1.691(a)-4(a). Where an IRD receivable is sold at a discount in an arms-length transaction that reflects market value (i.e., the discount does not represent a gift, disguised compensation, or the like), only the amount received should be taken into account because the consideration received should be the same as the fair market value of the IRD item. Where an IRD receivable is settled for less than its fair market value, fair market value is recognized. *Id.*

50. Code § 691(a)(5)(B).

51. Code § 691(a)(4).

52. *Findlay v. Comr.*, 332 F.2d 620 (2d Cir. 1964).

be recognized when the IRD is collected or it is transferred to a person who cannot recognize the IRD. The income amount recognized usually will be the amount collected, but special rules apply for installment obligations.

Questions

1. What are the tax consequences when a decedent bequeaths an installment obligation to the obligor?
2. Suppose a taxpayer sells his $1 million business for a ten-year installment note providing for annual principal payments of $100,000. The business consists of appreciated inventory and machinery:

	Inventory	Machinery
Tax Basis	200,000	100,000 ($400,000 of Code § 1245 gain)
FMV	400,000	600,000

Before the first payment is even made on the installment note, the taxpayer dies. How much income must the taxpayer report on his final income tax return?

Before the installment payments commence, the taxpayer's estate sells the note for $980,000. What is the amount and character of the estate's income?

IV. The § 691(c) Deduction — Avoiding Double Taxation

An IRD item that is included in the decedent's gross estate will be subject to estate taxation. If such item of IRD is recognized for income tax purposes, then such item also will be subject to income taxation.

Example (No IRD): On the day before his death, Kenneth receives his final paycheck of $10,000, which amount is reported in Kenneth's final income tax return. Kenneth's income tax liability related to this paycheck is $3,000, which tax liability will be a deduction against his estate tax. Thus, while Kenneth's final pay increased his gross estate, its corresponding income tax liability reduced his estate tax liability. The estate tax will apply to the net income of $7,000. If for sake of simplicity we assume a 40% estate tax, then Kenneth will have paid total income and estate taxes of $5,800 (i.e., $3,000 (income taxes) + $2,800 (estate taxes)).

Example (IRD): On the day after his death, Daniel's final paycheck of $10,000 is delivered. This pay will not be reportable on Daniel's final income tax return and, thus, incurs no income tax liability. This pay, however, will be included in Daniel's gross estate and will be subject to estate tax of $4,000, assuming, again, a 40% estate tax rate. In addition, this pay will be subject to income tax of $3,000, assuming, again, a 30% income tax rate. Thus, absent Code § 691(c), the estate would pay total tax on Daniel's final $10,000 paycheck of $7,000 (i.e., $3,000 (income taxes) + $4,000 (estate taxes)), or $1,200 more than the total tax paid on Kenneth's final paycheck of $10,000.

However, Code § 691(c) ameliorates this situation. Daniel's estate gets to deduct the estate tax attributable to his final paycheck so that the income tax applies to the net $6,000 (i.e., $10,000 – $4,000 (estate taxes)). At a 30% income tax rate, the estate pays income taxes of $1,800 and total income and estate taxes of $5,800 (i.e., $1,800 (income taxes) + $4,000 (estate taxes)), the same as Kenneth and his estate.

The § 691(c) deduction may be said to do only rough justice and is more concerned that the total income tax and estate tax be roughly the same as what would have been paid if the IRD item had been recognized by the decedent while alive. Thus, Code § 691(c) makes no attempt to balance any inequities that may arise between and among IRD beneficiaries or due to state income tax and estate tax laws. Furthermore, Code § 691(c) does not address deductions in respect of a decedent.

As a practical reality, because so few estates pay estate tax due the large size of the applicable exclusion amount (see Chapter 1), going forward, the deduction permitted under § 691(c) will have benefits only for the wealthiest among us.

A. Computation of the § 691(c) Deduction

1. Basic Structure

The basic structure of § 691(c) is to provide an income tax deduction equal to the federal estate tax attributable to the IRD items. In a nutshell, this amount equals:

The actual federal estate tax liability

MINUS

the hypothetical federal estate tax for which the estate would have been liable if all items of IRD and DRD (deductions in respect of a decedent) were removed from the estate.[53]

Each taxpayer who recognizes IRD will have a § 691(c) deduction for his or her proportionate share of the total § 691(c) deduction.[54] The IRD recipient can take the income tax deduction for the excess estate tax liability even if the estate tax has not yet been paid.[55]

53. Code § 691(c)(2).

54. Code § 691(c)(1)(A).

55. *See* F.S.A. 200011023 (concerning estate tax attributable to right to receive remaining payments on annuity for term of years).

2. Determining the Total § 691(c) Deduction

The first step in computing the total Code § 691(c) deduction is to determine the net value of all IRD items relating to the decedent. The net value is the excess of the value of all IRD items over the value of all DRD items.[56]

The second step in computing the Code § 691(c) deduction is to determine the estate tax that would have been payable if the estate tax was computed without including the net value of the IRD items in the gross estate.[57] Because the IRD net value is removed from the gross estate (as opposed to the taxable estate), it is necessary to compute a separate estate tax for the estate, using as a starting point the gross estate reduced by this net value.

In determining the hypothetical estate tax on a gross estate reduced by the net value of the IRD items, the regulations require that "any estate tax deduction (such as the marital deduction) which may be based upon the gross estate shall be recomputed so as to take into account the exclusion of such net value from the gross estate."[58] Where the marital deduction is based upon a percentage of the estate, whether by the governing instrument or by law,[59] the reduction of the gross estate results in a corresponding reduction in the marital deduction.[60] Where IRD items have been bequeathed specifically to the surviving spouse, the items are excluded from the gross estate and from the marital deduction.[61] The same result should follow for IRD items bequeathed specifically to a charity.[62]

> **Example:** Under her estate plan, Anna provided for one-half of her estate to pass to her husband Matthew (which qualifies for the estate tax marital deduction) and for one-half to pass equally to her three children from her prior marriage. At her death, Anna had net IRD items totaling $200,000 in value and had a gross estate of $18 million. In determining the hypothetical estate tax for purposes of determining the § 691(c) deduction, her gross estate would be reduced by the amount of her net IRD items, or to a gross estate of $17,800,000. In determining Anna's hypothetical estate tax, the marital deduction also is reduced from $9 million (one-half of $18 million) to $8,900,000 (one-half of $17,800,000).

---

56. Code § 691(c)(2)(B).

57. Code § 691(c)(2)(C).

58. Treas. Reg. 1.691(c)-1(a)(2). *See Estate of Cherry v. United States*, 133 F. Supp. 2d 949 (W.D. Ky. 2001) (applying Reg. § 1.691(c)-1(a)(2), the district court held that the hypothetical estate tax should be determined by reducing marital deduction by items of IRD; actual estate taxes were paid from marital deduction bequest, which was part of the residuary estate).

59. *See* pre-1982 § 2056 (limiting the marital deduction to the lesser of $250,000 or 50% of adjusted gross estate).

60. T.A.M. 9219006.

61. Rev. Rul. 67-242, 1967-2 C.B. 227 (explaining proper method for computing § 691(c) deduction). *See also* Treas. Reg. 1.691(d)-1(e) Ex. (2).

62. *See* M. Carr Ferguson, James J. Freeland & Mark L. Ascher, Federal Income Taxation of Estates, Trusts & Beneficiaries 3:171 (2d ed. 1993).

B. Allocation of § 691(c) Deductions

Over the course of one tax year, if all IRD items are recognized, the entire Code § 691(c) deduction is deducted by its recipient. However, in other cases, the Code § 691(c) deduction must be allocated between and among different taxpayers and/or across different tax years.

Section 691(c)(1)(A) allocates to each IRD item its proportionate share of the estate tax liability determined by multiplying the total Code § 691(c) deduction by the following fraction:

$$\frac{\text{The amount includible in gross income (but not more than the value of the IRD item for estate tax purposes)}}{\text{Total value of all IRD items for estate tax purposes}}$$

Example: Steven is survived by three children, David, Laura, and Robert. Steven bequeathed $25,000 in IRD items—$10,000 apiece to David and Laura and $5,000 to Robert. Assume the elimination of this $25,000 in IRD items from Steven's gross estate, taking into account all applicable estate tax deductions and credits, results in a net reduction of the federal estate tax of $10,300. If David receives his entire $10,000 of IRD in year one, he is entitled to a Code § 691(c) deduction of $4,120 [$10,300 × ($10,000/$25,000)]. If Laura also receives IRD of $10,000 in year one, she is similarly entitled to a Code § 691(c) deduction of $4,120. If Robert were to collect only $4,000 of his IRD in year one, then he will have a Code § 691(c) deduction of $1,648 [$10,300 × ($4,000/$25,000)] in that tax year and, if Robert were to collect the balance of IRD in year two, then he would have a Code § 691(c) deduction of $412 [$10,300 × ($1,000/$25,000)] in that tax year.

The foregoing example is a simple and equitable allocation. The total Code § 691(c) deduction is equal to 41.2% of the net value of the IRD items, and each IRD recipient gets a Code § 691(c) deduction equal to 41.2% ($10,300/$25,000) of the amount included both in his or her gross income and in the decedent's gross estate. However, as the next example demonstrates, the allocation of the total Code § 691(c) deduction ignores disparate estate tax burdens borne by IRD recipients and their status. Disparities arise, because the statute focuses on the total IRD received by all taxpayers and the total estate taxes paid, and does not make adjustments for the impact on particular taxpayers.

Example: Kenneth is survived by his wife, Lindsay, and two children, Laura and William. Kenneth bequeathed $25,000 in IRD items to them—$10,000 to each of Lindsay and Laura and $5,000 to William. The $10,000 bequeathed to Lindsay qualifies for the marital deduction and, thus, it is excluded from the taxable estate base in determining the estate tax attributable to the net value of the IRD items. Assume that the elimination of this $10,000 in IRD items from Kenneth's gross estate results in a net reduction of the federal estate tax of $6,180 ($15,000 × 41.2%). When Lindsay receives her $10,000 of IRD, she will be entitled to a Code § 691(c) deduction of $2,472 ($6,180 × $10,000/$25,000); Laura will be entitled to the same Code § 691(c) deduction; and William will be entitled to a Code § 691(c) deduction of $1,236 ($6,180 × $5,000/$25,000). Thus, Lindsay gets a Code § 691(c) deduction for estate taxes borne by Laura and William. In other words, Laura and William bore the entire tax burden of $6,180 attributable to the items of IRD, but will only get a Code § 691(c) deduction in the aggregate of $3,708.

A person is entitled to a Code § 691(c) deduction for any tax year in which he or she receives IRD that is includible in his or her gross income, subject to the other rules discussed.

C. Allocation to and through an Estate or Trust

When dealing with a trust or estate, one must cope with the division of the Code § 691(c) deduction between and among the trust and estate and its beneficiaries. Section 691(c)(1)(B) provides that, in the case of a trust or estate, solely for purposes of computing the amount of the Code § 691(c) deduction allowed to the trust or estate, the portion (if any) of the IRD items that are properly paid, credited, or to be distributed to the beneficiaries during the tax year are excluded from income. In other words, the Code § 691(c) deduction follows the IRD — if IRD is deemed distributed to beneficiaries, then the beneficiaries receive the appropriate portion of the Code § 691(c) deduction; conversely, if the IRD is deemed retained by the trust or estate, then the trust or estate receives the appropriate portion of the Code § 691(c) deduction. This section does not change the IRD determination amount.

The statute presents a problem of circularity. The following four determinations must be made:

(1) To determine the IRD properly paid, credited or distributed to the beneficiaries, one must determine the DNI of the trust or estate.

(2) To determine the trust's or estate's DNI, one must determine its taxable income.

(3) To determine the trust's or estate's taxable income, one must determine the Code § 691(c) deduction allowable to the trust or estate.

(4) To determine the Code § 691(c) deduction allowable to the trust or estate, one must determine the IRD properly paid, credited or distributed to the beneficiaries.

And we are back at the beginning.

The regulations eliminate our need to chase our tails. More specifically, the regulations provide that the DNI of the trust or estate is to be determined without taking into account the Code § 691(c) deduction ultimately allowable to the trust or estate.[63]

63. Treas. Reg. 1.691(c)-2(a)(2).

Thus, the trust or estate can compute its DNI without difficulty. Accordingly, where the trust or estate makes a distribution in the year of IRD receipt, each beneficiary who is deemed to receive IRD will effectively share, pro rata, in both the IRD and the Code § 691(c) deduction.

> **Example:** Assume that in the first year of an estate, the estate collects interest income of $50,000 of which $5,000 represents interest accrued to the date of the decedent's death and, thus, is an item of IRD. Also assume that the estate tax attributable to this $5,000 is $2,000 (the § 691(c) deduction). The estate will allocate the $2,000 between itself and the beneficiaries based on the amount of interest income deemed distributed to the beneficiaries pursuant to the rules for determining DNI and the amounts of the items comprising DNI deemed distributed to the beneficiaries (see Chapter 3). For example, if the beneficiaries receive one-half of the interest income, then the beneficiaries will receive one-half of the § 691(c) deduction.

Summary: When a person recognizes IRD income, Code § 691(c) allows a deduction equal to the estate tax liability attributable to such IRD. The estate tax attributable to IRD is determined by taking the actual estate tax liability and then subtracting a recomputed estate tax liability based upon removal from the decedent's gross estate the total value of all IRD included in the gross estate reduced by the total items of deductions in respect of a decedent (DRD).

Questions

Assume we have the following information with respect to an estate:

Total value of all items of IRD	$16,000
Total value of all items of DRD	6,000
Federal estate tax payable	40,000
Federal estate tax payable if all items of IRD are removed from the gross estate	36,000

1. What is the maximum § 691(c) deduction available?
2. Assume that during the tax year, the decedent's child collects all the IRD. What is the § 691(c) deduction that the child can take? What if the child had only collected $4,000 of the IRD?
3. Assume that during the tax year, beneficiary A collected $4,000 of the IRD and beneficiary B collected $8,000 of the IRD. What is the § 691(c) deduction that each can take?

V. Open IRD Issues

Notwithstanding that the current IRD regime has been in place since 1942, certain issues remain unanswered. One day, perhaps Congress or the IRS will address these issues and provide guidance.

A. The Date for Determining the Existence of an IRD Item

The question implied by the above heading is whether post-death events can affect the character of a receivable as IRD. This issue is most evident and, perhaps, is only of concern in the sales area and was well illustrated by the case of *Sidles Est. v. Commissioner.*[64] In *Sidles*, the decedent, who was a company's sole shareholder, had begun to liquidate the company when he died. Had he lived to complete the liquidation, he would have recognized income. As the sole shareholder, however, he could have stopped the liquidation of the company at any time. The court held that the liquation proceeds were IRD, but this decision was not unanimous and generated widely differing opinions from the judges.

The confusion in *Sidles* and other similar situations can be avoided if the date on which an item is to be characterized as IRD is known. The most logical date for this purpose would be the decedent's date of death. And, both *Sidles* and the Fifth Circuit decision in *Trust Company of Georgia v. Ross*[65] used the decedent's date of death to identify the existence of IRD.[66]

If post-death events play a role in IRD determinations, in essence a wait-and-see approach, then uncertainty is infused into the tax laws. While case law suggests that post-death events are irrelevant, it would be helpful if the IRS explicitly stated this. Using the date of death as the date to determine IRD existence leads to its own unanswered issue discussed in the next section.

> **Example:** Lillian enters into a contract to sell property, and at her death, all material acts have been performed, and her estate has a legal right to the sales proceeds. The sale has not yet been consummated, and Lillian has not recognized any portion of the gain from the sale. Thus, the right to the sale proceeds under the contract is an IRD item. At the time of Lillian's death, the closing is still two months away. If post-death actions can affect the characterization of the property as an IRD item and if Lillian's estate and the prospective buyers can alter the contract or terminate it completely, her estate does not know the full extent of its IRD items unless and until the contract is finally consummated. For example, if the buyer and Lillian's estate cancel the contract, does that retroactively eliminate the IRD? What if the buyer and Lillian's estate then enter into a new contract substantially similar to the canceled contract? What if no new contract is entered into?

---

64. 65 T.C. 873 (1976), *aff'd by unpub. opin.*, 553 F.2d 102 (8th Cir. 1977), *acq.* 1976-2 C.B. 2.

65. 392 F.2d 694 (5th Cir. 1967).

66. In footnote four of the opinion in *Sidles*, the Tax Court stated, "It is clear that the determination of whether a right or entitlement existed is to be made at the date of decedent's death." Similarly, the Fifth Circuit in *Trust Company of Georgia* proclaimed, "It is implicit in the statute and in the definition that this condition or limitation [that is, IRD] has reference to the date of death of the decedent."

If IRD identification is not determined at the date of death and if such characterization can be negated by post-death events, then, in the sales arena, an estate would benefit by canceling and renegotiating the transaction. To illustrate, assume that the decedent had entered into a contract to sell an item for $1,000,000 in which the decedent's basis was $600,000. Had the decedent lived to consummate this transaction, he would have recognized $400,000 of capital gains and, let us assume he would have paid $100,000 in federal and state income taxes on such gain. By way of comparison, assume that after the taxpayer's death, his estate nullifies the original contract and seeks the application of Code § 1014(a) to obtain a new basis in the property equal to its fair market value ($1,000,000). If the taxpayer's estate were successful and it then enters into another contract for the purchase and sale of the same item at a purchase price of $950,000, then both parties are $50,000 better off because of the IRD elimination.

Using the date of death as the determination date fosters certainty. Under a wait-and-see approach, it may not be known for some time whether receivables resulting from a sale are an IRD item.

B. IRD When the Sale Does Not Occur

Pursuant to Code § 691(a)(3), the character of the IRD is determined by reference to the decedent. In the sales area, this works fine if the transaction is completed and the IRD is recognized. What happens if the transaction is not completed?

> **Example:** Clark enters into a contract to sell commercial real estate. All material aspects of the transaction have been completed, and a date for closing has been set. Clark dies before the closing, and his estate and the prospective buyers mutually agree to terminate the agreement. The real estate that was the subject of the agreement passes to Lois, who is the residuary legatee of Clark's estate. How should § 691 apply to this situation? At the time of Clark's death, the real estate ought to be deemed to be an item of IRD, because Clark had a contract right to the sales proceeds in exchange for the real estate. But, with the post-death events, such rights have ceased to exist. Once Clark's estate determined that the real estate was an item of IRD, no step-up in basis is allowed. But after the contract was terminated, § 691 should then cease to apply on a going-forward basis. That is, tax consequences of any subsequent dealings with the land by Lois must be based on Lois's dealings and not based on any dealings by Clark.

If the determination of IRD is to be made on the date of death and if post-death transactions should not alter that determination, then the basis in the property that was the subject of the contract should not be subject to § 1014(a) because of § 1014(c). It should then follow in the above example that Lois receives the subject real estate with a carry-over basis, but any future transaction should not and cannot be determined by reference to the decedent Clark.

However, if post-death events can affect whether a receivable is an item of IRD, so that, for example, canceling a sales contract post-death would eliminate what otherwise would have been IRD, then the character rule should not be a problem. If post-death events can affect the determination of IRD and if the sale is not consummated, then there is no item of IRD, and there is a step-up in basis under § 1014 for the item (for all intents and purposes, it is as though the involved parties were ignorant of this fact at the date of death).

C. Trust and Estate Final Distributions Less Than DNI

One would think that in the last year of a trust or estate, when all of its income and principal is distributed, that the total amount distributed could never be less than DNI. But IRD items make this strange result possible.

Example: Sarah is unmarried and has no children. She dies with the following probate assets and liabilities:

Assets	
Automobile	$5,000
Checking account	3,200
Unpaid salary and vacation time	8,000
Retirement plan	150,000
Household and personal effects	2,000
Liabilities	
Credit card debts	42,000
Car loan	1,800
Miscellaneous monthly bills	2,000

Sarah has never designated a beneficiary under her retirement plan and, as a result, the plan provides that her estate is the beneficiary. Sarah dies intestate, and her entire estate passes to her surviving mother, Miriam. The administrator of Sarah's estate distributes Sarah's household and personal effects to Miriam. The administrator collects the $8,000 for Sarah's unpaid salary and vacation time and collects the retirement benefits so to have funds to pay debts, funeral bills, and administrative expenses. The administrator sells the car for $5,000 (which sales price was used to establish its fair market value above).

In the estate's first and final tax year, Sarah's administrator takes the estate's cash of $166,200, and makes payments to satisfy (1) all of Sarah's liabilities of $45,800; (2) funeral expenses of $6,000; and (3) administrator fees, legal fees, court costs, and other administrative expenses of $14,400. Sarah's administrator pays the remaining $100,000 balance to Miriam.

Sarah's administrator prepares the income tax return, reflecting the following information:

Income in respect of a decedent	$158,000
Less deductible administrative expenses	14,400
Tentative taxable income before the distribution deduction	$143,600
Distribution deduction	100,000
§ 642(b) deduction	600
Taxable income	$43,000

Sarah's administrator is puzzled and does not understand how the estate can have $43,000 of taxable income when all the estate assets were distributed to Miriam.

This problem can arise when there are substantial IRD items in an estate and is more likely to arise in modest estates where, as in the example above, retirement benefits may represent a substantial percentage of the estate. To ameliorate this problem, a suggested solution would be to modify Code § 661 to provide that, in a trust's or estate's final year, all of its DNI would be deemed distributed regardless of the amount actually distributed. This would shift the income tax liability to the persons who receive the estate assets and who should truly bear the responsibility for such taxes.

D. Sections 661 and 662 and IRD Distributions

Prior to the enactment of Code § 643(e), Treas. Reg. 1.661(a)-2(f) provided a way for a trust or estate to distribute property in kind and to have the recipient beneficiary receive the property with a tax-free step-up in basis. In *Rollert Residuary Trust v. Commissioner,*[67] the decedent died with significant items of IRD. The taxpayer assigned significant items of IRD and argued that pursuant to Treas. Reg. 1.661(a)-2(f), the recipients of the items of IRD received such items with a new basis equal to their fair market value so that when they collected the IRD no income would be recognized. This argument did an end run around the idea of IRD, but, yet, the actions by the taxpayer fit within the language of the regulation. To prevent this result, the court held that a distribution of an item of IRD did not fall under the reach of § 661 and, thus, the regulation relied on by the taxpayer did not apply. But, to hold that distributions of items of IRD did not fall under § 661,

67. 80 T.C. 619 (1983), *aff'd* 752 F.2d 1128 (6th Cir. 1985).

the court had to find that the language in § 661 addressing distributions of "any other amounts" did not include items of IRD. The court reached the right conclusion for purposes of IRD, notwithstanding its need to contort the language of § 661, but the court's holding eliminates the possibility of a distribution deduction under § 661.

With the enactment of Code § 643(e), what the taxpayer attempted to do in *Rollert Residuary Trust* could not happen today; the regulation relied on back then no longer exists. Thus, should distributions of IRD be allowed to carry out DNI?

> **Example:** The executor of a will distributes an item of IRD with a basis of zero and a fair market value of $1,000,000 to a residuary beneficiary. Under Code § 643(e), if the executor does not make any election to treat such transfer as a sale, then the recipient will receive the item of IRD with a basis of zero and no amount will be treated as being distributed for purposes of Code § 661. However, if the executor elects to treat the transfer as a sale to the recipient, the estate will recognize $1,000,000 of IRD, the estate will be treated as having made a distribution of $1,000,000 for purposes of Code § 661, and the recipient will have a basis in the item of IRD of $1,000,000 so that such IRD will not be taxed twice.

Arguably, with the enactment of Code § 643(e) and the elimination of old Treas. Reg. 1.661(a)-2(f), undoing the holding of *Rollert Residuary Trust* does no harm to the IRD scheme. However, the IRS has not stated that it will no longer follow the holding of *Rollert Residuary Trust* and, so, practitioners should continue to treat distributions of items of IRD as not carrying out DNI under Code § 661. This can lead to unexpected results where the transfer results in the estate recognizing the IRD but is not entitled to a distribution deduction.

> **Example:** The trustee of a trust distributes an item of IRD to partially fund a pecuniary-formula marital deduction trust. The transfer of the item of IRD results in the trust recognizing the IRD for income tax purposes. However, the trust is not entitled to a distribution deduction so that the trust has recognized income, but has transferred an asset (the item of IRD) that it may need to help pay its income tax liability.

E. IRD Amounts from Qualified Retirement Benefits

For many individuals, qualified retirement benefits represent a significant portion of their net worth. These benefits are IRD items. Often these benefits will be paid over a period of years, earning income and potentially appreciating after the participant's death. Although any post-death income and appreciation will be recognized as ordinary income to the recipient, such income will not be IRD.

The question, therefore, arises, with respect to post-death distributions of qualified retirement benefits, what portion represents pre-death IRD and what portion represents post-death income? The only relevance of this question is the allocation of the § 691(c) deduction.[68] In response to this question, there are three possible approaches:

(1) All IRD is distributed first. This simplistic approach avoids the complexity of the other two approaches.

(2) All IRD is distributed last. That is, whenever the value of the retirement account is greater than (a) the amount included in the gross estate or (b) the amount of IRD yet to be deemed received, the distribution of such excess is not IRD. This approach could result in an inequity if the value of the qualified retirement benefits decreased in value in that the recipient may be taxed on retirement benefits at least equal to the amount subject to estate tax but, yet, not receive a Code § 691(c) deduction for such amount.

> **Example:** Plato had an IRA at his death worth $1 million and payable to Socrates. Plato dies before his required beginning date, and Socrates must withdraw all the benefits within 10 years. Socrates' first distribution is $30,000 at a time when the account is worth $1,030,000. Because IRD is assumed to be distributed last, none of this distribution is deemed to consist of IRD. In the following year, the value of the account decreases to $970,000, and Socrates decides to withdraw all of it. The entire distribution of $970,000 would be IRD. Although Socrates has received distributions of $1 million in total, he would be deemed to have received only $970,000 of IRD.

(3) Assume a fractional share of IRD distribution. The numerator of such fraction would be the IRD remaining, and the denominator would be the value of the account immediately before the distribution. Although this approach appears equitable, its complexity makes it unappealing.

For practical purposes, one suspects that taxpayers have been applying the first approach, which is administratively manageable. That being said, it would be helpful if the IRS provided guidance.

---

68. As the applicable exclusion continues to increase, fewer and fewer decedents will owe estate taxes and, thus, the answer to the question will become academic only. If the estate tax ever is repealed, this question will be academic for all decedents.

Chapter 9

Foreign Trusts

In general, the income earned by a foreign trust (or estate) is taxed in the same manner as a domestic trust. This chapter explores the key differences between the income taxation of domestic and foreign trusts. Yet, before delving into this material, the chapter begins with the seminal tests to determine whether, for U.S. income tax purposes, a trust is a foreign or domestic trust.

I. Definition of Domestic Trust

Paradoxically, the Internal Revenue Code assumes all trusts are foreign trusts unless the trust can meet a two-prong test found in Code § 7701(a)(30)(E): (A) the Court Test (Code § 7701(a)(30)(E)(i)) and (B) the Control Test (Code § 7701(a)(30)(E)(ii)). Both tests contain numerous intricacies, which are explored below.

A. The Court Test

Trusts will satisfy the Court Test if "a court within the United States is able to exercise primary supervision over the administration of the Trust." Code § 7701(a)(30)(E)(i).

The Treasury regulations explain certain terms in the statute and provide examples of trusts that will satisfy the Court Test. The key definitions are:

- The term "administration" means "the carrying out of the duties imposed by the terms of the trust instrument and applicable law, including maintaining the books and records of the trust, filing tax returns, managing and investing the assets of the trust, defending the trust from suits by creditors, and determining the amount and timing of distributions." Treas. Reg. 301.7701-7(c)(3)(v).
- The phrase, "is able to exercise" means that a court "has or would have the authority under applicable law to render orders or judgments resolving issues concerning administration of the trust." Treas. Reg. 301.7701-7(c)(3)(iii).
- Finally, the words "primary supervision" means "that a court has or would have the authority to determine substantially all issues regarding the administration of the entire trust." Treas. Reg. 301.7701-7(c)(3)(iv).

The Treasury regulations also contain a nonexclusive list of four types of trusts that are deemed to satisfy the Court Test. The list includes the following:

1. Trusts registered in a court within the U.S. by an authorized fiduciary under a state statute that has provisions substantially similar to Article VII of the Uniform Probate Code;
2. Testamentary trusts where all Trustees have been qualified by a court within the U.S.;
3. *Inter vivos* trusts where the fiduciaries and/or beneficiaries take steps with a court in the U.S. to cause the administration of the trust to be subject to the primary supervision of such court; or
4. Trusts where a court within and without the U.S. can both exercise primary supervision over the administration of the trust.

Treas. Reg. 301.7701-7(c)(4)(i).

Finally, the Treasury regulations provide the following three-part "safe harbor" whereby a trust will be deemed to have automatically satisfied the Court Test: (1) the trust instrument does not direct that it be administered outside of the U.S.; (2) the trust is, in fact, exclusively administered in the U.S.; and (3) the trust is not subject to an automatic migration provision. Treas. Reg. 301.7701-7(c)(1). The Treasury regulations offer the example of a trust which meets the foregoing safe harbor:

> *A* creates a trust for the equal benefit of *A*'s two children, *B* and *C*. The trust instrument provides that *DC*, a State *Y* corporation, is the trustee of the trust. State *Y* is a state within the United States. *DC* administers the trust exclusively in State *Y* and the trust instrument is silent as to where the trust is to be administered. The trust is not subject to an automatic migration provision. . . .

Treas. Reg. 301.7701-7(c)(2).

With respect to the latter part of the safe harbor, an automatic migration provision is a provision in the trust instrument that would cause a trust to automatically migrate outside of the U.S if a court within the U.S. attempts to assert jurisdiction or otherwise, directly or indirectly, supervises the administration of the trust. Treas. Reg. 301.7701-7(c)(4)(ii).[1]

B. The Control Test

Trusts satisfy the Control Test if "one or more United States persons have the authority [(by veto, affirmative vote or otherwise)] to control all substantial decisions of the Trust." Code § 7701(a)(30)(E)(ii). This single sentence contains three important terms that must be understood: "United States person," "substantial decision," and "control."

1. However, the Treasury regulations also contain a narrow exception providing that an automatic migration provision that applies only if there is a foreign invasion of the U.S. or widespread confiscation or nationalization of property in the U.S. will not cause a trust to fail the Court Test.

A United States person is based on the definition set forth in Code §7701(a)(30)(E), defining one to be "a citizen or resident of the United States." Although citizenship can by readily identified, a person is a U.S. resident if they meet the green card or substantial presence tests in Code 7701(b)(1)(A).

The Treasury regulations define "substantial decision" as decisions that are non-ministerial in nature. Examples of ministerial decisions include "decisions regarding details such as the bookkeeping, the collection of rents, and the execution of investment decisions." Treas. Reg. 301.7701-7(d)(1)(ii). The Treasury regulations provide the following non-exclusive list of powers that are deemed to be substantial decisions of a trust: (a) power over whether, when, and how much income or principal to distribute to any beneficiary; (b) power to determine whether a receipt is allocable to income or principal; (c) power to terminate a trust; (d) power to arbitrate, litigate, or settle claims on behalf of a trust; (e) power to remove, add, or replace a trustee; and (f) power to make investment decisions (provided, however, a foreign advisor's power to make investment decisions will not cause the trust to fail the Control Test if a United States person can terminate the foreign investment advisor at will). Treas. Reg. 301.7701-7(d)(1)(ii)(A)–(J).

Finally, the Treasury regulations define "control" as an individual or entity "having the power, by vote or otherwise, to make all of the substantial decisions of the trust, with no other person having the power to veto any of the substantial decisions." In addition, "[t]o determine whether United States persons have control, it is necessary to consider all persons who have authority to make a substantial decision of the trust [(i.e., a grantor with retained powers over the trust, a beneficiary with the power to remove/replace a fiduciary, a trust protector's authority to act in a non-fiduciary capacity, etc.)], not only the trust fiduciaries." Treas. Reg. 301.7701-7(d)(1)(iii).

It is important to note that if any foreign person controls a single substantial decision, the trust will fail the Control Test. This includes a decision held by a foreign person in a non-fiduciary capacity or as settlor or protector of a trust. For example, if a foreign individual creates a trust that satisfies the Court Test and names a U.S. bank as Trustee, but retains the power to remove and replace Trustees, that trust will fail the Control Test and be classified as foreign trust. Treas. Reg. 301.7701-7(d)(4), Ex. 2.

Finally, it may be possible for a foreign person to serve as Trustee without failing the Control Test, provided there are at least two other Trustees, both of whom are United States persons, and all substantial decisions are made by majority vote. Treas. Reg. 301.7701-7(d)(4)(v), Ex. 2. However, if the trust requires unanimity or confers on the foreign person decision-making power over a single substantial decision, the trust will fail the Control Test. Treas. Reg. 301.7701-7(d)(4)(v), Exs. 1 and 3.[2]

2. In situations such as this, one must ensure that the trust will not subsequently fail the Control Test if one of the United States person trustees fails to qualify, ceases to act, or ceases to be a

Questions

1. Gerald creates a trust governed under Delaware law that names his friend Tracy, a U.S. income tax resident, as sole Trustee with full decision-making power over every aspect of this trust.
   a. Is this trust a domestic or foreign trust?
   b. What if Tracy does not meet the test for income tax residency but meets the test to be a resident for gift tax purposes?
   c. During the administration of the trust, suppose Tracy ceases to meet the test for income tax residency.
2. Sasha creates a trust governed under Nevada law that names three individuals as co-Trustees. Will the trust be classified as a foreign or domestic trust in the following circumstances?
   a. The trustees are all U.S. citizens and the trustees must act by majority vote on all decisions.
   b. Two trustees are U.S. citizens, and one trustee is a non-resident alien; the trustees must act by majority on all decisions.
   c. Two trustees are U.S. citizens, and one trustee is a non-resident alien; the trustees must act by unanimity on all decisions.
   d. Two trustees are U.S. citizens, and one trustee is a non-resident alien; the non-resident alien's responsibility is limited to investment decisions including the power to hire and fire an investment manager.
   e. The trustees are all U.S. citizens; the trustees must act by majority vote on all decisions. However, the trust also appoints a trust protector with the sole power to remove and replace trustees. The trust protector is a non-resident alien and does not act in a fiduciary capacity.

II. Tax Consequences Associated with Being a Foreign Trust

There are several important tax consequences associated with being deemed a foreign trust. Such consequences include (A) DNI computation of a foreign trust; (B) gain recognition when transfers are made to a foreign trust or a domestic trust

---

United States person. In the event of an inadvertent change that would cause the trust to fail the Control Test, the trust is provided with a twelve-month safe harbor to make any changes necessary to ensure the trust satisfies the Control Test. Treas. Reg. 301.7701-7(d)(2)(i). If the trust fails to make the necessary changes to satisfy the Control Test, the trust will convert to a foreign trust, and the conversion of the classification of the trust may be deemed a sale for U.S. income tax purposes, causing gain recognition (as discussed further below). Code § 684(c).

becomes a foreign trust; (C) application of grantor trust rules to foreign trusts established by foreign grantors; (D) application of grantor rules to foreign trusts created by U.S. persons; and (E) application of the throwback rules. Each of these differences is discussed seriatim below.

A. DNI Computation of a Foreign Trust

For foreign trusts, the Code prescribes the following three salient DNI computation modifications:

i. Capital gain is always included in DNI. Code § 643(a)(6)(C) (By comparison, with respect to domestic trusts, capital gain is only included in DNI in certain situations.)

ii. Income from sources outside the U.S. is included reduced by amounts that would be deductible in connection with such foreign income if Code 265(a)(1) did not apply.

iii. DNI includes income excluded from gross income under any income tax treaty. Code § 643(a)(6)(B).

Question

1. Horace died with all of his assets owned by a revocable trust governed by New York law. The sole trustee of the trust is Horace's cousin, Caroline, who resides in the U.K. and is not a U.S. citizen. In the year following Horace's death, during the administration of the trust, Caroline sells stock recognizing a significant capital gain. Is that capital gain included in the DNI of the trust?

B. Gain Recognition When Transfers Are Made to a Foreign Trust or a Domestic Trust Becomes Foreign

Section 684 contains a rule that creates a deemed sale when a U.S. person transfers property to a foreign trust. In such a situation, the U.S. person recognizes gain on this deemed "sale" in an amount equal to the excess of the property's fair market value over its adjusted basis. Code § 684(a). The Regulations prohibit a U.S. person from recognizing losses on such deemed "sales." Treas. Reg. 1.684-1(a)(2). When Code § 684 applies, the U.S. person must comply with the reporting requirements specified under Code § 6084. Treas. Reg. 1.684-1(c).

In addition, Code § 684 applies when a domestic trust becomes a foreign trust. Code § 684(c). In such cases, the domestic trust recognizes gain in the manner described above. This rule applies to domestic trusts that, for income tax purposes, are treated as grantor trusts, but in these cases, the transfer is treated as having been made by the U.S. person who is considered the owner of the trust. Treas. Reg. 1.684-2(d)(1).

Questions

1. Seth created a domestic non-grantor trust for the benefit of his descendants. The sole trustee recently expatriated from the U.S. and became a citizen of France, making the trust a foreign trust for income tax purposes. What are the income tax consequences when the trust becomes a foreign trust?

2. The facts are the same as in Question 1, except that Seth is considered the owner of the trust under the grantor trust rules. What are the income tax consequences when the trust becomes a foreign trust?

The Treasury regulations prescribe a broad definition to the term "transfer" to include both direct, indirect, and constructive transfers. Treas. Reg. 1.684-2(a). Under these rules, an indirect transfer is deemed to occur when a U.S. person for a "principal purpose" of avoiding tax uses an intermediary to transfer property to a foreign trust. For example, assume A, a U.S. person, transfers money to B, a non-resident alien, based on an understanding that B will transfer the money to a foreign trust. Because B is a non-resident alien, B's transfer to the foreign trust will not trigger gain recognition under Code § 684. If it can be established that A transferred property to B for a principal purpose of avoiding gain recognition under Code § 684, B's transfer to the foreign trust will be treated as an indirect transfer from A to the foreign trust and A will be subject to tax under Code § 684. Treas. Reg. 1.679-3(c)(3).

Treasury regulation 1.684-1 incorporates the Regulations under Code § 679 in determining whether the use of an intermediary is presumed to be used for the purpose of avoiding tax:

(a) When the U.S. person is related to a beneficiary of the foreign trust. For the definition of related for this purpose, see Treas. Reg. 1.679-3(c)(4).

(b) When the U.S. person cannot demonstrate that (i) the intermediary has a relationship with the beneficiary of the foreign trust establishing a reasonable basis for the intermediary's transfer; (ii) the intermediary acted independently of the U.S. person; (iii) the intermediary is not an agent of the U.S. person under generally applicable U.S. agency principles; and (iv) the intermediary timely complied with the reporting requirements under Code § 6048.

Question

1. Francesco, a U.S. citizen, makes a gift to her cousin, Ferdinand, who is a non-resident alien. Three months later, Ferdinand creates a foreign non-grantor trust for the benefit of his cousin, Felix, who is Francesco's brother. *Will there by any income tax consequences when Ferdinand creates and funds the trust for Felix's benefit?*

C. Application of Grantor Trust Rules to Foreign Trusts Established by Foreign Grantors

Section 672(f) severely limits the situations in which a foreign person can be considered the owner of a trust for income tax purposes. This section eliminates a potential abuse that could occur if a foreign person created a trust for the benefit of a U.S. person. If such a trust were deemed a grantor trust, the income earned by the trust would be excluded from the normal rules of trust income taxation that would carry out income tax obligations to this U.S. beneficiary. Thus, the foreign person would be responsible for reporting all income on that individual's personal return (which may not be subject to U.S. income tax) and the U.S. beneficiary would receive a tax-free distribution (even though the distribution would carry out an income tax obligation if the trust was a non-grantor trust).

Thus, Code § 672(f) provides all trusts created by non-resident aliens will be deemed non-grantor trusts other than in two limited situations:

1. If the grantor has the authority to revest trust property in the grantor, either without any approval or with the consent of a related or subservient party. Code § 672(f)(1)(A)(i). This is a traditional revocable trust.
2. If the sole beneficiaries of the trust during the grantor's lifetime are the grantor and/or the grantor's spouse. Code § 672(f)(1)(A)(ii).

Question

1. Harry, a non-resident alien, created an irrevocable trust. During Harry's life, the Trustee, who is an independent third party, can distribute income to his wife, Harriet, and has discretion to distribute principal to Harriet and the descendants of Harry. Will Harry be treated as the owner of this trust under Code § 671?

D. Application of Grantor Trust Rules to Foreign Trusts Created by U.S. Persons

Through Code § 679, the tax law makes it challenging for U.S. persons to avoid the reach of federal income tax by transferring income-producing assets to a foreign trust. Section 679 specifically provides, "[a] United States person who directly or indirectly transfers property to a foreign trust . . . shall be treated as the owner for his [or her] taxable year of the portion of such trust attributable to such property if for such year there is a United States beneficiary of any portion of such trust."

Question

1. What is the policy reason for limiting the situations in which a U.S. person can create a foreign non-grantor trust?

Section 679 applies regardless of whether any other power or interest in the trust causes the trust to be a grantor trust with respect to the grantor (*see* Code §§ 673 to 677) or a beneficiary (*see* Code § 678). Additionally, a trust that meets the requirements of Code § 679 with respect to the grantor, but that would be considered owned by a beneficiary under Code § 678, will be considered as owned by the grantor of the trust and not by the beneficiary. Treas. Reg. 1.679-1(b). Simply said, Code § 679 trumps the application of Code § 678.

Additionally, prior to transferring assets to a foreign trust that would be deemed a grantor trust, one must be cognizant of the additional reporting requirements with respect to the grantor. For example, any trust deemed to have at least one U.S. owner must file an annual Form 3520-A with the IRS and, to the extent that the trust fails to file such form, it is the U.S. owner's obligation to ensure that such form is completed and filed.

For Code § 679 to apply, the following four conjunctive criteria must be met: (1) a U.S. person; (2) who transfers property, directly or indirectly; (3) to a foreign trust; (4) with a U.S. beneficiary for the year. Below, there is an elaboration of each criterion.

1. U.S. Person Transferor

Section 679 uses the income tax definition of U.S. person, namely, either a U.S. citizen or resident (*see* Treas. Reg. 1.679-1(c)(2)), based entirely upon the objective criteria in Code § 7701(b) (i.e., if the person is a lawfully admitted permanent resident or if the substantial presence test is satisfied).

Section 679 will also apply to a grantor who becomes a U.S. resident within five years of the date that individual establishes a foreign trust. Under Code § 679(a)(4)(A), a non-resident alien who becomes a U.S. resident within five years of transferring, either directly or indirectly, assets to a foreign trust will be treated as having made the transfer on the date that the individual becomes a resident and the transfer will include the property initially transferred to the trust plus any undistributed income on such property. This rule prevents individuals expecting to become U.S. residents from avoiding the reach of Code § 679 by establishing a foreign trust before their relocating to the U.S. *See also* Treas. Reg. 1.679-5(c), Ex. 1.

Question

1. Clarissa, a non-resident alien, creates a foreign non-grantor trust in 2022. To her complete surprise, she receives an offer of employment requiring her to move to the United States. She accepts the job and moves in 2023. Will

Clarissa be considered the owner of the trust under Code § 679? Would your answer change if Clarissa moved to be closer to family who lived in the United States? What if Clarissa moved in 2028?

---

2. *Transfer of Property*

For Code § 679 to apply, the U.S. person (or person who becomes a U.S. person within five years of a transfer), must transfer property to a foreign trust. There are two categories of transfers that are excepted from the reach of Code § 679. First, Code § 679(a)(2)(A) excepts transfers "by reason of the death of the transferor." The second and more complicated exception is transfers "for consideration of at least fair market value." Code § 679(a)(2)(B). Transfers will be at fair market value provided they reflect an arm's-length price for property or for services rendered to the trust. Treas. Reg. 1.679-4(b)(1).[3]

Section 679 applies both to direct and indirect transfers. These rules were covered in the preceding section regarding Code § 684.

In addition to these rules, the regulations also provide that a transfer will occur when a U.S. person transfers property from a domestic trust owned by that person to a foreign trust. For Code § 679 to apply in this situation, the foreign trust must be one described in Code § 679 (i.e., it has at least one U.S. beneficiary). If not, Code § 684 would apply and would tax the transfer from the domestic to foreign non-grantor trust as if the domestic trust sold property to the foreign non-grantor trust. The same rules apply if the domestic trust becomes a foreign trust. Treas. Reg. 1.679-6(a).

Question

1. Jeremy is considered the owner of a domestic grantor trust for the benefit of his descendants, all of whom are U.S. persons. The trustee changes the governing law of the trust to the Cayman Islands and only the courts of that country have jurisdiction over the trust. Is Jeremy still considered the owner of the trust under the grantor trust rules? Is there immediate gain recognition under Code § 684?

---

3. However, an obligation or a guarantee of an obligation by the trust, any grantor, owner, or beneficiary of the trust, or anyone deemed related to such a person under the definition of related in Code § 643(i)(2)(B) will not be considered at fair market value unless it meets the requirements of a "qualified obligation." To be considered a qualified obligation, certain requirements must be met, including, the obligation must be made pursuant to a written agreement with a term of five years or less with payments in U.S. dollars. Additionally, the yield to maturity must not be less than 100% of the applicable federal rate (AFR) and not greater than 130% of the AFR, and the U.S. transferor must report the loan annually on Form 3520. Treas. Reg. 1.679-4(d).

3. Foreign Trust

Section 679 applies only when the transfer is being made to a foreign trust as defined in Code § 7701(a)(30)(E), the details of which were discussed earlier in this chapter.[4]

4. U.S. Beneficiaries

The final requirement under Code § 679 is that the trust must benefit one or more U.S. beneficiaries. The Code and Treasury regulations prescribe a general presumption that a trust has a U.S. beneficiary unless the taxpayer can demonstrate both that (1) no part of the income or corpus of the trust may be paid to or accumulated for benefit of a U.S. person during that taxable year, and (2) if the trust terminates, no part of the income or corpus would be paid to or applied for the benefit of a U.S. person. Code § 679(c); Treas. Reg. 1.679-2(a).

The Treasury regulations broadly prescribe a number of rules to determine whether income or corpus can be paid or applied for the benefit of a U.S. person. First, this determination must be made annually. Second, the mere possibility that income or corpus could benefit a U.S. person is sufficient even when there is no guarantee the U.S. person will ever benefit from the trust. Indeed, even a U.S. person's contingent beneficial interest will be sufficient unless the U.S. person's interest is highly remote. Treas. Reg. 1.679-2(a)(2)(ii).

The following examples from the Regulations demonstrate that even when it is unlikely that U.S. person may ever receive trust property, the very possibility of a distribution is usually sufficient to trigger this section's application:

1. A U.S. person funds a foreign trust for the benefit of a foreign individual. At the U.S. person's death, the remaining trust property is distributed to the foreign individual. However, if this foreign individual is not alive, under the laws of intestacy, the remaining property would be distributed in equal shares to two individuals, one of whom is a U.S. citizen. This trust is treated as having a U.S. beneficiary in the year of its funding. Treas. Reg. 1.679-2(a)(2)(iii), Ex. 8.
2. A U.S. person funds a foreign trust for the benefit of his uncle, who is a non-resident alien. At the U.S. person's death, the property is distributed to the uncle, if then living, or if not, to his descendants. One of uncle's grandchildren is a U.S. resident. This trust is treated as having a U.S. beneficiary in the year of its funding. Treas. Reg. 1.679-2(a)(2)(iii), Ex. 9.
3. A U.S. person creates a foreign trust providing for discretionary distributions of income to a non-resident alien. When the trust terminates, the remaining property is directed to be distributed to that non-resident alien; however, a

4. Transfers to domestic trusts are not captured by Code § 679, regardless of whether such trusts are grantor trusts based on the rules in Code §§ 673 to 678, discussed in detail in Chapter 6 of this book.

different person can appoint property to other remainder beneficiaries. This trust is treated as having a U.S. beneficiary in the year of its funding. Treas. Reg. 1.679-2(a)(2)(iii), Ex. 11.

On the other hand, there are some situations, where the contingent interest of a U.S. beneficiary is so remote that this interest can be disregarded:

> A U.S. person creates a foreign trust for the benefit of a non-resident alien. At that individual's death, the remaining trust property is directed to be distributed in equal shares to that individual's three children. Under the law of intestacy, if all three of these children are deceased at the time of that individual's death, the remaining property is distributed to the U.S. individual's heirs, which could potentially result in a distribution to a U.S. person but only if a number of non-resident alien heirs were deceased. *This foreign trust is not treated as having a U.S. beneficiary.* Treas. Reg. 1.679-2(a)(2)(iii), Ex. 7.

Finally, the Treasury regulations address the change of "U.S. person" status of a beneficiary. If all potential U.S.-person beneficiaries cease to be U.S. persons, the assets of the trust will be deemed to be transferred to a foreign trust, and the creator of the trust will be subject to tax under Code § 684. Conversely, if a beneficiary of a trust without any potential U.S.-person beneficiaries becomes a U.S. person, that trust will be treated as owned by the creator only if the change in U.S.-person status occurs five years or less after the transfer of assets to the trust. Treas. Reg. 1.679-2(a)(3).

Questions

1. Ulam, a U.S. citizen, created and funded a domestic trust naming himself as sole Trustee with the power to revoke the trust for any reason. Subsequently, he creates a foreign trust for the benefit of his daughter, Ulama, a U.S. citizen. A week later, Ulam transfers property of the domestic trust to the foreign trust. Will Ulam be considered the owner of the foreign trust under Code § 679? Would Code § 684 also apply to tax this transfer?
2. Ursula, a U.S. citizen, creates a foreign trust for the benefit of her daughter, Ariel, who is a non-resident alien. For twenty years, the trustee may distribute (or withhold) income or principal to Ariel. After twenty years, the trust will terminate and the remaining principal (if any) will be distributed 95% to Ariel and 5% to Ariel's cousin, William, a U.S. citizen. Is Ursula considered the owner of this foreign trust under Code § 679?

E. The Throwback Tax

The throwback tax and the rules associated thereunder are a complicated set of rules that apply when a foreign non-grantor trust makes an "accumulation distribution" of undistributed net income ("UNI") to a U.S. beneficiary. Such rules are intended to compensate the U.S. government for income taxes it otherwise would have received had an income distribution been made to the U.S. beneficiary in the year in which the trust realized the income. When the throwback rules are implicated, not only may the U.S. beneficiary be subject to a significant throwback tax on such distribution, but also an interest charge. This section provides (1) an overview of the throwback tax, (2) the applicable rules, and (3) methods to avoid or minimize its impact.

1. Overview of the Throwback Tax

To understand the throwback tax, one must first understand the definitions of UNI and an accumulation distribution.

Section 665(a) defines UNI for any tax year as "the amount by which distributable net income of the trust for such taxable year exceeds the sum of (1) the amounts for such taxable year [required to be distributed or discretionarily distributed], and (2) the amount of taxes imposed on the trust attributable to such distributable net income."

By way of example delineated in Treas. Reg. 1.665(a)-1A(a)(2), Ex., consider the following fact pattern:

> Under the terms of a trust, $10,000 of income is required to be distributed currently to A and the trustee has discretion to make additional distributions to A. During the taxable year 1971, the trust had distributable net income of $30,100 derived from royalties, and the trustee made distributions of $20,000 to A. The taxable income of the trust is $10,000 on which a tax of $2,190 is paid. The undistributed net income of the trust for the taxable year 1971 is $7,910, computed as follows:

Distributable net income:	$30,100
Income currently distributable to A:	($10,000)
Other amounts distributed to A:	($10,000)
Taxes imposed on the trust attributable to undistributed net income:	($2,190)
Undistributed net income:	$7,910

In addition, Code § 665(b) defines an accumulation distribution for any taxable year of the trust as "the amount by which (1) [the amounts properly paid, credited or required to be distributed other than accounting income required to be distributed] exceed (2) the distributable net income for such year reduced (but not below zero) by the amounts of accounting income required to be distributed."

By way of example delineated in Treas. Reg. 1.665(b)-1A(d), Ex.3, consider the following fact pattern:

> Under the terms of a trust instrument, the trustee may either accumulate the trust income or make distributions to A and B. The trustee may also invade corpus for the benefit of A and B. During the taxable year, the trust

had income as defined in Code § 643(b) of $22,000 and expenses of $5,000 allocable to corpus. Distributable net income amounts to $17,000. The trustee distributed $10,000 to each A and B during the tax year. There is an accumulation distribution of $3,000 computed as follows:

Total distribution:	$20,000
Other amounts distributed:	$20,000
Distributable net income:	$17,000
Less income required to be distributed:	$0
Balance of distributable net income:	$17,000
Accumulation distribution:	$3,000

However, pursuant to the flush language of Code § 665(b), notwithstanding this rule, an accumulation distribution can only occur to the extent the trust distributes in excess of its accounting income for the year.

2. The Applicable Rules

When an accumulation distribution is made to a U.S. beneficiary from a foreign non-grantor trust and the throwback rules are implicated, a complex calculation under Code §§ 666 and 667 must be undertaken to determine the tax amount. For this purpose, there is no difference in the character of income included in DNI—including long-term capital gain—all of which is effectively taxed to the beneficiary at the highest marginal income tax rate for the year in which the income or gain was earned by the trust.

In addition to such tax, when an accumulation distribution is made to a U.S. beneficiary from a foreign non-grantor trust and the throwback rules are implicated, the beneficiary is also subject to an interest charge on such distribution, and such interest charge is calculated as provided under Code § 668. The interest charge essentially attempts to offset the benefit of the tax deferral; the interest charge accrues for the period beginning with the year in which the income was realized by the trust and ending with the year in which the UNI is distributed, and such interest charge is assessed at the applicable underpayment rates (*see* Code § 6621).

In order to make such calculations, the Trustee must have maintained sufficient records regarding the trust's income and distributions. To the extent that the Trustee failed to maintain such sufficient records, Code § 6048 and Form 3520 provides a "default" method to determine the applicable tax and interest charge. Of course, depending upon the facts and circumstances, the default method could produce a punitive or beneficial result.

3. Methods to Avoid or Minimize Its Impact

There are a number of methods to avoid or minimize the impact of the throwback tax when a U.S. person is a beneficiary of a foreign non-grantor trust:

1. The foreign non-grantor trust can distribute on annual basis an amount equal to its fiduciary accounting income or DNI without the distribution being subject to the throwback rules. Code § 665(b)(2).
2. In addition, a distribution made within the first 65 days of the next taxable year may be deemed to have been distributed on the last day of the preceding taxable year, and subject to the parameters discussed in point 1 above, will not be subject to the throwback rules. The "65-Day Rule" of Code § 663(b)(1) is discussed in detail in Chapter 5.
3. If the trust instrument requires that a specific sum or property be paid to a beneficiary, and such property is actually paid all at once (or in no more than three installments), such transfer is not deemed a distribution subject to the throwback rules. The "Three-Installment Rule" of Code § 663(a)(1) is discussed in detail in Chapter 5.
4. The grantor (or even the Trustee) could consider establishing a dual-trust structure, wherein a foreign non-grantor trust and a domestic trust are both established. Thereafter, each year, if the foreign non-grantor trust distributed all DNI to the domestic trust, no UNI would accumulate in the foreign non-grantor trust and any subsequent distribution to the U.S. beneficiary from the foreign non-grantor trust would not be an accumulation distribution subject to the throwback rules. However, in establishing this type of structure, one must be cognizant of the multiple trust rule in Code § 643(f). Under such rule, two or more trusts will be treated as one trust if (i) such trusts have substantially the same grantor(s) and the same primary beneficiaries, and (ii) a principal purpose of such trusts is tax avoidance.

In addition, it is also important to be cognizant of two throwback traps:

1. Similar to the rules associated with Code § 684, if a distribution to a U.S. beneficiary from a foreign non-grantor trust is made indirectly through a nominee or an intermediary for the principal purpose of tax avoidance, such distribution will be deemed to be a distribution directly from the trust to the U.S. beneficiary. Code § 643(h). For the purposes of this Code §, a transfer through a nominee will be deemed to be for the principal purpose of tax avoidance if the U.S. beneficiary: (i) "is related . . . to a grantor of the foreign trust, or has another relationship with a grantor of the foreign trust that establishes a reasonable basis for concluding that the grantor of the foreign trust would make a gratuitous transfer . . . to the United States person; (ii) receives from the intermediary, within the period beginning twenty-four months before and ending twenty-four months after the intermediary's receipt of property from the foreign trust, either the property the intermediary received from the foreign trust, proceeds from such property, or property in substitution of such property; and (iii) cannot demonstrate to the satisfaction of the Commissioner that: (A) the intermediary has a relationship with the United States Person that establishes a reasonable basis for concluding that the intermediary would

make a gratuitous transfer to the United States person; (B) the intermediary acted independently of the grantor and the trustee of the foreign trust; (C) the intermediary is not an agent of the United States person under generally applicable United States agency principles; and (D) the United States person timely complied with the reporting requirements of Code § 6039F, if applicable, if the intermediary is a foreign person." Treas. Reg. 1.643(h)-1(a).

2. If the foreign non-grantor trust makes a loan of cash or marketable securities to a U.S. beneficiary (or permits such U.S. beneficiary to use trust property), the amount of the loan (or the value of the usufruct interest) will be deemed to be a distribution to such U.S. beneficiary. Code § 643(i).

Finally, it is important to note that the mere domestication of a foreign non-grantor trust that holds UNI will not cleanse the trust of its UNI. Although the throwback rules were repealed in connection with domestic trusts in 1997, such abrogation does not apply to a domestic trust that was at one time a foreign trust. Code § 665(c); Rev. Rul. 91-6.

Questions

1. In year 1, Haiden, a U.S. person, creates a trust for the benefit of his daughters, Ella, a U.S. person, and Sara, a foreign individual residing abroad. The trust appoints Trust Co., a Delaware trust company, Tom, a U.S. person, and Frank, a foreign individual residing abroad, as trustees, and the trustees are required to act by majority. The trustees are all independent third parties. The trust provides that the trustees may distribute as much income and principal to Ella and Sara as the trustees determine in their sole discretion. On January 1st of year 2, Haiden dies and the trust becomes a non-grantor trust. On January 15th of year 2, prior to the trustee's receipt of any income in such year, the Trustees distribute $1,000,000 to Ella. On January 1st of year 3, Tom dies and no successor is appointed in his stead.

    a. During years 1 and 2, would the trust have been deemed a foreign trust or a domestic trust for U.S. income tax purposes?

    b. Following Tom's death in year 3, would the income tax classification of the trust have changed?

    c. Is the distribution to Ella in year 2 a distribution that will be subject to the throwback rules?

    d. Would the analysis differ if the distribution was made to Ella in year 4? What if the trustees were directed under the trust agreement to make such distribution to Ella, but the trustees were given the discretion to determine when and how much to distribute at any given time and the trustees satisfied such distribution in 5 installments?

    e. Are there any other adverse tax consequences the trustees should be made aware of?

2. In year 1, Marco, a U.S. person, creates a trust for the benefit of his sons, Vinny and Giacomo, U.S. persons, and his niece, Aren, a foreign individual residing abroad. The trust appoints R.L. Trust Company, an Alaska Trust company, and Peter and Lucas, foreign individuals residing abroad, as trustees, and the trustees are required to act by majority. The trustees are all independent third parties. The trust provides that the trustees may distribute as much income and principal to Vinny, Giacomo, and Aren, as the trustees determine in their sole discretion. The trust has no U.S.-sitused assets. Marco died 30 days after the establishment of the trust.

   a. Is the trust deemed to be a foreign trust or a domestic trust for U.S. income tax purposes?

   b. If, in year 2, the trustees distribute $500,000 to each of Vinny, Giacomo, and Aren, are these distributions subject to the throwback rules?

   c. Is there any adverse U.S. tax consequences if Aren were to first gift $500,000 to each of Vinny and Giacomo, and then receive a $1,500,000 distribution from the trust one month later?

   d. Would there be any U.S. tax consequences if the trust loaned $500,000 of cash to each of Vinny and Giacomo, rather than making a distribution?

   e. What if the trustees permitted Vinny and Giacomo to use real property held by the trust in the Virgin Islands, without the payment of rent?

Conclusion

For those students who endured an entire semester immersed in Subchapter J and this textbook, we hope that your efforts have proved worthwhile and that mastery of the course material has been achieved. If you have truly given this course the time and energies it warrants and deserves, you're ready to practice what you've learned in the classroom.

Before concluding, we nevertheless want to take a moment and apologize for any mistakes we have in this textbook. Bear in mind that this is only a second edition textbook and, as such, there is still a steep learning curve for all of us involved, none of whom have ever participated in such an endeavor. Please bear further in mind that we had to address two difficult obstacles. The first is that Subchapter J itself has a whole coterie of unique challenges that does not lend itself to a natural progression akin to the lifecycle of a business enterprise (e.g., corporation or partnership) and, in addition, attempts to coalesce difficult accounting and tax concepts. The second is that Congress's most recent foray into reforming the Code embodied in the Tax Cuts and Jobs Act ushered in significant changes to the tax landscape, many of which have not yet been completely distilled. Whatever the case, we hope that future editions of this textbook will shed these errors, so we invite our readers — both professors and students — not to be bashful and send e-mails to us that call attention to our blunders (albeit, we know we are undoubtedly destined to make other mistakes in future editions).

A final word of advice. Circumspection is in order — the fact you have excelled with the course material will not substitute for practical experience. Our message is therefore a simple one: be careful, don't be lulled by your classroom success, and when it doubt, reach out to seasoned veterans in your network system. If you do make a mistake, join the crowd, clean off your "uniform," and then get back into the game. As the five of us routinely tell our children, it's far better to participate and possibly win a race and lose than to sit the race out entirely; the former is much more admirable than the latter. Now, off you go!!!

JAY SOLED, jaysoled@business.rutgers.edu
ALAN ACKER, alansacker@gmail.com
JERE W. DOYLE, jere.doyle@bnymellon.com
STEVEN G. SIEGEL, steve@siegel.net
SEAN R. WEISSBART, sean.weissbart@blankrome.com

Appendix: Supplemental Questions[1]

1. Gerry created an *inter vivos* trust for his daughter, Bradia, which provides that all annual income is to be distributed to Bradia for her life, and upon her death, the principal is to be distributed to New York University. Last year, Thomas, the Trustee, collected $100 of rental payments, which he distributed to Bradia. Thomas also sold stock, recognizing a $200 capital gain.
   a. Who are the possible taxpayers for the trust's income?
   b. Could the income earned by the trust be fairly taxed using the rules for taxing the income earned by corporations, partnerships, or individuals?
2. A trust is created under a decedent's will. The trustee is directed to pay all income to A at least annually. At A's death, the principal is to be paid over to B. During the year, the trustee receives $6,000 of dividends and sells real property for $30,000, recognizing no gain, but under that state's underproductive property statute, 10% of the gross sales proceeds are allocated to income. The trust has no other expenses or receipts for the year. What is the amount of the trust's taxable income?
3. A trust is created under a decedent's will. The trustee is directed to pay all income in equal shares to A and B at least annually. At A's death, the principal is to be paid over to C. During the year, the trustee receives $18,000 of dividends. In addition, the trust's gross income includes $9,000 of original issue discount ("OID") from a zero-coupon bond issued by XYZ Corp. The trust has no other expenses or receipts for the year. What is the character of the amounts included in each of A's and B's gross income?
4. A trust is created under a decedent's will. The trustee is directed to pay one-half of the amounts received as dividends to A and pay the remaining income in equal shares to A, B and C. At A's death, the principal is to be paid over to D. During the year, the trustee receives $12,000 of dividends and $15,000 of interest. The trust also recognizes $6,000 of capital gain from the sale of stock. During the year, the trustee sells real property for $30,000, recognizing no gain, but under that state's underproductive property statute, 10% of the gross sales proceeds are allocated to income. The trust has no other expenses

1. Questions created by Austin Bramwell and Sean R. Weissbart.

or receipts for the year. What is the character of the amounts included in A's, B's, and C's gross incomes?

5. A trust is created under a decedent's will that directs that all income shall be paid over in equal shares to the decedent's children beginning in 2011. In January of that year, the decedent's posthumously conceived child, PCC, brings a lawsuit claiming a one-third share of the income. The decedent's other two children, A and B, contest PCC's claim. Pending the outcome of the litigation, the trustee retains one-third of the income until the court resolves who is entitled to it. In 2016, after five years of litigation, a trial court resolves the dispute in favor of PCC, and directs that the accumulated one-third be paid over to PCC. Must PCC include income from the trust from 2011–2015?

6. The trustee of a trust created under a decedent's will is required to distribute all income to A at least annually. The decedent died in the state of Looking Glass, which has enacted the Humpty-Dumptyist Principal and Income Act. Under that Act (which governs the administration of the trust), all interest and dividends are allocated to principal and all proceeds from the sale of property are allocated to income. During the year, the trust has $15,000 of interest, $7,500 of dividends and sells a parcel of real property for $30,000. The trustee distributes $30,000 to A.

    a. Is the trust simple or complex?

    b. What is the trust's personal exemption deduction?

7. A trust is created under a decedent's will. The trustee is directed to pay one-third of the income at least annually to each of A and B. The trustee is authorized (but not required) to distribute any of the balance of the income or any principal to C. In year 1, the trustee receives $18,000 of dividends and $36,000 of interest and recognizes $60,000 of capital gain. In addition, the trust is a partner in a partnership, and the trust's distributive share for the year of that partnership's income is $18,000, all of which is rental real estate income. The trustee distributes $48,000 to C. There are no other receipts or disbursements in year 1. What is the character of the amounts included in each of A's, B's and C's gross income?

8. Nicole dies with an estate (after debts and administration expenses) of $200,000. Under her will, she makes a cash bequest of $100,000 to her husband, Keith, and bequeaths the residue of her estate to her first husband, Tom. Would you rather be Keith or Tom?

9. Which of the following bequests are ascertainable?

    a. Share certificate numbers 103 through 110 of XYZ Corporation.

    b. Eight shares of XYZ Corporation.

    c. Cash equal in date-of-death value to eight shares of XYZ Corporation.

    d. First edition of the reference book Necronomicon.

    e. All of the decedent's tangible property.

f. One-third of the residue of the decedent's estate.

g. Cash bequest of $200,000, but capped at one-third of the value of the decedent's gross estate for estate tax purposes.

h. Cash bequest of $200,000, but capped at one-third of the net value (after expenses of administration) of the decedent's estate.

i. Cash bequest of $200,000, where the estate only has $150,000 remaining to distribute after debts and expenses.

10. Which of the following bequests satisfies the requirements of section 663(a)(1) of the Code?

    a. $20,000 to A in year 1, $20,000 in year 2, and $20,000 in year 3.

    b. $20,000 to A in year 1, $20,000 in year 2, $20,000 in year 3, and $200 in year 4.

    c. A decedent makes a $60,000 cash bequest to A. To preserve liquidity, the executor satisfies the bequest by paying over $15,000 to A in year 1, $15,000 in year 2, $15,000 in year 3, and $15,000 in year 4.

    d. A decedent bequeaths to A $200,000 cash, 8 shares of XYZ Corporation, all the decedent's birdfeed, and his vintage Mickey Mouse cufflinks.

    e. A decedent bequeaths to A the decedent's four automobiles, but directs that A shall receive the Buick in year 1, the Oldsmobile in year 2, the Dodge in year 3, and the Stanley Steamer in year 4.

    f. A decedent bequeaths $20,000 to A. The decedent also creates a trust under the decedent's will under which A is to receive $20,000 when A turns 35, $20,000 when A turns 45 and $20,000 when A is first married.

11. A trust is created under a decedent's will. The trustee is authorized under the will, in the trustee's discretion, to pay over or apply any amounts to A or for A's benefit for A's support and maintenance. The trustee is also authorized to make distributions to B for any purpose. Which of the following amounts are deductible under Section 661(a)(1) and in what years?

    a. During the year, the trustee, intending to set aside an amount to be distributed to A, writes a "memo to file" saying that $6,000 shall be distributed for that year to A. In fact, the amount isn't distributed until the next year.

    b. During the year, the trustee writes to A a letter and says that the trustee intends to distribute $6,000 to A but asks A to acknowledge receipt first by countersigning and returning the letter. A countersigns and returns the letter during the year, but the $6,000 is not actually paid over until the next year.

    c. Same as in (b), except that the trustee doesn't ever pay over the $6,000, since it turns out the trustee needs it to pay legal fees. The trustee promises to make it up to A in the future. A does not object.

d. Same as in (b), except that A agrees in writing to refund any amount of the $6,000 that is required to discharge debts of the trust.

e. A rents a small apartment in midtown. The trustee pays $9,000 of monthly rent on A's behalf directly to the landlord.

f. The trustee buys a small apartment in midtown and permits A to use the apartment without paying rent.

g. The trustee pays $9,000 in maintenance charges on the apartment that the trustee has acquired for A.

h. A rents a 6-acre beach house in East Hampton, replete with a three-story water slide. The trustee pays $600,000 of rent directly to the landlord.

i. The trustee buys a car for A's use. It turns out that A does not want it, so the trustee gives the car to the trustee's sister.

j. The trustee resigns and the court appoints A as sole trustee. A's typical living expenses are $60,000.

k. B decides to start a literary magazine, The Questing Vole. The trustee believes that the magazine will fail, but decides to use trust funds to encourage B's endeavors. In lieu of making a distribution to B, the trustee invests $80,000 in B's magazine to cover start-up costs. The trust is given an equity interest in the magazine, and the interest becomes worthless within a year.

12. The trustee of a testamentary trust is directed to pay all income at least annually to Bob and Caroline. The trustee is given discretion to determine what amounts (if any) of the income each of Bob and Caroline will receive. The trustee has $50,000 of fiduciary accounting income in 2018. In September 2019, the trustee decides to distribute all of 2018's fiduciary accounting income to Caroline. In what year does Caroline include gross income?

13. A decedent creates a trust under the decedent's will that requires one-half of all income to be paid over to A at least annually. The trustee is also directed to pay $27,000 annually to B. The trustee has discretion to distribute income (other than income paid to A) or principal to C. During the year, the trust has $90,000 of fiduciary accounting income and $72,000 of DNI. The trustee distributes $45,000 to C out of principal. What amounts are included in each beneficiary's gross income? Would your answer be different if the trustee made the distribution to C out of fiduciary accounting income?

14. A trust is created under a decedent's will. The trustee is directed under the will to pay one-half of the income at least annually to A. The trustee is authorized to distribute principal to B. During the year, the trustee receives $45,000 of rents from a building and $45,000 of tax-exempt interest. The trustee pays $9,000 of building maintenance expenses. The trustee pays itself a commission of $9,000, one-half of which is charged to income. The trustee distributes $36,000 to B. There are no other receipts or disbursements in year 1.

a. What is the trust's taxable income?

b. What amounts are included in A's and B's gross income and what is the character of those amounts?

15. In which of the following circumstances are capital gains included in DNI?

a. The trust instrument directs that proceeds from the sale of a building shall be paid over to the beneficiary.

b. Unproductive property having a zero basis is sold by the trustee of a simple trust. Under the law governing the administration of the trust, a portion of the proceeds from the sale must be allocated to income.

c. Unproductive property having a zero basis is sold by the trustee of a trust whose income or principal may be distributed (or retained) in the discretion of the trustee. Under the law governing the administration of the trust, a portion of the proceeds from the sale must be allocated to income.

d. The trustee exercises a power to terminate the trust and pays over all of the trust property to the beneficiaries.

e. A trustee receives from a partnership, in lieu of a cash distribution, a distribution of corporate stock. The trustee then sells the stock and recognizes capital gain.

f. A trust is a shareholder in an S corporation. The S corporation has capital gain income for the year but does not make distributions to its shareholders.

16. A trust created under a decedent's will requires all income to be paid over annually to A. The will directs that one-quarter of principal be paid over to B when B turns 50. The trust is not governed by the laws of a state that has passed the Uniform Principal and Income Act, but the decedent has directed in the will that the Act shall govern allocations between principal and income. In the year that B turns 50, the trustee makes an adjustment of income to principal pursuant to the adjustment provisions of the Uniform Principal and Income Act that are incorporated by reference into the trust instrument. The trustee doesn't pay over B's share of principal until the year after B turns 50. What are the tax consequences in the year that B turns 50?

17. A decedent creates a trust under the decedent's will that requires one-half of income to be paid over to A at least annually. The balance of the income or principal may be paid over to B in the trustee's discretion. In year 1, the trust has $5,400 of fiduciary accounting income and $13,500 of DNI. The trustee distributes $4,500 to B on September 1 of year 1 and $7,200 to B on January 31 of year 2. The trustee makes a timely 65-day election to treat the year 2 distribution to B as made in year 1.

a. What amount of gross income is carried out to B in year 1?

b. What amount (if any) will be treated as distributed to B in year 2?

c. Now suppose instead that, in year 1, the trust has $13,500 of fiduciary accounting income and $5,400 of DNI. As before, the trustee distributes $4,500 to B on September 1 of year 1 and $7,200 on January 31 of year 2, and the trustee makes a timely 65-day election to treat the year 2 distribution to B as made in year 1. What amount of gross income is carried out to B in year 1?

18. A decedent creates a trust under the decedent's will that requires one-half of income to be paid over to A at least annually. The balance of the income may be paid over to B in the trustee's discretion. The will directs the trustee to transfer a reasonable portion of rental receipts to principal as a reserve. In year 1, the trust receives $18,000 of rents from a building, one-half of which the trustee transfers to principal. The trustee distributes $2,250 to B. A $45,000 depreciation deduction is allowed with respect to the building. The trust has no other receipts or disbursements for the year.

    a. How is the depreciation deduction allocated?

    b. Would the answer change if the decedent did not direct the trustee to set aside a reserve?

    c. In year 2, the trust has no rental receipts and no fiduciary accounting income. The trust still has a $45,000 depreciation deduction. The trust has no other receipts or disbursements for the year. How is the depreciation deduction allocated?

19. In 2018, Jeremy, a U.S. citizen, created a revocable trust, governed under the laws of the State of New York, naming his cousin, Ann, a U.S. citizen, as sole Trustee with all decision-making powers. In 2023, Jeremy expatriates, thereby relinquishing his U.S. citizenship and becomes a citizen of a foreign country. Upon Jeremy's expatriation, will the trust's assets be subject to tax under Section 684? Would your answer be different if Jeremy was sole Trustee?

20. In 2014, Angela creates a domestic trust for the benefit of her descendants and retains no powers that would cause the trust to be a grantor trust. The trust provides that all income must be distributed to Angela's child, Nick, and that the trustee has discretion to distribute principal to any beneficiary. In 2021, the trust becomes a foreign trust. In 2023, the trust sells stock generating capital gain; the trust's only other source of income for the year is dividends. The trustee distributes an amount equal to the dividend income to Nick, who is a U.S. citizen. Will Nick's distribution be considered an accumulation distribution subject to the throwback rules? What is the character of the income included in Nick's gross income from the trust?

Index